New York City Folklore

OTHER BOOKS BY B. A. BOTKIN

The American Play-Party Song

Edited:

Folk-Say: A Regional Miscellany, 1929, 1930, 1931, 1932

A Treasury of American Folklore

Lay My Burden Down: A Folk History of Slavery

A Treasury of New England Folklore

A Treasury of Southern Folklore

The Pocket Treasury of American Folklore

A Treasury of Western Folklore

A Treasury of Railroad Folklore (with Alvin F. Harlow)

Sidewalks of America

A Treasury of Mississippi River Folklore

NEW YORK CITY Folklore

Legends, Tall Tales, Anecdotes, Stories,

Sagas, Heroes and Characters,

Customs, Traditions and Sayings

Edited, with an Introduction, by

B. A. BOTKIN

RANDOM HOUSE NEW YORK

First Printing

 Published in New York by Random House, Inc., and in Toronto, Canada, by Random House of Canada, Limited. Library of Congress Catalog Card Number: 56-8815. Manufactured in the United States of America.

The editor and publisher wish to thank all authors or their representatives, publishers and publications for special permission to reprint the material credited to them at the foot of the page on which the material appears. An exhaustive effort has been made to locate all persons having any rights or interests in material and to clear reprint permissions. If any required acknowledgments have been omitted or any rights overlooked, it is by accident and forgiveness is requested.

Contents

4. Struggles and Triumphs

5. Peacocks on Parade

6. Old Saloon Days

7. City Fathers, Bosses and Servants

8. Sucker's Paradise

9. "You Walk Around a Corner, and It's a Different World"

10. Sins of New York

11. An Honest Living

12. Playtown and Playboys

13. Eight Million Stories

Illustrations

Front end paper

"Humbug's American Museum," lithograph (drawn by A. Weingaertner?), Nagel & Weingaertner, N. Y., 1851. *The Amos F. Eno Collection of New York City Views, New York Public Library, Prints Division.* (*Upper left*)

Detail from "Central Park, N. Y., Winter Sports," lithograph in color, H. Schile, N. Y., about 1872. *Eno Collection.* (*Lower left*)

"New Amsterdam (Now New-York), as it appeared about the year 1640, while under the Dutch Government, copied from an etching of the same size published by Justus Danckers at Amsterdam." *Collection of Daniel deKoven.* (*Upper center*)

"New-York & Environs," a bird's-eye view, lithograph in color, drawn and published by Bachman, N. Y., 1859. *Eno Collection.* (*Lower center*)

" 'I'm Bound Not to Run wid der Machine Any More,' F. S. Chanfrau in the character of Mose, as originally written for and performed by him at the Olympic and Chatham Theatres, 1848," photo by James Brown. *New York Public Library, Theatre Collection.* (*Upper right*)

Title page of "Jim Fisk, He Never Went Back on the Poor," written and sung by William J. Scanlon, F. W. Helmick, Cincinnati, O., 1874. *New York Public Library, Music Division.* (*Lower right*)

Following page 174

"The Terrors of America and Their Doings," lithographs in color, cigarette cards packed in Duke Cigarettes, Knapp & Co., N. Y., about 1890. Collection of Edward B. Marks, Jr.

Buy Me a Balloon, Mother, from "New York 'Street Arabs,'" *Harper's Weekly*, Sept. 19, 1868. *New York Public Library.*

"The Auctioneer in Public Streets," from a series of water color drawings, "Cries of New York," by Nicolino V. Calyo, 1840–44. *Museum of the City of New York.*

When Brooks Brothers Was Downtown, Catharine Street, 1845, lithograph in color by G. Hayward for D. T. Valentine's *Manual,* 1864. *The Mercaldo Archive.*

Introduction

The people are the heart of a city—great people and little people. We must know them all. . . . We must catch the rhythm, the color, the smells—the feel of it all. In short we must know the high of it and the low of it—and the middle of it.

—Frank Monaghan and Marvin Lowenthal

"Al Smith made the sidewalks of New York popular," said a Sawkill poultry farmer to me, "but we sent them in from here." He was referring to the Ulster County bluestone, quarried by Irish workers toward the middle of the last century, and worn by the feet of immigrants who came here expecting instead to find streets paved with gold.

Like much of its population and its resources, much of the city's folklore has come in from outside. In the broad sense, New York City folklore is all lore found in the city, regardless of origin. But this book is concerned with the lore that is *of* as well as *in* New York, and a clue to what New Yorkers think about and how they came to be that way.

"What people say is history," observed Joe Gould, in explanation of his "Oral History of Our Time." What people say about themselves in their own way and words—folksay—is folklore if said often enough and interestingly enough to be listened to and remembered. And what makes a thing folklore is this tellable, listenable, and repeatable quality, close to mother wit and common experience, heightened by popular fantasy.

The folklore of modern life, especially in the big city, is buried under the complicated overlay of modern industrial society (folklore itself being "extra-technological" and "extra-institutional"), its voice drowned out by louder and more urgent traffic and trade. To get under the collective skin of New Yorkers, to feel their traditional pulse and heartbeat, and to catch the folk "voice of the city" is the aim of this book.

The heart of New York City folklore consists of the anecdotes, sayings, and allusions that have grown up about the city's streets, neighborhoods, centers, landmarks, buildings, characters, occupations, pastimes, festivals, architecture, foods, customs, and beliefs. A cross between what happened and what people imagine or believe to have happened is not always pure folklore any more than it is always true history or true local tradition. Though much of it is indigenous, much of it is the localized versions of migratory tales and traditions, attached and adapted to the time, the place, and the person. Although frequently historical in origin or intent, it is not always historical in effect, since folklore, like history in Lessing's phrase, begins with the fact and ends with the symbol. Some so-called "historical" traditions, like the tall tales of unnatural natural history, are simply myths, hoaxes, and mass delusions, based on erroneous perception or artful deception and spread by rumor. More nearly historical are the "little" or hidden history of anecdotes and jests and the lost chapters in the lives of the great and near-great. More nearly folklore are the urban tales, fantasies and wisecracks of the "grapevine" and cracker barrel.

For my sources I have gone to out-of-the-way, off-beat, off-the-record and off-the-cuff accounts by contemporaries or near-contemporaries, participants or eyewitnesses.

These sources range from journals, diaries and memoirs to newspapers and magazines, including gossip columns, feature stories and letters to the editor; from guidebooks and travel books to individual works and collections dealing with special phases of New York City life; from ephemera and collectanea of all kinds to studies in literature, history, politics and economics. If recovery from print seems to run counter to the common conception of folklore as unwritten tradition, it should be borne in mind that in an age of print, folklore, even when originally oral, sooner or later finds its way into print and does not therefore cease to be folklore. In fact, print may be the only record we have of what is said by or about those who have gone before us.

Within the larger outer circle of all folklore found in New York City are two smaller concentric circles. The middle circle is made up of urban ways of life and looking at life common to American metropolitan communities. The inner and smaller circle is made up of traditions indigenous or peculiar to the city—the stories that New Yorkers like to tell about themselves; their heroes, badmen, tricksters, jesters, boasters, boosters, and knockers; their high life and low life and everything in between; their daydreams and nightmares, their wonders and absurdities, their greatness and meanness, flowering in the New York "personality" of a Jimmy Walker, an Al Smith, a Fiorello La Guardia, and a Jimmy Durante.

In geographical area, New York City is a circle or wheel whose center or hub is Manhattan and whose radii or spokes are the boroughs of the Bronx, Brooklyn, Queens, and Richmond radiating into the metropolitan hinterland.

The heart of this book is the folklore of the inner circle and center—Manhattan, the heart of the city and the "New York" of common usage. While Manhattan itself is a collection of ethnic, linguistic, and occupational groups, mostly centered in neighborhoods, the focus of the book is on the quintessence of New York, on the composite "identity" or "homogeneity" resulting (in O. Henry's phrase) from the "conjunction of so many units into so small a space." If like the island, the book is heavier on the lower and older end, it is because that is where most of the folklore is. As one gets further uptown and into the periphery, including the essentially separate cities of the "bedroom of New York," the lore gets less and less New Yorkish and more and more suburban or extraneous.

A certain number of functional neighborhoods are included (not only in "You Walk Around a Corner, and It's a Different World" but also in "An Honest Living" and "Playtown and Playboys") as samples of "cities within the city" and of the old neighborhood spirit. The latter still survives, as Mary Simkhovitch writes of the Old Ninth Ward (Greenwich Village), wherever a "certain character which animated [the neighborhood's] origin . . . works in and out of the social structure of today, coloring present modes of life." Even when the old neighborhood has changed, as in the case of the Village and Times Square, the legend remains, kept alive by and for the tourist trade—the last refuge of regionalism and local color.

The folk spirit or ethos of the city lies in this very spirit of change, which, from the point of view of the folklorist, is the most distinctive and central aspect of the city's unity-in-diversity (both historical and geographical). Though change would seem to be inimical to the growth and preservation of folklore, it is inherent in the element of invention or fantasy which, supplementing the conservative factor of tradition, is the creative factor in the folklore process. For every form of folk fantasy that dies, a new one is created, as folklore in decay is balanced by folklore in the making. As a place to study the folklore of change, changing, fantastic New York has an obvious advantage over other places in that it is at once a laboratory and a barometer of change and fantasy. In this sense New York may not be America, but it is a microcosm and a heightening of American traits, both as traditional Siren City, drawing to itself people and ideas from everywhere, and as Nerve Center, transmitting impulses to all parts of the country and world.

Change is thus inseparable from New York's two-way flow of national and world influence. It is also a corollary of the pressure of mass living on a crowded island, where people who have "too much of everything" find in change (novelty, diversion) a relief from tension and the rat-race. Change is also an integral part of the growth and decay of the city in its development from village to metropolis, from Little Old New York to New York Not So Little and Not So Old, but never, one hopes, Not So New York.

If like other great cities of the world, New York may be said to have an epic mission or destiny, then that lies in its progressive receptivity to change and its dynamic initiation of change. This is an epic in which all New Yorkers, if only vicariously, can participate, as part of the passing show, the greatest free show on earth, in which the spirit of Barnum mingles with that of Madison Avenue. A sense of this epic dominates and binds together kaleidoscopic daily changes in an overall pattern of historic, long-time change, just as the everyday images and symbols of the city's folklore heritage combine in a myth made up of what the city thinks of itself, what it thinks of the rest of the country and world, and what the rest of the country and world thinks of it.

So the more New York changes, the more it remains itself. Where everything is in a state of flux, change is the most constant and consistent trait and even becomes a tradition. The faster the present slips into the past and future, the faster the legends grow, and the more charged they become with associations and associative power. "No doubt," notes Ford Madox Ford, who, like every visitor, is impressed by the evocative aura and spell of the city, "because one thinks—or at least feels—quite twice as fast in front of the buildings of Fifth Avenue as before the stones of the Avenue de Wagram, Tiffany's, say, will clothe itself with the shimmer of more remembered emotions than will all that Paris avenue and the Avenue Hoche added to it." In fact, adds another visitor, Arnold Bennett, even the "numbers grow into names," and "that curt word, 'Fifth,' signifies as much to the New Yorker as 'Boulevard des Italiens' to the Parisian."

The folklore of New York got off to a good start with the origin tale of the purchase of Manhattan Island from the Indians by Peter Minuit for trinkets worth sixty guilder or twenty-four dollars—a bargain with as many implications for New Yorkers who are always trying to get something for nothing as for New York folklore, which is rich in tricks and treats. According to a legend as old as Queen Dido, the Dutch agreed to take as much land as could be contained by a bull's hide and then proceeded to shave the hide into a razor-thin thong that enclosed several score acres. According to a doubtful folk etymology, "Manhattan" is derived from a Spanish colloquial word for "drunk," which got into the Manhattan Indians' vocabulary by way of their first taste of Henry Hudson's liquor at the place of the "Big Drunk."

Perhaps because they live in a state of constant emotional intoxication, New Yorkers have become excessively attached to (if not inordinately proud) of their fabulous Twenty-Four-Dollar Island, where one can still make a good buy and a fast buck, in spite of the cynicism of the second-hand clothing-store proprietor encountered by Hyde Partnow, a writer on *PM,* back in 1921. On the corner of Bayard and Elizabeth Streets, where the "big rivers of Manhattan profits . . . give out into several small tributaries that end in a few trickles," Bill greeted him with a New Yorkese pitch:

"Here. Today's special. A la chic de Paree. A two-piece, no vest, but like a rock. A pair of pants like an ox. Fresh. No charge for looking. Yes, indeedy. Cheap, cheap, cheap. Come on, don't waste your time. It's a Saks-Fifth Avenue. Take it. Quick come, quick go. It's new, new, newy. Slip off your coat and try it on."

Then Bill confided:

"Customers are looking for good buys today. But the Dutchmen got the last bargain when they bought Manhattan for twenty-four bucks."

The second-hand clothes dealer to the contrary notwithstanding, Twenty-Four-Dollar Island was the *biggest,* not the *last* bargain; and folklore—from the Dutch to the Dutch Treat Club—is still a good buy and one of the best gimmicks in the "Wonder City."

Thanks are due to the following libraries for their many services and courtesies: American Jewish Committee, Columbia University Libraries, Croton Free Library, the Field Library of Peekskill, the General Society of Mechanics and Tradesmen of the City of New York, Library of Congress, New York Historical Society, New York Public Library, Ossining Public Library, Westchester County Historical Society, and White Plains Public Library.

In addition to the foregoing, the following have been of invaluable help in my picture research: Daniel deKoven, Herbert E. Marks and Edward B. Marks, Jr., the Mercaldo Archive, the Museum of the City of New York, Seidman Photo Service, the public relations department of the Standard Oil Co. (New Jersey), Wide World Photos, Inc.

I am especially grateful to the following friends and colleagues for advice, assistance, encouragement, and criticism: Therese Benston, Meyer Berger, Daniel deKoven, Evan Esar, Nathan Frankel, Harry Henderson, Moritz Jagendorf, Bella Landauer, Vincent Mercaldo, Mamie J. Meredith, George Milburn, Gilbert Millstein, Pageant Book Company, Gunther E. Pohl, Gene Rose, Ruth Rubin, Tony Schwartz, Leo W. Schwarz, Jay Scott, Phil Sterling, Sylvester L. Vigilante, Carl Withers, and others too numerous to mention.

To my editors, Hiram Haydn and Bertha Krantz, and the rest of the Random House staff, and to my wife and partner, Gertrude Botkin, who made this book possible, I am greatly indebted.

B. A. B.

1

Stranger's Guide

New York is not America, but it is plain to all beholders that all America would like to be New York.—Paul Morand

"A Nice Place to Visit—" [1]

"Where are you going, Sam?"

"Going to the city to get drunk, and God how I dread it."

George Walters went to New York for a few days and when he got back to the country a neighbor asked him how he liked the big city.

"To tell you the truth," said George, "there was so much going on in the depot, I never did get up to the village."

It has frequently been observed that New York hasn't got what you call a climate—just samples of weather.

Grant's tomb is the only perfect architectural structure in the world—you couldn't alter one detail without improving it.

Fifth Avenue is a street where a lot of people spend money they haven't earned buying things they don't need to impress people they don't like.

"If you don't like the Empire State building, why have you got your offices in it?"

"It's the only way I can avoid seeing the damn thing."

[1] From *New York and the State It's In,* Stories and pictures arranged by Keith Jennison, pp. 6–22, 30–34, 40–42, 60–62, 80–82. Copyright, 1949, by Keith Jennison. New York: William Sloane Associates, Inc.

"Here's where we change to the express; we save five minutes."

"What are you going to do with them?"

According to some people, the reason a subway had to be built to Brooklyn was so the people who lived there could get home without being seen.

Seeing New York[2]

. . . Three gentlemen from South America . . . called one day on Mayor O'Dwyer. The Mayor was born and raised in Ireland—and has the Irish gift of easy conversation, and he studied in Spain and speaks Spanish beautifully. So he made pleasant conversation with the gentlemen from South America.

And how long, he asked, did they intend to stay in New York?

"A week," said the man from Bogotá.

"Fine!" said the Mayor. "New York is a wonderful city, and undoubtedly you will manage to see all of it."

The traveler from Carácas said that he meant to stay for a month.

"Good," said the Mayor. "I am sure that you will see most of the things you should."

Then the man from Buenos Aires declared that he had fallen in love with New York, and intended to live here forever.

"Ah, then," said the Mayor, "I am afraid that you never will see New York at all!"

Talk New York[3]

It is futile to quibble with academicians who deny that New Yorkers speak English, since herewith is presented sufficient evidence to prove

[2] From *New York Holiday,* by Eleanor Early, p. 340. Copyright, 1950, by Eleanor Early. New York and Toronto: Rinehart & Co., Inc.

[3] By C. D. Harvey and James Reed. From *Almanac for New Yorkers 1938,* Accommodated to the Five Boroughs but May without Sensible Error Serve for the Entire Metropolitan District and Even More Distant Points, Compiled by the Workers of the Federal Writers' Project of the Works Progress Administration in the City of New York, pp. 114–115. Copyright, 1937, by the Guilds' Committee for Federal Writers' Publications, Inc., Franklin P. Adams, Bruce Bliven, Morris Ernst, Lewis Gannett, Travis Hoke, Margaret Marshall. New York: Modern Age Books, Inc.

that New Yorkese, however the savants may classify it, is at least as fruity and full-flavored as ever proper English could be.

Assawayigoze: Philosophical interjection for conversation lulls.
Braykidup, braykidup: Policeman's suggestion to any group of loiterers.
Domebeeztoopid: Expressing specific disagreement, with undertone of disparagement.
Domeblokadoor: An usher, or guard, in full cry.
Donkar-goyndon: One third of the vocabulary necessary to operate an elevator.
Duhshuh-ul: An underground railway connecting Times Square and Grand Central Terminal.
Filladuppigen: To a sympathetic bartender. Eventually elicits the response: *Yoovadanuffbud* from the same sympathetic bartender.
Hootoadjuh? "Please give the source of your information."
Ladderide: Warning not to pursue the subject further.
Nyesplayshagottere: On first looking into a friend's apartment. See *Welyecut.*
Ollowayback-fayzagate: Another third of the vocabulary necessary to operate an elevator.
Onnafyah: "A short order is being prepared."
Oppkar-goynop: The remaining third of the vocabulary necessary to operate an elevator.
Plennyaseatsnabalkny: Optimism outside a motion picture theater; not entirely trustworthy.
Saddy: Last day of the week.
Scramltoowisydafrench: A short-order is given.
Sowaddyasaybabe or *Hozzabotutbabe?* Prelude to romance.
Statnylant: The place on the horizon where good ferries go.
Steptiddyrearidybuspleez: Bus driver's request whenever two or three passengers are gathered together.
Sumpmscroowie: A note of suspicion.
Takadiway: "Please remove it from sight immediately."
Tsagayg: Sophisticated expression of polite incredulity.
Waddadajintzoodisaft: "Did the New York National League baseball team win today, I hope!" (Except in Brooklyn.)
Wahgoozidoo? Cynical dejection.
Wannamayksumpnuvvit? Invitation to a brawl.
Wattitcha? To a gentleman with facial contusions or (colloquial) a shiner.
Wazzitooyuh? Delicate rebuff to an excessively curious questioner.

Welyecut: Antiphonal response for host and hostess (to guest's comment, *Nyesplayshagottere*).

Whuzzup? Request for information, any information.

Whyntchalookeryagoyn? Rhetorical expression of relief used (by motorists especially) after a near-collision.

What Brooklyn Laughs At [4]

No matter how much Brooklynites are ribbed and kidded, they always come up laughing. Their sense of humor is out of this world.

They laughed with delight when Eddie Foy remarked, in discussing the engineering feat of the Brooklyn Bridge: "All that trouble, just to get to Brooklyn?" When a doctor was examining a soldier in a recent picture and asked him, "Where were you born?" and the kid answered "Brooklyn," they screamed as the doctor asked, "Any other defects?"

They loved the story of Peter Minuit, who bought Manhattan from the Indians for $24. As Earl Wilson tells it, Minuit had closed the deal and was standing on the banks of the East River, staring across. "Say, wait a minute," he said, "isn't that Brooklyn over there?" "For $24," said the Indian chief, a lower East Side boy, "are you expecting the place to be perfect?"

Brooklynites kid about their own community, too. One soldier from the Flatbush section of Brooklyn was in London seeing the sights after a heavy battle, when an Englishman, who was making the rounds with him, asked, "How do you find our English women?" His answer was straight to the point: "The same as in Flatbush, by whistling."

* * * * *

The people from "over the river" have a language all their own. When the great pitcher, Waite Hoyt, now a Cincinnati radio announcer, got hurt in Brooklyn, papers headlined the story, "Hoyt hurt." Brooklynites reading the headlines excitedly pronounced it in their native tongue just the reverse, "Hurt Hoyt."

[4] From *From Gags to Riches,* by Joey Adams, pp. 58–60. Copyright, 1946, by Joey Adams. New York: Frederick Fell, Inc.

"Everything Outside of Broadway Is Bridgeport" [5]

The official sensibilities of the Chamber of Commerce of Bridgeport, Conn., an industrial city of 159,352 [in 1951] persons on Long Island Sound, were inflamed not long ago by three lines in paragraph four of a determinedly light-minded article in *The New York Times Magazine.* "What frightens a Broadway man," it was reported, "is Bridgeport; everything outside of Broadway is Bridgeport." This is a *vieux canard,* or old duck, of show business, and is a sign of what sociologists call a marked cultural lag, since all that most Broadway people know about Bridgeport is what they can see from a train on the way to New Haven for an out-of-town opening. It also compares favorably with a yellowed libel on Philadelphia: "I spent two weeks in Philadelphia last Sunday." It is impossible, a number of knowledgeable people have said, to spend more than a week in Philadelphia even on Saturday.

The remark about Bridgeport was made by Arthur (Bugs) Baer, the columnist, who admitted it. As it happens, Baer is a native of Philadelphia but has nothing against that city. "That crack about Bridgeport," he said the other day, "has been credited to so many people, I wouldn't know how to start taking it back. And besides, it's lost its meaning. These days, Broadway is Bridgeport, what with the five-and-tens, the shooting galleries and the orange-juice stands. There aren't any more Bridgeports—not even in Bridgeport." Baer said it was his recollection that he had conferred immortality of a sort on Bridgeport in 1915, somewhere in the neighborhood of the Friars Club and the late George M. Cohan. What he said was: "When you're not on Broadway, everything is Bridgeport." Some years later, after a visit to the West Coast, he added a footnote: "Hollywood is just Bridgeport with palms."

The columnist was under the impression that his contribution was a modest switch on something Cohan had said, to the effect that when he wasn't in New York he felt he was camping out. This turned out not to be the case. To begin with, Cohan was fond of Bridgeport and once said so, while passing through to Boston, in the presence of an old

[5] From "And Now Bridgeport Looks at Broadway. 'It's a Fine Place to Visit,' the City Thinks, 'but One Really Wouldn't Want to Live There,'" by Gilbert Millstein, *The New York Times Magazine,* February 18, 1951, pp. 21, 48. Copyright, 1951, by The New York Times Company.

friend, John B. Kennedy, the newscaster, who added that the only place Cohan liked better than Broadway was Killarney. In the second place, the line about camping out comes from a song entitled "Good-Bye Sweet Old Manhattan Isle," which was written in 1905 by Billy Jerome and Jean Schwartz for a McIntyre and Heath musical called *The Ham Tree*. The last two lines of the chorus read: "For when you leave old New York town, You're only camping out." *This* was discovered by John F. Royal, a vice president of the National Broadcasting Company and another old friend of Cohan's.

Asked why he had picked on Bridgeport rather than Hartford, Danbury or Stamford (where he has a farm), Baer rummaged around in the depths of his subconscious and came up with this explanation: Between the ages of fourteen and twenty he had worked in a carpet mill in the Kensington section of Philadelphia, designing carpets and lace curtains. "It wasn't hard work," he said, "just work." The experience was a traumatic one and gave him nightmares. After he got into the newspaper business, he acquired a sideline doctoring up flop shows. "I did a dozen," he remarked. "Didn't save one." Among the cities in which these turkeys were tried out was Bridgeport. It occurred to Baer that there were more factories there than anywhere else and that the smokestacks seemed to be closer together. "For me," he went on, "Bridgeport, more than any other place in the country, symbolized work, and for a writer it's disheartening to see anyone working." Baer concluded forthrightly by offering to go to Bridgeport and address any Chamber of Commerce.

Thirty-six years of Bridgeport gags cause no more than flickering annoyance in the city, which looks upon itself as "The Arsenal of Democracy," "The Industrial Capital of Connecticut," or "The Park City," and the home of 250 known members of Phi Beta Kappa. Mayor Jasper McLevy, who is a Socialist and has a certain show business tradition behind him (as a boy, he was booted out of the winter quarters of the circus, which were then in Bridgeport, by ex-Mayor P. T. Barnum himself), said recently, with the air of a man who has been through it before:

"Broadway is America. It's a great place. Why should we feel any resentment against it? But, remember, we're the ones who make Broadway Broadway and put the life into it. I don't know that there's ever been a bigger hick town in the world than New York, right from the Mayor down—he's from Connecticut; he's an Ansonia boy. Evidently the majority of the voters weren't afraid of boys from hick towns." . . . He wished Broadway "all the success in the world."

What's Up? [6]

. . . Let one person stop and look attentively, all will stop to look. Having heard of this foible, I tried it out one day by standing on the curb on Broadway and looking fixedly at the cornice of a tall building opposite. Several people lined up following the direction of my eyes. One said: "What is it?" I answered: "I don't know," and walked on. Five minutes later when I came back, there was still a knot of people standing on the curb staring at the cornice. As fast as one drifted away another came up and stopped. "What is it?" they asked, and the answer always was: "I don't know." Any excuse will serve to start the kids charging down the street crying delightedly: "Somepin t'matteh! Somepin t'matteh!" A couple who lived in Stamford had a local girl for maid-of-all-work who had never been to New York. When her day off came around they persuaded her to spend it in town. She returned looking exhausted. "Well, Annie," said her mistress, "what did you see?" "Oh, ma'am, all the people start to run down the street and I run too." "What was it, a fire?" "No, ma'am. A lady got a fish-bone stuck in her throat!"

Live and Let Live [7]

I remember a fellow, a quiet young man with a quiet young wife, who gave up a good job in some Middle Western town and moved to New York. He had saved a handful of money for the venture and he had added to it by selling the furniture in his small rented bungalow in a respectable suburb. Coming to the city, he hunted desperately to find work and indeed found it after a few weeks. It paid him about the same salary he had earned at home. Now he was a New Yorker.

He lived in lower Manhattan, in an old dingy house that had been

[6] From *New York, City of Cities,* by Hulbert Footner, pp. 12–13. Copyright, 1937, by Hulbert Footner. Philadelphia, New York, and London: J. B. Lippincott Company.

[7] From *This Country of Yours,* by Morris Markey, pp. 294–296. Copyright, 1932, by Morris Markey. Boston: Little, Brown and Company.

converted into makeshift apartments. He lived on the top floor, a long walk up creaking stairs, past gloomy walls and the gloomy faces of his neighbors who stamped in and out, all night and all day. His front windows looked into the front windows of an Italian laborer, twenty feet across the street. His back windows looked into a forbidding courtyard that was alive at night with screaming cats. His wife had bought odds and ends of furniture on the installment plan, but they did not have to live with it very much, for they rarely spent an evening in their home. The air was too full of the bedlam of radio music and shouting children and thunderous motor trucks. They generally went to a moving-picture theater and saw the identical film that was showing in their neighborhood playhouse back home.

For this residence, he paid nearly a third of his income. It was utterly uncomfortable, sordid, and in any place other than New York it would have made a revolutionist of him. But he was happy and his wife was happy. "Oh," they said to me, "we're crazy about New York. Dreamed all our lives of coming here to settle. Wouldn't go back for a million."

I asked them why, but they had great difficulty in answering. I said, "Is it business? Do you think there is a better chance of becoming rich here?"

"No," they said. His chances were no better with the New York firm than with the Middle Western firm.

"Is it amusement you come for? Theaters and music and art galleries—things like that?"

Not exactly. They could not afford the theater, anyway.

"To be near celebrated people, then? To be in the shadow of the big shots—in the town where the big news is made and the mighty events happen?"

Oh, no. Hardly that.

"Well, in Heaven's name, what?"

Freedom, they said. But freedom from what bonds and freedom to gain what ends they could not say at once. What freedom was vouchsafed them in a sordid New York walk-up that was denied them in a neat white bungalow, they were quite unable to define for a long while. But gradually it became a little clear. They came to New York and put up with its miseries to escape something, rather than to attain something: to escape the kindly, well-meant bondage of parents and uncles and aunts; to escape, above all, the grubby little certainties of existence—the certainty that Monday would be wash day and Tuesday ironing day, that the Lodge would meet on Friday night and the Ladies' Auxiliary on Saturday afternoon, that the gentle old preacher would lay down for them on Sunday morning a mild and amiable pattern for existence, the certainty that the young fellow would be promoted when the man above him died. These things, these small securities, had palled upon their youth and their hunger for living. And so they had come to New York, as if New York were a sea of adventure, not a goal to be attained.

2

Twenty-Four-Dollar Island

"I'm the ninth generation," [*A. Van Horne Stuyvesant, millionaire recluse,*] *said. "The direct descent dies with me. Mine will be the last interment in this vault* [*in the old Stuyvesant family church, St. Mark's in-the-Bouwerie*]. *After that it will be sealed forever. How many are buried in our vault? Nobody knows. Some say eighty-three."—Helen Worden Erskine*

What the Indians Thought of the Dutch [1]

"Why do you stand saying so many words that no one but you may speak?" listening Indians asked a Dutch pastor.

"I have crossed the ocean," he replied, "to tell these white men about God, and that they must not swear, nor steal, nor be drunk, nor commit adultery, and, when I know your language better, I will come and preach to you."

[1] From *New York's Making Seen Through the Eyes of My Ancestors,* by Mary de Peyster Rutgers McCrea Conger (Vanamee), p. 15. London: Methuen & Co., Ltd. 1938.

It was David de Vries and Adriaen van der Donck and others living in New York . . . who studied Indian political organization and ideas of psychology and religion, and noted the Indians' clear-sighted criticism of white men.—M. de P. R. McC. C.

The Indians stood silent, then replied, "You do well to tell the white men, but why do so many of your people do these things?"

"We know," they added, "that there cannot be one God. If your God were our God we too must have known how to build ships."

When a Dutch trader found himself a hundred miles from his base in a "long house" with thirty armed chiefs, he wondered when they would talk of trade; for they talked and talked beside the mark. Presently an old chief laid his hand on the white man's heart and found it beating quietly.

"He is not afraid," the chief cried aloud. "Now we can speak of beaver skins. It is useless to make agreements with cowards."

Indian Account of Henry Hudson's Visit to Manhattan Island [2]

The Lenni Lenape claim the honor of having received and welcomed the Europeans on their first arrival in the country situated between New England and Virginia. It is probable, however, that the Mahicanni or Mohicans, who then inhabited the banks of the Hudson, concurred in the hospitable act. The relation I am going to make was taken down many years since from the mouth of an intelligent Delaware Indian and may be considered as a correct account of the tradition existing among them of this momentous event. I give it as much as possible in their own language.

A great many years ago, when men with a white skin had never yet been seen in this land, some Indians who were out a-fishing, at a place where the sea widens, espied at a great distance something remarkably large floating on the water, and such as they had never seen before. These Indians, immediately returning to the shore, ap-

[2] From *History, Manners, and Customs of the Indian Nations Who Once Inhabited Pennsylvania and the Neighbouring States,* by the Rev. John Heckewelder, of Bethlehem, Pa., New and Revised Edition, with an Introduction and Notes by the Rev. William C. Reichel, of Bethlehem, Pa., pp. 71–75. Memoirs of the Historical Society of Pennsylvania, Vol. XII. Entered . . . 1876, by the Historical Society of Pennsylvania. Philadelphia.

prised their countrymen of what they had observed, and pressed them to go out with them and discover what it might be. They hurried out together, and saw with astonishment the phenomenon which now appeared to their sight, but could not agree upon what it was; some believed it to be an uncommonly large fish or animal; while others were of opinion it must be a very big house floating on the sea. At length the spectators concluded that this wonderful object was moving towards the land and that it must be an animal or something else that had life in it; it would therefore be proper to inform all the Indians on the inhabited islands of what they had seen and put them on their guard. Accordingly they sent off a number of runners and watermen to carry the news to their scattered chiefs, that they might send off in every direction for the warriors, with a message that they should come on immediately. These arriving in numbers and having themselves viewed the strange appearance, and observing that it was actually moving towards the entrance of the river or bay, concluded it to be a remarkably large house in which the Mannitto (the Great or Supreme Being) himself was present, and that he probably was coming to visit them.[3]

By this time the chiefs were assembled at York Island, and deliberating in what manner in which they should receive their Mannitto on his arrival. Every measure was taken to be well provided with plenty of meat for a sacrifice. The women were desired to prepare the best victuals. All the idols or images were examined and put in order, and a grand dance was supposed not only to be an agreeable entertainment for the Great Being, but it was believed that it might, with the addition of a sacrifice, contribute to appease him if he was angry with them. The conjurers were also set to work, to determine what this phenomenon portended, and what the possible result of it might be. To these and to the chiefs and wise men of the nations, men, women, and children were looking up for advice and protection. Distracted between hope and fear, they were at a loss what to do; a dance, however, commenced in great confusion. While in this situation, fresh runners arrive declaring it to be a large house of various colours, and crowded with living creatures. It appears now to be certain that it is the great Mannitto, bringing them some kind of game, such as

[3] Henry Hudson, a British navigator and discoverer in the employ of the Dutch East India Company, sailed from Amsterdam in command of the *Half Moon,* in April of 1609, in search of a north-eastern passage. Foiled by the ice in the higher latitudes, he turned southwards, and in September anchored in New York bay.—W. C. R.

he had not given them before, but other runners soon after arriving declare that it is positively a house full of human beings, of quite a different colour from that of the Indians, and dressed differently from them; that in particular one of them was dressed entirely in red, who must be the Mannitto himself. They are hailed from the vessel in a language they do not understand, yet they shout or yell in return by way of answer, according to the custom of their country; many are for running off to the woods, but are pressed by others to stay, in order not to give offence to their visitor, who might find them out and destroy them. The house, some say, large canoe, at last stops, and a canoe of a smaller size comes on shore with the red man and some others in it; some stay with his canoe to guard it. The chiefs and wise men, assembled in council, form themselves into a large circle, towards which the man in red clothes approaches with two others. He salutes them with a friendly countenance, and they return the salute after their manner. They are lost in admiration; the dress, the manners, the whole appearance of the unknown strangers is to them a subject of wonder; but they are particularly struck with him who wore the red coat all glittering with gold lace, which they could in no manner account for. He, surely, must be the great Mannitto, but why should he have a white skin?

Meanwhile, a large Hackhack [4] is brought by one of his servants, from which an unknown substance is poured out into a small cup or glass, and handed to the supposed Mannitto. He drinks—has the glass filled again, and hands it to the chief standing next to him. The chief receives it, but only smells the contents and passes it on to the next chief, who does the same. The glass or cup thus passes through the circle, without the liquor being tasted by any one, and is upon the point of being returned to the red-clothed Mannitto, when one of the Indians, a brave man and a great warrior, suddenly jumps up and harangues the assembly on the impropriety of returning the cup with its contents. It was handed to them, says he, by the Mannitto, that they should drink out of it, as he himself had done. To follow his example would be pleasing to him; but to return what he had given them might provoke his wrath, and bring destruction on them. And since the orator believed it for the good of the nation that the contents offered them should be drunk, and as no one else would do it, he would drink it himself, let the consequence be what it might; it was better for one man to die than that a whole nation should be destroyed. He then took the glass, and bidding the assembly a solemn farewell, at once drank up its whole

[4] Hackhack is properly a gourd; but since they have seen glass bottles and decanters, they call them by the same name.—W. C. R.

contents. Every eye fixed on the resolute chief, to see what effect the unknown liquor would produce. He soon began to stagger and at last fell prostrate on the ground. His companions now bemoan his fate, he falls into a sound sleep, and they think he has expired. He wakes again, jumps up and declares that he has enjoyed the most delicious sensations, and that he never before felt himself so happy as after he had drunk the cup. He asks for more, his wish is granted; the whole assembly then imitate him, and all became intoxicated.

After this general intoxication had ceased, for they say that while it lasted the whites had confined themselves to their vessel, the man with the red clothes returned again, and distributed presents among them, consisting of beads, axes, hoes, and stockings such as the white people wear. They soon become familiar with each other, and began to converse by signs. The Dutch made them understand that they would not stay here, that they would return home again but would pay them another visit the next year, when they would bring them more presents, and stay with them awhile; but as they could not live without eating, they should want a little land of them to sow seeds, in order to raise herbs and vegetables to put into their broth. They went away as they had said, and returned in the following season, when both parties were much rejoiced to see each other; but the whites laughed at the Indians, seeing that they knew not the use of the axes and hoes they had given them the year before; for they had these hanging to their breasts as ornaments, and the stockings were made use of as tobacco pouches. The whites now put handles to the former for them, and cut trees down before their eyes, hoed up the ground, and put the stockings on their legs. Here, they say, a general laughter ensued among the Indians, that they had remained ignorant of the use of such valuable implements, and had borne the weight of such heavy metal hanging to their necks for such a length of time. They took every white man they saw for an inferior Mannitto, attendant upon the supreme Deity who shone superior in the red and laced clothes. As the whites became daily more familiar with the Indians, they at last proposed to stay with them, and asked only for so much ground for a garden spot as, they said, the hide of a bullock would cover or encompass, which hide was spread before them. The Indians readily granted this apparently reasonable request; but the whites then took a knife, and beginning at one end of the hide, cut it up to a long rope, not thicker than a child's finger, so that by the time the whole was cut up, it made a great heap; they then took the rope at one end, and drew it gently along, carefully avoiding its breaking. It was drawn out into a circular form, and being closed at its ends, encompassed a large piece of ground. The Indians were surprised at the superior wit of the whites,[5] but did not wish to contend with them about a little land, as they had still enough themselves. The white and red men lived contentedly together for a long time, though the former from time to time asked for more land, which was readily obtained, and thus they gradually proceeded higher up the Mahicannittuck, until the Indians began to believe that they would soon want all their country, which in the end proved true.

The Name "Manhattan"[6]

The name Manhattan, spelled in almost half a hundred ways in Dutch, French, and English writings of colonial times, has been very variously interpreted. "People of the Whirlpool" [Hell Gate] and "Place of In-

[5] These Dutchmen were probably acquainted with what is related of Queen Dido in ancient history, and thus turned their classical knowledge to a good account.—W. C. R.

Cf. Irving's version of the bullock hide legend:

. . . Here let me give the true story of the original purchase of the site of this renowned city, about which so much has been said and written. Some affirm that the first cost was but sixty guilders. The learned Dominie Heckewelder records a tradition that the Dutch discoverers bargained for only so much land as the hide of a bullock would cover; but that they cut the hide in strips no thicker than a child's finger, so as to take in a large portion of land, and to take in the Indians into the bargain. This, however, is an old fable which the worthy Dominie may have borrowed from antiquity. The true version is that Oloffe Van Kortlandt bargained for just so much land as a man could cover with his nether garments. The terms being concluded, he produced his friend Mynheer Ten Broeck as the man whose breeches were to be used in measurement. The simple savages, whose ideas of a man's nether garments had never expanded beyond the dimensions of a breech-clout, stared with astonishment and dismay as they beheld this bulbous-bottomed burgher peeled like an onion, and breeches after breeches spread forth over the land until they covered the actual site of this venerable city.

This is the true history of the adroit bargain by which the island of Manhattan was bought for sixty guilders; and in corroboration of it I will add that Mynheer Ten Breeches, for his services on this memorable occasion, was elevated to the office of land-measurer; which he ever afterwards exercised in the colony.—Washington Irving, *A History of New York* (New York, 1850), pp. 121–122.

[6] From *History of the City of New York in the Seventeenth Century,* by Mrs. Schuyler Van Rensselaer, Vol. I, pp. 55–56. Copyright, 1909, by The Macmillan Co. New York.

toxication" are fanciful and foolish readings based upon perversions of linguistic analogies and disproved by the testimony of the earliest maps and descriptions. The soundest belief seems to be that Manhattan was derived from a mutable Algonquin term, meaning "island," which was by no means limited in its application to the one island that perpetuates it. Possibly, in the form that survives, it meant "Island of the Hills." By the white men the name was sometimes applied in early days to the aborigines of the neighborhood, but Juet, the very first who set it down in writing, gives it a geographical meaning, saying "on that side of the river that is called Manna-hata." Which side he meant, whether the island itself or the opposite western bank, the context does not make clear. On the earliest English map, the one called the Velasco or Simancas Map, the river bears no name, but "Manahata" is written along its western and "Manahatin" along its eastern shore. The paper Figurative Map, which does not show the island, puts "Manhattes" on the mainland to the northeast of the harbor while the parchment map sets "Manhates" on the island itself. De Laet wrote that the river was called by some "the Manhattes River from the people who dwell near its mouth"; and Wassenaer called the island "the Manhates" and "the Manhattes" and explained that it was occupied by "a nation called the Manhates."

The Dutch commonly used the name in a plural form and gradually extended its significance. Augustine Herrman, whom Governor Stuyvesant sent on an embassay to Maryland in 1659, then explained:

> They commit a grave mistake who will confine the general name of Manhattans . . . to the particular city, which is only built on a little island; . . . it signifies the whole country and province, or at least the same particular place in the province: as, for example, it is frequent with many still at this day, to say—To go to the Manhattans, or, To come from the Manhattans—when they mean the whole province, as they do by the name of Virginia or Maryland, for the particular town itself is never named the Manhattans, but New Amsterdam.

This broader significance died out when the English secured the province. In documents of the English colonial period Island of Manhattan and Manhattan Island serve as interchangeable terms with the meaning they bear today. . . .

The Price of Manhattan[7]

At some time during the summer of 1626 Minuit bought from the Indians the island of Manhattan. This is told in a letter written from Amsterdam to the States General at the Hague by the delegate who represented them in the Assembly of the XIX. It is the oldest known manuscript that relates to the local history of Manhattan, and the oldest manifest of a trading vessel cleared from the port. . . .

HIGH AND MIGHTY LORDS,

Here arrived yesterday the ship Arms of Amsterdam which on the 23rd September sailed from New Netherland out of the Mauritius River. They report that our people there are of good cheer and live peaceably. Their wives have also borne children there. They have bought the island Manhattes from the savages for the value of sixty guilders. It is 11,000 *morgens* in extent. They had all their grain sown by the middle of May and harvested by the middle of August. They send small samples of summer grain, such as wheat, rye, barley, oats, buckwheat, canary seed, beans, and flax.

The cargo of the aforesaid ship is:

7246 beaver skins,
178 half otter skins,
675 otter skins,
48 mink skins,
36 wildcat skins,
33 minks,
34 rat skins,
Much oak timber and nut-wood.

[7] *Ibid.*, pp. 72–73.

It has sometimes been said that Minuit cheated the savages, buying as they thought only a plot for a garden and then claiming the whole of the island. Schaghen's letter disproves this, and so does the record of the prices willingly accepted by the Indians elsewhere in New Netherland for great stretches of their soil. Even though money at that period was much more valuable than it is to-day, sixty guilders (about $24) may seem a small price for an island almost twenty-two square miles in extent—thirteen miles and a half in length and two and a half in width at the broadest part. But it would have been an absurd price for a garden plot. Land, it should be remembered, was the Indians' one plentiful possession. Moreover, they were not dispossessed of their island but were only pledged, like tenants-at-will, to yield from time to time such portions of it as the white men might need—if, indeed, many of them used Manhattan as an actual abiding-place. Here and there on the island sites of Indian villages have been somewhat doubtfully identified; for the most part it seems to have been uninhabited although constantly frequented by the savages who lived on the neighboring shores. Of course Minuit gave, instead of useless money, articles that had an immense value in the Indians' eyes.—Mrs. S. Van R., *ibid.*, pp. 73–74.

Herewith

High and Mighty Lords, be commended to the grace of Almighty God.

At Amsterdam, the 5th of November, Anno 1626.

Your High Mightinesses' Obedient

P. Schaghen

"Spouting Devil" or "In Spite of the Devil"

I[8]

The Indian name of the stream connecting the East and the North Rivers was Muscoota; but from the very earliest days the part of the Harlem River nearest the Hudson was called Spuyten Duyvil creek, though how it received that name is still a question. Many reasons have been given, but none that is entirely satisfactory. The most likely is that the name was given from the spring of water which "spouted" from the hill near the end of the island; and mention is made of this spring in several of the early English grants. Another, offered by Riker, is that the Indians of this neighborhood, remembering their first encounter with the *Half-Moon* off the mouth of the creek and the firing of the falcon that killed several of them, called the creek "Spouting Devil"; but this explanation would presume on their part a knowledge of English which they could not have possessed until sixty years afterward. Before the construction of the ship canal, the tides used to race through the creek with great rapidity, and when the two tides from the Harlem and Hudson Rivers met, the tide rips thus formed caused a great turbulence in the creek, so that the water "spouted" or was thrown into the air, a fact that will be remembered by those acquainted with the creek in those days. Upon ancient maps and records we find many variants of the name; as "Spitting devil," "Spiking devil," "Spitten devil," "Spouting devil," "Spiken devil"—but many of these we may lay to bad spelling, as colonial orthography was no better than that of the present-day schoolboy. It is to Irving that we must go for a picturesque origin of the name.

[8] From *The Greatest Street in the World,* The Story of Broadway, Old and New, from the Bowling Green to Albany, by Stephen Jenkins, pp. 335–336. Copyright, 1911, by Stephen Jenkins. New York and London: G. P. Putnam's Sons, The Knickerbocker Press.

II [9]

Resolutely bent . . . upon defending his beloved city [of New Amsterdam against the English], in despite even of itself, [Peter Stuyvesant called unto him his trusty Van Corlear, who was his right-hand man in all times of emergency. Him did he adjure to take his war-denouncing trumpet, and mounting his horse, to beat up the country night and day —sounding the alarm along the pastoral borders of the Bronx—startling the wild solitudes of Croton—arousing the rugged yeomanry of Weehawk and Hoboken—the mighty men of battle of Tappan Bay—and the brave boys of Tarry-Town, Petticoat-Lane, and Sleepy-Hollow —charging them one and all to sling their powder-horns, shoulder their fowling-pieces, and march merrily down to the Manhattoes.

Now there was nothing in all the world, the divine sex excepted, that Antony Van Corlear loved better than errands of this kind. So just stopping to take a lusty dinner, and bracing to his side his junk-bottle, well charged with heart-inspiring Hollands, he issued jollily from the city gate, which looked out upon what is at present called Broadway, sounding a farewell strain that rung in sprightly echoes through the winding streets of New Amsterdam. Alas! Never more were they to be gladdened by the melody of their favorite trumpeter!

It was a dark and stormy night when the good Antony arrived at the creek (sagely denominated Haer-lem *river*) which separates the island of Manna-hata from the mainland. The wind was high, the elements were in an uproar, and no Charon could be found to ferry the adventurous sounder of brass across the water. For a short time he vapored like an impatient ghost upon the brink, and then bethinking himself of the urgency of his errand, took a hearty embrace of his stone bottle, swore most valorously that he would swim across in spite of the devil (Spyt den Duyvel!) and daringly plunged into the stream. Luckless Antony! Scarce had he buffeted halfway over when he was observed to struggle violently, as if battling with the spirit of the waters—instinctively he put his trumpet to his mouth, and giving a vehement blast—sank forever to the bottom!

[9] From *A History of New-York,* from the Beginning of the World to the End of the Dutch Dynasty, Containing, among Many Surprising and Curious Matters, the Unutterable Ponderings of Walter the Doubter, the Disastrous Projects of William the Testy, and the Chivalric Achievements of Peter the Headstrong—the Three Dutch Governors of New Amsterdam: Being the Only Authentic History of the Times that Ever Hath Been or Ever Will Be Published, by Diedrich Knickerbocker, pp. 429–431. Entered . . . 1848, by Washington Irving. New-York: George P. Putnam. 1850.

The clangor of his trumpet, like that of the ivory horn of the renowned Paladin Orlando, when expiring in the glorious field of Roncesvalles, rang far and wide through the country, alarming the neighbors round, who hurried in amazement to the spot. Here an old Dutch burgher, famed for his veracity, and who had been a witness of the fact, related to them the melancholy affair; with the fearful addition (to which I am slow in giving belief) that he saw the duyvel, in the shape of a huge moss-bonker, seize the sturdy Antony by the leg and drag him beneath the waves. Certain it is, the place, with the adjoining promontory, which projects into the Hudson, has been called *Spyt den Duyvel* ever since; the ghost of the unfortunate Antony still haunts the surrounding solitudes, and his trumpet has often been heard by the neighbors, of a stormy night, mingling with the howling of the blast. Nobody ever attempts to swim across the creek after dark; on the contrary, a bridge has been built to guard against such melancholy accidents in future; and as to the moss-bonkers, they are held in such abhorrence that no true Dutchman will admit them to his table, who loves good fish and hates the devil.

The Storm Ship[10]

In the golden age of the province of the New Netherlands, when under the sway of Wouter Van Twiller, otherwise called the Doubter, the people of the Manhattoes were alarmed one sultry afternoon, just about the time of the summer solstice, by a tremendous storm of thunder and lightning. The rain fell in such torrents as absolutely to spatter up and smoke along the ground. It seemed as if the thunder rattled and rolled over the very roofs of the houses; the lightning was seen to play about the church of St. Nicholas, and to strive three times, in vain, to strike its weathercock. Garret Van Horne's new chimney was split almost from top to bottom; and Doffue Mildeberger was struck speechless from his bald-faced mare, just as he was riding into town. In a word, it was one of those unparalleled storms which only happen once within the memory of that venerable personage known in all towns by the appellation of the "oldest inhabitant."

[10] From "The Storm-Ship," *The Works of Washington Irving,* Fulton Edition, *Bracebridge Hall,* pp. 374–379. New York: The Century Co. 1910.

Great was the terror of the good old women of the Manhattoes. They gathered their children together, and took refuge in the cellars; after having hung a shoe on the iron point of every bedpost lest it should attract the lightning. At length the storm abated; the thunder sank into a growl, and the setting sun, breaking from under the fringed borders of the clouds, made the broad bosom of the bay to gleam like a sea of molten gold.

The word was given from the fort that a ship was standing up the bay. It passed from mouth to mouth, and street to street, and soon put the little capital in a bustle. The arrival of a ship, in those early times of the settlement, was an event of vast importance to the inhabitants. It brought them news from the old world, from the land of their birth, from which they were so completely severed; to the yearly ship, too, they looked for their supply of luxuries, of finery, of comforts, and almost of necessaries. The good vrouw could not have her new cap nor new gown until the arrival of the ship; the artist waited for it for his tools, the burgomaster for his pipe and his supply of Hollands, the schoolboy for his top and marbles, and the lordly landholder for the bricks with which he was to build his new mansion. Thus every one, rich and poor, great and small, looked out for the arrival of the ship. It was the great yearly event of the town of New Amsterdam; and from one end of the year to the other, the ship—the ship—the ship—was the continual topic of conversation.

The news from the fort, therefore, brought all the populace down to the Battery, to behold the wished-for sight. It was not exactly the time when she had been expected to arrive, and the circumstance was a matter of some speculation. Many were the groups collected about the Battery. Here and there might be seen a burgomaster, of slow and pompous gravity, giving his opinion with great confidence to a crowd of old women and idle boys. At another place was a knot of weather-beaten fellows, who had been seamen or fishermen in their times, and were great authorities on such occasions; these gave different opinions, and caused great disputes among their several adherents; but the man most looked up to, and followed and watched by the crowd, was Hans Van Pelt, an old Dutch sea-captain retired from service, the nautical oracle of the place. He reconnoitered the ship through an ancient telescope, covered with tarry canvas, hummed a Dutch tune to himself, and said nothing. A hum, however, from Hans Van Pelt, had always more weight with the public than a speech from another man.

In the meantime the ship became more distinct to the naked eye; she was a stout, round Dutch-built vessel, with high bow and poop, and bearing Dutch colors. The evening sun gilded her bellying canvas, as she came riding over the long waving billows. The sentinel who had given notice of her approach declared that he had first got sight of her when she was in the center of the bay, and that she broke suddenly on his sight, just as if she had come out of the bosom of the black thunder-cloud. The bystanders looked at Hans Van Pelt, to see what he would say to this report; Hans Van Pelt screwed his mouth closer together, and said nothing; upon which some shook their heads and others shrugged their shoulders.

The ship was now repeatedly hailed, but made no reply, and passing by the fort, stood on up the Hudson. A gun was brought to bear on her, and, with some difficulty, loaded and fired by Hans Van Pelt, the garrison not being expert in artillery. The shot seemed absolutely to pass through the ship, and to skip along the water on the other side, but no notice was taken of it! What was strange, she had all her sails set, and sailed right against wind and tide, which were both down the river. Upon this Hans Van Pelt, who was likewise harbor-master, ordered his boat, and set off to board her; but after rowing two or three hours, he returned without success. Sometimes he would get within one or two hundred yards of her, and then, in a twinkling, she would be a half-mile off. Some said it was because his oarsmen, who were rather pursy and short-winded, stopped every now and then to take breath and spit on their hands; but this it is probable was a mere scandal. He got near enough, however, to see the crew, who were all dressed in the Dutch style, the officers in doublets and high hats and feathers; not a word was spoken by anyone on board; they stood as motionless as so many statues, and the ship seemed as if left to her own government. Thus she kept on, away up the river, lessening and lessening in the evening sunshine, until she faded from sight, like a little white cloud melting away in the summer sky.

The appearance of this ship threw the governor into one of the deepest doubts that ever beset him in the whole course of his administration. Fears were entertained for the security of the infant settlements on the river, lest this might be an enemy's ship in disguise, sent to take possession. The governor called together his council repeatedly to assist him with their conjectures. He sat in his chair of state, built of timber from the sacred forest of the Hague, smoking his long jasmin pipe and listening to all that his counsellors had to say on a subject about which they knew nothing; but in spite of all the conjecturing of the sagest and oldest heads, the governor still continued to doubt.

Messengers were dispatched to different places on the river; but they returned without any tidings—the ship had made no port. Day after day and week after week elapsed, but she never returned down the Hudson. As, however, the council seemed solicitous for intelligence, they had it in abundance. The captains of the sloops seldom arrived without bringing some report of having seen the strange ship at different parts of the river; sometimes near the Palisadoes, sometimes off Croton Point, and sometimes in the Highlands; but she never was reported as having been seen above the Highlands. The crews of the sloops, it is true, generally differed among themselves in their accounts of these apparitions; but that may have arisen from the uncertain situations in which they saw her. Sometimes it was by the flashes of the thunderstorm lighting up a pitchy night and giving glimpses of her careening across Tappaan Zee or the wide waste of Haverstraw Bay. At one moment she would appear close upon them, as if likely to run them down, and would throw them into great bustle and alarm; but the next flash would show her far off, always sailing against the wind. Sometimes, in quiet moonlight nights, she would be seen under some high bluff of the Highlands, all in deep shadow, excepting her topsails glittering in the moonbeams; by the time, however, that the voyagers reached the place, no ship was to be seen; and when they had passed on for some distance and looked back, behold! there she was again, with her topsails in the moonshine! Her appearance was always just after, or just before, or just in the midst of unruly weather; and she was known among the skippers and voyagers of the Hudson by the name of the "storm ship."

These reports perplexed the governor and his council more than ever; and it would be endless to repeat the conjectures and opinions uttered on the subject. Some quoted cases in point, of ships seen off the coast of New England, navigated by witches and goblins. Old Hans Van Pelt, who had been more than once to the Dutch colony at the Cape of Good Hope, insisted that this must be the Flying Dutchman, which had so long haunted Table Bay; but being unable to make port, had now sought another harbor. Others suggested that, if it really was a supernatural apparition, as there was every reason to believe, it might be Hendrick Hudson and his crew of the *Half-moon;* who, it was well known, had once run aground in the upper part of the river in seeking a northwest passage to China. This opinion had very little weight with the governor, but it passed current out of doors; for indeed it had already been reported that Hendrick Hudson and his crew haunted the Kaatskill Mountain; and it appeared very reasonable to suppose that his ship might infest the river where the enterprise was baffled, or that it might bear the shadowy crew to their periodical revels in the mountain.

Other events occurred to occupy the thoughts and doubts of the sage Wouter and his council, and the storm ship ceased to be a subject of deliberation at the board. It continued, however, a matter of popular belief and marvelous anecdote through the whole time of the Dutch government, and particularly just before the capture of New Amsterdam and the subjugation of the province by the English squadron. About that time the storm ship was repeatedly seen in the Tappaan Zee and about Weehawk and even down as far as Hoboken; and her appearance was supposed to be ominous of the approaching squall in public affairs and the downfall of Dutch domination.

Since that time we have no authentic accounts of her; though it is said she still haunts the Highlands and cruises about Point-no-point. People who live along the river insist that they sometimes see her in summer moonlight; and that in a deep still midnight they have heard the chant of her crew, as if heaving the lead; but sights and sounds are so deceptive along the mountainous shores and about the wide bays and long reaches of this great river that I confess I have very strong doubts upon the subject.

"Old Silver Nails"

Petrus Stuyvesant, a native of Friesland, had formerly been a director of the [Dutch West India] Company's colony at Curaçoa, whence, having lost a leg in an attack on the Portuguese settlement at Saint Martin's, he had been obliged to return to Europe for surgical aid. . . . [He] replaced his leg by a wooden one with silver bands, which gave rise [to the nickname "Old Silver Nails" and] the tradition that he wore a silver leg. . . .[11]

The [Rembrandt] portrait (owned by the New-York Historical Society) . . . is half-length and therefore does not record which of Pieter's legs was the "silver leg." This was a mystery, even to his re-

[11] From *History of the City of New York,* by Mary L. Booth, pp. 127–128. Entered . . . 1867, by W. R. C. Clark. Copyright, 1880, by E. P. Dutton & Co. New York.

mote descendants, for some two centuries, until, in 1926, Victor H. Paltsits, historian and linguist, read a group of Dutch versified manuscript letters, written to Stuyvesant by his English friend Johan Farret. Therein is a playful allusion to the amputation and burial in Curaçoa of Pieter's *right* leg.[12]

The Ghost of Peter Stuyvesant [13]

This last and most picturesque Dutch governor died in 1672, on the farm which he had maintained in semi-hermit fashion after the English conquest. His body was laid in a vault in the chapel he had built in 1660, which has been rebuilt since into St. Mark's in-the-Bouwerie. Almost immediately, family servants vowed fearfully that they had seen the governor's ghost prowling his old haunts. To the present day that story remains.

Any tampering with the graves, even the cutting of a street close by, has evoked strange and sometimes frightening phenomena. Tapping, as if by the famous wooden leg of the old warrior, sounds from the depths of his tomb.

The visitations continued and even grew in weird interest. In 1774 his old manor house burned to the foundations, and at dead of night a shadowy form was seen limping around the ruins—the angry wraith of the long-dead Stuyvesant, inspecting the damage. Again in the early nineteenth century, when houses were built and roads cut around the graveyard, strange and frightening phenomena—ghastly grumbling and rappings, with occasional apparitions of the phantom itself. In the sixties a church sexton visited the chapel late at night, to flee in wild alarm; he had seen Stuyvesant, flame-eyed and timber-toed, advancing upon him. Several times the church bell has

[12] From *The Battery:* The story of the adventurers, artists, statesmen, grafters, songsters, mariners, pirates, guzzlers, Indians, thieves, stuffed-shirts, turncoats, millionaires, inventors, poets, heroes, soldiers, harlots, bootlicks, nobles, nonentities, burghers, martyrs, and murderers who played their parts during full four centuries on Manhattan Island's tip, by Rodman Gilder, p. 12. Copyright, 1936, by Rodman Gilder. Boston: Houghton Mifflin Company.

[13] From *Look Behind You!* Ghosts, Demons, and Haunted Houses of the Metropolitan Area, by Manly Wade Wellman, from Researches of the Federal Writers' Project, pp. 6–7. Manuscripts of the Federal Writers' Project of the Works Progress Administration in New York City. 1938.

tolled loudly when no visible hand touched the rope. When impious commissioners began to cut Second Avenue through the graveyard itself, more than sixty years ago, the bell began tolling at midnight. The sexton and others, roused by the angry song, hurried to the scene. The church was securely locked and nobody could enter; yet, as the searchers produced a key and hurried through the door, the ringing ceased. Under the suddenly silent belfry hung a short length of rope, broken as if by a mighty jerk. The remainder of the cord was produced next day by the sexton, who insisted that he found it in Stuyvesant's vault.

How "Coney Island" Got Its Name

I [14]

During a lull in the decisive Indian War of 1643–45, Dutch officials offered to let dissenters from New England, led by Lady Moody, establish a colony at Gravesend. They figured that it would serve as a buffer for themselves.

Lady Moody was interested but cautious. What about the Indians supposed to be lurking at the seaside? She had been told they belonged to the big-animal Bear Band known as Konoh. Indians who called themselves bears sounded dangerous to her.

No danger at all, replied the Dutch. The Indians used the ocean-front area as a hideout for women and children, not as a lair for warriors.

"We call it Konijn Hok, the rabbit's hutch or breeding place," said one of the Dutch officials, punning on the fact that genuine rabbits—or coneys—shared the beach with the Indians.

But Lady Moody had lingering doubts. Were any Indians still around?

[14] From *Sodom by the Sea,* An Affectionate History of Coney Island, by Oliver Pilat and Jo Ranson, pp. 8–9. Copyright, 1941, by Oliver Pilat and Jo Ranson. Garden City, New York: Doubleday, Doran & Co., Inc.

Some historians traced Coney to Colman. Others, like Judge Egbert Benson, who presented a memorandum on the subject in 1816 to the New York Historical Society, argued that "Coney" came from "Conyn," the name of a Dutch family that took up residence at the beach. Neither explanation had the dramatic quality of a third theory.—O. P. and J. R.

"Oh no, they must be all gone by now," rejoined the Dutchman. "We scared them away. After hearing the guns, the Konoh ran like a coney!"

II [15]

About two hundred years ago [as of 1900] the King of England granted a patent or deed of land on the southwest end of Long Island to an English woman belonging to a noble family. Embraced within this deed of land were what are now known as Gravesend and Coney Island.

The lady who owned the land was of an enterprising character, and she sought to turn it to account, offering great inducements to parties who would settle and help develop the locality; and it was in this way that what is now known as Gravesend got its first start. But no one save a man named Cooney, or Coney, and his family—then a wife and child—and a New Yorker named Schenck, who boarded with them, could be induced to inhabit the sandy strip of land now so thronged with visitors from New York, Brooklyn, and vicinity every pleasant day during the months of July, August, and September.

Cooney and his "social circle" occupied a rude hut, which he erected on the edge of the marshes, and used to spend all his time fishing and gunning; but as there was no Fulton Market at which to sell the outcome of his luck with gun and fishing-line, he had a hard struggle to make enough to clothe his little family and himself.

One day, while Cooney was on a trip to Gravesend, in search of a stray job, a tremendous storm arose, accompanied by a terrific tidal wave, which swept everything before it, including the hut of poor Cooney, containing his wife and two children and the man Schenck. They were all washed out to sea, and were never seen or heard of more. Not a vestige of his hut could be found by Cooney, on his return to the island; he could not even locate exactly the spot where it had been placed.

From that day, Cooney, bereft of wife and children, and of everything he had in the world—though "monarch of all he surveyed"—became a helpless idiot. He found a temporary home with a kind-hearted soul at Gravesend, but every day he would wander round the spot where he believed his little hut and family had been destroyed, and look toward the sea beseechingly, as if expecting it to give back

[15] From "Coney Island as It Was, The Pioneer Who Gave It Its Name—A Disastrous Tidal Wave—Uses of the Island in Fugitive Slave Law Times—How Negroes Kidnapped in the Metropolis Were Disposed Of," *New York Evening Post,* September 8, 1900.

its dead; but the sea is not in the habit of giving back anything or anybody, and one day Cooney himself disappeared, and was never again seen. But the name of the poor, heart-broken, desolate idiot is still attached to perhaps the most popular watering-place on the face of the earth.

The "East" and "North" Rivers [16]

The apparent illogic of the popular designations, East and North Rivers, is explained away when we remember that the names were conferred at a time when all of New York lay well below Grand Street (the point where the East River turns north) and consequently, while the incoming tide flows north in the Hudson, it flows at the start almost due east in the East River.

Captain Kidd on Wall Street [17]

This remarkable man is intimately connected with Wall Street. He sailed on his remarkable voyage from the foot of the street when he entered on that career of infamy which has made him immortal. An association exists in Wall Street whose purpose is to dig for Kidd's money, and to search for his buried treasure. The belief that his name was Robert Kidd, and not William; that he buried his treasures on Gardiner's Island, and up the Hudson; that those treasures can be secured is entertained by large numbers in and around New York. Fortune-tellers have pointed out the exact location repeatedly; clairvoyants and dreamers have made the discovery; coin is occasionally found in different localities to keep up the drooping spirits of the

[16] From *Rider's New York City,* A Guide-Book for Travelers, compiled under the general editorship of Fremont Rider by Frederic Taber Cooper and others, pp. 137–138. Copyright, 1923, by the Cumulative Digest Corporation. New York: Henry Holt and Company.

[17] From *Twenty Years among the Bulls and Bears of Wall Street,* by Matthew Hale Smith, pp. 301–305. Entered . . . 1870, by J. B. Burr and Company. Hartford. 1871.

faithful, and assessments are regularly called in that the good work may go on. Investing in Kidd's stock is about as valuable as many other investments offered in the street.

Kidd had a house and lot on Wall Street. He was a wild adventurous fellow, when he was young, and ran away to sea. He passed through the various grades, and sailed from New York as Captain of a privateer in 1691. He married a respectable lady and moved into a commodious house, in the then upper part of New York, which was located in Liberty Street, then known as Crown Street. Piracy was then common, and was less disreputable than now. The war between England and France filled our waters with corsairs. Pirates with the black flag, daring and cruel, ravaged, destroyed, and pillaged on the high seas and on the land. They were numerous on the American coast. They ran into the creeks and inlets, and up the small rivers, and sold to merchants the spoils they took from the ships which were crossing the main. The people of New York and Boston connived at the crime, and profited by the depredations of these outlaws. The authorities were charged with being in complicity with the pirates. Desperadoes, known to belong to piratical craft, swaggered about the streets of the city unmolested. They squandered their money in taverns, filled the streets with rioting, and made the nights hideous with brawling and revelry. Trade with foreign ports was broken up, and unless the piratical trade was ended, honest business must come to a standstill.

From being a privateersman, Kidd secured the command of a packet ship between New York and London. The English ministry were troubled about the prevalence of piracy in the North American waters. It was proposed to fit out a privateer, fully armed, to defend commerce, and scourge the pirates from the coast. The colonial Governor Bellomont secured for Kidd the command of this privateer. It is believed that with the commission given to Kidd, to clear the coast of pirates, there was a private enterprise organized, to seize and take ships, vessels and goods, belonging to the French king and his subjects, and bring the gain to London. Kidd bound himself in the penalty of £20,000 sterling, to honestly fulfil the contract, and render fair account of the prizes he might take. Colonel Livingston, owner of the lordly manor on the Hudson, became Kidd's bondsman. The pirate evidently, at that time, stood high in the confidence of the best men in New York. He was shrewd, daring, competent, and was supposed to be honest. Distinction and untold wealth were within his grasp. He took an affectionate leave of his family, whom he left in his house in Crown Street, was attended to his vessel by merchants, whose trade the pirates had ruined, and by the authorities, whose honor was deeply involved in the suppression of unlawful traffic. Dressed in the handsome uniform of a British naval officer, he anticipated the day when he would return, loaded with wealth and honor. His crew was a picked one, made up of steady men, mostly of those who had families. To complete his force, however, he took the river sailors, and, with one hundred and fifty-five men, sailed beyond the Narrows for the Indian Ocean.

It is even in doubt, today, whether Kidd was or was not a pirate. That he captured vessels, was deserted by his crew, and denounced in England as a traitor, is unquestioned. His name became a terror in England and America. Ships arriving at any port brought thrilling stories of Kidd's black flag, his boldness, atrocity, and bloodthirstiness. French and Spanish vessels alike were seized, treasures taken, victims murdered, and vessels burned. Moors and Christians, English and Americans, were his victims. He tortured their persons to find hidden treasures. He made raids on the land, burned houses, pillaged and slaughtered, and was as much a terror on shore as on the sea.

These rumors were generally believed. His noble friends abandoned him. The government issued a proclamation denouncing his piracy, and offering a heavy reward for his capture. In the midst of the excitement, Kidd arrived in our waters. His vessel was loaded with coin and jewels, the fruits of his piracies. At the extreme end of Long Island, Kidd landed, and buried his treasures on what is known as Gardiner's Island. A family occupied the Island, and gave the spot its name. The story is that Kidd came ashore, and demanded of Mrs. Gardiner that she should cook his supper for him. He presented her with a cradle blanket, made of gold thread and silk. In the orchard, on the Island, he buried his treasure, threatening the family with massacre, if they revealed the spot, or touched the gold. The portion of his wealth that he did not bury, he divided with his crew. Having done this, he sailed for Boston, and then came to New York. He appeared boldly in the streets, and was confronted by Bellomont, who ordered him to be seized. The governor took from him all his private papers, memoranda, and a list of his treasures. Kidd was put in irons, sent to England as a pirate, and confined in Newgate Prison. He was tried and convicted as a pirate, and hung at the dock in May, 1701.

The curious doggerel printed and circulated at the time of the execution still survives, and hands his name and atrocities down to coming time. For over a hundred years, persons have been digging for Kidd's treasures. It is estimated that over thirty thousand people have embarked in this enterprise. There are men in and around Wall Street, who get a very respectable living from the dupes who are ready to invest in the attempts to find the pirate's treasures. Public meetings have been held in the city by parties interested in the search. At one meeting it was gravely stated that the spirit of Kidd watched his treasures, and succeeded in blinding the diggers. One of the popular traditions about Kidd was that the pirate was chased up the North River by a man-of-war. He sunk his ship with its precious freight near the Dunderberg mountains. A company was formed, a coffer dam thrown across, and professional divers employed at a large expense. Traces of the vessel were found, but no treasure. Dupes and fools who are willing to be swindled abound in New York and the vicinity, who are ready to continue the search for the lost treasures of Kidd the pirate.

The Legend of Captain Billopp[18]

After Staten Island had been discovered by Hendrick Hudson, there followed years of Dutch colonial government in it, during which this fine tidbit of land, in what came to be Tottenville, belonged to Nova Caesarea, the name of that period for New Jersey.

[18] From *Old Roads from the Heart of New York,* Journeys Today by Ways of Yesterday Within Thirty Miles Around the Battery, by Sarah Comstock, pp. 127–129. Copyright, 1915, by Sarah Comstock. New York and London: G. P. Putnam's Sons, The Knickerbocker Press.

During the administration of Governor Dongan, the claim of the Proprietors of East Jersey to Staten Island occasioned much correspondence. This claim arose from the wording of a grant made in 1665 by the Duke of York of land westward of Long Island, "bounded on the east by the Hudson River"; if the Hudson River emptied through Arthur Kill, Staten Island was east thereof and in New York; but if the Hudson emptied through the Narrows, it was not.

In 1672 Governor Cartaret of New Jersey attempted to cut hay on Staten Island despite the purchase in 1670 from the Indians by Lovelace. In 1675 and again in 1681, Governor Cartaret renewed his claims, but unsuccessfully; and once more in 1684. In 1704 an equally unsuccessful attempt was made, interesting because, in conjunction with those of 1681 and 1682, it shows that the question was not settled by Captain Billopp sailing around the Island in 1676 and thereby earning the Manor of Bentley. Staten Island was never, in fact, a part of New Jersey. It was part of the Dutch possessions which passed into the possession of the Duke of York. It was definitely purchased from the Indians by Governor Lovelace in 1670. Throughout the English period it was part of New York. The final adjustment of the boundary between the States

Now James, the Duke of York, and brother to Charles the Second, was given a sort of rulership over all the King's possessions in America. Provinces which had been under Dutch control passed into English hands. Staten Island became a scene of discord; to the English and Dutch dissensions the French added their quarrels, and matters began to look somewhat like a Kilkenny-cat controversy.

To settle matters, the Duke finally came to a decidedly original decision. He ordained that if the islands in the harbor of New York could be circumnavigated in twenty-four hours they should belong to the colony of New York; otherwise, Nova Caesarea, or New Jersey, was to possess them. The next thing was to find the right man to attend to the circumnavigation.

It happened at the fortunate time that Captain Christopher Billopp was stopping at Perth Amboy. His vessel, called *The Bentley,* was a small one, probably belonging to the British navy, although there seems to be a question as to whether it was of the merchant service or not.

Billopp was chosen to perform the Duke's task. He was accounted an excellent seaman; but the feat did not promise to be easy, even so. He did not start out until he had thought over the matter carefully, to determine how he would be best able to accomplish it.

And thus he hit upon the idea of the empty barrels. If he were to cover his deck with them, he argued, he would gain much sailing power. Thus laden, he set out, and we can picture the excitement which held New Yorkers and New Jerseyites in throbbing suspense.

Captain Billopp performed his feat. Nay, he more than performed it; a trifle over twenty-three hours sufficed for his sail, and Staten Island was New York's.

The Duke had a reward ready. So much pleased was he with Billopp's success that, instead of letting him return to England to make his home, he presented the Captain with [962] acres of land on Staten Island and invited him to remain there.

This land was at [Tottenville]. So fine a plum had fallen into the worthy seaman's hands that he determined to make the most of it, and [in 1676?] he set himself at once to building a suitable residence

---

of New York and New Jersey was made by a Boundary Commission after the Revolution. . . . Many interesting details of the correspondence on the subject in the seventeenth century will be found in "The Disputed Claims of the Proprietors of East Jersey to Staten Island," by Edward C. Delavan, Jr., in *Proceedings of the Staten Island Association of Arts and Sciences,* Vol. III, pp. 37–48.—Charles W. Leng and William T. Davis, *Staten Island and Its People, A History, 1609–1929* (New York, 1930), I, p. 132.

[still standing]. He named it, for the vessel which had won him his laurels, the Manor of Bentley.[19]. . .

Mrs. Murray's Madeira

I [20]

. . . It was the purpose of the British, when they landed at Kip's Bay, [September 15, 1776] to make their camp on the heights of Inclenberg, midway between New York and Harlem. The way thence led past the country-seat of Robert Murray, a Quaker merchant of large wealth and known loyalty to the crown. The shrewd merchant's wife and daughters, on the other hand, were ardent patriots, and the day before had had Washington for their guest. When Howe and his staff reached this Quaker homestead, near the junction of the present Fifth Avenue and Thirty-seventh Street, they were delighted to find Mrs. Murray and her beautiful daughters ready to greet them with a warm welcome and to renew an acquaintance made in other and more peaceful days. "William, alight and refresh thyself at our house," was the greeting of the Quaker matron. "I thank you, Mrs. Murray," said Howe; "but I must first catch that rascally Yankee, Putnam." The patriot general was not to be caught, however, if woman's wit could

[19] . . . The village of Tottenville was once known as the Manor of Bentley, and the peninsula at its farthest point, later called Ward's Point, was originally Billopp's. . . .

The Captain . . . disappeared in the early seventeen-hundreds, before the Revolution came on; it is believed that his vessel, *The Bentley,* went down with him while he was making a voyage to England to visit his old home. . . . The old cellar [of the house] has . . . a room like a cave, solidly walled. . . . Here, during that period of the Revolution when the house was held as a British outpost . . . our own American patriots are supposed to have been held captive. . . . When Cooper wrote *The Water Witch,* he laid one of its scenes in this mysterious cellar.

. . . It was after the Battle of Long Island in 1776 that Howe went to the Billopp House to meet Benjamin Franklin, John Adams, and Edward Rutledge, who were chosen to confer upon the issues of the war. They hoped for peace, but when they found that Howe's offer was merely to resume old conditions, as before the war, the conference came to an end without results.—S.C., *ibid.,* pp. 129–132.

[20] From *New York: Old & New,* Its Story, Streets, and Landmarks, by Rufus Rockwell Wilson, Vol. I. pp. 228–229. Copyright, 1902, by J. B. Lippincott Company. Philadelphia & London. 1903.

save him. "Didst thou not hear that Putnam had gone?" rejoined Mrs. Murray. "It is too late to try to catch him. Thee had better come in and dine." With Putnam out of reach there was no need of haste, and so, promising to pursue the Yankees after he had dined, the British commander alighted and entered the house, where the warmth of his welcome made him unmindful for hours of the task he had in hand. . . .

II[21]

. . . [Then, refreshed by Mrs. Murray's] good homemade cakes, her heady homemade wine, and her sprightly homemade conversation, the British officers rose at last, wiped their lips, and shook out the laces of their sleeves. But Dame Murray had still another trick in her bag. The little serving-maid, to whom the officers had been paying superior attention, sang beautifully. She knew a song just over from London—"Sally in Our Alley." Would the gentlemen like to hear it? Warmed with wine and flirtation, they settled down, listened through the seven long stanzas, even encored the performance. When they emerged, the battle-roar was dying down, and the clouds of black smoke were clearing away from the hilltops below. The British army, for lack of sharp staff direction, had let the Continentals slip through to their stand at McGowan's Pass—even that virulent gentleman rebel, George Washington of Virginia. . . .

[21] From *Highlights of Manhattan*, by Will Irwin, pp. 240–241. Copyright, 1926–1927, by New York Herald-Tribune; 1927, by The Century Co. New York and London.

3

Metropolis in the Making

[New York] is a fairly successful competitor of the Tower of Babel. . . . And that is why a picture of the Statue of Liberty is the best-known picture of New York by an overwhelming majority.—Henry Collins Brown

The High Stoop [1]

A custom which [the Dutch] brought with them and which was destined to become an outstanding feature of New York residential architecture, up to and including the brownstone-front era, was the raising of the "best rooms" in the house to a level well above the street, with the resultant steep flight of steps and the inevitable high stoop. The original idea was, of course, to protect the family in case a hole should develop in the dikes and the tulip beds go under water.

[1] From *Money Town,* The Story of Manhattan Toe, That Golden Mile Which Lies between the Battery and the Fields, by Frederick L. Collins, p. 38. Copyright, 1946, by Frederick L. Collins. New York: G. P. Putnam's Sons.

Why the North-South Streets Are Wide Apart [2]

The city fathers who laid out the plan for the streets of Manhattan anticipated that the heavy traffic would be east and west between the two rivers and that the north and south movement would be less. With this in view they spaced the cross-town streets close together and the longitudinal streets wide apart, and their plan has remained, for the most part until today, with only Madison and Lexington Avenues giving relief to the great north and south bound traffic; Broadway existed before the plan. . . . Lexington was the last north-south avenue to relieve the congestion caused by the widely spaced avenues of the city plan. . . .

Brillât-Savarin's Drinking Bout [3]

During the French Revolution there were many Frenchmen who had been driven from France and had taken refuge in New York City. One of these was the famous gastronome, Anthelme Brillât-Savarin, author of *La Physiologie du Gout,* who tells us something of the way they enjoyed themselves while here. He says: "I sometimes passed the evening in a sort of café-taverne, kept by a Mr. Little, where he served in the morning turtle soup, and in the evening all the refreshments customary in the United States. I generally took with me Vicomte de la Massue and Jean Rodolphe Fehr, formerly a mercantile broker at Marseilles, both *emigrés* like myself. I treated them to Welsh-rabbit, which was washed down with ale or cider, and here we passed the evening talking over our misfortunes, our pleasures and our hopes."

[2] From *Ruggles of New York,* A Life of Samuel B. Ruggles, by D. G. Brinton Thompson, pp. 58, 59. Copyright, 1946, by Columbia University Press. New York.

[3] From *Old Taverns of New York,* by W. Harrison Bayles, pp. 376–381. Copyright, 1915, by Frank Allaben Genealogical Company. New York.

Michael Little's Tavern, or Porter House, as it was called, was at 56 Pine Street, a little below William Street, and it speaks well for the house that it should have been selected by Brillât-Savarin and his friends as a place for their suppers. Brillât-Savarin spent two years in New York, 1794–96, supporting himself by giving lessons in the French language and playing in the orchestra of the theater. He gives a very amusing account of a dinner party at Little's place, of which he and his two friends formed a part. He had met there Mr. Wilkinson, an Englishman from Jamaica, and his friend, whose name he never knew, whom he described as a very taciturn man, with a square face, keen eyes, and features as expressionless as those of a blind man, who appeared to notice everything but never spoke; only, when he heard a witty remark or merry joke, his face would expand, his eyes close, and opening a mouth as large as the bell of a trumpet, he would send forth a sound between a laugh and a howl, called by the English horse-laugh; after which he would relapse into his habitual taciturnity. Mr. Wilkinson appeared to be about fifty years of age, with the manners and all the bearing of a gentleman (*un homme comme il faut.*)

These two Englishmen, pleased with the society of Brillât-Savarin and his friends, had many times partaken of the frugal collation which was offered them, when, one evening, Wilkinson took Brillât-Savarin to one side and declared his intention of engaging all three of them to dine with him. The invitation was accepted and fixed for three o'clock in the afternoon of the third day after. As they were about to leave, the waiter quietly told Brillât-Savarin that the Jamaicans had ordered a good dinner and had given directions that the wine and liquor be carefully prepared, because they regarded the invitation as a challenge or test of drinking powers, and that the man with the big mouth had said that he hoped to put the Frenchmen under the table.

For such a drinking bout Brillât-Savarin had no relish, but the Frenchmen could not now very well avoid it without being accused of being frightened by the Englishmen. Although aware of the danger, following the maxim of Marshal de Saxe, "As the wine was drawn they prepared to drink it." (*"Le vin était tiré, nous nous preparâmes à le boire."*)

Brillât-Savarin had no fear for himself, but he did not wish to see his two friends go down with the others; he wished to make it a national victory, and not an individual one. He, therefore, sent for his friends and gave them a lecture. He instructed them to restrain their appetites at the beginning so as to eat moderately with the wine throughout the whole dinner, to drink small draughts and even contrive to get rid of the wine sometimes without drinking it. They divided among them a quantity of bitter almonds, recommended for such an occasion.

At the appointed time they all met at Little's Tavern, and soon after the dinner was served. It consisted of an enormous piece of roast beef, a turkey (*dindon cuit dans son jus*), vegetables, a salad and a tart (*tarte aux comfitures*). They drank after the French fashion, that is to say, the wine was served from the commencement. It was very good claret. Mr. Wilkinson did the honors of the table admirably. His friend appeared absorbed in his plate and said nothing.

Brillât-Savarin was charmed with his two friends. La Massue, although endowed with a sufficiently good appetite, was mincing his food like a delicate young lady, and Fehr was adroitly succeeding in passing glasses of wine into a beer pot at the end of the table. He himself was holding up well against the two Englishmen, and the more the dinner advanced the more confident he felt.

After the claret came Port, after Port, Madeira, at which they stuck for a long time. On the arrival of the dessert, composed of butter, cheese and nuts, was the time for toasts. They drank to the power of kings, the liberty of the people and the beauty of women; particularly to the health of Mr. Wilkinson's daughter, Mariah, who, he assured his guests, was the most beautiful person in all the island of Jamaica.

After the wine came spirits—rum, brandy and whiskey—and with the spirits, songs. Brillât-Savarin avoided the spirits and called for punch. Little himself brought in a bowl of it, without doubt prepared in advance, sufficient for forty persons. No such vessel for drink was ever seen in France.

Brillât-Savarin says that he ate five or six slices of buttered toast (*roties d'un beurre extrêmement frais*) and felt his forces revived. He then took a survey of the situation, for he was becoming much concerned as to how it would all end. His two friends appeared quite fresh and drank as they picked the nuts. Wilkinson's face was scarlet, his eyes were troubled and he appeared to be giving way. His friend said nothing, but his head smoked like a boiling caldron. The catastrophe was approaching.

Suddenly Mr. Wilkinson started to his feet and began to sing "Rule Britannia," but he could get no farther than these words; his strength failed him; he felt himself drop into his chair and from there rolled under the table (*coula sous la table*). His friend seeing him in this state, emitted one of his noisiest laughs, and stooping to assist him fell by his side.

Brillât-Savarin, viewing the scene with considerable satisfaction and relief, rang the bell, and when Little came up, after addressing him the conventional phrase, "See to it that these gentlemen are properly cared for," with his friends drank with him their health in a parting glass of punch. The waiter, with his assistants, soon came in and bore away the vanquished, whom they carried out, according to the rule, *feet foremost,* which expression is used in English to designate those *dead* or *drunk,* Mr. Wilkinson still trying to sing "Rule Britannia," his friend remaining absolutely motionless.

Next day seeing in the newspapers an account of what had happened, with the remark that the Englishmen were ill, Brillât-Savarin went to see them. He found the friend suffering from a severe attack of indigestion. Mr. Wilkinson was confined to his chair by the gout, brought on probably by his late dissipation. He seemed sensible to the attention and said to Brillât-Savarin, among other things: "Oh! dear sir, you are very good company, indeed, but too hard a drinker for us."

The Great Center Market Hoax: "Sawing the Island Off" [4]

About this period [of the 1820's] there were several butchers in this [Center Market] as well as one or two other markets engaged in, or who at least encouraged, an affair which perhaps was one of the most ridiculous as well as one of the most perfect "hoaxes" ever introduced to the public, originating in a few playful remarks made by a near relative [of the author], in a joking conversation.

In the neighborhood of Mulberry and Spring Streets almost every afternoon congregated a number of butchers and others, to learn and talk about the current news of the day. Among the number was an old retired carpenter, whom we shall call Lozier (a name that he afterwards assumed in carrying out this "hoax") who was full of fun and

[4] From *The Market Book,* containing a Historical Account of the Public Markets in the Cities of New York, Boston, Philadelphia, and Brooklyn, with a Brief Description of Every Article of Human Food Sold Therein, the Introduction of Cattle in America, and Notices of Many Remarkable Specimens, by Thomas F. De Voe, Vol. I, pp. 462–464. Entered . . . 1862, by Thomas F. De Voe. New York: Printed for the Author.

"dry sayings," and his equal was seldom found in carrying a long face with them.

In the year 1823 or '4, one fine afternoon, this old carpenter, as usual, sought the current news of the day of this relative, whom we shall call Uncle John [De Voe].

"Well," says Uncle John, "we have had a long conversation about New York Island, and have come to the conclusion that the Island is getting too heavy on the Battery end, where it is altogether too much built upon, and we therefore consider it dangerous; so our intention is to have it sawed off at Kingsbridge, and turn that end down where the Battery is now located. But the question is, how shall it be done, as Long Island appears in the way? Some think it can be done without moving Long Island at all; that the bay and harbor are large enough for the Island of New York to turn around in; while others say, Long Island must be detached and floated to sea far enough, then anchored, until this grand turn is made, and then brought back to its former place."

Lozier at once took hold of this enormous job, and daily he was in consultation with the many visitors in relation to it, which generally took place before strangers, who, of course, overheard the conversation, usually appearing to be carried on in great earnestness; and, poor frail human nature! they would believe, and ofttimes suggest an opinion on some difficult point.

This subject, for some two or three months, appeared to be the question of the day—*"sawing the Island off";* and Lozier, having the job, was waited upon by numerous persons, and among them were several mechanics. Some were engaged to build barracks, which were to accommodate the hundreds of workmen; others to make the large sweeps, about twenty-four in number, of 250 feet in length, which were to be used on the opposite sides of the extreme ends of the Island, to sweep it around after it was sawed off. The iron-work on these sweeps was to be made in a peculiar but substantial manner, and an excellent neighboring blacksmith was very anxious to do the work, as he said: "There was no work in his line that he could not do"; and although his wife had no faith in this job, he every few days presented himself to Lozier to receive the dimensions of each part or piece, that he might properly estimate on it. Laborers and others who were seeking work, and happened to meet those who were acquainted with this job, and more especially with some of the butchers in this market, sent them to Lozier, who questioned them particularly as to their being long-winded, as he wanted a good many "pitmen," or those who could go below, to saw; he having engaged sufficient sawyers for the work above.

They very generally would engage and even assert that they could stay below as long as they might be wanted.

In this manner a great many were engaged who soon became anxious to be set at work; but Lozier had not engaged a sufficient number, and he could not think of going on with this large job until he had. This led those who were engaged to seek others, and at last the numbers became so thick and pressing that it got too warm for Lozier. He was forced to name a certain day, and thought it best to divide them; and on this particular morning one party were directed to be at the "forks of the Broadway and Bowery," near the present Union Park; and the other portion to be at No. 1 Bowery, corner of Spring Street, where a large number of live hogs was expected to be ready, which they were to drive up. Others were to carry provisions, tools, &c., in wagons and carts; and a few wagons were to carry up the wives of several of the workmen, who were to do the cooking, washing, &c., for all.

The day came, when great numbers presented themselves, but Lozier was nowhere to be found, and more particularly at No. 1 Bowery, corner of Spring Street. Soon, however, some of the more knowing ones got hold of the merits of this great job, and felt as if they had been "handsomely sold." Yet they desired to appear as if they had not engaged in it, and began to cast ridicule upon the excited and angry ones, and very soon there were but few who would confess they had been engaged "to saw the Island off." Lozier, in the meantime, lay quietly housed up; and so he stayed several weeks, not daring to venture forth even to the rendezvous; and when he did so, he was disguised into the general appearance of a different person, and assumed his proper name; as some of the most excited had not only used hard words, but also threatened, if they ever got hold of Lozier, they would "saw him off."

Barnum and the Glorious Fourth [5]

About the first of July, 1842, I began to make arrangements for extra novelties, additional performances, a large amount of extra advertising, and an outdoor display for the "Glorious Fourth." Large particolored

[5] From *Struggles and Triumphs:* or, Forty Years' Recollections of P. T. Barnum, written by himself, pp. 136–138. Author's Edition. [Biography Complete to April, 1872.] Entered . . . 1871, by P. T. Barnum. Buffalo, New York: Warren, Johnson & Co. 1873.

bills were ordered, transparencies were prepared, the free band of music was augmented by a trumpeter, and columns of advertisements, headed with large capitals, were written and put on file.

I wanted to run out a string of American flags across the street on that day, for I knew there would be thousands of people, passing the Museum with leisure and pocket-money, and I felt confident that an unusual display of national flags would arrest their patriotic attention, and bring many of them within my walls. Unfortunately for my purpose, St. Paul's Church stood directly opposite, and there was nothing to which I could attach my flag-rope, unless it might be one of the trees in the churchyard. I went to the vestryman for permission to so attach my flag-rope on the Fourth of July, and they were indignant at what they called my "insulting proposition"; such a concession would be "sacrilege." I plied them with arguments, and appealed to their patriotism, but in vain.

Returning to the Museum I gave orders to have the string of flags made ready, with directions at daylight on the Fourth of July to attach one end of the rope to one of the third-story windows of the Museum, and the other end to a tree in St. Paul's churchyard. The great day arrived, and my orders were strictly followed. The flags attracted great attention, and before nine o'clock I have no doubt that hundreds of additional visitors were drawn by this display into the Museum. By half-past nine Broadway was thronged, and about that time two gentlemen in a high state of excitement rushed into my office, announcing themselves as injured and insulted vestrymen of St. Paul's Church.

"Keep cool, gentlemen," said I; "I guess it is all right."

"Right!" indignantly exclaimed one of them. "Do you think it is right to attach your Museum to our Church? We will show you what is 'right' and what is law, if we live till tomorrow; those flags must come down instantly."

"Thank you," I said, "but let us not be in a hurry. I will go out with you and look at them, and I guess we can make it all right."

Going into the street I remarked: "Really, gentlemen, these flags look very beautiful; they do not injure your tree; I always stop my balcony music for your accommodation whenever you hold week-day services, and it is but fair that you should return the favor.

"We could indict your 'music,' as you call it, as a nuisance, if we chose," answered one vestryman, "and now I tell you that if these flags are not taken down in ten minutes, *I* will cut them down."

His indignation was at the boiling point. The crowd in the street was dense, and the angry gesticulation of the vestryman attracted their attention. I saw there was no use in trying to parley with him or coax him, and so, assuming an angry air, I rolled up my sleeves, and exclaimed, in a loud tone: "Well, mister, I should just like to see you dare to cut down the American flag on the Fourth of July; you must be a 'Britisher' to make such a threat as that; but I'll show you a thousand pairs of Yankee hands in two minutes, if you dare to attempt to take down the stars and stripes on this great birthday of American freedom!"

"What's that John Bull a-saying?" asked a brawny fellow, placing himself in front of the irate vestryman. "Look here, old fellow," he continued, "if you want to save a whole bone in your body, you had better slope, and never dare to talk again about hauling down the American flag in the city of New York."

Throngs of excited, exasperated men crowded around, and the vestryman, seeing the effect of my ruse, smiled faintly and said, "Oh, of course, it is all right," and he and his companions quietly edged out of the crowd. The flags remained up all day and all night. The next morning I sought the vanquished vestrymen and obtained formal permission to make this use of the tree on following holidays, in consideration of my willingness to arrest the doleful strains of my discordant balcony band whenever services were held on week days in the church.

Beecher's Slave Auction [6]

Slavery since the early days of New York was the source of frequent discussions. Slave markets had been established and abolished, and pulpit and press had never ceased to discuss the all-important subject. When in 1847 Mr. [Henry Ward] Beecher became the pastor of Plymouth Church, Brooklyn, he frankly stated that he intended to oppose slavery. The majority of the church members agreed with him, but the majority of the people of New York and Brooklyn sympathized with the Southerners, regarding slavery as a patriarchal institution that gave the people of the South leisure to develop into charming ladies and eloquent politicians. Mr. Beecher encountered bitter

[6] From *The New Metropolis,* 1600–1900, Memorable Events of Three Centuries, From the Island of Mana-hat-ta to Greater New York at the Close of the Nineteenth Century, edited by E. Idell Zeisloft, p. 88. Copyright, 1899, by D. Appleton and Company. New York.

opposition, and was abused as a Negro worshiper. He was threatened with personal violence, and a mob was formed in New York to tear down his church. Amid these excitements he conceived the idea of giving to the people who came to hear him preach an object lesson in Southern slavery. His idea was that he would sell a slave in Plymouth Church, so that everybody could see what slave dealing really meant, and might be stirred to help to pay for the liberation of some victims of the system.

The first slave auction in Plymouth Church was held on June 1, 1856. Mr. Beecher's intention had become known, and although the service did not begin until after ten o'clock, people had gathered by hundreds two hours before, until the streets on both sides of the church were literally jammed and carriages had to stop a block distant. Thousands had to turn away without gaining admission. When Mr. Beecher appeared on the platform a deathlike stillness fell upon the great audience, and after a short Scriptural introduction Mr. Beecher informed the congregation that a young woman had been sold by her own father, to be sent South.

"She was bought by a slave trader for twelve hundred dollars, and he has offered to give you the opportunity of purchasing her freedom. She has given her word of honor to return to Richmond if the money be not raised, and, slave though she be called, she is a woman who will keep her word.—Now, Sarah, come up here, so that all may see you."

When the young woman ascended to the pulpit and sank into a chair by Mr. Beecher's side, he assumed the look and manner of a slave auctioneer calling for bids.

"Look," he exclaimed, "at this marketable commodity—human flesh and blood like yourselves! You see the white blood of her father in her regular features and high, thoughtful brow. Who bids? You will have to pay extra for that white blood, because it is supposed to give intelligence. Stand up, Sarah! Now look at her trim figure and her wavy hair! How much do you bid for them. She is sound of wind and limb—I'll warrant her! Who bids? Her feet and hands—hold them out, Sarah—are small and finely formed. What do you bid for her? She is a Christian woman—I mean a praying nigger—and that makes her more valuable, because it insures her docility and obedience to your wishes. 'Servants, obey your masters,' you know. Well, she believes in that doctrine. How much for her?—Will you allow this praying woman to be sent back to Richmond to meet the fate for which her father sold her? If not, who bids?"

The impression produced by these words is indescribable. Mr. Beecher once told Mr. Robert Bonner that he could have been an actor, and his acting as auctioneer was perfect. People held their breath as he proceeded:

"Come now! We are selling this woman, you know, and a fine specimen, too. Look at her; see for yourselves. Don't you want her? Now, then, pass the baskets and let us see."

The congregation was wrought up to the highest pitch. Women became hysterical; men were almost beside themselves. For a half-hour money was heaped into the contribution boxes; women took off their jewelry and rings, bracelets and brooches were piled one upon the other. Men unfastened their watches, and some threw coin and bank notes upon the pulpit; and above all the confusion Mr. Beecher's powerful voice rang out:

"In the name of Christ, men and women, how much do you bid?"

At this point a gentleman arose and shouted that several members would make up the deficiency whatever it might be. The wildest demonstrations of enthusiasm followed. The collection was found to be more than sufficient to purchase the freedom of Sarah, who was established in a little home of her own at Peekskill, New York. This slave auction was the most remarkable of the many that later took place in Plymouth Church, and undoubtedly was a very effective means of opening the eyes of the people to the horrors of slavery.

Tweed, the Sailor, and the Water-Throwing Contest [7]

[William Marcy] Tweed's election as Foreman of *Big Six* [in 1850] made him a petty political power. There was a freemasonry among the volunteer firemen that knew no partisanship. This fraternalism was so deep-rooted that it long survived the abolition of the old non-paid force. When legislated out of existence, the volunteers had laws passed giving them an equal footing with the veterans of the wars in matters of public appointments. These acts were placed in the stat-

[7] From *"Boss" Tweed,* The Story of a Grim Generation, by Denis Tilden Lynch, pp. 58–62. Copyright, 1927, by Boni & Liveright, Inc. New York.

ute books by lawmakers who had once worn red shirts. They fought with one another. But they closed their ranks and formed an unbreakable hollow square when menaced by an outside force. *Big Six* numbered seventy-five men, each with a vote. Political mathematicians multiply by five to obtain the minimum strength of an active partisan in the ranks. This arbitrary formula—a fair one—raised the voting strength of *Big Six* to 375. Tweed was a successful businessman, with a name identified with the life of the [Cherry Hill] neighborhood for three generations. To cap all this, he had a personality that inspired confidence. And he was fast growing in popular esteem.

* * * * *

A favorite sport of the volunteer firemen was to engage in water-throwing contests. These were usually held on a Saturday afternoon when the men would be enjoying a half-holiday from their regular employment. Rivalry was keen at these tournaments which were conducted in the street, in front of a saloon boasting a Liberty Pole. All the pretentious beer gardens in the vicinity of a fire house went to considerable expense to obtain the tallest of pines to set before their doors. The more prosperous of these places had standing orders with local shipyards for a mast that topped their present possession.

The year Tweed was made Foreman of *Big Six,* the town had a hearty laugh at the expense of the red shirts of the entire West Side of the city. Engine company after engine company had vainly tried to throw a stream of water over the new Liberty Pole that had been raised in front of Riley's saloon on the irregular plaza formed by the junction of Franklin Street and West Broadway. The proud owner announced that he would not adorn the Liberty Pole with the Phrygian cap until a stream of water had been thrown over its top.

After the firemen of the West Side failed, the challenge was taken up by the engine companies on the East Side. Tweed, ever with an eye for the dramatic, waited until all the rivals of *Big Six* had had their chance and failed. Not a stream of water had struck within seven feet of the top of the pole.

Tweed and his red shirts clattered out of their headquarters on Gouverneur Street on a balmy Saturday afternoon in late September. All the small boys of the neighborhood knew where their own *Big Six* was headed, and its purpose. And they raced behind the gleaming engine drawn by their seventy-five idols, at whose head ran Tweed, his face aglow, and his silver trumpet glistening encouragement to his perspiring followers.

No halt was made until the engine had been drawn west of Riley's Liberty Pole. The wind was from the Hudson River, and Tweed wanted the breeze at his back. Thousands were present to see *Big Six* succeed where its rivals had failed. While his men were making ready, Tweed scrutinized the tall pine that had defied every other engine company in the city. He had to admit that it seemed taller than any other, but then *Big Six* had cleared the tallest on the East Side by at least two feet. And other units had failed to come within spattering distance of the Phrygian cap. Tweed had little doubt of the outcome.

A cheer rose from the crowd as the stream of water left the nozzle of the hose. At the end of fifteen minutes a thundering roar of applause went up as *Big Six* ceased its efforts. Tweed and his red shirts had outdistanced their rivals, but they did not throw the stream over the top. They failed by less than three feet.

"We'll try again tomorrow afternoon at three o'clock," Tweed announced to the crowd.

"The engine won't make it," said Johnson, the artist, when *Big Six* returned to its headquarters. Johnson was Assistant Foreman of the company under Tweed.

"The men were not up to their usual mark today," replied Tweed.

Johnson shook his head. Men couldn't have striven harder. The fault was not theirs. They had worked the apparatus to capacity. There wasn't an engine in the town capable of the feat.

"Wait till tomorrow," said Tweed, doggedly.

Tweed did not eat at home that night. He went down to the waterfront. One of his boyhood chums accompanied him. They boarded a clipper ship where one of the crew was a brother of Tweed's companion. Fortunately he was on board. Tweed outlined his plan. It was simple. He wanted the sailor to climb Riley's Liberty Pole between two and three the following morning and saw six feet off the top. And for his labors he would receive ten dollars. A princely sum in those days. Tweed gave him five dollars on the spot, the balance to be paid the following evening at the headquarters of *Big Six*. Tweed's parting word to the sailor was to leave no evidence behind him, urging him to return after he had disposed of the sawed-off top and remove any tell-tale traces of sawdust.

The following morning the sailor's brother examined the ground and reported to Tweed that there was not a single speck of sawdust to be seen anywhere near the Liberty Pole. Highly elated, Tweed led *Big Six* in the afternoon to the scene of their defeat of the day before.

The plaza was thronged. And again when *Big Six* sent the water streaming skyward, it was to the accompaniment of inspiring cheers.

In five minutes' time *Big Six* gave up the futile struggle, and Tweed quietly, yet eloquently, condemned a particular sailorman to the nether regions. Tweed had been tricked. Of course there could be no traces of sawdust, as not an inch had been taken off the Liberty Pole. Tweed eventually laughed. He always enjoyed a good joke, even when it was on himself.

A year later Tweed met the sailor again. He demanded to know why the sailor had not played fair with him. The man of the sea calmly replied that as he had received only half of the amount he felt that he would even up the account by climbing halfway up the pole. And this he had done. Tweed, amused at the coolness of the explanation, went on his way.

While Tweed was at the height of his power, nearly twenty years after the Liberty Pole incident, the sailor called on the Boss and said that misfortune had been his lot ever since he had played false. He was now down and out, and lacked even the price of the next meal.

"There," said Tweed, as he handed the sailor a five-dollar bill, "that will keep you from starving, and it squares our account. I promised you ten dollars for the job and you tricked me. Now I am going to try to make an honest man of you. Come and see me tomorrow and I will give you work."

Tweed gave the man work. We must pardon the Boss for his seemingly unctuous preachment on honesty. Tweed was sincere. The sailor had violated a cardinal tenet of Tweed's moral code. The game must be played in accordance with the rules. The sailor had cheated.

The Christening of the Little Church Around the Corner [8]

The useful career and unblemished character of George Holland will be recalled by all who knew him. He lived, a bright and cheerful spirit, in this world for eighty years, for time could not age his youthful heart.

[8] From *The Autobiography of Joseph Jefferson,* pp. 336–340. Copyright, 1889, 1890, by Joseph Jefferson. New York: The Century Co.

The two churches, together with their rectors, involved in this account were the Church of the Atonement, on the corner of Madison Avenue and Twenty-

He was the merriest man I ever knew. Practical joking was a passion with him, and though his pranks were numerous, by some good fortune they always ended innocently and with harmless mirth. I remember that on one occasion, when some goldfish had been placed in the ornamental fountain in Union Square, Holland dressed himself in a full sporting suit, and with a fish basket strapped upon his shoulder, a broad-brimmed hat upon his head, and a rod in his hand, he unfolded a campstool, and quietly seating himself in front of the fountain, began to fish, with such a patient and earnest look in his face that no one could have supposed that it was intended as a practical joke. This strange spectacle soon attracted a curious crowd about the sportsman, who, with a vacant and idiotic smile, sat there quietly awaiting a nibble. A policeman soon forced his way through the crowd and arrested Holland, who explained with a bewildered look that he was fishing in his own private grounds. The policeman naturally concluded that the intruder was some harmless lunatic, and, patting him kindly on the shoulder, bade him go home to his friends. Holland burst into a flood of tears, and while affectionately embracing the guardian of the law contrived to fasten the fish-hook into the collar of the policeman's coat, who walked slowly and sympathetically away, unconsciously dragging the line and rod after him. The crowd, seeing the joke, roared with laughter as Holland quickly made his way to the nearest omnibus, which he reached before the infuriated policeman could catch him.

Upon the announcement of the death of George Holland [in 1870], I called at the house of his family, and found them in great grief. The sister of Mrs. Holland informed me that they desired the funeral to take place from the church, as many of Mr. Holland's friends would like to mark their love and respect for him by their attendance, and that the house in which the family lived was too small to receive the large gathering of people that would be likely to assemble. The lady desired me to call upon the pastor of her own church, and request him to officiate at the service. I at once started in quest of the minister, taking one of the sons of Mr. Holland with me. On arriving at the house I explained to the reverend gentleman the nature of my visit, and the arrangements were made for the time and place at which the funeral was to be held. Something, I can scarcely say

---

eighth Street, from which the actor George Holland was refused burial by the Rev. William T. Sabine, and the Church of the Transfiguration, at 1 East Twenty-ninth Street, where the funeral service was read on December 22, 1870, by the Rev. Dr. George Hendric Houghton.

what, gave me the impression that I had best mention that Mr. Holland was an actor. I did so in a few words, and concluded by presuming that probably this fact would make no difference. I saw, however, by the restrained manner of the minister and an unmistakable change in the expression of his face that it would make, at least to him, a great deal of difference. After some hesitation he said that he would be compelled, if Mr. Holland had been an actor, to decline holding the service at the church.

While his refusal to perform the funeral rites for my old friend would have shocked under ordinary circumstances, the fact that it was made in the presence of the dead man's son was more painful than I can describe. I turned to look at the youth, and saw that his eyes were filled with tears. He stood as one dazed with a blow just realized; as if he felt the terrible injustice of a reproach upon the kind and loving father who had often kissed him in his sleep, and had taken him on his knee when the boy was old enough to know the meaning of the words, and told him to grow up to be an honest man. I was hurt for my young friend, and indignant with the man—too much so to reply; and I rose to leave the room with a mortification that I cannot remember to have felt before or since. I paused at the door and said: "Well, sir, in this dilemma is there no other church to which you can direct me, from which my friend can be buried?"

He replied that "there was a little church around the corner" where I might get it done; to which I answered: "Then, if this be so, God bless 'the little church around the corner' "; and so I left the house.

The minister had unwittingly performed an important christening, and his baptismal name of "The Little Church Around the Corner" clings to it to this day.

Humor of the Blizzard of '88 [9]

. . . As always happens in great emergencies, the meanness and sordidness that seem to be human nature, and are but its disguise and old clothes, vanished. Everybody wanted to help everybody else.

[9] From *From Sandy Hook to 62°*, Being Some Account of the Adventures, Exploits and Services of the Old New York Pilot-Boat, by Charles Edward Russell, pp. 184–185, 192–193. Copyright, 1920, by Charles Edward Russell. New York and London: The Century Co.

And in the midst of the calamity the irrepressible New York spirit of humor broke out. For some reason that I do not understand the neighborhood of Sixth Avenue and Twenty-third Street seemed to be a conspicuous center of the tempest. A merchant in West Twenty-third Street that had watched all day the growth of an alpine range in front of his door came out in the afternoon with a hugh placard that he stuck on the end of a pole on the mountain top. It read:

IMPORTANT NOTICE
THIS IS TWENTY-THIRD STREET

* * * * *

. . . You never find your New York wholly daunted of its characteristic and cynical good humor. The comedian and his signs now appeared everywhere. A huge drift at Third Avenue and Thirty-first Street was adorned with one of some size and splendor that said:

TAKE SOME!

At 105th Street another such drift bore this announcement:

WANTED—A CASHIER FOR THIS BANK

At another place:

THIS LOT TO BE RAFFLED JULY 4
CHANCES $10

At Barclay and West Streets was this:

WANTED—
ONE THOUSAND MEN TO CHEW SNOW

At Fifth Avenue opposite the Union League Club:

SNOW FOR SALE!
COME EARLY AND AVOID THE RUSH!

The First Steel Skeleton Skyscraper [10]

"There is no limit to the skyscraper, as it is called. I am now at work on a thirty-story building for the Wall Street district that will be as original a departure from the present type of steel skeleton structure as the first one of that type was from the old style of office building when I put it up. There will not be an inside room in the edifice. It will cover a much greater floor area than any office building of its size in the world. I am not at liberty to give details. Just as a photographer who wants to get a composite type of a race of people places negative upon negative until he attains the desired result, I have amalgamated one plan with another until I believe I have evolved the most perfect office building yet in existence. But it will in many respects be essentially different from what is now commonly known as the skyscraper."

So declared Bradford Lee Gilbert, architect of the first steel skeleton building in New York, or in the world, for that matter, when he was asked how he came to construct the first skyscraper nearly a generation ago, one soon to be torn down to make way for a larger building.

"It was a case of the boy, the chipmunk, and the minister coming for dinner," said Mr. Gilbert. "During the spring of 1887, John L. Stearns, who owned the first skyscraper in New York, found himself in possession of a double plot in New Street, just south of Exchange Place, with a Broadway frontage of only twenty-one feet. He was unable to dispose of this non-income property except at a considerable loss. He came to me to devise a plan that would enable him to build upon this property on a paying basis. I puzzled over the matter for six months or more. The building laws were explicit as to the required thickness of the walls for superstructure. Anything higher than the existing buildings on the plot could only be built at an actual loss. It would not pay to erect a high building on the Broad-

[10] From "The Birth of the New York Skyscraper," *New York Times,* May 21, 1905.

According to the commemorative tablet, the Tower Building, erected in 1888–9, was the "earliest example of the skeleton construction, in which the entire weight of the walls and floors is borne and transmitted to the foundation by a framework of metallic posts and beams."

way plot to reach the larger rear building, when the thickness of the walls required would leave a passageway only on the three main Broadway floors a little over ten feet in width. A low entrance building on Broadway for a higher office building in New Street would benefit only the abutting property. The problem grew perplexing and interesting in proportion.

"One day the idea came upon me like a flash that an iron bridge truss stood on end was the solution of the problem. The building laws did not limit the height of the foundations of a building either below or above the curb line. This was evident from the first-floor level of the prevailing high stoop, or English basement. I saw no reason why it was not feasible to carry the foundations up seven or eight stories, or even to the roof itself, in order to obtain floor space where it was most desirable. There was no reason why I should not begin the superstructure six stories above the curb. Having demonstrated to my own satisfaction the safety and practicability of such a construction I went to Superintendent D'Oench, who was then at the head of the Building Department in New York. While he agreed that my plan was feasible, he said, frankly, that no law existed under which the construction could be approved. It required the tedious negotiations with a Board of Examiners before the plans were approved in April, 1888. Meanwhile, the newspapers had made my 'idiotic building,' as some of them called it, talked about all over the United States. Architects came from as far away as Portland, Oregon, first to examine my plans, and then to denounce them as unsafe and impracticable. I was told, time and time again, that the building would blow over with the first stiff gale that came up the bay from Sandy Hook.

"The construction throughout the narrow portion of the building, as filed and erected, called for a twelve-inch curtain, or non-bearing inclosing walls between the foundation columns below the eighth story, and in some sections the entire height of the thirteen stories in the building, or about 160 feet, the weight of the curtain walls and floors being transmitted by girders to the wall columns at initial points, and there cared for by cement pile footings. Thus, out of a total available width of 21 feet 6 inches, 20 clear feet was obtained (on account of the party wall on the south) through the most valuable and rentable of the Broadway floors and offices. In fact, this wall space as saved and rentable, over the previous style of construction, proved worth upward of $10,000 a year.

"When the actual construction of the building began, my troubles increased tenfold. The mere suggestion of a building 21½ feet wide, rising to a height of 160 feet above its footings, filled everybody who had no particular concern in the matter with alarm. Finally, an engineer with whom I had worked for many years came to me with a protest. When I paid no attention to him he wrote to the owner. The owner came to me with the letter. He was afraid the building would blow over, and that he would be subject to heavy damages. My personal position in the matter, and that of the Building Department that had given me the permit, never seemed to strike him at all. Finally, I drew out my strain sheets, showing the wind bracings from cellar to roof, and demonstrated by analysis that the harder the wind blew the safer the building would be; as, under one hundred tons under hurricane pressure, while the wind was blowing seventy miles an hour, the structure was cared for by its footings, and was safest. And that is as true of the twenty-story skyscraper of today as it was of the thirteen-story skyscraper then. 'You must trust somebody,' I said, 'and you would better trust your architect for the sake of your peace of mind. To show my faith in the building I will make my offices in the two upper floors of the Broadway end. If the building falls, I will fall with it.'

"This seemed to satisfy him, and we went ahead. One Sunday morning, when the walls of the building were ready for the roof, I awoke to find the wind blowing a hurricane. That gale is a matter of record in the Weather Bureau. With a friend who had implicit faith in my plans I went downtown to the skyscraper. A crowd of persons who expected it to blow over stood at a respectful distance to watch the crash. Janitors and watchmen in adjoining buildings and structures across the street moved out. They were afraid of being crushed to death, and said unpleasant things about my steel frame building. I secured a plumb line and began to climb the ladders that the workmen had left in place when they quit working the previous evening. My friend went with me as far as the tenth story. The persons who looked at us from below called us fools.

"When I reached the thirteenth story the gale was so fierce I could not stand upright. I crawled on my hands and knees along the scaffolding and dropped the plumb line. There was not the slightest vibration. The building stood as steady as a rock in the sea. In my enthusiasm I was rash enough to stand erect and wave my hat. The wind caught me and carried me toward the end of that scaffolding. It is in emergencies like that that a man prays, if he ever prays. I prayed, not only giving thanks to God that my building was weathering that awful strain, but I prayed for safety. Just as I reached the end of the platform a rope that was swaying in the wind from an upright beam of the tower was swept within my reach. I grasped it, held on, dropped to my knees, and crawled back to the ladder. My friend and I descended to the street and walked arm in arm up Broadway singing the Doxology.

"There is nothing to fear about the safety of the skyscraper[s]. The Baltimore fire has put them to the severest test. I went there to watch them. They were not found wanting when weighed in the balance. Some attempt has been made to confound the steel-frame building with the cage-constructed building, like the Pulitzer Building and the Home Insurance Company Building. There is a radical difference. While steel was used in construction of these buildings, and the inner weight supported by the columns, the outer walls were thick enough to be self-sustaining. In the Tower Building, the first skyscraper, everything depended on the steel framework, outer walls and all.

"It has been demonstrated over and over again that the longer iron or steel is buried in cement the stronger it is. The men who tear down the first skyscraper ever built in New York are going to have a run for their money, long as the building has been standing. The Pabst steel-frame building, which was torn down to make way for the new home of *The New York Times,* was a new structure. This one has stood the wear of years. It cost only $250,000, as against the two-million-five-hundred-thousand-dollar skyscrapers of today. The skyscraper idea brought in $90,000 a year in increased rental. I am sorry I did not copyright it. The royalties would have amounted to millions. I should have done so, but I was scared off by lawyers who said lawsuits about infringements would outweigh the possible advantages."

4

Struggles and Triumphs

I think Gotham Society may be said to be composed of two great bodies—the "Wall-Streeters" and the "Knickerbockers." The former is chiefly noted for the wealth, enterprise, and "dash" of its members . . . who delight in "cornering stocks," or getting up a "squeeze" in cotton, or, possibly, "wrecking a railroad". . . and win or lose a fortune with the nerve and coolness of a Napoleon.—Heinrich Oscar von Karlstein [*F. C. Valentine*]

The Astor Story

GETTING A START[1]

John Jacob Astor, first, . . . lived at No. 81 Queen (now Pearl) Street (1786), and sold musical instruments. . . . New York wasn't a century old when the first Astor came here from his father's home in Baden, with a settled conviction in his mind that the town of his adoption had a great future and that he would link his destiny with it. Young Astor had fifteen guineas ($75) and a suit of Sunday clothes

[1] From *Seeing New York,* A Brief Historical Guide and Souvenir of America's Greatest City [by Julius Chambers], pp. 12–13. Copyright, 1908, by American Sight-Seeing Coach Co. New York: American Sight-Seeing Boat & Transportation Co.; American Sight-Seeing Car and Coach Co.; American Sight-Seeing Bus Co.

when he set out. He voyaged in the steerage, because he needed all his capital. On the sea he made the acquaintance of a fellow-countryman who had been here and had made enough money in the fur trade to revisit his native land. Astor wrote down in a memorandum book (which exists in the family archives) every suggestion regarding the fur business that he gathered from his unknown traveler.

The ship was caught by the ice in Chesapeake Bay and its loss seemed inevitable. Every other traveler put on his oldest clothes, but Astor appeared in his best suit. When asked a reason for this act, he answered: "If I'm saved I'll have my good clothes; if I'm drowned it will not make any difference how I'm dressed."

When the young man reached New York he began as a journeyman baker, being too proud to accept a clerkship under his brother Henry, who was the head of the existing "Beef Trust." He was an excellent baker, and "Astor rolls" are known to this day. After trying several trades he became a clerk to Robert Brown, a fur dealer, at $2 per week and board. He was sent up the Hudson to buy skins from the hunters and trappers. He learned the languages of the Mohawks, Senecas, and Oneidas.

At last he started in trade on his own account, with $500 borrowed from Henry Astor and a dowry of $300 from his bride, Sarah Todd. He organized his business, and within ten years had a regiment of Indians and white men killing wild game for him. He became the pioneer American in the China trade. One of his ships visited the Sandwich Islands and carried a cargo of sandalwood to China that netted nearly a hundred thousand dollars profit. Meanwhile his interests had been pushed to the mouth of the Columbia River, to Puget Sound, and to Hudson's Bay, in the far North.

He began to buy real estate, not farms, for building sites. Then it was that he laid down the principle, adhered to with very slight deviation, that "Astor bought property, but did not sell!" And so the financial giant grew until he became the wealthiest man of his century. He left to the people of New York a marvelous heritage in the Astor Library and the first good hotel, opposite City Hall Park, and to his heirs $20,000,000, which has grown today to fully half a billion dollars.

STORM'S HOTEL[2]

. . . Upon the point of land between Park Row and Centre Street stood Storm's Hotel, with which the name of John Astor was curiously asso-

[2] *Ibid.*, p. 26.

ciated. A faithful clerk in his employ was retired at the age of sixty, and the fur merchant asked him whether he would choose free board at Storm's for the rest of his life or $1,000 in cash. The clerk chose the former offer, and lived there in one of the best rooms for twenty years, much to Astor's chagrin at his own liberality.

JOHN JACOB ASTOR IN THE MILLINERY BUSINESS[3]

. . . They say that [John Jacob Astor, the elder] had a mortgage on a millinery store. I never reach this point without thinking that the ladies will say that "Fools rush in where angels fear to tread.". . . But John Jacob Astor had a mortgage on a millinery store, and foreclosed the mortgage and went into business with the same people who had failed on his hands. After he entered into partnership, he went out and sat down on a bench in the Park. What was the successful merchant doing out there, in partnership with people who had just failed on his own hands? Ah, he had the most important, and to my mind, the pleasantest part of that partnership. He was out there watching the ladies as they went by—and where is the man who would not get rich at that business? As he sat upon that bench, if a lady passed him with her shoulders thrown back and her head up, and looking straight to the front, as though she didn't care if all the world did gaze on her, then John Jacob Astor studied the bonnet she wore; and before it was out of sight, he knew the shape of the frame, and the curl of the lace, and crimp of the feathers, and lots of intricate things that go into a bonnet which I cannot describe. Then he went to his millinery store and said: "Now put in the show window just such a bonnet as I describe to you, because I have just seen a real lady who likes just such a bonnet." Then he went and sat down again. Another lady, with another form and complexion came, and, of course, she wore another style of bonnet. He then went back and described that and had that put into the window. He didn't fill his show window full of hats and bonnets to drive the people away, and then sit down in the back of the store and bawl because people went somewhere else to trade. . . . He didn't have a hat or a bonnet that some lady didn't like. That has since been the wealthiest millinery firm on the face of the earth. There has been taken out of

[3] From "Acres of Diamonds," by Russell H. Conwell (copyright, 1901, by Russell H. Conwell), in *Modern Eloquence,* editor Thomas B. Reed; Justin McCarthy, Rossiter Johnson, Albert Ellery Bergh, Associate Editors, Vol. IV, Lectures, A-E, pp. 321–322. Copyright, 1900, by the University Society. Philadelphia: John D. Morris and Company.

the business seventeen millions of dollars and over, by partners who have retired. Yet not a dollar of capital have they ever put into that business, except what they turned in from their profits—to use as capital. Now, John Jacob Astor made the fortune of that millinery firm not by lending them money, but by finding out what the ladies liked for bonnets, before they wasted any material in making them up. And if a man can foresee the millinery business, he can foresee anything under Heaven! . . .

THE BANK CLERK'S OPINION[4]

It was [John Jacob Astor's] instinctive abhorrence of ostentation and waste that enabled him, as it were, to glide into the millionaire without being observed by his neighbors. He used to relate, with a chuckle, that he was worth a million before any one suspected it. A dandy bank clerk, one day, having expressed a doubt as to the sufficiency of his name to a piece of mercantile paper, Astor asked him how much he thought he was worth. The clerk mentioned a sum ludicrously less than the real amount. Astor then asked him how much he supposed this and that leading merchant, whom he named, was worth. The young man endowed them with generous sum-totals proportioned to their style of living. "Well," said Astor, "I am worth more than any of them. I will not say how much I am worth, but I am worth more than any sum you have mentioned." "Then," said the clerk, "you are even a greater fool than I took you for, to work as hard as you do." The old man would tell this story with great glee, for he always liked a joke.

A DEAL IN LAND[5]

. . . It was neither his tea trade nor his fur trade that gave Astor twenty millions of dollars. It was his sagacity in investing his profits that made him the richest man in America. When he first trod the streets of New York, in 1784, the city was a snug, leafy place of twenty-five thousand inhabitants, situated at the extremity of the Island, mostly below Cortlandt Street. In 1800, when he began to have money to invest, the city had more than doubled in population, and had advanced nearly a mile up the island. Now, Astor was a shrewd calculator of the future. No reason appeared why New York should not repeat this doubling game and this mile of extension every fifteen years. He

[4] From *Life of John Jacob Astor, to Which Is Appended a Copy of His Last Will*, by James Parton, p. 50. Entered . . . 1865, by James Parton. New York: The American News Company.

[5] *Ibid.*, pp. 60–61.

acted upon this supposition, and fell into the habit of buying lands and lots just beyond the verge of the city. One little anecdote will show the wisdom of this proceeding. He sold a lot in the vicinity of Wall Street, about the year 1810, for eight thousand dollars, which was supposed to be somewhat under its value. The purchaser, after the papers were signed, seemed disposed to chuckle over his bargain.

"Why, Mr. Astor," said he, "in a few years this lot will be worth twelve thousand dollars."

"Very true," replied Astor; "but now you shall see what I will do with this money. With eight thousand dollars I buy eighty lots above Canal Street. By the time your lot is worth twelve thousand dollars, my eighty lots will be worth eighty thousand dollars." Which proved to be the fact.

ASTOR'S JOKE[6]

[John Jacob] Astor dearly liked a joke, and occasionally indulged in a sly bit of humor himself. On one occasion a committee called upon him to solicit a donation for some charitable object. The old man took the subscription list, and, after examining it, signed it and gave the committee a check for fifty dollars. They had expected much more, and one of them ventured to say: "We did hope for more, Mr. Astor. Your son gave us a hundred dollars."

"Ah!" replied the old man drily. "William has a rich father. Mine was very poor."

The Commodore

STATEN ISLAND FERRY[7]

. . . [When] Vanderbilt [was] . . . fifteen years old, it seems that he had entertained fantastic and boyish visions of going to sea and adventuring; to make these dreams practical, his mother offered him a reward of one hundred dollars with which he might buy a boat, provided

[6] From *Great Fortunes, and How They Were Made;* or, The Struggles and Triumphs of Our Self-Made Men, by James D. McCabe, Jr., p. 93. Cincinnati: E. Hannaford & Co. 1871.

[7] From *Old Roads from the Heart of New York,* Journeys Today by Ways of Yesterday Within Thirty Miles Around the Battery, by Sarah Comstock, pp. 103–104. Copyright, 1915, by Sarah Comstock. New York and London: G. P. Putnam's Sons. The Knickerbocker Press.

he accomplished an almost impossible farm task. Young Cornelius immediately laid the project before some of his boy friends, promised them sails in the boat if they would help him win it, and the task was forthwith accomplished. Instead of seeking treasure islands or playing hooky to loaf in his boat, he conceived the idea of ferrying passengers back and forth to the island, which he did for eighteen cents a trip. By the end of the first year he not only paid his mother for the boat, but had cleared one thousand dollars. By the end of the next year he had cleared another thousand and had secured a fractional interest in some more boats. He often went without his meals to carry excursion parties across. During the War of 1812 his business became tremendous. And so begins a story of transportation.

"CORNELE" AND THE HARLEM RAILROAD[8]

It was ten o'clock of a Sunday morning in June, 1863. The place was the bedroom of Commodore Vanderbilt, the new president of the Harlem Railroad. The speakers were Commodore Vanderbilt, still in bed, and I. D. Barton, his first freight-agent, formerly a Harlem Railroad conductor. The story is told in Barton's words.

"The commodore had a habit of lying in bed late Sundays, although he was an early riser week-day mornings. Railroading was comparatively new to him; he had just got hold of the Harlem road; but he had a faculty of asking questions, and it was with this object in view that he sent for me to discuss freight-rates.

"I was ushered into his bedroom. The old commodore pulled himself up and began firing queries at me.

" 'What does it cost to ship a ton of coal from here to White Plains?' he asked, pointing his index finger first to the right and then to the left. He had a habit of doing that when he talked.

"I told him.

" 'Umph! Huh!' he sort of groaned, and, after a pause: 'And how much for a horse and buggy?'

"Again I gave him the amount.

"There was another pause. Finally: 'And how much for a barrel of flour to White Plains?' I told him the rate. Without hesitation, the old commodore, now in a sitting posture, said gruffly: 'Put your rates down on flour and coal; poor people use those things; but anybody

[8] From "With the First Vanderbilt," by C. P. Greneker, *The Railroad Man's Magazine,* Vol. II (February, 1910), No. 1, pp. 147–150. Copyright, 1910, by the Frank A. Munsey Company. New York.

that can afford to have a horse and buggy can afford to pay high freight-rates. Put your rate up on horses and buggies.'

"That ended the 'freight meeting,'" commented Barton, "and the next day I had a new tariff. When I read of this teapot tempest which is being raised over rate legislation, I often wish that the old commodore, with his common sense, were here to spread oil on the troubled waters. Horse sense is what he had, and a heart as big as this sofa."

We were seated on a plush-covered divan of tremendous proportions, in one corner of which half reposed the figure of the commodore's first freight-agent, a man now seventy-six years of age, who had seen service on several roads as general superintendent. His last position, which was given up on account of advanced years, was in charge of operation of the Brooklyn Rapid Transit.

"Yes, he had the kindest disposition of any man I ever knew," continued the veteran. "One day we were standing near the ticket window of the Twenty-sixth Street station—that was at Fourth Avenue—when a woman with four or five children came up and asked for tickets to Chatham. She lacked one dollar of having enough money.

"The commodore never missed anything. He overheard the woman's conversation with the ticket-agent and, calling me aside, told me to pay the difference and charge it to 'profit and loss.' Before carrying out his wish, I ventured to ask the woman why she wanted so many tickets and the cause of her financial embarrassment.

"She replied that her husband could not get work in New York or, at least, I should say she began to tell me that when the commodore, who I thought was some distance away, broke in with: 'What? Can't get work in New York? Your husband must be a fine specimen,' he thundered. He had followed me up to hear what I said.

"'No, yure rivirince,' explained the woman, 'it was this way.' And with that she led up from around the corner of the station a one-legged man, who was her husband. 'He wure run over by er train on this very road.' The man nodded, as though to confirm his wife's story.

"'When?' demanded the commodore with some passion. He had just taken possession of the road.

"'Some years ago,' answered the woman. 'And he niver got a cint.'

"'Then he'll be my first pensioner,' said the commodore, 'and,' he added, thoughtfully, 'I trust, my last.'

"Yes, indeed," commented Barton, heaving a great sigh, "those were great days. Dick Croker, Tammany's old boss, was a machinist in the Harlem shops at Thirty-second Street; his brother George drove a horse-car on the Fourth Avenue line; and another brother, Ed, was an engineer on the Harlem.

"In those days, just after the commodore got hold of the road, his son, W. H. Vanderbilt, was farming over on Staten Island—a regular country farmer—and he used to sell hay to the Harlem road for the horses that pulled our trains from Tryon Row.

"I can't just recollect the year, but the commodore got tired of mule-power through the tunnel and ordered me to run the trains from Twenty-sixth Street up with engines. Yes, I was general freight-agent at the time and I was also assistant superintendent, but for both jobs I got only seventy-five dollars a month.

"I did as I was told, and soon the city authorities were after us, as all of the property-owners objected to the smoke and noise from the engines. This tunnel was the one under Fourth Avenue, and both sides of the avenue were lined with fine dwellings.

"The commodore defied the authorities until at last a squad of policemen was sent to capture any engine that went through the tunnel pulling a train. The commodore saw to it that I was on that engine. There were about ten policemen and they started for us at Twenty-sixth Street. Four or five were daring enough to climb on the tender, and I tell you we gave them the ride of their lives, and a free bath from the tender tank into the bargain. When we reached Forty-second Street, there wasn't one of them left to tell the tale.

"At the end of the tunnel the commodore was waiting for us. I jumped off, and the train went on. Presently the police squad came charging through the tunnel with an Irish sergeant in command. He was one of the four whom we had first drenched and then discarded. He was a sorry spectacle.

"There the commodore was, in white stove-pipe hat and long black frock coat. A most commanding figure he was. At the sight of him the policemen halted. Before the sergeant had time to say anything, the commodore turned upon them with: 'What do you impertinent rascals mean by trespassing in this tunnel?'

" 'Trespassing do ye call it?' snorted the Irishman. 'A dum foine name it be for murther.'

"The remark so amused the commodore that he laughed until I thought he would burst. The bedraggled appearance of the drenched policemen helped matters along, and soon the sergeant, realizing how he had been worsted, joined in the laughter. The situation suddenly dawned upon the Irishman. He walked up close to the commodore and in a whispered tone said: 'Ye won't mintion it, will ye, yure honor—between two gintlemen?'

"The latter remark I thought would result fatally with the commodore—he laughed so long and heartily. But 'between two gintlemen,' enough had been said, and the incident was closed. The secret was not divulged.

"I was saying I got seventy-five dollars a month. I was handed down, as it were, when the commodore bought the Harlem road, for I had served under five presidents of the same company before Cornele—that's what we sometimes called the commodore—got hold of it. He never thought to inquire as to my salary.

"The road was making money—you remember, a year after the commodore was elected president of the New York Central he declared a stock dividend of eighty per cent—and one day, while out driving with him, he asked, somewhat abruptly: 'What salary are you getting, young man?'

"I told him 'seventy-five dollars' as meekly as I possibly could. 'More than you're worth' was his curt reply. But at next pay-day, I think it was less than a week off, I found that my salary had been doubled.

"I shall never forget this particular ride I took with Cornele. I think it was a Sunday morning. At any rate, we were going up to 103rd Street to look at the new stock-yards. I got in the buggy at Twenty-sixth Street, and before we started, the commodore says to me: 'Young man, they tell me this tunnel leaks.'

"I knew it only too well, but I wouldn't admit it. So I thought by giving an evasive answer he would forget.

" 'I think I'll drive through and see for myself,' said he.

"I remonstrated with him, not that I cared so much about the leaks, but on account of the danger of driving a blooded pair and a light runabout through the tunnel. He appeared not to hear me.

"Whipping up the horses, we started bumping over the ties. Did he find any leaks? If you had known the commodore, you wouldn't ask. As I said, the leaks were there and he found them.

"After emerging from the tunnel at Forty-second Street, the commodore turned into Fifth Avenue. It was then a dirt road above Forty-second Street, and the thoroughfare was lined with boulders. He drove around them so recklessly I feared that we would meet with an accident, but he simply laughed when I told him to be careful. They were very fine horses, that team, and I complimented the commodore on owning such fine stock.

"'By George!' he replied. 'I wouldn't swap them for the whole Long Island Railroad.' At that time I don't know that the commodore was putting too high a valuation on his horses."

TELLING THE COMMODORE OFF[9]

"Commodore Vanderbilt, I wish your daughter in marriage?"

"Hey?" quoth the money king.

"I want your daughter."

"You mean you want my money?" growled Vanderbilt, seated.

"You and your daughter be d——d," said the young lawyer, leaving the room.

"Hold on," said Vanderbilt, raising himself to his feet, and looking suave and paternal. "I rather *like* you. I didn't say you should not have my daughter. You may have her. I rather like you, young man."

Clark never got much of the commodore's money. It is said Vanderbilt even used Clark one day, and his son-in-law lost thousands on thousands. So he boldly told his father-in-law what he thought of him, and after a time the losses were made good.

Even William Vanderbilt, the commodore's pet, did not escape. One day his father said to him: "Sell Hudson, William."

"Thank you," said the son.

Nevertheless, William concluded to look around him. The stock seemed remarkably steady. He discovered by peculiar ways that his father was buying quietly. William covered his movements, and followed suit.

When the day closed, the commodore rode round to the son's office. "Well, William, how much did you lose?"

"I went in at 110 on 10,000 shares, that makes me $260,000."

"Very bad luck, William," soothingly; "very bad luck."

"But then, I bought, you know."

"Hey? What sent you doing that, sir?"

"Why, learning that was your little game, I concluded *short* meant *long* with you."

"Ahem," croaked the benignant commodore, *sotto voce,* buttoning up his fur overcoat.

The commodore has had a high opinion of William ever since that.

[9] From "Representative Men of Wall Street," in *Men and Idioms of Wall Street,* Explaining the Daily Operations in Stocks, Bonds and Gold, pp. 62–63. Entered . . . 1875, by John Hickling. New York: John Hickling & Co., Bankers and Brokers. March, 1875.

THE COMMODORE'S FEINT[10]

There is a story told, with several variations, in regard to a sensational interview between Mr. Gould and Commodore Vanderbilt. The scene is laid in the parlor of the commodore's house. It was about the time that the latter was making desperate efforts to get a corner in Erie, and at that particular juncture when, having been defeated in his purpose by the astute policy of the able triumvirate of Erie—Gould, Fisk, and Drew—he had applied to the courts as a last resort to get even with them.

They had used the Erie paper mill to the best advantage, in turning out new securities of Erie to supply the Vanderbilt brokers, who vainly imagined that they were getting a corner in the inexhaustible stock. Mr. Vanderbilt was wild when he discovered the ruse and had no remedy but law against the perpetrators of this costly prank. These adroit financiers usually placed the law at defiance, or used it to their own advantage, but this time they were so badly caught in their own net that they had to fly from the State and take refuge at Taylor's Hotel in Jersey City.

It seems that during their temporary exile beyond the State, Gould sought a private interview one night with the commodore, in the hope of bringing about conciliatory measures.

The commodore conversed freely for some time, but in the midst of his conversation he seemed to be suddenly seized with a fainting spell, and rolled from his seat onto the carpet, where he lay motionless and apparently breathless.

Mr. Gould's first impulse was to go to the door and summon aid, but he found it locked and no key in it. This increased his alarm and he became greatly agitated. He shook the prostrate form of the commodore, but the latter was limp and motionless. Once there was a heavy sigh and a half-suffocated breathing, as if it were the last act of respiration. Immediately afterward the commodore was still and remained in this condition for nearly half an hour. Doubtless this was one of the most anxious half-hours that ever Mr. Gould has experienced.

If I were permitted to indulge in the latitude of the ordinary story teller, I might here draw a harassing picture of Mr. Gould's internal emotions, gloomy prospects in a criminal court and dark forebodings. His prolific brain would naturally be racked to find a plausible explanation in the event of the commodore's death, which had occurred while

[10] From *Twenty-Eight Years in Wall Street,* by Henry Clews, pp. 623–624. Copyright, 1887, by Henry Clews. New York: Irving Publishing Co.

they were the sole occupants of the room; and at that time, in the eyes of the public, they were bitter enemies.

I can imagine that, in the height of his anxiety, he would have been ready to make very easy terms with his great rival, on condition of being relieved from his perilous position. It would have been a great opportunity, if such had been possible, for a third party to have come in as a physician, pronouncing it a case of heart disease. No doubt Mr. Gould would have been willing to pay an enormous fee to be relieved of such an oppressive suspicion.

The object of the commodore's feint was evidently to try the courage and soften the heart of Mr. Gould, who never seemed to suspect that it was a mere hoax. His presence of mind, however, was equal to the occasion, as he bore the ordeal with fortitude until the practical joker was pleased to assume his normal condition and usual vivacity. If Mr. Gould had been a man of common excitability he might have acted very foolishly under these trying circumstances, and this doubtless would have pleased his tormentor intensely.

Daniel Drew's Handkerchief Trick [11]

[Daniel Drew] was wonderfully prolific in resources for the purpose of getting advantage of those who attempted to overreach him.

A good story, illustrative of this trait in his speculative character, is told of the time that he was so severely squeezed in Northwestern stock. He was greatly grieved at his ill luck, while the brokers and operators who had been prosperous at his expense were highly elated. They considered it a great thing to have caught the wily old Daniel napping. He was accordingly made the victim of much ribaldry and jesting for several days in Wall Street. Some of the young men carried the joke so far as to meet him and laugh significantly and irritatingly in his face. He seemed to take it all in good part, for he had a happy flow of animal spirits, but he had a terrible rod in pickle for these young men who were making him an object of ridicule.

He watched for his opportunity, and one evening as several of them were enjoying themselves in an uptown club, Uncle Daniel walked in, *sans cérémonie*. He appeared to be looking after some man, and though

[11] *Ibid.*, pp. 121–122.

invited to remain, seemed to be in a great hurry to get away, and was apparently excited and warm. He seemed to have something important on hand. He drew a big white handkerchief out of his pocket a few times and wiped the perspiration from his heated brow. When he was about to depart, there came out of his pocket with the handkerchief a small slip of white paper which floated around apparently unseen by him, and alighted at the feet of one of the bystanders, who quickly set his foot upon it. When Mr. Drew made his exit the white scrap of paper was instantly scanned. It contained these ominous words in his own handwriting: "Buy me all the Oshkosh stock you can at any price you can get it below par."

Here was a speculative revelation for the boys, for everybody believed at the time that Oshkosh had already gone too high, and the point had been circulated to sell it "short." The mysterious words written on this erratic slip of paper, however, convinced these operators that there must be a new deal to give Oshkosh another "kiting." There was no time to be lost in taking advantage of the unexpected and highly valuable information. They formed a pool to purchase 30,000 shares the next day. They bought the stock according to pre-arrangement, and a new broker of Daniel Drew's was the man who sold it to them. They only discovered how badly they themselves had been sold by Mr. Drew's handkerchief trick when Oshkosh began to decline at the rate of a dozen points a day, and Uncle Daniel soon raked in from the jokers and their friends more than he had lost in Northwest.

The Erie

MORRISSEY AND FISK[12]

Morrissey and Prince Erie were friends till Black Friday. He had sold to Fisk, believing his word. Fisk, having ruined hundreds, took refuge in his citadel, the Grand Opera House. Morrissey, putting his muscles in order, repaired to that stronghold. He passed the cordon of Fisk's bodyguard, and stood in the presence of the astonished Prince.

[12] From "Representative Men of Wall Street," in *Men and Idioms of Wall Street,* Explaining the Daily Operations in Stocks, Bonds, and Gold, p. 64. Entered . . . 1875, by John Hickling. New York: John Hickling & Co., Bankers and Brokers. March, 1875.

"Well, Morrissey, what is it?"

"Simply your check, certified, for $83,000, in that little matter of — —— ———."

"I never bought that gold. It's only a lawsuit anyway."

"Bah! We are not going to law," said the Prince of the P.R., tightening his fist. "Pay me that money without more bother."

"See my lawyer," stammered Fisk.

"Not at all; your signature is what I want to see."

"Well, this interview had better be ended. If you can't find the door, I will ring for someone to show it to you."

Morrissey didn't care to clean out a regiment of Erie roughs. Lightly brushing back the terrified Prince, [he] broadened his shoulders, threw back his arms into position, and said: "Draw that check."

The role was decided. Fisk saw it. Morrissey got his pay. The bell was not rung, and there was at least one account with Erie which was squared.

FISK AND THE IRISHMAN [13]

An Irishman in his cups told me the following story, so its authenticity can't be exactly vouched for. However, it is just the sort of trick Jim Fisk would have tried.

The Irishman had a heavily mortgaged farm in Scarsdale, New York, and Fisk knew about it. At that time Fisk was deep in trouble with his Erie Railroad deal and needed to dispose of the books of the company. So he told the Irishman to load up a cart with hay, drive in to Washington Market with a yoke of oxen, sell all of the load but two hundred pounds at the usual hour of four A.M., and then drive back and around to the back entrance of the Erie Railroad offices. This the fellow did, and picked up some packages at the office, put them under the hay remaining in his wagon, and drove up Broadway, and so home, where he buried the packages.

Then he received his mortgage—cancelled: reward for his work! I myself do know that his mortgage was satisfied, and that the books for the Erie never were found. . . .

[13] From *Recollections of an Old New Yorker,* by Frederick Van Wyck, pp. 170–171. Copyright, 1932, by Frederick Van Wyck. New York: Liveright, Inc., Publishers.

DEPEW DAMNS ERIE [14]

Illustrating the wild speculative spirit of one financial period, and the eagerness with which speculators grasped at what they thought points, the following is one of my many experiences.

Running down Wall Street one day because I was late for an important meeting, a well-known speculator stopped me and shouted: "What about Erie?" I threw him off impatiently, saying: "Damn Erie!" and rushed on. I knew nothing about Erie speculatively and was irritated at being still further delayed for my meeting.

Sometime afterwards I received a note from him in which he said: "I never can be grateful enough for the point you gave me on Erie. I made on it the biggest kill of my life."

W. H. Vanderbilt's Park Avenue Pasture [15]

New York has completely forgotten the original use of the ground west of the [Grand Central] station, now [occupied] by the Hotel Biltmore. The space was kept beautifully green and enclosed with a picket fence to serve as the pasture for the most famous horse of the day, "Maud S." The famous trotter was owned by William H. Vanderbilt, the head of the New York Central Railroad, who arranged the field so that he might see his favorite horse grazing, from his office window.

J. P. Morgan Wipes Out a Deficit [16]

A certain Mr. ——, though his family was of considerable social importance, had been employed as cashier in a J. P. Morgan bank, and at his death his balances were found to be incorrect. Large sums of money were lacking. This fact came as a thunderbolt to his son. Help-

[14] From *My Memories of Eighty Years,* by Chauncey M. Depew, pp. 353–354. Copyright, 1921, 1922, by Charles Scribner's Sons. New York. 1924.

[15] From *The Romance of Park Avenue,* by F. A. Collins, p. 61. Copyright, 1930 [by the Park Avenue Association, Inc.]. New York.

[16] From *New York's Making Seen through the Eyes of My Ancestors,* by Mary de Peyster Rutgers McCrea Conger (Vanamee), pp. 108–109. London: Methuen & Co., Ltd. 1938.

less and overwhelmed, this son rushed to my father. And, even as he came into my father's presence, pressmen, hot for the scandal, seethed in behind him. As the son gasped out his distress at an inner office door, my father returned to the pressmen and said, "Gentlemen, I sympathize with your position. If you will keep silence till four o'clock today and return to me then, all of you together, I will promise to give you the facts." Thereupon, leaving the young man, he walked to Mr. J. P. Morgan's office. Mr. Morgan's generous swiftness equaled my father's faith. "There will be," Mr. Morgan said, "no deficit." At four o'clock my father gave his promised interview to the newspapermen. He told them that Mr. Morgan said there was no deficit; and though they grasped the course of the morning's events, they completely forwent their story—so completely forwent it that, in the sixty years gone by since then, no hint of it has come to the public or even to Mr. ——'s family.

Hetty Green [17]

There we were [at the St. George in Brooklyn], under the same roof with that famous woman financier, Hetty Green, and having our meals at an adjoining table. Evening after evening, Hetty held court in the foyer with ladies dressed in frilly muslins. She herself was always dressed in musty, fusty black, which stood out like a very dark chocolate drop in a box of pastel-tinted candy. Hetty usually held forth on the subject of Joseph Choate, who had got the better of her in a lawsuit. Outside the pages of Dickens, I had never come across bombazine, black bombazine. It seemed more a state of mind than a material, but Hetty's clothes always looked to be the bombazine of Miss Murdstone, Miss Pipchin, and other grim ladies come to life from Dickens' pages.

The beauty parlor, at that time, did not bloom on practically every city block, and making the best of a woman's appearance had not become one of the nation's great industries. A five-dollar bill would have converted grim Hetty Green into a very handsome old lady—that, and control of her dreadful habit of squinting.

But there were generous things about her, despite her reputation.

[17] From *Ladies Now and Then,* by Beatrice Fairfax (Marie Manning), pp. 85–87. Copyright, 1944, by Beatrice Fairfax. New York: E. P. Dutton & Co., Inc.

For instance, she had the least expensive room in the hotel. It was common knowledge that she paid only eleven dollars a week for it. Her husband, who never appeared in the dining room, had one of the best suites, and her daughter, Miss Sylvia Green, was equally well-housed.

She had other economies, too, unappetizing ones. "Do you mind Hetty, now?" our mutual waiter warned out of the side of his mouth. We minded. Hetty was engaged in strange table rites. Into a half-pint pitcher she poured cream and coffee, dropped in a couple of lumps of sugar; broke and buttered a hot roll, jammed in a slice of bacon. With this she corked the pitcher, slipped the mixture under her black basque, and left the room. The headwaiter bowed her out with the unction reserved for their six-figure clientèle.

"For her little Scotch terrier?" I ventured.

"Divil a bit, 'tis for Miss Sylvia. She ain't coming down this morning."

Her daughter never joined the muslin-clad group that listened to the maternal diatribes against Joseph Choate. Hetty never seemed to have any other line. The talk might start about the weather, or the Floradora sextette, or anything else, but always slid into the iniquitous behavior of Joseph Choate.

That summer Hetty's son, Colonel Edward Howland Green, came to visit his mother. There were two salient points about the Colonel: he had a game leg and a roving eye. But his mother sternly shepherded the roving eye as it lingered on the muslin-clad group in the foyer. Despite little attempts on the part of the ladies to make room for the Greens, Hetty never stopped, nor glanced toward her erstwhile acquaintances. She took no chances with her big boy. The Green gift for making money must not be cluttered up with romance.

The Colonel's private apartment, in the Texas town where he lived, beggared anything New York had to offer in the way of luxury, rumor said. He entertained glamorous actresses and lovely visiting firewomen. Anything asked for could be had at his private bar. Yet, when his mamma descended on him, he turned the key on his Babylonian splendors, took rooms at the Young Men's Christian Association, put on ready-made clothes, and surpassed old Great-great-grandfather Howland in parsimony. These were current tales, and may indeed be just another bit added to the Green saga.

I'm a dog addict, a weakness dogs never fail to realize, and Hetty's little Scotch terrier would make for me whenever we met. I suppose it must have been curiosity that made me put the question to the old lady: "Why do you love this little dog so much, Mrs. Green?"

She looked at me out of those curiously puckered eyelids, and answered: "He doesn't know how rich I am."

Cool Operator: Jim Fisk Speeds the Parting Passenger [18]

Among the expresses of recent date, no company has been formed on such a scale of liberality in equipments as the one started by James Fisk, Jr., and called the New York and Boston Express. This express commenced with the running of the Narragansett Steamship Company's boats between New York and Fall River, about three years since [as of 1872]. The feasibility of this route for a first-class express was very apparent to Mr. Fisk, and he lost no time after the line passed into his hands in carrying out his plans. . . .

. . . He was born to command, and possessed the rare faculty of inspiring others to almost impossible achievements. His capacious brain grappled with projects of overwhelming dimensions, and mastered them without apparent effort. Operations involving immense outlays, which an ordinary manager would require days and weeks to digest, were decided and acted upon with such rapidity that they excited distrust, and seemed to border upon recklessness; yet results showed them to be the shrewd combinations of a mathematical brain, marvelously conceived and marvelously executed.

An amusing instance of his promptness and audacity was once witnessed by the writer. One of the large steamers of the Narragansett Company was just leaving her dock in New York. The gangway planks had been hauled in, and Fisk stood on the dock waving an adieu to some friends on board, when an individual, valise in hand, rushed down to the landing, exclaiming, "I must go! I must go!" "Go you will," said Fisk, grasping him under the arms, and giving him a toss towards the moving boat. "Look out for him, boys," shouted Fisk, as the astonished traveler alighted safely on board, followed by his valise. This audacious transaction occupied but a moment, yet it was characteristic of the cool operator, who, during the affair, had not ceased

[18] From *Waifs from the Way-Bills of an Old Expressman,* by T. W. Tucker, pp. 115–117. Entered . . . 1872, by Lee and Shepard. Boston and New York.

to smoke his cigar, nor did a smile disturb the self-complacency of his countenance.

A. T. Stewart

FLOORWALKER[19]

. . . The A. T. Stewart store was a woman's store. In hiring salesmen the owner picked only gentlemen of presence. The "floorwalker" had his rise in A. T. Stewart. Once a woman asked a floorwalker this question, "Do you keep stationery?" and the answer was, "If I did I'd never draw my salary." This is a silly story, and if it ever happened, it did not transpire at A. T. Stewart's. There the floorwalker was always as a cow that is being milked. For the first fifteen years of his career Stewart made it a rule to meet and greet every customer, personally.

The floorwalker—or "head usher," as he was called—was either the proprietor or his personal representative.

Stewart never offered to shake hands with a customer, no matter how well he knew the lady, but bowed low, and with becoming gravity and gentle voice inquired her wishes. He then conducted her to the counter where the goods she wanted were kept. As the clerk would take down his goods, Stewart had a way of reproving the man thus: "Not that, Mr. Johnson, not that—you seem to forget whom you are waiting on!"

When the lady left, Stewart accompanied her to the door. He wore a long beard, shaved his upper lip, and looked like a Presbyterian clergyman making pastoral calls.

Silks, dress-goods, and laces gradually grew to be the A. T. Stewart specialties. That the man had taste and never ran stripes around a stout lady or made a very slim one look more so, is a matter of history. "I have been hoping you would come, for we have a piece of silk that seems to have been made for you. I ordered it put aside until you could see it. Mr. Johnson, that silk pattern, please, that I told you not to show to anyone until Mrs. Brevoort called. Thank you; yes, that is the one."

Then there were ways of saying, "Oh, Mr. Johnson, you remember

[19] From *Little Journeys to the Homes of Great Business Men, A. T. Stewart,* by Elbert Hubbard, Vol. 25 (October, 1909), No. 4, pp. 107–108. Copyright, 1909, by Elbert Hubbard. East Aurora, N. Y.: The Roycrofters. 1909.

the duplicate of that silk-dress pattern which was made for Queen Victoria— I think Mrs. Astor would like to examine it!"

Thus was the subtle art of compliment fused with commerce and made to yield a dividend.

COST SALE[20]

. . . The first man in New York to work the "Cost Sale" scheme was A. T. Stewart. In eighteen hundred thirty he advertised:

> Mr. A. T. Stewart, having purchased a large amount of goods soon to arrive, is obliged, in order to make room for these, to dispose of all the stock he has on hand, which will be sold at Actual Cost, beginning Monday at eight A.M. Ladies are requested to come early and avoid the crush.

At another time he advertised:

> A. T. Stewart is obliged to raise a large amount of money to pay for silks and dress-goods that are now being made for him in Europe. To secure this money he is obliged to hold a Cost Sale of everything in his store. This sale will begin Friday at noon, and end at midnight on Saturday, the day after.

* * * * *

During those first years he used to have a way of opening cases on the sidewalk and selling from the case to the first person who made an offer. This brought him good luck, especially if the person had cross-eyes or was a hunchback. The messy clutter in front of the store and the pushing crowds advertised the business.

Finally, a competitor next door complained to the police about Stewart's blocking the sidewalk. The police interfered and Stewart was given one day to clear off the walk. At once he put up a big sign:

> Our neighbors to the right, not being able to compete with us, demand that we shall open no more goods on the sidewalk. To make room we are obliged to have a Cost Sale. You buy your goods, pay for them and carry them away —we can't even afford to pay for wrapping-paper and string.

* * * * *

If A. T. Stewart sold goods at an average profit of, say, thirty per cent, he could well afford to sell a small portion of his stock at cost, or even at ten per cent below cost. He knew his stocks, and he made it a point never to carry goods over from one year to another.

[20] *Ibid.*, 109–110, 114–115.

Before he held one of his famous "Cost Sales," he would personally work all night, taking down from the shelves and out of drawers and showcases everything in the store. Then he himself would dictate what each article should be sold for. Here was exercise for a mind that worked by intuition.

The master decided instantly on how much this thing would bring.

* * * * *

Dry-goods deteriorate in quality when kept on the shelves for several months. Worse than that, they cease to attract the buyers. People go where there is life, activity, and are moved by that which is youthful, new and fresh. Old stocks become dead stocks, and dead stocks mean dead business and dead men— bankruptcy.

When it came to selling old stocks, Stewart paid no attention to the cost. He marked the tag in big, plain figures in red ink at the price he thought would move the goods. And usually he was right.

We hear once of his marking a piece of dress-goods forty-nine cents a yard. A department salesman came and in alarm explained that the goods cost fifty-three.

"That has nothing to do with the case," replied Stewart; "we would not buy it today at fifty-three, and we do not want the stuff on our shelves even at forty-nine."

"But," said the manager, "this is a Cost Sale, and if we sell below cost we should explain that fact to the customers."

And the answer was, "Young man, you must tell the customer only what she will believe. The actual truth is for ourselves."

"TEN PER CENT OFF"[21]

To all charitable objects [A. T. Stewart] gave liberally. He gave to all churches, and was recognized as a sort of clergyman himself, and in his dress he managed to look the part.

The ten per cent off to clergymen and school teachers was his innovation. This ten per cent was supposed to be his profit, but forty per cent would have been nearer it. Of course the same discount had to be given to any member of a clergyman's or a teacher's family. And so we hear of one of Stewart's cashiers saying, "Over half of the people in New York are clergymen or teachers." The temptation to pass one's self off for a clergyman at Stewart's was a bait that had no lure when you visited Girard College.

[21] *Ibid.*, p. 110.

All this was but a part and parcel of the times—an index of the Zeitgeist. Bear-baiting, dog-fighting, and open gambling had given way to milder excitements, and the sweet desire to smuggle or get an unauthorized discount was the lingering joy of the chase.

Macy's

RED STAR

I[22]

. . . The first [Macy trademark] occurred in 1860, when Macy sold hoopskirts to his order and bearing his name stamped by the maker. In 1862 or 1863, if not earlier, he began to use the five-pointed red star which is the general trademark that the firm has used ever since, but the extent of its use at that time on particular articles is not known. . . .

A legend of long standing attributes Macy's adoption of the red star to an experience which he had at sea. According to this story, he was trying to make port through a fog on a dark night and had no bearings by which to steer until he discovered a single star shining through a rift in the clouds. With this as a guide he made port safely, and he later took the red star as a symbol which would guide him to business success.

Since Macy was never in command of a ship, the story is doubtless apocryphal; certainly it will not bear close scrutiny from the point of view of navigation. Possibly the idea came to him when he composed the advertising verse . . . in which the Star of Empire and the Star of Fashion are mentioned.[23] Another suggestion is that he simply took as his trademark the red star which had, in whaling days, been tattooed on his arm.

[22] From *History of Macy's of New York*, 1858–1919, by Ralph M. Mower, pp. 112–113. Harvard Studies in Business History, 7. Copyright, 1953, by the President and Fellows of Harvard College. Cambridge: Harvard University Press.

[23] "Westward the Star of Empire takes its way!"
So does the Star of Fashion and of graces,
Judging, at least, by the vast crowds each day
Rushing to MACY'S.

Broadway no longer tempts with costly glare,
With fancy shop fronts and still fancier prices,
Cheapness—if good and tasteful for the fair—
Is what entices. . . .

Whatever the origin of the trademark, its use meant that Macy, rather than the manufacturer, assumed responsibility for the merchandise on which the star appeared, and its adoption at so early a stage of the store's development is additional evidence of Macy's business genius. Many of the steps which have been taken by the firm since the 1860's mark a growing realization of the responsibility which such private branding entails.

II[24]

In his store in Haverhill, Mr. [Rowland H.] Macy had adopted as his trademark a rooster bearing the motto in his beak, "While I live, I'll crow." For his nascent enterprise in New York, however, he adopted a different and, to him at least, a far more significant device, which to this day remains the symbol of the great enterprise which still bears his name.

It was a star, a star of red, if you will. And back of that simple symbol rests a story: It seems that in the days of his youth when he sailed the northern seas in a whaling ship he had gradually acquired such proficiency that he was made first mate and then master. It was in the earlier capacity, however, and upon an occasion when he was given a trick at the wheel that Macy found himself in a thick fog off a New England port—one version of the story says Boston, the other New Bedford. To catch the familiar lights of the harbor gateways was out of the question. The cloud banks lay low against the shore. Overhead there was a rift or two, and in one of them, well ahead of the vessel's prow, there gleamed a brilliant star.

For the young skipper this was literally a star of hope. His quick wit made it a guiding star. By it he steered his course and so successfully into the safety of the harbor that the star became for him thereafter the symbol of success. With the strange insistency that was inherent in the man, he was wont to say that the failure of his Boston store was due to the fact that he had not there adopted the star as his trademark. He made no mistake in his New York enterprise. The star became the forefront of his business. And to this day it is a

---

"Westward the Star of Fashion takes its way!"
That it should poise o'er MACY'S is not funny;
'Tis that he SELLS GOODS EQUAL TO BROADWAY
FOR MUCH LESS MONEY.

—*Ibid.*, p. 60.

[24] From *The Romance of a Great Store,* by Edward Hungerford, pp. 22–24. Copyright, 1922, by Robert M. McBride & Co. New York.

prominent feature of the main façade of the great establishment which bears his name.

Mr. Macy never lost his boyhood affection for the sea—the one thing inborn of his ancestral blood. It is related of him that one morning on his way to the store he found a small silver anchor lying on the sidewalk, picked it up, placed it in his pocket and thereafter carried it until the day of his death, regarding it as a talisman of real value. There was one souvenir of his early connection of which he was greatly ashamed, however. As a boy he had permitted his shipmates to tattoo the back of his hands. In later years he regretted this exceedingly, and developed a habit of talking to strangers with the palms of his hands held uppermost, so that they might not see the tattoo marks.

"ODD PRICE"[25]

There was still another merchandising idea born of that great and fertile New England brain that needs to be set down at this time. For many years a notable feature of the advertising of the Macy store has been in the peculiar shading of its prices—at forty-nine cents or ninety-eight, or at $1.98 or $4.98 or $9.98 rather than in the even multiples of dollars. A good many worldly-wise folk have jumped to the quick conclusion that this was due to a desire on the part of the store to make the selling price of any given article seem a little less than it really was. As a matter of fact it was due to nothing of the sort. With all of his respect for the honesty of his sales-force, the Yankee mind of R. H. Macy took few chances—even in that regard. He felt that in almost every transaction the money handed over by the customer would be in even silver coin or bills. To give back the change from an odd-figured selling-price the salesman or the saleswoman would be compelled to do business with the cashier and so to make a full record of the transaction. With the commodities in even dollars and their larger fractions, the temptation to pocket the entire amount might be present.

It required a good deal of logic, or long-distance reasoning, to figure out such a possibility and an almost certain safeguard against it. But that was Macy. His was not the day of cash-registers or other checking devices. The salesman or the saleswoman in a store was still apt to find himself or herself an object of suspicion on the part of his or

[25] *Ibid.*, pp. 26–27, 41.

her employer. Business ethics were still in the making. A long road in them was still to be traversed.

* * * * *

[Once a] partner (Mr. Wheeler) worried himself almost into a nervous breakdown for fear that there would not be enough pennies for the cashier's cage during the forthcoming holiday season. Mr. Macy's odd-price plan was something of a drain upon the copper coin market of New York. And at this particular time, the local shortage being acute, Mr. Wheeler took a night train and hurried to Washington, to see the Secretary of the Treasury. Late the next evening he returned to New York and went to the house of Miss Abbie Golden, his head cashier, at midnight, just to tell her that he had succeeded in getting an order upon the director of the Philadelphia Mint for $10,000 in brand-new copper pennies. After which he went home, to a well-earned rest.

TEAR IT DOWN[26]

In [the] summer of 1901, while the architects and contractors were busy at their plans and specifications [for the new Macy store in Herald Square] there was wholesale and systematic devastation upon such a scale as New York has rarely ever seen. Such pullings down and tearings away! The scene was not without its drama at any time. . . .

* * * * *

. . . A restaurant-keeper who had a small eating place on the Broadway side of the site sought obdurately to hold out in his location—seeking an advantageous cash settlement from the store owners. His lease, perfectly good, still had from sixty to ninety days to run. He felt that the store could not wait that length of time upon him—that, in the language of the street, it would be forced to "come across." But it did not "come across." It was not built that way. It was built on either side of the restaurant. Its steel girders were far above its tiny walls and spanning one another across its ceiling before its disappointed proprietor moved out—at the end of his perfectly good lease—and without one cent of bonus money in his pocket; after which it was almost a matter of mere hours to tear the flimsy structure away and remove a small segment of earth that held it up

[26] *Ibid.*, pp. 75–76, 77–78.

to street level. A barber around the corner in Thirty-fourth Street caught his cue from the restaurant. He, too, was going to stand pat. But he was not in the same strategic position as the *restaurateur*. He had no lease. He merely was going to stay and defy the wreckers. They would not dare to touch his neat, immaculate shop.

They did dare. On the very night that his lease expired something happened to the business enterprise of the razor-wielder. A cyclone must have struck it. At least that was the way it looked. The barber, coming down to business on the morrow, found his movables upon the sidewalk, neatly piled together and covered by tarpaulins against the weather. But the shop was gone. Where it had stood on the close of the preceding day was a deep hole in the ground; and three Italian workmen were whistling the Anvil Chorus.

"DOES MACY'S TELL GIMBELS?"[27]

Gimbels is less than half the size of Macy's, but is organized for merchandising scoops which can be aggressively promoted. Unlike Macy's, it has a bargain basement where price is frankly highlighted. Periodic price wars on specific items find comparison shoppers posted in the enemy store, and when the cuts come thick and fast they complain of running out of change to phone back their reports. Since Macy's does a complete job of checking all stores, Gimbels can get by with a shopping force just large enough to check Macy prices. During the price war of 1951, Gimbels comparison-shopping department was headed by a woman appropriately trained in Macy's—a clear case of Macy's telling Gimbels. Both stores have on occasion bought peace at any price by buying out the other's complete supply of an item at issue.

During the war, the competition turned on availability of scarce merchandise. Macy's promised a brighter future with copy asking, "When will Macy's have it?" In reply, pugnacious Miss Fitz-Gibbon featured Gimbel exclusives under the headline "Gimbels *has* it!" The two stores occasionally vary the battle with friendly gestures. In 1946, they buried the hatchet long enough to adopt a well-publicized uniform outdoor decorating scheme for Christmas. In 1953, Gimbels called attention to Macy's flower show with an advertisement which trumpeted, "Does Gimbels tell Macy's? No. Gimbels tells the world!"

[27] From *The Great Merchants,* The Stories of Twenty Famous Retail Operations and the People Who Made Them Great, by Tom Mahoney, pp. 166–167. Copyright, 1947, 1950, 1951, 1952, 1955, by John Thomas Mahoney; 1949, by the Curtis Publishing Company. New York: Harper & Brothers.

Macy's responded politely with a thank-you: "Nobody but nobody said it more prettily than Gimbels." Customers loved it as much as British sports fans love the way tennis contenders shake hands at the net.

Brooks Brothers' "See-You" Customers [28]

Possibly the most important feature of the Brooks [Brothers] tradition is the personal service given regular customers. Brooks salesmen refer to these people as "see-you" customers. Because of a policy of "open book" selling, whereby one clerk may serve all the needs of a customer, strong relationships are established. These customers are frequently reluctant to be served by any other than their favorite salesman, and should he be on vacation, the customer waits until his return. "Mr. So-and-So wants to see you," goes the word. Many customers never bother to learn their own measurements but rely wholly on the little black book of their favorite salesman.

So unswerving in their loyalty to the store are these "see-you" customers that four or five generations from one family is not uncommon. One salesman, the late Frederick Webb, served five generations of Morgans, calling them by their first names. It is doubtful if any store in the world can equal such continuous patronage as that given Brooks Brothers by the late John R. Voorhis, one-time Grand Sachem of Tammany Hall and noted for his immaculate dress. When he was ten, his mother bought him his first long pants at Brooks Brothers and, until his death at one hundred and two, he never bought a suit elsewhere.

How Lane Bryant Was Born [29]

In 1904, the year that New York opened its first subway, young Mrs. Bryant moved to 1489 Fifth Avenue. This was between 119th and 120th Streets and only a short walk from Mount Morris Park,

[28] *Ibid.*, pp. 35–36.
[29] *Ibid.*, pp. 242–243.

where there was a playground for her son. For $12.50 a month, the household of three rented the first floor of a new six-story building. They lived in the rear and used the front room as a shop, hanging garments from the gas fixtures.

Enough trousseau finery was made to cause the place to be known as a bridal shop. An early sign misspelled it "bridle." But Mrs. Bryant soon earned more than a neighborhood reputation for fine work of all kinds, especially for women of unusual proportions. She estimated lengths by eye, ignored tape measures and patterns, kept few records but turned out better-fitting garments than many of her customers had previously worn. More carriages began to arrive at the door and the earrings made fewer trips to the pawnshop.

Into the modest shop one day walked an attractive young woman for whom Mrs. Bryant had previously done some sewing. After exchanging greetings, the customer announced: "I am going to have a baby, Mrs. Bryant. What shall I do?"

For an instant the young widow thought that her visitor was asking medical advice, but this was not the case.

"You make all kinds of things," continued the visitor; "can't you make me something that will be both pretty and practical and in which I can entertain at home?"

While the Empress Eugenie had been recorded as having worn a maternity dress in Europe, such a garment was unknown in New York in 1904, but Mrs. Bryant met the challenge. She created a comfortable and attractively concealing tea gown by the simple device of an elastic band attaching an accordion-pleated skirt to a bodice. The result was the famous No. 5 maternity gown, so called because it was given this number when the business grew large enough for a price list.

The first purchaser was grateful and enthusiastic. She was happy to pay $18 for the gown and praised it continually to her friends. She volubly told them about the ingenious little widow who made it. More expectant mothers ordered the tea gowns.

Word of Mrs. Bryant's talent and popularity reached the big downtown stores and two of them offered her jobs. But she preferred independence and the opportunity to rear her son. Her sister had married, and her new brother-in-law offered to lend the young widow $300 with which to open a bank account and to use as working capital for the purchase of fabrics.

Formalities required that Mrs. Bryant appear in the ornate quarters of the old Oriental Bank at 182 Broadway. She was so unaccustomed to the grandeur of the surroundings and the awe of having so much money that she filled out the deposit slip not as Lena Bryant but as *Lane* Bryant.

Thus was born Lane Bryant. The young widow was at first too timid to rectify the mistake and later grew to like the euphonious name. She used it when she opened a new shop in a loft at 19 West Thirty-eighth Street, a few yards off Fifth Avenue. . . .

The Missing Wanamaker Label[30]

It was [Mr. Rodman Wanamaker's] custom when I was General Manager to call me when he reached the store about one P.M. and invite me to have luncheon in his private dining room. After luncheon he would make a brief inspection of the store, singling out the floors he was particularly interested in on that particular day. One day when we had a large hat sale going on in our downstairs store, Mr. Rodman and I went down in the elevator and then through the tunnel into the basement of the old building, where the hat buyer had assembled a great display of women's hats at five dollars. There were so many customers crowding the basement for the sale that we had trouble walking through from the Fourth Avenue side of the store. Mr. Wanamaker didn't mind this a bit, however. The success of the sale made him fairly glow with pleasure.

He turned to me and asked if we had John Wanamaker labels in all the hats. I told him that not only were our labels in every hat, but that I had instructed the buyers never to sell any merchandise in the apparel line unless the name of the store was in it. As we were leaving the hat department, Mr. Rodman picked up a hat and looked inside it. He smiled, handed it to me and said, "I thought you told me every hat on these counters had John Wanamaker labels in them."

I looked inside the hat and could find only a size label. Quickly I picked up two or three hats from different counters. All carried the Wanamaker label, as I showed Mr. Rodman. But he kept on holding the unlabeled hat in his hand. When I asked him for it, he said he was going to keep it as a souvenir.

We continued on our inspection of the other floors. When we fin-

[30] From *Mr. New York,* The Autobiography of Grover A. Whalen, pp. 165–167. Copyright, 1955, by Grover Whalen. New York: G. P. Putnam's Sons.

ished I left Mr. Rodman off at his office on the fourth floor and proceeded back up to mine on the eighth floor. Sitting sobbing inside my office waiting for me was the buyer of the downstairs hat department. She had observed the scene with Mr. Rodman over the label.

"I worked all night, Mr. Whalen, with twenty of my girls sewing in labels because I know how strict you are about that," she said tearfully. "I went through almost every hat we had out after you and Mr. Rodman left, and every one had a label in it," she continued.

"Now, now, Miss Walsh," I said, "pull yourself together. That could very easily happen with the large stock you're handling." She left my office somewhat reassured.

At the close of each day all the buyers were requested to come to Mr. Rodman's office and hand him their sales slips for purchases and returns during the day. That night Mr. Rodman greeted them with the hat still under his arm. When Miss Walsh came before him with her sales slips, he asked her to wait until he had finished "taking sales," as it was called. That was all she needed. She was so exhausted from the strenuous sale and from working the previous night preparing for it that she burst into hysterical tears. Of course from my own early experiences I appreciated her problem very well indeed, so I walked over to her and asked her to step into the next office.

When Mr. Rodman was through taking sales, I explained to him that the label probably had fallen out of the hat during handling by the customers. I asked him if perhaps I could speak to the buyer for him. He gave me a quizzical look and handed me the hat. I went back into the next room and gave Miss Walsh the good news that she could go home. This is a typical example of the sort of pressure undergone by department store buyers during their business day, at Wanamaker's and elsewhere. I don't think anyone works much harder than a good buyer.

Sherry Never Disappoints a Patron [31]

. . . There came a time . . . when a certain New Yorker decided to honor an important social occasion upstate with a gift of a large and most wonderful cake. Sherry's got the order. As sometimes hap-

[31] From *The Story of Louis Sherry and the Business He Built,* by Edward Hungerford, pp. 20–21. Copyright, 1929, by William Edwin Rudge. New York.

pens, it got it at the eleventh hour. That was the hour at least when that same manager of the New York establishment, arriving at his office, found the huge cake still unfinished; with the order imperative that it go to the state capital on the one o'clock train out of the nearby Grand Central Terminal. . . . There was a deal of confusion. And some excuse for it:

The favors—thirty lovely gold bracelets that were to have been imbedded deep within the cake—had not yet arrived. The masterpiece could not be completed until they had been inserted. "Finish baking that cake," ordered the manager, "but do not put on the decorations."

Then he set out in a taxi to get the favors. He found them in the shipping-room of the jeweler's, took them with him to the station, and there, by appointment, met two of the chef's crew. A drawing-room in a Pullman had been engaged. In it, between New York and Albany, the cake was finished. Slits were cut down into it, the bracelets were inserted, and the candles and the icing were fitted as the swift train made its way. It was ready and on time. . . . "Never disappoint a patron," was an early tradition of Louis Sherry. "Get a special train, a special boat— anything— but never disappoint a patron."

5

Peacocks on Parade

Ye dandies of Gotham; I've seen fools and fops in forty different cities, but none to compare with you.—Dow's Sermons

Peacock Alley [1]

. . . [Peacock Alley] originally was the corridor forming the Thirty-third Street lobby of the [Waldorf] hotel, where women of fashion were supposed to play the peacock and strut in their fine frocks for the delectation of the other sex and the envy of their own. When the Astoria opened, the Thirty-fourth Street Corridor claimed the promenaders and inherited the name. It was a corridor three hundred feet long. At first nobody ever thought of it as anything but just a corridor; a grand one, of course, in the biggest hotel in America. But this is how Oscar explains how it got its name:

The first corridor ran between the Palm Room and the Empire Room. The Palm Room was perhaps New York's most lavish and exclusive restaurant. Not even Delmonico's surpassed it. It was there that the most prominent people of the town—that social dynasty including the Vanderbilts, the Goulds, and the Twomblies—dined. Tables were engaged long beforehand; otherwise you didn't get in. There usually was not a table to be had after seven o'clock in the evening. You saw the women come in, their long trains draping the

[1] From *Peacock Alley,* The Romance of the Waldorf-Astoria, by James Remington McCarthy, pp. 60–61. Copyright, 1931, by James Remington McCarthy and John Houghton. New York: Harper & Brothers.

floor, the diamonds and pearls and necklaces gleaming, or their generously feathered hats bobbing up and down as they moved with stately tread along the corridor.

People from the outside used to jam the corridor every night just to see this parade of fashion, beauty, and importance. Those who did not come to be seen came to see. Since there was prestige attached to staying at the hotel, it was but natural that guests would want to show themselves off. So they strolled through the corridor. Finally somebody—Oscar never learned just who it was—and nobody knows to this day, for that matter—remarked that the corridor seemed like an alley of peacocks. Then newspapers picked up the label, "Peacock Alley." Nobody protested it, because it really wasn't irrelevant; the people of wealth who dined in the Palm Room rather liked it, for they were not ashamed of their pride.

The Hyphen [2]

The public mind refused to consider the Waldorf and the Astoria as two separate hotels, though the new building had been put up as a separate entity and the old retained its own engine room and machinery for many years, in case coolness between the Astor cousins should dictate that the two hostelries be operated separately. [George C.] Boldt, of course, did not invent the hyphen; he did, however, receive credit for first putting it into a hotel's name. Who would wish to say "the Waldorf and the Astoria"? The hyphen was handy; besides, the compound name had a definite advertising value. It was sonorous. Few syllables have more inflectional possibilities than "or," and here it was . . . repeated. "We are going to stop at the Wald-o-r-f-Astor-r-ia!" How impressive it must have sounded back in the home town when a prospective patron thrilled the Sewing Circle or the Civic Improvement Club with the announcement! And, however blasé New York professed to have grown by this time, its average citizen must have felt that as the city could now boast what was by far the world's biggest and most luxurious hotel, its claim to being the world's

[2] From *Peacocks on Parade,* A Narrative of a Unique Period in American Social History and Its Most Colorful Figures, by Albert Stevens Crockett, pp. 86–87. Copyright, 1931, by Sears Publishing Company, Inc. New York.

greatest city—if not actually its largest—had gained substantiation.

The joke-makers took up the name and it flew about on potent wings of humor.

"Where shall I meet you?" one might ask a wag who had heard "the latest."

"At the Hyphen."

"What do you mean?"

"Aw, between the Waldorf and the Astoria, of course!" [3]

Mrs. Astor's Ball [4]

. . . Queen of the Four Hundred as [Mrs. Astor] was, in New York society she reigned supreme, and her decisions as to things social were final, from which there was no appeal. She could make or mar the ambitious climber.

The annual ball at the Astor house was the greatest social event of the year. It was also the occasion for much heartburning. Several weeks beforehand Mrs. Astor and Harry Lehr, as her lieutenant, would sit in solemn conclave scanning the columns of the Social Register, deciding who should and who should not be invited. The Astor ballroom only held four hundred, therefore [as Ward McAllister declared for all time] New York society must be limited to Four Hundred. One name after another was brought forward and rejected. Mr. and Mrs. X——? No, they were too blatantly in trade. . . . "I buy my carpet from them, but then is that any reason why I should invite them to walk on them? . . ." said Mrs. Astor.

The process of elimination went on. The lists were written and rewritten at least half a dozen times until the guests had been brought within the limits of the four hundred. Then the invitations were sent out. This was always done by Maria de Baril, who acted as a sort of social secretary to all the great hostesses of New York and Newport, where she took up her abode during the season. The moment an en-

[3] By the spring of 1899 somebody was singing on the stage a song called *The Waldorf-Hyphen-Astoria,* whose words various New York papers printed. —James Remington McCarthy, *Peacock Alley* (New York, 1931), p. 92.

[4] From *"King Lehr" and the Gilded Age,* with Extracts from the Locked Diary of Harry Lehr, by Elizabeth Drexel Lehr, pp. 80, 86–90. Copyright, 1935, by Elizabeth Drexel Lehr. Philadelphia and London: J. B. Lippincott Company.

velope addressed in her delicate handwriting, embellished with the Gothic scrolls which no one dreamt of imitating, appeared on the breakfast tray, one knew that here was an invitation of importance. For Maria de Baril was exclusive, as befitted one who claimed descent from the Incas. Her handwriting was by no means at the disposal of any one who could pay for it. She had to make certain that invitations emanating from her pen would only be received by people of eminence before she would condescend to despatch them. She would arrive at the great houses of Fifth Avenue, a stout dumpy little figure, always bedizened with a weird assortment of bead necklaces and amulets, receive her list of guests and depart to send out her invitations, perfectly worded to suit the occasion.

Weeping and gnashing of teeth on the part of those who did not receive the coveted slip of cardboard, "Mrs. Astor requests the pleasure. . . ." Life could hold no more bitter mortification. There remained only one course open to them—to hide the shameful truth from their friends. They did it at all costs. Doctors were kept busy during the week of the ball recommending hurried trips to the Adirondacks for the health of perfectly healthy patients, maiden aunts and grandmothers living in remote towns were ruthlessly killed off to provide alibis for their relations . . . any and every excuse was resorted to. Not a man or woman in society who would let their friends jump to the dreadful conclusion that their absence from the greatest social event of the year was due to lack of an invitation!

Even after all the acceptances had been received, there remained another problem whose solution almost demanded the judgment of Solomon: Who should sit on "The Throne"?

Even after all these years I have only to close my eyes to conjure up a vision of the Astor ballroom in all its splendors. The massive candelabra that William Astor had brought back from Italy, the walls lined with pictures of the nineteenth century French school, New York's last word in European culture, the long rows of chairs tied together in pairs with ribbons, the musicians' gallery with the band in the familiar Astor blue liveries. And on a raised platform at one end was an enormous divan—"The Throne." No one ever dreamt of calling it anything else. But alas, capacious as were its depths, it could only accommodate a limited number on those ample red silk cushions and there was acute disappointment every year when the seats were allotted. Once I remember Mrs. John Drexel ("Cousin Alice," as Harry Lehr christened her and every one else called her thereafter) bursting into noisy tears when she saw the names on the Throne list and found her own not included among them. Sobbing, she seized upon Mrs. Orme Wilson. . . . "Your mother doesn't like me. She has given me the most dreadful humiliation. . . . Oh, I have never been hurt so in my life. . . ."

"But what has Mother done?" asked Mrs. Astor's daughter in astonishment. . . .

"My name is not on the Throne. . . . She does not love me. . . . I won't stay one minute longer in a house where I am not loved. . . ."

And she rushed out to the entrance hall in her white satin ball dress and ran to the cloakroom pursued by Harry Lehr. It was several minutes before he succeeded in bringing her back to the ballroom and persuading her that no slight had been intended.

The occupants of the Throne outside the family were generally chosen in consideration of their social claims. One lady, however, was debarred from the privilege on account of her enormous hips. . . . "How can I have her when you have to allow at least two ordinary seats for her?" asked Mrs. Orme Wilson plaintively. There was a harrowing legend of how on the one occasion when she had sat in the row upon the seat of honor her neighbor had been a young Englishman. Feeling her massive hips in their tight steel corsets running into him he turned to her and asked in all innocence. . . . "I wonder if you would mind taking that book out of your pocket? . . ." She rose in outraged majesty. . . . "Young man, you are grossly impertinent . . ." and left the house mortally offended.

There was an amusing incident at the ball which Mrs. Astor gave in Newport immediately after the Spanish War. As usual she had left all the arrangements in the hands of Harry [Lehr]—he had chosen the cotillion favors, issued instructions to the caterers and musicians. When she arrived in the ballroom she was amazed to see the members of the orchestra wearing, in place of their smart blue and gold uniforms, travel-stained suits of khaki. . . .

"What is the meaning of this?" she asked Harry. He was just as puzzled as she. Suddenly the explanation dawned on him. He had wired instructions to the orchestra. "Wear regular uniforms . . ." and as they had all been serving with Colonel Jack Astor in Roosevelt's Rough Riders, they had interpreted his instructions as a command to appear in their military uniforms!

The Seeley Dinner [5]

. . . For years [the Seeley dinner] was the subject of quip and wisecrack; the stage travestied it; the pulpit rolled it under its tongue as a sweet morsel and then spat it out as one of the depravities of the age. Today such a festivity as the "Seeley Dinner" might almost be done in the open and attract only momentary interest. But that was in a time when closed doors and "peeping elders" made many things wicked whose mention as happening these days would hardly serve to lift an eyebrow.

When the shouting and the tumult had begun to recede, the notoriety Mr. Seeley's little party attained was ascribed to the jealousy of a Broadway theatrical agent—not, however, a press agent. Certainly, the host was not anxious that certain features of his dinner be advertised in the public prints, although he himself was a nephew of that most noted of free advertisers and circus men, the late Phineas T. Barnum, and the agent who, in reportorial phraseology, spilled the dope, was not paid by him.

Herbert Barnum Seeley had certain social ambitions. He wanted to be known as a man-about-town. A fortune, partly inherited from the gentleman who first discovered and capitalized the fact that the American people liked to be bamboozled, enabled the nephew to head in that direction. An occasion for Mr. Seeley properly to challenge the attention of those with whom he would mingle was furnished by the pending marriage of his brother Clinton. So Herbert announced a bachelor dinner in honor of the prospective bridegroom, to take place at Sherry's on Saturday night, December 19, 1896.

As originality was promised—and something about just what form that originality might take was permitted to leak out to those invited—he had no difficulty corralling a lot of the young bloods of the time who rated as men-about-town, and a few approaching middle age, some of them belonging to families of well-established social positions. "Among those present," as reported, were Clarence A. Postley, Commodore of the Larchmont Yacht Club, Horatio R. Harper, Alfred Marshall and Wilson Marshall, later to attain yachting fame as the

[5] From *Peacocks on Parade,* A Narrative of a Unique Period in American Social History and Its Most Colorful Figures, by Albert Stevens Crockett, pp. 183–190. Copyright, 1931, by Sears Publishing Company, Inc. New York.

owner of the *Atlantic,* winner of the German Kaiser's international yacht race, from Sandy Hook to the Lizard, in 1905. Others were Marmaduke Tilden, H. W. Harris, Charles Tobias and the elderly father of the two Seeleys.

Bachelor dinners at Sherry's, according to surviving witnesses, were memorable events. The intendant voyager on uncharted matrimonial seas must be toasted not once, but many times, and his bride as well. The toastmaster would stand up, glass in hand, and would call, "Bumpers!" or "Bottoms up!" and everybody must drain his cup. Then each must hurl his "empty" towards the opposite wall, with magnificent disregard for delicately frescoed walls, or gold-banded wine-glasses. Proceedings grew fast and furious as enthusiasm waxed, but the main damage was to the glasses. For, after costly experience, Sherry's men would always measure the manly aim when it was soberest, and to that height carpenters would build, before such a festivity, a padding so decorated that the drinkers would not readily discover it was not the real wall; otherwise they would have considered themselves cheated out of a share of due enjoyment. Seldom were fewer than ten rounds of toasts drunk during one evening.

To amaze as well as please his guests, Mr. Seeley's bachelor party must offer spice, as well as anything and everything fancy could dictate in the way of drink. To produce the necessary nutmegs, the host went to Broadway. A theatrical agent agreed to furnish the best talent on his booking-list and named as his price a sum a third-rate booking-agent would turn up his nose at nowadays. According to report, it was one thousand dollars. The agent later asserted it was only two hundred and seventy-five. "Damn the expense!" said rich young Mr. Seeley, in effect, at the mention of whatever was the sum. "Go ahead!"

News of the contract seeped to other Broadway theatrical sanctums. Whichever was the correct figure, it was big money. It set rival agents thinking. One of them called upon Mr. Seeley and made him aware that he was to pay an exorbitant price. Why, the bearer of the tidings would furnish talent even better and more numerous for considerably less! A stroke of what proved to be misguided thrift made Seeley lend his ear to the tempter and the agreement with the first agent was canceled.

Now, the jealousies of Broadway have always kept apace with the illuminations. Other agents listened to the lamentations of the first and made common cause with him. They decided to squeal.

The night of the dinner, an emissary of the vaudeville bund sought the officer in charge of the Tenderloin police station, in West Thirtieth

Street. He was the famous Captain Chapman, whose ferocious mien and landscaped side-whiskers were familiar in New York as those of the "Czar of the Tenderloin." Sherry's was in his precinct, and "unlawful and disorderly practices" were his concern. The envoy of the disgruntled agents confided to the autocrat that at Sherry's an "obscene" entertainment was even then going on, with women dancing naked—or, as was the novel and polite expression of the time, thanks to Du Maurier's *Trilby,* "in the altogether." Chapman's sympathy was won by the plea of an alleged father—later unmasked as a vaudeville agent—to protect his "daughter," one of the performers engaged, from being made to strip—"do a Trilby"—against her will, before a lot of men.

The Czar of the Tenderloin went into action immediately, but whatever that action was, it happened too late to make the Sunday morning papers. On Monday, however, almost everybody in New York was scrambling to get hold of a copy of the *World,* which had "blown the lid off," as the saying was—a phrase originating from the action of steam upon the lid of a pot, but also ascribed to similar effects of sewage gas upon manhole covers. Not yet had screaming headlines four inches tall been seized upon to add emphasis to a scandal. True, the story was on the front page of the *World.* There it needed no four-inch type for emphasis. In space just one ordinary column wide was a text that for two months was to furnish the greatest sensation of its time.

In modern eyes, how tame that heading! "FUNNY RAID ON SHERRY'S," it read. And below: "Capt. Chapman and a Squad Invaded a Private Dinner Party; Heard of a Naughty Dance; Report that a Woman Was to Entertain Fifty Revellers in a Shocking Way."

Not many particulars were given in the story, which besides the heading, occupied not more than half a column. It was mostly based on the information given Chapman. In substance: "A woman was to pose and dance. She would be in the altogether. It was to be the gayest, raciest dinner ever given in New York." And it was told that Chapman and half a dozen detectives had forced their way into Sherry's and burst upon Mr. Seeley and his astonished guests. But Chapman had not found the naked lady he was looking for.

The *Morning Journal* now went after the story, but the *World* was not to be outstripped. And the soberer newspapers had to take up the tale. Inside a day or two, it was revealed that the dancer Chapman had sought was "Little Egypt," a specialist in the coutchie-coutchie, or coochee-coochee—the *danse du ventre* which had first shocked and thrilled Americans on the Midway Plaisance of the Chicago World's Fair, in 1893. The spelling of the name originally was apt to depend much, in the language of Sam Weller, "upon the taste and fancy of the speller." Later it became standardized, apparently, as "hootchy-kootchy." The "sinuous Oriental dancing woman, who should be permitted to dance only in the darkness of Egypt," readers were told, had stripped before Mr. Seeley and his guests, in exclusive Sherry's, "sacred for matriarchs and patriarchs," and, clad in what was variously described as a piece of gauze, or a pair of stockings and slippers, or nothing at all, had not only done her wicked stomach dance, on a table or a stage, but after drinking a lot of champagne, had executed the same dance for guests individually. In Sunday "feature stories" and pages of space, everybody interviewable was interviewed and sworn statements were printed. And, of course, a big part of the story was "those present," and the fact that some of them were married men.

Theodore Roosevelt was Police Commissioner of New York at that time and he was making a record that was soon to focus national attention upon him. For one thing, he was doing what was humanly possible to clean up New York—a very dirty place, indeed, according to the Rev. Dr. Charles H. Parkhurst and other reformers of that time, who were probably right. Every association for the purification of public morals was willing to lend "Teddy" voluntary assistance in his effort. Seeley himself, the host at the dinner, was indignant over the scandal involving himself and his guests, all thus made targets for nation-wide notoriety. Charges were preferred against Chapman, which were equivalent to "unlawful entry." Roosevelt was urged on the one hand to ventilate the whole incident and, if necessary, to decapitate Chapman; on the other, to dismiss the charges lest the scandal become too notorious. However, Chapman's trial took place upon his own insistence, and apparently everything that could be produced in the way of soiled linen was washed in public. Little Egypt herself made a statement in which she said that, while she had not appeared in the nude, she had intended to do so, and after Chapman left Sherry's she had really done a dance in a Zouave jacket and a pair of lace knickerbockers, and was preparing to "throw everything overboard" for her second act when, in consequence of Chapman's threat, the idea was abandoned, and she repeated the first dance.

Anybody who scans newspaper files of those days of the Seeley dinner scandal is apt to retain at the end only a confused impression of what really must have happened. Anyhow, Oscar Hammerstein, enterprising impresario, saw a chance to crowd his New York theater, and put on a skit entitled *The Silly Dinner,* in which were caricatured divers performances at its namesake. One man who saw both avers that the skit was many times more suggestive than the original. But if you mention the Seeley dinner to almost any old-timer, who thinks his recollections of the late Nineties are keen, he is apt to say: "The Seeley dinner? Well, I should say so! Why, that was where she got out naked and danced upon the table before a lot of men!"

Some of the details ascribed to the Seeley celebration would perhaps have fitted better a dish later served at a dinner given in his home in Twenty-third Street by James L. Breese, a wealthy bachelor. There, it was told, the centerpiece was a huge pie, the bottom of which, hidden in flowers, was cleverly arranged as a trap. When the festivities had reached a certain stage, the trap was wound up, the pie opened, and from it sprang, to dance among the guests, a beautiful girl, described by one who claimed to have been present as "covered only by the ceiling."

Bishop Potter Says Grace [6]

Going to church was a social function. Everyone was religious. The more successful in business you were during the week, the more devoutly you attended church on Sunday. Pierpont Morgan took up the collection at Saint [George's],[7] the Vanderbilt men roared out the hymns untunefully at Saint Thomas's. Everyone lionized the popular preachers; they were invited to the smartest houses in New York.

Bishop Henry C. Potter was one of them. He was stately and magnificent, a man of the world, a lover of rich food and rich houses. He had actually two forms of saying grace before meals. The first which he used at the table of Mrs. Fish and other wealthy hostesses was delivered in a rich and fruity voice. "Bountiful Lord"—rolling the words round his tongue—"we thank Thee for all these Thy blessings. . . ." In the homes of lowlier parishioners where the fare was of

[6] From *"King Lehr" and the Gilded Age,* with Extracts from the Locked Diary of Harry Lehr, by Elizabeth Drexel Lehr, pp. 77–78. Copyright, 1935, by Elizabeth Drexel Lehr. Philadelphia and London: J. B. Lippincott Company.

[7] The original erroneously has "St. Bartholomew's."

uncertain quality he would begin meekly, in a minor key, "Dear Lord, we give thanks for even the least of these Thy mercies. . . ."

"Like a Part of the Saddle"[8]

. . . Efforts of "climbers" to attain the heights of the crumbling structure of [Society] were . . . amusing.

A certain wealthy widow, both attractive and ambitious, came out of the West with her fortune and proceeded to lay siege to New York's social citadel. Direct action availing nothing, she sought to achieve her goal through persistent personal publicity. It was at this time that Society was beginning to adopt the habit of riding along the newly made bridle paths of Central Park. Daily, the climber, perched on a magnificent horse, rode demurely along the upper reaches of Fifth Avenue to Forty-ninth Street, a pleasant and alluring sight for the bored eyes of men of fashion idling at club windows.

These men, observing her daily progress, began to ask who she was. They also remarked that she sat her mount with a sure, confident air, "as though she were part of the saddle." That is precisely what she was, temporarily. She had never ridden until she had come to New York, but her ambition had surmounted this difficulty. She, or some accomplice, had invented an elaborate system of straps and loops of leather, whereby she was attached to the saddle before venturing forth and released by a servant on her return home. Thus attached, she gave every appearance of being a confident and skilled horsewoman, and drew much comment from the socially elect.

All went well until, one day, while she was riding through the park, a thunderstorm broke. She could not dismount and take shelter. Fifth Avenue club windows witnessed her downfall. Through the gusts of rain she rode, her horse trotting fast, her hat awry. She was weeping tears of rage and mortification; her clothing was soaked, but she still sat her mount "like a part of the saddle." So she passed, and New York knew her and her efforts at social advancement no more.

[8] From *The Social Ladder,* by Mrs. John King Van Rensselaer, in Collaboration with Frederic Van de Water, pp. 187–189. Copyright, 1924, by Henry Holt and Company. New York.

The Lost Week-End [9]

Among the social leaders of years ago there was a great lady who had a vast estate near New York. To be invited there was to be "made," socially, overnight. To be asked for a week-end was the constant dream of every climber.

A friend of mine, who need never worry about his position in that mysterious world of society, went with several others of equal importance to spend the first week-end of September, long, long ago. They arrived on Friday evening at the palace in the country, with its spreading lawns and great trees, which their hostess, for some reason that no one has ever been able to discover, had christened (perhaps in her one moment of dry humor) "The Shack." It was a gay young crowd, and they hoped to make the welkin ring, even in these marble hills, and, because the wine-cellar was good, they succeeded. They were all jaded and tired, and had looked forward to these long days of tennis, golf, dinners, and dancing.

But promptly at nine o'clock on Monday morning they found themselves, bag and baggage, out on the marble terrace en masse, with the motors coming up the drive to take them to the railway station. They were furious. They held a guests' rebellion then and there. The haughty English butler heard their treacherous whisperings, but paid not the slightest attention to them. He had his orders, and he would carry them out.

Finally one of the men in the party handed him a five-dollar bill and told him to go to the great lady and say that they had all expected to remain until Tuesday morning, as this was Labor Day. This guest spoke in a tone which commanded obedience. A servant always knows when a gentleman is addressing him.

White, and even ashen, the butler disappeared within those stately walls. Five minutes later he returned, a look of triumph upon his ancient face. He addressed the waiting group:

"Mrs. Twimbler's answer is that she has never heard of Labor Day."

[9] From *This New York of Mine,* by Charles Hanson Towne, pp. 205–206. Copyright, 1931, by Charles Hanson Towne. New York: Cosmopolitan Book Corporation.

Death in the Night [10]

Yes, there were beaus and belles; and personalities, too; and strange stories floated about the city. If one thinks that romance did not flourish then; that a woman's name was not protected; that mysteries were not hushed up, then, as now, listen:

Down on lower Fifth Avenue there dwelt a highly respected gentleman. He and his wife were among the very first to be listed among the noble Four Hundred. But like many another gentleman of his middle years, he had taken unto himself a mistress. And one summer when his family were absent in Newport, he remained in town for a week, business being the excuse. But of course the real reason was that he wished to see as much as he could of the actress he adored before she sailed for Europe—at his expense—a few days later.

And so it was that while New York—a much less crowded city at that time—drowsed in the heat of a sultry July night, practically a deserted village, Mr. Blank and his mistress were alone in her apartment, then far uptown in the West Fifties. There were few uniformed doormen and ubiquitous bellboys in those quiet days, and on such a night as this, in the very heart of summer, an almost bucolic hush lay over the city. A hansom lurched against the arc-lights down on the corner, and tired horses pulled the empty cars up and down Sixth Avenue and Broadway.

These two were happy and serene in each other's company, yet wistfully sad over their approaching separation. They had no premonition of how close their eternal separation would be. For at midnight the man dropped dead—clothed only—grotesque and anticlimactic as it must sound today—in his nightshirt.

Horror seized the actress when she realized that her lover, so highly regarded in the community, lay motionless in her bed. She too was well known in her world. It would never do—it could not be—that a scandal should occur. One can picture her alone, distracted, horrified, feeling New York's hot breath pouring in at her windows; sensing that aching silence of the streets, as the great monster of the city turned slowly in its sleep.

[10] *Ibid.*, pp. 199–202.

She thought rapidly. She must have help—but not the paid help of the servants in the building. She remembered two men-about-town whom she had known in the past, and known well. They were still her friends. One was a doctor, and she knew he was in town, living at his club. He might be there. With trembling hands she reached for the telephone. An awful moment of suspense. The night operator's sleepy voice at the club. "I'll see if he's in." Silence. And then, in her panic, she heard his answer, roused from slumber. "Who is it?" he said.

She told him to come to her at once. "I am ill—desperately ill," she whispered over the wire. And she added, "I need you."

Within ten minutes he was at her door. And he saw a woman, white, terrified, but in full control of her emotions, since she had to be calm until she put through her desperate plan.

"You must take him out of here. You must dress him and take him down the stairs, and in a cab to his home. His keys are in his pocket. If any one sees you, you must pretend that he is drunk. It's awful. But it must be done. Then you must take him into that house, undress him, and put him in his own bed, and come back here to tell me that you have done it. Oh!" And for the first time she sobbed.

"Be calm. I see it all. Yes, I'll do it," said the doctor. "You know you can trust me."

He set about his grim business. Down the stairs he carried his awful burden. Fortunately, the one servant on duty was asleep in the basement. On the sidewalk he hailed the one open fiacre which chanced to loll down the street. The unsuspicious driver was glad of any fare at this late hour. "Just one more drunk being carried home," he thought. He was used to such experiences.

And to that proud door on lower Fifth Avenue the dead man was taken, and the cabman dismissed.

The next evening, the papers told how the respected and respectable Mr. Blank had been found by the housekeeper who came in to prepare his late breakfast, dead of heart disease in his bed. And for years no one, in all our town, knew the true story of that terrible night. The actress died—long afterward, abroad; and columns were printed about the perfection of her art, and regret was expressed that she had retired from our stage at the height of her career.

The Death of Jim Fisk [11]

The differences between Edward S. Stokes and James Fisk, Jr., were of long standing. One night, in the month of January, 1871, Stokes, after having been followed from place to place by detectives, was arrested on a charge of embezzling money from the Brooklyn Oil Refining Company, of which he was Secretary, the arrest being instigated by Fisk. This was the beginning of bad blood between the parties. In 1868 Fisk met in this city Mrs. Helen Josephine Mansfield Lalor, a very fascinating Boston woman, who had been, a few years before, divorced from her husband, Frank Lalor, an actor; and the moment Fisk laid eyes on her, she captivated him. He gave her an elegant establishment in Twenty-third Street, near the Grand Opera House, and fitted it up without regard to expense. Her horses and carriages were the finest in the city, and the four-in-hand which she used at Long Branch and in the Central Park were much admired wherever seen. Fisk spent the greater part of his leisure time with his *chère amie,* and seemed to be bound up in her. One day, he received a note from "Josie," as he called her, requesting him to remove all his personal effects from her home, and advising him that she wished to know him no more. This was a severe blow to Fisk. Knowing that Stokes was a frequent visitor at Mrs. Mansfield's house, he at once divined the cause of her change of heart toward him and, having some money trouble, the two admirers of the siren became bitter enemies, each swearing savage vengeance upon the other.

On Saturday, December 31, 1871, there had been an examination, in the Yorkville Police Court, of Edward S. Stokes and Josie Mansfield on a charge of attempting to blackmail James Fisk, Jr. Mrs. Mansfield admitted that she had given to Stokes the letters written by Fisk to her, but not for blackmailing purposes; and also admitted that Mr. Stokes had visited her two or three times a week for a year and a half. Mr. Stokes acknowledged his frequent calls, but said the acquaintance was an ordinary one between a lady and a gentleman; and he denied, as charged, that he had ever talked with Mrs. Mansfield about the amount of money Mr. Fisk ought to pay for the letters he had written

[11] From *Thirty Years of New York Politics Up-to-Date,* by Matthew P. Breen, pp. 495–499. Copyright, 1899, by Matthew P. Breen. New York: Published by the Author.

to her. At the termination of the examination the Court postponed the further hearing of the case for a week, and Stokes accompanied Mrs. Mansfield to her residence in Twenty-third Street. He was seated with her in the parlor, when the doorbell rang, and a friend entered and told Stokes he had been indicted by the Grand Jury and that a bench-warrant was out for his arrest. He sprang from his seat with an oath and, hastily donning his hat and overcoat, hurried from the house. He went directly to the Grand Opera House and inquired for Col. Fisk (I omitted to mention that James Fisk, Jr., was a Colonel, for in the midst of all his other excitements, he "dearly loved the military," and accepted the Colonelcy of the Ninth Regiment, New York State Militia). When Stokes learned that the Colonel was not at the Opera House, he hailed a coupé, sprang in, slammed the door, and told the driver to proceed at once to the Grand Central Hotel, on Broadway. Arriving there, he jumped out of the coupé, and bidding the driver to wait for him, went up the stairs of the establishment, made a search through the parlors of the house, and was about to descend the stairs when he encountered Fisk, who was on his way up.

Stokes had been informed that his examination, which I have so briefly referred to, was but the prelude to a much more damning kind of testimony to be adduced the ensuing Saturday. Ex-Judge William A. Beach, the counsel for James Fisk, Jr., he was told, was prepared to prove him a most disreputable character, the companion of gamblers and thieves, and a swindler and scoundrel himself; and counsel claimed he had testimony to show that Stokes had boasted that he could have sold Fisk's private letters to prominent politicians and that he intended to make a million dollars out of them. Stokes's motive was to be proven to have been nothing but disgraceful blackmail from the start. Moreover, it had been rumored that Fisk had, through counsel, concluded a compromise with Mrs. Mansfield, whereby she was to receive fifteen thousand dollars and go to Europe, and Stokes was to be left out in the cold.

All of these causes, and the fact that his avowed enemy had thus far beaten him at every step, had ruined his character and made him a comparative pauper, combined, it was believed, to drive the unhappy Stokes to desperation. He insisted, on his defense, that the rencontre between him and Fisk at the Grand Central Hotel was totally unpremeditated on his part; that he had not the remotest thought of meeting Fisk on that day and at that place; but, as he was going down, or turning in the act of going down the ladies' staircase, he suddenly perceived Fisk coming up and looking toward him; that as soon as Fisk saw him, Fisk pulled a pistol and was bringing it up to a level when Stokes, to save himself, discharged two chambers of his own weapon, and immediately jumped to one side to get out of the range of Fisk's pistol.

The evidence on both sides was conflicting. Stokes had arrived at the Grand Central Hotel at four o'clock, and passed up the stairs by the private entrance, as sworn to. At a quarter past four, Fisk drove up to the same entrance, and, stepping out of his carriage, inquired of the door-boy if a Mrs. Morse and her daughters were in. This Mrs. Morse was said to have been the widow of the man who gave Fisk his first start in business, in Boston, and Fisk had provided for her and her family since her husband's death. The hall-boy answered that he thought Mrs. Morse and her eldest daughter had gone out, but that the younger Miss Morse was in her mother's room. Fisk requested the boy to show him up, and the two started, Col. Fisk leading.

At that moment and before Fisk had mounted more than two steps, Stokes suddenly made his appearance, and a shot rang out which struck Fisk in the abdomen, passing downward, backward, and to the left, and inflicting a terrible wound. Fisk fell, shouting, "Oh!" but immediately scrambled to his feet again, when Stokes again leveled the revolver and fired another shot, the ball passing through Fisk's left arm without touching the bone. Fisk turned to run, but fell a second time, and slid to the bottom of the stairs, where he was picked up by those who had congregated on hearing the report of the pistol, carried upstairs to a room, where he was laid upon a bed, and the house physician was summoned. Stokes, meantime, had passed quietly downstairs into the office, where he made the remark that a man had been shot on the stairs. The hall-boy said: "Yes, and you are the man that did it." Stokes made no reply, but calmly awaited arrest; and Captain Byrnes and Officer McCadden, having been sent for, took him into custody.

In the meantime, three prominent surgeons were sent for, as were also Jay Gould, Wm. M. Tweed, John Chamberlain, Col. Fisk's brother-in-law and sister, and several other relatives. The surgeons were obliged to administer chloroform before they could proceed with an examination of the wounds. While under the influence of the anesthetic, Fisk suddenly arose to a sitting position, and they were compelled to jump upon him and hold him down. The hole in his abdomen, it was found, was large enough to have been made with a Minié ball. The chances were thought to be ten to one against his recovery. Coroner Young summoned a jury, and Fisk made an ante-mortem deposition, the substance of which was in accordance with the foregoing statement, he fully identifying Edward S. Stokes as the person who shot him; and John T. Redmond, the doorkeeper, corroborated Fisk's evidence. Whereupon the jury found a verdict that "James Fisk, Jr., had received his injuries by a pistol shot, at the hands of Edward S. Stokes," and they were temporarily discharged to await the result of Col. Fisk's injuries.

David Dudley Field, another of Col. Fisk's counsel, having been sent for, soon arrived, and under the Colonel's directions, drew up a will, in which he devised the whole of his property, whatever it might be, to his wife, his father and his sister. This done, it was thought best to put him under the influence of morphine, and he was soon sound asleep. He never recovered consciousness, and passed out of the world at an early hour the next morning, Sunday.

And thus ended the career of a man who had all the dash and audacity of a Napoleon of finance, and but for whose early help, perhaps, Jay Gould would not have been able to amass the many millions he left behind when he, many years afterwards, departed this life.[12]

[12] Convicted of manslaughter on the third trial, after a long court fight waged by his wealthy and influential family, Stokes served four years in Sing Sing and was discharged.

6

Old Saloon Days

[The bartender] presented an inspiring spectacle as he leaned upon the polished mahogany of his bar, amid the gleam of polished silver and cut glass, and impressively pronounced the immemorial greeting, "What will it be, gentlemen?"—Herbert Asbury

Why Saloons Became Political Centers [1]

. . . It was part of the original charter of New York, according to old-time records, that the officials of the city government should be paid from an excise tax. It can therefore be seen that, from the beginning, it was the policy of the city authorities to encourage, not to oppress, taverns and public houses. In New Amsterdam the taverns were under the special control and protection of the city government, which regulated all their details and protected their proprietors in all their rights. The law even regulated the precise amount of liquor which was given or could be demanded for a drink. Any man who "beat" the barkeeper, or did not pay his bill, was ostracized as well as punished. Originally, the New York taverns were, in fact, used as District Courts. The magistrates decided local disputes at the local taverns. And as the Court held its sessions and rendered its decisions at the taverns, so the fines imposed by the courts were often taken out in drinks. The Judges, wit-

[1] From *Thirty Years of New York Politics Up-to-Date,* by Matthew P. Breen, p. 112. Copyright, 1899, by Matthew P. Breen. New York: Published by the Author.

nesses, and all concerned, including the plaintiff and defendant, would order their drinks, and take them together, and then the party against whom decisions were rendered would pay for them—a pleasant way of paying a fine, especially for the landlord! When the Dutch surrendered New Amsterdam to the English, the courts became more dull and dignified. Regular halls of justice were established, and the tap-room ceased to be a court-room; nevertheless, under the English as under the Dutch, the New York tavern continued to be a political center, and it has so remained down to our own day.

The Origin of the Corner Saloon [2]

From the time that the very first market was established, there were laws which compelled those who dealt in meats and vegetables to sell in the public markets and nowhere else. As the town grew larger and larger, there was determined opposition to this state of affairs, and the climax came in 1841, when an ordinance was passed permitting the sale of meat and vegetables anywhere in the city, in shops as well as in the markets.

Of course, the market people fought the passage of the ordinance, but it was passed for all that, and very soon a new institution, in the form of the corner green-grocer's stand and meat shop, came into existence. But although there had seemed to be a general demand for the doing-away with the markets as exclusive places for meat-selling, they were too firmly established to be suddenly abolished. So the corner shopkeepers had a hard time of it for a while, and, in order to make business pay, they combined with the regular trade rear-barrooms for the sale of spirituous and malt liquors. Later, when the corner storekeepers decided that they could carry on trade in the middle of a block as well as on corners, they removed when they saw fit, but they left the corner barrooms to look out for themselves. These, in due time, became full-fledged saloons, and there they are to this day, one on every corner.

[2] From *When Old New York Was Young,* by Charles Hemstreet, pp. 275–276. Copyright, 1902, by Charles Hemstreet. New York: Charles Scribner's Sons.

The Greatest Bartender in America [3]

It was Jerry Thomas—rise, please—who invented those celebrated cold weather beverages which have come down to us as the Blue Blazer and the Tom and Jerry, the former a powerful concoction of burning whisky and boiling water which, if properly employed, would render the hot water bottle obsolete. And it was Jerry Thomas who, a few years before the Civil War, gave the aid and encouragement of his genius to the cocktail, then a meek and lowly beverage pining for recognition and appreciation, and by self-sacrificing work in the laboratory raised it to its rightful place among the drinks. A perfect flood of new mixtures soon showered upon a delighted world, and the Metropolitan Hotel at Prince Street and Broadway, in New York, where Jerry Thomas was Principal Bartender in the days when the metropolis was the scene of the soundest drinking on earth, became the first great cocktail house. As a mark of gratitude for his invention of the Tom and Jerry and the Blue Blazer and for his researches in the field of the cocktail, Jerry Thomas's host of admirers invested him with the honorable, if honorary, title of Professor, by which he was thereafter known, and which he carried with becoming dignity through the remainder of his earthly pilgrimage. Thus he fulfilled one of the ambitions which his father had expressed for him as he lay, a helpless little one, in the cradle of the New Haven cottage [where he was born in 1825]. . . .

* * * * *

A few historians have expressed the opinion that the Tom and Jerry was an English drink, and that Professor Thomas merely chanced to be the first bartender of importance to prepare it in America. This impression probably grew out of the fact that after 1821, when Pierce Egan published his famous novel, *Life in London, or Days and Nights of Jerry Hawthorne and His Elegant Friend Corinthian Tom*, the lower class of London public house became known as Tom and Jerry. . . .

[3] From *The Bon Vivant's Companion, or How to Mix Drinks*, by Professor Jerry Thomas, Formerly Principal Bartender at the Metropolitan Hotel, New York, and at the Planters' House, St. Louis, edited, with an Introduction, by Herbert Asbury, pp. xix–xx, xxxi–xxxii, xxxvi–xxxviii, xli, xlvi, 72–73. Copyright, 1927, 1928, by Alfred A. Knopf, Inc. New York.

Concoctions of hot rum, but unspiced, had been favorite tipples in the English barrooms for many years, and for that matter in America as well, but I have been unable to find authority for the belief that any beverage was specifically entitled Tom and Jerry until Professor Thomas introduced his mixture into St. Louis [at the Planters' Hotel] and subsequently throughout the land. Moreover, the Professor first called his invention the Copenhagen, perhaps wishing to acknowledge his indebtedness, so far as concerned the basic idea, to a rum-and-egg drink then in vogue in the capital of Denmark. But the patriotic Missourians refused to accept a foreign name for such a delectable drink, and it soon became known simply as Jerry Thomas. It was not called Tom and Jerry until Professor Thomas brought the secret to the Atlantic coast. The name, in this connection, is obviously a contraction of Professor Thomas's Christian- and sur-names.

* * * * *

After much research Professor Thomas concluded that the lowly estate of the cocktail was in part due to the faulty bitters employed in its composition. He therefore busied himself in laboratory work, and in due time appeared with Jerry Thomas's Own Bitters. This brilliant discovery was made soon after Professor Thomas had opened the first of his New York barrooms, and during the next few years cocktail drinking increased until the beverage had become the favorite morning tipple of all men of convivial habit, and few self-respecting New York businessmen would attempt to begin a day's work without one. However, very few of the myriad of present-day cocktails were known. The first edition of [Professor Thomas's] *The Bon Vivant's Companion* [1862] lists but ten different varieties—the bottle, the brandy, the fancy brandy, the whisky, the champagne, the gin, the fancy gin, the Japanese, the soda and the Jersey. They were all very simple mixtures, but potent, except the soda and the Jersey.

Professor Thomas's ballyhoo for the cocktail was carried on with great vigor for almost a score of years, and the last edition [1887] of his masterpiece contains formulae for no fewer than twenty-four different mixtures, including such well-known concoctions as the Manhattan, the absinthe, and the Martini, which was originally called the Martinez. He also gives directions for preparing the Saratoga and Coffee cocktails, and the Morning Glory, perhaps the most powerful of all. They were very popular for many years. . . .

Professor Thomas left the Metropolitan in 1859 to brave the dangers of a transatlantic voyage, but he was both seasick and homesick, and in less than a year he was again in New York, and at Broadway and Washington Place opened the most ornate barroom in the metropolis. But within another twelve months the wanderlust led him in a covered wagon to San Francisco, where he was Principal Bartender in the Occidental Hotel for almost two years. Then he joined a wagon train to Virginia City, Nevada Territory, where he introduced sound drinking practices and amassed another small fortune in gold dust. In 1865 he returned to New York, and thereafter roamed no more.

He opened a barroom at Broadway and Twenty-second Street which became one of the most celebrated saloons in the history of the city, and was frequented by the best citizens. Thomas Nast was then a young man struggling to find his place in the field of art, and Professor Thomas graciously extended a helping hand and opened his back room to the first exhibition of Nast cartoons. A hundred caricatures of prominent personages were displayed upon the walls, and Nast leaped into instant popularity. Later, Ned Mullin, a brilliant but dissipated caricaturist, also exhibited his work in Professor Thomas's art gallery, as did Theodore Wust and Junmp, clever draughtsmen who had been discovered in San Francisco by the Professor and brought to New York to make their little artistic splashes.

After seven years of continuous success and popularity, Professor Thomas sold his property and opened another and equally elaborate place at No. 1239 Broadway, where he remained for eight years. He finally disposed of this establishment to John Morrissey, a noted political and sporting figure, who was in turn a successful gang captain, a prize fighter with a victory over John C. Heenan to his credit, the owner of luxurious gambling houses in New York and Saratoga Springs, a member of Congress and finally, with the original Honest John Kelly (not the gambler of that name), co-leader of Tammany Hall. . . .

After John Morrissey had purchased the Broadway property Professor Thomas moved downtown, and in August, 1875, opened Thomas's Exchange at No. 3 Barclay Street, which soon became as popular as any of his other places. Morrissey operated the Broadway house as a pool room for a year or so, when it again came into the hands of the Professor, and was remodeled as a theater. It opened with a minstrel show in which Lew Dockstader made his first hit as a comedian. Dockstader's brother Charley was also a member of the company, as were Tommy Turner, Billy Bryant, Frank Kent, and Charley White, then the dean of minstrelsy. It was soon after he opened his Barclay Street bar that Professor Thomas began to form his notable collection of gourds, which soon crowded cartoons and caricatures out of his mind, and within a few months literally covered the walls of his back room.[4]

* * * * *

In Barclay Street, now largely devoted to the sale of religious images and literature, Professor Thomas spent the remainder of his professional career, surrounded by his gourds and warmed by the respect and admiration of all enlightened drinkers. He strove to the last to inculcate proper drinking habits in his clientele, and frowned sternly and disapprovingly upon drunkenness and other forms of dissipation. During his later years, as is the fashion of decaying men, he became just a bit finicky, especially about the Blue Blazer and the Tom and Jerry. He insisted that they were intended for cold weather only, and refused to prepare the Tom and Jerry until the first snowfall. It is related that he once smashed a punch bowl containing the mixture which he found in the bar of a business rival in early September. He was even more strict with the Blue Blazer, and would concoct it for no man until the thermometer registered ten degrees or less above zero.

* * * * *

TOM AND JERRY

Use punch bowl for the mixture

Five pounds of sugar.
Twelve eggs.
One-half small glass of Jamaica rum.
One and one-half teaspoonful of ground cinnamon.
One-half teaspoonful ground cloves.
One-half teaspoonful ground allspice.

Beat the whites of the eggs to a stiff froth, and the yolks until they are as thin as water, then mix together and add the spice and rum, thicken with sugar until the mixture attains the consistency of a light batter.

To deal out Tom and Jerry to customers:

Take a small bar glass, and to one tablespoonful of the above mixture, add one wine-glass of brandy, and fill the glass with boiling water; grate a little nutmeg on top.

Adepts at the bar, in serving Tom and Jerry, sometimes adopt a

[4] He owned more than three hundred gourds, of every conceivable shape and size, the finest and most important group of these natural curiosities in the United States, if not in the world. Indeed, the collection may well have been unique.—H.A., *ibid.*, p. xx.

mixture of one-half brandy, one-fourth Jamaica rum, and one-fourth Santa Cruz rum, instead of brandy plain. This compound is usually mixed and kept in a bottle, and a wine-glassful is used to each tumbler of Tom and Jerry.

N.B. A teaspoonful of cream of tartar, or about as much carbonate of soda as you can get on a dime, will prevent the sugar from settling to the bottom of the mixture.

Old John McSorley and the Oldest Saloon in New York City [5]

McSorley's occupies the ground floor of a red brick tenement at 15 Seventh Street, just off Cooper Square, where the Bowery ends. It was opened in 1854 and is the oldest saloon in New York City. In eighty-eight years it has had four owners—an Irish immigrant, his son, a retired policeman, and his daughter—and all of them have been opposed to change. It is equipped with electricity, but the bar is stubbornly illuminated with a pair of gas lamps, which flicker fitfully and throw shadows on the low, cobwebby ceiling each time some one opens the street door. There is no cash register. Coins are dropped in soup bowls —one for nickels, one for dimes, one for quarters, and one for halves— and bills are kept in a rosewood cash box. It is a drowsy place; the bartenders never make a needless move, the customers nurse their mugs of ale, and the three clocks on the walls have not been in agreement for many years.

The clientele is motley. It includes mechanics from the many garages in the neighborhood, salesmen from the restaurant-supply houses on Cooper Square, truck-drivers from Wanamaker's, internes from Bellevue, students from Cooper Union, and clerks from the row of second-hand bookshops just north of Astor Place. The backbone of the clientele, however, is a rapidly thinning group of crusty old men, predominantly Irish, who have been drinking there since they were youths and now have a proprietary feeling toward the place. Some of them have tiny pensions, and are alone in the world; they sleep in Bowery

[5] From *McSorley's Wonderful Saloon,* by Joseph Mitchell, pp. 3–8. Copyright, 1943, by Joseph Mitchell. New York: Duell, Sloan and Pearce. Originally published in *The New Yorker.*

hotels and spend practically all their waking hours in McSorley's. A few of these veterans clearly remember John McSorley, the founder, who died in 1910 at the age of eighty-seven. They refer to him as Old John, and they like to sit in rickety armchairs around the big belly stove which heats the place, gnaw on the stems of their pipes, and talk about him.

Old John was quirky. He was normally affable but was subject to spells of unaccountable surliness during which he would refuse to answer when spoken to. He went bald in early manhood and began wearing scraggly, patriarchal sideburns before he was forty. Many photographs of him are in existence, and it is obvious that he had a lot of unassumed dignity. He patterned his saloon after a public house he had known in Ireland and originally called it the Old House at Home; around 1908 the signboard blew down, and when he ordered a new one he changed the name to McSorley's Old Ale House. That is still the official name; customers never have called it anything but McSorley's.

Old John believed it impossible for men to drink with tranquillity in the presence of women; there is a fine back room in the saloon, but for many years a sign was nailed on the street door, saying, "Notice. No Back Room in Here for Ladies." In McSorley's entire history, in fact, the only woman customer ever willingly admitted was an addled old peddler called Mother Fresh-Roasted, who claimed her husband died from the bite of a lizard in Cuba during the Spanish-American War and who went from saloon to saloon on the lower East Side for a couple of generations hawking peanuts, which she carried in her apron. On warm days, Old John would sell her an ale, and her esteem for him was such that she embroidered him a little American flag and gave it to him one Fourth of July; he had it framed and placed it on the wall above his brass-bound ale pump, and it is still there. When other women came in, Old John would hurry forward, make a bow, and say, "Madam, I'm sorry, but we don't serve ladies." If a woman insisted, Old John would take her by the elbow, head her toward the door, and say, "Madam, please don't provoke me. Make haste and get yourself off the premises, or I'll be obliged to forget you're a lady." This technique, word for word, is still in use.

In his time, Old John catered to the Irish and German workingmen—carpenters, tanners, bricklayers, slaughter-house butchers, teamsters, and brewers—who populated the Seventh Street neighborhood, selling ale in pewter mugs at five cents a mug and putting out a free lunch inflexibly consisting of soda crackers, raw onions, and cheese; present-day customers are wont to complain that some of the cheese Old John laid out on opening night in 1854 is still there. Adjacent to the free lunch he kept a quart crock of tobacco and a rack of clay and corncob pipes—the purchase of an ale entitled a man to a smoke on the house; the rack still holds a few of the communal pipes. Old John was thrifty and was able to buy the tenement—it is five stories high and holds eight families—about ten years after he opened the saloon in it. He distrusted banks and always kept his money in a cast-iron safe; it still stands in the back room, but its doors are loose on their hinges and there is nothing in it but an accumulation of expired saloon licenses and several McSorley heirlooms, including Old John's straight razor. He lived with his family in a flat directly over the saloon and got up every morning at five; he walked to the Battery and back before breakfast, no matter what the weather. He unlocked the saloon at seven, swept it out himself, and spread sawdust on the floor. Until he became too feeble to manage a racing sulky, he always kept a horse and a nanny goat in a stable around the corner on St. Mark's Place. He kept both animals in the same stall, believing, like many horse-lovers, that horses should have company at night. During the lull in the afternoon a stablehand would lead the horse around to a hitching block in front of the saloon, and Old John, wearing his bar apron, would stand on the curb and groom the animal. A customer who wanted service would tap on the window and Old John would drop his currycomb, step inside, draw an ale, and return at once to the horse. On Sundays he entered sulky races on uptown highways.

From the time he was twenty until he was fifty-five, Old John drank steadily, but throughout the last thirty-two years of his life he did not take a drop, saying, "I've had my share." Except for a few experimental months in 1905 or 1906, no spirits ever have been sold in McSorley's; Old John maintained that the man never lived who needed a stronger drink than a mug of stock ale warmed on the hob of a stove. He was a big eater. Customarily, just before locking up for the night, he would grill himself a three-pound T-bone, placing it on a coal shovel and holding it over a bed of oak coals in the back-room fireplace. He liked to fit a whole onion into the hollowed-out heel of a loaf of French bread and eat it as if it were an apple. He had an extraordinary appetite for onions, the stronger the better, and said that "Good ale, raw onions, and no ladies" was the motto of his saloon. About once a month during the winter he presided over an on-the-house beefsteak party in the back room, and late in life he was president of an organization of gluttons called the Honorable John McSorley Pickle, Beefsteak, Baseball Nine and Chowder Club, which held hot-rock clambakes in a picnic grove on North Brother Island in the East River. On the walls are a number of photographs taken at outings of the club, and in most of them the members are squatting around barrels of ale; except for the president, they all have drunken, slack-mouthed grins and their eyes look dazed. Old John had a bull-frog bass and enjoyed harmonizing with a choir of drunks. His favorite songs were "Muldoon, the Solid Man," "Swim Out, You're Over Your Head," "Maggie Murphy's Home," and "Since the Soup House Moved Away." These songs were by Harrigan and Hart, who were then called "the Gilbert and Sullivan of the U. S. A." He had great respect for them and was pleased exceedingly when, in 1822, they made his saloon the scene of one of their slum comedies; it was called *McSorley's Inflation.*

Although by no means a handshaker, Old John knew many prominent men. One of his closest friends was Peter Cooper, president of the North American Telegraph Company and founder of Cooper Union, which is a half-block west of the saloon. Mr. Cooper, in his declining years, spent so many afternoons in the back room philosophizing with the workingmen that he was given a chair of his own; it was equipped with an inflated rubber cushion. (The chair is still there; each April 4th for a number of years after Mr. Cooper's death, on April 4th, 1883, it was draped with black cloth.) Also, like other steadfast customers, Mr. Cooper had a pewter mug on which his name had been engraved with an ice-pick. He gave the saloon a life-sized portrait of himself, which hangs over the mantel in the back room. It is a rather appropriate decoration, because, since the beginning of prohibition, McSorley's has been the official saloon of Cooper Union students. Sometimes a sentimental student will stand beneath the portrait and drink a toast to Mr. Cooper.

Old John had a remarkable passion for memorabilia. For years he saved the wishbones of Thanksgiving and Christmas turkeys and strung them on a rod connecting the pair of gas lamps over the bar; the dusty bones are invariably the first thing a new customer gets inquisitive about. Not long ago, a Johnny-come-lately infuriated one of the bartenders by remarking, "Maybe the old boy believed in voodoo." Old John decorated the partition between barroom and back room with banquet menus, autographs, starfish shells, theater programs, political posters, and worn-down shoes taken off the hoofs of various race and brewery horses. Above the entrance to the back room he hung a shillelagh and a sign: "BE GOOD OR BEGONE." On one wall of the barroom he placed portraits of horses, steamboats, Tammany bosses, jockeys, actors, singers, and statesmen. Around 1902 he put up a heavy oak frame containing excellent portraits of Lincoln, Garfield, and McKinley, and to the frame he attached a brass title tag reading, "THEY ASSASSINATED THESE GOOD MEN THE SKULKING DOGS." On the same wall he hung framed front pages of old newspapers; one, from the *London Times* for June 22, 1815, has in the lower right-hand corner a single paragraph on the beginning of the battle of Waterloo, and another, from the New York *Herald* of April 15, 1865, has a one-column story on the shooting of Lincoln. He blanketed another wall with lithographs and steel engravings. One depicts Garfield's deathbed. Another is entitled "The Great Fight." It was between Tom Hyer and Yankee Sullivan, both bare-knuckled, at Still Pond Heights, Maryland, in 1849. It was won by Hyer in sixteen rounds, and the prize was $10,000. The judges wore top hats. The title tag on another engraving reads, "Rescue of Colonel Thomas J. Kelly and Captain Timothy Deacy by Members of the Irish Revolutionary Brotherhood from the English Government at Manchester, England, September 18, 1867." A copy of the Emancipation Proclamation is on this wall; so, inevitably, is a facsimile of Lincoln's saloon license. An engraving of Washington and his generals hangs next to an engraving of a session of the Great Parliament of Ireland. Eventually Old John covered practically every square inch of wall space between wainscot and ceiling with pictures and souvenirs. They are still in good condition, although spiders have strung webs across many of them. New customers get up on chairs and spend hours studying them.

Although Old John did not consider himself retired until just a few years before he died, he gave up day-in-and-day-out duty back of the bar around 1890 and made his son, William, head bartender. Bill McSorley was the kind of person who minds his own business vigorously. He inherited every bit of his father's surliness and not much of his affability. The father was by no means a lush, but the son carried temperance to an extreme; he drank nothing but tap water and tea, and bragged about it. He did dip a little snuff. He was so solemn that before he was thirty several customers had settled into the habit of calling him Old Bill. He worshipped his father, but no one was aware of the profundity of his worship until Old John died. After the funeral, Bill locked the saloon, went upstairs to his family flat, pulled the shutters to, and did not come out for almost a week. Finally, on a Sunday morning, gaunt and silent, he came downstairs with a hammer and a screwdriver and spent the day painstakingly securing his father's pictures and souvenirs to the walls; they had been hung hit or miss on wires, and customers had a habit of taking them down. Subsequently he commissioned a Cooper Union art teacher to make a small painting of Old John from a photograph. Bill placed it on the wall back of the bar and thereafter kept a hooded electric light burning above it, a pious custom that is still observed.

The Bronx Cocktail[6]

Johnnie Solon [who came to the Waldorf Bar in 1899, shortly after the close of the Spanish-American War] is the inventor of the original Bronx cocktail.

Other claimants may have arisen to the title. Publicists and propagandists may have endeavored to shove forward the name of some other favorite barman as the creator of a cocktail whose name, masking a variety of curious concoctions, has been set before disgusted Americans in many parts, when they demanded a Bronx. Even in the United States there are many conceptions of a Bronx. But Johnnie's claim to parenthood, while modestly put forth, is nevertheless a Waldorf tradition.

Unfortunately, I have found it impossible to establish the date of its creation. Johnnie invented so many drinks that he never put down the dates. But to the best of his recollection it was early in the century. This is the story as he told it to me:

"We had a cocktail in those days called the Duplex, which had a pretty fair demand. One day, I was making one for a customer when in came Traverson, head waiter of the Empire Room—the main dining room in the original Waldorf. A Duplex was composed of equal parts of French and Italian Vermouth, shaken up with squeezed orange peel or two dashes of Orange Bitters. Traverson said, 'Why don't you get up a new cocktail? I have a customer who says you can't do it.'

" 'Can't I?' I replied.

"Well, I finished the Duplex I was making, and a thought came to me. I poured into a mixing glass the equivalent of two jiggers of Gordon

[6] From *Old Waldorf Bar Days,* With the Cognomina and Composition of Four Hundred and Ninety-one Appealing Appetizers and Salutary Potations Long Known, Admired and Served at the Famous Big Brass Rail; *also* A Glossary for the Use of Antiquarians and Students of American Mores, by Albert Stevens Crockett, pp. 79–81. Copyright, 1931, by Albert Stevens Crockett. New York: Aventine Press.

gin. Then I filled the jigger with orange juice, so that it made one-third of orange juice and two-thirds of gin. Then into the mixture I put a dash each of Italian and French Vermouth, shaking the thing up. I didn't taste it myself, but I poured it into a cocktail glass and handed it to Traverson and said: 'You are a pretty good judge. [He was.] See what you think of that.' Traverson tasted it. Then he swallowed it whole.

" 'By God!' he said, 'you've really got something new! That will make a big hit. Make me another and I will take it back to that customer in the dining room. Bet you'll sell a lot of them. Have you got plenty of oranges? If you haven't, you better stock up, because I'm going to sell a lot of those cocktails during lunch.'

"Up to that time we never used more than one dozen oranges per day in the Bar. I sent down to the storeroom and got two dozen. The storeroom keeper came up himself and wanted to know what I meant by ordering so many oranges. 'What the hell are you going to do with them?' he demanded.

" 'Well,' I said, 'maybe I will take them home if I can.' But I didn't.

"The demand for Bronx cocktails started that day. Pretty soon we were using a whole case of oranges a day. And then several cases.

"The name? No, it wasn't really named directly after the borough or the river so-called. I had been at the Bronx Zoo a day or two before, and I saw, of course, a lot of beasts I had never known. Customers used to tell me of the strange animals they saw after a lot of mixed drinks. So when Traverson said to me, as he started to take the drink in to the customer, 'What'll I tell him is the name of this drink?' I thought of those animals, and said, 'Oh, you can tell him it is a Bronx.' "

Tom Flynn's Temperance Lecture [7]

. . . When the old Chatham Theater [just above Roosevelt Street] was in the height of its popularity, Tom Flynn and Charley Thorn were its owners. Flynn was one of the best of the old-school actors, and

[7] From *Reminiscences of the Old Fire Laddies and Volunteer Fire Departments of New York and Brooklyn,* Together with a Complete History of the Paid Departments of Both Cities, by J. Frank Kernan ("Florry"), pp. 34–35. Copyright, 1885, by J. Frank Kernan ("Florry") and Michael Crane. New York: M. Crane.

the most successful Irish comedian that ever stepped upon a stage. He was a heavy drinker, though he managed always to promptly attend to business and play his parts without a blemish. It was along in the early Forties that a crusade against rum was organized in this city, and the movement was known as the "Washingtonian Battery against Rum." Though organized and for a time confined entirely to doing good in this city, the work gradually spread itself throughout the whole country, and no temperance movement ever before or since met with such enthusiastic success. Entire engine companies in this city were known to sign the pledge in a body, and beautiful silk banners were presented to each company when they joined the crusade. . . . It was during the excitement consequent upon these meetings that it was suggested that the old Chatham be secured for revival meetings.

"I have been seriously thinking over this tippling business," said Flynn to the committee who waited upon him, "and I cannot fail noticing the great good which this temperance revival is causing among thousands in this city. Its good effects have reached even so rum-soaked a sinner as myself, and I am desirous of doing something for the cause. You can not only have the theater on certain occasions for meetings, but I will address the first gathering that is called together there under the auspices of the Washingtonians."

When the announcement was made public that Tom Flynn was to address a temperance meeting, it created the greatest surprise and wide-spread comment. The day, or rather afternoon, finally arrived when the great actor was to renounce rum and tell his audience the reason why. The theater was packed from pit to dome, the very aisles being jammed almost to suffocation with solid humanity. The stage was set with a scene from *The Drunkard's Home,* and near the footlights was placed a table, upon which rested a half-filled glass pitcher and a tumbler. At the appointed hour Flynn, wreathed in his most genial smile, came upon the stage, and the thunder of applause which greeted him never awakened such echoes before in the old theater. Filling his glass from the pitcher, Flynn drank the contents in one draught, and then proceeded with his lecture. He was a brilliant and voluble talker, and his fund of anecdotes never seemed to be exhausted. The pathos and eloquence with which he pictured step by step the drunkard's path down the abyss of moral ruin, I will never forget; neither will I forget the laughter I enjoyed while listening to his side-splitting anecdotes. Such an audience was never seen. One moment the sobs of men and women were distinctly audible throughout the whole building while Flynn drew one of his inimitable pictures of the curse of rum. At the next moment everybody was holding his or her sides in a strong effort to save themselves from bursting with laughter. Flynn finally reached the peroration of his lecture, and a finer burst of eloquence I never listened to. The audience was fairly worked to the highest pitch of seemingly religious enthusiasm, and the lecturer continued for two hours to talk uninterruptedly. At the end of that time, he was seen to totter at the close of one of his sentences and then fall fainting upon the stage. Such excitement was never manifested in a public gathering before or since; and while some attendants carried Flynn around to the old New England Hotel, the audience dispersed to their homes, loud in their praises of the reformed actor. Some of the temperance people, however, managed to get upon the stage, and in nosing about discovered that the pitcher which was supposed to contain water actually contained gin—old swan gin, which was Tom's favorite beverage; and putting two and two together, they concluded that Flynn had been drawing inspiration for his lecture from the camp of the enemy, and that his exhaustion and final collapse were not due so much from the mental strain of the lecture as from the seductive and exhausting contents of the pitcher. The story soon got out, and though it caused many to laugh, it made Flynn very unpopular with some at the time. The object of the joke was to prevent the temperance people from again asking for the use of the theater, and they never did.

The Smasher [8]

I

Here is what Carry Nation did during a six-hour stay on Manhattan Island yesterday:

Gave Police Commissioner Murphy the most uncomfortable quarter of an hour in his life.

Scared Chief Devery into dodging her.

Gave John L. Sullivan a bad attack of the frights.

Kept Acting Mayor Guggenheimer in a state of nervous agitation.

Had a row with her manager and left town as happy as a lark.

With a two-foot hatchet strapped to the girdle under her linen jacket, her beaded black poke bonnet pushed down firmly on her head,

[8] From New York *World,* August 29 and September 2, 1901.

her broad jaw set at its most pugnacious angle, the Smasher strode into Colonel Murphy's room at Headquarters at eleven A.M., plumped into a chair close to him, and in ringing tones demanded: "Don't you think New York is an awful bad place."

"I don't think anything of the kind," testily said the Colonel.

"Yes, it is," insisted the Smasher. "It's full of hellholes and murder factories."

"Stop right there. I don't want to listen to you or to hear that kind of talk in this place," almost shouted the Commissioner.

"You won't listen to me?" queried the Smasher in surprise. "Why, I came here a-purpose to discuss these matters with you. Do you mean to say you won't discuss these murder shops, these hellholes, these sinks of depravity in New York?"

"That's just what I mean."

"Now, now, now," said Mrs. Nation patronizingly, "I want to know why the saloons are permitted to open on Sunday."

"I won't discuss that matter with you."

Mrs. Nation laid a pudgy forefinger on the Colonel's arm. He angrily brushed it away, but in her sweetest tones the Smasher went on: "I only came here to do New York good. I want to do good for humanity. I want to do something for you."

"You don't know what you're talking about," said the Colonel, in a rage. "Go back to Kansas. If you want to do something, why don't you do it for your husband?"

"I have no husband now," said the Smasher in a tone of regret. "I supposed you knew all about [our divorce]."

"Oh, yes," said the Commissioner, with a grin. "All I have to say is that I congratulate Mr. Nation. He ought to be a happy man now."

Unabashed, the Smasher took hold of the saloon question again.

"I won't sit here and be lectured. I don't want to talk to you. You are not in your right mind," said the Colonel.

"Do you think I am crazy?" shouted the now-furious Smasher.

"Yes, I do."

"You say, then, just what those wicked, riotous, rum-soaked, bedeviled Republicans in Kansas City say. They say that when they know that forty hellholes are closed in Topeka."

Murphy beckoned to Detective Linden to eject Mrs. Nation. Linden hesitated, and the Joint Smasher, undaunted, added new misery by saying: "Now, father, be calm. I want to talk with you without quarreling."

"Don't call me father," said Murphy in a voice of agony.

"I will call you father. You are old enough to be my father. I'm only fifty-four and you are at least eighty, and I'll call you father anyway. Now, father, do you think a little 'hatchetation' would do a lot of good in New York?"

"If you violate the law I'll have you locked up," shouted the Commissioner.

The Smasher kept a crafty eye on Linden, and as she saw the detective had got his nerve up to the ejecting point she bounced out of her chair, saying: "Now, father, we could have had a nice long talk if you didn't quarrel with me. We will all of us have to give an account of our stewardship—remember that."

All this time Deputy Commissioner Devery was hiding in a corner where he could listen without being seen. As the Smasher went out she passed a man smoking a cigarette. Turning to him, she shouted: "You horrid, nasty man! Don't you know that your fate will be an eternal smoking?"

"Now take me to see John L. Sullivan," said the Smasher to her manager. "He once said some mean things about me."

Up to the Forty-second Street saloon formerly owned by the ex-champion the Smasher went. The saloon was recently closed, but John L. still had a room on the upper floor. A messenger took up word to the pugilist, who said: "Not on your life. Tell her I'm sick in bed."

Word came from City Hall that the Joint Smasher was coming, and, much perturbed, Acting Mayor Guggenheimer called in the policeman at the door and said: "If Carry Nation comes here don't let her in. Tell her the Mayor's office cannot be used for advertising purposes."

The Smasher, however, did not visit the City Hall. Instead she had a pleasant row with her manager. He had contracted for her to deliver a lecture last night at Ocean City, New Jersey. She had contracted to lecture tonight at College Green, Ohio, and at Dyckman, Illinois, tomorrow night. So she took the one P.M. train for Ohio while the manager fretted and fumed.

Mrs. Nation will return to New York Saturday and will lecture in Carnegie Hall Sunday.

Proprietor Caddigan, of the Hoffman House, was in a nervous frenzy last night. He did not know that Mrs. Nation had left the city, and jokers had told him she intended to invade the café at nine P.M., smash the famous $10,000 painting, *Nymphs and Satyr,* and rip to pieces the $100,000 worth of art treasures. Mr. Caddigan posted a man at all the entrances until someone told him Mrs. Nation was on her way to Ohio.

II

A deafening medley of voices that merged into a terrific "Hurrah for Carry Nation!" A mob of thousands, beating this way and that, tearing, trampling each other for a sight of that squat, determined little figure, marching on with the exaltation of a conquering hero, and the Kansas Smasher was steered straight into the arms of three burly New York policemen and promptly "pinched."

It happened at Devery's corner, Twenty-eighth Street and Eight Avenue, at 5:30 yesterday afternoon. The dauntless Carry unmolested had:

Precipitated a riot in three saloons.

Invaded two Sunday concert halls.

Paraded the highways and byways with a tumultuous rabble at her heels.

It was only when she invaded the district of the Big Chief that the arm of the law became effective.

"I am not disturbing the peace," asserted Mrs. Nation indignantly, whisking about in her Quakerish linen gown with its quaint cape, and fixing on the bluecoats an invincible eye.

"You are raising a crowd and creating a riot, and I arrest you," was the response of one of her captors, while the two others closed in about her and the procession started for the West Twentieth Street Station.

At Twenty-fourth Street, satisfied by Mrs. Nation's friends that she was about to return to her hotel, the policemen released her and put her on a car amid a volley of "Hurrahs!"

Mrs. Nation arrived from Danbury, Illinois, at 9:30 yesterday morning to fulfill her lecture engagement at Carnegie Hall last night. She went immediately to the Victoria Hotel, loudly declaring that she had traveled in a "saloon on wheels."

Giving herself only time to exchange her linen duster for a fresh white piqué frock (plain in cut and finished with the invariable cape, with a small hatchet in her buttonhole) and fortifying herself with a service at the Cathedral, the crusader started out to purify New York. With characteristic directness she went straight to the Democratic Club.

* * * * *

"I want to get in," she said to the servant who barred her path.

"No ladies admitted!"

"But I want to see a member who can admit me," went on the imperturbable Carry, while a crowd gathered about the steps.

"I'm one, madam," from an elderly gentleman just inside the door, "and I repeat it is against the rules."

"Break 'em," responded the Smasher, one foot on the threshold.

The Superintendent rushed forward to the rescue.

"Have you got anything in here you don't want me to see? I would like to hold a Sunday-school lesson and a Bible reading in here."

"The club was not organized for that purpose," put in the Superintendent hastily.

"Don't you know," and she pushed her way past, only to be politely thrust out again, "that God said it isn't good for men to be alone?"

"Who are you, madam?" in wrathful tones.

"I'm Carry Nation, and I tell you that this must be a mighty bad place if you can't let a woman in."

At Fiftieth Street and Seventh Avenue, Mrs. Nation saw the side door of a saloon open, and dashed in, attended by a crowd that filled the place.

"Oh me! Oh my!" she cried, making way for the "barkeep," who, paralyzed with terror at the unexpected onslaught, turned a sickly white.

"Look at him! Look at his white face! Nervous, ain't you?" and with a gleeful laugh Carry launched out for a bottle of whisky and raised it to hurl it to the floor, but the man was too quick for her, and disarmed, she turned to the loungers drinking at the tables.

"Ain't you 'shamed, boy, to be drinking up what you ought to give to your family?" she inquired from a bullet-headed youth.

"Ain't got none," was the laconic reply.

"Give her a highball, Peter, and I'll stand treat," cried a voice from the rear before the employees of the place could come to their senses and endeavor to clear the place.

The Smasher's progress down Broadway after this escapade was a veritable triumphal procession.

A short luncheon, and Mrs. Nation was in fine fettle for her afternoon campaign.

"Take me to some more hellholes," she demanded of her escort. Darting into a saloon at Twenty-ninth Street and Sixth Avenue, she cried: "Ain't this against the law? Where are the police? I am Carry Nation, and I protest against the selling of that hell broth."

"We are selling lemonade," insisted the barkeeper.

"Lemonade!" echoed the reformer scornfully. "It's beer!" and walking over to a table where some sailors were drinking, she seized one of the steins and took a sip. "I know the taste of beer as well as you do, and you men are disgracing Uncle Sam's uniform every drop you drink."

At Thirty-first Street and Sixth Avenue she effected an entrance and intrepidly faced the danger of a rough handling.

Her further progress was "tipped off." Wide-open places were mysteriously closed at a moment's notice, and the Smasher was confronted by a series of closed doors, with anxious faces peeping from behind drawn curtains.

Half a dozen times en route she was obliged to take a car to escape the crowds, but her enthusiasm never flagged, and while her escort lagged and faltered she never turned a hair.

At the Apollo Music Garden—the French quarter of Eighth Avenue, with a legend that reads *Entrée libre au Café Chantant*—she went in search of women sinners, but quiet reigned and an irritable proprietor turned her out of his "private house."

Further down she investigated The Abbey, No. 416, another music hall, with similar results. It was here that the crowds running from every direction swelled into a mighty sea of humanity that brought about her encounter with the police.

Mrs. Nation did not confine her attention to the saloon abuse and cigarettes. She discovered in the lobby of the Victoria Hotel a subject for her hatchet that roused her to fury.

"Look at that image," she cried, pointing to a figure of Diana, clothed simply in a bow and arrow—"she ain't got a thing on. Where's the hotel proprietor?"—and she rushed up to the desk.

"There's a woman over there," she announced to the astonished clerk, "without any apparel on her. It ain't respectable. Would you like your wife to see that?" pointing an accusing finger. "Now, I'd like you to put a little something on her right away or there may be a little 'hatchetation' around here."

The clerk hurriedly promised the matter should be looked to, and Carry retired to rest for her lecture.

Corsets came in for her denunciation from the platform of Carnegie, where her talk was constantly interrupted by shouts of laughter, storms of applause, and audible comment. She bade girls avoid making their "hearts and livers into one solid lump." She likened herself to Moses, who, she said, was the first smasher when he broke up the golden calf.

Today she goes to Steeplechase Park, Coney Island, and will make the Bowery her chief concern while here.

Free Lunch and the Bum's Rush [9]

. . . Considine's [Metropole] had three entrances and a man thrown out of one door could always come in another. George Considine was a very husky citizen and usually acted as master of ceremonies in his own barroom. He ejected one intoxicated gentleman who was too boisterous and told him not to come back again. Considine took him on a personally conducted tour to the door and dropped him for a field goal on the sidewalk. Then he walked back, rubbing his hands in the reflective manner of a man who has just done something well worth doing. To his surprise he saw the drunk coming in another door opening on the side street.

Considine grabbed him by the scruff and tossed him out, saying, "Didn't I tell you not to come back?" Five minutes later the same well-lubricated lad staggered through a third door, and as Considine started for him he backed out, exclaiming, "Good heavens, do you own all the places in town?"

Considine and the other café owners experienced great difficulties with the itinerant actors and Broadwayites who came in to sample the free lunch without first going through the formality of sampling the beer. The barkeeps kept an eagle eye on the food show and woe to the man who tried to eat himself fat after buying one or no beers. It was another of those famous unwritten laws that no client could attack the lunch counter until he had purchased two beers at five cents apiece. Having complied with this invisible mandate a man could stroll casually over to the free lunch, pick out a reasonably clean fork, and start stabbing at the tomatoes, scallions, beans, radishes, sausages, and sliced ham. After he got his load he was expected to step back to the bar and contribute another ring to the cash register. You could eat and drink very well for fifteen cents.

There were free lunches served that were famous all over the town. The buffet of the Hotel Knickerbocker paraded a marvelous collection of snicks and snacks on its free-lunch counter. The lunch counter ac-

[9] From *The Girl from Rector's,* by George Rector, pp. 184–187, 188–190. Copyright, 1927, by Doubleday, Page & Company; 1926, 1927, by The Curtis Publishing Company. Garden City, New York.
By permission of Louise Fraser Lensky and Loew's Incorporated.

tually had chicken salad, lobster salad, lobster Newburgh, melted cheese on toast, cold corned beef, Virginia ham, and even chafing dishes. Unfortunately the beer in the Knickerbocker café was ten cents a scoop. This outrageous price was resented by the better class of lunch grapplers, who seemed to consider a five-cent glass the standard price. The Waldorf, Biltmore, and Plaza hotels all supplied free lunches to their bar patrons, and this method of distributing rations seriously interfered with the restaurant business.

Thousands of bachelors subsisted entirely on the free-for-all banquet style of feeding. However, it was then impossible for a man to bring his family into the barroom and have a basket picnic. Rector's didn't suffer much from the two-beer dining. We had no barroom, and if we had, we would have been too smart to give away lunches to prospective patrons. The man who lived on free lunch was the same kind of citizen who will look at a circus procession but will never pay to see the circus itself. He lived from hand to mouth—and got most of it on his vest.

The competition among saloon proprietors grew very keen in their individual efforts to attract bar flies by spreading tremendous repasts on the lunch shelf. The buffets with the most free groceries usually got the biggest play from the crowd. A man could get a New England boiled dinner and two beers for ten cents. It got so bad that six or seven of us restaurant owners had an emergency meeting to decide on ways and means of combating the free-lunch evil.

America was free and united in those days. The lunch was free and the cigar stores were united. We decided that we couldn't find anything in the Constitution that declared generously donated food to be aiding and abetting the enemy, and therefore treasonable. So we adjourned the meeting and went over in a body to the Knickerbocker and sampled the lunch ourselves.

* * * * *

Rector's was connected with free lunch in a very direct manner. One of our patrons complained that any man who had picked up a dinner check in Rector's would be compelled to live on free lunch for the rest of the month. Our charges may have been a trifle high, but were not to be compared with the prices of today. If a man wants to dine frugally nowadays he must go to a feed-and-grain store and do his best. There is no more free lunch. In fact, as I have explained, there never was. You always had to buy the customary two beers before you could stuff yourself like a turkey on Thanksgiving. The hobo who tried to crash the lunch without purchasing the schooners which came sailing over the bar was generally grasped by a husky bouncer and streeted. The process of being streeted meant that you were grasped by the slack of the trousers and the back of the neck and tossed out on the street. Sometimes the uninvited guest turned the tables on the bouncer.

I once saw a burly hobo sneak into Silver Dollar Smith's, a saloon famous for its shining floor of mosaic composed of Uncle Sam's bright dollars. He made a balk motion toward the bar to fool the proprietor and then turned to the lunch, where he wolfed down the entire exhibit, which consisted mostly of American cheese, Schweitzer, and Limburger. He had all the cheese stowed away before the boss woke up and started for him. The hobo grappled the proprietor and tossed him back over the bar. He did the same thing to the bartenders and then threw the bouncer through the window. With all opposition removed, he then proceeded to chase out the patrons and drank their deserted beer. Completely refreshed and invigorated, he watched the owner and his three assistants struggling to their feet and read them a fine piece of advice. He said, "Don't think that men are mice because they eat cheese."

Third Avenue Medicine [10]

There's a kind of medicine practiced by old veteran bartenders among old veteran drinkers along Third Avenue, not tourists, and probably the Mayo Brothers out in Rochester have never got wind of it.

Perhaps it isn't exactly medicine, but it's medical observation, anyway, and the main part of it is summed up in two things they say at the proper times. One is "The snake is out." The other, which they say in reverent tones, is "The elevens are up." Neither of these sayings has anything to do with the ordinary, everyday bartender school of medicine, which has to do with overpowering a hangover.

First of all, about the snake. The snake is an ordinary little vein, or maybe it is an artery, that runs along the left temple of a man's head. Most of the time you don't see it, but it's there, and it runs along, a

[10] From *A Man Gets Around,* by John McNulty, pp. 171–174. Copyright, 1945, 1946, 1947, 1949, 1950, 1951, by John McNulty. Boston: Little, Brown & Company, Inc.
Originally published in *The New Yorker.*

little slantwise, from up around his hair to above the left-hand corner of his eye.

Take a man gets in his late thirties, into his forties, and then, of course, as time goes on, into his fifties, and he still keeps coming into this saloon or that, wherever he always goes, and after a while this vein, the snake, gets to acting up.

One day this man goes on drinking one after the other—nobody is talking about beer but about hard stuff, and especially, out of all, brandy. No use trying to tell him to take it easy; that only gets him sore and he probably says, "Nobody's going to tell me take it easy, I know what I'm doing, I know what I'm doing," and all that kind of guff.

But after a while—and it has to be understood the bartender is his true friend—why, the bartender leans over the bar and takes a good look at him, staring.

"What's the matter with you?" the man probably says. "Have you gone nuts, looking at me like I was some kind of a bug sitting on a leaf? Give me some more of the same. The glass is empty."

"Oh, no, I'm not nuts," the bartender will say, but not for anyone else to hear. "I was just going to tell you the snake is out."

"Oh, oh!" says the man. "The little son of a bitch come out of his hole, did he?"

And he leans over the bar and stares hard into the mirror. Or if he can't see well that far, he's almost sure to go back in the men's room and study his forehead in the mirror. There will be the snake, pulsing and beating away. It must be blood pressure or something.

Time and time again this happens, in a quiet way, and it seldom fails that it halts up the man that's drinking—slows him up, anyway—when no amount of talk or lecturing could do it. Mostly, they come back from the men's room and tell the barkeep they guess they'll take a little walk, and go over to the park and sit for a while, or else they might even go home and lie down. That's what the snake coming out of his hole does, although it's probably nothing serious in the minds of regular doctors.

"The elevens are up" is as serious as anything could be, and there is no joke about it. This is not said to a man to his face at all. It comes about when there's been an old codger around for years and years, long enough to have arguments about is he seventy-one years old or is he up to seventy-eight or even more. Everybody talks of how healthy he is and he can go on for years yet, as the saying has it.

Then one time comes along and he doesn't drop in for a few days or a week. Every one (except the tourists, of course) asks for him and some one passes word he's under the weather a little. Then he shows up one day, usually when there's only one or two in there. Such a man, in such a fix, hardly ever comes bouncing back into the place while the crowd is there. He visits for a few minutes and says he's all right, a little weak, but he'll be all right in a week or so, and then he leaves.

No sooner has he gone than those of his friends who are there—including the bartender, of course—look at each other.

"The elevens are up," says the bartender, quietly and sadly, like a priest or a judge or the like.

"They are, they are!" say the others, and they all nod their heads.

It means that the two cords on the back of the man's neck have begun to stick out, the way they have never stuck out before his illness. The space on each side of each cord has sunk away—wasted, you might say—so the two cords, from his collar to his hair, stick out like two "1's," making a number "11." That's why they say "The elevens are up" when it happens to an old codger. It means he hasn't a chance and there's not much more time for him. They never let him hear them saying it, but the word passes around, one to another, and for a little while every one is nicer than usual to the man, until what they're sure will happen does happen.

7

City Fathers, Bosses and Servants

A reformer is a guy who rides through a sewer in a glass-bottomed boat.—Mayor James J. Walker

Father Knickerbocker [1]

The idea of a living symbol for the city was born in the nimble reportorial mind of Frank Lee Donoghue, director of the municipal Department of Commerce in 1949. His choice for the job was Dr. James J. O'Brien, former Professor of Modern and Romance Languages at Fordham University and now secretary of the Public Works Department, a learned gentleman with a burry brogue that carries over into the many tongues he speaks.

When Dr. O'Brien drew the assignment in 1945, he got no time to do Father Knickerbocker research. The city rented a more or less proper rig for him from the Brooks Costume Company, piled him into a plane at La Guardia Airport, and sent him on an eighteen-day world tour to publicize New York's World Trade Week. He had been

[1] From "About New York," by Meyer Berger, *The New York Times*, May 29, 1953. Copyright, 1953, by The New York Times Company.

Mayor William O'Dwyer's official greeter, anyway, and had met a multitude of foreign dignitaries. Mr. Donoghue figured that was qualification enough.

Dr. O'Brien finds some facets of his job a little tiring. In Calcutta, he wilted in the heat and reduced his Knickerbocker outfit to the black three-cornered hat and linen shorts, which wasn't quite what the script called for. Even at that, Indian small fry shrilled and whooped at his heels wherever he went. In Damascus, Arab soldiery and Arab citizenry gaped at his snuff-brown Colonial jacket, his four-tiered jabots, his gold-buckled slippers and his tight knee breeches.

He had his happiest moment in Dublin, on the way home, when he dropped his Dutch form of greeting and lapsed into a more natural Gaelic as he sipped good ale.

Of course, there were laundry difficulties on the trip. He had to wash his long white cotton stockings each night, and the heat and dust dealt unkindly with the six jabots. Most of his Knickerbocker clay pipes broke and put him in the habit of using a wooden facsimile, which he still carries. He also packs a Colonial writing pouch, quill pen, sandbox blotter, a few rounds of snuff.

The city never got around to buying a complete Knickerbocker outfit for Dr. O'Brien because of budgetary pinches here and there, and because one change would come to about $200. Dr. O'Brien still rents either from Brooks, or from Eaves, at $15 a rental. He gets his gray periwig from Birnstein & Migliore, and he owns two pairs of square-rimmed spectacles done to his prescription by Schoenig & Co. He's given up Colonial slippers for modern loafers, but so far no stickleback seems to have caught on. He finds the loafers more comfortable.

Dr. O'Brien, pulling gently out of his fifties, is six feet high, tips the scale at 200 pounds. He concedes that these are gigantic proportions for a Knickerbocker; Washington Irving's mythical Diedrich Knickerbocker who inspired the symbol was a tiny, shriveled ancient.

There's another Father Knickerbocker in town, who poses for beer ads—actor chap named O'Neill—but Dr. O'Brien has never met him, has just seen his image in subways and billboards. "He's a commercial Knickerbocker," the doctor will tell you. "We don't recognize him down here at City Hall."

The real Knickerbockers in New York, the doctor has discovered, trace back to Harmen (or Herman) Jansen Knickerbocker, who came here from Holland in 1674. Originally the name was Knikkerbakker, which means "baker of marbles."

Herald of the City [2]

During the blue days and fair of what Westbrook Pegler likes to call the era of wonderful nonsense a frequent ornament of the Mermaid Tavern of the Tenderloin [Bleeck's Artists and Writers Restaurant in Fortieth Street] was Hector Fuller, herald of the City of New York, scroll reader to Mayor James J. Walker, and major-domo of City Hall in an age when civic receptions and municipal barn raisings achieved a magnificence unknown since the fabled extravagances of the Field of the Cloth of Gold. A stately and plausible fellow, Fuller, with his silk hat, cutaway, and resonant oratory often enough defective in content but never orally, was vastly admired at a time when it was a lean week that lower Broadway didn't toss telephone books and cartons of lily cups out of the windows at triumphant channel swimmers or returning round-the-world fliers. Fuller was handsome, seventy, always thirsty, and could recite more English verse than any one in Bleeck's except Dick Maney, and bemused reporters, weary of precinct stations and sidewalk suicides, would listen by the hour, pausing only to refresh the minstrel's glass, while he recited Swinburne, Dowson, Dobson, and Tennyson with unfailing memory and persuasive enunciation. Plain-clothes men from Center Street and whiskered gaffers from the rim of the copy desk would maintain a deathly hush while the stanzas of "Locksley Hall," "The Triumph of Time," and "Cynara" were forthcoming as long as there was a highball handy.

Fuller dreamed up the scroll which, in that halcyon era, was presented by the city, through his hands, to distinguished visitors. It was when Captain George Fried was returning to the country after one of his heroic sea rescues that the Mayor, Rodman Wanamaker, and Grover A. Whalen were sitting around the Stork Club, then located uptown near Seventh Avenue, and wondering what to do about it, that the scroll came into being. Then and there on the back of a menu Fuller devised the text of the testimonial, which, suitable in gold leaf and hand lettering, became the standard Manhattan award of chivalry or swimming prowess.

"It cost twenty-one hundred dollars," said Fuller later, "but what the hell! New York is rich!"

[2] From *Snoot If You Must*, by Lucius Beebe, pp. 155–157. Copyright, 1943, by D. Appleton-Century Company, Inc. New York and London.

He composed other scrolls at Bleeck's, and reporters, press-agents, and actors in rehearsal at near-by playhouses contributed their bits to their ornate and flowery mannerisms.

Sometimes, after a prolonged session at Bleeck's with a Roget's *Thesaurus* handy, Fuller would give his plug hat a brush, step into a municipal limousine, and head for city hall and oratorical disaster. He got names and titles wrong and once publicly saluted Premier Pierre Laval as "Prime Minister Paul Claudel." On another occasion he hailed Queen Marie of Romania as "Your Imperial Highness," a lapse of protocol which passed practically unremarked in the happy confusion of the moment.

After Mayor Walker met his Wellington in the person of Judge Samuel Seabury, and after the departure for high office in Washington of his other patron, William H. Woodin of the American Car and Foundry Company, times grew lean for Fuller. Scrolls were no longer in municipal requisition, and a usurper held the throne at City Hall. Fuller never batted an eye or turned a hair. He paid his last bar check at Bleeck's one winter afternoon and went home and turned on the gas. His friends last saw him, distinguished even if silent, at Campbell's Funeral Home, his ledger-ruled morning trousers creased to a knife edge and in his lapel a single gardenia cabled to him from his friend, Mayor Walker, an exile in England.

How Grover Whalen Started the Ticker-Tape Welcome[3]

. . . The really distinctive mark of a New York welcome is the ticker-tape blizzard. Contrary to what most people imagine, this custom did not grow up spontaneously. In fact, I thought it up.

It was back in 1919. We had been having some trouble preparing a welcome for the Prince of Wales, now the Duke of Windsor, making his first visit to the U. S. It was hard to convince some of my Irish friends that we should honor the Prince, who they felt represented the British troops who had been occupying Ireland, then seeking its

[3] From "Top Hats and Ticker-Tape," by Grover Whalen, *This Week Magazine,* July 11, 1954, p. 20. Copyright, 1954, by the United Newspapers Magazine Corporation.

independence. Mayor Hylan was advised to call the whole thing off. With Irish blood in my own veins, I felt qualified to come out strongly for what I knew was right.

Wishing to make the Prince's welcome a spectacular one after the struggle I had had to get it put on at all, I hit on the ticker-tape idea. I simply started a word-of-mouth campaign at City Hall, and the idea swiftly filtered all through the thousands of offices that line the lower Broadway canyon. Many office workers promptly carried the thing beyond ticker-tape—they tore up phone books, waste paper, and almost any kind of paper and tinsel they could get their hands on and threw it in great volume from tens of thousands of windows. Since that day no New York welcome would be complete without the confetti snowstorm.

Seth Low and the Law [4]

One who acted as Seth Low's legal adviser while he was Mayor of New York tells the following story. A young fireman lost his life in a fire. Since he had not completed a full year's service, his family was not entitled to the customary insurance. However, his friends became active in the matter; secured powerful political backing; went to Albany and obtained a special act of the legislature giving the Mayor of New York discretion to waive the objection and grant the insurance. They then descended upon Mayor Low, in a body. He met them, cool and aloof, as they came crowding into his office. When they had stated their case, he turned to his legal adviser and said: "Aside from this special discretion vested in me by act of the legislature, what is the law?" "I am compelled to advise your Honor," the latter replied, "that a full year's service is a prerequisite." Turning to the petitioners, Mayor Low said: "You hear the law, gentlemen. I can do nothing for you." They went out, boiling mad. Whereupon Seth Low, the private citizen, sat down at his desk, wrote his personal check for the entire amount of the insurance, and sent it to the bereaved family. "I begged him," adds the teller of the story, "to make it public. But he never would."

[4] From *Seth Low,* by Benjamin R. C. Low, pp. 86–87. Copyright, 1925, by Benjamin R. C. Low. New York and London: G. P. Putnam's Sons.

Jimmy Walker

HIS PRESENCE OF MIND[5]

Walker and I have been a team as after-dinner speakers at possibly a thousand different affairs, including churches, synagogues, and every conceivable charity, regardless of race, creed or color. Jimmy is the greatest impromptu speaker of his or anybody else's time. The greatest example of his presence of mind happened during his last campaign for the mayoralty, with Dudley Field Malone, Collector of the Port of New York and myself. The three of us made a series of political speeches in the Bronx, from seven o'clock in the morning to midnight. Tired as we were when we returned downtown, Jim suddenly remembered that there was one more affair we had neglected to attend. It was a dinner or something at the Biltmore. He had forgotten what it was all about, but we could not disappoint the people who were expecting us. Malone's voice had stayed in the Bronx by this time, and the Mayor and I were hoarse, but into the Biltmore we marched. We hurried up to the Cascade Room, where a group of men was seated, and somebody was making a speech. What and who these men were, neither Jim nor I knew. We were rushed to the dais and the speaker stopped immediately at our entrance. There was applause, and Jim whispered to me, "Start talking, stall for a few minutes till I find out what this is all about."

I began in the customary vein: "Gentlemen, this is an evening to be remembered, a memory to conjure with." (I have always said this at the beginning of my speeches when I'm not sure of the audience, because the word "conjure" sounds as if I've had an education.) Then I went into a couple of set gags. "A funny thing happened on the way down here tonight, etc. etc. . . ." The group of men I was addressing didn't crack a smile. I had no idea what nationality they were. I had never seen them before. I turned to Jim and whispered, "It's all yours, Jim." Relief gave a ring of sincerity to my voice as I said, "Now, gentlemen, I bring you the Magistrate of this, our great city, Father Knickerbocker's truly begotten son, James J. Walker."

The Mayor took his time, cocked his head to one side and began with this routine opening: "Gentlemen, in this kaleidoscopic era that

[5] From *So Help Me,* The Autobiography of George Jessel, pp. 74–76. Copyright, 1943, by Random House, Inc. New York.

we live in, this great melting pot, where from all walks of life men come closer together, it is needless for me to tell you what the people of Polish birth have meant to the progress of the city of New York. I can take you back to the great General Kosciusko in 1776. . . ." There was no reaction from the audience to all this. They were definitely not Poles. Undaunted, Jim continued: "And the simple Italian ditchdigger, imbued with the spirit of freedom handed down to him by the memory of the great Garibaldi, has been more helpful to greater New York, than anyone I can think of. . . ." This brought no cheering either. They were *not* Italians. Jim kept this up until there were no countries left, except Denmark and a few then-unknown South American countries. He took a long chance, and mentioned that the streets of New York would soon be as clean as those of Copenhagen, the great capital of Denmark. That was it! They were a group of Danish-Americans. He was all right from then on; he had their votes. . . .

LONG-WINDED SPEAKERS[6]

Apt humor is always a sharp weapon against Ciceronian orations. Jimmy Walker in a dozen ways was the peer of them all when it came to impromptu, sophisticated wisecracks. He was no paragon to hold up to youth. He was the product of a crazy age, impish, urbane, polished, sardonic. He was at his best when he was dependent solely on his wits, when he was unprepared, unrehearsed and seriousness was purely coincidental.

At the one-hundredth anniversry of the Erie Canal, the Port Authority put on a big lunch to celebrate the union of New York City and the Great Lakes. Frothing rivers flowed. Filet mignons were piled up like flapjacks. Oratory flowed, too. The guest speaker was a charming old gentleman from Buffalo, a grandson of the DeWitt Clinton who built the big ditch, resting peacefully after an honorable local career, unknown to fame and vastly astonished to find himself so honored. He determined to do the occasion full justice and read quietly, historically and monotonously for forty-five minutes. This was after lunch.

He was followed by counsel for the Port Authority, an estimable lawyer who claimed to have invented the Authority idea and also the extraordinary legalistic device known as "and/or," with the 45-degree line in between. This gentleman, with the precedent before him, also spoke forty-five minutes!

[6] From *Working for the People,* Promise and Performance in Public Service, by Robert Moses, pp. 28–29. Copyright, 1956, by Robert Moses. New York: Harper & Brothers.

As the audience began to filter out, deterred only by curiosity as to how the Mayor would get himself out of this situation, Beau James lifted himself lightly to his feet, pointed to the clock and said: "I see before me the busiest and most powerful leaders of the world of industry. They must get back to their desks. Neither wind, nor snow, nor rain, nor gloom of night, nor Jimmy Walker shall keep them from their appointed rounds. Gentlemen, this meeting is adjourned for one hundred years." It is an art which few possess.

The "Little Flower" and the Pushcart Peddlers[7]

Rarely did La Guardia miss the chance to dramatize his ideas. Due to the fact, perhaps, that he was of Italian descent, and because so many pushcart peddlers in the lower East Side were Italians, he was especially sensitive to the problems of these peddlers and the spectacle they created. He decided to abolish the pushcarts and establish enclosed public markets. He was opposed by taxpayers' lobbies. The plan was held to be too expensive. Besides, many sentimental people argued that the peddler with the rusty scales hanging from the side of his cart (which were in many cases giving short weight to housewives) was one of the quaint sights of New York City. They hated to see him go.

I shall never forget how, during a similar campaign to clean up the streets of organ-grinders (most of whom were simply licensed beggars), a woman came up to La Guardia at a social function and begged him not to deprive her of her favorite organ-grinder. "Where do you live?" he asked her. "On Park Avenue."

La Guardia successfully pushed through his plan to eliminate the organ-grinders and the peddlers, despite the pleas of the penthouse slummers. I accompanied him to the dedication of the first public market, and I shall always remember the event. The peddlers were attired in neat white coats. Each stood by his indoor stand, his wares in orderly array. La Guardia launched into his address, and suddenly, in

[7] From *Let the Chips Fall,* My Battles against Corruption, by Newbold Morris, in Collaboration with Dana Lee Thomas, pp. 119–120. Copyright, 1955, by Newbold Morris and Dana Lee Thomas. New York: Appleton-Century-Crofts, Inc.

the middle of it, stooped and picked up an apple from one of the stands. "There will be no more of this," he said, as he pretended to spit on the apple, polishing it up on his coat sleeve and putting it back on the stand. This was his way of demonstrating that the new public markets were in the interest of public health. Pointing to his listeners in their crisp white coats, he concluded, "I found you pushcart peddlers. . . . I have made you *merchants!*"

Let the Aldermen Sleep [8]

[Harrigan and Hart's] entertainment is still an unforgettable memory in the minds of all old-time New Yorkers. Their sketches were humorous pictures of those phases of local life that they all understood so well. . . . All their plays were marvels in the way of local detail and rich in homely wit. I remember one scene in which the members of the Board of Aldermen visited Dan Mulligan's house and were so well entertained that they all fell asleep in the dining room.

"Whatever will I do?" demanded Mrs. Mulligan of her husband. "The aldermen are all sound asleep. Will I wake them?"

"Lave thim be," said Mulligan. "While they sleep the city's safe."

Al Smith

F.F.M. [9]

The [New York state assembly] session of 1911 had a moment when partisanship on both sides of the house was running high. Ed Merritt, Fred Hammond, and Jesse S. Phillips, representing the Republican side, and I, representing the Democratic side, were engaged in a cross-fire of debate on a bill that had to do with the removal of the Com-

[8] From *Forty-Odd Years in the Literary Shop,* by James L. Ford., pp. 97–98. Copyright, 1921, by E. P. Dutton & Company. New York. 1922.

[9] From *Up to Now,* An Autobiography, by Alfred E. Smith, pp. 111–112. Copyright, 1929, by Alfred E. Smith. New York: The Viking Press.

Here [at Fulton Market] Smith picked up some homely similes. Describing a person he did not like, he referred to him as having "an eye as glassy as a dead cod." Of another person he said, "He shakes hands like a frozen mackerel."—Norman Hapgood and Henry Moskowitz, *Up from City Streets: Alfred E. Smith* (New York, 1927), p. 23.

mission of Jurors in Niagara County. There was considerable hard feeling on both sides of the chamber when Assemblyman Wende from Buffalo arose in his place and asked the privilege of interrupting. It was readily granted.

Mr. Wende said, "Mr. Speaker, I have just heard that Cornell won the boat race."

Merritt said, "That doesn't mean anything to me. I'm a Yale man."

Hammond said, "It doesn't mean anything to me. I'm a Harvard man."

Phillips said, "It doesn't mean anything to me. I am a U. of M. man."

I was all alone, the only one of the quartet left standing, so I said, "It doesn't mean anything to me because I am an F.F.M. man."

Assemblyman Hoey shouted out, "What is that, Al?"

I said, "Fulton Fish Market. Let's proceed with the debate."

POLITICAL CHOWDERS[10]

Political chowders, which were quite an institution in old New York, have entirely died out. Nearly every assembly district leader, it seemed, at one time or another during July and August, gave an annual outing. These were for men only. . . .

The biggest chowder of the year was given by the Timothy D. Sullivan Association with headquarters in the Bowery. Big Tim Sullivan led the parade, and after passing through the district, the parade would head toward the dock, where the boats would be ready to take the picnickers to the picnic grounds. As many as seven thousand men have attended one of these outings. The old steamer *Grand Republic* could carry only about thirty-five hundred. It was impossible for the steamboat inspectors to keep track of the guests, as they were jumping on the boat along its length and many times it pulled out from the dock with as many as six thousand men aboard.

When it arrived at Donnelly's Pavilion on College Point, Long Island, the parade would form again and march from the boat to the pavilion, where breakfast was immediately served. Six or seven thousand people could be seated at a single time. When the head waiter rang a large bell, waiters would appear on all sides with clam fritters, ham and eggs, fried potatoes, rolls and coffee.

After breakfast there would be games. There would be a fat man's race, a hurdle race, an obstacle race, and three or four different games

[10] *Ibid.*, pp. 31–33.

of baseball. Kegs of beer would be on tap around the entire place. Strange to say, in those days, out of a gathering of six thousand men, there would not be a dozen who drank anything stronger than beer. When evening came along, dinner would be served, which consisted usually of clam chowder, roast beef, lamb chops, ice cream and coffee.

Returning home at night, the picnickers would again parade through the district, and there was great rivalry in the various parts of the district as to which would give them the greatest reception. Fireworks were so freely used that on the morning after one of the chowders I found my best suit and my straw hat covered with burns from stray sparks.

In those days political leaders had very little spare time to themselves in the summer. They were expected to attend one another's outings, and leaders of the prominence of Tom Foley, Tom McAvoy, John F. Ahearn, Timothy D. Sullivan, and The McManus spent a large part of their summers sailing from Manhattan to Donnelly's or Witzell's Point View Island, eating clam fritters and parading through a shower of fireworks at night.

"TOWN-LOT" AL SMITH[11]

. . . The presidential bee having settled under his brown derby, and started its work, [Alfred E.] Smith began to face the criticism that his outlook did not extend beyond the limits of New York State, that he was, in the unkind words of William Allen White, "a town-lot Sir Galahad who never fared afield." Numerous solemn people started to demand his views, if he had any, on the tariff, the League of Nations, international debts. There were two reasons why Al did not look with favor on these queries: the first was that he was still Governor and had promised that he would devote all his time to the job instead of seeking the presidency; the second reason was that he had really not thought about these weighty matters at all.

So, again he was bland and suave with an undernote of hostility when a serious soul journeyed to Albany with a questionnaire in his brief case. One by one Al evaded the questions on national issues. Finally, exasperated, the visitor lost his temper.

"But, Governor," he demanded, "tell me just one subject you think is important to people living in states west of the Mississippi."

"What states *are* west of the Mississippi?" asked Smith, as if for information.

[11] From *Alfred E. Smith,* A Critical Study, by Henry F. Pringle, p. 97, Copyright, 1927, by Macy-Masius, Inc. New York.

Tricks of Campaign Club Strikers [12]

"Striking" nominees, in the [Tweed] Ring days, was carried to extremes. It was, in fact, a systematic form of brigandage. Those running for office would have been glad to ignore it, but few regarded it as good policy so to do. The operations of the strikers were indeed characterized by so much adroitness and skill as almost to excite admiration from their victims.

Of course there were all kinds of "strikers," or, more properly speaking, there were strikers who sought to impose upon candidates for office in all kinds of ways. At an exciting Presidential election it was customary to organize what were called "campaign clubs" in almost every election district of the city, for the purpose of arousing the enthusiasm of the voters in small neighborhoods; and often these organizations became permanent institutions. The known existence of these clubs afforded the political brigands an excellent opportunity to pursue their nefarious practices.

* * * * *

It was the custom among almost every branch of skilled mechanics, as well as among the members of the fire engine companies, to have a day's outing in October of each year, when, to add interest to the occasion, they would shoot at targets for prizes contributed by the friends of the members; and the better to carry out the semi-military appearance of the turn-out, would organize themselves as companies, marching to their chosen locality with a band of music; and after the shooting and distribution of prizes they would have a regular picnic with their families, and a dance to wind up the festivities of the occasion. These were enjoyable, and generally well-conducted affairs.

But this target-shooting feature, occurring just before the annual elections, was also made use of by the striking fraternity as a means to "bleed" candidates for office.

A story is told of an impecunious politician of military fame, showing how, when once he was running for Congress, he was waited upon and victimized by strikers who represented themselves as an authorized

[12] From *Thirty Years of New York Politics Up-to-Date,* by Matthew P. Breen, pp. 236, 238–241. Copyright, 1899, by Matthew P. Breen. New York: Published by the Author.

committee from a target-shooting organization in the candidate's district.

When the bogus committee called upon their intended victim and made known their mission, the candidate, who had doubtless been overrun with many similar applications, pleaded poverty, and vowed that, just then, he did not have a five-dollar bill in his pocket.

"But, perhaps, your wife has some money with her," suggested the spokesman of the alleged target-shooters' committee, who happened to know that the lady had at least the reputation of possessing ample means. "The shooting comes off day after tomorrow," he added, "and we are hard pressed for time to arrange matters."

The candidate's first impulse was to knock the impudent fellow down, but realizing that he was in a close contest, and needed every vote he could get, sober second thought advised him to go and see his wife. While discussing the situation, he "arranged" with her that there was only twenty dollars in her possession, and received that amount from her. Returning to his visitors, he told this fact to the target committee. The spokesman of the party took the matter very coolly, however. He was equal to any emergency. He did not seem touched in the slightest degree by the candidate's pecuniary trouble.

"Twenty dollars," said he. "Well, General, let us have the twenty dollars for the boys, and I will explain how you are fixed," and he stretched out his hand for the $20, which the candidate unhesitatingly delivered to him.

"Now, General," said the striker, when he had counted the money and put it in his pocket, "this $20 is all good enough for beer money for the boys, but you must give us something worthy of yourself as a prize—something the boys can show—a watch or a diamond ring—something to shout for and make them feel they are appreciated, so they can work all the harder for you. Don't you think so, Jim?" he continued, addressing one of his associates.

"Of course! The boys will expect something real nice from the General," responded Jim.

The candidate, who could hardly restrain his indignation at this cool proceeding, had his breath nearly taken away, when the spokesman of the party, walking toward a valuable mosaic carved table in a corner of the room, which was a wedding present to his wife, said: "What a splendid committee-room table this would make for the boys! We will be satisfied with this table, General; and to save time and expense, we will take it right along with us now. When the boys see that table, they will go for you sure, and never forget you."

"That's so," the man known as Jim chimed in; "the boys will rally round you, General, for that table, and no mistake."

"Bet your life on that," exclaimed the third committee man, who thought it was now time for him to say something.

Each of the scoundrels had at a glance gauged the value of the table, and was mentally calculating how large a ransom the General would pay rather than part with it; for that was the scheme of the trio.

The candidate, while ready to burst with rage, at this climax of cheek, could not help admiring the monumental impudence and persistency of the gang of would-be marauders, though he did not propose to let them despoil him of his property. But it cost him, as he afterwards freely admitted, about half an hour more of talk, and his wife's check for $50 to save the table.

This incident will give you an idea of the "gall" and impudence of some of the strikers who flourished in the flush days of the Tweed Ring. There are plenty of deceptive rogues ready to take advantage of and "bleed" aspirants for office nowadays, but, like a good many of our present-day politicians, in comparison with their prototypes of thirty years ago, they are mere pigmies.

Waring's White Wings [13]

In the late Nineties, Colonel George Waring was about the most talked of and the best talked of man in New York. This was not due to the fact that he had written several good books, and was a very exceptionally accomplished and attractive gentleman, but because he was the first man who had ever cleaned the streets. Many men of all sorts of ability and eminence, from Judge Whiting down, and possibly sometimes up, had tried it and failed, until everybody thought the task impossible. It was harder then than now; for when walking even on Fifth Avenue, on a windy day, one was covered with clouds of dry horse dung. The automobiles have remedied that, but Waring remedied it before them.

One agency of his miracle was his leading the men to take a pride in their work. Before his day, "street cleaner," was a term of degradation.

[13] From *Garrulities of an Octogenarian Editor,* with Other Essays Somewhat Biographical and Autobiographical, by Henry Holt, pp. 157–158. Copyright, 1923, by Houghton Mifflin Company. Boston and New York.

Waring began by putting his men in uniform—and of all things, white uniforms at that. In their beneficent task, they were known as "Waring's White Wings." And strange to say, notwithstanding the soiling to which the white duck was subjected, it always gave an impression of cleanliness. Then instead of leaving his men to carry the dirt to its piles a shovelful at a time, he gave them the little tanks on wheels still in use, which were great labor savers.

After a year or so of revolutionary experience, he got up a parade of his street cleaners, carts and all, reviewed by the mayor. He rode at the head. He had been a colonel of cavalry in the civil war, and was a superb horseman. When he got opposite the reviewing stand, he turned his horse to face it, and sidestepped its whole length amid thunders of applause. All this of course reacted on the spirit of his men, and ever since, the impossible has been accomplished and, helped by the substitution of the automobile for the horse, New York streets, because Waring taught how to do it, have been kept clean.

Street Name Crises [14]

The squalls [of 1945] over changing the name of Sixth Avenue to the Avenue of the Americas represent only the most recent chapter in the long, uneasy history of the names and numbers of New York streets. Just a hundred years ago, in 1845, New Yorkers were bickering about the street numbers of Wall Street—both odd and even numbers appeared on both sides of the street—and the city directory of that year referred to Wall Street as "a regular state of beautiful confusion." At the moment the bartenders of Sixth Avenue are roused, asserting that confused sailors will be unable to find their favorite saloons under the new dispensation.

* * * * *

It is clear that the changing of street names requires a very delicate technique. Skilled practitioners are seldom found. Instead, city officials, trade associations, antiquarians, real estate promoters and veterans meddle and blunder along from generation to generation.

[14] From "On Fitting a Name to a Street, It's Ticklish Business, The Risks Are Great, and The Results Often Don't Please Anyone," by George R. Leighton, *The New York Times Magazine,* October 21, 1945, pp. 16, 53. Copyright, 1945, by the New York Times Company.

Occasionally, by lucky chance, they hit on an acceptable name; often the public simply smothers the new name to death. If you ask a New Yorker where the West Side Elevated Highway is, he will tell you it runs along the edge of Manhattan from Seventy-second to Duane Street. On the maps this is the Miller Highway, named after Julius Miller, [since] New York Supreme Court Justice, but not one New Yorker in a thousand knows this and the name has no standing in everyday usage.

Sometimes the issue sways in the balance for a long time. The suspension bridge that crosses the Hudson River from 179th Street to the New Jersey Palisades was originally called the Hudson River Bridge. At this juncture Congressman Sol Bloom, who had made the veneration of George Washington into a life work, insisted that the new artery be called the George Washington Bridge. Finally he had his way. Both names have persisted, but it looks as though the Congressman will win in the end. It is different with the Bronx thoroughfare that starts out at 138th Street as the Grand Concourse and then, at 161st Street, suddenly bellies out into the Grand Boulevard and Concourse. Bronx residents put this monstrosity through the wringer and it came out simply "the Concourse."

The chief place for street name manufacture used to be the Board of Aldermen. One of the most imposing of latter-day aldermen was Peter J. McGuinness, now assistant commissioner of borough works for Brooklyn, and district leader and boss of Greenpoint. Commissioner McGuinness could with ease sit for the portrait of the urban statesman as Mr. Dooley used to describe him. He is over six feet, weighs 240 pounds and has white hair, a ruddy complexion and a tremendous jaw. The Commissioner is an authority on many subjects, New York street names among them.

"The true instinct for street names," says Mr. McGuinness, "lies in the heart of the people. If your life depended on it could you tell me where Rigelman's Walk is? That you could not. Rigelman's Walk was the official name for the Boardwalk at Coney Island, in honor of Harold Rigelman, once borough president of Brooklyn, and a mighty fine man he was. But the people knew better. Something told them that the right name was the Boardwalk, and that's the way it stayed.

"What politician in his right mind will attempt to oppose the sound instinct of the people? Why will they say okay to Pulaski Skyway for the big bridges over in Jersey, and nix the Kosciusko Bridge here in Brooklyn? Sure, both the two heroes was Polish. But Kosciusko Bridge the people will not have and they call it the Meeker Avenue Bridge to this day.

"Well do I recall," says Mr. McGuinness, "when Isidor Frank, the alderman of the Twenty-third District, was acting chairman of the Committee on Thoroughfares. He was bound that Stone Avenue should be renamed after Hyman Schorenstein, the leader of Brownsville. Such a storm as that caused you would not believe. 'Twas not that Schorenstein was not deserving. He started life working on a truck for the American Ice Company; from that he moved up to be United States marshal and then higher yet, but that made no difference. The people would have it Stone Avenue.

"As for myself, did I not read the hearts of my constituents right when I called Greenpoint the 'Garden Spot of America'? That I did. And who named Greenpoint? Ah, that is lost in the mists of histhry [sic]."

The street-naming functions of the old Board of Aldermen are now exercised by the City Council and the business is taken seriously, if not expertly. There is generally some proposition before the Council which involves the Roosevelt name. It took a hard fight a century ago to change the name of Roosevelt Slip to Peck Slip; a few weeks back there were bitter words over the change of East River Drive to Franklin D. Roosevelt Drive. At the present moment there are nine Roosevelt street and place names in the city, not to mention the Theodore Roosevelt High School in the Bronx. These include Roosevelt Street and Roosevelt Square in Manhattan; Roosevelt Court in Brooklyn; Roosevelt Plaza and Roosevelt Avenue in Queens and Roosevelt Avenue in Richmond.

Often, just as the aldermen used to do, the Council deals with proposals to glorify living politicians. Mayor La Guardia smiled sweetly when La Guardia Airport was first named. He was not incensed at the idea of transferring the name to an even larger airfield. Then came the explosion; there were mutterings about Caesarism, and so on.

Unfortunately the opposition had no first-class name to suggest and so, by default, the most magnificent airport in the world will be named after a golf course that once occupied part of the site—Idlewild. A name that originated in the brain of some real estate promotor when elegantly rustic names were popular for high-toned suburban speculations.

Sometimes the City Council loses its nerve in a street-naming crisis. Five years ago it got entangled with two Brooklyn racial groups who lived on the edge of a small park. The Irish residents wanted the place called Callahan-Kelly Park; the Italians preferred Amerigo Vespucci Park. The Council weaseled and dodged and then went to pieces altogether. It passed bills approving both names and left the problem up to Mayor La Guardia. He solved it by vetoing both bills and the park is nameless to this day.

Saved from Potter's Field [15]

If any Jewish person ever goes to Potter's Field, it is only through an oversight on the part of The Hebrew Free Burial Association. This extremely efficient society was founded and organized in 1888 by a Mr. Barnett Friedman for the purpose of providing a resting place and free burial for persons of the Jewish faith who lacked the necessary funds at the time of their death. . . .

* * * * *

If a body in any of our city mortuaries has something on it to indicate the person is of the Jewish faith, the authorities notify the Association. Not infrequently representatives of the Association, whom they station at the morgues, spot a Jewish body even before the authorities. Thereupon the body, if unidentified and unclaimed, is turned over to this admirable society for burial.

* * * * *

There is a legend at the Bellevue morgue that the Association was once shamefully hoaxed. The morgue attendants at that time were a harum-scarum lot, poorly paid and habitual drinkers. One of them was an Irishman, a good-natured soul who was extremely popular with his fellows. He got drunk once too often and was brought in dead one morning. His comrades knew there was no money to save him from Potter's Field. The circumstances worried them. They debated what to do, until finally one of them went out quietly, bought two copies of Jewish newspapers and carefully thrust them into the side pocket of the dead man's coat. Shortly afterward the Association's representative turned up, reviewed the bodies awaiting his inspection and came to the man with the newspapers. He said: "Tsk-tsk! Poor fellow! Poor fellow!" He stooped reverently and tagged the body in behalf of his

[15] From *The Murdered and the Missing,* by Armstrong Livingston and Capt. John G. Stein, pp. 115–116. Copyright, 1947, by Armstrong Livingston and Capt. John G. Stein. New York: Stephen-Paul Publishers.

society. Somewhere in a Jewish cemetery today rests this Son of Erin, and quite comfortably, no doubt, beneath the Star of David.

Always a considerate man, when Stein tells this story he makes it clear it relates to long ago. It could never have happened, he says, under our present efficient administration.

A Cop's Yarns [16]

. . . In the Station House, the back room is always the clearing house of all that goes on in the city and the dormitories are the cops' playground. What stories are told from one bed to another! Every one exchanges his experiences with his neighbor. Human interest, nonsense and scandal. What secrets are buried in the walls of the station houses of New York City! Except when reputations are at stake and homes might be blasted if the truth were known, these yarns are told among the gang after the day's rounds, but the others . . . well, they're buried somewhere in the dim reaches of the cop's memories, and if he's wise, he keeps what he knows to himself. I consider the necessary qualifications of a good cop to include friendliness to the good and a tough attitude toward the bad, with generous wisdom keeping his head on his shoulders all the time.

When bed time came the yarns began to fly around.

"Say, boys, I had a funny one today," one of the boys began. "A woman, swinging a heavy cane, said, 'Officer, do you see that hotel there?' 'Yes, madam,' I answered. 'Well, my husband is in there with another woman. I followed them and I know which room they have and all I need is protection, and I'll handle the case myself. You can't get any information in the hotel but I know just where they are and I want you to walk in with me and protect me.' We went over there and she headed straight for the room. She broke in the door with a few good hard kicks and in she went. She chased a naked blonde out of the closet and, boy, how she did whack that dame. The blonde dashed out of there and ran into another room and the old girl turned on hubby. What a lacing she gave him! Then she turned to me and said, 'Name and shield number, Officer. You were very kind and I may need you as

[16] From *A Cop Remembers,* by Captain Cornelius W. Willemse, pp. 76–79. Copyright, 1933, by E. P. Dutton & Co. New York.

a witness.' Why that woman thought she needed protection is beyond me. What a polisher she was with her feet and her cane both working!"

Another corner was heard from. "I had a good one today. A gang of kids was swimming without bathing suits in the North River at Twenty-second Street. They'd put their clothes and shoes in a big box and I came along and threw the box on a truck and dropped it off in front of the car barns. What a mix-up! The kids began running in all directions and found themselves right smack in the middle of the late afternoon crowd of women shoppers. Some of the big fellows ran to a vegetable stand and stole some carrots, decorating themselves with the greens. They sure looked funny with strings around their middles and the greens for fig leaves. What a fine moving picture that would have made!"

"Well, I had a hot one on the late tour." This from another bed. "The engineer of an apartment house called me in and said there was someone acting strangely in the back yard. I took a look and found a poor guy out there with hardly a stitch on trying to hide himself in an empty ash barrel. I brought him into the engine room and he explained his troubles. One of those 'out the window you must go' cases. I certainly had a good laugh. The husband came back an hour too soon."

Then I told about the burglar scare of an old maid on my post. They're always funny. This one had called me in saying she was sure there was a man under the bed. I searched every nook and corner and found nothing. When I turned to go she asked me if I wouldn't stay and have a cup of tea. She wouldn't take no for an answer, so when I hesitated she grabbed my helmet, and began pulling off my coat. Then she took off my jacket and collar. I said, "Whoa, what's this?" and she said, oh, she just liked to undress men. She was very coy and I had to laugh at her because she was at least twenty years older than I. Just lonely I suppose but it's a shame when women act that way on a late tour and lead us into temptation.

Some women see ghosts. Others hear noises and you've got to be patient with all of them. I got along with these cases on my post, all except one old crank on Twenty-fifth Street. She was a window-peeper. She used binoculars and was always looking for trouble. Across the street were furnished room houses and what she could see between ten P.M. and four A.M. was plenty. She called me in one night. We had a great silhouette show and I thought I'd die laughing. A couple of very affectionate people were having a big evening and a crazy mutt of a dog was the whole show. The light was evidently behind them and every move was seen on the shade. I couldn't keep a straight face and this old woman said, "Shame on you, Officer, for making light of such a performance. They ought to be put in jail." I left, for the show was too much for me, and she yelled down after me to know what I was going to do about it. I told her I'd do what I could, then I sent word to the people that they had an audience. I thought they might like to know it.

We had a fine mix-up at the Station House one night. I sneaked up to the section room ahead of the gang and put a piece of limburger cheese under the pillow slip on the bed of a grouchy Irishman who never could take a joke. As soon as Paddy came in and sat down on his bed he began to sniff. He looked long and hard at the man alongside of him and shouted, "Hey, you damned Dutchman, don't you ever take a bath?" The Dutchman was a Down East Yankee named Cobaugh and he was getting hot under the collar, when Paddy added, "You're not fit to sleep among men, you ought to go and sleep in a stable." Cobaugh wasn't in on the joke and I don't blame him for being mad, so he advised Paddy in no uncertain terms to wash his own feet, that the trouble with him was that he was smelling himself. Paddy grumbled but went on preparing for bed and as he got another strong whiff he got up and looked under the bed and under his mattress. He sniffed and sniffed, looking madder every minute, then he investigated his pillow.

What a roar went up! Waving the limburger around he challenged everybody in the section room, then someone turned off the gas jet, our only light, and threw an old shoe at Paddy. That was a signal for a general riot and there was no sleep that night for anybody.

"Shoo Flies" and "Coops"

I [17]

The sergeant of today, as was the old roundsman, is the most important superior officer in the police service. He's the active field commander, the man directly responsible for the discipline and efficiency of the uniformed force. While captains are in command and lieutenants

[17] From *Behind the Green Lights*, by Captain Cornelius W. Willemse in Collaboration with George J. Lemmer and Jack Kofoed, pp. 96–99. Copyright, 1931, by C. W. Willemse. New York and London: Alfred A. Knopf.

are performing the desk duties, the sergeant goes out on patrol in uniform to check up on the individual patrolmen. It's a close supervision, often rasping to tempers of officers and men alike. The sergeant is the most important boss to the foot patrolman. He's respected and liked or detested and feared according to his temperament. The top sergeant of a company of soldiers has a job much the same.

But there's one great distinction between the sergeants of the present and the roundsmen of about thirty years ago. The sergeant has obtained his rank as the result of competitive examination under the Civil Service system. He goes higher only when he is able to qualify by examination. The roundsman was a political appointee—and his efficiency was measured by the number of complaints he could make against his men!

In my early police years, the department operated upon the theory that proper discipline could be obtained only when the roundsmen were hounding the patrolmen and preferring charges against the latter on the slightest provocation. The more complaints the roundsman was able to make against his men, the quicker the roundsman's chances of promotion.

In self-defense, the patrolmen of every station banded together to protect themselves from the watchful eyes of the roundsmen. There was another worry, besides. Headquarters had its own method of "checking up." A force of "shoo flies"—roundsmen in civilian clothes —were sent out regularly from Headquarters to sweep into a precinct and look over the men. The "shoo flies" were expected to make complaints—or "didos," as the policemen call them—and they did their jobs uncomfortably well. The double-check may have been good for discipline, but it raised the devil with a man's peace of mind.

Every incoming policeman was "put wise" to the need for watchfulness. The fun began soon after I entered the old 17th Precinct as a rookie. The escapade of Tom Egbert taught me that patrolmen had to think fast to keep out of trouble.

At that time, Roundsmen Londrigan and Harrigan were the two most feared "shoo flies" in the city. One night, when I was on post, the word was passed along from patrolman to patrolman that Londrigan and Harrigan were in the precinct "looking for meat." Within ten minutes, everybody was on the alert except Patrolman Tom Egbert.

Tom was taking a rest for himself in the undertaking rooms of Stephen Merritt. The "shoo flies," having seen a uniformed patrolman enter the place, were covering the entrance to nab him when he came out.

The policeman on the adjoining post saw the two sergeants and hurried to phone the undertaking parlor.

"The 'shoo flies' are at the door, Tom. Stay inside out of sight."

The warning aroused the whole Merritt staff. The undertaker's assistant got on the phone. In a few minutes, a wagon drove up to the door, the driver stepping out and swinging wide the doors before he stepped into the shop. In a moment the driver and two of the Merritt employees came forth carrying the basket always used in the transportation of corpses. They handled it with the care and reverence only undertakers know how to show. In the presence of death, the "shoo flies" stepped back and watched as the corpse was placed carefully in the wagon and driven away. At the other end of Tom's post, the wagon stopped, the basket was opened, and the "corpse" stepped out in person, the sweating, much worried Tom.

Then Tom strolled back along the sidewalk, swinging his club as an officer should, apparently without a care in the world. Londrigan and Harrigan stared in amazement.

"Where've you been?" they demanded.

"Why, on the post where I belong."

Londrigan remembered the hearse and the basket.

"Done in," he snapped, looking at Tom wrathfully. There was nothing the "shoo flies" could do. They didn't know Tom personally and weren't able to identify him positively as the officer they'd seen entering Merritt's. But ever afterwards, when Londrigan and Harrigan visited the precinct, Tom had to watch his step even more carefully than usual.

I had a close call myself with the same "shoo flies" shortly after Tom's escape. I had entered a restaurant on Eighth Avenue between 24th and 25th Streets and was having a bite to eat in the kitchen when my side partner on post sent in word by a boy that Londrigan and Harrigan had seen me enter and were covering the outside.

It was a tough spot. There was no back door and no chance to escape by way of the cellar. The only way out was the front door where the "shoo flies" were parked.

I did some fast and furious thinking in that kitchen. I took off my uniform blouse, folded it and placed it on a large tray. On top of the blouse I laid my hat and nightstick, covering the whole with a white tablecloth. Then I slipped into a long white apron, balanced the tray on one hand and marched straight out the front door of the restaurant, managing to hide my face somewhat with my uplifted arm. I must have handled that tray like a born waiter, for the two "shoo flies" never even gave me a tumble. I marched up 8th Avenue to 25th Street and turned the corner. Then I flew into the nearest areaway. In a matter of seconds, I had discarded the tablecloth, apron and tray and was patrolling along the line in full regalia.

I reached 8th Avenue and the roundsmen spotted me. They muttered quickly to themselves and then came up.

"Where are you on post?" Londrigan demanded.

"On Twenty-fifth Street, Seventh to Tenth Avenues."

"What were you doing in the restaurant around the corner?"

"Why, I wasn't in any restaurant."

"You look just like the policeman we saw go in there!"

"Well, it couldn't be me because I am outside."

The "shoo flies" hurried into the restaurant and found there was no back door. They looked puzzled when they hit the sidewalk again.

"By God, I've got it," Londrigan shouted suddenly. "You were the fellow who went by us in the waiter's apron!"

"Who, me?" Injured innocence on the outside but quaking inside.

They looked at me sternly and I figured the game was up. But they had never seen me before and couldn't swear to my identity. Also, they might have realized that it wouldn't look so good for two smart "shoo flies" to admit that a rookie had fooled them.

"Get back on post," Londrigan growled suddenly. It was a mighty close shave.

II[18]

John Hoffman had a grocery store between Bleecker and Minetta on Carmine Street, in what is now the Italian quarter of New York, and it was a great hangout for cops, for John was good to them and they liked him. I can see a grin creeping over the faces of a good many policemen and even inspectors retired or still active who will recall this spot when I mention it.

* * * * *

I had a key to the side door of John Hoffman's grocery store and on late tour it was a great coop. After seeing the boss and satisfying myself that all was serene in the neighborhood, I used to go into John's back room and shove him over to the wall and go to bed with him for a short snooze. At 5:30 in the morning, when he opened up shop, I used to cook breakfast. When Nutsy Carroll was on, it was different. John used

[18] From *A Cop Remembers,* by Captain Cornelius W. Willemse, pp. 134, 135–137. Copyright, 1933, by E. P. Dutton & Company, Inc. New York.

to cook the breakfast and Nutsy would put on his apron and wait on trade.

One morning a colored woman looked carefully at Nutsy and said, "Mistah Groceryman—you shuah do look like de cop on de Lane."

"Yes, ma'am," said Nutsy politely. "He's my twin brother."

A day or so later he met this same woman in the Lane and she said, "Offisah, your brother look a heap like you, but you is a mite taller."

Nutsy was equal to the occasion. He nodded his head and looked wise and replied, "Yes'm. He's a little bit older than I am. That is, he was born first." The woman flashed a wide smile at him and went her way. I guess the neighborhood was onto most of our tricks.

* * * * *

Getting into a coop is easy, but getting out of it when the boss is outside is not so pleasant. I know of a cop who was carried out of a bakery in a large basket with loaves of bread sticking out all over him. It took him a long time to get the flour dust off his uniform.

One time I was in Getty's sawmill on Ninth Avenue during a late tour with Andy Brady, the one-armed night watchman of the mill. He discovered a fire while making his rounds, and as he couldn't handle the fire hose and turn on the water with his one arm, he yelled for me. I ran up the stairs and grabbed the hose while he turned on the water, and by the time the fire engines got there in response to an alarm turned in by some passer-by, the fire was out. A few minutes' delay and that place would have caused a blaze that would have meant a four-alarm fire. Mr. Getty was so grateful for my part in helping to put out the fire he gave me a month's pay as a present.

I'm not telling this to prove the merits of "cooping," but it has its good as well as its bad aspects, although I must admit they are usually bad. But under the two-platoon system it was almost impossible in a busy precinct to get a moment's relaxation while on reserve. The station houses were noisy, filthy, vermin-ridden and foul and a clean board somewhere on post was preferable to a bed behind the green lights.

The Fire Laddie's Revenge [19]

. . . I want to portray something of the exciting interest which so attached the "old boys" to their favorite companies; and perhaps I cannot better do so than by relating an incident, showing the intense earnestness to which the competition between the rival companies gave rise, although I cannot hope to do this with the Homeric simplicity and art displayed by the old ex-Chief, Assemblyman Decker, when he narrated the facts to me.

For a long period a "grudge" existed between Engine companies No. 34 and No. 27. The famous David C. (or "Dave") Broderick, afterwards United States Senator from California, was foreman of No. 34. On the side of No. 27 as foreman was John R. Mount, afterwards Police Captain, with Ely Hazleton, assistant foreman. Before attaining the position of foreman, Mount had figured in various "episodes" in the annals of the Department; while Hazleton, always "full of the devil" (as Decker emphatically expressed it), and priding himself on his muscle, contrived to have some kind of a tussle with No. 34's men whenever, during Mount's absence, he was in command of the company. The rival companies were located not many blocks apart, and, whenever possible, they would "race" each other to a fire. After the fire was out and the companies homeward bound, if they happened to reach the same street at the same time (and when Hazleton was in command they somehow invariably did so), the "runners" or outside attachés of each machine would manage to collide. Altercations were thus of frequent occurrence, and the scene of contest was generally in the vicinity of Duane and Chatham Streets, which locality was kept in a state of commotion whenever there was an alarm of fire in that district. The two companies were pretty equally matched, and when they did have a "controversy," it was hard to tell which got the better of the argument.

One Sunday, No. 34, having made due preparations, caught No. 27 somewhat short-handed, "went for" her like an avalanche, and not only "washed" but "licked" her. In elucidation of these expressions, so pat with the ex-Chief, but which needed some translation for me,

[19] From *Thirty Years of New York Politics Up-To-Date,* by Matthew P. Breen, pp. 74–77. Copyright, 1899, by Matthew P. Breen. New York: Published by the Author.

I may say that, before the introduction of steam fire apparatus, the old hand-power engines, in order to utilize the street hydrants, some distance apart, had to form lines; one apparatus, taking water from a hydrant, would supply through several lengths of hose another apparatus, and so on till the scene of conflagration was reached, the last apparatus through its hose and pipe doing the best execution possible on the fire; the men on the brakes of the several engines working at the rate of about one hundred and sixty strokes a minute, each man working only half a minute, and then retiring exhausted, while another jumped in and took his place, at the risk of having his fingers cut off or his head broken by the descending brakes. Whenever one engine pumped water into another faster than the receiving engine could get rid of it, the water would of course overflow her box, and she got "washed"; and then there was a "Hurrah, boys!" time very humiliating to the "washed" company. On the occasion spoken of, No. 34 had not only succeeded, as I have stated, in "washing" No. 27, but (in Decker's expressive phrase) had "licked" her, meaning that on her way home the runners of the triumphant engine had so flouted and irritated the humiliated company that a row ensued, and the adherents of No. 27 had got soundly thrashed, in the bargain!

About three weeks after this "licking," No. 27's fellows (who had meanwhile been preparing for an "emergency") met No. 34's boys at a fire in what was then Van Renwyck Street. So well had Hazleton drilled his men to conceal their hostile intention from 34's company that the latter felt, up to the very moment when the "charge of the light brigade" was made on them in Hudson Street, that there would be no "fuss" that day; that No. 27's boys had got enough at the last encounter to satisfy them; and, secure in such confidence, "Dave" Broderick, foreman of No. 34, was walking along a little distance in the rear of his engine, on its return home, when, suddenly, someone from behind knocked his fire-cap from off his head. Turning quickly, he saw a big strapping fellow, with the figures "27" on his shirt front, who, as Broderick made an effort to secure his cap, jumped upon and threw him to the ground, and then, with a wild war-whoop of victory, picked up his fire-cap and ran off with it as a trophy.

What his enemy's scalp was to an Indian, the fire-cap of an opponent was to a fireman fighter; it was a trophy of his foe's defeat, a badge of his own glory. As Broderick's assailant, on the run, held the captured fire-cap aloft and gave a yell of triumph, as if this were a preconcerted signal, No. 27's "fellows" rushed the fight all along the line, and the "engagement was general." Broderick never felt so badly in his life. He had been taken completely by surprise—by a "fire in the rear," as it were; and as he gazed upon the lively melee ahead of him, he felt like Sheridan, in Buchanan Read's poem, "miles away." Bareheaded as he was, he threw himself, trumpet in hand, into the midst of the fray, hoping to transform threatened defeat into victory; but he did not; he could not. No. 27's leader had laid his plans too well; Ely Hazleton was "too many" for him. After about half an hour of terrific fighting, resulting in broken bones, broken heads, and one fatal injury, No. 34's fellows were bodily driven from the scene of conflict, leaving their apparatus behind them. It was a Waterloo defeat. No. 27 had had its revenge.

Next day there was a grand jubilee at the headquarters of Engine No. 27, in Desbrosses Street; while, with fife and drum to lead the way, Ely Hazleton and "Dave Broderick's assailant, arm in arm, bearing aloft the top of a pole "Dave" Broderick's fire-cap, piloted the fighting element of No. 27 in a parade around the vicinity of the house of their favorite engine, and past the engine house of No. 34, as if inviting somebody or anybody to "tread on the tails of their coats." For a climax they fastened the pole (surrounded by their trophy of victory), on the top of their engine house, with three cheers and a tiger that swelled the hearts and heads of the members of Engine Co. 27, as they gazed upon the fire-cap of the discomfited "Dave." Never again was there any serious trouble between the two companies. No. 34's boys had really "got enough."

High-Ladder Boys[20]

Although today virtually every American city and town, including those with volunteer fire companies, has aerial-ladder trucks, this particular type of apparatus is a New York specialty. It was first developed in Manhattan back in the horse-drawn days because the tenements kept getting higher and higher—and the loss of life more staggering. Finally a law requiring any structure of more than seven stories to be fireproof—or provided with fireproof escape towers—put

[20] From "The High-Ladder Boys," by Harry Henderson, *Argosy*, Vol. 335, (December, 1952), No. 6, pp. 81–83. Copyright, 1952, by Popular Publications, Inc. New York.

a ceiling, so to speak, on tenement height. That's why the New York fire department's trucks carry ladders that are 75 or 85 feet when fully extended.

New York "truckmen," as hook-and-ladder men are called, have acquired remarkable deftness in taking these hurtling 25,000-pound trucks through bumper-to-bumper traffic and in using the aerial ladder at fires.

"What makes H & L No. 26 the top truck company in New York is the neighborhood," a veteran fireman told me. "They get more practice than anybody else does anywhere in the city."

Spanish Harlem is a tense, teeming, ghetto-like area between 100th and 125th Streets, lying between Fifth and Third Avenues. Its tenements seem to have been designed as firetraps. All have narrow halls, steep, dark stairways, inadequate fire escapes. In addition, they are equipped with dumbwaiter, air and light shafts that provide perfect flues and spread the fire rapidly from floor to floor.

The people themselves constitute an additional problem. Like previous immigrant waves, from Italy, Poland, Ireland and Germany, they are strangers in a foreign land, miserably exploited, uneducated and unaccustomed to American ways. Unable to speak or understand English, they are easily panicked by fire. Often they jump needlessly to their death when the fire is nowhere near them. They allow dirt and rubbish to accumulate in the hallways and often the dumbwaiter shaft is packed with refuse up to the third floor—before it catches fire. They use kerosene stoves which they do not know how to operate and maintain properly. Frightened by New York's hoodlums, they put steel bars over their windows so they can't be robbed—and can't be saved. Jealous husbands sometimes padlock their wives in their rooms, and those from the rural areas of Puerto Rico, where dirt floors are customary, sometimes build fires in the middle of a wooden tenement floor. This invariably results in a holocaust.

The fishing-pole technique of ventilating a fire with the big ladder is a specialty with H & L No. 26. They keep their eyes on the engine company's hose line and when it swells with water, they tap the 75-foot ladder against the blackened, smoking windows gently, one by one, shattering the glass and letting the heat and smoke mushroom out. One of the company veterans told me: "You can get that ladder up there faster than you can get men there. In some of these crowded tenements, it's the only way the fire can be ventilated." He pointed out that by holding off on the window-breaking until they see water fill the hose, they do not create a flue until there is water there to attack the fire directly and immediately; at that point the lifting of the heat and smoke becomes imperative.

What gives the men of H & L No. 26 their greatest trouble is that, when a fire breaks out, everyone immediately starts out in the narrow hallways with his dearest possession. Often these old tenement halls are literally clogged with people and furniture. The truckmen particularly feel this because the New York technique of tenement fire fighting calls for the two men on the running boards to "ventilate" the fire immediately. This means that they must get to the roof, open all skylights and bulkhead doors to allow heat and smoke and gas to escape; otherwise, experience has shown that the top floor is liable to explode.

Once they have opened up the roof, the men then go down, one working the front of the building and the other the rear, searching for occupants and getting them out. However, the hallways are often so jammed with people that the truckmen cannot get up to do their ventilating job. Therefore, H & L No. 26 sometimes throws up its aerial ladder as the fastest way of getting men to the roof. It also puts the ladder up, ready for rescue.

Against all these special hazards the men in H & L No. 26 pit their speed in reaching the scene, and their skill in rescue work. The backbone of any aerial ladder's crew are, of course, the driver and tiller man. In New York, these two men not only drive the apparatus, but put it up. The "chauffeur," to use the department's title for driver, must be an "MPO"—that is, a graduate of the department's school for motor and pump operators. The tiller man can be anybody, and from time to time every man handles the tiller wheel. Some men, however, are better at it than others, and in actual practice, teams are found or developed which work well together. . . .

* * * * *

The truck carries, in addition to the big aerial ladder, two 35-foot truss ladders and five other truss ladders—of 30, 25, 20, 15, and 10 feet. In addition, it carries a 16-foot extension ladder and a 12-foot hook ladder, which can be hooked over a window sill. It also carries four Pompeiian scaling ladders. These consist of a long, saw-toothed hook attached to a slender strip of wood into which thin crosspieces have been fitted for footholds. Although fascinating to look at, these ladders are, in the opinion of members of H & L No. 26, wholly impracticable.

To replace damaged and sprung ladders, the New York Fire Department maintains its own ladder-building shops in Long Island City. Since the damage rate is high, the shops have built most of the ladders on New York trucks.

Merely learning how to match wood properly for ladder construction takes time and practice. "A man comes in here a union carpenter," according to Michael Horan, head of the ladder shops for more than thirty years, "but it takes two years before he's ready to build a ladder." No nails, screws or glue are used in the ladders, the rungs being tightly fitted by hand.

All the ladders are expected to have a certain amount of spring in them, especially the big aerial ladders. Before leaving the shops, each aerial ladder is tested for its "deflection," or bending qualities, by being fully extended at a 45-degree angle with a 200-pound weight on the tip. An 85-foot ladder is expected to bend as much as 25 inches under these conditions.

H & L No. 26 carries, in addition to the scaling ladders, one other item which the men classify as useless. This is a gun which can fire a heavy cord over a building preliminary to setting up a breeches buoy; it has never been used and is considered something of a joke. The truck also carries an assortment of hose couplings, chemical extinguishers, floodlights, axes and hooks, which get considerable use in knocking down tenement walls and ceilings concealing fire. The most useful tool on the truck is a new one designed several years ago by Deputy Chief Hugh Halligan, called the "Halligan tool." About 30 inches long, it is an ugly bar of forged steel with crowbar teeth at one end and a three-sided combination hook, axe and sledge at the other end. It is used to rip open skylights, bulkhead doors, punch holes in the roof, knock down cornices, pry open doors and flooring.

"The thing we all like about it," says Mike Sisty, "is that it weighs only eight pounds, can be used in a tight place, and can do anything."

To roll this 25,000 pounds of equipment to a fire safely requires smooth driving from both chauffeur and tiller man. The tiller man drives in a co-ordinated movement with the chauffeur, but he steers in the opposite direction from that taken by the chauffeur. This carries the tail end in a wide arc away from the corner or parked car they are rounding—and then the tiller man "recovers," i.e., straightens out his wheels so that the whole rig is lined up. Artie Bartunek, one of the most experienced tiller men in the city, says, "The chauffeur carries the tiller man. If the driver's good, the tiller man has no problems; if he's no good, it doesn't matter how good the tiller man is. A good driver cuts wide enough to make the turns easy for the tiller man and then he travels slow enough to give him time to recover."

The H & L No. 26 driving teams believe all drivers should begin as tiller men so that they'll be conscious of his problems. "Basically," says Danny Ford, who is rated as an excellent driver, "the problem is that the driver knows where he is going, while the tiller man has to guess where he's going. If the driver's been a tiller man, he makes allowances to take care of the tiller man, and the tiller man learns his style of driving so that he knows how to anticipate things."

One of the firemen's oldest jokes concerns a tiller man who, having turned in the opposite direction all week, got into his own car on his day off and promptly smashed into the corner drugstore.

Accidents with these big trucks, whose extreme length offers a perfect target for a car shooting out of a side street, occur periodically. To protect themselves from side-street cars the truckmen hanging on the side of the truck do not stand on the running board proper, but on tool boxes as far back as they can get. This puts them up an extra foot, giving them better visibility, and puts them in a better position to jump—either atop the big ladder or outward into the street. Safety is always a primary consideration. "We can't do anything," says Captain O'Reilly, "if we don't get there."

* * * * *

Somewhat ironically, the greatest threat is being hit by another piece of apparatus going to the same fire. This is what firemen fear most because both trucks are certain to be traveling fast. Not long ago a police emergency truck hit a big aerial truck almost exactly in the middle and bent its iron frame into a U-shape; the big ladder bent, too—without springing its rungs.

The problem arises because certain fireboxes draw apparatus from several firehouses. Each has a definite route to follow with a minimum number of turns and it is timed down to the second. This means that the routes sometimes intersect. Since each is traveling at high speed, and neither can hear the other's bell because of the racket of their own, the chances of their knocking one another for a deathly loop are high. Therefore, everyone knows the other company's route on certain boxes and keeps a sharp lookout. If H & L No. 14 is expected to pull out into Madison Avenue just ahead of H & L No. 26 at 110th Street, everyone on H & L No. 26 holds his breath until the other company's truck has been sighted. Then everyone cries, "There's

Number Fourteen!" and rides easier. If the truck isn't sighted, the intersection is approached with extreme caution.

Not the least of the driver's headaches is positioning the truck at the fire. . . . The distance from the base of the burning building to the truck may determine whether you get someone down safely. If the fire is on the top floor, the calculations are simplified; you get in as close as you can. But when the fire and trapped people are on the third, fourth, or fifth floor, you have to get exactly the right distance out in the street. Consequently, the driver must make fast, accurate distance judgments. Most NYFD drivers figure on a 25-foot sidewalk, seven feet for a parked car, and get down to fine points by sighting off manhole covers, which they know to be in the middle of 30-foot streets.

8

Sucker's Paradise

In New York Reuben does not come to town.
He lives there. Remove the spats and monocle
and behold the apple-knocker.—O. O. McIntyre

The Country Merchant and the City Merchant [1]

The East Side from the earliest time was the cradle of mercantile life. The old Dutch founders of the city settled by locating their canal on Broad Street and anchoring their vessels in the East River, on whose banks their primitive wharves and storehouses were built. There is not a street between the Battery and the City Hall Park which is not redolent with the romance of the old merchants of the metropolis. They were a social power in the colonial days, a political power in the years that saw the struggle for independence, a progressive power in the building up of the young republic. To write their story would be to give the history of the rise and prosperity of the city. Yet their social, business, and domestic life in the earlier part of this century is a theme to tempt sorely the saunterer's pen.

I remember when a boy frequently visiting the store of Valentine & Bartholomew, on Front Street, in which one of my uncles was the youngest clerk. It was a dingy place. The front was filled with coffee and sugar in bags and barrels, and in the rear was a bare, bleak office,

[1] From *A Tour Around New York and My Summer Acre,* Being the Recreations of Mr. Felix Oldboy, by John Flavel Mines, pp. 187–189. Copyright, 1892, by Harper & Brothers. New York. 1893.

containing high desks with spindle legs, wooden stools and chairs, and neither carpet nor anything else approaching luxury. In winter a small fire of Liverpool coal made a dismal attempt to heat the atmosphere. As for the clerks, they were expected to work early and late. The junior clerk had to be on hand by seven o'clock to admit the porter, and help him and set things to rights. The modern clerk would think himself insulted if set to such tasks. Yet out of just such work our great merchants were moulded. In the case above quoted the junior clerk was president of a bank in Wall Street at thirty years of age.

It would not do, in those days, to judge of the prosperity of a firm by its surroundings. A story told me by Jehiel Post, many years ago, illustrates this aptly. His father and uncle were in business in William Street, and their office and store (in which they kept only samples) were as bare and comfortless as an empty barn. It happened that a country merchant had received a note of theirs in course of trade, and as he was in the city he thought it would do no harm to look them up and find how they stood. On entering the store he was astonished to find their stock apparently very low, and everything bearing the appearance of a lack of trade. Beginning to grow alarmed, he entered the back office, and was still more disheartened by its appearance of poverty. At last he mustered courage to remark that he held a note of the firm. "Very well," answered the senior Jehiel, "it will be paid when due." But this did not satisfy the countryman, and he ventured to inquire if the firm would not discount the note. "We don't do business that way," was the cold reply. "But, gentlemen," stammered the man, "I'll take off 10 per cent, for cash—yes," with a burst of terror, "I'll take off twenty." "Brother Jehiel, do you hear that?" whispered the other partner; "let's take him up." The bargain was made and the money paid down. "Now," said one of the brothers, "if you please, tell us the meaning of this strange transaction." The countryman made his confession, and the brothers roared. They were vastly more tickled by the joke than by the profit. Calling one of their clerks, they sent him around with the visitor to the bank where the note was to be paid, and there the latter was informed by the cashier that he would cash the check of the firm any day for $50,000.

A Kentucky Colonel in New York [2]

[A] . . . Kentucky Colonel who used to loom large—or at least tall —thereabouts was John C. C. Mayo, who, starting his career as a poor country school teacher, had amassed a fortune through sagacity in acquiring huge tracts of coal or lumber land. Colonel Mayo liked Bourbon. He also liked to gamble, and the "House of the Bronze Doors," or some other establishment of similar type conveniently near the hotel, found him a steady patron during his New York visits. Mayo had a habit of obtaining what money he wished from the hotel cashier on the strength of an I.O.U. One day he got deeply interested in play and the wheel, or the cards, or whatever it was at the moment, persisted in running the wrong way, so that he kept coming over and giving the hotel cashier notes of hand for five hundred dollars at a time, and running back with the cash. On one of his trips he could not gain immediate attention because another man was arguing with the man in the cage over a check he had just presented. The cashier did not know the other and was asking him questions. Mayo became impatient.

"The man's all right," he interposed. "Give him his money. Why, I'll O.K. his check myself." This he did, and the money was passed over.

The check came back. Mayo's account was charged with the money the cashier had paid for it. When he got his bill at the end of his stay, he started in right there to raise a rumpus. However, the cashier was able to produce the check he had honored and to show Mayo his own signature on the back of it.

Not all Waldorf spenders were as frank in later years about their lack of sophistication when they first came to New York as Mayo proved to be. One story he was fond of telling on himself. He had got his first glimpse of Manhattan shortly before the Waldorf was built, and when in certain portions of the South the best known and most popular of New York bonifaces was the late James H. Breslin, whose Gilsey House was long a favorite resort for people coming from below Mason and Dixon's Line. So that when the lank young Kentucky

[2] From *Peacocks on Parade,* A Narrative of a Unique Period in American Social History and Its Most Colorful Figures, by Albert Stevens Crockett, pp. 144–147. Copyright, 1931, by Sears Publishing Co., Inc. New York.

school teacher, pausing in his efforts to obtain options on mineral land, came to New York to look about and figure just whom he could interest and how, he knew just where he wished to stop.

"I arrived at the ferry wearing a wide-brimmed hat, and was immediately spotted by the cab drivers," was the way Mayo told the tale. "As I looked about uncertainly, I was asked where I wished to go.

" 'The Gilsey House,' I replied.

" 'Right here, sir,' said one of the drivers, motioning with his whip. 'Mr. Breslin himself sent me down for you.'

"This was an honor I had not anticipated. I knew that Mr. Breslin was the proprietor of the hotel, but I did not know how he had got wind of my coming. However, I climbed into the vehicle and in due time was landed at the hotel.

" 'Five dollars,' said the cabman. I was amazed, but as Mr. Breslin had personally sent him down to meet me, I paid it. Then I went in and registered.

" 'Do you want a room with bath?' asked the clerk. I fancied I detected a sort of sniff in his tone.

" 'Of course,' I replied. 'How much?'

" 'Seven dollars,' was the answer. This was spreading it on rather thick, but I reflected that, after all, Mr. Breslin had singled me out for special attention, and I had an idea that the seven dollars included meals.

"Well, I went in to breakfast the next morning and ate pretty much what I wanted from the bill of fare, without noticing that each dish was priced separately. The bill came to $2.75. In those days you could get a good breakfast almost anywhere I had known about for fifty cents. However, I gulped down my emotions, reflecting that Mr. Breslin, the proprietor, had especially sent to meet me, and it would be discourteous to question his prices. So I paid the bill.

"But," added Colonel Mayo, "I kept puzzling all day because Mr. Breslin, who had seemed to evince such a particular interest in my advent, had not made any effort, so far as I was aware, to seek my personal acquaintance. I was too proud to ask questions that might betray my ignorance. But late that afternoon, after a day spent down in the financial district, seeing people, and finding my wits working a little faster than their wont, I said to the room clerk, as casually as I could, 'Does Mr. Breslin happen to be about?'

" 'Why, no,' he replied, 'Mr. Breslin went down to the Jersey Coast last Saturday, and as the races are on at Long Branch, we hardly expect he'll get back before Sunday night at the earliest.' It was not until then that light really dawned upon me, and I began to realize that the first man I had met in New York, a cabman, had trimmed me."

And, thanks to Colonel Mayo's trustful disposition, the cabman was not the last.

The Talking Owl [3]

Two young fellows were "on a racket," or "painting the town red," as "going on a spree" is called—if the explanation be accepted as less slangy than the other phrases. Between them they had a dollar and ten cents. With the dollar they bought an owl from a street vendor, and then entered a beer saloon to spend the rest of their fortune.

"Swei beah!" called the one who carried the owl, as grandiloquently as if his reserve capital would suffice to purchase several hundred saloons.

"Only two?" said the owl. "Where am I?"

"You don't want beer, do you?" asked the new master.

"Of course I do," responded the owl emphatically.

"I'll give you some of mine, if you'll only keep still," pleaded the young scamp.

"All right," responded the owl, looking grave—if an owl ever looks otherwise.

It is unnecessary to say that the young fellow was a ventriloquist.

By a skillful twist of his arm he poked the owl's beak into the foaming glass, and all this comedietta was enacted for the benefit of a countryman, who evidently was "taking in the town," as people who come to Gotham have a way of doing.

"Say, mister," said the hayseed gatherer, "I'll give yer four shillin' for that bird."

"Four shillings!" exclaimed our friend, as if he were mortally of-

[3] From *Gotham and the Gothamites* (*New York and the New Yorkers*), by Heinrich Oscar von Karlstein [F. C. Valentine], translated by F. C. Valentine, pp. 150–152. London: Field & Tuer, The Leadenhall Press, E. C.; Simpkin, Marshall & Co.; Adams & Co. 1887.

The mention of owls recalls a naughty little story I heard in Gotham; it will bear repetition in a modified form. . . . The story was not told me exactly this way; but it will have to do as it is.—H.O.v.K.

fended. "Four shillings—fifty cents for a talking owl—I wouldn't sell him for four hundred dollars."

However, he agreed to part with his pet for fifty dollars, after much haggling.

"I say, my bucolic wanderer," he added as a parting injunction, "if the beast won't speak, just blow into his ear."

The countryman carried the owl home, and introduced it "with much pomp and circumstance" to the good wife, with minute instructions how to make the bird speak. Then he left home to look after some cows that his wife told him had strayed.

He had hardly left when the parson, who had slipt into a closet on his entrance, came out, and the farmer's wife and her friend at once proceeded to develop the owl's loquacity. The result was that the owl grasped the woman's lips with his claw and the parson's nose with his beak, and despite their screams refused to release either.

The farmer returned, and seeing the state of affairs, sang out in joy: "I'd have given a thousand dollars for the owl, had I known that he could find out in a minute what I've wanted to know these ten years."

Diamond Cut Diamond[4]

A noted race-course man, taking a drink at the bar of [Charley Johnston's famous sporting house], exhibited a diamond ring of great beauty and apparent value on his finger. An acquaintance present, who has a penchant for faro, had a great passion for diamonds. After drinking several times and much bantering, the owner consented to barter the ring for the sum of six hundred dollars. As the buyer left the room a suppressed tittering struck his ear. He concluded that the former owner had sold both the ring and the purchaser. He said nothing, but called the next day upon Hart, the jeweler, where he learned that the dia-

[4] From *Brooklyn's Guardians,* A Record of the Faithful and Heroic Men Who Preserve the Peace in the City of Homes, by William E. S. Fales, pp. 380–382. Copyright. 1897, by William E. S. Fales. Brooklyn.

[Detective John F.] Burns, from his long experience around the City Hall, is well acquainted with all the "sporting men" of Brooklyn and familiar with all their deeds and misdeeds. He tells one good story which concerns a group of men who "hang out" at Charley Johnston's famous sporting house.—W. E. S. F.

mond was paste and the ring worth about twenty-five dollars. He examined some real diamonds and found one closely resembling the paste in his own ring. He hired the diamond, pledged twelve hundred dollars, the price of it, and gave twenty dollars for its use for a few days.

He went to another jeweler, had the paste removed, and the real diamond set. His chums, knowing how he had been imposed upon, impatiently waited for his appearance the next night. To their astonishment they found him in high glee. He flourished his ring, boasted of his bargain and said if any gentleman present had any twelve-hundred-dollar ring to sell for six hundred dollars he knew of a purchaser. When he was told that the ring was paste, and that he had been cheated, he laughed at their folly. Bets were freely offered that the ring did not contain a real diamond. Two men bet a thousand dollars each. Two bet five hundred dollars. All were taken, umpires were chosen. The money and the ring were put into their hands. They went to the first-class jeweler who had loaned the stone and who applied all the tests. He said the stone was a diamond of the first water and was worth, without setting, twelve hundred dollars. The buyer put the three thousand dollars which he had won quietly into his pocket. He carried the diamond back and recalled his twelve hundred dollars, and with his paste ring on his finger went over to a New York sporting house. The man who sold the ring came in later, heard the news and departed. He wanted to get the ring back. He attempted to turn the whole thing into a joke. He sold the ring, he said, for fun. He never wore false jewels. He knew that it was a real diamond all the time. He could tell a real diamond anywhere by its peculiar light. He would not be so mean as to cheat an old friend. He knew his friend would let him have the ring again. But his friend was stubborn—said that the seller thought it was paste and intended to defraud him. At length, on the payment of eight hundred dollars, the ring was restored. All parties came to the conclusion, when the whole affair came out, that when diamond cuts diamond again, some one less sharp will be selected by the original seller.

The Ring Trick[5]

Besides downright thievery and robbery through schemes into which strangers are entrapped by sharp decoys, there are other means for swindling verdant visitors in New York, a few of which may be mentioned as examples. The "patent safe" and "pocket-book dropping" games were once very popular and successful, but charlatans have made rapid progress and their ingenuity is kept busy inventing new devices and planning different strategies with which the police and public are unfamiliar. Here is one:

A rustic, watching the lascivious dance in a Bowery beer garden or walking along Chatham Square, conscious only of the novelties displayed about him, looking into some show-window, perhaps, may be accosted by a clever faced gentleman as follows: "See here [holding up before the visitor's gaze a beautiful gold ring set with a large sparkling diamond] did you drop this?"

The rustic knows he did not, and answers: "No, sir; why?"

"Why, I found it right under your feet, and I felt sure that you had dropped it. It's a beautiful ring and I am certainly a lucky man to find such a treasure, it must be worth at least one hundred dollars. Why, see here, there is an inscription inside, 'H.L. to Carrie.' I'll bet a round sum that this is an engagement ring, and tomorrow every paper in the city will publish Carrie's reward for its return to her."

All this conversation is to get the visitor interested, and it rarely fails of the purpose. Still holding the ring before his victim's eyes, sharper continues: "This is singularly unfortunate; I would like very much to get the large reward which I know will be offered tomorrow for the ring and at the same time see the owner get it, but a business engagement in Buffalo compels me to leave New York tonight. I am sorry, but see no way out of the dilemma except to keep the ring, which my sense of honor almost forbids."

With this, sharper starts off, but turning suddenly, as if a happy thought had just been forged from his brain, he again accosts our rustic: "Say, I can't do this, my honor absolutely forbids, but we can

[5] From *Metropolitan Life Unveiled;* or the Mysteries and Miseries of America's Great Cities, Embracing New York, Washington City, San Francisco, Salt Lake City, and New Orleans, by J. W. Buel, pp. 145–147. Copyright, 1882, by Historical Publishing Co. St. Louis.

perhaps fix this between us so that both will be profited by my lucky find, and the owner will obtain the ring also. You will be in the city for a day or two yet? Yes; well, suppose you give me $10 and I'll leave the ring with you, and whatever reward may be offered, which I dare say will be $25 or more, shall be yours."

Our pastoral friend thinks he has struck a decidedly honest gentleman, and now fully convinced of the ring's value, thinking what a nice present it would make for Maria, or that he might realize at least $50 from it at a pawnbroker's, he gives sharper the $10 and the two part. On the following day he eagerly scans the "Lost" column of the morning papers, but sees no notice of any reward for a lost ring. So much the better, he thinks, for this gives his conscience a little ease; he then repairs to a pawnbroker, where the cruel fact is revealed that his ring is of German silver, plated with gold and set with a Brazilian pebble; the whole thing is not worth twenty-five cents, so he naturally gets mad and does not stop short of calling himself a fool.

Bunco-Steering and the Sawdust Game[6]

A local pastime that flourished unabated in these days [of the Eighties] and does still with altered externals is the gentle art of bunco-steering. Certain masters of this art used to practice with considerable success at the railway terminals and ferry houses of the City. Such a professor as "Grand Central Pete" took his title from his activities at that station. "Ike" Vail, a noted confidence man, frequented the steamboat and ferry landings. It was difficult to secure convictions against these gentry as their schemes were worked with a full knowledge of the cupidity of their victims and the latter were not prone to get into the newspapers and their stories thence transmitted to the folks to hum. The green goods game and the gold brick swindle which were worked with vast profits for years by numerous gangs were especially unsavory in their implications. . . .

The gentle art of swindling is not, however, a game entirely played out. A case in point was a recent newspaper story detailing a transaction in which a newly arrived Greek parted with a considerable

[6] From *Valentine's Manual of Old New York,* 1927. edited by Henry Collins Brown, pp. 85–92. Copyright, 1926, by Henry Collins Brown. New York: Valentine's Manual, Inc.

sum of money for the privilege of selling fruit in the Information Bureau of the Grand Central Terminal. Earlier concessions of a similar kind involved the bandstand in Central Park, Brooklyn Bridge terminals, and other allurements to unsophisticated capital.

But real estate was ever the most active commodity. The City Hall, Post Office, and Woolworth Building are daily sold to the credulous for trifling sums and the supply of suckers seems inexhaustible. Although these swindlers rarely suffered reprisals at the hands of their victims, there were occasional exceptions. And in the case of Tom Davis . . . , punishment was swift and terrible. Davis was a notorious practitioner of the sawdust game and had an "office" at Reade Street and West Broadway. Tom and his brother "The" had inveigled one Holland, a Texan, into the office for the ostensible purpose of selling him $10,000 worth of counterfeit banknotes for $500 of good money. Davis produced $10,000—the "stall" in genuine banknotes—which he placed in a handbag, and then asked for Holland's bag with the other money and remarked to Holland that as the premises were being watched by detectives, it was best to leave the bag in safekeeping for a while, at the same time attempting to pass it through a sliding panel to his brother "The" in an adjoining room. Mr. Holland, besides bringing the $500 to the place of appointment, also carried that conventional Texas utility, a "Colt .45," which, without more ado, he discharged—one bullet into the panel and another into the body of Tom Davis, thereby terminating the latter's interest in high finance for good and all.

Holland's trial before Judge Van Brunt was a curious mingling of frontier jurisprudence with that of local procedure.

His counsel were Gen. Roger A. Pryor, the distinguished ex-Confederate soldier and New York barrister, and the Hon. Tom Grady, also a member of the bar, and a valiant warrior in many a hard-fought election-day battle for Tammany Hall. The District Attorney was Col. Fellows, also a Confederate veteran. The courtroom thronged with the military elite of the South, intermingled with a large congregation of "sawdust workers," "short card men," and other variegated swindlers.

Mr. Holland, on the stand, acknowledged with the delightful naïveté of a hardy plainsman, that he was fully cognizant of the esoteric workings of his tryst with Mr. Davis. He had gone there on purpose to buy the legal tender. When his $500 had been passed over, he considered the deal consummated. His subsequent proceedings, he declared dramatically, were "in defense of my life and property." He exhibited his capacity in this direction by a demonstration in court of his speed "on the draw," to the admiration of the local spectators, who at that period regarded such an exercise a superfluous accomplishment for a New

"Watch him kick it"

Get onto the Dude

"Get onto me spread de eagle"

"The Terrors of America and Their Doings" (about 1890)

Buy Me a Balloon, Mother (1868)

"The Auctioneer in Public Streets" (Chatham Square, 1840-44)

When Brooks Brothers Was Downtown (Catharine Street, 1845)

"The Marriage of General Tom Thumb" (Grace Church, Feb. 10, 1863)

Rake's Progress in a Low Groggery (1868)

"Ye Jolly Brokers of Ye New York Stock Exchange" (about 1870)

"Taking in" P. Green of Arcadia, N.Y. (Chatham Square, 1875)

When Grand Street Was Main Street (Bowery and Grand, 1879)

Mixing Advertising with Politics (1880)

Perils of the Streets on the Way to the East Side Slaughter Houses (1851)

The *Police Gazette* Exposes Some Firehouse Frills and Furbelows

Dancing on "The Sidewalks of New York" (1897)

The Wide-Awake Bowery Boy in the Nickel Weekly (1907)

Yorker. He had left as a matter of precaution his scarfpin and watch and chain in the care of Mr. Hill, City Marshal of Abilene, his traveling companion, who with considerable self-control had abstained from participation in his friend's enterprise, and appeared in court as corroborating witness. Mr. Holland, with righteous indignation, disclaimed any intention of purchasing and circulating counterfeit money among his guileless friends and neighbors of the Texas ranches.

Mr. Holland offered as character witnesses such distinguished officers as General Macy of Houston, Col. Paddock, ex-Senator from Texas, and Col. Frost. The jury, evidently impressed by Mr. Holland's social background, and perhaps in reprobation of the deceit involved in substituting sawdust for counterfeit money, acquitted him after a discussion of only ten minutes. He shook hands with every one within reach, with the cordiality born of a warm Southern nature, and expressed his entire satisfaction with the bench, bar, and jury system of our effete Eastern civilization, and vanished, minus his $500 and that cherished Texas talisman, the "Colt .45."

Creep and Panel Houses [7]

"Creep" and "panel" cases were extremely difficult to handle, for the victims seldom dared to complain, thereby admitting that they had visited a disorderly house.

The robbery was simplicity itself. The man was taken to a house by the girl. If the "panel" stunt were being tried, he was induced to hang up his clothing on hooks attached to the panel of the door. Then, when his attention was diverted, or while he slept, the panel revolved noiselessly, the side which held the clothing disappearing into an adjoining room, where the girl's confederates went to work at their leisure. The victim's roll was removed and stripped. One or two bills were left to be wrapped around carefully cut sheets of paper. Then the "weeded" roll, just the same in size and exterior appearance as before, went back into the pockets and the panel revolved once again. The victim never would suspect that his clothing had been disturbed, and usually didn't discover his loss until hours afterward.

[7] From *Behind the Green Lights,* by Captain Cornelius W. Willemse, in Collaboration with George J. Lemmer and Jack Kofoed, pp. 71–72. Copyright, 1931, by C. W. Willemse. New York and London: Alfred A. Knopf.

There was a bigger element of risk—for the victim—in the "creeper" game. While the girl held the man's attention, the lower part of the door would come open without sound to a height just sufficient for a man or woman to slip through on hands and knees. The intruder would crawl forward on stockinged feet until he could rifle the man's pockets, retiring the way he had come. Outside, the roll was stripped and doctored, and replaced in the way in which it had been taken.

In the sporting Negro quarter, the creepers frequently were armed with razors. In one house which I investigated, the Negro matron herself was the creeper. Powerful in build, she would crawl into a room in bare feet with a razor between her teeth. She could do a neat job of carving, too.

All victims were tracked when they left a "creep and panel" place, a "trailer" watching to see what would happen when the theft was discovered. If the victim proved to be a "rapper"—a man who squealed to the police—the trailer gave warning in time for the girl and her confederates to disappear. If, as was most usually the case, the man made no complaint or he headed home unconscious of his loss, the trailer kept with him to find out just where he lived. Later, if the case were brought to the police, the victim was intimidated by threats of exposure before his wife or family, and usually was shaken down into the bargain. Blackmail was a lucrative side-line for the "creep and panel" houses.

A Gaming Hell Romance [8]

For some weeks past, one of the most fashionable Broadway gambling houses had been honored with the presence of a dashing young man, apparently not more than nineteen or twenty years of age. The gentleman gave his name as Dick Harley, and professed to hail from New

[8] From *The Secrets of the Great City:* A Work Descriptive of the Virtues and the Vices, the Mysteries, Miseries, and Crimes of New York City, by Edward Winslow Martin (James Dabney McCabe), pp. 382–385. Entered . . . 1868, by Jones Brothers & Co. Philadelphia, Pa.; Cincinnati, Ohio; Chicago, Ill.; St. Louis, Mo.; Boston, Mass.; Atlanta, Ga.: National Publishing Company.

One of the city journals recently published the following account of an affair, which occurred some time since, at one of the best-known gaming hells of Broadway. The parties referred to are members of one of the wealthiest and most fashionable families in the city.—E. W. M.

Orleans. As he displayed a well-filled pocketbook, he was welcomed, of course.

In play he was remarkably lucky, for a time, at least. This attracted additional attention, and not only made him an object of envy but of jealousy. Many of the most expert resorted to all the known arts of the game in order to pluck the youngster, but were themselves sold.

During all these visits, young Harley appeared to feel an especial interest in one of the visitors, who was known to hold a responsible position in a downtown banking house. This person was nearly always a loser, and his manner plainly told the fact that those losses greatly affected him. He was always uneasy, his eyes inflamed, and his hand trembling, while he would often start to his feet, and walk up and down the apartment, in a manner bordering on frenzy. It soon began to be whispered around that the man was utterly ruined—that there would soon be another bank defalcation sensation, and perhaps a suicide.

For some time, young Harley had made efforts to gain the exclusive attention of the bank officer, but had failed to do so. At length, however, he was successful, and the New Orleans buck and the ruined gamester sat down together.

Fortune now appeared to change. Harley had fifty thousand dollars in his possession, which he had won. But he began to lose now, and the bank officer was the winner. The game continued, and still Harley lost. He remained perfectly calm in the meantime, while the winner became even more excited than while he was unfortunate.

At length the fifty thousand dollars changed hands, and the banker asked: "Shall we continue the game, sir?"

"No," replied Harley.

"But you want a chance for revenge?"

"No, I will play no more with you. However, I would like to make one condition."

"What is it?"

"Step aside with me, and you shall know."

Harley and the winner stepped a little apart, when the former whispered: "Sir, your manner has spoken only too plainly that your losses were about to involve you in trouble. Those losses have but just commenced; but if you continue your play, they will soon be very great, and yourself and family will be crushed. You have won sufficient tonight to save your honor, have you not?"

"Thank God, yes," was the earnest reply.

"Then the condition I would make is this: leave this place and never enter it again."

"I'll do it," was the almost frantic response, and the banker turned to leave the room.

At the same time those around had no idea of losing such an opportunity as now presented itself. That fifty thousand dollars must again change hands. One of the men presently advanced, and, laying his hands upon the shoulder of Harley, said: "Look you, youngster, you are going a little too far. You have won from us largely."

"Aye, and lost again," was the calm reply.

"So have we; and you must not stand in the way of our making good that loss."

"How can I possibly do so?"

"By persuading the winner of your money to play no more."

"Have I not a right to do it?"

"No."

"Then I shall assume that right."

As Harley said this he caught the bank officer by the arm, and led him toward the door. But the little fellow was instantly seized, and hurled to the opposite side of the room, where he fell with considerable violence.

Instantly he sprang to his feet, while his eyes flashed fire. At the same time he drew a revolver, and exclaimed: "Stand from that door, or there will be blood shed here."

On occasions of this kind, revolver generally answers revolver. It was so on this occasion; and Harley received two shots, which sent him reeling upon the carpet. A crimson spot appeared near his temple, and he clutched his breast with his hands.

Of course, there were those present who did not like the idea of murder, and such sprang forward to the aid of the wounded lad. A black wig fell from his head, and then long golden locks were exposed to view. The vest was opened, and the bosom palpitating beneath the spotless linen was that of a woman.

The surprise of all was very great, and none more so than that of the young bank officer, when he discovered in Dick Harley no other than his own sister. She had learned of the gaming, and had followed him in order to save him from ruin. She had succeeded, for no person now attempted to molest her. The wound upon the head was but slight, although it stunned her for a few moments.

She left the house with her brother, and it is not likely that either of them will ever enter it again.

Matrimonial Brokers of the Sixties[9]

The [matrimonial brokers'] advertisements—we advertise everything in New York—are usually after the following fashion:

MARRIAGE—Young ladies and gentlemen desirous of being wisely and happily married will consult their interest by applying to the undersigned, who gives all his attention to this branch of business, and who has already been very successful in bringing together persons adapted to each other by similarity of taste, temperament, and sympathy. Terms reasonable. All communications strictly confidential.

HENRY HYMEN, No. —— Broadway

WEDDED HAPPINESS DESIRED—It is well known that nothing conduces so much to happiness in life as a proper marriage. To avoid all mistakes in selecting partners, persons of either sex, who contemplate matrimony, should call at once on

GEORGE JACOBS
Matrimonial Broker, No. —— Bleecker Street

N.B.—Mr. Jacobs has the best of opportunities and the amplest facilities for accommodating his patrons. He has had large experience, and can say without vanity that he has made matches for which hundreds of ladies and gentlemen are eternally grateful to him. They have acknowledged their gratitude in autograph letters, which will be shown to his patrons if desired.

MATRIMONIAL BROKERS—John Johnson & Co., No. —— Bowery, offer their services to ladies wishing agreeable and wealthy husbands, or to gentlemen desiring beautiful, rich, and accomplished wives. They arrange interviews or correspondence between parties, and leave nothing undone to insure a marriage that will result to the satisfaction of all. The success that has heretofore crowned their efforts induces them to believe they have a firm hold upon the public confidence. They respectfully solicit a continuance of patronage.

* * * * *

Matrimonial brokerage is merely match-making systematized. The brokers do for money what amateurs do for excitement and from a

[9] From *The Great Metropolis,* A Mirror of New York, A Complete History of Metropolitan Life and Society, with Sketches of Prominent Places, Persons and Things in the City as They Actually Exist, by Junius Henri Browne, pp. 588–594. Entered . . . 1868, by American Publishing Co. Hartford.

passion for managing. They have an uncertain trade, but yet more business than would be supposed. They don't expect much custom from home, or from cities generally; but look for it from the country people, to whom they send circulars soliciting patronage. The marriages arranged by brokers rarely turn out well; but that happens so frequently under all circumstances that it may be unjust to the profession to make them responsible for it. There have been instances of what are known as happy marriages brought about by these gents, whose mode of procedure is interesting.

Peter Pindar lives in Chenango or Cataraugus County, and comes to town. He has often read Jacobs's or Johnson & Co.'s circulars and advertisements, and they have put the notion of a wife into his head. He has a small farm; is thirty-five or thirty-six years of age, is in ordinarily comfortable circumstances; likes women; but is shy—afraid of them, indeed; and consequently, he has never gotten along with them. It has often occurred to Peter that it would be convenient to have a wife; but the trouble and difficulty, as he imagines, of procuring one, have always stood in his way. "If I could get some fellow to do the courting," Peter has said to himself, never recalling, because he has never read, the sad story of Paolo and Francesca—"I'd been a husband long ago. But this popping the question I'm not equal to. It requires a chap of more courage than I can muster."

He reads over the advertisements until he has them all by heart. They impress him deeply. The opportunity he has sought seems to be at hand. He goes to the broker's and announces the object of his visit. The broker is always distrustful of strangers, fearing they are not sincere. But after a few minutes' talk he sees that Peter is too unsophisticated to be guilty of a ruse. The broker soon puts his customer at ease; says he knows a number of elegant and accomplished ladies who will suit him exactly.

"Perhaps I don't know what an elegant and accomplished lady is," observes Peter, "but I'm afraid it is not exactly the sort I want. I'd like a kind o' nice, good wife, that wouldn't put on too much style, and look down on a fellow because he wasn't quite as good as her."

"Certainly; you need a good, domestic woman who loves her own fireside and is bound up in her children."

"Well, if I had it my way," hesitatingly remarks Pindar, "I'd rather she wouldn't have any children that wasn't mine."

"Precisely. I mean yours, my dear sir. I wish to say when she had made you the happy father of a beautiful offspring, that she would devote herself to the family; be an angel in her home; a presence of love and peace, filling it with sunshine, and all that sort of thing."

"Oh, yes, that is it," responds Pindar, caught by the cheap rhetoric of the broker; "that's what I want and will pay for."

"I have a lady in my mind, now—I saw her this morning—who will be all you desire. I shall charge you $10 for this interview. If we consummate the marriage, you will of course pay more. Our regular price is—"

"I'll do the handsome thing. I'll give $100 cash down."

"Come day after tomorrow, Mr. Pindar, and I'll tell you the result of my negotiation. Be here at eleven o'clock."

Soon as Pindar has gone, the broker takes a letter from a drawer and reads:

DEAR SIR—I should be willing to accept a husband who could come well recommended; who could provide for me handsomely; who had good habits; was well educated; and was of a domestic turn. I have some reputation for beauty and accomplishment; am young, although no longer a silly girl, and would, I think, be an ornament to a well-regulated household.

Sincerely,

BESSIE BAKER

The broker drops a line to Miss Baker, soliciting an interview. She comes, and is not what might be anticipated from her note. She is probably four or five-and-thirty; has a thin face, faded blue eyes, high cheekbones; is freckled, and anything but handsome or elegant. She talks rapidly and is intelligent, though not very delicate or sensitive. She has been a teacher and a seamstress; has had a hard struggle with life; and, seeing the broker's advertisement one day, was tempted to write him by way of experiment.

An interview is arranged for her and Pindar in the private office. They meet and are both disappointed.

"I would never have him," she thinks.

"I would not marry her for anything," he says to himself.

After half an hour's conversation, they find themselves mistaken. They rather like each other. He proves to be candid, upright, independent, good-hearted; she, amiable, affectionate, loyal, truthful. When they have been acquainted three days, they believe they can get along together. Pindar pays his $100 to the broker most willingly; takes Bessie Baker to Chenango as his wife; and they have lived comfortably, rearing pumpkins and babies ever since.

Not seldom, men who have mistresses they wish to get rid of apply to the matrimonial broker, and pay handsomely for the procurement of husbands. This branch of the business, it is claimed, requires unusual exertion and adroitness, and $500 is asked for the service. The man who is a candidate for marriage has no suspicion of the woman. She tells an ingenious story; proclaims herself a widow—the broker indorses all her stories—and, by her tact and shrewdness, completely deceives him. The marriage is consummated, and strange to say, is sometimes happy; the wife resolving upon, and adhering to, a change for the better, after being invested with the dignity and bearing the responsibility of wedlock.

The brokers are not men of very high principle. They are willing to make money in almost any way. When they have an application for a wife, they are certain to supply the demand. They usually enjoy the acquaintance of a number of adventuresses—women of doubtful reputation and uncertain character. The broker makes an appointment for them; and, as they have city manners, style in dress, and much self-assertion, they are likely to make an impression upon some honest countryman's heart. He marries one of them, perhaps; or, if he does not, he forms a relation that he afterwards regrets. He is threatened with exposure and punishment, and is compelled to compromise by liberal payments. Sometimes he is surprised by a fictitious husband, who demands blood, but is finally persuaded to take money instead. The broker makes sure of his commission, and, after that, he does not concern himself about the future or the status of the couple he has introduced to each other.

The unions made by the brokers are, as I have said, unfortunate for the most part. The parties enter into them without understanding each other's character or antecedents. They quarrel and go apart, denouncing the means used to bring them together. In a number of divorce cases in the courts, it has been shown that the couple seeking separation became acquainted through the matrimonial brokers.

The broker is always a pretender and a trickster; tells more falsehoods than is needful for his trade; describes fine women he never saw; boasts of his correspondence with the members of the best society; contradicts and condemns himself—or would in dealing with a man of the world—fifty times an hour. He is perpetually tempted to become a maker of assignations; to dupe honest rustics; to palm off demireps and wantons for ladies; to swindle all who trust him; and, I am sorry to say, he almost invariably yields to the temptation without a struggle.

A Corner in Rusty Knives: How George Stivers Invented Pitch [10]

It was in 1869 or thereabouts, according to the meager traditions of the pitchman tribe, that George Stivers, a newsboy, hesitated for a moment in a hardware store at Wall and Nassau Streets, New York, where he had gone as usual that day to deliver a paper to Joseph Prince, the owner of the store, a regular customer. The original thing which caused the pause was a large showcase full of knives—and the failing in the heart of a boy to window-wish in front of every display of cutlery. But as Stivers looked, a new element entered—the fact that a great many of the knives were rusty. Following which he learned that while knives with bright shining blades could be retailed for a dollar or more apiece, those which were specked with rust merely remained in the showcase unwanted. It gave the boy an idea. He asked for a price on rusty knives in wholesale lots, and received it—a dollar a dozen. Then he purchased twelve, hurried to the nearest cigar stand, begged a cigar box, marked "Twenty-five cents apiece" on the lid, and started out.

In all this George Stivers didn't know that he was dealing with a fundamental selling principle as regards men. Whether the principle stands good with stores in general I do not know. But as regards the pitchman, the theory has held water and procured dollars for more than a half century now—the fact that the boy spirit never dies in a man, that the things he likes in boyhood he will like in manhood, and that if dangled before him, like the proverbial worm before the proverbial fish, he is sure to take the bait. One of the most important of these things is a knife; and upon various forms of cutlery have thousands of pitchmen made a living ever since the days of the Reconstruction.

However, all that George Stivers knew was the fact that he, a boy, liked knives and that other persons should like them also, especially if they could be purchased at a bargain price which incidentally would give him a profit of 200 per cent. He was right. Before he had

[10] From "High Pitch—Low Pitch," by Courtney Ryley Cooper, *The Saturday Evening Post,* Vol. 195 (August 5, 1922), No. 6, pp. 8, 58. Copyright, 1922, by the Curtis Publishing Company. Philadelphia.

gone a block the entire stock was gone, and Stivers was bulbous-eyed with a big idea. If he could sell one dozen rusty knives in a block, how many could he sell in an all-day session?

The matter had progressed to one of high finance now, with a necessity for more dollars than the newsboy possessed. So he hurried to a friend, known as Dutchy Lehman, for the necessary financial backing, and told him of his newfound pocketknife gold mine. Lehman listened, and Lehman gave his assistance. The result was that within a few hours Stivers had purchased the entire stock of rusty pocketknives which the hardware store possessed, and then cornered every other discolored whittler that he could find in that section of New York. After which he took his stand at the corner of Ann and Nassau Streets and made the first authentic pitch in the annals of street fakery.

There was something new about it, something different. Here was a boy, lecturing on the good qualities of an oil-tempered, bone-handled, four-bladed knife, with a sample sharpened to a razor thinness, and the slivers flying in all directions as he whittled a piece of soft pine to demonstrate the cutting ability of an edge which could be purchased for twenty-five cents. The crowd gathered, the crowd watched him whittle; then the crowd bought. Nor was it long before George Stivers scoured the city of New York in vain. The stocks of rusty nonreturnable bargain knives were gone.

Then another element entered—again with fortune on the side of the first pitchman. This time it was another thing to appeal to the boy in man—lead pencils.

A big pencil factory had burned, with practically every pencil in stock damaged by scorching, blistering or by water. The firm of Stivers and Lehman hurried to the place and purchased the salvage for almost nothing. Then Stivers went a step higher in his operations. He bought a pushcart, loaded it with pencils, sharpened a dozen or two of them for demonstration purposes, and began to extol their virtues. Any one at all who desired to test the writing qualities of the offerings could step right up and scribble to his heart's desire on pads furnished for the purpose, and then buy half a dozen pencils for the price that one would cost in a stationery store. There never was a small boy without a stub of a lead pencil in one of his pockets. There never was a man who didn't feel lost without a pencil or a fountain pen. Stivers had bumped headlong into another masculine failing, and a few days later the entire stock of pencils was gone, while the combination of

Stivers and Lehman split a gross profit of more than six thousand dollars.

By this time Stivers had learned the psychology of the spiel and of the personal recommendation and demonstration in selling. . . .

"Everybody Likes to Be Humbugged"[11]

The street vender has a good knowledge of human nature, and very often he does not hold his fellowmen in high esteem. Some people think he relies upon the stranger for the most of his patronage, but if you talk with one of them, after getting into his confidence, he will very likely tell you such is not the case.

"The city's full of muffs," said one of these fellows recently when I "interviewed" him. "Talk about the hayseeds from the country!" he continued; "the city jay is the readiest of 'em all to be gulled. There's men standin' round on every corner, or passin' along by here every minute, just waitin' for somebody like me to come along and sell 'em anything. Nobody need starve in New York if he's got any grit about him, I can tell you that. Let me tell you what I did.

"One day last week I went in to play policy just for the fun of the thing, you know, and when I come out of the place, kind of dazed like, I had just twenty cents left; everything else was gone, and I wondered for a minute what on earth I'd do. It didn't take me more'n a minute, though, to make up my mind.

"I went into the fust grocery I come across and bought two cakes of common laundry soap and three cents' worth of blue tissue paper. I borrowed a knife and cut up my soap into thin slices, and wrapped each slice up nice and tidy-like, as though it had been done in a

[11] By Thomas W. Knox. From *Darkness and Daylight; or, Lights and Shadows of New York Life,* A Woman's Story of Gospel, Temperance, Mission, and Rescue Work, "In His Name," with Hundreds of Thrilling Anecdotes, and Incidents, Personal Experiences, Sketches of Life and Character, Humorous Stories, Touching Home Scenes, and Tales of Tender Pathos, Drawn from the Bright and Shady Sides of City Life, by Mrs. Helen Campbell, with an Introduction by Rev. Lyman Abbott, supplemented by a Journalist's Description of Little-Known Phases of New York Life; and a Famous Detective's Thirty Years' Experiences and Observations, by Col. Thomas W. Knox and Inspector Thomas Byrnes, Part II, by Thomas W. Knox, pp. 626–627. Entered . . . 1891, by A. D. Worthington and Company. Hartford, Conn. 1892.

big shop. Then I went down on the Bowery jest as men were comin' out for their hour at noon, and grabbed hold of the fust one I see with grease on his coat-collar, and I didn't have to wait long to find him, you bet. I told him I'd clean his coat up nice for nothin' if he'd only give me five minutes. Well, sir, before the five minutes was up I had a big crowd around me, and I did his coat up so's you couldn't see a bit of grease on it; 'twas jest as clean as though it had come spick and span new from the tailor's. Perhaps you don't know, but you can wet a grease-spot and it won't show for two hours or so; only if you give it time to dry it'll be out again about as plain as ever.

"When I got the feller's coat fixed all right I turned to the crowd, and says, says I—

" 'Here yer are, gents, yer see what the great chain-lightnin', double-refined, centennial, night-bloomin' serious soap will do. Invented by a Frenchman who spent twenty years findin' out what it ought to be made of, and spoiled thirteen thousand coats before he hit it exactly right. A British syndicate's been after the secret and offered him ten thousand pounds cash down and no back talk for the rights for New York City, but he refused it, and him and me's in partnership for two years, and nobody else hasn't any right to sell it.

" 'Here yer are, the great patent grease-eradicator, make a coat or carpet as good as new, and all in five minutes with a twist of your wrist that anybody 'as only to try and find out he can do it. Only twenty-five cents a cake, gents, and will save you five dollars in havin' your clothes cleaned and made good as new, no matter if they's a dozen years old.'

"Well, sir, I kept right on talkin' in that style, sayin' anything that come into my head and jest beatin' the angels for lyin'. In less than half an hour I'd sold out my whole stock and made eight dollars and a half, and back I went to the grocery and got more soap, and was sellin' it like hot cakes when a cop took me up fur sellin' without a license. I let him start off with me, and a big crowd a-follerin', and then I hauled my license on him and he let me go. I've worked the soap racket pretty well out jest now, and I am goin' into the cheap pocketbook and pencil line. The pocketbooks look fust-rate and they sells well, and d'yer know why?"

I acknowledged my ignorance and asked to be enlightened.

"They look well and they're cheap, and that's what catches the gulls," said the vender. "I tell you everybody likes to be humbugged, though there ain't many as'll acknowledge it."

Beggar Dodges

I [12]

Beggars noted among their fellows for sobriety often hold up belated revelers to request the price of a drink. It was such a beggar who approached a typical Kentucky colonel with these words: "Boss, for Heaven's sake, gimme a dime to buy some whisky! S' help me, I haven't had a drink today!" The Southerner threw up both hands. "Bless my heart, all day without a drink? The misery and suffering in this great city is awful to contemplate!" And the wily mendicant departed a quarter richer.

Beggars often find that an air of *bonhommie* and familiar jocularity meets with better returns than the pitiful tale and the woebegone countenance. A case in point was that of a jolly old beggar who once held me up on West Forty-second Street with the statement that he was a worthless old drunkard, but that I looked like a sport, and he felt sure I would "stake" him. When I took him to task for his abrupt and cheeky request, his reply showed him to be a believer in the maxim, "Laugh, and the world laughs with you." "Cap," he replied in a confidential and alcoholic whisper, "Cap, de great American public won't stand for hard-luck stories any more!"

Near Union Square, year in and year out, an old man, familiar to frequenters of Fourteenth Street, stands beside a glass case which rests upon a wooden frame, inside which he has the model of a full-rigged ship. A lettered sign says that the whole affair—the ship, the seething cambric waves, the fort in the background—is all "the work of a poor old sailor." A wooden box with a slot receives the pennies of his admirers. This man owns a fine block of houses in Harlem as a result of his careful business methods.

* * * * *

A stout, able-bodied Frenchman, who haunts the west side of the city, is chiefly noted for the fact that he carries reversible signs. On one side is the legend "I am deaf and dumb," and on the other "I am

[12] From *The New Metropolis,* 1600–1900, Memorable Events of Three Centuries, from the Island of Mana-hat-ta to Greater New York at the Close of the Nineteenth Century, edited by E. Idell Zeisloft, pp. 199–201. Copyright, 1899, by D. Appleton and Company. New York.

paralyzed." He is a hard drinker, and upon several occasions has been found lying insensible from alcohol, with the "I am paralyzed" side of the sign uppermost on his breast.

[One of the best-known beggars] is the old Frenchman who with his camp-stool and little organ which he holds on his knees is a steady occupant of the sidewalk in front of the Broadway Tabernacle. A humorous story is told of his son, who applied for a position, and upon being asked his father's business, replied, "Oh, he is the organist of the Broadway Tabernacle."

II[13]

The beggars' cant has names for all types of practitioners. There are the "nibblers," who gaze wistfully into a restaurant or bakeshop while they gnaw at a prop bread crust. They never speak to prospects and depend simply upon their attitude to appeal to passers-by. In the same category are the "divers," who dip hungrily into ashcans when they see a prospect approaching. The "flickers" are beggars who throw fits or pretend to have fainted from hunger. One of these once told a detective that he had pretended to have fits thirty-five times in one month and usually collected enough after each act to pay for a day's food and lodging. It was easy, he said, except when the public insisted that he lie on the sidewalk until an ambulance surgeon arrived. When that happened he had to go through the routine of being taken to a hospital and being dismissed after an examination. "Pillinger" (the etymology is obscure) is the name for beggars who operate in front of big shops and public buildings, and "P.D.'s" are punch-drunk prize-fighters who beg at the doors of places like Madison Square Garden. The Jamaica Kid, a Negro pugilist, who was a pretty good boxer some years ago, belongs in this class. Fight promoters occasionally put "P.D.'s" on small allowances to stay away from their clubs. They sometimes make ambitious young fighters think too much.

Once in a while a beggar hits on a new dodge and does pretty well at it. One posed as a leper. He would emerge from a shadowy areaway on a side street late at night and walk toward a prospect with arms raised above his head to show that he wasn't carrying a weapon. In a hollow voice he would warn the passer-by not to come close because he was a leper, and then entreat him to drop money on the sidewalk.

[13] From *The Eight Million,* Journal of a New York Correspondent, by Meyer Berger, pp. 308–311. Copyright, 1942, by Meyer Berger. New York: Simon and Schuster.

This was frequently good for a quarter, and sometimes for as much as a dollar. The man who worked this game kept shifting his ground and the cops never caught up with him. They were sure he was a fraud, however, and classified him as what beggars call a "weeper"—a panhandler with a hard-luck story.

In a class by themselves are the "dingoes," who really are small-time confidence men rather than beggars. They take pride in their work and like to get together to brag about the sly ones they have put over. One dingo got a dollar and one of the President's best cigars by "putting the arm" on Mrs. Roosevelt at the entrance of her own town house. Another is a well-dressed, dignified man who carries an empty violin case and shows prospects a few coins. His story is that he has been out of work, but that at last he has a job to play in a concert if he can get to Newark within an hour. All he needs, he says, is a few more pennies to make up the carfare.

One type of beggar keeps strictly within the limits of Jewish communities in the city. He is the *schnorrer,* a bearded mendicant, who begs at the doors of the synagogues, at the gates of Jewish cemeteries, and wherever a Jewish wedding is being held. On the East Side a good many storekeepers leave outside the door a handful of pennies in a small container, the *pushke,* from which the *schnorrer* takes his mite—a single cent. This type of beggar has tradition behind him; he survives chiefly because of the ancient Oriental belief that the giver is blessed for his generosity and by it stores up heavenly credit. Shopkeepers know the beggars operating in their neighborhoods and are rarely imposed upon by outsiders. The newer generation of Jews tends to ignore the *schnorrer,* but up to five years or so ago his take was fairly high. One bank in Grand Street even used to have a separate counter for *schnorrers* where they could make up their coppers, nickels, and dimes in rolls for deposit without delaying the lines at the regular tellers' windows. There were a great many women *schnorrers* among the Jews in the old days. Some of them would hire a neighbor's child and take it with them to increase their appeal, particularly in the shopping and market districts. The usual rental for a baby was twenty-five cents a day. Another trick was showing a landlord's dispossess notice, generally faked, to entice larger contributions.

A detective who has had a lot of experience on the Mendicant Squad says that slightly more than half the beggars who appear blind or crippled are frauds. He knew of one "blinkie" who tapped his way around Times Square for years, doing pretty well at begging until he took to supplementing his income by picking pockets at night.

When he was caught at it in a bar at Seventh Avenue near Forty-seventh Street, he explained that, being blind, he thought his fingers were in his own pocket. He wasn't blind and he got six months. Another blinkie simulated blindness by pasting his eyelids down with collodion before he left his flat each morning. He carried with him a small vial of alcohol and a cotton swab, with which he removed the collodion at the end of the working day. In the halfway phony class are "sitters," one-legged men who beg at fixed posts and leave their wooden legs at home when they are on the job because an empty trouser leg has more appeal.

Beckie the Malingerer [14]

. . . Probably every hospital has its oddities, but among those at Gouverneur Hospital in my day, Beckie easily led the list. She was a character that Balzac might easily have written about. Beckie was our prima donna of malingerers, and don't think that I am telling you about any ordinary performer. No, indeed! She had a method and technique so unique and productive of results that she fascinated us all. I knew nothing about Beckie's background, whether she had a home, family, or any friends. I presume she was a vagrant and because of her amazing ability to simulate almost any known disease and get away with it, she had achieved a very interesting life. When the outside world got too cruel she knew how to enter a hospital and secure the best skill and attention, food, and shelter.

Beckie was not too hard to look upon, fairly young, a squat little Jewish woman with an appealing expression and eyes which under duress of suffering could be so eloquent as to tear your heartstrings. She had an uncanny way of knowing when a young green doctor would be on the ambulance and in this way she got back many times into the hospital before she was recognized. The ailment she would fake depended on how long she wanted board and lodging. If a long period of time was needed to study obscure symptoms and differential diagnosis, this meant of course a bed, security, and food meantime.

[14] From *Bowery to Bellevue,* The Story of New York's First Woman Ambulance Surgeon, by Emily Dunning Barringer, M.D., pp. 163–167. Copyright, 1950, by W. W. Norton & Co., Inc. New York.

Beckie believed in the dramatic and when she had decided that the time had come for another hospital sojourn, she would invariably pick out a street corner where there was plenty of room for a sympathetic crowd to gather, and gather they always did. She would have to decide what ailment to fake. If it was something demanding surgery, there would be a post-operative stage where she would have more intensive nursing and sometimes her ego demanded this. When the decision was made, Beckie would become alarmingly ill on the street corner she had selected for her take-off. In fact, she would appear so ill that everyone would think she was dying and the policeman on the beat would become so impressed with the advice from the crowd, that he would send in a hurry call. Beckie did not want an ordinary call, it was much too slow and uninteresting. When her time came, she wanted to go to the hospital at top speed, bells clanging to give her the right of way. In this way almost every preceding member of the staff had brought Beckie to the hospital and for a long list of apparently sick-unto-death illnesses. On one occasion I was told she had produced indications of acute appendicitis so convincing that an immediate operation was performed, and rumor hath it that it was none other than John F. Erdmann himself who removed a perfectly normal appendix. This, however, was before my time.

It must be remembered that methods of diagnosis were more primitive then, and lacking all the tests of later days, greater reliance had to be put on the patient's own testimony. Was it surprising then that, in spite of the reputation of this malingerer, I, a green young doctor, should not have spotted Beckie when it was my turn to be called? I found the usual crowd, surrounding a pathetic little woman writhing apparently in death agonies. She seemed to have a great tumor mass in her stomach region suggesting an intestinal obstruction. In all the excitement of the street scene, with the solicitous bystanders offering advice from all sides, I didn't even think of considering that her symptoms might be feigned, through some power to control muscles in an unusual way, and that her pain might be simulated. From a medicolegal standpoint these problems are often difficult to decide. I had no time to even think of their existence. Instead the patient got at once my best care and was rushed to the hospital at top speed, put to bed immediately and with all the nurses on the service rushing with restoratives and sedatives for her pain. Immediately I reported this patient to my superior officer, and when he arrived he at once recognized Beckie, much to his glee and discomfiture. However, Beckie was equal to the occasion and now that she was in the hospital with a good bed, food, and shelter, she did not intend to convalesce too rapidly. There is always a chance that one of these malingerers may sometime really have something seriously wrong, and it is therefore necessary to give them the benefit of the doubt and watch them carefully. So Beckie took her time and several days elapsed before she allowed her phantom tumor to disappear. During this time she got the best of care and consideration from us all. When she finally was ready for discharge, I believed she could stand some straight talk and I said to her: "Beckie, you know you are a wonderful fake. This hospital is here to take care of really sick people, and it is not fair for you to come as you do and hold a bed, get free board and lodging and all kinds of medical care. Beckie, perhaps you do not know it, but when I am on the ambulance, I am a Sergeant of Police and I can arrest people. Now, if ever you throw a fit on a street corner again and I am on the bus, I'll arrest you and take you to the station house, not to the hospital. Do you understand what I am saying, Beckie?" Her eyes gave me a wary glance to see if I were just "talking big," but sharply I repeated, "Beckie, do you understand what I am saying?" This time her eyes focused full on mine with complete understanding. Yes, I was sure Beckie and I thoroughly understood one another.

Several months must have elapsed, and I had forgotten about Beckie, when one day an urgent hurry call came in. We were off in the bus in record time, little Rags running ahead to be present at the big moment of our arrival. As we neared the scene I could see an unusually large crowd ahead, massed around a street corner. Suddenly, I thought of Beckie. Certainly the crowd was worthy of her best efforts and instinctively I felt she must be the center of this dramatic scene.

As we neared the scene of action the crowd parted to make room for the ambulance, and leaning far out on the arm strap I made a quick survey of the situation before the bus had come to a stop. In those few seconds I caught the furtive eyes of Beckie and she knew perfectly well who I was. Before I could reach her she gave one mighty jump, and with the agility of a gazelle, began running in the opposite direction. So decisive was her action that the gaping crowd did not try to stop her, but meekly opened a path, bewildered as to what it was all about. As she fled she picked up speed and I doubt if any of the bluecoats on the police force could have caught her. She may be running still for all I know, for I never saw or heard of Beckie again while I was at Gouverneur Hospital.

The Tiffany Man and the Blonde [15]

. . . A Tiffany man was victimized by one of the oldest swindles in the confidence man's book. An attractive blonde entered the store and with the bored nonchalance of the rich, said her fiancé had asked her to select some rings. She chose two, a solitaire and a diamond wedding band, valued at $6,300, then told the clerk she would like her mother's approval before buying. She demurely asked the clerk to deliver the rings at her Riverside Drive apartment.

When the clerk arrived, she took the kid-covered box and walked through a door, calling, "Mother, the Tiffany man is here with the rings." When she failed to reappear after fifteen minutes, the clerk became alarmed. He knocked on the door, got no answer and turned the knob. The door was another exit into the hall. Tiffany's never saw the blonde or the rings again.

The Locker Trick [16]

Joseph and I left the subway at Grand Central and walked through the station toward Madison Avenue. As we passed a bank of self-service bag-checking lockers, he said to me, "There's another way to make a buck—those lockers. You hang around the lockers here or in Pennsylvania Station and wait until you see somebody—it's better if it's an old dame—who's just put her suitcase in a locker and is having trouble figuring out how the thing works. You walk up and say to her, 'Having trouble? Maybe I can get the key out for you.' You have a key in the palm of your hand that you just got by putting ten cents in the slot and locking the door on an empty locker, see? You start turning the old dame's key in the lock, and just as you get it unlocked you drop the

[15] From *The Great Merchants,* The Stories of Twenty Famous Retail Operations and the People Who Made Them Great, by Tom Mahoney, pp. 58–59. Copyright, 1947, 1950, 1951, 1952, 1955, by John Thomas Mahoney; 1949, by the Curtis Publishing Company. New York: Harper & Brothers.

[16] As told to Croswell Bowen by "Joseph Marin." From *They Went Wrong,* by Croswell Bowen, pp. 196–197. Copyright, 1954, by Croswell Bowen. London, Toronto and New York: McGraw-Hill Book Company, Inc.

key to the empty locker on the floor. Then you pick it up and hand it to the old dame.

"You start talking fast then and ask her is she from out of town, does she expect to stay long, what does she expect to see while she's here. If she happens to look at the key and notices it's not the same number as the locker she got her suitcase in, then you quickly put your hand in your pocket and take out her key and say, 'Maybe I picked up your key by mistake.' You give her back her key, and there's no beef. Generally, she goes off with the wrong key. You wait awhile and get the suitcase. The clothes you pawn, but mainly you hope to find money or a camera or jewels or something."

Clip Joints [17]

The worst creature, of all the army of parasites who carried on their trade along Broadway during the speakeasy period, was the proprietor of the "clip joint." Ever since the beginnings of Manhattan Island there have been resorts where it was not safe for a man to go unless he sought to be beaten up, drugged, or robbed, or all three. There are not a great many of these places, but the few which have been discovered are enough. The clip joint preys on the New Yorker and the out-of-town sport alike.

A crooked taxicab driver usually makes a suggestion to a likely-looking passenger that he can take him to a place where he can "have a good time." Many men who ought to know better, indeed, men who regard themselves as wise guys, able to take care of themselves in any emergency, have accepted such an invitation. Inside the place, they drink themselves into a stupor, usually talking to some of the girls who are a part of the staff of the place, and then, finally, the time comes to pay the bill.

Well, suppose the bill, outrageously high, comes to more than the customer thinks he owes. Of what use is argument, with at least four rough-looking customers leering on? Very well. He will pay. But he hasn't enough cash. The proprietor agrees to take a check. He examines the signature, pronounces it indistinct, pretends to tear up the check,

[17] From *The Night Club Era,* by Stanley Walker, pp. 218–220, 223. Copyright, 1933, by Stanley Walker. New York: Frederick A. Stokes Company.

and asks the customer to try again. In this fashion the clip joint proprietor may get several checks. In addition, he may say, "Never mind the checks. I'll tear 'em up. We know you're all right. Just give us an IOU and we can collect any time."

The next day, if the victim checks with his bank, he will find that he has been rooked. Moreover, a horribly hard-looking customer will likely as not call at his office to get cash for the IOU. Then comes remorse, anger and terror. Usually they pay, but not always. The sensible ones call the police, who, be it said to their credit, are death on "clip joints" when they have a definite complaint.

Achille Mirner, a jeweler, was beaten to death in a "clip joint" when he protested that he was being robbed. His murderers were sent to prison. Many of the joints have been raided and wrecked. Often it is difficult to convict the operators of these abattoirs, for the victim, even when he can identify the place and the people who robbed him, often fears that his family will hear about it, or, even worse, that he will appear silly before his friends. Recently a wealthy man from the South, stopping at the Waldorf-Astoria, was gypped of almost $2,000 one night, and a grim visitor the next morning was asking for another $1,000 on an IOU. He got in touch with a friend, who told him to tell the collector to go to hell, and that the police would be there soon. The Confederate visitor didn't have enough nerve to go through with it. He told the collector to come back in an hour. Then, in an utter panic, he checked out and took the next train out of New York.

Raiding a clip joint is one of the most exhilarating experiences which can befall any one. The police, even those who are not sadists at heart, throw all abandon aside when they are on such an errand. To the privileged witness the wrecking of the joint is as pleasantly exciting as having a ringside seat at one of the decisive battles of history. . . .

* * * * *

[On one such occasion] the bar was pulled up by its roots and broken. Every table and chair was splintered. Even the bottles and the glasses were smashed. There were horrendous sounds as the big mirrors crashed. Draperies and chandeliers were pulled down with a deafening clatter. Within half an hour the clip joint looked like one of those old pictures of devastated Belgium. . . .

Wilson Mizner on Suckers [18]

Early in 1905 Wilson Mizner arrived in New York and made his first contact with Broadway. It was less of a meeting than a head-on collision, for Broadway was just what this veteran of the wilds required—and a new and most amusing giant of the Arctic brotherhood got attention with his first burst of laughter.

All his natural contacts, through his California antecedents, would direct his steps to Fifth Avenue, but his Klondike and Nevada credentials led him straight to theatrical, newspaper, and gambling welcomers. And he had not reached the end of his first week of this fortuitous invasion of the Big Town when Broadway began to look up and pay homage to a genuinely absorbing personality.

* * * * *

Never disturbed about either his reputation or associations, the utter frankness of Mizner regarding matters usually cloaked in Victorian obscurity early distinguished him. Always regarding himself as a drifter and ne'er-do-well, Mizner had the sympathy and patience which attracted all sorts of unconventional people, and from such contacts came some of his keenest and most applauded mots.

He not only gave financial help but his good company to some of the strangest people to be met anywhere. At the height of his theatrical earnings in New York, he took over the Strand Hotel and invited fifty characters who depended on him for "flop money" to make their homes there.

Although Mizner coined the warning, "Never give a sucker an even break," he was known as the easiest touch on Broadway. "I never worry about money," he once explained, "unless a rich man comes anywhere near me. Then I can't sleep until I find a way to get in on the take."

It was Phineas Barnum who declared that "there's a sucker born every minute." To this Mizner added—"and two to take him." As far back as his Barbary Coast days in San Francisco, Mizner had used the greeting, "Hello, Sucker," which, during the prohibition era in New

[18] From *The Fabulous Wilson Mizner,* by Edward Dean Sullivan, pp. 141, 143-145. Copyright, 1935, by the Henkle Company. New York.

York, was the greeting of Texas Guinan in Manhattan's costliest *couvert* joints.

"In fact," Mizner said, "everyone in the world is a fall guy or sucker for nearly anything outside of his own racket. I've bitten off more than I could chew, or sign the check for, a thousand times and therefore anything I do is in self-defense. The first dawn of smartness is to stop trying things you don't know anything about—especially if they run to anything over a dollar."

When the theatrical writers interviewed Mizner in his Broadway days regarding his playwriting, they invariably came away with further feature stories regarding something quite apart from their set interview, with the result that the publicity of Mizner grew apace. Usually he was in bed when interviewed, but there were occasions when he went out into the byways to illustrate a point.

He had said, "The principal function of a sucker is police work. The law is always looking for swindlers, but it takes a sucker to find them."

"Where are all these easy marks, anyway?" asked his interviewer. "I never see anyone who seems much easier than the cautious average."

So Mizner dressed and went out into Broadway with the newspaperman. They stopped at a corner behind a man who was waiting to cross when traffic permitted.

"Do you know," said Mizner loudly to his interviewer, "what city outside of New York has the best fire department?"

"Springfield, Massachusetts," spoke up the stranger, "and I'll bet y' on it."

Mizner laughed.

"He's one," he said to the interviewer, moving off.

"Let's see the color of your money," yelled the man at the curb, still craving bankruptcy.

9

"You Walk Around a Corner, and It's a Different World"

"All the world is a village," papa [Anacleto] said, "even this great metropolis."—*Maria Sermolino*

Ellis Island Adventures of Immigrants en Route to Points Beyond New York [1]

. . . At that time all the leading railroads sold tickets at Ellis Island, but later this privilege was narrowed down to an Immigrant Clearing House of the Trunk Line Association.

The Trunk Line Association included the New York Central, West Shore, New York, Ontario and Western, Pennsylvania, Lehigh Valley, Delaware, Lackawanna and Western, B. and O., and the Central of New Jersey. . . .

In the flood-tide years the railroads got about fifty per cent of their

[1] From *In the Shadow of Liberty*. The Chronicle of Ellis Island, by Edward Corsi, pp. 123–126. Copyright, 1935, by The Macmillan Company. New York.

business in cash and the other half in orders from the steamship companies. It was not uncommon for the ticket sellers to take in forty thousand dollars per day, which meant that, including the orders from the steamship companies, their day's business had amounted to eighty thousand dollars from tiny Ellis Island. The present joint agent, Benjamin Sprung, who came to the Island as an office boy, has held the job twenty-seven years.

Strangely enough, many of the aliens destined to points beyond New York never saw the city. They were ferried to Jersey piers and there embarked for their destinations.

What a scene the old railroad room must have presented with aliens waiting all day for their tickets and hours of departure! What jabbering! Twelve men sold tickets at the windows, while linguists worked the floors separating the aliens into groups. The Germans were usually en route to Wisconsin, Illinois, North and South Dakota, there to work on the great northwestern farms.

The Hollanders and Germans always had the biggest families. Superintendent Baker recalls one Dutch family who paid nine full fares, eight half fares, and had three or four children too young to require any fares.

"The steamship companies," he recalled to me, "often advanced ten or fifteen dollars to aliens without money. And I have an idea they got most of it back."

On occasion it happened that women waiting for tickets would have babies born in the waiting room. Hurry calls would go forth to the hospital, and attendants with litters would come and carry them off. Others died in the waiting room; a few were murdered. It cost nine dollars to bury a dead alien.

Only the Jews, of all the races in the world, have a perfect record for burying and administering the last rites to their own dead from Ellis Island.

The railroad ticket business frequently caused repercussions in Superintendent Baker's office. Primarily, it was a concession, and as such was beyond his control except for his responsibility for supervising it along with other concessions in order to prevent or eliminate graft. The office now sells two hundred and fifty tickets a month, but there used to be that number in ten minutes. Each ticket seller had to have a number of languages at his command in order to ask the alien where he or she was going. Agent Sprung, then a ticket seller, could ask an alien where he was going in any language in the world except Chinese or Japanese, two which he could never master.

But the repercussions which fell upon Superintendent Baker were often the result of mistakes made by Sprung's men. Once fifteen Italians bound for Amsterdam Avenue in New York City wound up in Amsterdam, New York. The chief of police of that city wired:

"Get wise at Ellis Island. Fifteen Italians sent here want to go to Amsterdam Avenue, New York."

Sometimes the states were confused, as in the case of a party of Austrian laborers who got to Johnstown, Pennsylvania, when in reality they wanted to go to Johnstown, New York.

Once the leader of a group of Italians walked up to the window to buy a block ticket for himself and companions.

"Where are you going?" the ticket seller demanded in Italian.

"P-p-p-p-p-p-p-p-p—" stuttered the Italian in consternation and distress. Then he tried it again.

"P-p-p-p-p-poo-poo-poo-poo—"

But that was as far as he could get. Finally he reached into an inner pocket of his coat and produced a typed slip. The name of the town was Punxsutawney, Pennsylvania.

One immigrant in endeavoring to ask for a ticket to Detroit, Michigan, said something which was a variation of Detroit-a-Mich. Charley McCullock, the agent at the window, thought the alien had called him a dirty mick, and resented it.

In those days it cost thirteen dollars for a day coach ticket to Chicago. One morning about ten o'clock, an elderly Jew with a flowing black beard and a skull cap arrived in the railroad waiting room with his family. The wife, who appeared to be about his own age, had her hair bound in a handkerchief in typically foreign fashion. There were ten children, and each carried a basket.

Approaching the old man, the interpreter questioned him: "Yiddish? Russian? Deutsch? Italiano? English?" There was no answer. Merely an imperturbable countenance and a shake of the head. At four o'clock in the afternoon the family still occupied the same bench. Finally some one thought of asking the old man if he spoke Gaelic. With a big smile he replied that he did, and the interpreter learned that he wanted to go to Chicago.

George O'Donnoghue, formerly of the Cashier's Office at the Island, which handled financial matters and maintained a depository for alien funds, always had difficulty with orthodox Jews who would not sign for the receipt of their money on holy days. They would wait until after sundown before accepting their money from our office.

"Some aliens were reluctant to admit that they had money for fear of being robbed. It turned out that one Greek, who claimed he had no money, was carrying over five thousand dollars on his person.

"Some would squander money which relatives had sent to them in our care, while going to their destinations. On arrival they would contend that we had short-changed them, and soon we would receive threatening letters from attorneys. The cash business of our office was as high as five hundred thousand dollars monthly and for a time reached eight million dollars per year."

Suit-Hunting Avenue [2]

As I walked slowly up the street, munching one of my three-and-one-third-cent oranges, I passed hundreds of bright windows filled with suits, pants, shirts, hats and ties. Canal Street was known in those days as Suit Hunting Avenue. It was a man's street, quite exclusive. There wasn't a single store where a woman could have bought anything but a tie for her husband.

Many of the windows were filled with magnificent dummies, all reflecting the high life of society. They were dressed beautifully in suits of all shades. Some of them seemed to promenade in serene Fifth Avenue elegance. Others were sitting leisurely, smoking cigarettes in ivory holders, petting poodles, reading splendidly bound books. Still others sported magnificent derbies or were engaged in serious conversation, leaning nonchalantly on elegant canes.

Outside, in front of the stores, were the hawkers.

"Hey, mister," they barked, and their cries overcut each other and filled the street with a constant staccato of human voices. "Hey, mister, it's a suit you want. And if it's a suit you want this is the place to get it."

If you as much as hesitated the hawker would run over and grab your arm and place his arm around your neck and in friendly tones, but backed up by an overpowering embrace, would keep on talking while he marched you away.

And so, attracted at last beyond the call of prudence by a monocled dummy with a gray derby ($2.75) and a begloved right hand, I hesitated just one second too long. A hawker jumped. I was a goner.

[2] From *A Penny from Heaven,* by Max Winkler, pp. 89–95. Copyright, 1951, by Max Winkler. New York: Appleton-Century-Crofts, Inc.

He took hold of my left arm and we began to walk. As we entered the store I found that there was none. There was just a window with all the beautiful things to look at and a door that led down to the basement. As we climbed down the stairs the hawker cried out: "Abe! Customer!"

We had reached the cellar. The hawker didn't let go of my arm till a cigar-chewing man in shirt sleeves had gotten hold of the right one. Then he returned to the upper world. Abe escorted me deeper to the back of the storeroom, which was filled with all kinds of clothing.

"All right, pal," he said, and his voice that seemed to come out of a rusty barrel filled with gravel made me shrink back, "all right, pal, we have just the thing for you."

He pulled a suit from a pile.

"Take off your pants," he thundered. I took off my pants.

Abe watched me silently, chewing wildly at his cigar. He seemed to lose patience with me.

"Come on now!" he roared. "Give me your pants. Try these."

I put on the pants he had handed me. They were at least five inches too short.

"Mister," I said timidly, "these pants, don't you think they are a little bit short?"

Abe's face contorted in a vicious grin. "Short—well, you sure must be a greenhorn. Don't you know that's the way they wear 'em now in America?"

I looked again down my legs and tried to make a step forward. The trousers were as tight as cement.

"I don't want them," I said. "I don't think I want any new suit today. Let me have my pants."

Abe seemed unimpressed.

"O.K., O.K., pal," he said. "Take it easy now, don't get excited. Hey, Moe! Where are his pants?"

Moe—I hadn't seen or heard Moe before—emerged out of the dark. "What pants?" he said. "Whose pants?" He was tiny and thin, a fraction only of bulging Abe. But he had a flat nose and cauliflower ears and I didn't like Moe a bit.

"This fellow here," Abe said. "He says he can't find his pants."

"Look, mister," Moe said. Then he broke up in the middle of whatever sentence he had started to hurl at me. "Ah, what the hell!" he said, turned and vanished in the dark.

Abe spat out what was left of his cigar, took out a new one and lit it slowly.

"Don't worry, pal," he said at last. "Your pants must be around here some place, or maybe Philip sold them or maybe he put them some place. He just went out to make a delivery. Just wait here till Phil comes back—or maybe I'll find you in the meantime a suit with long pants. Look here: I got a good suit for you right here. Try on the jacket.

I put on the jacket. The sleeves barely covered my elbows

I extended my bare forearms towards Abe in a silent gesture of despair and protest.

"What's the matter now?" Abe said. "Aren't short sleeves nicer than short pants? What else do you want?"

"I want my pants back."

"Here we go again. What do you worry? We got lots of pants. Hey, Moe, come here, fix his coat."

Moe came back. He scarcely glanced at the coat. "It can take an inch or two more," he said. "Take it off."

He ripped the coat off my body, took it and departed.

Abe, too, strolled away in an evil cloud of cigar smoke. I was alone.

Cautiously I began moving around. I had to find my pants. I had to get out of here. I looked at the tables and the shelves, I looked at the floor and up at the hangers. Pants, pants, pants—but I couldn't find mine. I was a thirsty sailor, marooned in the middle of the ocean, dying from thirst with oceans of water surrounding him.

Suddenly I heard Moe yell somewhere in the dark, "Where is he, where is the fellow you were selling the suit to?"

"I don't know," gravel voice answered. "He must be around here somewhere. He couldn't have run out without his pants."

"Who says he couldn't? He probably ran out with half a dozen pants. If I catch him I'll murder him. Get him, you dope, before he takes the whole place."

By now I was lost somewhere between the tailor shop way back in the basement and a dozen tables loaded with stacks of boxes up to the ceiling. I tried to find my way back to the spot from where I had started. But Moe's voice had trailed off and there was nothing to guide me. The place was filled with a sinister silence. I stood there, without pants, trying to figure out what to do next. My situation, I realized, was dangerously balancing between the ridiculous and the catastrophic.

After a little while I heard steps. Moe and Abe had returned and I heard little Moe pouring out a stream of invectives against mighty Abe who had "let the dirty robber get away with half the store."

Suddenly he turned a corner and saw me.

He was still holding my new coat with the lengthened sleeves over his arm.

"What are you doing here in the dark?" he growled. "Here is your new suit. Let me have the money and get the hell out of here."

"Let me have my pants."

Abe extended a lazy hand and pushed one of the cardboard boxes off a table. There were my pants.

I took them. I slipped on the new suit. It was a sunbleached pale blue. The two inches at the end of the sleeves weren't quite so bleached and much more blue. I handed Moe the money, rushed up the stairs and with a deep breath stepped out into the bustle of the street. A man was offering oranges. But I just laughed at him, I wasn't buying any more. No, sir, not me. Not today and not tomorrow and not ever again.

The next morning at our regular 7:30 meeting I faced Clara in my new suit. She paled only slightly and then she smiled. We walked along our accustomed route. As we passed a big mirror in a furniture store I suddenly saw myself for the first time in my new American suit.

I looked at Clara with a reassured feeling of happiness. A girl that could see such a sight and still smile had passed the supreme test of love and affection. I took her arm and in the midst of the thunderous traffic of Third Avenue bent down and kissed her. Nothing that fate might ever have in store could ever tear us apart.

East Side Pushcarts

VENDERS AND THEIR WAYS[3]

The East Side takes its pushcart so seriously that you are greatly impressed with it, when you go down there and see and hear the hundreds of men engaged in the actual pushing and selling, and learn of the half-dozen or more pushcart headquarters, where the handcarts of all sizes and degrees of strength and running capacity are kept on hand, to be hired out by the day or week; and are told finally, of the scores of mimic living-room factories, where goods of an especial pushcart brand are made up, to be sold to the dealers at special pushcart prices.

[3] From "The Push-Cart Peddlers, The Swarms in and about Hester Street—Enormous Growth of the Trade—The Proposed Market-Place—Views of a Veteran—What Some Men Have Earned—The Police and the Venders," by Olive F. Gunby, *New York Evening Post,* August 20, 1898.

Then you learn of the not-very-well-defined depots and repositories, hidden away on side streets and back alleys, where scales, torch-holders, lanterns, trays, and other pushcart appliances may be had, at all rates, and hear of the late-running carts trundled back to quarters as late as half-past two in the morning. Plainly all edicts and enactments touching the pushcart directly or indirectly strike at the very root of East Side concerns. In other parts of the town the pushcart is a mere incident, abiding vagrantly on such uncertain footing as may be permitted for the moment by favor of a policeman or wagoner, and voted a nuisance by everybody who takes the trouble to think about him at all. Half-knave, half-scapegoat, altogether vagabond, may be his rating west of the Bowery and north of Fourteenth Street, but within that precinct he has distinct place and finding, and is rated, moreover, not all-of-a-piece on the lowest rung of the social ladder, but judged variously, according to desert or circumstance.

The pushcart man who owns his cart and whose wife stays at home while he pursues the calling, posting himself always in the vicinity of a certain corner, or in front of a certain building, is accounted much higher socially than his contemporary who hires his "equipage," by the week, and scuttles round from place to place, with no regular customers to depend on and no established business reputation to sustain. In turn, such a peddler is higher in neighborhood estimation than the one whose wife and children trundle out carts beside him, and who only manages to hire vehicles and secure stock for them between times, on odd days when trade is slack and the legitimate lessees are occupied with other things, or do not care to go out.

There are many women in the pushcart business, it turns out, many who rent their own carts at eight or ten cents a day, just as the men do, but who get them by proxy, delegating to some man the task, it being a law, unwritten but unacknowledged, that women should not undertake pushcart trundling. In addition to these women who have no husbands to take the initiative, or perhaps only such incapables as cannot be trusted, there are a whole army of pushcart women trained and habituated to the business, who from long custom or love of excitement follow their consorts about the streets and help in the selling, even if they do not have a cart to themselves.

"There are just three pushcarts out on the street now to every one that was there five or six years ago," said a veteran leader of the clan, who has attained prosperity and can take an all-round view of the situation. "Anybody can dip into the business as things are now, and a man can land in this country today, penniless and with no knowledge of the language or the customs, and start out with a pushcart tomorrow. Formerly it took $30 at least to set up a cart. There were not any for hire, so you had to own one and you had go to headquarters and buy your stock yourself, which, of course, called for some amount of intelligence and knowledge of business methods. Then you had to have a place to keep your cart and your goods. Now all these middle-men have stepped in, and if a fellow has a dollar or a dollar and a half, or can borrow that amount, he can strike out with the rest. Ten cents will get him a strong cart, which he can take out of the cellar at half-past five or earlier in the morning and keep out until two o'clock the next morning.

"Then goods, to suit the trade, can be got handy from the little factories or from storekeepers who get them from the factories for that purpose. The pushcart man today need not even have a roof over his head; he may sleep in the park or on a doorstep, if he has not the money to get a ten-cent lodging; but his goods, if not sold out, will be taken care of by the man he hires his cart from. License? Ah! there it is; he strikes out without a license, and comes in competition with those of us who pay our $15 a year—that is, when we are allowed to pay it or have anybody to pay it to.

"Since January there has not been a license issued to any of us, and the policemen can run us in as often as they like, and there's no help for it. I know men who have been, time and time again, to the city hall to get a license, men whose old licenses have run out, and others, new recruits in the business, but none of them get any, and if the officer on their beat takes a notion to nab them, up they go and pay their $2 or their $5, so as to go on with their business. Everybody knows that there are a lot of pushcarters without licenses, but there are also plenty with them. These last six months, though, the good and the bad are treated about alike, and it's no use explaining, because the police say 'tain't their place to listen to explanations. 'You ain't got a license, have you?' they say, and you answer 'No,' and that's all there is about it. No use saying how many times you've been to get a license and couldn't. You just step along with the officer, and the neighbors look and think you're a thief or a scalawag.

"You see that cart full of plums and peaches and one thing or another, over there in the corner; well, that fruit is all spoiled; the man was taken up yesterday for not having a license, left his cart just as it stood, and his wife trundled it in here, where he hires it for $1.50 a week. She's a delicate kind of woman, not fit to hustle with a cart, so there the stock stands while her husband waits trial. I know he's tried to get a license, but then that don't count.

"Ain't there a way of getting on the good side of the policemen? Oh, yes, I know them as pays in a quarter or fifty cents occasionally, and keeps out of a muddle, but it has to be done on the sly—slip the money in a pear or a plum and offer the fruit to the policeman, on account of its looking so tempting; that works sometimes; but all the same, when a policeman is sent out to make a raid he makes it and runs in all the pushcart men in sight, whether they merit it or not. Some of them take their carts to the station-house with them; and others turn them over to some friend or get word home. It's hard luck with the most of the boys right about now, and some of them are good, steady workers, who do the best they can, and give good weight, and are known to be square."

MERCHANT VS. CUSTOMER[4]

Buying and selling were not, as elsewhere, a mere affair of looking at a price mark and making up one's mind. The price asked was only meant as a declaration of war, the act of purchase was a battle of insult, the sale was a compromise of mutual hatred.

"*Weiberle* [ladies], *weiberle*," cries the merchant; "come by me and get good '*metsiah*' [bargain]."

The woman stops with a sneer, pokes contemptuously at the merchandise, insults it and the salesman, underbids him half. He tries to prove that he would die of starvation if he yielded to her disgusting bid. She implies that he takes her for a fool. In a moment he is telling her that he hopes her children may strangle with cholera for trying to make a beggar of him. She answers that he is a thief, a liar, a dog of an apostate Jew. She makes as if to spit on his wares; he grabs them from her and throws them back on the heap. At length a sale is made and she moves on to the next bout.

[4] From *The Real New York*, by Rupert Hughes, pp. 336–337. Copyright, 1904, by the Smart Set Publishing Company. New York and London.

Knishes and *Pasteles Calientes* on Delancey Street[5]

A sign outside a Delancey Street hot-dog stand points up more graphically than census figures the vast changes in New York City's ethnic picture in recent years. One line reads: "Knishes." And just below is the announcement: "Pasteles Calientes."

Well, knishes have been favored goodies since time began on Delancey Street, double-breasted main stem of the lower East Side. They're potato pies which give their aficionados that round, firm, fully packed look. But pasteles calientes? Something new on Delancey Street.

The counterman, who's been dealing knishes for years, finished his seltzer and said: "Pasteles calientes? That's Puerto Rican knishes, you might say. Chopped meat wrapped up in leaves and cooked. *They* like them, but not the regular knish-eaters."

"Pasteles calientes" means hot pies, and a Puerto Rican friend says most of them sold in New York are imported in cans from the island. The leaves in which the meat mixture is wrapped are plantain. Racial changes in the city are reflected more quickly in restaurants and food markets than in other ways. Puerto Ricans who have settled on the lower East Side are still in small minority in the Delancey Street throngs. But enter the huge Essex Market buildings which straddle it at Essex Street, and you realize the scope of the Caribbean influence.

An elderly grocer dozes on a stool near his counter in the market. Above him is a crayoned cardboard with this Spanish legend:

Por favor compren aqui que nosotros le llevamos la compra a la casa. Gracias. Tu amigo, MORRIS.

It means: "Please buy here. We deliver to your home. Thanks. Your friend, Morris."

"A smart Puerto Rican kid put up the sign for him," explained veteran Inspector Morris Scheier of the Department of Parks, indicating the dozing Morris. "This kid is a sort of interpreter between his people and the merchants. Keeps himself busy that way after school."

[5] From "Viva el Knish!" by Murray Robinson, *New York World-Telegram and The Sun, Saturday Feature Magazine,* October 31, 1953, p. 2. Copyright, 1953, by New York World-Telegram Corp.

Some of the market stands are loaded with articles of food Delancey Street never dreamed of ten years ago. In the fish stalls, where once the whitefish looked only at the pike and the pike looked only at the carp, you now see bacalao, the dried cod which Italians call baccala. Near the kosher butchers you find pork specialists, and one Spanish butcher has a big sign plugging lamp haslets (edible innards), favored by his clientele.

Tropical fruits and vegetables abound. Irving Samuels, a bored-looking merchant, pointed out mango and clabazza (pumpkin), nami (yams), marina de maiz (yellow corn meal), mabi bark (boiled for drinks), and the ever-popular plantain.

Grocers in the market stock strange bottles of syrup—tamarind, soursop, and sesame seed—which are mixed with water for cold soft drinks, along with canned pinto beans and pasteles calientes hard by the jars of gefuelte fish.

Bob Cooper, one of the grocers dealing to the new trade, said that only one East Side item has exerted any influence on his new customers. "They're crazy about 'galletas,'" he said. "That's matzos."

The Old Bowery from Vauxhall Garden to Big Mose[6]

The Five Points gradually declined as an amusement center as the green groceries invaded the district and the gangs began to abuse their privileges as overlords of Paradise Square, and the Bowery became increasingly important as a place of recreation. As early as 1752, when

[6] From *The Gangs of New York,* An Informal History of the Underworld, by Herbert Asbury, pp. 23–37. Copyright, 1927, 1928, by Alfred A. Knopf, Inc. New York.

Originally an Indian trail, the Bowery, which runs from Chatham Square to Cooper Square, was known in Dutch days as the "road to the *bouwerij*" (farm), Peter Stuyvesant's country estate, which extended to the East River, from Sixth to Eighteenth Streets. During the Revolution the Bouwerie Lane became the Bowery Road, and in 1807 it became the Bowery.

The original Mose has been traced to Moses Humphreys, a printer on the New York *Sun*. Richard M. Dorson ("Mose the Far-Famed and World-Renowned," *American Literature,* Vol. 15, November, 1943, No. 3, p. 298n.) quotes a letter from Herbert Asbury, saying: "The stories about Mose grew up as did those of Paul Bunyan. I started collecting them when I first came to

the waters of the Collect still covered the site of the Tombs and flowed sluggishly through Canal Street, the Bowery began to make some pretensions to being a street of pleasure by the opening of Sperry's Botanical Gardens, later Vauxhall Garden, at the upper end of the thoroughfare near Astor Place. Its claims were greatly enhanced in 1826 by the erection of the Bowery Theater on the site of the old Bull's Head Tavern, where George Washington had stopped to quench his thirst with Bowery ale on Evacuation Day in 1783. The new playhouse opened with a comedy, *The Road to Ruin,* but its first important production was in November, 1826, when Edwin Forrest played the title rôle in *Othello*. For many years it was one of the foremost theaters on the continent; its boards creaked beneath the tread of some of the greatest players of the time. It was then the largest playhouse in the city, with a seating capacity of 3,000, and was the first to be equipped with gas. The structure was burned three times between 1826 and 1838, and again caught fire some fifteen years before the Civil War, when the police, recently uniformed by order of Mayor Harper, appeared on the scene in all the glory of their new suits and glistening brass buttons. They ordered the spectators to make way for the firemen, but the Bowery gangsters jeered and laughed at them as liveried lackeys, and refused to do their bidding. The thugs attacked with great ferocity when some one howled that the policemen were trying to imitate the English bobbies, and many were injured before they were subdued. So much ill-feeling arose because of this and similar incidents that the uniforms were called in, and for several years the police appeared on the streets with no other insignia than a star-shaped copper shield, whence came the names coppers and cops. After weathering many storms the theater was finally renamed the Thalia, and [in 1927] still stands in the shadow of the Third Avenue elevated railroad, devoted to moving pictures and Italian stock, with occasional performances by traveling Chinese troups.

Several other theaters soon followed the Bowery, among them the

---

New York in 1915, when I used to spend considerable time on the Bowery talking to the old-timers in the saloons and lodging-houses. Some of these old men professed to remember the Bowery in the days before the Civil War, and from them I got most of the stories about Mose."

In *Fire-Fightin' Mose* (New York, 1955) Harold W. Felton has reconstructed the story of Mose; his engine, *Lady Washington,* known as the *White Ghost;* his girl, Lize; Linda, the cigar girl; and his friend, Sykesey. After the *White Ghost* had been "washed" by the rival *Old Maid* or (according to other versions) after he had been rejected by Lize, Mose went to the Sandwich Islands, where he married a princess and became king, raising forty children, and fighting volcano fires as chief of the local fire department.

Windsor, which became famous for its performances of *Hands across the Sea,* and for the remarkable acting of Johnny Thompson in *On Hand.* For many years these houses presented first-class plays and were frequented by the aristocracy of the city, but in time, as the character of the street changed and the dives and gangsters made it a byword from coast to coast, they offered blood and thunder thrillers of so distinct a type that they became known as Bowery plays, and could be seen nowhere else. Among them were *The Boy Detective, Marked for Life, Neck and Neck,* and *Si Slocum.* From these productions developed the "ten, twent', thirt'" melodrama which was so popular throughout the United States, until its place was taken by the moving picture. The dress circle and first balconies of the early Bowery theaters, after the first citizens had abandoned them for the playhouses farther uptown and along Broadway, were generally filled with respectable German families from the Seventh Ward, who drank pink and yellow lemonade and noisily devoured Ridley's Old Fashioned Peppermint Kisses. But the pit and topmost galleries fairly swarmed with ragamuffins of all degrees and both sexes who stamped and whistled and shouted "h'ist dat rag!" when the curtain failed to rise promptly on schedule time. "These places were jammed to suffocation on Sunday nights," wrote an author who visited the Bowery about the time of the Civil War. "Actresses too corrupt and dissolute to play elsewhere appear on the boards at the Bowery. Broad farces, indecent comedies, plays of highwaymen and murderers, are received with shouts by the reeking crowds which fill the low theaters. Newsboys, street-sweepers, rag-pickers, begging girls, collectors of cinders, all who can beg or steal a sixpence, fill the galleries of these corrupt places of amusement. There is not a dance hall, a free-and-easy, a concert saloon, or a vile drinking-place that presents such a view of the depravity and degradation of New York as the gallery of a Bowery theater."

Within a few years after the erection of the first theater the Bowery was lined with playhouses, concert halls, saloons and basement dives, and huge beer gardens seating from 1,000 to 1,500 persons at long tables running lengthwise of an enormous room. As late as 1898 the Bowery had ninety-nine houses of entertainment, of which only fourteen were classed as respectable by the police, and there were six barrooms to a block. Now [in 1927] the street can muster a bare dozen theaters, devoted to burlesque, moving pictures, and Yiddish, Italian and Chinese drama. Some of the dives which dotted the Bowery before and after the Civil War have never been equalled, even by Prohibition speak-easies, for the frightful and deadly quality of their liquor. In many of the lower-class places, in the early days, drinks were three cents each and no glasses or mugs were used. Barrels of fiery spirits stood on shelves behind the bar, and poured out their contents through lines of slender rubber hose. The customer, having deposited his money on the bar, took an end of the hose in his mouth, and was entitled to all he could drink without breathing. The moment he stopped for breath the watchful bartender turned off the supply, and nothing would start it again but another payment. Some of the Bowery bums became so expert at swallowing, and were able to hold their breaths for such a long period, that they could get delightfully drunk for three cents. One famous saloon, in Baxter Street near the Bowery, provided and extensively advertised a rear chamber called the "velvet room." When a good customer was reduced to a nickel, he was given an extra large bowl of liquor and escorted with considerable ceremony into the "velvet room," where he was permitted to drink himself unconscious, and sleep until the effects of the potation wore off.

The most famous of the early Bowery beer halls was the Atlantic Gardens, next door to the old Bowery Theater and now a palace of the moving pictures. Upstairs and down it provided seats for more than a thousand, and two four-horse drays, working ten hours a day, were scarcely able to keep the customers supplied with beer fresh from the brewery. In this and other similar establishments, there was music by pianos, harps, violins, drums and brasses; and dice, dominoes, cards and sometimes rifles for target shooting were provided. Everything was free except the beer, which cost five cents for an enormous mug. Most of the gardens were operated by Germans, and at first were frequented by men and women of that nationality, who brought their families and spent the day quietly. Beer was served by girls from twelve to sixteen years old, wearing short dresses and red-topped boots, which reached almost to the knees and had bells dangling from the tassels. The sale of the beverage was so profitable that the managers of the gardens bid against each other for the privilege of entertaining the large racial and political organizations, frequently paying as much as $500 to any association that would agree to hold an all-day picnic on their premises.

For many years these gardens were entirely respectable, but low-class thugs and hoodlums finally began to invade them, not to drink beer but to guzzle hard liquor from flasks, and in time they came to be the resorts of the gangsters and other criminals of the district, and the Bowery assumed the character which has made it one of the most renowned thoroughfares in the world. The most important gangs of the early days of the Bowery district were the Bowery Boys, the True

Blue Americans, the American Guards, the O'Connell Guards and the Atlantic Guards. Their membership was principally Irish, but they do not appear to have been as criminal or as ferocious as their brethren of the Five Points, although among them were many gifted brawlers. The True Blue Americans were amusing, but harmless. They wore stovepipe hats and long black frock coats which reached flappingly to their ankles and buttoned close under the chin; their chief mission in life was to stand on street corners and denounce England, and gloomily predict the immediate destruction of the British Empire by fire and sword. Like most of the sons of Erin who have come to this country, they never became so thoroughly Americanized that Ireland did not remain their principal vocal interest. The other gangs were probably offshoots of the Bowery Boys, and commonly joined the latter in their fights with the roaring denizens of Paradise Square. Their exploits earned them no place of importance in gang history.

For many years the Bowery Boys and the Dead Rabbits waged a bitter feud, and a week seldom passed in which they did not come to blows, either along the Bowery, in the Five Points section, or on the ancient battleground of Bunker Hill, north of Grand Street. The greatest gang conflicts of the early nineteenth century were fought by these groups, and they continued their feud until the Draft Riots of 1863, when they combined with other gangs and criminals in an effort to sack and burn the city. In these early struggles the Bowery Boys were supported by the other gangs of the Bowery, while the Plug Uglies, the Shirt Tails and the Chichesters rallied under the fragrant emblem of the Dead Rabbits. Sometimes the battles raged for two or three days without cessation, while the streets of the gang area were barricaded with carts and paving stones, and the gangsters blazed away at each other with musket and pistol, or engaged in close work with knives, brickbats, bludgeons, teeth and fists. On the outskirts of the struggling mob of thugs ranged the women, their arms filled with reserve ammunition, their keen eyes watching for a break in the enemy's defense, and always ready to lend a hand or a tooth in the fray.

Often these Amazons fought in the ranks, and many of them achieved great renown as ferocious battlers. They were particularly gifted in the art of mayhem, and during the Draft Riots it was the women who inflicted the most fiendish tortures upon Negroes, soldiers and policemen captured by the mob, slicing their flesh with butcher knives, ripping out eyes and tongues, and applying the torch after the victims had been sprayed with oil and hanged to trees. The Dead Rabbits, during the early forties, commanded the allegiance of the most noted of the female battlers, an angular vixen known as Hell-Cat Maggie, who fought alongside the gang chieftains in many of the great battles with the Bowery gangs. She is said to have filed her front teeth to points, while on her fingers she wore long artificial nails, constructed of brass. When Hell-Cat Maggie screeched her battle cry and rushed biting and clawing into the midst of a mass of opposing gangsters, even the most stout-hearted blanched and fled. No quarter was asked or given by the early gangsters; when a man fell wounded his enemies leaped joyfully upon him and kicked or stamped him to death. Frequently the police were unable to disperse the mobs, and were compelled to ask the National Guard and the Regular Army for aid. The city soon became accustomed to regiments of soldiers marching in battle array through the streets to quell a gang riot. Occasionally the artillery was called out also, but generally the gangsters fled before the muskets of the infantrymen. Much of this work was done by the Twenty-seventh, later the Seventh Regiment.

Little knowledge of the activities of most of the early Bowery gangs has survived, but the lore of the street is rich in tales of the Bowery Boys and the prowess of their mighty leaders. Sometimes this gang was called the Bowery B'hoys, which is sufficient indication of its racial origin. It was probably the most celebrated gang in the history of the United States, but before the eminent Chuck Connors appeared in the late eighties and transformed the type into a bar fly and a tramp, the Bowery Boy was not a loafer except on Sundays and holidays. Nor was he a criminal, except on occasion, until the period of the Civil War. He was apt to earn his living as a butcher or apprentice mechanic, or as a bouncer in a Bowery saloon or dance cellar. But he was almost always a volunteer fireman, and therein lay much of the strength of the gang, for in the early days before the Civil War the firemen, most of them strong adherents of Tammany Hall, had much to say about the conduct of the city's government. Many of the most eminent politicians belonged to the fire brigade, and there was much rivalry between the companies, which gave their engines such names as White Ghost, Black Joke, Shad Belly, Dry Bones, Red Rover, Hay Wagon, Big Six, Yaller Girl, Bean Soup, Old Junk and Old Maid. Such famous New York political leaders as Cornelius V. W. Lawrence, Zophar Mills, Samuel Willets, William M. Wood, John J. Gorman and William M. Tweed were volunteer firemen. In still earlier days even George Washington was an ardent chaser after the fire engines, and for a short time during his residence in the metropolis was head of the New York department. Before the formation of a paid fire fighting force one of the great events of the year was the Fireman's Parade, and great crowds lined the sidewalks and cheered the red-shirted, beaver-hatted brawlers as they pulled their engines over the cobblestones, while before them marched a brass band blaring away at *Solid Men to the Front*, a rousing tune which was a favorite for many years.

But the rivalry between the fire companies whose membership included men of substance was friendly if strenuous, while the Bowery Boy loved his fire engine almost as much as he did his girl, and considered both himself and his company disgraced if his apparatus was beaten to a conflagration. And the acme of humiliation was to roll to a fire and find that all of the fire plugs had been captured by other companies. To prevent this the Bowery Boy resorted to typically direct methods. When the fire alarm sounded he simply grabbed an empty barrel from a grocery store and hurried with it to the fire plug nearest the burning building. There he turned the barrel over the plug and sat on it, and defended it valorously against the assaults of rival firemen until his own engine arrived. If he succeeded he was a hero and his company had won a notable victory. Frequently the fight for fire plugs was so fierce that the Bowery Boys had no time to extinguish the flames.

The original Bowery Boy, who followed his chieftain in so many forays against the hated Dead Rabbits and other Five Points gangs, was a burly ruffian with his chin adorned by an Uncle Sam whisker—the type of American which is still portrayed by the English comic weeklies. On his head was a stovepipe hat, generally battered, and his trousers were tucked inside his boots, while his jaws moved constantly on a chew of tobacco as he whittled on a shingle with the huge knife which never left his possession. In later years, a little before the time of Chuck Connors, the type changed as new fashions in men's clothing appeared, and the Bowery Boy promenaded his favorite thoroughfare with his head crowned by a high beaver hat with the nap divided and brushed different ways, while his stalwart figure was encased in an elegant frock coat, and about his throat was knotted a gaudy kerchief. His pantaloons, cut almost as full as the modern Oxford bags, were turned up over his heavy boots. The hair on the back of his head was clipped close and his neck and chin were shaven, while his temple locks were daintily curled and heavily anointed with bear's grease or some other powerful, evil-smelling unguent. His downfall had begun in those days, but he was still an unruly and belligerent citizen, and it was unwise to give him cause for offense.

Some of the most ferocious rough-and-tumble fighters that ever cracked a skull or gouged out an eyeball fought in the ranks of the Bowery Boys, and from their rough school emerged many celebrated brawlers and political leaders. Butcher Bill Poole, a famous gangster and ward heeler, owed allegiance to the Bowery Boys, and so did his murderer, Lew Baker, who shot him to death in Stanwix Hall in 1855.

But the greatest of the Bowery Boys, and the most imposing figure in all the history of the New York gangs, was a leader who flourished in the forties, and captained the gangsters in the most important of their punitive and marauding expeditions into the Five Points. His identity remains unknown, and there is excellent reason to believe that he may be a myth, but vasty tales of his prowess and of his valor in the fights against the Dead Rabbits and the Plug Uglies have come down through the years, gaining incident and momentum as they came. Under the simple sobriquet of Mose he has become a legendary figure of truly heroic proportions, at once the Samson, the Achilles and the Paul Bunyan of the Bowery. And beside him, in the lore of the street, marches the diminutive figure of his faithful friend and counsellor, by name Syksey. . . . The present generation of Bowery riffraff knows little or nothing of the mighty Mose, and only the older men who plod that now dreary and dismal relic of a great street have heard the name. But in the days before the Civil War, when the Bowery was in its heyday and the Bowery Boy was the strutting peacock of gangland, songs were sung in honor of his great deeds, and the gangsters surged into battle shouting his name and imploring his spirit to join them and lend power to their arms. He was scarcely cold in his grave before Chanfrau had immortalized him [in Benjamin A. Baker's *A Glance at New York in 1848*, which opened at Mitchell's Olympic Theater on February 15, 1848].

Mose was at least eight feet tall and broad in proportion, and his colossal bulk was crowned by a great shock of flaming ginger-colored hair, on which he wore a beaver hat measuring more than two feet from crown to brim. His hands were as large as the hams of a Virginia hog, and on those rare moments when he was in repose they dangled below his knees; it was Syksey's habit to boast pridefully that his chieftain could stand erect and scratch his knee-cap. The feet of the great captain were so large that the ordinary boot of commerce would not fit his big toe; he wore specially constructed footgear, the soles of which were copper plates studded with nails an inch long. Woe and desolation came upon the gangs of the Five Points when the great Mose leaped into their midst and began to kick and stamp; they fled in despair and hid themselves in the innermost depths of the rookeries of Paradise Square.

The strength of the gigantic Mose was as the strength of ten men. Other Bowery Boys went into battle carrying brickbats and the ordinary stave of the time, but Mose, when accoutered for the fray, bore in one hand a great paving stone and in the other a hickory or oak wagon tongue. This was his bludgeon, and when it was lost in the heat of battle he simply uprooted an iron lamp-post and laid about him with great zeal. Instead of the knife affected by his followers, he pinned his faith on a butcher's cleaver. Once when the Dead Rabbits overwhelmed his gang and rushed ferociously up the Bowery to wreck the Boys' headquarters, the great Mose wrenched an oak tree out of the earth, and holding it by the upper branches, employed it as a flail, smiting the Dead Rabbits even as Samson smote the Philistines. The Five Points thugs broke and fled before him, but he pursued them into their lairs around Paradise Square and wrecked two tenements before his rage cooled. Again, he stood his ground before a hundred of the best brawlers of the Points, ripping huge paving blocks from the street and sidewalk and hurling them into the midst of his enemies, inflicting frightful losses.

In his lighter moments it was the custom of this great god of the gangs to lift a horse car off the tracks and carry it a few blocks on his shoulders, laughing uproariously at the bumping the passengers received when he set it down. And so gusty was his laugh that the car trembled on its wheels, the trees swayed as though in a storm and the Bowery was filled with a rushing roar like the thunder of Niagara. Sometimes Mose unhitched the horses and himself pulled the streetcar the length of the Bowery at a bewildering speed; once, if the legend is to be credited, he lifted a car above his head at Chatham Square and carried it, with the horses dangling from the traces, on the palm of his hand as far as Astor Place. Again, when a sailing ship was becalmed in the East River and drifting dangerously near the treacherous rocks of Hell Gate, Mose pulled out in a rowboat, lighted his cigar, which was more than two feet long, and sent such mighty billows of smoke against the sails that the ship was saved, and plunged down the river as though driven by a hurricane. So terrific was the force of Mose's puffs, indeed, that the vessel was into the Harbor and beyond Staten Island before it would respond to the helm. Occasionally Mose amused himself by taking up a position in the center of the river and permitting no ship to pass; as fast as they appeared he blew them back. But Mose was always very much at home in the water; he often dived off at the Battery and came up on the Staten Island beach, a distance which is now traversed by ferry boats in twenty-five minutes. He could swim the Hudson River with two mighty strokes, and required but six for a complete circuit of Manhattan Island. But when he wanted to cross the East River to Brooklyn he scorned to swim the half mile or so; he simply jumped.

When Mose quenched his thirst a drayload of beer was ordered from the brewery, and during the hot summer months he went about with a great fifty-gallon keg of ale dangling from his belt in lieu of a canteen. When he dined in state the butchers of the Center and Fly markets were busy for days in advance of the great event, slicing hogs and cattle and preparing the enormous roasts which the giant needs must consume to regain his strength; and his consumption of bread was so great that a report that Mose was hungry caused a flurry in the flour market. Four quarts of oysters were but an appetizer, and soup and coffee were served to him by the barrel. For dessert and light snacks he was very fond of fruit. Historians affirm that the cherry trees of Cherry Hill and the mulberry trees of Mulberry Bend vanished because of the building up of the city, but the legend of the Bowery has it that Mose tore them up by the roots and ate the fruit; he was hungry and in no mood to wait until the cherries and mulberries could be picked.

Steve Brodie[7]

Pugilists and sports who visited the Bowery were usually found at some time or other spinning yarns in the back room of Steve Brodie's saloon. Steve was one of the most renowned of Bowery characters, simply because he was a clever and tireless seeker of publicity. A native of the Five Points, a stocky, dark-haired, bright-eyed Irish boy, he blacked boots in front of French's Hotel, where the Brooklyn Bridge now ends, and later sold papers along Park Row and the Bowery. Isaac Myers, an old curio dealer at 205 Bowery, claimed to have given Steve the idea which made him famous and wealthy. The Brooklyn Bridge had been completed in 1883, and was one of the wonders of America. One R. E. Odlum of Brooklyn sought fame by jumping from it in 1885, but struck

[7] From *Old Bowery Days*, by Alvin F. Harlow, pp. 417–424. Copyright, 1931, by Alvin F. Harlow. New York & London: D. Appleton and Company.

the water on his side and was killed. Myers said that Steve, then in his early twenties, remarked to him one day several months later that he wished he knew how to make a name for himself.

"Jump off the Brooklyn Bridge," remarked Myers, carelessly.

"I'll do it," said Steve, after a moment's thought. He secured the interest of some sporting friends, and publicity was devised by a fake bet of one hundred dollars that Brodie would not dare the leap. Oddly enough, the date of the function was kept secret. But suddenly on July 23, 1886, it was announced that the leap had been made. An air of mystery surrounds the affair, and the facts probably still elude the historian. Steve's friends and backers claimed to have been present when he climbed over the rail, hurtled downward, and was picked out of the water by the crew of a barge which just happened to be passing. Then one or two persons, cudgeling their memories, seemed to remember having seen a body shooting downward. Scoffers assert that if anything fell, it was a dummy, and that Steve, a good swimmer, dived from concealment under a dock near by, swam under water and came up near the boat at the proper moment.

That brought him an engagement at Alexander's Museum, 317 Bowery, where he talked and danced, and then at other museums. Two years later he made a tactical error when he essayed to swim the Niagara rapids in winter, clad in a rubber suit. He was daunted by the wild, white, icy water; he would not release his hold of the rope which was to give him his start, and finally screamed to be drawn out. "I was kilt wit' the cold or I'd 'a' done it!" he sobbed as he lay on the bank. He did not make another mistake like that.

For such a famous character it was easy to find a brewery who would set him up in the saloon business. His place at 114 Bowery became a mecca for sports and slumming parties. Brodie saw to that. There were three rooms in a row, the two rear ones being the snuggery where Corbett, Sharkey, McGovern, and other boxers and sporting characters sometimes gathered to swap yarns and discuss congenial topics. If they weren't there when sightseers came in, other loungers must impersonate them. Owen Kildare tells of playing Jake Kilrain on one such occasion at Brodie's whispered request.

The barroom was a museum of oddities, souvenirs, and wise-cracking wall mottoes. The main feature was a large East River landscape in oil, showing Brodie halfway in the air from bridge to water. This was considered proof of the feat, even had there not been a framed affidavit from the barge captain who claimed to have pulled Steve out of the tide. When he was asked, as he frequently was, why he did not repeat the jump in the presence of witnesses, Steve's answer always was, "I done it oncet."

On the wall hung belts and trophies of various kinds, some presented to the hero, some picked up in pawnshops. One professed to be the diamond-studded belt for which Sullivan and Kilrain fought. The framed cards were mostly designed to forestall bromidic questioners and deadbeats: "The Clock Is Never Right"; "We Cash Checks for Everyone"; "If You Don't See What You Want, Steal It"; "If You Haven't Any Money, the Hydrant Is in the Rear"; "When the Bartender Is Awfully Busy, Then Is the Time to Bother Him"; "$10,000 in the Safe to Be Given Away to the Poor; Ask the Bartender for What You Want"; "If You Ain't Got Any Money, Steal a Watch." A battered bugle hung near the ceiling and on it a card reading, "If You Don't Blow Yourself, Blow This." Beside the clock was another card, "The Clock Ticks, but We Don't." Hanging over the door to the back room was, for undistinguished loafers, the familiar harbor warning: "Cable Crossing; Don't Anchor."

Swipes the Newsboy, pugilist and pride of the New York Dime Museum, was to be starred in a melodrama, but suffered eclipse when he inadvertently killed an opponent in the ring. The producers bethought them of the famous Brodie and diffidently approached him: Would he act? Would he! Did Steve ever miss an opportunity to bask in the spotlight? He demanded a share in the show and a salary which momentarily stunned the promoters, but they rallied and signed a contract.

The play—its modest title was *On the Bowery*—was rewritten so as to bring in Steve's leap from the bridge, but this time "to save the girl." The company opened at Philadelphia in August, 1894, and came via Brooklyn to the People's Theater—for of course Steve could not think of playing anywhere else in Manhattan than on the Bowery. The day of the opening, October 22, was like Inauguration Day in Washington. The theater was gorgeously decorated, and a big banner with "WELCOME HOME—STEVE BRODIE" swung across the street. All day long, wagons and trucks were unloading floral tributes at the door. A huge model of the Brooklyn Bridge in flowers (an opus of Le Moult, the Bowery florist, who hauled it around town on a truck for two or three hours as an advertisement) was tagged. "From your friend, Jim Shannon." Police Magistrate Paddy Diver, Fourth Ward boss, with characteristic modesty, sent a Gargantuan pillow of roses and chrysanthemums, with letters ten inches high worked into it, "WELCOME BRODIE —P. DIVER."

The jam that night was terrific. Harry Miner, owner of the theater, then a candidate for Congress, stood smiling in the lobby, pinkly barbered and flower-budded, while portraits of him were sprinkled on the walls, all cut low enough to show the *boutonnière*. To say that the play was a success is an absurd understatement. The setting of Act II, the interior of Brodie's saloon, was considered a triumph of realism—a real bar and fixtures, including that up-to-date device, a cash register, real painted women drinking real beer; and when Steve came on, the applause stopped the show. Bowery folk were evidently a musical lot, for they burst into song on the slightest provocation. In that act there was an aria in Bowery Italian, the Bridge Sweeper sang a moral ballad, Delaney the bum did a series of parodies and Brodie crowned the occasion by singing "My Pearl Is a Bowery Girl!" If memory fails not, his rendition of it ran, in part, something like this:

Of course ev'ry boy has a sweetheart,
An' some boys dey have two or t'ree.
Of all de goils in dis great city,
Dere is only one in it wit' me.
She lives wit' her folks on de Bow'ry,
A few doors away from Canal,
An' helps to support her old mother,
Does my little Bowery gal.

CHORUS:
My Poil is a Bowery goil,
She's all de woild to me.
She's in it wit' any de goils 'round de town,
An' a corkin' good-looker. See?
At Walhaller Hall she kills dem all,
As waltzing togedder we twoil.
She sets dem all crazy, a spieler, a daisy,
My Poil's a Bowery goil.

In that act Steve saved Hobart, the young aristocrat hero—hero only technically, for Brodie's was all the heroism—from arrest with the modest statement that the man who dared oppose the process of the law was "Steve Brodie, the King of the Bowery." But it was in Act III that the great climax arrived—first on the walkway of the bridge, whence Steve sees the caitiff tools of the villain Thurlow Bleeckman hurl the heroine Blanche into the river. Other horrified witnesses naturally turn to Steve as the only hope in the crisis. "There's one chance in a thousand that you can save her. Will you take it, Brodie?" "You bet your life I will!" the brave fellow answers elegantly, and over he goes. Quick change to the river level—not a tank, as it should have been, but a partially darkened, perfectly dry stage, with Steve plunging down through a trap, alighting with a muffled bump and eyes closed against the showers of rock salt thrown upward by stage hands from below to simulate spray. As the curtain fell, the house tottered with enthusiasm. A procession of ushers came down the aisles bearing floral offerings, which banked the whole front of the stage; and Steve appeared, astonishingly dry, considering the fact that he had just emerged from the river, and made a speech: "Friends and neighbors—I won't call you ladies and gents; everybody's that—I thank you. I feel proud of my reception on the old street."

Brodie was quite at ease, and justified his boast of histrionic talent, at least of a melodramatic sort. When he sang "My Pearl" in the second act, the audience would not let him go without an encore; so he finally obliged with a ballad which had been popular for some two years past, and over which the Bowery was inclined at that time to chuckle as a tribute to its own smartness and "toughness." It was called "The Bowery," and the comedian Harry Conor had first sung it in Charles M. Hoyt's comedy, *A Trip to Chinatown,* in 1892. Elderly folk will remember well how its popularity swept across the country in their youth.

* * * * *

When Brodie warbled it in 1894, the Bowery hadn't yet discovered that the song was detrimental to the street's prosperity. Ten years later complaints were arising that it had worked an injury, and today, veteran East Siders will swear that it was nothing else than that slanderous lampoon that "killed" the street. Poor Charlie Hoyt, before he lost his reason and died, was actually called upon to deny that he had harbored any animus against the Bowery, and that he wrote the thing only to provoke a laugh. And the fact was that he put into the doggerel only what was already common gossip in New York and in many places else besides. It is true that this immensely popular song spread the story of the Bowery's foibles more widely than ever. But for that matter, so did Steve Brodie and his play when they toured the country after their New York run, picturing low-browed Bowery thugs at their nefarious work and introducing to many who had never heard it before a pronunciation with which the language of most New Yorkers is generously tinged, together with a vocabulary which from that day to this has borne irremediably the categorical name of "Bowery dialect."

As Brodie became prosperous, he tried in vain to induce his old mother to move into a better lodging, one more worthy his own station in life. But she was as stubborn as flint and refused to leave the three little rooms where her old man had died and Steve had been born, and finally her son, in despair, went to the extremity of having her evicted. As she sat dolefully on the sidewalk amid her pathetic little household goods, with the neighbors around, commiserating her, Steve came opportunely along, hoping to find her in a more complaisant humor. But both the old lady and her neighbors fell upon him and berated him so soundly that he was glad to move back into her old rooms again, light a fire, and boil a pot of tea for her.

"And may the Divil fly away wid you, Steve," she grumbled, "but I'll niver go away from here until I'm waked and carried out."

Brodie knew the value of publicity—any kind of publicity—as well as Barnum had known it. "Say something about me," he begged McCardell and the other reporters whose beat was the Bowery. "Say I'm a crook, a faker, that I never jumped off a curbstone; anything, so you print my name"—for every time they did so, "the hayseeds and suckers" came in hordes, and the clang of the cash register made music in his ears.

He was a bright-faced, personable chap, always well groomed in his prosperity and with shirt front and plump fingers glittering with diamonds. Hero-worshipers were flattered if he would drink with them, and so he stood in front of his bar by the hour and drank whisky glasses of beer, mostly foam, so small that he thought they could not injure his health. His assertion that these tiny drinks for which customers paid at five cents each brought him in an average of thirty dollars a day is rather fantastic; but they were enough to bring on diabetes, and he died in 1901, aged somewhere from thirty-five to thirty-eight.

Rubberneck Stories [8]

. . . The show must go on for out-of-town visitors who wouldn't dream of leaving New York without a sightseeing tour of the missions and hostels on the Bowery—and the joss houses—carefully preserved replicas of Chinese temples—on Pell Street.

[8] From "The Cerfboard: The Bowery," by Bennett Cerf, *This Week Magazine,* August 3, 1952, p. 4. Copyright, 1952, by United Newspapers Magazine Corporation. New York.

In one teashop every busload of tourists is regaled with the story of old Loo Ching, the Chinese laundryman, who violated a fundamental law of his powerful Tong soon after his arrival in New York, and was condemned to death in a secret conclave. American law permitted no violent carrying out of the sentence, so the Tong leaders simply decreed, "We pronounce Loo Ching a dead man."

From that moment on, not one soul spoke to Loo Ching or revealed the slightest awareness of his presence. Shopkeepers ignored his attempts to buy or beg food. Children turned the other way when he shuffled down the street. His room was rented to another and his belongings deposited in a back alley. Loo Ching spoke not one word of English and knew nothing of American ways.

So each day he grew thinner and more desperate until finally his wasted body was found in the snow outside the teashop. His death sentence had been carried out.

Round the corner from the Chinese teashop long stood the Bowery eating place where once a penniless lad named Irving Berlin waited on table and picked out tunes on the piano for a living. Every guide included the spot in his itinerary before the building was torn down. The night I made the trip, our informant even declared that it was on that very battered piano that Berlin had composed "White Christmas."

One evening Irving Berlin himself decided to visit his old haunt. In a nostalgic glow, he seated himself at the piano and began to hum, "Oh, How I Hate to Get Up in the Morning." In the middle of the rendition, a busload of sightseers shuffled in, and their gravel-voiced guide began his spiel.

"Yes, sir, folks," he declared, "this is the very place the great Oiving Boilin began his career—singing songs on that same pianner you see standing in the corner. As a matter of fact, the song that Bowery bum is playin' this minute happens to be one of Boilin's own songs!"

The guide then walked over to the piano and dropped a heavy hand on Berlin's shoulder.

"Fella," he announced, "if Oiving Boilin could hear the way you're moiderin' one of his greatest songs, he'd toin over in his grave!"

Minutes of the Monthly Meeting of the Bowery Chamber of Commerce [9]

Gus Schaefer's hoary three-day growth of beard quivered as he rapped an ancient gavel on the long table. "Get away from that free lunch," he angrily warned two or three onlookers, "we ain't ready for that yet." Thus commenced the monthly meeting yesterday of the unchartered Bowery Chamber of Commerce in the "big room" of Sammy's Bowery Follies, 267 Bowery.

At least eighteen members of the chamber, each a veteran of many miles and years of "dinging," "boiling up" or just plain "bumming," sat in solemn session, ready to discuss and act upon such important projects as establishment of a Bowery College, requesting Mayor O'Dwyer for "improved, and more, city flophouses for this winter," and the coronation of Miss Hitchhiker of 1946. Sammy Fuchs, unofficial Mayor of the Bowery, welcomed the Chamber and prepared a table of cold cuts, potato salad and seidels of beer for his constituents.

First on the agenda was the election of new officers. Boxcar Betty, an ample ageless woman in gray pinstripe slacks, waved her cigar at the audience as she nominated Harry Baronian, editor of *The Bowery News,* for president. Following no rules of parliamentary procedure the chamber noisily accepted the suggestion. Similarly, Mayor Sammy was chosen secretary and Abie Wallstreet, described as a former stock market wizard, treasurer. That ended the election.

Brooklyn-born, sixty-two-year-old Gus Schaefer, who calls himself a "literary tramp" and freely quotes Spinoza and Marx, then proposed that "we ought to start a Bowery College. We gotta teach those scenery tramps the arts of dinging and stemming, and boiling up and jungling up techniques. Also back-door methods for getting lumps and setdowns."

(Rough translation of foregoing: "We have to teach those young green kids the arts of begging and panhandling, and cooking and camping out. Also how to get food at back doors.")

The project was set aside to be discussed in committee and brought up again next month.

[9] From "Bowery 'Chamber' Bravely Faces 'Dinging' and 'Boiling' Problems," *The New York Times,* August 23, 1946. Copyright, 1946, by the New York Times Company.

Then Miss Linda Folkard, who was born in Toronto nineteen years ago and who estimates that she has traveled—by thumb—15,000 miles, arose to be crowned Miss Hitchhiker of 1946. When Harry Slim shouted to ask if "being a young girl, she ever encountered trouble with strangers," she replied, "That's easy. I ask them if they like poetry. Then I recite to them. My own stuff mostly."

The question of housing an anticipated record number of hoboes who will migrate to New York this winter was discussed. By that time the Chamber was hungry, and Gus agreed it was "time for them cold cuts and beer."

Dave Gould, executive secretary of the organization, then described a number of types that still can be found along the storied hangout, under the shadows of the Third Avenue Elevated.

"Among them," he said, "are scizzorbills—small town characters who come to the Big City and can't make the grade; ex-newspaper men and writers who permanently lost their week-ends; doctors who wrote one prescription too many; brilliant eccentrics who find themselves unable to adjust to society's rules, and congenital jungle buzzards who are satisfied to live with and off their fellow misfits. Here and there are also found occasional philosophic types who are sincerely concerned with lifting the level of those who call the Bowery home."

He indicated the group around him. "There you are," he added, "see for yourself."

"Professor" [10]

The Bowery from Chatham Square to Cooper Union—a stretch of concrete known to its seedy denizens as "One Mile of Hell"—mourned yesterday the passing of one of its most illustrious residents, Walter Edwin Peck. His friends along Skid Row called him "Professor," a nickname which aptly suited the tall, gaunt gentleman's bearing and background. And a professor is what he once actually was.

In the Nineteen Twenties, after earning his Doctor of Philosophy degree from Oxford University in England, he taught at Columbia University and Hunter College. A romantic scandal abruptly ended his career in 1929, when he was forced to resign his assistant professorship

[10] From "'Leading Citizen' of Bowery Dead, Habitués Mourn Passing of Professor Peck, a Former College Teacher Here," *The New York Times,* January 16, 1954. Copyright, 1954, by the New York Times Company.

of English at Hunter. He landed on the Bowery not too long after that.

The professor's death was attributed to a heart attack. A policeman found him unconscious in a doorway and had him taken by ambulance to Columbus Hospital. His body was transferred to the Bellevue Morgue yesterday. If it is not claimed within the next day or so, authorities said, it will be buried in Potter's Field.

As word of the professor's death spread last night through a jungle of flophouses and saloons, his colleagues raised their glasses and bottles in one toast after another to his memory. A kind of wake was scheduled at the professor's favorite hangout, a bar called Mike's near Houston and Broome Streets, where the sixty-seven-year-old Bowery inhabitant often met with a group of Skid Row intelligentsia to discuss mathematics, physics, art, poetry, and literature.

Among the charter members of this literary circle—a sort of lower-depths version of the famous Round Table that met at the Algonquin Hotel some years ago—were many college graduates. They refer to their meeting place as "The Pitcher Joint," because it is there that they can order a pitcher of wine for only fifty cents.

Mr. Peck, once a prominent student of Shelley's poetry, was a familiar figure on the Bowery. He had gray flowing hair cut in the fashion of his romantic idol, Lord Byron. When he wasn't discussing literature, he earned some money selling and writing for *The Bowery News.* He also lectured frequently at the newspaper's office to visiting university sociological classes.

With his resonant voice, the Professor used to awe Bowery habitués with his dramatic recital of Kipling's "Mandalay." Harry Baronian, editor of *The Bowery News,* said last night that Mr. Peck numbered among his friends members of every Bowery social level—hoboes, floaters, and panhandlers—but did not fall into any of those categories. "He was in a class by himself," the editor remarked. "He was our most illustrious citizen."

A book he wrote in 1927, entitled *Shelley: His Life and Work,* received favorable notices in the book reviews of the metropolitan press. In 1925, he made a discovery for which he was hailed in literary circles the world over. Through his research in the Harvard Library he found in an old notebook two previously unpublished poems by Shelley. The two poems were "Translated from an Epigram on Plato" and "Verses Written on Receiving a Celandine in a Letter from England." A line from the latter might have served as his epitaph:

They were his hopes which he doth scorn.

Bowery Fairy Tales [11]

Christmas is bleak on the Bowery, warmed only fleetingly by the mission dinners and the boozily maudlin promises of the derelicts to "go home next year."

After the feasts have become news pictures captioned "Homeless Men Down Turkey 'n' Fixin's," the promises are forgotten. Next year becomes this year, and the splayed feet of the bums resume their aimless shuffling along gummy sidewalks until the next Christmas handout, the next spell of remorse. . . .

But there are shining exceptions to the hopeless Bowery pattern, and, fittingly, it is these which stand out in the Christmas memories of Captain Bert Noble. He's in charge of the Volunteers of America center at 65 East Houston Street, and a veteran worker among the displaced persons of Rummy Row.

Shortly after last Christmas, a proper lady (from Boston, Captain Noble guessed, and he was right) visited the center. She spread out a picture of "Homeless Men, etc.," taken there on the holiday and pointed to a shabby man wolfing turkey.

Explaining she had seen the picture in a Boston newspaper, she said, "That's my brother, I'm sure of it, even after twenty-five years. He started drinking after finishing Harvard Law School and soon disappeared. I want to take him home."

The Harvard man who'd made a career at the wrong bar was located in a Bowery flophouse. He went back to Boston with his sister, and last week Captain Noble heard from him. "I'm living with my sister now," he wrote, "and I've got a fine job. Tell everyone I'm having *this* Christmas dinner at home."

Call this one coincidence, luck or just another Miracle on East Houston Street. A few days before a recent Christmas, a shabby young man, shivering with cold, asked Captain Noble for help. He'd gone off on a long binge, lost his job, and had no home or friends. But he was sober.

A few hours later, a stranger type of client weaved his way into the center—after having erratically steered a gleaming Cadillac to a halt at the curb outside.

From his ensuing blurred monologue, Captain Noble gathered he'd

[11] From "Bleak Season of Maudlin Remorse Smogs Bowery," by Murray Robinson, *New York World-Telegram and The Sun,* December 23, 1955. Copyright, 1955, by New York World-Telegram Corp.

been to too many Christmas parties, could no longer drive, and wanted someone to see him home safely in his car. The shabby young man who had come to the center earlier was assigned to the job.

Next day, the Cadillac man, now brisk and clear-eyed, again showed at the center. He thanked Captain Noble, gave the Volunteers a plump check, and asked for the kid who had driven him home. He was told he was out looking for work. "Tell him to come see me," the man said. "He's got a job."

But Captain Noble's warmest Christmas memory is a fresh one. He got a call recently from a man who identified himself as an editor and said he wanted to serve as a street Santa Claus for the Volunteers for just a day. The surprised captain asked why, since editors are traditionally not the Santa type.

The editor explained that the first person he saw as a five-year-old when he came out of Grand Central Station with his mother on their first trip to New York was a Volunteer Santa. He was so kind to the little stranger in the Big Town that he always wanted to make other kids happy the same way.

Chuck Connors, Mayor of Chinatown [12]

The most celebrated of all the white hangers-on in Chinatown was Chuck Connors, who was born in Mott Street of a respectable Irish family and christened George Washington Connors. He acquired his sobriquet by his fondness for chuck steak, which in the wild days of his youth he cooked on a stick over gutter fires. A great deal was written about him in the newspapers of the period, especially after he had become the acknowledged King of the Lobbygows (or guides), and he was variously called the Sage of Doyers Street and the Bowery Philosopher. He was one of the originators of the dese, dem, and dose school of linguistic expression, and achieved a considerable reputation as a wit and story teller. In his teens and early twenties Chuck was a lightweight pugilist of much promise, but in his later years he became a bar fly and a tramp; he used to sit motionless for hours at a time in a chair tilted against a wall of the Chatham Club, while crowds of tourists gaped at him in awe.

[12] From *The Gangs of New York,* An Informal History of the Underworld, by Herbert Asbury, pp. 316–320. Copyright, 1927, 1928, by Alfred A. Knopf, Inc. New York.

It is very likely that most if not all of the smart sayings attributed to Chuck Connors had their inceptions in the brains of Frank Ward O'Malley and Roy L. McCardell, then writing for the *Sun* and the *World*. They found Connors a prolific source of copy; he would stand for anything, and he was always careful to read the newspapers and find out exactly what he was doing and thinking. When there was nothing else on which to build a feature story, there was always Chuck Connors, and with almost continuous publicity he was soon built up into a nationally known figure. His talk, or at least the talk that O'Malley and McCardell ascribed to him, found its way onto the stage, and even today is accepted as the sort of stuff that is spoken on the Bowery. Here is a typical specimen, published after Chuck had consented to grace the American theater in an act with Nellie Noonan, Queen of the Seventh Ward:

> To de woods fer mine. I bit so easy de jay must a t'ought he had a dead one on de string. Anyhow he had de show all fixed up an' me in a sleepin' car before even I turns me mind to de wagis for yours truly. Th' first time I goes to de box offis fer me dough I near drops dead. De guy behin' de bars passes me out a envelick wit' $15 in it.
>
> "W'at t' 'ell?" says I. "W'at t' 'ell is dis?" says I, like dat, to de bloke in de windy.
>
> "Dat's your wagis," says de guy.

Probably the only work that Chuck Connors ever did was during the year he courted the girl who later became his wife. He obtained a job as fireman on one of the little locomotives which hauled the elevated railroad trains before the lines were electrified, and remained a useful citizen until his wife died. Then he reverted to his former status and became a notable ornament of Chinatown. She had taught him to read and write, though imperfectly, and he delighted in displaying his erudition at the Chatham Club, reciting the alphabet backwards and answering questions about the multiplication table. Frequently he appeared in a Bowery skit at various theaters, and with road companies, and once was on the bill at Oscar Hammerstein's famous variety theater, the Victoria, on Broadway. Not long after the death of his wife Chuck was shanghaied by a Water Street crimp, and voyaged to England as an unwilling fireman. He promptly deserted when the ship docked, and remained for two weeks in Whitechapel, where he became enamoured of the manners and customs of the costermongers. He was particularly impressed by their dress, and when he returned to New York he had a Division Street tailor fashion a pair of wide sailor pants and a blue, square-cut pea jacket, adorned with two rows of very large pearl buttons. These he wore with a blue shirt and a sailor's silk scarf of vivid hue. He attempted to introduce a costermonger's pearl-buttoned cap as an article of gentlemen's wear in Chinatown and along the Bowery, but it failed to meet with favor and he soon abandoned it for the low-crowned black or brown derby which was then in vogue.

When he had been exploited by the newspaper reporters so that he had become well known, Chuck Connors organized the Chuck Connors Club and gave rackets at Tammany Hall several times a year. He became a power in the politics of Chinatown and the Bowery, controlling the votes of lesser Lobbygows, and was frequently consulted by such shining lights of Tammany Hall as Big and Little Tim Sullivan. Both of these statesmen were honorary members of the Chuck Connors Club, as were also Al Smith, [since] Governor of New York; Richard Mansfield, the actor; John L. Sullivan, champion pugilist; Honest Johnny Kelly, the gambler; Walt B. McDougall, the cartoonist; Jim Corbett, Bob Fitzsimmons, and many others. For many years during the latter part of his life Chuck Connors lived in a two-room apartment at No. 6 Dover Street, near the East River, in a tenement house which was called Fox's Flats because it had been constructed by Richard K. Fox, owner of the *Police Gazette*. He never paid any rent, and the fact that Fox made no effort to dispossess him gave rise to the report that the publisher had given him the flat rent free so long as he lived. But Chuck was seldom at home, except to sleep there occasionally; he spent his entire time in Chinatown, and generally could be found in the Chatham Club at any hour of the day or night.

At the age of sixty-one, in 1913, Chuck Connors died in the Hudson Street Hospital. The doctors said he had heart disease, but really it was neglect that killed him. He became old and garrulous and uninteresting; he complained of rheumatism, and frequently had to stay away from his accustomed haunts for several days at a time. The reporters, having exhausted him as a source of interesting copy, dropped him, and without publicity Chuck Connors was soon forgotten. The final nail was driven into his cross when Frank Salvatore, an Italian bootblack known as Mike the Dago, began to call himself Young Chuck Connors and organized the Young Chuck Connors Association. He acquired political influence as the prestige of the original Chuck declined, and when he announced that he would give a grand ball in opposition to the affair of the old Chuck Connors Club, the one-time King of the Lobbygows consented to abdicate, or at least share his throne with the newcomer. It was agreed that on the program of

Young Chuck's ball the name of Chuck Connors should appear as a patron immediately after that of Jim Jeffries, then heavyweight champion of the world, and before the name of Jim Corbett.

Chuck lingered on for several years after that, but his heart was not in his work, and finally he died. He was buried by members of the Press Club, and of the thousands upon thousands of persons who had known him fewer than forty attended his funeral.

The Mayor of the Fish Market [13]

Mr. Flood visits the [Fulton] fish market every weekday morning. He rises at five, has a cup of black coffee in the Hartford dining room, lights a cigar, and begins a leisurely tour of the fish stalls, the oyster sheds, the flounder-filleting houses, the smoking lofts, and the piers. When he reaches Fulton Street, the pandemonium in the market invigorates him. He throws his shoulders back, sniffs the salty air, and rubs his palms together. To him, the reek of the fish houses is not unpleasant. "I'll tell you a valuable secret," he once said. "The Fulton Fish Market smell will cure a cold within twenty minutes. Nobody that works in the market ever has a cold. They don't know what a cold is. The fishmongers are afraid the general public will find this out. It's too crowded around here as it is, and if the public took to coming down here to cure their colds, there wouldn't be room enough to turn around in." When making his tour, he dresses like a boss fishmonger, wearing a full-length white apron and knee-high rubber boots. The streets down there, as well as the floors of the stalls, are constantly being hosed down, and he believes in heeding the old market proverb, "Keep your feet dry and you'll never die." He goes first to the piers and looks on as the trawlers, draggers, and scallop dredges are unloaded. The fishermen treat him with respect and answer all his questions. They seem to think that he is an official of some kind. They call him Pop or Commissioner. One morning I was standing on the Fulton

[13] From *Old Mr. Flood,* by Joseph Mitchell, pp. 18–23. Copyright, 1943, 1944, 1945, 1948, by Joseph Mitchell. New York: Duell, Sloan and Pearce.

Originally published in *The New Yorker.*

Mr. Flood is not one man; combined in him are aspects of several old men who work or hang out in Fulton Fish Market, or who did in the past. I wanted these stories to be truthful rather than factual, but they are solidly based on facts.—J. M.

Street pier with Edmond Irwin, supervisor of the Fishery Council, when Mr. Flood came poking along. He looked down into an unloading trawler from New Bedford and yelled, "Hey, Captain, step over here!" The captain stopped what he was doing, obediently crossed his deck, and peered up at Mr. Flood, who asked, "What you got today, Captain?"

"Nothing to speak of, sir," the captain said. "Just a load of flounders —blackbacks and yellowtails."

"Fine, fine, Captain," said Mr. Flood. "You got enough filly of sole in that load for five thousand dinners. Where'd you go this trip?"

"We was up north of Brown's Bank."

"Up in The Gully?"

"That's right. We was up in The Gully."

"Fine, fine, Captain!" said Mr. Flood, beaming and rubbing his hands. "That's just fine!"

Mr. Flood moved on down the pier. The captain stared after him for a moment, obviously puzzled, and then turned to Mr. Irwin and said, "Ed, who in hell is that man, anyway? Does he work for the government, or what?"

"It's hard to say," Mr. Irwin said. "All I know he's an old boy who's trying to live to be a hundred and fifteen years old by eating fish."

"God bless us!" said the captain. "How far along is he?"

"He's way past ninety," Mr. Irwin said.

"I declare to Jesus!" the captain said. "Well, we live and learn. Maybe I ought to start eating fish."

After Mr. Flood has inspected the boats, he goes into the shed of the Fishmongers Association. He listens to the blasphemous haggling between the fishmongers and the buyers from the retail fish stores, asks scores of questions, peers into bins, hefts and admires a striped bass here and a red snapper there, and carries market gossip from one stall to the next. He has so much curiosity that a few of the fishmongers look the other way when they see him coming, but the others treat him considerately and sometimes introduce him to visitors as the Mayor of the Fish Market. Presently he leaves the shed and steps into one of the filleting houses on South Street and helps himself to a bucket of gurry, or fish scraps, with which to feed some one-legged gulls that he has adopted. The fish market supports a flock of four or five hundred gulls and at least two dozen of them are one-legged. "This condition," Mr. Flood says, "is due to the fact that sea gulls don't understand traffic lights. There's a stretch of South Street running through the market that's paved with cobblestones. And every so often during the morning rush a fish drops off a truck and is ground up by the wheels and packed down tight into the cracks between the cobbles. The gulls go wild when they see this. They wait until traffic gets halted by a red light, then drop out of the sky like bats out of hell and try to pull and worry the fish from between the cobbles. They're stubborn beasts. They get so interested they don't notice when the light changes and all of a sudden, wham bang, the heavy truck traffic is right on top of them. Some get killed outright. Some get broken wings and flop off and hide somewhere and starve to death. Those that lose only one leg are able to keep going, but the other gulls peck them and treat them as outcasts, and they have a hard, hard time." The gimpy gulls are extremely distrustful, but Mr. Flood has been able to make friends with a few of them. When he strides onto a pier toting a bucket of gurry they circle down and surround him. One or two will eat from his hands.

Mr. Flood finishes feeding his gulls around nine o'clock. Then he is ready for his first drink of the day. He is opposed to drinking alone—he says it leads to the mumbles—so he proceeds along South Street, hunting for company. He often goes to the freshwater branch of the market, in Peck Slip, and invites Mrs. Birdy Treppel, a veteran fishwife, to step into a bar and grill near her stand and have one. "I *do* need a little something," she usually says, "to thaw me out." Mr. Flood and Mrs. Treppel are old friends. She fascinates him because she is always cold. Mrs. Treppel specializes in pike, carp, buffaloes, red horses, and sturgeon, and her stand, a one-bin affair, half on the sidewalk and half in the gutter, is in Peck Slip, just below Water Street, right in the path of the wind from the harbor. "I am beautifully situated," she says, "on the corner of Influenza Street and Pneumonia Slip." In the wintertime, Mrs. Treppel lets an assistant handle the bulk of her trade, while she keeps a fire jumping in an old oil drum beside her stand, feeding it with barrel staves and discarded fish boxes. She says that it doesn't do much good. She hovers near the fire, shivering, with her arms in her apron, which she rolls up and uses as a muff. She has a nervous habit of hopping up and down and stamping her feet. She does this in the heat of summer as well as in the winter; she can't seem to stop. She appears to be unusually corpulent, but she says that this is misleading. "I'm really a thin little thing, nothing but skin and bones," she says, "but I got on twelve layers of clothes—thirteen, counting my shimmy. If you was to see me undressed, you wouldn't know me." One morning I was going through the market with Mr. Flood. We paused beside Mrs. Treppel's fire and he said,

"Birdy, tell the man how cold it gets in Peck Slip." "Well, son, I tell you," she said, hopping up and down as she talked, "if you went up to the North Pole in the dead of December and stripped to the drawers and picked out the biggest iceberg up there and dug a hole right down to the heart of it and crawled in that hole and put a handful of snow under each arm and sat on a block of ice and et a dish of ice cream, why, you wouldn't be nowhere near as cold as you'd be in Peck Slip in a sheepskin coat with a box fire in the gutter."

Washington Market [14]

"The beans how much?" the man asked at the corner of Jay and Washington Streets soon after one A.M. today. "How much the beans?"

"Five-fifty," said the man in the long white coat. "Five-fifty, don't tell me a cent less."

"One thing I'll tell you," the buyer said. "Good-by I'll tell you. Not a cent less, eat them yourself."

He picked a bean from the hamper, snapped it in two, sucked the juice from his knuckle and moved cautiously through the narrow sidewalk, picking his way north to Harrison Street.

Here is Washington Market, on the third day of summer [1947], stretching north from Barclay to Beach Streets, ablaze with lights and alive with people: buyers and sellers, drivers and handymen; a thousand trucks and as many horses.

Smell Washington Market in the hours from midnight to six A.M. with wares piled twenty feet above the sidewalk.

Smell scallions from Long Island, and watermelon from Georgia. Smell cantaloupe and honeydews from Texas, and cauliflower from California, green leaves hiding meat as white as the driven snow. Smell Roman Beauty apples and Delicious apples and hard, blood-red Winesaps from Wenatchee, Washington.

"How many, how many, *how many?*" yelled the man at the Georgia corn, one huge hand slapping the sack.

"One is too much," sniffed the buyer with the benzedrine inhaler.

[14] From "In Washington Market at 1 A.M.," by Norman Katkov, *The New York World-Telegram,* June 25, 1947. Copyright, 1947, by New York World-Telegram Corp.

See Washington Market with the strawberries from Germantown, New York, in Columbia County. Row and row and crate on crate of quarts of berries, bleeding a little where they've been squashed, waiting for tonight's shortcake.

See Bing cherries from Oregon, twelve rows of matched rubies, sparkling in the light, splendid in the night for today's pie.

Look at the peas from California, heavy, bulging pods, sweating a little from the refrigerator, and the Pennsylvania asparagus in the triangular boxes, standing primly behind the slats.

Look at the Santa Rosa plums, sweet and succulent, juice trickling on your lips, and the Green Gage plums and the Florida eggplant, awkward vegetables with the silk-smoothed skin of royal purple for today's Parmigiani.

"Call us night hawks down here," said Reginald Bell, 102 Convent Avenue. "I'm twenty years on the job," he added, wrapping rope around the bulging truck. "Eleven to eight, there's a whole life down here nobody knows anything about. Five days a week. No market Saturday morning."

Listen to the trucks. Their only gear in the jammed street is low and the groans never abate as the trucks inch forward. Trucks from Manhattan and Brooklyn and all the boroughs.

"I got five hampers squash!" a man shouted. "Five squash, the best."

"Your opinion," snorted the buyer and bent to the hamper, pressing thumbs against the skin, determining ripeness.

Thread through to the green gardens: Head lettuce and leaf lettuce, giant stalks of Pascal celery, spinach dirty from the field, squat lima beans, dill and parsley, mint and endive and cucumbers.

The sellers wear white coats, starched crisp as surgeon's trappings, for Washington Street is their operating theater and when dawn breaks, their frocks will carry the blood of the fruit they sell.

"Whatdysay huckleberries?" asked the man, lifting the cover from the crate, peering at swollen fruit, overripe.

"Buy 'em as is."

"As is you keep them," said the man. "As is take them to the wife for jam."

The man in the white coat reached over suddenly, slamming the cover shut with one stroke of his hammer, thrusting his face at the buyer's. "For advice I'll go on the radio," he snarled. "Advice I don't want on Washington Street."

Garment Center [15]

Five blocks long, three blocks wide, the garment center of New York is a world in itself, a world apart.

Sandwiched between 35th and 40th Streets, from Broadway to Ninth Avenue, the ready-to-wear industry provides some 300,000 people with their daily bread.

Thousands more work in the "suburbs," the streets south and avenues east, the peripheral area that feeds the trade its raw materials and trimmings, belts, buttons and bows, zippers, labels, linings—and everything else that goes to make up a dress, a suit, a coat.

It's the largest industry in the city, the largest in the state, tenth largest in the nation—and like no other on earth.

* * * * *

And it's a small world, really, with small-town talk, where nearly everyone knows everyone else—or knows somebody who knows something about somebody else.

"How's the wife, how're the kids? How's your mother's liver?"

"I want you should see my latest grandchild. Such a boy!"

"So when I meet him, he says this is my cousin. Cousin, my elbow!"

It's a jungle where the weak get slaughtered and the strong build empires. And advice is for free.

"All it takes is one. One good style and you're set."

"For how long? One bad season and you're through."

"So what? So you start again. . . ."

"It's timing, I tell you. If your timing is right, you're in."

"It's this lousy weather. How can you expect fall reorders when it's so damn hot for so damn long?"

It's a rat-race where nothing and nobody stand still.

Except the traffic.

[15] From "Fabulous Seventh Avenue, Garment Industry: A World within a City," by Muriel Fischer, *New York World-Telegram and The Sun,* August 23, 1955. Copyright, 1955, by New York World-Telegram Corp.

"C'mon, buddy, move it over."

"Grease it, boy, you can make it."

It's operation clockwork. Now is the time to design the line. Buy your fabrics early, before it's too late. Cut and cut and cut. And if you get stuck, them's the risks of the trade. Everybody's got to gamble.

Deadline for samples, for showings and shipments. And it's overtime for the workers when the deadlines draw near.

But when the two hands of the clock join in the split second of noon, the entire industry puts in a pin. Sewing machines pause in mid-seam. Cutting tables lie draped in silence. It's lunchtime.

And now the elevators bob up and down, carrying workers to the streets. Like an army of bees from an overturned hive, they pour forth. To sit in the cafeterias and shmooze. To squint in the sun, have a smoke—and shmooze.

The cutters, the sewing-machine operators, the pattern graders, the basters, the finishers, the fellerhands, the pressers, the pinkers—they flock to their favored spots along Seventh Avenue and make with the talk.

"At your age you shouldn't be working so hard."

"I'm asking you to tell me how old I am."

"So he tells me cut against the grain. Do I tell him his business he should tell me mine?"

"So when's the wedding?"

Around tables in Dubrow's, Gross' Dairy and the Midtown Cafeteria, world issues are settled, grievances discussed—and sometimes is whispered a matter of the boss' business.

"So, you hear, he builds a kitchen right in the plant. So the help should eat better? No! So they shouldn't be able to tell some one from next door what's with him."

A few minutes before one, the dictating hands of the clock signal the flock to return. One last glance at the sun, one more puff—and back they march.

And now the bosses eat. At Dunhall's and Morgen's, at Lou Siegel's and Al Cooper's, at Club 1407.

The talk is light and noncommittal. The frowns disappear when a competitor is near. And business is always good, good—never better. It's a world of sweeping success stories. A boy who sweeps floors gets promoted to shipping clerk, a shipping clerk becomes a salesman, a salesman teams up with a pattern-maker—and a partnership is born.

After all, "if I can do it for him, I can do it for myself!"

Partners are found at the cutting table, in the elevator, next door, upstairs, in the family, or in *Women's Wear Daily*. A three-line ad for three days costs $6.48 and 55,000 subscribe to the industry's own newspaper.

It's a world where they quibble over pennies, but dig deep into the pockets to give dollars to the poor.

It's a world of sweat and worry. Worry if you don't make it and if you do—worry you won't next year.

And it's a world of poets.

"Just think. Somewhere out West a sheep is grazing on the mountainside. Soon his wool goes to the mill to become fabrics. And here, from piece goods, a design, a form, a pattern—cutting, grading, sewing, lining, trimming, pressing and shipping—a coat is made. Tell me, when a woman goes into the store, tries on and buys, does she think of all this?"

The Great Columbus Day Parade Feud[16]

The first Columbus Day parade in New York City was held in 1900, under the auspices of the Benevolent Order of the Sons of Columbus. Columbus was a son of the north, born in Genoa, and no patriotic northerner could wholly ignore the anniversary of his discovery of America. On that day, some of the clubs and lodges of northern Italians condescended to join in a parade with the lodges, clubs, mutual aid societies, fraternal organizations, etc., etc. (there was one for every city, town, province, hamlet in Italy), of the southerners to make this the biggest and noisiest Italian celebration in New York City.[17]

* * * * *

. . . On . . . October 12, 1909, . . . Governor Hughes . . . at long last signed a bill, introduced by Big Tim Sullivan, making Co-

[16] From *Papa's Table d'Hôte*, by Maria Sermolino, pp. 90–92, 96–100. Copyright, 1952, by Maria Sermolino. Philadelphia and New York: J. B. Lippincott Company.

[17] "Campanilismo" is a patriotic concept even narrower than chauvinism. It was felt to an exaggerated degree by the Italians who emigrated to America about the time papa did. Each individual felt bound not so much to Italy, the country, but rather to his own town or village, of which the campanile, or church bell-tower, is the symbol.—M. S., *ibid.*, p. 89.

lumbus Day a legal holiday in New York State. Up to that time there had been no political connotations in the Columbus Day celebrations. They had been gala events spurred by patriotic fervor and the desire of parading and merrymaking. In addition, the festivities of the day had a charitable aspect because the profits from the picnic and bazaar held in the afternoon and the ball held in the evening were donated to the Columbus Hospital, founded by the now canonized Mother Cabrini. With the Governor's declaration, that henceforth Columbus Day would be an American holiday, the celebration seems to have lost its sincerity and became a tool of politicians and glory-seekers. The following year the parade was a fiasco, and papa, who had never taken part in a Columbus Day parade before, elected that year in which to be a participant.

Papa, Mr. Preti and the other ten members they had enrolled agreed to pay their annual dues of twelve dollars in advance so that the newly organized Partinengo lodge might make an honorable showing in the parade. . . .

* * * * *

Several days before the parade, the Partinengo lodge was all set to play its part. The priest had blessed the flags. Mr. Preti had "baptized" his uniform by wearing it while drinking several gallons of good wine with his lodge brothers. Each member had written his name in the empty space on [his] badge and they had agreed on their formation. But in the Italian press and in the secret sessions of the old established lodges a battle of major proportions was developing.

In every previous year there had been an understandable amount of bickering over the selection of a Grand Marshal to lead the parade, but a compromise had always been possible because the choice had always been between one Italian and another. The past dissensions seemed like petty family squabbles when compared with the current fracas. This year matters were not so simple. Fundamental principles were at stake. Through the chicanery and conniving of a few politically ambitious lodge officers, a foreigner, none other than the Irishman James March, had been secretly nominated and elected as Grand Marshal. Here was an insult which no loyal Son of Columbus could stomach. Parade behind an Irishman? When an Italian had led the whole world to a new land? Folly! Had they not sufficient leaders within their own ranks? Did they have to choose one from an *Irish* camp? In vain did the committee, who had appointed James March, argue that the honor had been tendered to him in recognition for his efforts in behalf of the bill making Columbus Day a legal holiday. Without the support of the Republican party in New York City, of which Mr. March was the leader, the bill would never have been passed. The honor of being Grand Marshal was the least that the Sons of Columbus could bestow on Mr. March to show their gratitude.

But the old guard in the Benevolent Society of the Sons of Columbus denounced the selection of Mr. March as treason. They fought his appointment up to the day before the parade and then, when they realized that the pro-March faction would not budge, they bolted and proclaimed they would hold their own parade led by the loyal Italian, Cav. Vito Contessa. But their defiance proved to be an empty gesture. Their eleventh-hour application for a permit to parade along the customary route—from south of Washington Square, through the Square, up Fifth Avenue to Fifty-eighth Street and then west to Columbus Circle—was rejected because the Irish-loving traitors had forestalled them, and two parades could not be permitted along the same route. They then mapped out a secondary route up First Avenue, but their hearts were not in it.

The controversy created a schism in every one of the five hundred or more independent Italian societies which customarily, at least on this one day, rallied behind one leader. A few of the lodges reached a decision which enabled them to march, as a unit, behind one or the other leader, but most of them did not. Only about two thousand joined the dissenting group up First Avenue. In the Fifth Avenue group there were less than twelve thousand men. The previous year there had been fifty thousand. The rest, however, did not stay home but jampacked the sidewalks along the line of march.

Papa and the other Partinengo lodge members had no strong feelings one way or the other, but since their fine new equipment would be displayed to best advantage along the Fifth Avenue route they decided to march behind the Irishman.

* * * * *

We did not hear about the parade's riotous finale until the next day when papa, nursing a bump as big as a beefsteak tomato on his head, told us about it.

It seems that as the marchers in the Fifth Avenue parade turned west on Fifty-eighth Street and approached Columbus Circle, they were greeted by a wildly shouting mob of the anti-Irish faction marching east from the circle towards them. The two factions met head-on. Lodge brother fought against lodge brother for possession of flags and standards. Men who had never drawn a sword instinctively pulled their costume swords out of their sheaths and used them to beat up their opponents. Officers in resplendent uniforms tumbled from their dray horses. Papa and his group were trying to push their way out of the melee—after all, they were a new lodge and there were no old-timers to question their right to march behind an Irish leader if they so pleased—when the police came galloping through the crowd, swinging their sticks this way and that. The police quickly put an end to the fighting, but not before papa had been hit on the head.

"And I'm quite sure it was an Irish policeman's stick," papa said with a that's-gratitude-for-you kind of air.

To Grandma, however, the episode was merely further proof of a deep-rooted conviction.

"That's what comes," she said, "of getting mixed up in a parade with a lot of *caffoni.*" [18]

The Four Faces of Greenwich Village [19]

Greenwich Village has four faces. There is that which it turns to the tourists—a place of interesting shops in which items ranging from rare foods to grotesque jewelry are on display, sleazy night clubs offering slightly off-color entertainment at outrageous prices, restaurants, often superior, which specialize in foreign dishes, outdoor art exhibits, sidewalk cafés, picturesque tree-shaded alleyways, the former homes of the great and the near-great literary figures of past decades. The tourist, too, may wander into the fag joints and bow-tie clubs, but unless he shows that he is an initiate, the "gaiety" will cease during his presence. As for the bars, each boasts of a few "characters"—eccentrics and lesser lights of the world of theater, art, and writing.

The Village presents another face to those who work and live there—the hard-working artists, writers, musicians, actors, and business people with artistic and literary leanings. These are men and women who have fallen in love with the Village's crooked streets, its small-

[18] . . . The uninformed Italians of northern Italy dubbed every one south of the Tiber River a *caffone,* meaning loutish, uncivilized, rough-mannered.—M. S., *ibid.*, p. 88.

[19] From *Monkey on My Back,* by Wenzell Brown, pp. 199-201. Copyright, 1953, by Greenberg, Publisher. New York.

town atmosphere, and its sudden glimpses of unexpected beauty. When a book has been finished, a portrait painted, or a play has closed its run, there is cause for celebration. At these parties, there are guests who drink too much and maybe a few who make a production of smoking reefers. Some will show up in eccentric garb or bring along a favored Village character. Even this type of mild Bohemianism is dying out as the old houses are being torn down to make way for swank apartments and university buildings. High rentals, too, have driven away those who are struggling for a living in the field of the arts. More and more the Village has been taken over by the successful, the moderately well-off.

The Village shows still a third face to the foreign-language groups, mostly Italian, who have settled there. These people love their homes, cherish their native tongues, and have little to do with those who are not of their own national background. The Italian restaurants, bakeries, and fruit stalls serve all comers, but those who run them have a special price for their own people. From the outside, the homes of the Italians may look like slums, but inside they are rich with color, warmth, and comfort. They represent the most solid element in the Village but their pattern of life is rarely shared with the outsider.

But the final face of the Village is one of unrelieved sordidness. Over the years, the Village has drawn to it the homosexual and the lesbian, the sadist and the masochist, the exhibitionist and the voyeur, sex perverts and psychopaths of every description. There are shabby bars that teem with prostitutes of both sexes and every race, "rose-tinted" rooms where the jaded may seek new thrills, and "joy clubs" where "caps" that sell in Harlem for fifty cents cost ten dollars.

Luke O'Connor's [20]

In those naïve days of 1895, when Village Square was a grimy triangle where Sixth Avenue, Greenwich Avenue, West Eighth Street, and West Ninth all foregathered under the shadow of the unsavory Jefferson Market Courthouse and Detention Home and the clanking, swaying El

[20] From *Greenwich Village, Today & Yesterday,* Photographs by Berenice Abbott, Text by Henry Wysham Lanier, pp. 125–127. Copyright, 1949, by Harper & Brothers. New York.

railroad structure, an upright and upstanding Irishman, Luke O'Connor, had a bar where Christopher Street and Greenwich Avenue crossed in angled disregard of the new-fangled Commissioners' Plan for north-and-south streets.

One need only look at the photograph that lies before me to understand the whole setup: mustached Luke O'Connor and his Irish cronies, lined up beside the shoeshine stand in front of the Columbian Gardens Restaurant and Bar, solemnly confronting the camera for the future record. A grand, self-respecting Irishman, Luke O'Connor, known throughout the Village as a tavern keeper who dispensed honest beers, ales, and stronger liquors. Just how this favorite resort for thirsty folk came to be nicknamed the "Working Girl's Home," nobody seems to know. Possibly it was a natural expression of the fact that a self-supporting young woman could have her restorative glass there and be as safe from annoyance as she wanted to be. (Archangels could do no more than that for the independent female.)

This Luke was quite a person. He used to cash checks for everybody, apparently. "One evening I found myself uptown without a dime," said a man who knew him admiringly. "I did have a check for $150. There wasn't even a nickel in my pocket. So I took a cab down to the Columbian Bar, almost hidden under the Elevated there. Though I didn't really know him well, Luke cashed the check without a moment's hesitation.

"I looked at him. 'You do this all the time?'

" 'Oh, once in a while, when a man needs it.'

" 'Don't the checks ever bounce?'

"Luke just grinned."

There was an odd Italian barboy, Julius, who was always talking to himself. Every now and then these two would quarrel and Luke would fire him. Presently Julius, who couldn't work for anybody else, would sneak in unobtrusively, and Luke, as unobtrusively, would take him back.

One of his peculiarities was that he couldn't bear noise in his place. There was a ramping Irish regular, McDonnell, who played the flageolet when he got uplifted. Luke would stand it till he'd explode and threaten to throw McDonnell out for good and all. Then the big fellow would pocket the offending flageolet and start singing—while Julius, behind the bar, would join in. Between them they'd drive the boss pretty near out of his mind.

"Altogether that was quite a place," says the artist, with a look of reminiscent regret on his face.

One September day there walked into this bar an English boy of seventeen. I've always suspected that he had jumped ship—doubtless with every justification considering what those times offered to a junior in a merchant vessel. Anyhow, he was broke or close to it; his plans were as indefinite as the future; he could do with a square meal and a tankard of ale.

Shrewd-eyed Luke looked him over. He knew quality when it stood before him. He tested this specimen by offering him a job as porter—which meant swamping out the barroom, helping with anything that needed to be done, plenty of work, in return for a living, and the experience this odd Herefordshire boy was evidently seeking.

For a year young John Masefield cheerfully did "potboy's" work in the Columbian Bar, while he and Luke developed a silent respect and liking for each other.

Then, in a September dawn, the boy took the Elevated to 155th Street, and from there the train to Yonkers—in quest of new experience in a great carpet factory, which he found not nearly so humanly satisfying as sweeping floors, and washing out spittoons, and being virtually an adopted son of the Irish proprietor of the Columbian Bar.

* * * * *

After he became England's most famous poet, he came to the United States to lecture. I had heard from the newspapermen who acted as liaison between him and the press that he was naturally somewhat perturbed to find that what most of the besieging reporters really wanted to know was just how often he cleaned out the spittoons in Luke O'Connor's Columbian Bar and how he felt about all that now.

The House of Frustration [21]

One block west of Madame Branchard's chambers [at 61 Washington Square South], Papa Strunsky operated the famous House of Frustration, where any one who paid room rent was under grave suspicion of insanity. Albert Strunsky always had what his daughter, Mrs. Emily

[21] From "Anything Goes in Greenwich Village," by Stanley Frank, *The Saturday Evening Post,* Vol. 223 (September 16, 1950), No. 12, pp. 125–126. Copyright, 1950, by the Curtis Publishing Company. Philadelphia.

Paley, calls "a pathological compulsion for charity." Years after arriving from Russia when he was nineteen, he spent Sundays at Ellis Island helping immigrants get settled in the new country.

Strunsky had a great, consuming appreciation of beauty which was given singular expression after he made a comfortable stake in the wine business. In 1921 he leased from Columbia University a square block of tenements and converted them into rooms for people vaguely associated with the arts, and no questions asked. He never asked for rent, either. The worst that happened to tenants who didn't pay was banishment to Strunsky's Siberia, a maze of rabbit warrens deep in the decaying innards of the property. His children regularly sent out bills and Strunsky padded after them, assuring his indignant roomers they weren't obliged to pay and soothing ruffled feelings by installing a skylight for an artist or buying a bottle of inspiration for a writer.

In 1932 Strunsky created a terrific sensation by dispossessing one Ernest Gutman, a sculptor, for nonpayment of rent. Gutman took the case to court, and the judge asked Strunsky one question after listening to both sides.

"None of your tenants seem to pay rent," his honor observed. "Why are you making Gutman leave because he is three months in arrears?"

"That's not the reason!" the old gentleman snapped. "I've kicked him out because he's a lousy artist!"

"Papa always carried a big wad of money, with each bill folded separately in the middle," Mrs. Paley recalls. "When I asked him why, he explained it was easier to peel off bills for handouts. He said it might embarrass a man to wait while he counted out the money."

Strunsky's philanthropies led to the default of the property in 1939. When he died broke three years later, his children found he had lost $100,000 in the House of Frustration.

Bob Clairmont and His Group [22]

Sellers McKees Chandler was a Pennsylvanian millionaire of the family after which the towns of McKees Rocks and McKeesport were named. He was a member of a rich men's club in Pittsburgh where a dreamy

[22] From *Garrets and Pretenders,* A History of Bohemianism in America, by Albert Parry, pp. 316–319. Copyright, 1933, by Covici Friede, Publishers. New York. By permission of Crown Publishers, Inc.

youth slaved his precious days away in the garb of a soda clerk. One day, in the middle 1920's, Chandler went into the club swimming pool and could not get out. He was drowning. Robert Clairmont, the dreamy clerk, saw the millionaire's trouble, plunged into the pool, and saved him. The grateful steel magnate conveniently died shortly after the rescue, having willed to Clairmont $350,000. Bob moved to New York, took journalism courses in Columbia, and then settled in Greenwich Village. By that time he had learned the game of Wall Street and was running up his fortune to the million mark. Rich men's sons at Columbia offered to effect his entry into fashionable society, but Clairmont was set on remaining amid the long hair and wild ideas of the Village.

Bob wrote good poetry, knew good music, and financed a few impudent but not cross-grained Village magazines, which stressed esthetics instead of economics. He leased a luxurious studio-apartment in West Fourth Street, which had been, only a short time before, vacated by Margaret Wilson, the novelist, the late President's daughter.

Bob walked, even on the frostiest days and nights, without a hat, and often looked the part of a penniless poet. His features were good to gaze at, and girls took pity on him, often loving him for the human being that he was, oblivious of his riches. Often, they offered to pay for his restaurant checks. The publishers of the Dial Press also took him for a poor poet, and paid him for a book of his poems.

But the news spread of the rich poet who had come to live in the Village. Soon, there was a circle of hungry eyes and mouths around Bob, the sugar daddy. The legend was that he fed the poets and the painters when they were hungry, paid their bills and their rent, took them with him on his rounds of the Village jazz-joints and Harlem dives. He spent as much as $10,000 on a single Christmas party, inviting some of the best Broadway and Harlem entertainers to his studio. But he would not allow any rich dullards into his Village group; the spending and the entertainment were only for those who could create or at least talk brilliantly. The elect of the Village, on getting into Clairmont's group, hailed the era as a renaissance and a millennium.

Bob's parties would last for three days and three nights with no intermission, having no connection with the outside world except for telephone orders for more wine. The studio was full but not overcrowded. Poets wrote poetry at the tables, artists drew, some guests recited, others discoursed on philosophy, and everybody theorized or practiced love. The five-gallon jug of wine was replenished now and then; some guests went to sleep in a corner for an hour or two, but others continued to drink and declaim with nary a nap. Sometimes, Bob Clairmont would leave his studio, but the guests stayed on, and the session flared forth without the host.

Often, after such parties or mere visits, Bob would discover that some of his rarest volumes were missing—and a few days or weeks later he would come across his own books in a Second or Fourth Avenue bookshop, his signature still gracing the flyleaf. Going through his wardrobe, he would find his ties and shirts and socks missing. Once, on coming home after a fortnight's visit in the country, he found the lock on his door broken. Entering, he saw pillows and blankets half-torn on his rich but bespattered carpets; he noticed a multitude of cigarette holes in his fine davenport; he sadly beheld his remaining books scattered on the floors, some of them mutilated. The closets were cleaned out, the chairs broken, the typewriter gone. There had been a grand party in his studio these two weeks while he was out of town. The party was arranged, without Clairmont's permission, by Hans Stengel, the cartoonist. It was Stengel's suicide party; he had hanged himself during this escapade.

The landlord was aghast. He sent Bob a special delivery letter, notifying him that the apartment was rented to one person and not to an army. Clairmont had to move. In his new place, on Perry Street, for a time, he tried not to answer the bell, but his insistent friends lifted each other to his apartment with the help of the ice chute.

Clairmont became abusive. He said that his boy friends were insincere in their quest for true art, that all they wanted was money. He said that the Villagers owed him as much as $25,000 in small loans ranging from five to fifty dollars. But the Villagers said that all this was bunk, that Bob had talked more about giving money to art and artists than he actually gave. Whatever the truth, there was a lot of drinking, noise, poetry writing, and love making. For all we know, the last real Bohemia of the Village may have been Bob Clairmont's.

This great hoopla went on for four or five years, all through the middle and late 1920's. Then came the famous Wall Street crash. Bob Clairmont lost all on that Black Thursday. He tried to be nonchalant to the reporters when they came to interview him in a municipal lodging house: "Black Thursday—hell! it was Red Monday, Tuesday, Wednesday, Thursday, Friday, Saturday, and Sunday, too. Wall Street was flooded in red ink, and I happened not to have my water wings along. It was rather embarrassing, but it's really nothing to get excited about, you know."

But he did not go to the very bottom, even though he found himself in a municipal lodging house. He found himself there as a clerk, counting loaves of bread to the more unfortunate drifters. "Yes," he said, "it could be plenty worse—I might have had to try selling apples at a medical convention. After all, there is a certain philosophical satisfaction in counting loaves of bread. Suppose there was no bread to count? Then one should start worrying." But he was not exactly fair to his former Village satellites when he sent a parting shot at them: "It cost me just $800,000 to learn that the only art which mattered vitally to those apostles of esthetics was the art of getting dollars for nothing. Education is rather expensive, isn't it?" As if the Villagers ate up and drank up all his fortune, or as if they and not the Wall Street brokers were responsible for the mad speculation and the sad crash!

But Maxwell Bodenheim once came to town, on his way to Europe, and looked up Bob in the lodging house to give him a good time of partying and drinking. So, perhaps, the Village can be forgiven its callousness if at least one of its denizens comes to the fallen caliph as a good Samaritan.

Poetry Mender [23]

The sign outside the door at 25 West Third Street, Greenwich Village, said "Ring bell loudly or knock hard and wait." But no one tugged at the bellpull—a piece of baling wire with clothespin attached—or knocked on the faded green door last night. For the Saturday night soirees of Anton Romatka were over forever.

Anton Romatka, self-styled "poetry mender" and one of the best-known of the versifiers who tack their wares on the fences around Washington Square, had been conducting his Saturday night sessions for as many years as most Village poets and artists can remember—seventeen years, some said; twenty-odd, according to others. Two weeks ago several of the poets came as usual and got no answer when they tolled the wire. They called the police, who broke into the two-room

[23] From "Ended Are Village Evenings of Poem Mending with Romatka; Poets Bid Last Farewell to Their Bohemian Host, Familiar Village Figure; Cluttered 3d Street Garret Was Scene of Saturday Soirees Nearly 20 Years," *New York Herald Tribune*, April 4, 1948. Copyright, 1948, by New York Herald Tribune, Inc.

cold-water flat on the third floor. There they found the seventy-some-years-old poet dead of natural causes.

Last Tuesday sixty Village poets filed into Bellevue Hospital's mortuary chapel and paid final tribute to the little old man who had been one of their leaders for so many years. One of them, George Simmons, conducted the last rites. Others recited poems, and one read a letter from the poet Otis Hanslick. Maxwell Bodenheim, Mary Samuel, John Cabbage, Joseph Cobb and a number of others dropped verses into the coffin before it was sealed. And twelve of them accompanied Mr. Romatka to his grave in Rose Hill Cemetery, Linden, N. J.

Mr. Romatka's tiny apartment was the kind of place which non-Villagers think of when they speak of the garrets of poets and artists in that romanticized section of lower Manhattan. It was cluttered with manuscripts when the police broke in; boxes of food hung from the ceiling by strings to keep them from mice; on the wall was a huge map, which the elderly poet once explained was not for the purposes of keeping track of his "verse-mending" customers but to cover up a hole on the wall.

In the dingy apartment each Saturday night a host of poets gathered, not only from the Village but from out of town. Sitting on chairs and soap boxes, they read their poetry and heard criticism from the others. They didn't always agree. "The usual argument," the soiree's conductor once said, "is: 'I can't change my poem, because it came to me that way. The inspiration would be killed if I altered a line. Besides it's my poem and I like it.' "

Some of those at the services were among the hundreds of verse-writers all over the country whom the Bohemian-born poet—Bohemian-born and Bohemian throughout life—had helped to make their creations salable to magazines and newspapers. It was this work that provided most of his meager livelihood. He charged a few cents to criticize or edit poems; he wrote verses to order, for five to fifteen cents a line, depending on the work and the customer; and he wrote, designed, lettered and published dozens of brochures on poetry-writing, which sold for anywhere from a quarter to $2.50. Typical were "Supreme Versification Course," only $2.50; "Patterns for Artistic Thought," $1; "Refrains, Tail Rhymers, Envois," 50 cents, etc., etc. His total income, he said, was $500 a year.

Mr. Romatka had a file of 10,000 persons who wrote poetry, but his list of active writers was only two or three hundred. Among them were such people as a Texas church worker, an Indiana life insurance executive, an Oklahoma attorney, a love-sick New York truck driver, a

Brooklyn school teacher and many others from many professions and occupations.

His clients came from various sources. The Texas church worker, a wife of a rancher, had read one of his ads in *Popular Mechanics*. The truck driver had read a card tacked on his door.

The cards and signs on his door were familiar to strollers in Greenwich Village. They bore such messages as: "Honest, Sympathetic, Efficient Service for Poets, by Anton Romatka, poet, critic, teacher of poetics, penman. Hundreds of pleased clients since 1925." Or: "Poetry Mags & Various Books for Sale Cheap."

His cards and verses also were familiar on the fence at Washington Square in the spring when the poets such as Maxwell Bodenheim and Frank McCrudden (president of the Raven Poetry Society) and Ellen Wood tacked up their works for the world to see and buy. Many of his were four-line verses neatly lettered on cards, like "Progress":

Who love shall live,
Who live must learn,
Who learn shall grow—
God willed it so.

On the sidewalk Mr. Romatka would pace up and down, his frayed brown hat pulled down over his brow, offering advice to fellow poets—or a piece of the apple pie some one had paid him for a verse.

The people who were close to him in Greenwich Village said that Mr. Romatka, who never married, was widely known for his generosity and kindness—and for his chivalry toward women. It was for the latter quality, they said, that poets placed a picture of Our Lady of Fatima on his breast, beside the poems and a group of red roses, before his coffin was sealed on Tuesday.

Hippolyte[24]

. . . Hippolyte had a personality which seemed to focus on himself the attention of any group in which he pursued his odd and whimsical career—really, I've concluded, something of a mask to conceal an es-

[24] From *Greenwich Village, Today & Yesterday,* Photographs by Berenice Abbott, Text by Henry Wysham Lanier, pp. 146–148. Copyright, 1949, by Harper & Brothers. New York.

sentially childlike nature, permeated with good will toward his fellowmen.

Among the legends which grew up was one that he was from Central Europe, Austria-Hungary perhaps, and that there was a dash of the Bohemian or Hungarian aristocrat in his ancestry, and this was confirmed to many by his *boulevardier* gallantry toward women, his assumption of a Don Juan attitude with a newcomer, his formal Continental dandyism in dress. Also he had a slight heart ailment, and had perhaps learned the value in feminine eyes of bearing the pain of such attacks with quite unconcealed fortitude.

For instance, one of his girl friends who was initiated by him into the inner circles of Greenwich Village when she arrived as a stranger years back recalls walking along the street with him one evening. Suddenly Hippolyte sank to the sidewalk and lay there evidently in the throes of some sort of seizure.

She tried to lift him to his feet.

"No, no!" he gasped. "You cannot. And I cannot. Anyhow—it is nothing."

But it was so patently something, the poor girl stood miserably, uncertain what to do. To call a doctor, or ask help from a stranger would, she felt sure, outrage her friend's prickly pride. How should a seasoned Villager behave in such a distressing emergency?

And then as she stood uncertainly, bending over to look down at the closed eyes, at the mouth resolutely closed against the pain, wondering about this Gallic man-of-the-world who openly proclaimed she was his daughter, Hippolyte's lips moved.

"Now, Hippolyte," he murmured, "die nicely."

But he was still quite self-possessed a few moments later when, instead of dying nicely or otherwise, he was helped up by strong young arms and resumed the interrupted stroll with her as if nothing had happened.

He developed one unvarying form of address . . . : "Don't be a damfool, give me a dollar." Everybody familiar with him expected this —and most of those who had an extra dollar complied with the demand. It was all one to Hippolyte whether they did or not.

Also, he called everybody "darling." Being a professed anarchist (but really a gentle soul who wouldn't have used a bomb on a rattlesnake), he was indulging in wild talk one evening when he had turned his dollar into wine. A policeman had to take him into custody.

The desk sergeant at the precinct station house knew him well, understood with Irish perception of human nature that there was no wickedness in him except words. Hippolyte rushed forward, threw his arms around the red-faced cop: "Darling, lend me fifty cents."

The encrimsoned sergeant sent two grinning patrolmen out of the room, gave Hippolyte a Dutch-uncle lecture, gave him fifty cents, told him to get out and keep his big mouth shut. As he disappeared happily into the night, the sergeant wiped his wet forehead. "Jesus!" he breathed. "What my name is going to be in the Police Department!"

Instead of a byblow of Continental nobility, Hippolyte was really the completely legitimate son of a Chicago newspaperman. He had lived in Berlin, Vienna, Paris, London, supporting himself as a correspondent to various papers, getting himself jailed as a Socialist in Berlin, where the authorities then lacked a sense of humor about radical speeches.

For a time, in secret, then publicly, he was desperately in love with Polly Halliday, most famous of the Village hostesses, whose restaurants were always the center of the inner groups, who at times equaled Papa Strunsky in her attitude of mother toward young painters and poets who had large appetites and no dollars.

Finally Hippolyte offered to act as chef at her popular eating place —and what housekeeper could resist such a proposal? Moreover, he was a good chef and all went happily for everybody save poor Hippolyte. Propinquity and the kitchen range inflamed his passion to such a degree that he fell into the habit of waylaying his goddess during business hours and pleading his cause in season and out.

At length, one night he came to her bedroom upstairs, after the last diner and drinker had been swept out. There was no violence in him except in the urgency of the feeling with which he implored and wept and begged her to marry him and stop all this foolish providing of meals to stupid people half of whom never paid.

Polly was tired. She wanted nothing except to go to sleep—and poor Hippolyte had become incapable of leaving her presence.

So next day she had him brought into court: disorderly conduct, breach of the peace, and a hard-working woman's rest—it had to stop.

The judge looked at the mild little bearded man who listened to his accuser's charge adoringly.

"Well, sir, what have you to say for yourself? What is your object in this performance?"

Hippolyte drew himself up. "Your Honor, what would you do if you had loved a woman most of your life and she wouldn't listen to you?"

He was dismissed on probation, fell to drinking more heavily, finally found haven at an anarchist colony in New Jersey. I saw him there and talked with him at length—a nice little man, with interesting mind and experiences, who wished all simple people well.

Joe Gould Says, "I Am Introvert and Extrovert"[25]

[Joe] Gould, ever since his childhood, has been perplexed by his own personality. There are scores of autobiographical essays in the Oral History [of Our Time] and he says that all of them are attempts to explain himself to himself. In one, "Why I Am Unable to Adjust Myself to Civilization, Such As It Is, or Do, Don't Do, Don't, A Hell of a Note," he came to the conclusion that his shyness was responsible for everything. "I am introvert and extrovert all rolled in one," he wrote, "a warring mixture of the recluse and the Sixth Avenue auctioneer. One foot says do, the other says don't. One foot says shut your mouth, the other says bellow like a bull. I am painfully shy, but try not to let people know it. They would take advantage of me." Gould keeps his shyness well hidden. It is evident only when he is cold sober. In that state he is silent, suspicious, and constrained, but a couple of beers or a single jigger of gin will untie his tongue and put a leer on his face. He is extraordinarily responsive to alcohol. "On a hot night," he says, "I can walk up and down in front of a gin mill for ten minutes, breathing real deep, and get a jag on."

Even though Gould requires only a few drinks, getting them is sometimes quite a task. Most evenings he prowls around the saloons and dives on the west side of the Village, on the lookout for curiosity-seeking tourists from whom he can cadge beers, sandwiches, and small sums of money. Such people are scarce nowadays. If he is unable to find any one approachable in the tumultuous saloons around Sheridan Square, he goes over to Sixth Avenue and works north, hitting the Jericho Tavern, the Village Square Bar & Grill, the Belmar, Goody's and the Rochambeau. He has a routine. He doesn't enter a place unless it is crowded. After he is in, he bustles over to the telephone booth and pretends to look up a number. While doing this, he scrutinizes the cus-

[25] From "Professor Sea Gull," in *McSorley's Wonderful Saloon,* by Joseph Mitchell, pp. 78–79, 80–81. Copyright, 1943, by Joseph Mitchell. New York: Duell, Sloan and Pearce.
Originally published in *The New Yorker.*

tomers. If he sees a prospect, he goes over and says. "Let me introduce myself. The name is Joseph Ferdinand Gould, graduate of Harvard, *magna cum difficultate,* class of 1911, and chairman of the board of Weal and Woe, Incorporated. In exchange for a drink, I'll recite a poem, deliver a lecture, argue a point, or take off my shoes and imitate a sea gull. I prefer gin, but beer will do." Gould is by no means a bum. He feels that the entertainment he provides is well worth whatever he is able to cadge. He doesn't fawn, and he is never grateful. If he is turned down politely, he shrugs his shoulders and leaves the place. However, if the prospect passes a remark like "Get out of here, you bum," Gould turns on him, no matter how big he is, and gives him a frightening tongue-lashing. He is skilled in the use of the obscene epithet; he can curse for ten minutes, growing more shrill and scurrilous by the minute, without repeating himself. When aroused, he is fearless. He will drop his portfolio, put up his fists, and offer to fight men who could kill him with one half-hearted blow. . . .

* * * * *

Inevitably, at every party Gould goes to, he gets up on a table and delivers some lectures. His lectures are brief, but he gives them lengthy titles, such as "Drunk as a Skunk, or How I Measured the Heads of Fifteen Hundred Indians in Zero Weather" and "The Dread Tomato Habit, or Watch Out! Watch Out! Down with Dr. Gallup!" For a reason he has never been able to make quite clear, statistics of any kind infuriate him. In the latter lecture, using statistics he maintains he has found in newspaper financial sections, he proves that the eating of tomatoes by railroad engineers was responsible for fifty-three percent of the train wrecks in the United States during the last seven years. When Gould arrives at a party, people who have never seen him before usually take one look, snicker, and edge away. Before the evening is over, however, a few of them almost always develop a kind of puzzled respect for him; they get him in a corner, ask him questions, and try to determine what is wrong with him. Gould enjoys this. "When you came over and kissed my hand," a young woman told him once, "I said to myself, 'What a nice old gentleman.' A minute later I looked around and you were bouncing up and down with your shirt off, imitating a wild Indian. I was shocked. Why do you have to be such an exhibitionist?" "Madam," Gould said, "it is the duty of the bohemian to make a spectacle of himself. If my informality leads you to believe that I'm a rum-dumb, or that I belong in Bellevue, hold fast to that belief, hold fast, hold fast, and show your ignorance."

"Well, Here We Are on Top of the Empire State—"

RASKOB'S DREAM[26]

In August, 1929, New York financial wizard John J. Raskob was walking down Fifth Avenue with H. Hamilton Weber, now executive vice-president of the Empire State Building Corporation. As they paused in front of the old Waldorf-Astoria, at Thirty-fourth Street, Raskob asked:

"What would you say if I told you that this hotel will be torn down and a 102-story office building erected in its place?"

"I might think," replied Weber, "some one was telling me a fib."

"Well," said Raskob, "it's true—we will announce it in the newspapers tomorrow."

Sure enough, plans were annnounced on August 30, two months before the stock market crash.

Raskob had just resigned as chairman of the Democratic National Committee, after ex-Governor Alfred E. Smith's unsuccessful presidential campaign. The "father of time payments" on General Motors cars, he was at one time reputed to be worth $100,000,000. A New York City bank was presently involved in negotiations over the ailing Waldorf-Astoria, which had to be put on its feet again or demolished and replaced. In search of a man of the caliber of Chrysler, whose 1,048-foot tower was completed in 1929, the bank found that man in Raskob. At that time the tide of office-building activity was moving uptown, with plans for Rockefeller Center already under way. But Raskob predicted, rightly, that when the wall of Central Park South was reached, the backwash would flow into the area between Thirty-fourth and Forty-first Streets.

Joe Bergin, assistant operating manager, recalls some of the tall-tale aspects of the building's construction. Less than nine months elapsed between the laying of the first steel for the foundation on March 17, 1930 (St. Patrick's day, in honor of Al Smith) and the completion of the masonry on November 13. When construction was in full swing, an average of four and a half stories were erected every week, and at top speed, fourteen and a half stories in ten working days. Because of the

[26] Compiled and edited from material prepared by Jay Scott, of the Benjamin Sonnenberg office, for the Empire State Building Corporation, New York 1956.

lack of ground storage space, steel (60,000 tons in all, enough to build a double-track railroad from New York to Baltimore) was set into place as soon as it was unloaded from the trucks. An industrial railroad was built to transport materials around the lot, and men were lifted to their places with a mine hoist. Food stations were set up at various levels, to which water was piped up.

When the fourth floor was reached, the builders, Starrett Brothers and Ekin, moved their offices from below and, between the shanties, laid out streets bearing such names as "Surf Avenue," "Sheepshead Bay Alley," "Bowling Green," "Hogan's Alley," and "Peacock Alley."

And what parties they had when the steel was "topped out!"

DEPRESSION AND STRIKE LORE[27]

In a high wind tenants sometimes hear ghost "typewriters" tapping away like mad in empty offices—but this is only the building's steel skeleton creaking and groaning. It happens in all tall towers.

* * * * *

. . . Two [months] after plans for the Empire State were announced, the stock market went whoosh, and the depression was on its way. It didn't look like a good time to throw an additional 2,158,000 square feet of space on the market, but nobody bothered about that.

* * * * *

. . . [By 1931] the depression was beginning to be felt, and tenants were scarce. [New Yorkers referred to the Empire State as the "Empty State Building" and said, "The only way the landlords will ever fill it is to tow it out to sea."]

The owners, however, considered the edifice a long-term investment, and preferred to keep rents at a pre-depression level. As a result, for almost ten years there were no tenants to speak of above the 60th floor.

Right away legends started to grow. Fiction writers used the empty floors [for settings] instead of haunted houses, castles in Europe, or lonely moors. The natives are convinced to this day that lights were strung artfully in vacant offices at night to make it look lived-in. The management insists lights were put in to help watchmen find their way about.

They still tell of King Prajadhipok of Siam, who was shown the sights of the city from the 102nd floor by [building president] Al Smith.

[27] From "Peak of a Skyline," by Creighton Peet, *Collier's*, Vol. 123 (February 5, 1949), No. 6, pp. 32, 60. Copyright, 1949, by the Crowell-Collier Publishing Company. New York.

"Reminds me of home," the king was supposed to have said.

"Why?" asked Smith in surprise. "You haven't anything like this in Siam."

"Oh, yes," the king replied, "we have white elephants, too."

Actually, the management insists, the building was 46 per cent rented when it opened, and even in the worst of the depression was 68 per cent full.

* * * * *

Every few years, some muscular lad climbs [the 1,860 steps] to the top, just to show off, but it is hard on the heart, and the building discourages that sort of stunt. Back in 1932 the Polish Olympic ski team climbed from the fifth to the 102nd floor in 20 minutes, but presumably they could take it. People really had a chance to climb, but not for fun, in September of 1945, not long after the bomber crash. Most elevator operators in New York City had gone on strike, and some 2,000 tall buildings were left without service. Since the Empire State was the tallest of all, it got a big play in the newspapers.

There was the loyal employee who plugged all the way up to the 46th floor, and was the only one who reported for work. And there were the NBC television engineers (cloud hermits) stranded on the 85th floor. They had provided themselves with cots and a refrigerator filled with food. Another man stayed on the 68th floor for three days waiting for an important phone call. He got it. A few who climbed to work on lower floors could get out for food. But a luncheonette operator toted 150 sandwiches and jugs of coffee way up to the 31st floor. He got a $75 tip from a brokerage firm.

* * * * *

Al Smith used to take tremendous pride in the building's height, and often showed distinguished guests around personally. They say that once a fearful old lady hesitated before stepping into the tower elevator. "Governor," she asked, "if something goes wrong, will I go up or down?"

"Lady," Smith answered, "that all depends on what kind of a life you've led."

* * * * *

If you go up and feel the folks back home are going to be skeptical, you can not only get your picture made by the official photographer at the top but you can make a recording of your voice. Half the visitors go home clutching a record beginning, "Well, here we are on top of the Empire State. . . ."

THE DAY THE BOMBER HIT THE EMPIRE STATE[28]

Saturday morning, July 28, 1945 . . .

A seventeen-year-old Coast Guardsman, Apprentice Pharmacist Mate Dan Malony, stood window-shopping in front of the Empire State Building. He was on a three-day pass from the Coast Guard Academy at New London. Although he had considered going up to the observatory, he had decided against it when he found that he couldn't see the upper reaches of the 1,472-foot structure through the thick fog.

"A little before ten o'clock," writes Creighton Peet in *Collier's,* "people in the streets suddenly saw an Army bomber skimming out of the overcast barely 900 feet above the sidewalk. As they watched [Dan Malony among them], horrified, the plane, a B-25, shot straight for the midtown skyscraper.

"For a fraction of a second the pilot appeared to be pulling up. But it was too late. He crashed into the Empire State with a shock that seemed to make it rock to its base. The plane's wings were sheared off, the gasoline tanks exploded, and brilliant flames enveloped the tower.

"The 78th and 79th floors were wrecked. Gasoline ran down corridors and stair wells, as far as the 75th floor. Thirteen were killed and twenty-six injured. One of the plane's engines lunged through two elevator shafts, shearing all cables and dropping the cars to the basement. The other engine went clear through the building and destroyed a studioful of sculpture in the next block."

Betty Lou Oliver (now married and mother of several children, residing in Oklahoma) was operating one of the elevators when the cables were sheared. Her car crashed to the basement, and as she hit bottom, she screamed.

Young Malony had dashed into the building pharmacy after the explosion.

"Give me hypos, needles, first aid kits, ointments, and distilled water," he yelled.

So equipped, he reached the lobby, where he heard Miss Oliver's scream. Followed by two firemen, who had been making an inspection tour of the vicinity, he rushed downstairs, and, guided by her screams, found the elevator. They cut a hole in the top and Malony climbed in. Lying covered with debris, Miss Oliver managed to say, "Thank God, the Navy's here!"

[28] By Jay Scott.

Malony applied unguents, put cold compresses over her seared eyes, and injected morphine. Then he handed her out to the firemen.

Malony treated others in the lobby. Then the word spread that others were dying high in the building. Malony grabbed his kit and with a priest began one of the weirdest climbs of all time. Not knowing what floor the bomber had hit, unaware whether the region was still dangerous, the two hastened upward, opening stair-doors every few floors, trying to find the scene of the crash. Fifty—sixty—seventy flights—then slippery oil, scorched walls, and brooding stillness told them they were nearing the spot. Finally, they came to the 78th floor, full of piled, twisted, smoldering wreckage and choking smoke. But there were no dying, only the dead, and Malony laid out the bodies so that the priest could administer the last rites.

The tragedy had its lighter side. An observatory staff photographer named Frank Wernli had been getting hell from Frank Powell for being continually late to work. This morning he had been late again, and he got off the elevator at the 85th floor so that he could sneak upstairs to the 86th and punch the time clock. At ten minutes to ten, just as he pushed the lever, there was a terrific crash, followed by the sound of an explosion. Wernli's first thought was that Powell had rigged a booby trap in the clock to frighten him. Scared to death, he ran all the way down to the lobby floor, eighty-six flights, and he might have been going still if they hadn't stood him against the wall to recover.

"ESB" WORKERS[29]

The Empire State Building employs about one thousand workers, including five or six hundred regular employees and the rest under contract from outside firms. A new employee will ride numbly in the elevators for a time. Then as he settles into the routine he will begin to say, "Nice day for the tower," or "Bad weather for the tower."

On account of the varying "coefficients of contraction" of the limestone, stainless steel, and aluminum, constant attention is required to prevent cracks from opening up. Vice-President John F. Garrety points out that there's no nice convenient building across the street where they can go to look across and see what repairs are needed. Ergo: they have to put up a scaffolding and go out and look for themselves.

Once or twice in ten years, the management has to replace the windows in the observatory on account of people scratching their initials, etc., on the glass with their rings. After new glass has been put in, it

[29] By Jay Scott.

stays clear for quite a time until one or two visitors venture to inscribe their initials. Once the ice is broken, initials follow thick and fast.

Aside from the defacing of the windows, there is remarkably little malicious damage or petty theft. Garrety once received a complaint from one office that cellophane bags full of water were being thrown from upper windows. He managed to discover the reason—to attract the attention of a pretty girl in the office. But how can you tell who in thirty or so floors is throwing things from his window? He finally tracked the culprit down through the cellophane bags. Another time, a passing pedestrian suddenly found himself encircled by a swirl of typewriter ribbon, tossed from somewhere in the building. When he demanded retribution, Garrety had a tough time convincing him that there really was no way of tracing the prankster.

Assistant Operating Manager Joe Bergin tells the story of the outside electricians who came in to fix the lights on the TV tower. They like to wait for good weather, of course, and showed up one sunny winter day to do the job. While Bergin and some others waited at the bottom of the tower, the men started up. When they were about halfway, a sudden snow storm developed, and the men were lost to sight in great big swirling flakes. Bergin was sure the men would come down, but there was no sign of them. After a long wait they reappeared, the repairs completed. They explained that it was just as far to come down as it was to go up, so they decided to keep on going and finish off the job.

The 6,500 windows are washed every two weeks by an outside firm. Richard O. Hart, who with six helpers has been keeping the more than five acres of glass clean since the building was erected, has never been injured on the job. (As a matter of fact, the only danger, according to Garrety, comes when window washers, against regulations, move from one window to another outside of the building.) While washing windows in his home, however, Hart fell three stories, a chicken-wire fence breaking his fall.

THE INQUIRERS[30]

Down through the years the one question that predominates in the thousands of letters addressed to the building from all over the world reads something like: "A friend and I were arguing the other day. He said the Empire State Building sways fifty feet in the wind and I say it's five feet. Which is correct?" [According to Jay Scott, inquirers call up from

[30] From "Biggest Building Can't Count Its Rooms, Empire State Has Other Mysteries," by Robert Prall. *New York World-Telegram and The Sun,* April 26, 1952. Copyright, 1952, by New York World-Telegram Corp.

as far away as Anchorage, Alaska, as early as seven A.M., usually with a heavy bet on.]

The answer is always the same. . . . Engineers have determined that if a 100-mile-an-hour wind blew against the building for two or more hours, it would sway 1.45 inches at the 1,250-foot-high tower.

People still want to know if it's true that the structure is built on steel springs, if the building is sinking into Manhattan Island or if the weight of the Empire State is making the entire island sink lower in the water. Each letter is carefully answered. The building is erected on bedrock. It is not sinking. Neither is Manhattan Island. Despite its weight of 365,000 tons, the building actually weighs less than the dirt and rock excavated for its foundation [fifty-five feet below street level].

TOWER TRICKS AND THRILLS[31]

The "vaudeville" aspect of the building is pretty well confined to the tower. There is, of course, the not-so-funny feature of suicides, although there haven't been any off the top since the suicide rail went up in 1947. In the years before that, according to observatory manager Frank Powell, there was a total of twelve who jumped from the tower. This doesn't include numerous attempts prevented by alert guards. Elevator operators and ticket takers, by the way, were trained to observe people going to the tower, and to pick out and report ones who looked suspiciously melancholy, who were alone, etc. Once on the tower no one is left standing all by himself—a guard will go up and converse.

Al Gordon, assistant observatory manager, tells of the calls he gets from the police tipping him off that Joe Blow has threatened his wife that he would jump off the tower. "A lot of this is baloney," he says, "but once they did talk a soldier out of jumping, after a tip-off."

Besides these tragic people, there is the usual spate of publicity seekers. There was the man who wanted to parade around in his leopard suit, but was stopped as he started to change in the men's room. There was a fellow from Barnum and Bailey who stood on the narrow space on the top of the building (pre-TV) on one finger.

There was the skating troupe who whirled and twirled on an eight-foot square platform built at the 87th floor setback. (Says Powell: "I like to die watching it.") There was a composer who had a piano brought up to the top and was photographed composing a "musical portrait" of New York eighty-six floors above the street.

There was a lady medium who insisted on holding her séance way up

[31] By Jay Scott.

in the building, in order to be nearer to the spiritual world. And there were six people who wanted the ashes of their loved ones scattered from the observatory tower. This is done, says Powell, before the tower opens to the public, and the wind has to be at least thirty-five miles an hour at the time. He admits to feeling something like a funeral-home employee as he stands by, hat to chest, while the bereaved empty out the contents of their little packages.

Every year hundreds of people are photographed for publicity and fashion purposes standing on the tower. During "Swim for Health Week" a special platform was built for twenty lovelies to stand on in their bathing suits.

Powell agrees that plays and movies (especially *The Thief,* made in the building) encourage more people to come, but he thinks the greatest business-getter of all was the policy of permitting service men to come up free during the war. Thousands of visitors have told him that they've come to see the view because their boy wrote them about it during the war. Young children also bring their parents. When the youngsters make a map of New York City, they simply draw a long horizontal line with a tall peak in the middle for the Empire State.

On West Forty-second Street, opposite Bryant Park, there used to be a man with a telescope who for a dime, when the moon wasn't out, would invite you to have a look at the Empire State tower and "see the people instead." Arnold Grant, secretary of the corporation, dug up a newspaper picture of the telescope man with his sign reading "Interesting View of Empire State Building, 10¢," and had it hung in one of the elevators, with the caption, "Man Bites Dog."

When Grand Central Depot Was the "End of the World"[32]

In 1857 steam locomotives were forbidden to run south of Forty-second Street and the railroad faced a difficult situation. Heretofore cars had been run south of Thirty-second Street by attaching horses to the cars at the foot of Park Avenue, but with the increase of railroad travel and the crowding of the streets the system became impracticable.

[32] From *The Romance of Park Avenue,* by F. A. Collins, pp. 58–59. Copyright, 1930, [by the Park Avenue Association, Inc.] New York.

To meet this situation, Commodore Vanderbilt conceived the "Grand Central Depot." From every point of view the enterprise was a daring adventure. The needs of the City were anticipated at least by a generation in designing the great terminus. Its position was so far up town that many derided the plan. The papers of the day, or most of them, suggested that the station should be called "End of the World," rather than "Grand Central." The trip from the center of the city to the "Forty-second Street" and return at the time was half a day's journey.

It Happens in Grand Central

I [33]

[The Stationmaster in Grand Central Terminal is speaking.]

. . . If anyone in the terminal loses his ticket, his money, his wife or his memory, he sooner or later comes to me. And whenever anything goes wrong for a passenger on any of the lines that operate out of Grand Central—the New York Central to Chicago and St. Louis with connections to the West Coast, and the New York, New Haven & Hartford to New England with connections to Canada—conductors and porters always say: "See the stationmaster when you get to New York. He'll take care of everything."

A Kansas wheat farmer came in one day and said he'd left his new set of false teeth on the train that morning. He hadn't remembered them until he'd ordered a steak sent up to his room in the Hotel Waldorf-Astoria. I took him up to the lost-property department and, sure enough, a set of teeth had been turned in. They looked like his, he said, and he put them in his mouth, muttering: "That's one thing we don't grow in Kansas—new teeth. Sure wish we did, because these feel like a pair of hip boots."

A few hours later a brakeman delivered another set of false teeth to Lost and Found. Just after he left, a minister walked up.

"I arrived from Boston this morning," he told the boys behind the counter, "and I think I left my dentures in a paper cup on the window ledge."

The Kansas man had taken the wrong set of teeth!

[33] From "Everything Happens at Grand Central Station," by Edward G. Fischer, with Wayne Amos, *Collier's*, Vol. 133 (March 5, 1954), No. 5, p. 88. Copyright, 1954, by the Crowell-Collier Publishing Company. New York.

"I thought something was wrong," the farmer said when one of the clerks reached him on the telephone at the Waldorf-Astoria. "I just spent ten dollars having these dern things filed down. But I'll take care of everything," he added. "The wheat crop was good this year."

So the Boston minister and the Kansas wheat farmer met by the information-booth clock and trooped off to the best dentist in town to get new choppers all around.

Late one Friday night I was just about to leave for home when a seventy-five-year-old man from Minnesota came in and said he had been walking all day trying to find his hotel. He had arrived at Grand Central that morning, taken a taxi to a hotel recommended by a train acquaintance, and gone out for a long walk. When he turned back, he realized he remembered neither the name of the hotel nor the street it was on. In the hotel room were all his belongings, a ticket on a ship leaving for Norway early the next morning, and $5,000—his life savings. He had been planning to go back to the old country to retire.

The taxi had cost 70 cents and the room $4. With those two clues, the Travelers Aid Society, which maintains a booth in the terminal, began telephoning all medium-rate hotels "70 cents away from Grand Central by taxi." The agency found the right one on the eighty-seventh call, just in time for the man to make his ship.

Every day many people come in frantic because they have lost a husband or a child. We hold the distracted person in the office and broadcast a plea over the amplifying system for the missing relative to come to the stationmaster's office. When the lost person arrives, the pair embrace fondly, and then give each other the dickens for being stupid enough to get lost.

Runaways, three or four a week, are regular customers. Old people, I've noticed, run away almost as often as children, and for the same reasons. They get peeved at their families and want to show their independence. One old man over eighty told me he had tried unsuccessfully to join the circus at Madison Square Garden as a water boy.

About once a year we get a real heartbreaker—a child deserted by its parents. One of my matrons in the ladies' waiting room, Mrs. Asonta Peterson, still thinks one woman must have been run over by an auto. She came into the nursery a year and a half ago with a cute six-month-old baby and asked a maid to watch the child for a moment while she went across the street. She never came back. The railroad police took the baby to the New York Foundling Hospital.

Every year or so one of my matrons comes to me with the same story: a man, usually between fifty and sixty, rings the bell outside the ladies' rest room and asks if his "wife" is in there. She said she'd be right out and she's been gone an hour; he describes her as young and pretty. The matron looks but the woman isn't there.

Then the maid tells him the ladies' room has another exit, leading to a back stairs to the other level. He tries to laugh. "She's gone, then," he says, "and with my watch." Or perhaps it is his diamond ring or wallet. The man met the girl on a train and she persuaded him to let her hold his valuables.

One of the chief duties of my crews and myself is to help people. But our aid is not always appreciated. One of my redcaps once noticed an elderly woman in a floppy straw hat stop at Gate 23 to light her cigarette. Suddenly the flame leaped to the brim and the entire hat blazed up. The redcap grabbed at it and tried to pull it off the woman's head, but it was anchored firmly with hatpins. He pulled out a big handkerchief and as he smothered the flames, the flabbergasted old lady, unaware of her danger, beat him on the head with her umbrella. Even when she found out he had saved her from possible serious injury, her dignity was so ruffled she walked off in a huff.

Another redcap told me he was carrying a suitcase for a lady who was in a terrific hurry. As they rushed across the concourse, he tried to tell her she had plenty of time for her train.

"My husband is after me," the lady said, "and I've just had six stitches taken where he cut me with a knife."

Just then, the redcap heard a man's deep voice call out right behind him: "Put that bag down."

"What happened?" I demanded.

"I put the bag down like the man said," he replied, shamefaced, "and kept right on goin'. I didn't even look back."

II[34]

. . . I had a friend once who was going for the first time to the Adirondacks to make a visit; and he was about the twenty-fifth person in line before the ticket window at the Grand Central Station. The line moved slowly forward, and every moment was precious. My friend is rather absent-minded, and was thinking of many important matters of business. When, finally, he triumphantly reached the window and faced the harassed ticket-seller, he forgot the name of the station to

[34] From *This New York of Mine,* by Charles Hanson Towne, p. 170. Copyright, 1931, by Charles Hanson Towne. New York: Cosmopolitan Book Corporation.

which he was going. In confusion he stammered, "It's some camp in the Adirondacks—Camp—" The words died on his lips. "Get to the end of the line!" shouted the man through his grille; and my poor friend, perspiring and distraught, had to begin all over again. But the moment he had stepped out of the way, he remembered the name of his station. Yet he was forced to step to his original place, twenty-five human beings behind. Needless to say, he lost his train.

III [35]

They're members of the Brotherhood of Railway Clerks, and they live in a blaze of questions.

"What time is the next train to Carthage?" "How do you get to Times Square from here?" "Can I get straight-through Pullman accommodations from Indianapolis to Asheville, North Carolina?" "Where can I get a subway to Brooklyn?" "Where can I get the bus to La Guardia Field?" "Where can I get a shot of whisky and still have time to catch that train for Syracuse?"

"What time is the next train for Greenwich?" "Did I just miss a train for Brewster?" "What time is the next train to Boston?" "Say, buddy, don't look now, but where do I go to get a marriage license in this burg?"

* * * * *

"What's the next train for Tonawanda?" "Where can I get my pants pressed around here in a hurry?" "Will the train from Springfield be on time?"

"When does the train leave?"

"What train do you mean?"

"I don't know—the boss is in a rage and he didn't tell me."

"Then where is he going?"

"He didn't tell me that either? Must I go back and ask him?"

* * * * *

"Is my niece's train in yet?"

"Where is your niece coming from, madam?"

"From college. I'm sure I've missed her. Do you think she'll know the way? She's never been in New York before."

"What college does she go to, madam?"

[35] From *Grand Central,* by David Marshall, pp. 102–104. Copyright, 1946, by David Marshall. New York and London: Whittlesey House, McGraw-Hill Book Company, Inc.

"Would that make a difference? Vassar, of course."

"Your niece's train has not yet arrived, madam. Train from Poughkeepsie is coming in now on Track Thirty-Seven."

"Oh, thank *you! . . . You said Track Twenty-seven, didn't you?"*

"Thirty-seven, madam. Track THIRTY-seven."

"Yes, that's what I said. TWENTY-seven. Thank you so much."

* * * * *

"Do you have a Rutland Railroad timetable?" "How do I get to New Jersey from here?" "What's the next train to New Haven?" "Is the *Knickerbocker* in yet?" "What kind of medicine should I bring in case my little boy gets sick on the train?"

"Are dogs allowed on trains going to Canada?" "How far is Saint Patrick's Cathedral from here?" "When is the next train to Rhinecliff?" "Would you please tell a stranger what's the best show to see on Broadway tonight?"

"Can I get a train to Pittsfield, Massachusetts, after seven o'clock tonight?" "Where's a good restaurant around here?" "If I take the *Century* from here tomorrow night, how soon can I be in San Francisco?"

"How much is a Pullman?"

"Where are you going, madam?"

"That's my business, ain't it?"

"In that case, madam, the answer to your question is fifty-two thousand dollars. Next."

They live in a blaze of questions, these railway clerks who man the Information Desk below the Golden Clock.

Short Cut [36]

Fifth and Sixth Avenues teem these days; the thronging pedestrians maneuver under rules skimpier than those of bagataway. As a service to readers who are too frail or shy for good-natured hurly-burly, we decided to plot a course from the Empire State Building to Rockefeller Center that would involve no contact with either Fifth or Sixth Avenue. So, early one morning, armed with a box lunch our

[36] From *The New Yorker,* Vol. 31 (February 11, 1956), No. 52, pp. 26–27. Copyright, 1956, by The New Yorker Magazine, Inc.

wife had insisted on packing for us, we found ourself in front of the Cantigny Printing & Stationery Corporation, on Thirty-third Street, facing the tallest structure in the world. Fifth Avenue was to the east, Sixth to the west. Indomitably, we charged into the Empire State's dimly lit and brownly marbled lobby, resisted the suave pleas of uniformed attendants to ascend with them to the Observatory, cleaved between the elevator banks, and emerged on Thirty-fourth Street, opposite the great bland façade of Ohrbach's. We threaded our way among handbags, gloves, and tailored cotton shirts ($1.99), took the escalator to the Budget Balcony, wriggled through a tight crevasse at the Customers' Accommodation Desk, and thus reached Thirty-fifth Street. There we bore west until we struck a Meyers Brothers System parking lot, feebly guarded by a sign reading, "NO WALKING OR TRESPASSING THRU THIS STATION." Crouching low between the automobiles, we attained the Thirty-sixth Street end of the lot, only to discover a tall wire fence. Would we, then, have to fall back? No; under the gate, a gap of around twenty inches permitted easy egress to anyone willing to crawl on his stomach. We did this. On Thirty-sixth Street, after futilely exploring a series of shallow luncheonettes and furriers' shops, we came to the Herald Square Garage, at whose farther end the light of Thirty-seventh Street gleamed. As slack-mouthed young men in coveralls stared, we exploited this tunnel.

Thirty-seventh Street resisted our advances. The sole block-deep building in this backward area is owned by Franklin Simon & Co. A door with the store's name on it and a tantalizing view of the men's clothing department, with salesmen pensively studying their reflections in three-way mirrors, promised quick triumph, but the door was painted black, the handles had been removed, and instructions to use the Fifth Avenue and Thirty-eighth Street entrances were lettered upon it. We tugged brutally at the recalcitrant portal, wedging our fingers in a crack left by the imperfection of the carpentry, until a spectator said, "There's a burglar alarm on that door, you know." Chastened and despairing, we backtracked and discovered, on Thirty-fifth Street near Sixth Avenue, a dismal cave mouth titled "Independent Subway System." We descended a crooked flight of stairs, turned right, and were appalled by the extensive cavern before us. The floor tilted Surrealistically; overhead, mammoth white beams suggested the molars of an unthinkably huge whale. A few ectoplasmic figures shuffled back and forth. At the faraway end, they could be seen dissolving in mist. Only our own footsteps made noise. Our panic mounted, and eventually we did also, at Thirty-eighth Street.

We walked east to Lord & Taylor's, whereby we passed over to Thirty-ninth Street. Near Sixth Avenue, we entered the back door of Schumacher's and continued through the store. The Schumacher passage is one of the trip's pleasantest; the deep repose of stacked carpets, uncut fabrics, and middle-aged couples turning the leaves of wallpaper books provides an appropriate prelude to the two-block open-air run of Bryant Park, fragile and silent in winter.

At Forty-second Street, the footsore traveler must not be dazzled into indecision by the variety of through passageways—Stern's, Woolworth's, the Salmon Tower arcade. We chose Woolworth's. The odors of cheap candy, cashews, cosmetics, and cookies, in that order, titillated our nostrils. Forty-third Street is simple enough. Arcades exist at our own 25 West Forty-third and at No. 37, though neither is as grand a throughway as that offered by the Association of the Bar of the City of New York, at No. 43. On Forty-fourth Street, the choice lies between the Berkeley Building and the Hotel Seymour, where a narrow corridor yields to vistas of affluence as the main entrance, on Forty-fifth Street, is approached.

In our chain of passageways, the link between Forty-fifth and Forty-sixth Streets demands the most hardihood and perseverance to forge. The correct procedure is: Ask for the superintendent at 45 West Forty-fifth Street. He is benign, though burly. Accompany him as he leads you through a second-story window onto a brick-and-tar projection he terms a balcony. Listen respectfully as he explains that an easy jump of about twenty feet will land you on a parking lot that fronts on Forty-sixth Street. Indicate to him that your ankles are not firm. Follow him into the basement, where deep-throated boilers chug. Slither through an infinitesimal window. Finding yourself in a kind of concrete well, with a ledge and rusty fence perhaps three feet above your head, leap strenuously, seize the ledge and then the fence, pull yourself up, wipe your hands, and stroll through the parking lot to Forty-sixth Street.

After this, cutting through the Hotel Wentworth to Forty-seventh Street will seem as easy as a promenade in Central Park. At Forty-seventh, we once again had recourse to the subway, and this time it cost us fifteen cents. After passing through the turnstile, we inched along the platform until we came to a sign pointing the way to the United States Rubber Building. Up silver sliding stairs, through vacant halls of pearl-pink and ash-blue marble, into the open air we moved. Where were we? There was no mistaking those momentous slabs, those quaint half streets, those flat-muscled bas-relief ladies so dear to the hearts of sculptors commissioned to body forth the concepts of Labor, Valor, and Communications. Rockefeller Center.

Madison Avenue Patchwork [37]

Madison Avenue, New York City, is a patchwork street. It has skyscrapers and it has grocery stores. It has St. Patrick's rectory and it has God-knows-how many banks. Its windows and its store fronts are heavy with wonderful names—Cassebeer, Jarazever, Dussourd and Filser, Schwarz and Forger, Mrs. R. Stricker and Nephew—a melting pot of merchants who sell everything from mink to miscellaneous. You wouldn't think of ambling over to Broadway to buy antiques, or to Park Avenue for a hamburger, or to Lexington for a saddle for the polo pony, or to Fifth for a fish. Madison Avenue sells antiques, fish, boots and saddles (M. J. Knoud, 716 Madison), and hamburgers, and shoes and ships (Abercrombie & Fitch), and songs and dances and funny sayings (Rodgers and Hammerstein, 488 Madison). One of the endearing charms of the street is that all this merchandise is peddled with dignity, all of it fits neatly into the patchwork pattern. Let the two-week tourists rattle on about the diverse delights of the shops of Paris, of the infinite variety of Rome, or the curiosities of London. If you're a true New Yorker, smile when you say that. You know that on a stretch of fifty blocks, containing some 630 retail stores, Madison Avenue has a market place to match any of them. It is, in a word, Manhattan's closest approach to a Main Street.

. . . In New York . . . there is no single Main Street, not even by name. It becomes a matter of choice, every man entitled to one vote. Big boulevards run up and down the limb of Manhattan as parallel as the stripes on a pair of pants (with diagonal Broadway a tailor's mistake). They're all loud, wide, busy, and bright—but all different, and the Manhattanite can take a pick to suit his own tastes. Broadway? Fifth? Park? Lexington? First or Second, or Sixth, or Tenth? Which gives you the greatest sense of kinship with the metropolis? Which fills you with pride and—yes—patriotism?

Nobody has ever polled the population in the matter. There's never been a need for a vote. It is generally known that most perspicacious

[37] From "Madison Ave.: The New York Manner," by Sidney Carroll, *Esquire, The Magazine for Men,* Vol. 37 (February, 1952), No. 2, pp. 43–46, 96. Copyright, 1952, by Esquire, Inc. Chicago.

New Yorkers, most Manhattanites of sense and sensibility, with intelligence and 20-20 vision, will pick Madison Avenue over all the others.

Why? Well . . . because.

Madison is an important big-business street. Its skyscrapers make many of the exclamation points in New York's skyline. Behind the million windows in the behemoths of stone and steel, function some of the biggest of the country's big firms. Big banks and big publications and very big boys like International Business Machines live on Madison Avenue. But these representatives of industry at large are suspended high above the street itself, and have little to do with its personality. Madison derives its real flavor from its stores; it is a shopkeeper's street. Skyscrapers you can find all over town. Bankers and editors and hucksters are nothing unusual in New York. But where else in town can you find the kind of shopkeeper who still flourishes on Madison Avenue?

He is expensive. By and large, Madison is probably New York's most expensive shopping street. But for the patrons who can afford it, the Madison store owner maintains an old-fashioned intimacy of contact—the old general store technique that has become a rarity in the big town. Some of the stores have been here, man and boy, for a hundred years. They are serving fifth and sixth generations of the original customers, and they look it, and they like it. . . .

* * * * *

In his mind's eye, the New Yorker divides Madison into three parts: Bottom, Middle, and Top. The bottom part, running from Madison Square to 42nd Street, is largely a wholesale business section, and has little to capture the imagination. The top part extends—roughly—from 86th Street northward to some indefinite point on the map (could be Montreal, figures the average New Yorker). This part is wholesale, retail and residential, but the mid-Manhattanite does little visiting up that way unless he has relatives in Harlem.

So the provincial, mid-town New Yorker pays no attention to the Top or the Bottom of Madison. His heart belongs to the Middle, the section that runs from 42nd Street to—approximately—86th. When he says "Madison," this is the part he means, the part with all the personality.

* * * * *

Every shopping street in New York is aimed predominantly at the female trade, but one of the delights of middle Madison Avenue is that it offers so much to the masculine shopper. It starts with a men's shop (Weber and Heilbroner, at 42nd), and from there on it's a constant zigzag of men's shops. On the northwest corner of 44th stands that citadel of the sack suit—the city's oldest men's store, the world's largest—Brooks Brothers. (Button down your collar, please, when you say the name.) A block farther uptown and you're face to face with the world's largest sporting-goods store (props.: Messrs. Abercrombie & Fitch), where you can get outfitted for anything from a shave to a safari. Another block and you're looking into Tripler's window, a favorite with the stiff-collar crowd. J. Press sits one flight up on the east corner of 44th. Clark Gable and Frank Sinatra and Cary Grant buys shirts at Wendley's, between 47th and 48th. Near the corner of 49th is Clyde's, where the shirts run puce, cerise, ebony, or egge, with vests and pants to match. If you favor a real touch of whimsy in your attire, Clyde's is featuring underwear shorts with Chinese hieroglyphics on the fly. Real rugged.

The men you see on Madison Avenue are a mixed lot. They come in all shapes and sizes and from all walks of life. The Madison Avenue man can be Mr. John, who makes ladies' hats just a step from The Street, or Cardinal Spellman, who enjoys a good brisk constitutional up Madison every once in a while. Stick around 57th and Madison long enough and you'll see Thomas J. Watson of IBM, whose salary check is probably the biggest on Madison Avenue—or any other avenue. The Madison Avenue man is also the radio-television actor standing in front of the Columbia Broadcasting building telling the sweet young thing with the hatbox what a dope his producer is. He might be Bennett Cerf, the well-known television star. The Madison Avenue man may be selling moose steaks, or Chippendale desks, or he may be a Soldier of the Lord.

There is no Madison Avenue "type" and no one profession monopolizes the street—but along about lunchtime, when the upstairs occupants of Madison Avenue file out in quest of food and drink, you can hear a good deal of talk about "space" and "sponsor" and "option" and "double truck." These are the radio men, the advertising men, the magazine men, the public-relations men—the whole glossy fraternity of word merchants, so many of whom work their wonders here on Madison Avenue. A large part of New York's advertising industry has settled here, and a hefty hunk of its radio and television world (the headquarters of CBS stands on the corner of 52nd Street). Some of the country's biggest magazines, a goodly portion of the city's book publishers, a flock of literary agents, toil and spin on Madison

Avenue. Of all the occupants of Madison Avenue only the men who belong to this fraternal order may be said to run to type. So many of them dress alike (be it the Brooks look or the Bold Look), and talk alike and eat alike. Comes lunchtime, these ulcerated hucksters and editors and account executives come out of their conference rooms to eat—at the Biltmore or the Weylin, the New Weston or Longchamps, or Hamburg Heaven, or Hamburg Bar, or Hamburg Grille, or Hamburger Barn, or Hamburger Hearth, or Hamburger Mary, or in one of the dozens and dozens of intimate and expensive French and Italian restaurants that have settled snugly on the side streets, as close to Madison as possible.

* * * * *

The closer a man gets to 57th Street, the more he finds himself surrounded by dainty underthings. He sees more linen and lingerie shops, more shops named for "milady," and cozy, costly gown shops with but one or two mannequins in the window.

When the wandering male passes the 57th parallel he moves into the sixties, seventies, eighties, New York's proudest residential district; and now the stores cater almost exclusively to milady's wants. Even the banks here drop all pretense of wooing the male animal. The Bank of the Manhattan Company, at the corner of 64th, has a special room for female depositors, a room with organdy curtains and a real fireplace.

"Charming" is still the inescapable word for Madison from 42nd to 86th, and even a few blocks beyond. But it becomes increasingly obvious that we won't be able to afford the charm much longer. Madison is costly real estate, and getting more so all the time. Between 23rd and 96th, Madison pays the city $10,000,000 a year in taxes. If those three-and-a-half miles were counted as a separate city, they would be the 25th wealthiest city in the United States. The day is coming, closer and closer, when every inch of this golden ground must be made to give its maximum yield. That symbol of elegance and charm, the Ritz, *used* to be on Madison Avenue. At this writing only the carcass of its ancient foundation remains. It leaves memories that flow through the mind as gin flows through the stories of Scott Fitzgerald and *Liebfrauenmilch* through the reminiscences of Ludwig Bemelmans. But the memory is all; they will never build hotels like the Ritz with its Ritz Gardens designed like a pagoda, its curving staircases, and the best damn Men's Bar in the world. It was very handsome, but it wasn't functional—so wait till you see the functional factory they'll put in its place.

The old order keeps changing and it makes Madison more and more a street of melancholy contrasts. The Wilke sisters (that's right —*sisters*) run the same old-fashioned pipe-and-tobacco shop they've been running here for seventeen years (their grandfather started the business), and 100,000 customers, including Lords Inverchapel and Halifax, have found its quaint, quiet air to their liking. But a lot of pipe smokers also patronize the new Wally Frank pipe shop on the corner of 44th, which has a layout so ultramodern that some wit has called it the Wally Frank Lloyd Wright shop.

One by one the old buildings are being torn down, the shops are being modernized. Perhaps the most conspicuous example of this headlong plunge into the brave new world is the case of the Parke-Bernet Galleries, America's largest auctioneers of fine art. They used to be down at the corner of 57th and Madison in a stately brown pile, a kind of Roman *palazzo,* that lent nobility and dignity to the whole neighborhood. It was torn down in 1950 to make room for the 25-story 575 Madison Avenue Building, which now gives the neighborhood the look of the inside of a submarine.

In its early days Madison was a residential section for the rich. Call it the Park Avenue of its day—the day before apartment houses. The aristocracy of the new democracy—Morgans and Reids and Pynes and Tiffanys and Villards—all built palaces on Madison and all built to stay. Down on Madison Square a group of culture-conscious sports hired the great Stanford White to design the greatest palace of them all. They wanted to use it as the burgeoning city's premier athletic arena. Mr. White created a building so beautiful that it was called a Garden, and everybody expected it to last as long as the Colosseum in Rome. But the old Garden is gone now, and the New York Life Insurance Company's mammoth pile stands in its place. Whitelaw Reid built a fabulous Florentine villa way up on 50th Street. The Reids no longer live there. Their former home has been divided into three parts—one-third occupied by Random House, publishers, and the remaining two-thirds the property of the Catholic Archdiocese. Directly across the street is the rectory of St. Patrick's Cathedral, and further down the block is the residence of Francis Cardinal Spellman. This is a distinction in itself because few people have residences on Madison Avenue any more. The old J. P. Morgan place on 37th Street is now the headquarters of the United Lutheran Church in America. This old brownstone still has a garden—the only garden remaining on Madison Avenue.

So very little of the old flavor clings to the city. Downtown they're tearing Washington Square to pieces and uptown they're destroying the Ritz. Madison, of all the city's streets, is the last reminder of the New York that used to be, and its nostalgic portions are shrinking every day. How much longer can they hold out against the pressure of taxation? Ten years? Five? In the meantime, of course, it's still nice to see a very old lady with a flowerpot hat doing her window-shopping along this street, while a chauffeur at the wheel of an immaculate old limousine pulls slowly along the curb to keep pace with her, and a cop winks at the effect on traffic. It's nice to see a drugstore like Cassebeer's, with Merlin's own collection of old jars and vials behind the counters, and the business of the house very plain on the window: "H. A. Cassebeer," it says, "Apothecaries, Chemists, Pharmaceuticals, Drugs." In other words, no ham on rye, no jumbo malt. Just a plain (and wonderfully handsome) old-fashioned drugstore. It is nice to see a laundry on this street advertising itself as a *"nettoyage à sec,"* on the blithe assumption that everybody knows what *that* means. It's nice to see the old clock-repair shops one flight up, and a firm like Aguilar-Ramirez which specializes in "Tailored Closets," and the old drinking trough for horses down in front of the old ASPCA building. It's nice to know that Mr. Gristede does a neighborly business in groceries, has ten stores on this street (plus a wines-and-liquors establishment), while the Great Atlantic and Pacific has only four—in other words, that Madison is not *yet* a supermarket street. The odor of lavender still clings to it—in spots. Madison is like the rich old aunt, still alive and kicking, with a room all her own in our shining new house. We are wise to savor her wit, charm, and gracious company while we can. The old girl can't last forever.

"Matches Mary" [38]

Every regular theatergoer in New York [in 1902] knows of "Matches Mary" or "Matchless Mary," as she is better known by those who have had occasion to incur her anger. She is as much identified with the theater district as the electric signs which make the day longer on Broadway than any other place on earth. She is interested in plays,

[38] From *The "Man in the Street" Stories from "The New York Times,"* Containing over Six Hundred Humorous After-Dinner Stories about Prominent Persons, p. 41. Copyright, 1902, by J. S. Ogilvie Publishing Company. New York.

and always gets a symposium review from those who leave between the acts on the first nights. Of each one she asks: "How is it going; will it be a success?" She is interested in successes, and failures have a great bearing upon her business.

One evening a short time ago it was snowing hard. The theaters were doing a light business, and the smokers in the audiences remained indoors. Mary was walking down Broadway when she met a well-known critic.

"Hello, Mary!" he called.

"Oh, hello, Mr. ——. This is a terrible bad night for our business, ain't it?"

Broadway Rose[39]

Faintly the rain strummed Broadway at four o'clock Sunday morning. Squatting there on a pile of Sunday papers sat my big, red-hot date of the evening, Broadway Rose, the straggly-haired little queen of panhandlers. As usual, she was bedecked in What the Well-Dressed Woman Would Not Be Caught Dead in—including a red stocking cap. Her toes punched out of her shoes, and her stringy hair got somehow into her mouth.

She surveyed me lovingly through her thick glasses, pinched me a couple of times on the cheek, and said, "Darling!"

But such sighs didn't fool me. Broadway Rose has heaved herself like a football player upon the necks of Abe Lyman, Earl Carroll, George Jessel, Harry Richman, and others. She is a fickle dame. Because earlier I saw her belly up to a subway turnstile and scream, "Good night, sweetheart," and throw many slobbery kisses to Orchestra Leader Ted Eddy of the Iceland Restaurant, her real passion. He's been kind to her and her twisted ideas. It's perhaps the wackiest romance on our wacky street.

"She's got a little peephole down there in a boiler room," a fellow told me. "She sneaks down there, puts her eye to the hole, and watches him on the bandstand in the Iceland. That makes her happy."

I went looking in the building at 1680 Broadway but she was as elusive as Garbo. "It's too oily for her," the white-haired newsdealer

[39] From *I Am Gazing Into My 8-Ball,* by Earl Wilson, pp. 163–166. Copyright, 1943, 1944, by the *New York Post;* 1945, by Earl Wilson. New York: Doubleday & Co., Inc.

said at midnight. "Come at three." He said she hangs around till seven A.M.

At three I found her down at her peephole, blinking at me, showing a semi-toothlessness, a little ring of froth occasionally around her mouth. Mistaking me for a detective, she trembled, and her hands toyed with a couple of sharp, dangerous-looking pins she wears in her coat sleeves. She was clutching fearfully at a Negro girl who shuddered and said, "Put those pins away, Rose, you scare me."

Out came Ted Eddy, and his big hello made me acceptable. She shuffled up in her tango slippers with tissue paper stuck around the edges and offered her mouth to be kissed—an offer he didn't accept.

Like children, we walked to the subway. She always escorts him to the turnstile; usually she meets him when he arrives for work, going right down to the turnstile to hurl herself upon him. When she can she sneaks into the Iceland; once she watched adoringly from a phone booth and flung herself at him as he came off the stand.

"Tell him," Ted Eddy said, "about the time I had a cold and you got my cold."

"A cold I had," she snorted indignantly. "A running fever I had!" She hung onto his arm. "I like him so much," she said, "I always snuggle up close and I caught his cold."

"Are you jealous?" he asked.

"What *chu* think?" she returned, doglike.

"He's my doll!" she announced to a woman she knew. "We're getting married, ain't we, sweetheart?"

He preferred to be vague, as he is happily married to a woman who understands and sympathizes with his predicament. Broadway Rose, whatever her mental state, seems to receive little affection. Once he gave her a ring containing a cluster of attractive colored glass which she often says is their engagement ring. "You gotta marry me fast, sweetheart," she says sometimes, "because Earl Carroll wants to marry me.'

Suddenly she dug a roll of bills from inside her clothes, removed it from a paper wrapping she had taken off a candy bar, and said, "Count it, darling!"

He counted $66 and gave it back. She wore a waitress' apron and in the pocket of this there was a fistful of silver. He watched anxiously for his train and then started for it. Clinging to him, she accompanied him to the turnstile, and waved and shouted at him after the train door had closed and the train had started to roll away.

"He's a doll," she told me, coming back. "He's a doll in my heart."

She sometimes warms herself in the early morning in the steam that comes up through the street. She is still kidded about her untidiness. One gag is that she is fashion editor of the *Hobo News.* It's also smart to say of a girl, "She's as pretty as a rose—Broadway Rose." Some storekeepers chase her by squirting seltzer water on her or sweeping under her feet. Most of the mere workers tolerate her and cheerfully say, "Hel-lo, Broadway!"

We were talking about this and she looked up meekly through thick-lensed glasses, with the toothlessness showing, and said, "Let's get out of the subway. It reminds me too much of him." That's why we went up and sat on the stack of newspapers there in the rain at 4 A.M.

Toots Shor

HIS SAYINGS[40]

"I ain't interested in bein' a millionaire," Shor remarked the other day. "What's the difference between makin' twenty-five thousand and fifty thousand? You can only sleep in one bed, eat three squares, and drink one bottle of whiskey a day. I don't need a million. I always say, 'I don't wanna be a millionaire, I just wanna live like one.' And I do. I go to all the ball games, I get the best seats at the fights, and I got the best friends in the world. What the hell! Rockefeller isn't any happier than me.". . .

* * * * *

. . . Unmarried women, in the Shorian society, are generally referred to, in descending order of beauty and respectability, as "dames," "broads," and "beasts." A member's wife is spoken of as his "missus." A member who has been married twice is called a "two-striper." One who is married but living apart from his wife is said to be "living in Splitsville," or, as Shor sometimes says of such a person, "He's married, but he ain't workin' at it." Wives of members are expected to conduct themselves decorously, because the males of the society have a sentimental respect for womanhood, which when combined with motherhood becomes sacrosanct. "They're old-fashioned guys," one

[40] From *The Wonderful World of Toots Shor,* by John Bainbridge, pp. 88–89, 90–91. Copyright, 1950, by John Bainbridge. Boston, Mass.: Houghton Mifflin Company.

Originally published in *The New Yorker.*

member who has drifted away has said. "They're knights with cauliflower ears."

TOOTS SHOR AND THE ARTS[41]

Most of the people who eat, drink, and make their social headquarters at Toots Shor's, which some of its patrons have called The Temple of Friendship, earn their living by contributing in one way or another to the diversion of the masses. At the top of the Shorian society are the athletes and sportswriters, the aristocrats whose income derives from their ability to play or write about games that interest large sections of the public. At the bottom are the shoestring press agents, the society's peasantry, who turn a dollar by exploiting small-time night clubs and undistinguished strip-teasers. In between is the large middle class, composed of actors, singers, gag writers, cabaret, radio, and television performers, columnists, ticket brokers, music publishers, bookmakers, motion-picture executives, and a variety of other people whose income depends directly or indirectly on entertainment. The Shorians' occupational similarity lends homogeneity to their society and is one of the important determinants of its culture, which has the charm of primitiveness.

The members, taking their cue from Shor, their revered leader, have a frank and almost aggressive lack of interest in aesthetic and intellectual pursuits. "You don't seem to know anything about opera, Mr. Shor," Elsa Maxwell once remarked when the two titans were appearing together on a literary radio program. "That makes us even, Miss Maxwell," Shor replied. "You don't seem to know anything about baseball." Shor went to the opera once, when he was dragooned by a friend into seeing *Faust*. Afterward, at the restaurant, he was asked if he had enjoyed it. "Nah," he said. "Too much singin'." As a favor to his friend James Conzelman, Shor attended a cocktail party given by Doubleday for Elizabeth Janeway, a friend of Conzelman's, to celebrate the publication of one of her novels. Leonard Lyons, another guest, asked Shor what he was doing there. "Just drinkin' and bein' literary," he said. Later, as his eye roved over the gathering, Shor said to Conzelman, "I don't see nobody here I'd want to be with at two o'clock in the morning." In 1945, Shor and his wife attended the Broadway opening of Maurice Evans' shortened version of *Hamlet*. Shor had never seen any Shakespeare, but the Evans *Hamlet* was produced by Shor's friend Michael Todd, and Shor showed up in the interests of friendship. As the bell rang at the end of the first

[41] *Ibid.*, pp. 78–83.

intermission, Shor said to the friends he was with, "I bet I'm the only bum in the joint that's going back just to see how it comes out." Because of his friendship for Todd, Shor later told all his friends that *Hamlet* was a fine show and Evans a great actor. "Some creep says to me, 'Evans spits,' " Shor remarked. "I said to this creep, 'You don't have to sit ringside for Evans. Sit back in the side arena and he can't spit on you. And if he does, it's worth it.' "

Shor has been in Carnegie Hall twice. He was forced to make his first visit by losing a bet on a football game with his friend Paul Draper; in compliance with the terms of the wager, Shor, in white tie and tails, was obliged to attend one of Draper's recitals. After the performance, Shor got into a taxi and said, "Take me to Toots Shor's." The driver looked stunned. "Mister," he said, "I been working this stand for ten years, and this is the first time I ever took anybody from here to there." About a year after that, Shor was given—and faithfully promised the donor he would use—a pair of tickets to a symphony concert conducted by Leopold Stokowski. As his guest, Shor took his friend the late Rags Ragland, a burlesque comedian. After they had been seated, Shor looked around the hall and said to Ragland, "There ain't a crumb here I know." After the first number, Stokowski returned to the podium again and again to acknowledge the applause. Shor turned to Ragland and said, "Look at that creep! I saw Hubbell pitch a no-hitter and he didn't take no bows. Let's leave at the half." They did.

Shor, who sometimes points out that the only five-syllable word he knows is "delicatessen," is dimly aware that his world is somewhat circumscribed, but he is perfectly contented in it. Shortly before V-J Day, he wrote a letter to his friend Jack Mahon, then a war correspondent in the Pacific. "You know, Jughead," Shor said, "gradually all our boys are coming home, and I know it won't be long before we have our Friday nights together again. We will have our same good festivities and our usual arguments about sports and no talking about world affairs. The reason I say this, Jug, is guys like us here are born to have fun and discuss the little things in life and not get mixed up in discussions of heavy, big-time arguments."

HIS INSULTS[42]

Maybe Toots is a little sadistic about the Great. Maybe he's just extra proud of his good restaurant. Louis B. Mayer, a minor god to

[42] From *I Am Gazing into My 8-Ball,* by Earl Wilson, pp. 136–137. Copyright, 1943, 1944, by the *New York Post;* 1945, by Earl Wilson. New York: Doubleday & Co., Inc.

Hollywood, came in one night and while Toots was glad to serve him, he saw in Mayer not a regular patron but a transient who might get in two or three times a year. Mayer, who was only trying to be friendly, and didn't appreciate how sensitive the big two hundred and fifty-pounder can be, said, "This is a nice room you have here. I hope the food is good."

"I've seen some of your pictures," Toots quietly replied.

The dinner and service pleased Mayer, and on the way out he tried to patch it up. "The food is very good," he said to Toots.

"I don't need you to tell me that," Toots said. "The people"—he indicated with his hamlike hand the crowd in the room and outside the rope—"tell me!"

* * * * *

Toots is a special friend of people such as Jimmie Walker, Quentin Reynolds, Frank Sinatra, Joe E. Lewis, Bill Corum and others, and they make his place their hangout, so it vexes him a lot when somebody demands some special attention, as a big radio producer recently did, by saying, "I bring a lot of important people in here."

"Yeah?" said Toots. "What do you want me to do—buy that building next door just to take care of you and your important people? Nobody's important."

The producer didn't come back, and would get a chilly welcome if he did.

One of radio's most celebrated stars dropped in on a meatless day and brought a guest along. The radio star urged Toots to break his meatless-day rule, to give the guest some hamburger. "Couldn't you do it for this special customer?" asked the star.

That inflamed Toots, who said, "See all these people in here? They're regular customers. They're not getting it. Why should a special customer get it?"

Damon Runyon's Ashes [43]

November 17, 1946

My dear Son:

These are your instructions for the disposal of my remains and you are not to permit any one to dissuade you from them on any grounds.

[43] From *Father's Footsteps*, by Damon Runyon, Jr., pp. 162–163, 176–177. Copyright, 1953, by the Curtis Publishing Company; 1954, by Damon Runyon, Jr. New York: Random House.

Have Campbell's . . . take charge of body immediately on being advised of my death.

No funeral services. No display of my body. No flowers.

I desire that my body be cremated and my ashes scattered without publicity over the island of Manhattan, the place I have truly loved and that was so good to me.

I think you can get Captain Eddie Rickenbacker of Eastern Airways to get his boys to perform this service for me. If you like you may have my name added to the stone over your mother's grave in the family plot at Woodlawn.

I have often expressed these wishes about my disposition in my column and other writings so there is nothing new about them save as addressed to you personally.

In Affection,

Dad

P.S. There is a copy of these instructions in my box in the hotel office or the vault box in the Chase National Bank branch at 143 57th.

Dad

* * * * *

My father's expressed hope . . . was that he would be in a happy state if he "woke up dead" and found himself at a big poker game with his departed pals—"TAD" Dorgan, Sid Mercer, Matty Matthewson, Hype Igoe, and all the rest. He hoped, my father said, that they would have held a seat open for him.

December 18, 1946, my wife and I went secretly to Campbell's, where I was handed a bulky package, wrapped in brown paper tied with thick twine, carefully prepared to conceal the shape. Inside was a heavy bronze urn containing the ashes of Damon Runyon. At Eastern Airlines headquarters in Rockefeller Center we met Captain Rickenbacker.

From La Guardia Airport we went up in a big twin-engine transport with chief pilot John F. Gill at the controls along with co-pilot Captain Eddie Rickenbacker, both of whom had known my father. Rickenbacker, my wife and I, with the urn on my lap, sat in bucket seats in the rear of the plane.

The ship droned north and banked over Woodlawn. Then it bore through the dreary day down the Hudson River and turned at 3,000 feet over the Statue of Liberty. Captain Rickenbacker took the urn and went forward to the co-pilot's seat on the right of the cockpit. I stood right behind, bent over in the little companionway.

The plane steadied north over Broadway. Captain Rickenbacker tied the wrapping twine from his wrist to the heavy bronze container as insurance against a slip. At Times Square I nodded and Captain Rickenbacker tipped the urn out the cockpit window.

Nothing was said aloud.

Numbers in Harlem [44]

Playing numbers is the most flourishing clandestine industry in Harlem. It is the first and foremost of the rackets and the oldest. Exciting the masses' imagination to easy "hits" by the placement of tiny stakes with glittering quick returns, it squeezes Harlem in its powerful grip. To the Negro operators it is not so enormously profitable today as in its halcyon period, when its foundations were laid and it spread with impunity, not fearing white competitors and the action of the law. At that time the operators ("kings" and "queens" as they were called) each had a turnover of a quarter of a million dollars yearly. But after a span of unbelievably fabulous gold-years, the law of the land at last became aware of them and Federal and Municipal investigations compelled well-known operators to retire to private, comfortable and even luxurious lives. Through fear or careless management the business of some slipped from their hands and they were reduced to penury. And others were driven from the field by white overlords.

Through all the changes Harlemites have played the game increasingly and apparently will as long as Harlem exists. Numbers is a people's game, a community pastime in which old and young, literate and illiterate, the neediest folk and the well-to-do all participate. Harlemites seem altogether lacking in comprehension of the moral attitude of the white world towards its beloved racket.

In its early years these whites in and around Harlem who were aware of the game were tolerantly amused, and contemptuously called it "the nigger pool," or "nigger pennies"! "Numbers" was the only game on which a penny could be put up as a wager. But a lucky penny makes six dollars for the player, minus the small percentage for the collector who places the bet. The white world never imagined that the pennies

[44] From *Harlem: Negro Metropolis,* by Claude McKay, pp. 101–102, 106–114. Copyright, 1940, by E. P. Dutton & Co., Inc. New York.

of Harlem's humble folk were creating fortunes of thousands of dollars and "kings" and "queens" in Harlem.

* * * * *

. . . The avid playing of numbers enormously multiplied the appetites of the credulous in the science of numerology. Harlem was set upon a perpetual hunt for lucky numbers. House numbers, car numbers, letters, telegrams, laundry, suits, shoes, hats, every conceivable object could carry a lucky number. Any casual thing might become unusual with the possibility of being endowed with a lucky number: a horse in the street, the first person you meet, an automobile accident, a fire, a fight, a butterfly fluttering on the air, a funeral, even a dog posing against a wall! And dreams! Harlem is haunted by numbers.

Dreaming of numbers is an inevitable condition of the blissful state of sleeping. And so the obsession of signs and portents in dreams as interpreted by numbers created a business for local numerologists. They compiled books of dreams interpreted by playing numbers. Dream books of numbers were published by Prince Ali, Madame Fu Futtam, Professor Konje, Red Witch, Moses Magical and many others. Such are the best sellers of Harlem.

"Hot" lucky numbers are peddled on the streets. Some are offered with a phial of oil or a box of incense to elude the curiosity of the police. But many are brazenly sold in a little piece of folded paper. And the occult chapels have multiplied and increased their following by interpreting dreams by numbers and evoking messages from the dead with numbers attached to the messages and by figuring out signs and portents by numbers.

The religious playing of numbers naturally increases the development of mysticism in Harlem. The numbers must be guessed and played at hazard. When such numbers do not win, the addicts of the game will readily resort to those psychic types of persons who profess to be mediums of numbers. It may be crudely manifested in Harlem, but this mystical abnegation is not a Negroid monopoly. It exists among the international gamblers of Monte Carlo as well as the *aficionados* of the Spanish lottery. In fact I have been amused in foreign parts by some gamblers taking me as a kind of fetich and touching my skin before placing a bet.

Harlem Occultists [45]

In Harlem . . . [the occultists] have refined their work and enlarged their scope. The former basement dives of the obeahman and the conjure-woman, once weird with the accumulated relics of animals' skins and bones and feathers and the black pot brewing evil-smelling stuff, are now transformed into mystic chapels in which burn candles and oils and incense.

Distraught persons resort to them for solace, to get information on finding jobs, love, friendship and conjugal felicity, lucky playing numbers, charms to ward off evil. It is not so strange that these occult establishments should exist in Harlem. Like gypsies, they may be found in every place. But it is significant that such an increasingly large number should flourish there. Many of them advertise in Harlem's newspapers. But the exclusive and successful ones do not advertise. And these constitute the majority.

An indication of their luxuriant growth is the unusual springing up of sacred shops in Harlem. These are the depots which supply the ritualistic paraphernalia of the occult chapels. At first glance they appear no different from similar establishments downtown which furnish special religious articles for priest and altar.

But a little investigation discloses astounding differences. Behind the pictures and the statuary of biblical figures, there are the more important appurtenances of mumbo-jumbo. The shelves look like a pharmacist's, loaded with vari-colored jugs of oils with euphemistic labels such as: Jupiter, King Solomon, Felicity, Love-charm, Commander, Concentration, High John, Rosemary, Chapel Bouquet.

There are candles of every hue which are used in the mystic rites of candle-lore. Divination is done by the flicker of the flame or the shape of the tallow after the wick has burned out. The color of the candle is of special importance, as also the day on which it should be burned.

Yellow candles are burned for true devotion; green for material gain; purple for self-mastery, power and domination over others; red to win and increase love; pink to invoke celestial happiness; white for communion with the departed; orange for lucky dreams; blue for peace

[45] *Ibid.*, pp. 75–79.

and harmony; black to ward off evil. Incenses, magic herbs and roots and an array of dream books of numbers complete the stock.

There is no connection between the occult chapels and the open cults, such as Mother Horne's and Father Divine's. The chapels are designed for intimate séances. Most of them are hidden away in apartments and known only to special devotees. There is as much difference between the occultists and the cultists as there is between the human ghost and the human soul.

Cultists, such as Father Divine, somehow follow the tradition of the prophets. But the Harlem occultists are the true descendants of the fetich priests. They attract their following by exploiting the method of a deft combination of cosmic mysteries and jungle apprehensions. Upon their altars in Harlem, pagan and Christian symbols are ranged together. But the priest or priestess is partial to oriental vestments, either Hindu or Persian, Arabian or Egyptian.

Over their pagan apparel the cross hangs upon their breasts. But they appease the wishful thinking of their devotees, telling their thoughts with roses and stars and birds' feathers and the symbol of the serpent, even as with the symbol of the cross. The lavish use of incense, oil and candles is a powerful opiate to the senses. And in that close atmosphere a rosary of meaningless words may seem beautifully true to those who recoil from facing forever the drab reality of their existence. Messages from the dear dead, interpretation of dreams and lucky numbers are eagerly accepted. And adequate remuneration is given in return. Like drug addicts accustomed to their special stimulant, the devotees must have their occult medicine.

I am drawn to Harlem's occult chapels by the same curiosity which impelled me to visit the candle-lit shrines of marabouts in Africa. One I visited recently is situated in the middle sector of Harlem, on the third floor of a tenement. Half the flat has been transformed into a chapel. It was suffocatingly crowded. I found standing room at the back. The atmosphere was narcotic with the heavy aroma of burning oils and incense. In the audience women predominated. They whispered excitedly, eyes strangely glittering, like pentecostal pilgrims awaiting a miracle. The walls in light blue were covered with mottoes and rubrics—"Trust and Hope," "Love and Live," "Life Is Mystery"—and embellished with stars, crosses, crescents and hearts cut out of colored paper.

Up front there was a white altar, loaded with colored candles burning in little glass jars, and behind it, on the wall, a crude painting of an elaborate Tree of Life and Hope. The priestess was a brown woman of commanding height and bulk. She was robed in black and white, with voluminous sleeves and a long white train. Her headdress was fitted like that of a woman of ancient Egypt and all her movements were sidelong. She was assiduously assisted by a tall black man, costumed in red and gold. He straightened the train whenever the priestess seemed in danger of becoming entangled. He handed her the magic-making items she needed. On the altar were set the symbols of divination: a cross, a star, a crescent and roses.

When I entered, the priestess was engaged in a pantomime before the altar, clasping and unclasping her hands, bowing her head and stretching her large-sleeved arms to look like wings. At intervals she glided around the altar. Then she started an unintelligible incantation. When she stopped, she picked up a star and gazed intently at it. And in dark deep tones she declared: "I can see the limitless dimensions of omniscience. It is a long straight stroke. Is it the divine whip of the archangel of retribution? Or is it a staff? I feel interference. Let mine eyes be as the sight of the serpent."

Slowly she began gliding again around the altar, one hand thrust out before and the other behind her as she said: "I see through the rose of revelation and I discern a pattern of lightning. It is a bright triangle. There is the letter Y. I hear sweet voices singing. I see little children dancing. The grass is green and tender, oh, I glimpse a silver M. Oh, I see another M clear as the sunny water of the stream of heaven! It is the month of May."

The women sighed together. "But there is a shadow," the priestess intoned. "There is a hand and a long finger pointing at May. Oh, clear like the jewel of the Madonna, I can see R. Yes, it is a name, Mary—a message for Mary." Five women, each named Mary, showed their hands. "But it is one message for one person only," said the priestess. "And it isn't you, and it isn't you and it isn't you," she sing-songed pointing at each Mary. She swayed back and forth and glided around the altar. She clasped the star to her forehead. Then she flung back her head and threw her hands straight upwards.

"I see a garden in the sky, a beautiful garden. Now there is a lady walking in the garden. Oh, but it is painful, painful. She walks with crutches. Oh, she is very painful, but she must walk in that garden. Now she is stooping—it is painful, very painful, but she picks a rose." As she chanted, moaning, the priestess acted out the part of the lady in pain in the garden. She was a good actress. And now she cried: "Oh, light of my vision! My eyes are dazzled by a wonderful flash in the sky. And it brings me the name, Rosemary! Rosemary!"

A good-looking brown girl fell out of her chair in the front row and writhed on the floor: "Oh, mother, my mother, my mother in pain!" she wailed. The women started keening and moaning, but in subdued voices, like persons sobbing in a sickroom. The priestess lifted up the girl, embraced and comforted her: "Don't cry. Your mother is no longer in pain. But the good spirits revealed her to me by her former life here on earth. Those are the ways of the spirit to convey hidden secrets. I saw your mother in pain, but I have also seen her uplifted from pain. She is happy and laughing with honey on her tongue. Her message to you is, walk straight and beware of the joy-riding lovers in Harlem."

"Thank you, mother, for your message," said the girl. Composing herself, she extracted a five-dollar note from her purse and handed it to the priestess. "This is mother's gift," said the priestess, holding the note before the altar. "And any of you who feel compensated by the action of my spirit, in contacting and revealing the unknown tonight, may contribute something for the good spirits. I feel that my inspiration is boundless tonight and those who desire more personal and secret revelation may wait and see me after the meeting. The fee is only one dollar for a private revelation. And I am giving you two consecrated numbers, 618 and 901."

The women crowded round the altar with contributions.

The Barefoot Prophet[46]

In the years gone by . . . prophets have appeared in Harlem representing the whole list of Biblical oracles, all of them with "calls" and supernatural credentials. Martin was the first to be known simply as "The Prophet." He was probably Harlem's most picturesque figure. Watching him stroll along the avenue was a pleasant thing to behold. His luxuriant mane of gray hair and flowing beard made him look as if he had just stepped from the pages of the Bible.

Prophet Martin was a beloved man and a one-man institution. He carried the word daily to stranger places than street corners. Patrons were seldom surprised to see him in gin mills, cabarets, bars or buffet

[46] By Abram Hill. Manuscripts of the Federal Writers' Project of the Works Progress Administration in New York City, "Negroes of New York." Schomburg Collection, New York Public Library.

flats. Usually he would quote a few passages of the Scriptures, take up a small collection, and then vanish. Small children followed him through the streets, touching his robe for "good luck." Confused parents would stop him in the streets and seek advice about their wayward offspring. Hustlers and number runners treated him with respect and unsmilingly accepted his benedictions.

Legends grew. It was rumored that he was rich; that he owned several apartment houses and that he traveled over the country in an expensive automobile. This Prophet Martin denied emphatically. He pointed out that he never accepted a church. He had no income other than the small change that he received from his listeners. He preached on the street corners for fifty years in twenty-five different states. When he died his family was on relief.

"The Prophet" was born Clayburn Martin in Henry County, Virginia, in 1851. At an early age he had a vision. "Take off your shoes, for this is holy ground. Go preach My gospel," a voice told him. He obeyed. His first audience was a group of crap shooters on a street corner. He succeeded in influencing the crap shooters so well that he continued his mission.

Mary, his wife, was over twenty years his junior. He had four daughters and one son. The latter was born when he was sixty-one years of age. Once he grew weak and listened to Mary. She told him to cut his hair and wear shoes. Like Samson he cut his locks. Illness followed. He realized his error. He let his hair grow back and again trod his way in bare feet. His health was restored and he never cut his locks nor wore shoes again.

The vagabond preacher maintained a sanctum sanctorum at 217 West 134th Street. He received callers every evening from 6 to 8:30. Brother Russell, himself a living witness to the healing power of Prophet Martin, would assist him. Here "The Prophet" would ask whether the trouble was of the soul or of the body. If it was of the soul, confession and prayer were enough. If God's Temple—that is what he called the body—was broken down, he would administer a few drops of the ointment or drugs which he prepared himself, then console the ailing person with a few words of prayer. Once he was arrested in Newark, New Jersey, for practicing medicine without a license.

"I will make you ruler over the Nations. I will lift up my people through you," he would begin. Though he could not read nor write, God gave him his messages. "You are the temples. Every man is the dwelling place of the Almighty. He's not in the buildings we call churches." Thus he justified his non-belief in church buildings.

The title of Elder was bestowed by "The Church of God, Pillar, Ground of Truth, House for all people, Holy and Sanctified."

Prophet Martin's short messages showed a great lyrical quality, somewhat in the style of James Weldon Johnson's "Creation." Following is one of Martin's typical sermons:

Our world is like a fox, brethern. Like a fox that catch his foot in the trap of the Devil. Fox knows, bretherns, that if he stays long enough in the Devil's trap the Devil will kill him with a long stick. So the fox gnaws off his foot and leaves the foot for the Devil and goes home on three legs and praises God he's gittin' home at all.

Now brethern, you see what I mean. We got sin and we got sinners, and better than that the sinners should lead us into the Devil's trap we must cut them off. Sin ain't no part of God, my brethern, but we righteous are part of God Himself. We got to save all we can, and let the rest go. But now, brethern, before we let 'em go, let's pray hard and long for them with His omnipresence.

Prophet Martin died in July, 1937. He was eighty-six years old. Barefooted in death as he was in life, his bushy head resting on a royal purple cushion, the aged evangelist lay in state. Hundreds heeded a last message pinned to a box, resting on his chest. The appeal written in his own shaking hand as he lay dying in Harlem Hospital read:

"Help bury the prophet."

Harlem House-Rent Parties [47]

[In the 1920's] house-rent parties began to flourish—and not always to raise the rent either. But, as often as not, to have a get-together of one's own, where you could do the black-bottom with no stranger behind you trying to do it, too. Non-theatrical, non-intellectual Harlem was an unwilling victim of its own vogue. It didn't like to be stared at by white folks. But perhaps the down-towners never knew this—for the cabaret owners, the entertainers, and the speakeasy proprietors treated them fine—as long as they paid.

The Saturday night rent parties that I attended were often more amusing than any night club, in small apartments where God knows who lived—because the guests seldom did—but where the piano would

[47] From *The Big Sea,* An Autobiography by Langston Hughes, pp. 228–233. Copyright, 1940, by Alfred A. Knopf. New York & London.

often be augmented by a guitar, or an old cornet, or somebody with a pair of drums walking in off the street. And where awful bootleg whisky and good fried fish or steaming chitterling were sold at very low prices. And the dancing and singing and impromptu entertaining went on until dawn came in at the windows.

These parties, often termed whist parties or dances, were usually announced by brightly colored cards stuck in the grille of apartment house elevators. Some of the cards were highly entertaining in themselves:

We got yellow girls, we've got black and tan
Will you have a good time? - YEAH MAN!

A Social Whist Party

—GIVEN BY—

MARY WINSTON

147 West 145th Street Apt. 5

SATURDAY EVE., MARCH 19th, 1932

GOOD MUSIC REFRESHMENTS

H U R R A Y

COME AND SEE WHAT IS IN STORE FOR YOU AT THE

TEA CUP PARTY

GIVEN BY MRS. VANDERBILT SMITH

at 409 EDGECOMBE AVENUE
NEW YORK CITY

Apartment 10-A

on Thursday evening, January 23rd, 1930

at 8:30 P. M.

ORIENTAL - GYPSY - SOUTHERN MAMMY - STARLIGHT
and other readers will be present

Music and Talent — — Refreshments Served

Ribbons-Maws and Trotters A Specialty

Fall in line, and watch your step, For there'll be
Lots of Browns with plenty of Pep At

A Social Whist Party
Given by
Lucille & Minnie
149 West 117th Street, N. Y. Gr. floor, W,
Saturday Evening, Nov. 2nd 1929

Refreshments Just It Music Won't Quit

If Sweet Mamma is running wild, and you are looking
for a Do-right child, just come around and
linger awhile at a

SOCIAL WHIST PARTY
GIVEN BY
PINKNEY & EPPS
260 West 129th Street Apartment 10
SATURDAY EVENING, JUNE 9, 1928

GOOD MUSIC REFRESHMENTS

Railroad Men's Ball

AT CANDY'S PLACE

FRIDAY, SATURDAY & SUNDAY,

April 29-30, May 1, 1927

Black Wax, says change your mind and say they do and he will give you a hearing, while MEAT HOUSE SLIM, laying in the bin killing all good men.

L. A. VAUGH, *President*

OH BOY **OH JOY**

The Eleven Brown Skins

of the

Evening Shadow Social Club

are giving their

Second Annual St. Valentine Dance

Saturday evening, Feb. 18th, 1928

At 129 West 136th Street, New York City

Good Music Refreshments Served

Subscription 25 Cents

Some wear pajamas, some wear pants, what does it matter just so you can dance, at

A Social Whist Party

GIVEN BY

MR. & MRS. BROWN

AT 258 W. 115TH STREET, APT. 9

SATURDAY EVE., SEPT. 14, 1929

The music is sweet and everything good to eat!

Almost every Saturday night when I was in Harlem I went to a house-rent party. I wrote lots of poems about house-rents parties, and ate thereat many a fried fish and pig's foot—with liquid refreshments on the side. I met ladies' maids and truck drivers, laundry workers and shoeshine boys, seamstresses and porters. I can still hear their laughter in my ears, hear the soft slow music, and feel the floor shaking as the dancers danced.

Market Songs of Harlem [48]

THE STREET CHEF

Ah'm a natu'al bo'n cook
An' dat ain't no lie,
Ah can fry po'k chops
An' bake a low-down pie
So step right up
An' he'p yo'se'f
Fum de vittles on
Mah kitchen she'f!

THE SORREL WOMAN

Sorrel! Oh, sorrel!
'e tehste lak Granny's wine,

[48] Recorded by Frank Byrd, New York. From *American Stuff,* An Anthology of Prose & Verse by Members of the Federal Writers' Project, pp. 158–160. Copyright, 1937, by The Guilds' Committee for Federal Writers' Publications, Inc. New York: The Viking Press.

Sorrel! Oh, sorrel!
'e sweet an' 'e too fine!

Sorrel! Oh, sorrel!
'e sure a 'trengh'nin' t'ing,
Sorrel! Oh, sorrel!
'e med to suit de king!

THE AH-GOT-UM MAN

Ah got pompanos!
Ah got catfish!
Ah got buffaloes!
Ah got um!
Ah got um!

Ah got stringbeans!
Ah got cabbage!
Ah got collard greens!
Ah got um!
Ah got um!

Ah got honeydews!
Ah got can'lopes!
Ah got watermelons!
Ah got um!
Ah got um!

Ah got fish,
Ah got fruits,
Ah got veg, yes 'ndeed!
Ah got any kind o' vittles,
Ah got anything yo' need!

Ah'm de Ah-Got-Um Man!

DE SWEET PERTATER MAN

See dese gread big sweet pertaters
Right chere by dis chicken's side,
Ah'm de one what bakes dese taters
Makes dem fit to suit yo' pride.
Dere is taters an' mo' taters,

But de ones ah sells is fine
Yo' kin go fum hyeah to yondah
But yo' won't git none lak mine
'Cause Ah'm de tater man!
(Ah mean!)
De sweet pertater man!

THE CRAB MAN

Ho! Cra—ab man!
Ho! Cra—ab man!
Ho! Crabs, I say!

Fresh crabs! Hyeah!
Fresh crabs! Hyeah!
Fresh crabs, today!

THE PEPPER-SAUCE SONG
(West Indian Song Poem)

Make's no diff'ence what yo' eat
Whether rice or greens or meat
All de flavah sho am los'
'Less yo' got some pepper-sauce

When yo' pass by this-a way
Keep a lis'nin' fo' mah call
Pyo [49] *Jamaica pepper-sauce!*
Fresh red pepper-sauce!
Dat's all.

Harlem Children's Rhymes and Gags [50]

I

When you see a guy got on brown pants you say:

Buster Brown
Went down town

[49] Pure—F. B.
[50] Recorded by Ralph Ellison at playground at East 139th Street and Lenox Avenue, New York City, 1939. Manuscripts of the Federal Writers' Project of the Works Progress Administration. Deposited in the Folklore Section, Library of Congress, Washington, D. C.

With his britches
Hanging down.

Other members of the group chimed in with the following, each voice following the other in rapid succession, giving an antiphonal effect as varied as the colors named. While most of the jingles appear to have a set formula, there were many attempts at improvisation.

Yellow, yellow,
Kiss a fellow.

Blue, blue,
I love you.

Black, black,
Sit on a tack.

Green, green,
Eat ice cream
Stick your nose
In kerosene.

White, white,
You can fight.

II

Hey, Mister, if you shut up in a iron house without any windows and you didn't have nothing but a baseball bat—

In an iron house?

Yeah, yeah, that's right. Come on, Mister. What'd you do?

Well, I guess I don't know.

Gee, don't you know how to play baseball? Anybody who can play baseball knows how to get outa there.

Well, how *would* I get out?

Three strikes, and you out, Mister. . . .

You see what he means? Three strikes an' you out!

III

The following is said by children on noticing a stranger or an out-of-town license on a car driven by a Negro:

I'm a square from Delaware,
Just come in town to see the Fair.
Boom da dee ah dee
Boom! boom!

The last two lines, to the tune of "Shave and a Haircut," were used by Herbert Lambert to end each stanza he gave. Thus:

Once upon a time, goose drink wine.
Monkey chewed tobacco on the street car line.
Street car broke, monkey choke,
And that was the end of the monkey joke.
Boom da dee ah dee
Boom! boom!

IV

You know this one, Mister? See, you meet a guy you know and he's doing something good and you say, "Gee, that's fine." And the other guy says, "Wine!" And you say,

Sho nough, that's fine as wine,
As a Georgia pine,
Two old grandmothers drinking wine.

In the West Bronx

KOSHER BUTCHER[51]

Whereas on other days the patronizing of the various food stores is a matter requiring only an ordinary degree of acumen, tact, and watchfulness, a certain air of solemnity settles over the West Bronx on Thursday. Thursday is devoted to shopping for the weekend, since Friday is given over to cooking and cleaning so that Saturday can be the day of rest ordained on Mount Sinai. Even emancipated young housewives

[51] From "West Bronx: Food, Shelter, Clothing," by Ruth Glazer, in *Commentary on the American Scene,* Portraits of Jewish Life in America, edited by Elliot E. Cohen, pp. 306–308. Copyright, 1945, 1947, 1948, 1949, 1950, 1951, 1952, 1953, by The American Jewish Committee. New York: Alfred A. Knopf.
Originally published in "From the American Scene" in *Commentary.*

have been caught up in the tyranny of this custom. This is the day when the housewife descends to do battle with the butcher in earnest. Small purchases during the week of "a few veal cutlets" or "a piece liver" can be regarded as minor skirmishes. The one point that must be firmly grasped is that one does not buy meat from a butcher, one negotiates. One lives in a state of armed truce.

The young bride, for example, goes through a long period of training before she dares ask for so much as a single lamb chop. This rigorous course includes elements both scientific and psychological. To know the cuts of meat derived from the cow, the calf, and the lamb is, of course, primary. (For to what end all this fencing if one simply gives away one's hand by asking for two pounds of meat for pot roast?) Even more important are the little professional tricks suspected of every butcher by every well-versed housewife. This information is generally delivered *sotto voce* as the butcher disappears to get the cut of meat requested; viz., "If he asks you what you want it for, tell him you want to broil it. It's *his* business that you want to use it for chopped meat?" or, "Make sure when you ask for *mittel* chuck, that he doesn't give you single chuck."

This masked antagonism, this deep-lying mutual suspicion between the kosher butcher and his customer, is symbolized by the customarily empty showcase. The only function of this elaborate testimonial to refrigeration seems to be to set a restraining barrier, a neutral zone between the two contending parties. Every piece of *flanken,* every shoulder steak must be custom-cut, and each piece of meat is held up for inspection with the furtive glances, the special avowals which only a butcher knows how to utter. Occasionally a timid young woman will attempt to influence his mysterious choice as he disappears into the refrigerator. "A small piece of calf's liver," she'll say, "I hope it'll be good. It's for the baby." To dissipate the illusion that the prospective cut is not already predestined, the butcher will respond, "Whaddya mean 'good'? Would I give you a piece of liver that isn't good?" Is there a reply?

Unlike other stores, too, there is a leisurely, almost clublike atmosphere here as the women gather of a Thursday morning. Then the butcher holds court, announcing his opinions on the world, commenting on departing customers. There are no small private conversations between neighbors. No. There is an easy general public discussion and everyone is included. "Well, Mr. Pizetsner" (not "Sam," as she might say to the grocery-store man), will begin an older and more favored customer, "and how are your sons these days?" "All right, thank God;

the new business in Flatbush is doing fine." "So, how do you like living in Brooklyn, Mr. Pizetsner?" "Well, it's not so bad. We have our own house. . . ." "It must be a terrible trip for you every day. How come you don't move the store to Brooklyn?" "Listen," says the butcher, as he prepares to quarter a chicken, "everyone says the same thing. My wife wants me to give up the business. (*chop*) The boys have a good spot for me there. (*chop*) But you know what I say . . . ? (*The cleaver is suspended.*) I tell 'em, I couldn't give up my business here. Where would I ever find such customers? They're not customers. They're dolls!" (*chop, chop*) Really, could you buy in the A & P?

FURNISHINGS[52]

Perhaps it is because in her youth the present-day housewife slept most of her nights on a folding cot put up in a hallway or a dining room or in the kitchen. Whatever the reason, today both sides of Jerome Avenue are lined with stores specializing in bedding: special extra-thick mattresses, extra-curly coiled springs, super-warm and light quilts made of 100 per cent imported white European goose down. Macy's, which is capable of packing a quilt with simple lamb's wool, is somehow not good enough. But it doesn't stop here. A girlhood spent sitting on hard kitchen chairs, or worse, on stiff-backed, gloomy dining-room chairs, bears fruit in the Bronx living room filled with the softest of down-cushioned chairs and sofas upholstered in the brightest of "cherry-red" or "chartreuse."

* * * * *

The delight with the soft and sumptuous does not end with pillows and coverlets. Everywhere straight lines are abhorred. Lamps are preferred in the form of baroque vases, their shades adorned with poufs and swaths of ruffling; the drapery is of a weight and quantity calculated to set a luxurious barrier between the beholder and the University Avenue view. Wherever there is an upholstered surface, it is tufted; wherever a wooden one, it is carved into sinuous outlines and adorned with gilded leather.

* * * * *

. . . Even the draperies fall in little puddles or the floor in the prevailing manner indicating (1) opulence—"Let it be a little longer"—(2) superlative housewifery—"Her floors are so clean you could eat off them."

[52] *Ibid.*, pp. 312–313, 314.

CLOTHING[53]

Bronx style extends to clothing, too, for undeniably there *is* a Bronx style, the result of an appreciation for, even a reveling in rich fabrics, in sumptuous textures, in elaborate folds, in dense colors, and in complex designs. This emerges in the extravagant hats, the weighty fall of a dress, the dark and brilliant nail polish, and the sculptured, appliquéd, and platformed shoes.

Even men can taste a little of this sheer exuberance of costume, now that it has been semi-legalized as "California style." They can have silky gabardines (just a bit more silky than Brooks Brothers would approve), smooth, rich flannel shirts, of an altogether different nature from the scratchy, plaid, woodsman's type, and brilliant, broadly knotted ties. And so—a suit is not a suit, but an experience, just as a fur coat is the achievement of a decade of yearning. It would be a shame if people didn't notice.

For Sunday afternoons the men have developed a special style suitable for airing the baby, milling about on the Concourse, visiting relatives in the neighborhood, and not inappropriate for local parties or poker sessions. This costume, often the cause of hidden, or sometimes energetically expressed, distress on the part of the wife, enables the Bronx husband to indulge his liking for informality (no tie), color (!), and comfort (sport shirt). With the aid and abetment of local haberdashers, the men have gained their first victory in a decade over the delicate sensibilities of Bronx taste which draws a sharp distinction between what is proper for every day and what is required for occasions. The women, however, will not be deterred from their knowledge that Sunday is the day to be straitened by corsets, pinched by shoes, hobbled by skirts, and burdened by furs.

ARCHITECTURE[54]

The role of the Concourse in Bronx life, like its geographical location, is central. Its once aristocratic buildings have become shabby and it no longer has its former prestige. But as the longest and broadest avenue in the Bronx it is still a name to conjure with. . . .

. . . The architecture of the Bronx is basically characterized by the long sober lines of six-story apartment houses, built some twenty to thirty years ago, running in a northerly and southerly direction, intersecting the main avenues. The majority of these edifices are built in

[53] *Ibid.*, pp. 314–315.
[54] *Ibid.*, pp. 315–316, 319.

a plain, unpretentious style vaguely suggesting Italian Renaissance fortresses. In harmony with their solid construction are the gloomy but magnificent hallways that even the marauding hands of three or four generations of children have not been able to disfigure. There are black-and-white tiled floors, laid out in formal patterns to resemble marble; there are gilded, pilastered walls, heavy mirrors, tables and chairs of an indefinite but regal historical period, and rococo flambeaux on the walls, unfortunately requiring the prosaic aid of electricity. The arrangement and interior architecture of the apartments also suggest palace chambers. The entrance to a meanly proportioned living room, for example, will be guarded by two elaborate French doors; the walls imitate wood paneling; the floors are parqueted; once again, there are flambeaux on the walls. Most buildings front directly on the street, but many, built on a larger scale, have center courts frequently ornamented by a pirouetting nymph or a cupid cut in stone.

The "new" houses of the Bronx (some are more than fifteen years old) are all built in a uniform "modern" style, with white or cream brick façade, casemented windows, and chromium-decorated doorways. Their interiors are likewise constructed smoothly, with a minimum of doorways, mouldings, and decoration. Despite their great number, these houses always seem exceptional, and, somehow, frivolous, appearing at random among the "regular" apartment houses, and practically never in solid blocks.

* * * * *

Elsewhere in this country, the mechanics of living comprise only the framework within which other events are supposed to occur—like making money or belonging to a golf club, or playing bridge, or doing all the other things that handsome American families are shown doing in automobile ads. But in the West Bronx . . . there it *is* life.

10

Sins of New York

The City has sins enough to answer for, Heaven knows; but it is painted blacker than it deserves, and the bright hues that belong to it are hidden under the veil of censure.—J. H. Browne

The Colt Case

COLT'S CONFESSION[1]

Samuel Adams called on Friday [September 17, 1841] at my office, as near as I can recollect, between the hours of three and four o'clock. Whether he had any especial object in view in coming at that time or not I cannot say. When he entered my office I was sitting at my table, as usual, and was at that time engaged in looking over a manuscript account book, as I had been engaged in this work for one or two days previous—that is, I was reading over the entries, and reconsidering the arithmetical calculations belonging to the entries, etc. Mr. Adams seated himself in a chair near the table, and within an arm's length of myself—so near that had we both leaned our heads forward towards each other, I have no doubt but that they would have

[1] From *The New York Tombs,* Its Secrets and Its Mysteries, Being a History of Noted Criminals, with Narratives of Their Crimes, as Gathered by Charles Sutton, Warden of the Prison, edited by James B. Mix and Samuel A. McKeever, pp. 69–77. Entered . . . 1873, by Charles Sutton. New York: United States Publishing Company.

John C. Colt, a professional bookkeeper and teacher of ornamental penmanship, with an office at Chambers Street and Broadway, was the author of a work on bookkeeping, for which he owed money to the printer, Samuel Adams.

touched. I spoke of my account, which he had, at my request, handed to me ten or twelve days before. I stated to him that his account was wrong, and read to him at the same time the account, as I had made it out on another piece of paper, and requested him to alter his account as I had it. He objected to it at first, saying that I did not understand printing. He, however, altered his figures as I read them from my account, as I made the remark that I would give $10, or some such sum, if I was not right; after he had altered his figures, and on looking it over, he said he was right at first. He made the remark that I meant to cheat him. In the meantime, we both had been figuring on separate papers parts of the account. Word followed word until we came to blows. The words "you lie" were passed, and several slight blows, until I received a blow across my mouth, and more, which caused my nose slightly to bleed. I do not know that I felt like exerting myself to strong defense. I believe I then struck him violently with my fist. We grappled with each other at the time, and I was shoved against the wall, with my side next to the table. There was a hammer on the table, which I then immediately seized hold of, and instantly struck him over the head. At this time I think his hat was nearly in my face, and I think his face was downward. I do not think he saw me seize the hammer. The seizing of the hammer and the blow were instantaneous. I think this blow knocked his hat off, but will not be positive. At the time I only remember of his twisting my neck handkerchief so tight that it seemed to me as if I lost all power of reason, still I thought I was striking away with the hammer. Whether he attempted to get the hammer away from me or not I cannot say. I do not think he did. The first sense of thought was, it seems, as though his hand or something brushed from my neck downward. I cannot say that I had any sense or reflection until I heard a knock at the door, yet there is a faint idea remains that I shoved him off from me, so that he fell over, but of this I cannot say.

When I heard the knock on the door I was instantly startled, and am fully conscious of going and turning the key so as to lock it. I then sat down, for I felt very weak and sick. After sitting for a few minutes and seeing so much blood, I think I went and looked at poor Adams, who breathed quite loud for several minutes, threw his arms out, and was silent. I recollect at this time taking him by the hand, which seemed lifeless, and the horrid thrill came over me that I had killed him. About this time some noise startled me. I felt agitated and frightened, and I think I went to the door to see if I had fastened it, and took the key out and turned down the slide. I think I stood for a minute or two listening, to hear if the affray had caused any alarm. I believe I then took a seat near the window. It was a cold, damp day, and the window had been closed all day, except six or eight inches at the top, which I let down when I first went to the office, and which remained down all the time I occupied it. I remained in the same seat for at least half an hour without moving, unless it was to draw close the curtains of the window, which were within reach. My custom had been to leave the curtains about one-third drawn from the side of the window towards Broadway. The blood at this time was spreading all over the floor. There was a great quantity, and I felt alarmed lest it should leak through into the apothecary store. I tried to stop it by tying my handkerchief around his neck tight. This appeared to do no good. I then looked about the room for a piece of twine and found in a box which stood in the room, after partially pulling out some awning which was in it, a piece of cord, which I tied tight around his neck, after taking his handkerchief off, and his stock too, I think. It was then I discovered so much blood, and the fear of its leaking through the floor caused me to take a towel and gather with it all I could, and rinse it in the pail which stood in the room. The pail was, I should think, at that time about one-third full of water, and the blood filled at least another third full. Previous to doing this I moved the body towards the box and pulled out part of the awning to rest it on, and covered it with the remainder. I never saw his face afterward. After soaking up all the blood I could, which I did as still and hastily as possible, I took my seat near the window and began to think what it was best to do. About this time some one knocked at the door, to which, of course, I paid no attention. My horrid situation remained at this time till dark—a silent space of time, with still more horrid reflection.

At dusk of the evening, and when some omnibuses were passing, I carefully opened the door and went out as still as possible, and was, as I thought, unheard. I crossed into the Park and went down to the City Hotel, my purpose being to relate the circumstance to a brother who was stopping at that house. I saw him in the front reading room, engaged in conversation with two gentlemen. I spoke to him; a few words passed between us, and, seeing that he was engaged, I returned to the Park. I walked up and down, thinking what was best to do. I thought of many things, among others of going to a magistrate and relating the circumstance to him. Then I thought of the horrors of the excitement, the trial, public censure, and false and foul reports that would be raised by the many that would stand ready to make the best appear worse than the worst for the sake of a paltry pittance, gained to them in the publication of perverted truth and original, false, foul, calumniating lies. All this, added to my then feelings, was more than I could bear. Besides, at this time, in addition to the blows given, there would be left the mark or evidence of a rope drawn tightly around the neck, which looked too deliberate for anything like death caused in an affray. Firing the building seemed first a happy thought, as all would be enveloped in flames and wafted into air and ashes; then the danger of causing the death of others, as there was quite a number who slept in the building, the destruction of property, etc., caused me to abandon the idea. I next thought of having a suitable box made, and having it leaded, so the blood would not run out, and then moving it off somewhere and burying it; then the delay of all this, and the great liability of being detected.

After wandering in the Park for an hour or more, I returned to my room and entered it as I had left it, and, as I supposed, unobserved. Wheeler's door was open, and he was talking to some one, quite audibly. I went into my room, entering undetermined and not knowing what to do. After I was seated in my room I waited silently until Wheeler's school was out and his lights were extinguished—and during this suspense it occurred to me that I might put the body in a cask or box and ship it somewhere. I little thought at this time that the box that was in the room would answer; I thought it was too small and short, and unsafe, as it was quite open. Wheeler's school being out, I still heard some one in his room, and, as I then thought, whoever it was lay down on the benches. The noise did not appear exactly like a person going to bed; there was no rustling of bed clothing. I felt somewhat alarmed. The thought then occurred to me that it might be the person who Wheeler had stated was going to occupy the room which I then held as a sleeping room as soon as I gave it up, which was to be in about ten days. The party in question was temporarily occupying Wheeler's room. Relieving myself by this thought, I soon lit a candle, knowing that something must be done; there was no time to lose.

This was about nine o'clock, I should think. Having closed the shutters, I went and examined the box to see if I could not crowd the body into it. I soon saw that there was a possibility of doing so, if I could bend the legs up so it would answer, and if I could keep some of the canvas around the body, so as to absorb the blood and keep it from running; this I was fearful of. It occurred to me, if I bury or send the body off, the clothes he had on would, from description, establish his identity. It became necessary to strip and dispose of the clothes, which

I speedily accomplished by ripping up the coat sleeves, vest, etc. While doing so, the money, keys, etc., which he had in his pocket, caused a rattling; I took them out and laid them on one side, and then pulled a part of the awning over the body to hide it; I then cut and tore a piece from the awning and laid it in the bottom of the box; then cut several pieces from the awning for the purpose of lessening its bulk, supposing it was too much to crowd into the box with the body; I then tied, as tight as I could, a portion of the awning about the head, having placed something like flax, which I found, in the box with the awning; I then drew a piece of rope around the legs at the joint of the knees and tied them together; I then connected a rope to the one about the shoulders or neck, and bent the knees toward the head of the body as much as I could, which brought it into a compact form.

After several efforts I succeeded in raising the body to a chair, then to the top of the box, and, turning it around a little, let it into the box as easy as I could, back downward, with head raised. The head, knees, and feet were still a little out, but by reaching down to the bottom of the box and pulling the body a little towards me, I readily pushed the head and feet in. The knees still projected, and I had to stand upon them with all my weight before I could get them down. The awning was then all crowded into the box, excepting a piece or two, which I reserved to wipe up the floor. There being still a portion of the box next to the feet not quite full, I took his coat and after pulling up a portion of the awning, crowded it partially under him, and replaced the awning. The cover was at once put on the box and nailed down with four or five nails, which were broken, and of but little account. I then wrapped the remainder of his clothing up, and carried it downstairs to the privy and threw them into it, together with his keys, wallet, money, pencil cases, etc.; these latter things I took down in my hat and pockets, a part wrapped in paper and a part otherwise. In throwing them down I think they must have rattled out of the paper. I then returned to the room, carried down the pail which contained the blood, the contents of which I threw into the gutter—into the street. I pumped several pails of water and threw them in the same direction. The pump is nearly opposite the outer door of the building. I then carried a pail of water upstairs, and, after rinsing the pail, returned it clean, and two-thirds full of water, to the room, opened the shutters as usual, drew a chair to the door, and leaned it against it on the inside as I closed it, locked the door, and went at once to the Washington Bath House, on Pearl Street, near Broadway.

On my way to the bath house I went to a hardware store, for the purpose of getting some nails to further secure the box. The store was closed. When I got to the bath house, I think, by the clock there it was eight minutes past ten o'clock. I washed out my shirt thoroughly in parts of the sleeves and bosom that were somewhat stained with blood from washing the floor; my pantaloons, in the knees, I also washed a little, and my handkerchief in spots. I then went home. It wanted, when I got home, about five minutes of eleven o'clock. I lit a light as usual. Caroline wished to know why I came in so late. I made an excuse, saying I was with a friend from Philadelphia, I think, and that I should get up early in the morning to see him off. I went to the stand and pretended to write till she became quiet or went to sleep, then put out the light and undressed myself, spread my shirt, etc., out to dry, and went to bed.

In the morning, about half past five, I got up, put my shirt and handkerchief, which were not yet quite dry, in the bottom of the clothes basket, under the bed. I always change my shirt on going to bed. In the morning I put on a clean shirt and handkerchief, and was nearly dressed when Caroline woke up. I stated to her it was doubtful if I would return for breakfast; did not return; went to the office, and found all, apparently, as I had left it. I went after some nails and got them at Wood's store. The store was just opened. I returned to the office, nailed up the box on all sides, and went down to the East River to ascertain the first packet to New Orleans. I then returned to the room, marked the box, and moved it, with great difficulty, to the head of the stairs. I did not dare to let it down myself, but went to look for a cartman. I saw a man passing the door as I was going out, and requested him to help me down with the box. He got it down without any assistance, preferring to do it himself, and I gave him ten or twelve cents. I then went down Chambers Street for a cartman whom I saw coming towards Broadway, and hired him to take the box to the ship at the foot of Maiden Lane. I went with him. While he was loading the box I went to my office for a piece of paper to write a receipt on, and wrote the receipt to be signed by the captain on my way down the street. I did not offer the receipt to be signed; requested one, which the receiver of the box gave me. The clerk was by at the time, and objected to the form of the receipt, and took it and altered it, wishing to know if I wanted a bill of lading. I at first remarked, as there was but one box it was not very important, adding, however, that I would call at the office for one. I did not go for the bill of lading. I tore up the receipt before I was two squares from the ship. I returned to my office by way of Lovejoy's Hotel, opposite the Park. I went to the eating room and called for a hot roll and cup of coffee; I could not eat, but drank two cups of coffee. Went to my office, locked the door, and sat down for some time. I examined everything about the room, wiped the wall in one or two places, and then went home and to bed.

[The ship did not sail as advertised, and when rewards were offered for information regarding the whereabouts of Adams, a cartman reported to the authorities that he had taken a box from the Chambers Street building to a packet lying in the East River. Thereupon the box was fished from the bottom of the hold, and disclosure of its contents led to the arrest of Colt, whose subsequent trial, despite the efforts of able counsel, ended in a verdict of murder and a sentence to the gallows. Colt's friends and counsel made a strenuous fight for him after conviction, but appeals proved fruitless.[2]]

WEDDING IN THE TOMBS[3]

. . . During the time that Colt lay in the Tombs he was repeatedly visited by one Caroline Henshaw, who had been his common-law wife. As they had never been legally married, Colt expressed a wish that they should be made husband and wife before his execution. The authorities at first refused to give the necessary consent, but afterwards gave permission and agreed that it should take place on the day of his execution, which was fixed for November 18th, 1842. At 11:30 on the fatal day, the bride appeared at the condemned cell, neatly attired in a straw bonnet, green shawl, claret-colored cloak trimmed with red cord, and a muff.

Colt was remarkably cheerful for a man who was to die four hours afterwards, but it was his wedding day, and when should a man be cheerful if not that day? The ceremony, which took place in the con-

[2] Rufus Rockwell Wilson, *New York: Old & New* (1902–1909), Vol. II, pp. 114–115.

[3] From *The New York Tombs Inside and Out!* Scenes and Reminiscences Coming Down to the Present—A Story Stranger than Fiction, with an Historic Account of America's Most Famous Prison, by John Josiah Munro, pp. 256–258, 271. Copyright, 1909, by John J. Munro. Brooklyn, N. Y.: Printed and Published by the Author.

Marriages have been performed in the Tombs Prison since it was first opened in 1838, by clergymen of all denominations, Protestant, Catholic, and Jewish, without the least objection. . . .

. . . These Tombs weddings are of two kinds: voluntary and involuntary. . . . But the marriages that attracted the most attention during these years were of persons who really wished to be man and wife, from choice. Of course, their wish is not always granted, for reasons best known to the authorities. The first marriage of this character which excited the people of the city was that of John C. Colt, who was convicted of the murder of Samuel Adams.—J. J. M.

demned cell, was witnessed by Judge Merritt, the Sheriff of the County, Colt's brother, John Howard Payne, the author of "Home, Sweet Home," and several others. The bride and groom were allowed to be alone for one hour, after which he must prepare for death.

Two hours after she left him to change orange blossoms for somber weeds, the Sheriff and his deputies went to his cell to escort him to the scaffold, which was all ready, when to their amazement they found that Colt was dead. The gallows had been cheated of its victim. The honeymoon of an hour was past, and he was cold in death.

* * * * *

. . . Just then the cry of fire was raised, which caused intense excitement among the officials and prisoners in their cells.

The lurid glare which came from the burning cupola, and which cast a shadow on all sides, attracted wide attention and a great crowd of people. After the fire was extinguished and order once more restored, Colt was found in his cell in a pool of blood. Many persons in the city believed that the burning of the cupola was a well-designed scheme to save Colt from the gallows, and in the midst of the excitement Colt escaped through one of the side doors by the aid of powerful friends and a dead body from one of the hospitals was substituted in his place. . . .

The Mystery of Mary Rogers [4]

On the corner of Fifth Avenue and Fifty-second Street, during the Seventies, there stood a dignified residence that commanded unusual attention. "Upon 'most any day that was inviting to the outdoors, a grim-visaged but elegantly dressed woman might be seen making her way down the high front stoop with a stride that was firm, for all her advancing years and a bearing that flaunted a callous defiance. At the walk waited a glittering equipage and a prancing pair of horses ready to join fashionable Gotham on wheels. A liveried coachman held open the door of the carriage to bow his mistress into the interior. No sooner had he resumed his seat and the reins and started the afternoon drive,

[4] From *Sins of New York,* As "Exposed" by the Police Gazette, by Edward Van Every, pp. 91–98. Copyright, 1930, by Edward Van Every. New York: Frederick A. Stokes Company.

with the first roll of the wheels, around the corner there came scurrying a band of unkempt street urchins, who only turned on their heels sufficiently long to chorus in derision: 'Yah! Your house is built on babies' skulls!' "

For a way these ill-mannered boys would chase after the carriage the while they kept up their offensive yelling. There was no change of expression in that grim-visaged countenance, even while the carriage occupant was within hearing of her tormentors. There was something about the woman that suggested she was utterly adamant to public regard as her shocking vocation would make her seem—and she was an abortionist of most unenviable reputation. So when finally she came to the end of her hardened existence, and with an estate officially inventoried at over $1,000,000, it came as amazing news that "she merely added one more life, that of her own, to the many she had taken, by committing suicide in the bathtub in her palatial home."

Madame Restell, or Mrs. Ann Lohman, . . . carried to her grave secrets that would have wrecked the peace of many a respected household, and that would have affected the names of many of the powerful and widely known of New York and even throughout the entire country. Madame Killer, the Abortionist, as she was long known, was one of the most noted birth control practitioners, so to put it, in all the land for many years. While she saved many fine reputations from disgrace through her handiwork, she made her own name one of the most hated. Anthony Comstock is generally credited with having driven Madame Restell to do away with herself in 1878. The *National Police Gazette,* however, which was harrying her with vigor almost as soon as Comstock was permitted his first glimpse of this immoral sphere, puts quite a different motive back of this sensational suicide case. One year after Anthony Comstock opened eyes on a world that he was to find such an offending one, the *Gazette* of February 21, 1846, printed the following torrid editorial:

RESTELL, THE FEMALE ABORTIONIST—The exposures which we have recently made of this base woman's practices have excited the profound attention of the community; and moved by the deep necessity of providing a punishment adequate to her horrid and unnatural crimes, an association is already in the process of formation, whose intention it is to petition the legislature to make abortion a State Prison offense; and also to take such measures as may lead to the punishment of its practices, and the prevention of any future murders at hand.

It is well known that Madame Restell keeps a large number of apartments in her golgotha in Greenwich Street for the accommodation of females in *accouchement,* and the number that avail themselves of such facilities in a city where licentiousness stalks abroad at midday may be guessed at, but not counted. It is well known that females frequently die in *ordinary* childbirth. How many, then, who enter her halls of death may be supposed to expire under her execrable butchery? Females are daily, nay, hourly missing from our midst who never return. Where do they go? What becomes of them? Does funeral bell ever peal a note for their passage? Does funeral train ever leave her door? Do friends ever gather round the melancholy grave? No! An obscure hole in the earth; a consignment to the savage skill of the dissecting knife, or a splash in the cold wave, with the scream of the night blast for a requiem, is the only death service bestowed upon her victims. Witness this, ye shores of Hudson! Witness this, Hoboken beach!

We do not wish to speak in parables. There is a mystery yet to be cleared up which sent a thrill of horror and a sensation of profound excitement through the length and breadth of the land! We speak of the unfortunate Mary Rogers. Experience and futile effort have proved that we have heretofore followed a wrong trail. The wretched girl was last seen in the direction of Madame Restell's house. The dreadfully lacerated body at Weehawken Bluff bore the marks of no ordinary violation. The hat found near the spot, the day after the location of the body, was dry though it had rained the night before! These are strange but strong facts, and when taken in consideration with the other fact that the recently convicted Madame Costello kept an abortion house in Hoboken at that very time, and was acting as an agent of Restell, it challenges our minds for the most horrible suspicions. Such are these abortionists! Such their deeds, and such their dens of crime!

We now ask again, if a community professing to be civilized will any longer tolerate this wholesale murder under their very eyes? Will a city, possessing courts and a police, wink at such an atrocious violation of the laws, and if it will, and the demon murderess Restell be too rich to be within the power of the law, will the community, in the last resort, suffer her to go on unrebuked by some sudden application of popular vengeance?

We are not now demanding justice upon the perpetratress of a single crime, but upon one who might be drowned in the blood of her victims, did each but yield a drop, whose epitaph should be a curse, and whose tomb a pyramid of skulls.

This was inflammatory stuff to be printed in a paper of the already considerable circulation owned by the *Gazette*. But before setting forth what followed the publication of this editorial, which sounds as though it might have been phrased by a William Jennings Bryan, it would be well first to give some attention to the inference that the Restell woman may have been in some way connected with the death of Mary Rogers, "the beautiful cigar girl," a case that goes down in the history of crime as one of the greatest of the unsolved death mysteries.

Less than four years previous to the appearance of the above editorial the city of New York knew no other topic of conversation than the assassination of Mary Rogers, whose beauty back of the cigar counter of John Anderson, well-known snuff manufacturer, played havoc with many masculine hearts and made her the bright attraction of the store at 319 Broadway. She lived with her mother, who kept a boarding-house at 126 Nassau Street. Sunday morning, July 25, 1842, she knocked at the door of one of the young lodgers, Daniel Payn, to whom she was engaged to be married. She told Payn she was going to the house of her aunt and requested that he call for her that evening if she had not returned home by supper-time. She never crossed the threshold in life again. The following Wednesday her murdered body was found on the shore of Weehawken Heights.

"The annals of crime are gorged with mysteries. The red band of murder has set its mark on many of its pages, but left no other sign of its identity. Of all the episodes enshrouded in this somber vagueness, there is none more tantalizing than the case of Mary Cecilia Rogers." Thus wrote the *Gazette* in review of the mystery when it was again brought to attention through the death of John Anderson, Mary's employer. This was in 1881.

The corpse that was buried over in New Jersey after a primitive inquest was not immediately known, according to most versions, to be that of the beautiful cigar girl. But, shortly after, a New York newspaper demanded that the remains be dug up, and the disinterred body was laid out in the dead-house in City Hall Park, New York, and though decomposition had already set in, portions of the attire were positively identified and all doubt was removed that the corpse was that of Mary Rogers. The search for the murderer was next in order. Newspapers started an untiring pursuit of the mystery and the unsatisfactory results worked the public mind to fever-heat. Meetings were held and public and private subscriptions made as rewards for the unveiling of the death secret. Various suspected persons were arrested, yet, as the *Gazette,* long years after, commented: "In this case murder will not out. The murderer of Mary Rogers never was and never will be definitely known. His crime is buried forever in the grave in which its victim long ago mouldered to dust, so thoroughly forgotten that today no one knows where she is buried."

Mary Rogers did not go to the home of the relative toward which she was supposed to have been headed the Sunday she left her abode. She was last seen in New York in company of an unknown young man in the vicinity of Barclay Street not far from the Restell dwelling on

Greenwich Street, but she was presumably walking toward the Hoboken Ferry. Her companion was supposed to have been a young naval officer, who was among her legion of admirers. But somehow his identity remained ever somewhat vague, for all his undoubted importance in this puzzling tragedy.

Of the various suspects there was none on whom the crime was ever fastened, and few death mysteries have ever been kept so long alive. No sooner had interest commenced to flag than something happened to give it a fresh start. Some boys roaming close to where the body had been found discovered in a thicket a white petticoat, parasol, silk scarf, gloves and a handkerchief on which, for all the discoloration and rot of mildew, the initials of Mary Rogers worked in silk thread were still legible.

Some months later, and to further add to the mystery, young Payn, who had been her betrothed, contributed no small share. After the death of Mary he had taken to dissipation and seemed obsessed by a settled melancholy. He drank hard and deep and one day he staggered out of a saloon and was seen no more until his dead body was found in the thicket where the relics of his dead sweetheart had been found. There was an empty laudanum bottle by his side and in his pocket a letter which read:

"Here I am on the very spot. God forgive me for my misspent life."

And then came two other incidents shortly after and almost at the same time that further helped to sustain interest. Edgar Allan Poe, who had written an amazing mystery story, "The Gold Bug," which in the year 1843 had won the $100 prize offered by The Dollar Newspaper of Philadelphia, wrote a short story which purported to be the solution of the murder, and which was entitled, "The Mystery of Marie Roget." In this Poe paraphrased the events of the Mary Rogers tragedy, only giving the actors different names and locating the crime in Paris instead of New York. His theory was that there had been an indiscreet intimacy with her mysterious sailor lover which had resulted in her pregnancy, and finally her murder.

It is in order to insert here, there is a standing *Gazette* tradition that Poe, some time between 1846 and 1849, the year of his death, had been temporarily on the staff of this journal. How much actual foundation there is to this tradition remains a question. The same year that the *National Police Gazette* came into existence, the firm of Wiley & Putnam, 161 Broadway, brought out the first edition of a book, *Tales by Edgar A. Poe.* It included "The Gold Bug," yet the book did not enjoy much in the way of success, though its author was, too late for his satisfaction, to be accepted as a genius. More attention was attracted to the author by his poem, "The Raven," which saw print in 1845, the year the *Gazette* came into existence. That year Poe was for a time the assistant editor of the *Broadway Journal,* a weekly paper published in New York, but he did not prosper in the connection. In fact, the closing years of Poe's life were such a discouraging struggle for existence that it is easily possible that he may have been pressed to do some hackwork for such a successful weekly as was then the young and robust *Gazette.* If such was the case, Poe never attached his name to any scrivening that he may have been driven to do for Messrs. Wilke & Camp.

Coming back to the other happening that livened interest in the Rogers case, the very month in which the Poe story of the crime was published, over in Weehawken a woman was fatally wounded through the accidental discharge of a gun. The woman was Mrs. Loss, who kept an inn which was close to the scene where the body of the beautiful cigar girl had been found. Mrs. Loss was the mother of the children who had made the discovery of the Rogers girl's handkerchief and other belongings. She made a deathbed confession that would lead to the assumption that the objects found in the thicket had been specially planted there by herself. According to the dying words of Mrs. Loss, Mary Rogers had come to breathe her last through the performance of a criminal operation. Why no special credence was placed in this confession is something of an enigma, but such seems to have been the case. Yet, it obviously came nearer to the truth than any of the various surmises that were offered instead. It was probably the basis for the *Gazette* charge that the Rogers girl was a victim of the abortionist, Restell.

Red Leary's Jailbreak [5]

Halfway between the Hermitage and Moran's stood a modest inn operated by Kate Leary, the Joan of Arc of the [Coney Island] colony [of crooks and unfortunates, in the '80's]. Kate was the wife of John

[5] From *Sodom by the Sea,* An Affectionate History of Coney Island, by Oliver Pilat and Jo Ranson, pp. 60–62. Copyright, 1941, by Oliver Pilat and Jo Ranson. Garden City, N. Y.: Doubleday, Doran & Company, Inc.

(Red) Leary, chief lieutenant of Shang Draper, who was probably the most successful American gang leader in the nineteenth century. Draper and his friend, Alex McCoy, were among the first New York criminals to establish joints specializing in liquor and prostitution at Norton's Point, but Draper soon put his obvious talents to wider use.

Neighborhood gangs had flourished in New York slums as early as the Civil War, but none like Shang Draper's group, which specialized in bank robbery. They were the aristocrats of the underworld. According to the reliable estimate of George W. Walling, one-time New York police commissioner, they committed 80 per cent of all bank robberies between 1860 and 1884 in the United States, getting away with fully $7,000,000. Much of the loot proved unnegotiable, some was kicked back in the form of bribes or recovered by the authorities, but enough stuck to the fingers of the gang to establish as high spenders those members who from time to time hid out at Coney Island.

Red Leary participated in the Northampton (Mass.) bank robbery of January, 1876. Members of the Draper gang, including Shang himself, woke up the cashier at his home, marched him to his own institution to open up the vaults, and escaped with $1,500,000 in securities and cash. So tremendous did the hue and cry become that Red decided on a jaunt to Europe and Kate Leary left her Coney Island establishment in the care of Shang Draper's mistress. While Red and Kate Leary were looking at French cathedrals, the identity of all the robbers became known to police through the confession of a minor member of the gang. Much of the missing money was recovered, two of the thieves got twenty-year jail sentences, and even Shang Draper was under arrest briefly until he exerted his political influence.

Red and Kate Leary returned to Coney Island in 1877 and lived quietly in the colony of unfortunates for two years, until Red got careless and went to New York and was picked up by the police.

Kate was a bold girl with hair as red as that of her husband. When political efforts and bribery failed to win his release, she decided on direct action. Posing as the wife of a longshoreman, she leased a fifth-floor room in a tenement at 76 Ludlow Street, New York, adjoining the Ludlow Street Jail, where Red was being kept, pending extradition to Northampton, Mass. Then she brought in Shang Draper and Fatty Dolan with a hydraulic jimmy to challenge brick walls totaling five feet in thickness. Kate shopped and cooked meals and piled brick in the room, while the men worked almost continuously in their tunnel, struggling against time and the threat of noise or an error in calculation.

On May 7, 1879, Kate visited her husband at the prison until eight P.M. This was a formal visit, full of whispered last-minute instructions. An hour later she saw him again, informally, as Shang Draper holed through the tunnel to the third-tier toilet where Red was sitting.

No alarm was raised, nor was the tunnel leading to the room with its neatly piled ton of excavated brick discovered until 10:30. By that time the fugitive was on his way to Coney Island in a light truck owned by Ed (Goodie) Gearing, a thief who co-operated with the gang. Leary didn't arrive until next day, according to Charley Kaiser. Kaiser had a variety of jobs in later years and in 1941 was serving at Steeplechase Park in Coney Island as a watchman, but on May 8, 1879, he was just a carefree kid driving a meat truck. At Neptune Avenue and Ocean Parkway he was hailed by Shang Draper, who said his sorrel horses were almost exhausted by the trip from New York. With a gesture of his thumb, Draper indicated two packages in the rear of the truck, which he said were very heavy, but Kaiser didn't bother to look. He was content to give the other man a tow up the hill into Coney Island with his powerful team and to accept a cigar as reward. Later, when he learned that he'd been involved in an escape discussed from coast to coast and that the supposed packages had been Kate and Red Leary, he merely shrugged, more proud than displeased.

So celebrated did the exploit become that it passed into baseball slang. A coach who wanted to instruct a player to break loose and steal a base simply yelled: "Red Leary!"

Chicago May [6]

While I was on the *World* I knew the Tenderloin. I was a Tenderloin reporter. I was a friend of thieves, counterfeiters, harlots, police captains, and I knew big Chicago May. There were a great many distinguished things about May. At one time in her career she had been married to two men and lived with them both at the same time—one working in the daytime and one at night, and May moving from one flat to the other. She was the woman who helped her lover, Eddie Guerin, escape from Devil's Island. She invented the system of taking

[6] From *The Fun I've Had,* by Bayard Veiller, pp. 39–40. Copyright, 1941, by Bayard Veiller. New York: Reynal & Hitchcock.

men into the halls of flat houses and there, burying her face against their chests, she bit the stones out of their scarf pins and went blithely on her way. She was a big Irish girl with fair hair—not bad-looking. She had been married years before to a man named Churchill, so her real name was Churchill, and she always claimed that she was the divorced wife of Police Captain Churchill, to the intense rage of that very able officer.

I remember one time she picked up a man on the street and took him home with her. She was rather attracted to him. He woke the next morning raging with typhoid fever. May wouldn't let them move him. In some queer way she felt that the man was her guest. God knows why she should pay any attention to this particular guest—she had had many others. But May took care of this man—he didn't amount to much—a telegraph operator—but this big Irish girl tramped the streets at night and spent the money she earned on this man. Eventually he got well. He left her flat and went back to his own home and two or three days later, feeling that he owed his life to May, he went to her and proposed marriage. May wasn't flattered. I wish I could put in print her language as she described the scene to me later, but she was a big, husky Irish woman, strong as a man, and she picked this suitor up by the seat of his pants and the back of his neck, and threw him down two flights of stairs. That night, as I was making my rounds through the Tenderloin, I ran into May as she came staggering out of Paddy the Pig's. And there's the story just as she told it to me.

Who Killed Kid Dropper? [7]

In the summer of 1923 the New York police received a tip and raided the Putnam Building in Times Square, on the site where the Paramount Theater now stands.

The haul brought into the clutches of the law a score of criminals and among them a prize catch, Nathan Kaplan, better known as Kid Dropper, the king of the East Side racketeers.

Between the Kid and Little Augie (Jacob Orgen), another gang leader, there was a standing feud and it was assumed that the tip had

[7] From *Jimmie Walker,* The Story of a Personality, by Louis J. Gribetz and Joseph Kaye, pp. 100–105. Copyright, 1932, by Louis J. Gribetz and Joseph Kaye. New York: Lincoln MacVeagh, Dial Press, Inc.

come from the latter. The important thing, however, was that Kid Dropper was now behind prison bars and the police set themselves to keeping him there as long as they could.

The last-resort charge of carrying concealed weapons was lodged against him and an accomplice, George Katz, and in due time both men were brought into Essex Market Court for trial. But to the intense disappointment of the police the gangsters were discharged for lack of evidence.

The problem now was to get the two "innocent" men away without creating trouble. A number of flashy youths with well-known faces were hanging around the court and the police were apprehensive. A squad of fifty detectives and many uniformed policemen were ordered out and placed at strategic points around the building. They were under the charge of Captain Peter Tighe, an old and trusted hand at such gatherings. In command of the escorting of the Kid and his partner to the waiting taxicab was Captain of Detectives Cornelius Willemse, another veteran of criminal warfare.

When all preparations had been made, the procession from the courtroom started. With Kid Dropper was his wife Irene Kaplan. Captain Willemse led the way. Mr. Kaplan was delighted with the outcome of the trial and smiled and nodded approvingly as he noted the state of siege in which Essex Market Court had been placed for his benefit.

When they reached the curb Captain Willemse placed the Kid and Katz into the cab and then stepped in himself. As Mrs. Kaplan was about to follow him a little runt of a fellow, drab and undistinguished, ran to the back of the cab and before any one could do more than gasp fired three shots through the window. The Kid collapsed in his seat and the neighborhood of Essex Market Court was thrown into an uproar.

Mrs. Kaplan shrieked and leaped at the assassin. But after she had seized him she stupidly let go and continued shrieking. At this very moment Detective Sergeant James Marron was coming out of the court after having arraigned a prisoner. He saw the shooter drop his pistol and run. Tighe shouted to him: "You get the gun—I'll get the man!"

Both the gun and the man were retrieved. By that time it was found that Kid Dropper had passed on to a quieter life. No one could believe that the execution had actually taken place in the open street, amidst an army of policemen and detectives. It was an astounding crime. Only a madman or a person stupefied by drugs could have attempted it.

The killer was Louis Kushner, alias Louis Cohen, an insignificant member of Little Augie's gang and a truck driver for a laundry when he was ostensibly working for a living. Cohen freely admitted that he had killed the Dropper because he knew it was either his life or the other's. How he could have hoped to save his life by a public killing and thereby invite the penalty of a march to the electric chair was unexplained.

Cohen was probably the most unheroic figure in gangland and lived with his mother, three brothers and a sister in a squalid tenement at 164 E. 7th Street. It was obvious that he had been induced to kill the Kid. He was very proud of it, too, but when brought up for arraignment he was shocked to find that his good friends were all absent. He had been abandoned, and not even a lawyer was there to safeguard whatever rights he might still have under the law. Thus he was thrown on the protection of the court and Senator [James J.] Walker and Hyman Bushell were appointed by the judge to defend him.

The trial took place in December of 1923. Cohen, the forsaken, still remained faithful to the gangster code and stuck to his story that he had killed to save himself. He related that a day before Kid Dropper's trial he had been told by a friend, Willie Silverman, that the Dropper believed it was through him, Cohen, that the police had been tipped off for the raid.

"He said," Cohen testified, "that the Dropper told him he would get me and I became so frightened that I went to a Turkish bath that night but couldn't sleep. I went out and walked the streets, went back to the baths but couldn't sleep. The next day I went down to the court to see the Dropper arraigned. I heard the Judge say 'discharged.' The Dropper gave me a look when he reached the sidewalk. I went behind the taxicab and began the shooting."

Mrs. Kaplan, however, testified that two days before the killing she had seen Cohen in company with Little Augie and two other members of his gang near the courtroom, evidently planning the murder.

The defense work at the trial had been left largely to Walker. It was practically a water-tight case—water-tight for the prosecution. The best Walker could do was to obtain a second-degree murder verdict. But how was this to be done with a self-confessed murderer, and one who readily repeated his confession whenever asked? His one loophole, Walker decided, was in the law itself, which makes it impossible to convict a person of first-degree murder, even if a confession is obtained, unless the murder is proven.

Walker carefully planned his defense. First of all he built up a foundation of testimony to prove that the Dropper was one of the most bloodthirsty ruffians in the history of American crime. He described his favorite method of branding his enemies—a slash across the face with a can-opener (such a slash as Little Augie was stamped with for life), and went into details about the disappearance of several men imputed to him and the vicious cruelty of his rule, which created terror even in the underworld. Thus the jury could understand that little Cohen, under the circumstances, had ample cause to fear for his life.

Now he made use of something that had been ignored by every one connected with the case. Three bullets had been found in the cab: one in the body, one in the floor and one in the ceiling. The ways of bullets, Walker observed, were stranger than that of women and jewels, but why should one have climbed to the ceiling and the other buried itself in the floor when all three were fired at close range by Cohen? The merest pistol novice would have had a straighter aim. Still, that was more or less beside the point. There was a more important fact. Captain Willemse, the officer who guarded the gangsters in the car, reported that a bullet had passed through his hat. In proof, he exhibited a straw hat which did have a bullet hole drilled through it. Consequently, argued Walker, there were *four* shots fired, not three.

Four shots fired and only three bullets found. Where was the fourth bullet? And who fired it? It could not have been Louis Cohen, for he was seen and heard by several people to have shot only three times.

With fine, dramatic eloquence Walker bombarded the jury with that fourth bullet. Who was the man that fired it? Who killed Kid Dropper?

"We know Cohen *attempted* to kill the Kid," he declared. "But to sustain a charge of first-degree murder you must prove it. If you convict him of second-degree murder, or"— he took a chance— "manslaughter, we will concede it. But when you consider first-degree murder—there was a man sitting next to the Dropper in the cab; four bullets were fired and only three of them by Cohen. The bullet that went through Willemse's hat might have come from Cohen's revolver — but from whose revolver came the fourth shot? The shot that may have killed the Dropper?"

The jury reacted as Walker had hoped and brought in a verdict of second-degree murder.

The judge presiding at the trial . . . Alfred J. Talley . . . was outraged by the verdict and denounced it bitterly. The evidence, he told the jury, had been clear enough to send Cohen to the chair. But he was helpless and so imposed on the murderer the limit sentence of twenty years to life.

As to the mystery of the fourth bullet, it was unsolved. Some of those familiar with the details of this case were mean enough to suggest that Captain Willemse fired the shot through his hat in the alley after the murder was committed, as a prank, and boasted afterward how narrowly he had escaped death.

The Downfall of the "Patchen Avenue Gang" [8]

The criminal annals of these times are rich in anecdotal lore, showing the cunning and courage that marked so many deeds of darkness, among which was the novel enterprise of the so-called "Patchen Avenue gang" composed of high-grade crooks, every one of whom was known by sight and record to the New York police and some of them to the sophisticated public as well. The operations of these men were hampered by the constant surveillance of the police to whom their various haunts, homes and "hang-outs" were well known, nor did frequent changes of address lessen the "shadowing." Heretofore their migrations had always been from one shady spot to another, and when they sought to escape attention by establishing new headquarters in the suburbs they were wont to select a house whose very remoteness was suggestive of mystery.

In order to escape this continued espionage they determined to defy all criminal tradition by establishing a rendezvous in some locality to which no sinister suspicion could attach, and the house that they selected was one with an ample garden in Patchen Avenue, a quiet residential street in Brooklyn. For a time the scheme worked well. The wife of one of the gang was a very presentable woman and to her were assigned the duties of mistress of the house. It was agreed from the first that an atmosphere of quiet respectability should be carefully maintained. Neighbors called and were graciously received by an amiable hostess. Neither peeking through shutters nor the furtive scurrying of wary feet was allowed on these occasions and in due time the calls were returned in a manner that confirmed the belief that the newcomers were desirable acquaintances. They had many visitors of their own kind who invariably came and went in broad daylight, for by common consent all mysterious, midnight flitting to and fro was strictly forbidden.

[8] From *Forty-Odd Years in the Literary Shop,* by James L. Ford, pp. 51–53. Copyright, 1921, by E. P. Dutton & Company. New York. 1922.

And under cover of this mask of decorum all sorts of nefarious, predatory schemes were hatched and later carried to successful fulfilment. A sense of complete security, to which they were utterly unaccustomed, grew upon the little household, and as spring advanced they set out a croquet set on the lawn and played openly within sight of their neighbors. But it was this innocent diversion that proved their ruin, for religious prejudice was a stranger to them and one fatal Sunday morning passing churchgoers were amazed and shocked at the sight of their supposedly decent neighbors busy with mallet and ball. Never since the battle of Long Island was fought had such an abhorrent spectacle been seen in the staid City of Churches. Suspicion was instantly aroused; the New York police were notified and plainclothes men paid a domiciliary visit to Patchen Avenue which resulted in the closing of the house and the disappearance of its inmates from the scene.

The Mobster and the Night Club [9]

The glamorized racketeers of the day were . . . good parties but they only spent with reason. They only showed off and played the sucker when their own odd social code demanded it. If a mobster opened a night club, the top men and lieutenants of all other mobs which were at peace with the entrepreneur considered it imperative, socially, to give their business contemporary a "big play" or to drop around dutifully and "spend a dollar in Joe's joint."

Thus, when a combination of "the boys" opened The Silver Slipper on Broadway, the opening night audience was well larded with hard guys exhibiting friendship. One of these racketeers, presiding over a table of six well-rodded assistants, called one of the Slipper owners to his festive board.

"How much did it cost you to open this trap?" he asked.

"About $18,000," said the boss. The racket guy summoned a captain of waiters.

"Serve $18,000 worth of champagne," he said imperiously. There

[9] From *No Cover Charge,* A Backward Look at the Night Clubs, by Robert Sylvester, pp. 168–169. Copyright, 1956, by Robert Sylvester. New York: The Dial Press.

was no doubt he meant every word of it, the Slipper alumnus says today in fond memory.

"But we talked him out of it," he says, "because we felt the talk would get around that he pulled us off the hook all alone. We had other factions who felt more responsible for us. We only let the guy spend $4,800 that night. We weren't worried. We took in over $35,000 before we closed the doors."

A Perfect Fit for Frankie Yale [10]

. . . [It was] the era when no highly successful hoodlum would be caught dead unless he was wearing two-hundred-dollar suits, ten-dollar ties, twenty-five-dollar shirts, fifty-dollar shoes, monogrammed silk shorts, English imported socks, and a streamlined, palm-caressing gat individually forged by a fashionable gunsmith. The two main characters in [a yarn related by Pat Caruso, the Fifth Avenue custom tailor] are a tailor friend and the late Frankie (Yuale) Yale—Frankie being the New York mobster who suggested that his bodyguard, a swarthy punk named Al Capone, hop a Pullman and take over Chicago's rackets—a piece of "Go West" advice "Scarface" took advantage of with great gusto.

Yale never ordered anything but brown or gray suits from his tailor, at about the same price asked for rubbing out an enemy. He wouldn't even attend a murder unless he was wearing one or the other of these two hues. One dark day a couple of the boss's shadows ankled into the shop and said, "You've got Frankie Yale's measurements—hustle up a blue serge suit for him."

"Frankie doesn't wear anything but browns and grays," the craftsman remonstrated.

"Look, wise guy," the henchmen hissed, "do like we tell you, see. Make a neat, well-fitting blue serge for the chief; he's dead and his Mrs. wants to bury him with dignity."

The tailor put his entire staff to work and within twenty-four hours the suit was finished and sent to the mortuary. "You didn't do so good," the mourners complained to the tailor after they took a gander

10 From *Champagne before Breakfast,* by Hy Gardner, pp. 66–67. Copyright, 1954, by Hy Gardner. New York: Henry Holt and Company.

at the corpse, "that ain't such a good fit in the shoulder." The puzzled merchant nodded. "I don't get it, they're the same measurements as usual—he couldn'ta lost that much weight already."

The little group studied the problem when one brain-twister tightened his lips. "I know what it is, it ain't your fault, schneider, you can run along, we can handle this ourselves." That's how come Frankie Yale looked as sartorially perfect in death as he had in life—he was buried wearing a shoulder holster complete with rod—all loaded, just like his friends at the wake.

White Powder and White Slavery [11]

. . . The wife of the chauffeur of a prominent New Jersey iron founder, after having made a professional call on her dentist, went for luncheon at a popular restaurant above 34th Street near Fifth Avenue, and took a seat at one of the small tables. At a nearby table a young lady was lunching. A few minutes later a young woman came in and sat down in the empty chair on the other side of the table and ordered something, which was immediately served and the attendant paid. As the newcomer sat there, the young lady at the table let fall her glove, and as she stooped to pick it up, the newcomer quickly and dextrously emptied a white powder into her cup. The young lady, having finished her lunch and paid for it, left the restaurant. The newcomer then immediately arose and followed her. The procedure was so peculiar that the woman observing it decided to follow and see what might occur. When the young lady reached the corner of Fifth Avenue, she suddenly collapsed on the sidewalk as though in a faint. The person who had put the powder in her cup immediately stepped forward and exclaimed to those who proceeded to help her: "The young lady is my niece and I will take care of her," and called a taxi. The chauffeur's wife came forward at once, and said to a policeman who had been attracted by the commotion, "Officer, arrest this woman. She is not the aunt of this young lady, and I saw her just now drug her drink in the restaurant." Accordingly the policeman interfered, and during the struggle the suspect's head gear became displaced and dis-

[11] From *Then and Now*, by Jacob Knickerbocker, A New Yorker, pp. 434–435. Copyright, 1939, by Bruce Humphries, Inc. Boston.

closed that it was not a woman but a young man disguised. The young lady, the policeman, and the party arrested were then driven to the station house of that precinct. I intended to inquire as to what followed, and I looked for a notice of the affair in the newspaper, but none ever appeared. My supposition is that the family of the young lady had the matter dropped to avoid the comment and wide publicity the case would incur. But I consider it one of a very serious character, for if this man had obtained possession of the girl and had kept her drugged and hidden away in some house, her future fate would have been of a character sad to contemplate. It is in such ways that the detestable crime called "White Slave Traffic" is managed. The victim is drugged and kept drugged in some house and finally carried off to some distant city or country. This suggests that a companion or chaperon is advisable for a young lady, considering the heinous crimes that have been perpetrated in the past, and still are at times in the present. . . .

How Magistrates Studied Human Nature in 1844 [12]

. . . The simple and unsuspecting, who only look upon a police officer as a minister of justice and on a magistrate as the pure and dignified dispenser of the law, imagine that the former thrive simply upon six shilling fees for every arrest they make; and are by no means aware that a large number of them are the pensioners of brothels and derive four-fifths of their income either directly or indirectly from female prostitution. In their ignorance of this, they are also strangers to the luxury of laughing at the ridiculous spectacle of these fellows pretending to be arrayed against a class which puts clothes upon their backs, money in their pockets and furnishes them with their bread and butter. This revenue is collected in different ways. One prostitute may have a difference with another which results in blows. An officer arrests each party at the complaint of the other and each pays five or ten dollars to be released. A landlady retains the clothes

[12] From *The Mysteries of the Tombs,* A Journal of Thirty Days' Imprisonment in the New York City Prison, for Libel, by George Wilkes, pp. 39–41. New York. 1844.

of a delinquent for board. An officer recovers them and receives in pay a liberal fee and perhaps a *tender favor* in [addition]. Balls are given in palaces of pleasure and two officers receive five dollars each, for maintaining peace and protecting the *filles des joies* in the quiet enjoyment of [their] licentiousness.

But the most lucrative depredations which are made upon this unhappy class are obtained by foray; or, in other words, a general descent of the magistrate and a posse of officers upon a house, and a sweep of all its inmates into the Tombs. This is done on pretext of the aforesaid house being "disorderly," and some familiar devil of the Tombs is made to previously swear out a complaint to that effect as a sort of justification of the outrage. The women are then seized and dragged rudely to prison and locked up. On their way, each officer who has one in charge pledges his victim his eternal friendship, and receives in lieu all the money she has about her as an earnest for his good offices with the magistrate in getting her discharged. In the morning, the terrors of her confinement have rendered her willing to any sacrifice, and she then takes out her earrings and strips her fingers to urge his aid again. The officer pockets this lawful plunder, but still makes no effort to release her, for there is yet another source which will yield a tribute, if she is kept a little longer. She has a *cher ami* outside who is interested in her fate and he will come down handsomely for the deliverance of his lady-love. The lover found and sounded, there is no further reason for her detention, and she is accordingly discharged on sham bail, with an admonition, which, if meant, would be suicidal to the interests of him who gives it, to "never do so again." Sometimes one of these poor victims of official tyranny will be betrayed into an outburst of indignation, and if this should happen to be accompanied with a refusal or inability to pay, she is sent to Blackwell's Island by the indignant magistrate as a vagrant, and then, good night to her forever.

I know a most aggravated case of this kind of extortion. A party of French girls, the mistresses of some military officers at Quebec, came on to this city on a frolic. Two of them were only sixteen years of age, and knew nothing of the world beyond what they had gained through their connection with the officers who had seduced them. All put up together in a house somewhere up town, but had been there only four days, when word reached the police officer that a party of French girls, with plenty of money, had just arrived and stopped at such a number in such a street. The magistrate to whom it was told was in ecstasies. It was a pecuniary godsend, which would enable him to pay a shortly coming bill, and he fervently thanked Providence for the blessing. A complaint against them was sworn out at once, for fear some other magistrate should get the start of him, and about five o'clock in the afternoon the descent made. Almost ignorant of our language, trembling and terrified, the wretched girls were seized unceremoniously and marched, shivering in their gossamer indoor dresses, through the chill of a bleak October day, to the Tombs. They were thrust all together into a cold, damp cell, ignorant of their offense, and left to the terrors of an imagination which had never yet conceived a scene so horrible as this. The magistrate who committed them went home to a comfortable supper and snored sonorously between the softest blankets; the poor girls, who were his superiors in everything, who had been reared in luxury and always had been the object of tenderest solicitude, wept in a shivering circle upon a dungeon floor. By special favor, some humane keeper had given them a light, and they enjoyed its meager cheer till ten o'clock, when a huge rat, apparently inspired with a spirit congenial to the magistrate's, jumped suddenly through it, and knocked it out. This was a signal for redoubled terror, and huddling closer together they clasped themselves in each other's arms for protection. In this position, worn out with weeping, they at last fell asleep. Their repose lasted until four o'clock in the morning, when they awoke and found four or five inches of water which had overflowed into the cell, welling against their sides. They ate no breakfast, but at breakfast time received the visits of the officers who arrested them—tempted them to humanity with all the money and valuables on their persons, and informed them of the names of some who might interest themselves in their release. This necessarily delayed matters until a late hour in the afternoon, when all the strings having been pulled and all the contributions being in, the magistrate wiped the recent traces of venison steak and Scotch ale from his lips, and called them out for examination. He took them into a privy chamber, one by one, and there, in the widest sense of the term, examined them. As the public may have some curiosity as to the nature of Star Chamber examinations in such cases as these, I will describe this one for their especial edification.

The magistrate approached the trembling girl, with his arms clasped magisterially behind him and his brows bent upon her in a most magisterial manner. He asked her her name, age, place of birth and business, and after receiving answers to these questions, relaxed a little, and in a softer tone inquired who seduced her. He relaxed a little more, made his tone softer still, and then asked her *how?*

She blushed, hung down her head and made no answer.

The representative of justice laid his hand softly on her shoulder with the insinuation of a cat, and relaxing his countenance still further, till he became positively amiable, remarked, as he slightly compressed his fingers in the moulded beauty between them—"You are very pretty."

"Oh, sir!"

"Indeed you are! (Another amorous compression with a slight change of latitude.) "Why, what a pretty foot you have! What a pretty ankle, too, and—"

"For shame, sir!" cried the outraged girl, coloring scarlet and repulsing him with indignation.

"Come, come!" said his honor, resuming his sternness and adding to it with a most formidable frown, "recollect where you are, and who I am! I am informed that you have been engaged in passing counterfeit money."

"Oh, *mon Dieu!*"

"Yes; I have been informed that you have been engaged in passing counterfeit money, and I intended to search you in as delicate and gentlemanly a manner as possible."

"Counterfeit money!" exclaimed the astonished girl in surprise, and forgetting her delicacy in her terror at the charge, told his honor he might search her and see; and in the impulse of unthinking innocence, pulled forward her dress and revealed to him the treasures of her bosom.

His honor peeped into it, as eager as a Turk would into the seventh heaven, and inspired by this into extraordinary diligence (though he found no spurious indications there), he continued his search in a most faithful manner.

She hoped his honor was satisfied.

Not quite; French women were very adroit in concealing their money; they did not only trust to the intricacies of their *clothes,* but sometimes—

* * * * *

The magistrate continued his search, and after protracting it for several minutes, Justice was satisfied. Hard luck if it wasn't! I might attempt and succeed in getting up an indignation on this subject, but I suppose it was all meant in a joke, and so we might as well laugh it off.

After his honor was through, he discharged the prisoner on condition that she should not repeat the circumstances of her examination, and that she should leave the city within three days. The same ceremony was then performed, in detail, with the other three, and they were released upon the like condition.

These magistrates have fine opportunities for studying human nature, but they sometimes carry their researches to extremes.

The "Tenderloin" [13]

In the May, 1944, issue of AN&Q, "S.H.A." explained "Tenderloin" as a name first applied to a particular New York City precinct "because of its resemblance in shape to a tenderloin steak." But the term, he added, "soon became synonymous with the demimonde life of the West Thirties. . . ."

I had always assumed that the name had sprung up in the early nineties and had come from the passing remark of a policeman transferred to that precinct. But when "S.H.A." wrote me that he had joined the Tenderloin Club in about 1891, I began to see that the date of its source was considerably earlier.

Herbert Asbury's *The Gangs of New York* . . . (N. Y., 1928) defines the area and states that it was so named by

> . . . Captain, later Inspector, Alexander S. Williams. After long and unrequited toil in outlying districts, Captain Williams was transferred to the command of the Twenty-ninth in 1876. A few days later a friend meeting him on Broadway and seeing his expansive smile, asked the cause of his merriment.
>
> "Well," said Williams, "I've been transferred. I've had nothing but chuck steak for a long time, and now I'm going to get a little of the Tenderloin."

Mr. Asbury told me that most of his source material was either lost or temporarily inaccessible. But fortunately, at this juncture, I was steered to the report (Albany, 1895) of the Lexow Committee [for investigating New York City Police Department]; and on pages 5569 and 5570 of Volume 5, I found this friendly exchange between Inspec-

[13] By H.M.L. From *American Notes & Queries,* A Journal for the Curious, Vol. V (August, 1945), No. 5, pp. 72–74. Copyright, 1945, by Walter Pilkington. New York.

tor Alexander S. Williams and Recorder Goff, of Friday, December 28, 1894:

Q. And in fact that the Tenderloin district is the most notorious district in New York; that is also a lie? A. No.

Q. It was the most notorious? A. It had some reputation.

Q. You gave it that name, the Tenderloin? A. No.

Q. How did it originate? A. Through a newspaper reporter, a man that was on the *Sun* that used to call on me in the Fourth precinct; when I was transferred to the Twenty-ninth he came up there and asked me how I liked the change: I said, I will have been living on rump steak in the Fourth district, I will have some tenderloin now; he picked it up and it has been named that ever since. . . .

Q. This is the first time a waiting and anxious public have had an opportunity to hear from your lips your understanding and your reasons [for] calling the Fourth precinct the "rump steak"? A. No; I said I had been living on rump steak.

Q. What did you mean by that? A. Well, I got better living in the Twenty-ninth.

Q. Why? A. Better saloons; better hotels.

Q. You were having your police captain's pay while you were in the Fourth? A. Yes.

Q. . . . you could not expect to get your living in the saloons or hotels without paying for it? A. No.

Q. And did you expect to pay out of your captain's salary the high prices charged by the hotels in the Tenderloin? A. I might.

Q. Did you? A. They don't charge very high prices there.

Q. Did you? A. I might if I got a meal there, certainly, I would have to pay for it.

Q. Don't you know you had it in your mind at that time [that the] reason why you had made use of that apt and descriptive term was that you could not make so much money in the Fourth as you could in the [Twenty-ninth]? A. No.

A letter from Mr. George Ormsby, Acting Chief Clerk of the Police Department, dated November 9, 1944, sets down the essential facts about Williams:

appointed to the Force on August 31, 1866 . . . retired May 24, 1895 . . . died March 25, 1917 . . . boundary of the 29th precinct in Captain Williams' time was . . . from Seventh to Park and Fourth Avenues; from 42nd to 14th Streets. . . .

Augustine E. Costello's *Our Police Protectors* (N. Y., 1885) is the earliest printed reference to the term that I have been able to find:

> the . . . "Tenderloin Precinct". . . embraces nearly all the great caravansaries, parks, clubs, theatres and stores . . . Its population is mainly the "upper ten" and those who serve them. . . . It . . . is infested with people who live viciously. . . .

Two years later *Harper's* (March, 1887, p. 500) carried an article on the New York Police Department by Richard Wheatley; here the term is ambiguously defined, but the nature of the context marks it as relatively common at that time.

From the publication of the Lexow report onward, the allusions to this famous and infamous region are ever on the increase. Funk & Wagnalls *Standard Dictionary* picked it up almost immediately (1895 ed.), but only as a statement of physical boundaries and without explanation or connotation; for a full set of references and a good outline of how cautiously the full meaning emerged in print, see, of course, all editions of Webster and the OED, Thornton's *An American Glossary* (1912), and the DAE. Of these I will quote only one, the OED's treatment of this expression in its 1919 edition. At the end of the routine definition it adds:

> Understood to have reference to the large amount of "graft" said to be got by the police for protecting illegitimate houses in this district, which rendered it the "juicy part" of the service.

Here, then, is at least a part of the record. Because that (now) meaningful chat between Williams and the unnamed *Sun* reporter was only a matter of a passing remark, the case for "the Tenderloin" will presumably never enjoy a complete documentation.

Police Commissioner Devery

I[14]

. . . Great power lodged in the hands of the Police Commissioner, whose sway extended over all the new borough [of Queens]. "Dick" Croker was then the ruler of the city. He had made Robert Van Wyck mayor who, at his request, appointed one William Devery to this high office. Uncouth, illiterate to a degree unusual even in New

[14] From *From Alley Pond to Rockefeller Center,* by Henry Collins Brown, pp. 76–79. Copyright, 1936, by E. P. Dutton & Co., Inc. New York.

York, Devery soon began to attract attention by his unusual conversational gifts. "Touchin' on an' appertainin' to" marked the opening of every remark he was about to make and the phrase passed into the vernacular of the day.

It was at Police Headquarters where his oratorical gifts shone to the greatest advantage. Devery himself had served in the ranks, and no "rookie," as he expressed it, could shove the queer on him. He was holding trial at the sessions called to reprimand or punish those members of the finest who had committed some breach of the rules. To a patrolman who said he had taken whisky for cramps, he said, "Look-a-here, young man! You've been three months on the force and havin' cramps already! You're a quick learner you are. Ten days' pay!"

To a policeman who was found dazed in front of a cigar store, "You ought to hire out as a cigar-store Indian. I know you, an' I know what you're doin'! You're bendin' yer elbow too much. You stop bendin' yer elbow!"

"Where's your moustache?" he asked a cop.

"I shaved it off for the summer."

"Um—I—see—I see. Gettin' too *warm* for ya, eh?" And then Devery showed in what sense it was getting too warm. For very good reasons the man was trying to hide his identity. It seemed, sometimes, indeed as though the caliph knew the inside history of every bluecoat from the Battery to the Bronx.

To a young man who complained that a policeman refused to arrest a young woman on his charge of soliciting: "It takes two to solicit—a lady and a gentleman—an' that lady wouldn'ta solicited you unless you'da made those goo-goo eyes."

A policeman had been given a civil sentence by Justice Jerome. As soon as Devery heard Jerome's name mentioned he blurted out: "There's a lot of little tin soldiers with guns on their shoulders shootin' 'em off in the streets and raisin' riot and rebellion an' degradin' the positions they hold. Complaint's dismissed! Justice Jerome ain't goin' to run New York."

He tells a cop accused of kissing a girl in a dark hallway that he is fined, not for being off post but for getting caught. "I would kiss a girl myself; there's lots of things I'd do and do do, but I'll never get caught. And so I can and I do herewith fine you good and plenty for getting caught. Two days' pay."

Upon another occasion he remarked: "There ain't no law against a policeman thinking."

Mulberry Street Looks at the Camera (1903)

RED DEVIL RIDER
ERSON'S
ND RESTAURANT
DROP THE DIP
STAUC
WACKE'S
PIEL'S BEER
LUNCH
RHEINGOLD BEER
COLLEGE ARMS
DANCING
10¢
5¢

A Streetcar Named
ridge Only" (Greenpoint,
Brooklyn, 1947)

"All That Trouble, Just to Get to Brooklyn?"
(The Bridge, about 1890)

Horse and Delivery Wagon in the Snow
(Rockefeller Plaza, 1947)

he Bowery," Coney Island (about 1909)

Lunching al Fresco (Outside Pier 32, North River, 1947)

Out-of-Towners on the Town (Radio City, 1947)

"Little Paganini": Professor Giuseppe Ravita in front of Carnegie Hall (1952)

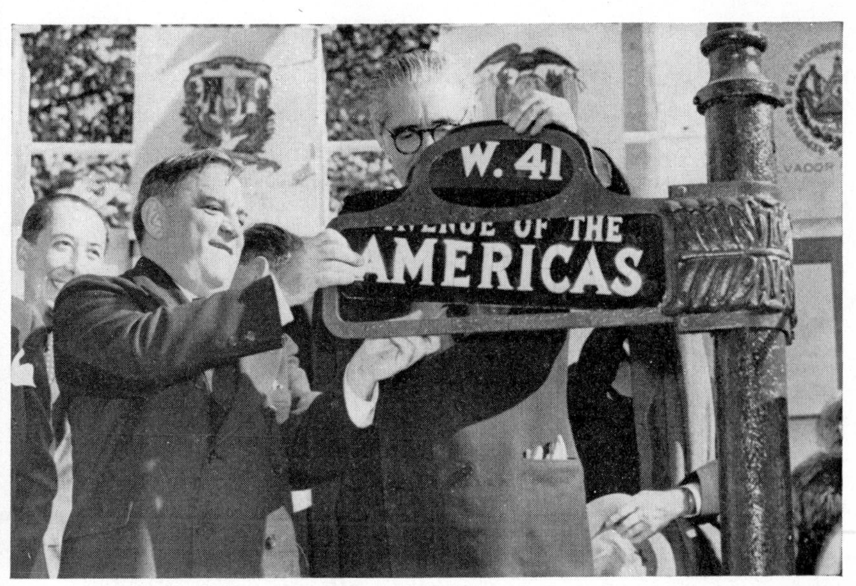

Lost Cause: The "Little Flower" Renaming Sixth Avenue (1945)

Sunshine and Shadow on Third Avenue: Looking Downtown from 53rd Street (1946)

Skater's Waltz at the Rockefeller Plaza Rink (1945)

Seal-Feeding Time at the Bronx Zoo (1951)

Boat Basin and Clover-Leaf Intersection: Henry Hudson Parkway at 79th Street (1949)

United Nations: A Roof's-Eye View (1951)

To a culprit accused of grafting, Devery pounded his fist on his desk and roared: "That's got to stop! If there's any graftin' to be done, I'll do it—leave it to me. What I want to know is, have you noticed any stray grafts runnin' around loose that I have overlooked?"

Information was leaking out of police headquarters and getting into the press. Devery said: "I'm out for the guilty party that's got a leak in my office that I can't stop up."

"Well," said a reporter, who knew the chief despised plain-clothes men, "why don't you put a detective on the job?"

The chief exploded: "Detective. Detective! Hell! What I need is a plumber."

"I don't like to ride," he said one day as he stepped out of his carriage to enter his office; "I'm more used to walking and I feel better on my two nice big police feet, but it's the fashion in my set, when you're getting rich, to show it forth and not be hiding your light under no bushels, whatever in hell they are."

Notwithstanding a certain amount of horse sense in his office, Devery was the joke of the town, although Van Wyck said he was the "best Police Commissioner New York ever had." The papers were constantly hounding him, and at last the Society for the Suppression of Vice succeeded in having him indicted for allowing disorderly houses to operate openly. He was convicted and resigned.

When he was all packed up and ready to leave his office, he called in all the reporters at police headquarters and said: "Gentlemen, I have summoned you to bid you good-by and to ask you politely to tell your editors to go to hell; all except you, Moran. Give my compliments to the city editor of *The Commercial Advertiser*."

* * * * *

After his dismissal Devery held court at a pump on Seventh Avenue, and some of his most entertaining remarks were born there. He was a product of the times, of an era rapidly drawing to a close, which ended with the century that produced it.

II[15]

In March, 1893, William S. Devery, then a captain, took command of the Eldridge Street police station. It was a district then, as now, in which a great many poor people were closely crowded together. There

[15] From *Touchin' on an' Appertainin' to Mr. Deputy Commissioner Devery*, pp. 3–4. [No publisher or date.] The New York Public Library, Local History and Genealogy Division, New York City Election Material, 1859–98.

were, too, a number of wicked men and women who knew that by taking a little money from a great many poor people they could get rich just as fast as if they picked the pockets of a few rich people, and without running as much risk. To do this they needed police help. When Captain Devery took command of the station he told his men that he expected them to be obedient, industrious, and fearless; he concluded his remarks thus:

"They tell me there's a lot of graftin' goin' on in this precinct. They tell me you fellers are the fiercest ever on graft. Now," [pounding his fat fist on the edge of the desk] "that's goin' to stop. If there's any graftin' to be done, I'll do it. Leave it to me!"

The patrolmen laughed dismally. The man who doesn't laugh, when Devery cracks a joke, weeps. The doors were unlocked and the men marched out to their posts. The day of Devery the Grafter had begun. What a day it was! Well might the Deputy Commissioner, looking back over his own career, voice his reminiscences thus:

"I've been charged with everythin' on the calendar except murder. I'm here yet."

Byrnes' Third Degree [16]

. . . [Thomas F. Byrnes] started the famous third degree. Now in the general mind, as I gather from time to time, the idea of the third degree is that it is a method of taking the prisoner and beating him with a rubber hose, which leaves no bruises. Byrnes' third degree was something entirely different.

A butcher in Williamsburg was suspected of murdering a man and cutting up the body and packing it carefully in a trunk and shipping it to a fictitious name in care of the American Express Company in Baltimore. The murderer had, as we subsequently found out, tried to prevent identification by severing the head, which normally weighs thirty to thirty-five pounds, wrapping it in cloth, and gently but firmly tossing it over the Brooklyn Bridge. In the course of time the trunk made itself discovered, because after all you can't leave a putrefying body in an express office for very long. So all the evidence that Byrnes

[16] From *The Fun I've Had,* by Bayard Veiller, pp. 77–80. Copyright, 1941, by Bayard Veiller. New York: Reynal & Hitchcock.

really had was a neatly dismembered body. The murdering butcher had left just this clue. He had worked with a butcher's skill. Byrnes described his find like this: "So help me God, boys, it looked like a lot of chops and steaks."

And here began Byrnes' third degree. The butcher was arrested and taken to a cell at 301 Mulberry Street. No one struck him; no one spoke to him. No one answered any of his questions. He was given a comfortable supper and then at ten o'clock that night he was moved out of his dark cell into a much better cell, pleasantly lighted. The transition from the dark room to the light one left him temporarily blind, and when he opened his eyes, or rather regained his sight, he found himself in a much larger cell with the bloodstained sofa on which he had cut up his victim, and the saw he had used and a butcher's cleaver thrown in for good measure.

Now that was Byrnes' third degree. About nine o'clock the next morning they let out a chattering, screaming murderer, and all he wanted to do was to talk. He talked for hours. Not a blow had been struck, not an unkind blow spoken. If I had been that murderer, I would rather have been beaten half to death.

Then, in another instance, there was a man named Hanrahan, and if that's not his name, it's near enough. He had shot and killed and robbed a wine dealer on West Twenty-eighth or Twenty-ninth Street. There were no real clues, but after four or five weeks he was suddenly arrested and brought down to Police Headquarters, and in those days Byrnes' office was a sort of court which led to the cells downstairs, so that any one sitting in a certain position in that office could look through the window and see what was happening in the courtyard below. Hanrahan was put in a chair facing the windows. The shades had already been pulled up. Byrnes sat at his desk writing—his back to the windows, facing the prisoner. There was an ugly and a short pause, and then Hanrahan said: "Well, now, Inspector—"

Byrnes didn't look up from his writing at all. He kept on writing and said: "I'll talk to you in a moment." Then suddenly he made his pen scratch as he wrote. That was the only sound to be heard in the office. Occasionally there was a nervous cough from the man under arrest. And then, across the courtyard below, Hanrahan saw pass before his frightened eyes, one after the other, first the woman he was living with, who knew about the murder and might have talked—but hadn't. She was handcuffed to a detective. And then his best friend, who knew about the murder, and he hadn't talked either; and one by one he saw his friends dragged to cells, and all that was heard was the scratching of Inspector Byrnes' pen. And as the last man passed, Byrnes threw his pen down on the desk and said, "Now"—and the man confessed.

Years later this scene was the big confession scene in *Within the Law,* which brought me a great deal of praise for my inventiveness in devising a scene which could not possibly have happened.

Inspector Byrnes Extracts an Inadvertent Confession[17]

. . . The sagacity with which the red Indian follows the trail of his enemies, in Fenimore Cooper's works, is not greater than the eager keenness with which a New York Detective scents his prey. Sometimes he watches under the shadow of a wall a whole winter night, under heavy snow, cutting sleet, drenching rain, or piercing wind; or stands for a day before one of our fashionable hotels, theaters, or big dry goods or banking houses; wherever his duty calls him, waiting and watching for the favorable opportunity to lay a firm and relentless hand on the shoulder of the transgressor, who, desperado as he generally is, and armed, finds himself overmatched and overreached at the game at which he has played in his warfare on society. The perseverance born of such experiences is extraordinary, and only equals their sagacity and penetration. It happens with some mental talents as it happens with the muscles of the body; through continual exercise they become developed beyond measure. Habitual close observation and great experience enable them, from the most insignificant signs, to construct a complete theory, which is seldom incorrect; just as the practiced physician sees at a glance the nature of a patient's malady. It is related of Cauler (a celebrated French Detective) that, from four words written on a piece of paper in which some butter was wrapped up, he discovered the clue to a murder. This is characteristic of detectives as a class. They, in time, acquire a wonderful memory, and

[17] From *Our Police Protectors,* History of the New York Police from the Earliest Period to the Present Time, published for the benefit of the Police Pension Fund, by A. E. Costello, pp. 411–414. Copyright, 1884, by A. E. Costello. [New York:] Published by the Author. 1885.

they never fail to recognize a face they have once seen, however altered or disguised it may be.

A single instance of this may be cited. One day Inspector [Thomas] Byrnes and the writer left the public thoroughfare of Broadway, in the vicinity of Police Headquarters, and strolled into the less frequented by-ways, while the Inspector, who was on his way home, was explaining the facts in the case of a recent arrest of some importance, the writer being then attached to the *Herald* Police Bureau as a reporter. The Inspector is an inveterate smoker. As usual, he was enjoying the weed, and in his peculiarly earnest way he was, while talking, seemingly absorbed in his subject, and apparently oblivious to all things else. Without raising his eyes, altering his tone, or changing his gait, he remarked: "See that fellow on the other side of the street; isn't he a dandy? I'll bet five dollars I know him." The reporter looked and beheld a "solitary figure," a nobby young man with a silk "tile," a silk-lined overcoat, and carrying a cane. His face was not within view, as he was walking in the same direction, but faster, and he was some yards in advance.

"One of your friends, eh?" queried the reporter, languidly and mechanically, the interruption not being relished.

There was a queer twinkle in the Inspector's eye. Removing his cigar, he uttered a low but penetrating sibilant sound with his half-closed lips. The man heard it, started, looked back over his shoulder, turned pale, and stood still. "I told you so," said the Inspector, with a quiet and amused smile, addressing himself to the reporter, who was now wide-awake and interested. "Sam," said the Inspector, still moving ahead in a half-abstracted manner, as before. The petrified statue again heard, and regaining animation, he slowly crossed the street diagonally and stood by the side of the Inspector and reporter, looking nervous, but remaining silent. "You are looking splendid, Sam; times must be good," said the Inspector, with a chilling sarcasm in his tone. The man's teeth were chattering now; his tongue refused to give utterance to his thoughts, and the change that had come over him in a brief moment was both radical and remarkable. From being the rakish-looking, light-hearted sport, he was now metamorphosed into a cringing, frightened, abject creature, with pallid cheeks, downcast eyes, and cowering form. The three men were standing still now. The Inspector, critical and austere, the stranger, cringing and frightened, and the reporter, curious and observant. "It is a long time since I saw you, Sam; I thought you dead or—"

Sam at last found his tongue. "I know what you want to add, Inspector. The latter supposition is the correct one. I have been in a tight snap; did my bit and have been out a few months. For God's sake don't run me in. I swear to you I have been keeping straight."

The man's knees shook under him, and his voice was husky with emotion.

"Sam," said the Inspector, very quietly and almost gently, only for the frigidness of the tone. "It is a long time since we've met. You did not look quite so dapper then; and there have been times since when I would have given a fingernail to have found you. How long is it since the night you shot at the officer and escaped over the housetops?"

"Six years, going on seven, Inspector," said the man thus interrogated.

"Call at my office at ten o'clock tomorrow morning, Sam," said the Inspector, moving a step forward. "I want to have a word with you privately."

The man bent his head, stood still a second, and then darted forward in a rapid walk, never once looking back.

"This is the second time I have ever met or seen that man in my life," said the Inspector, in a reminiscent way and reflectively. "The first time, he and two other men were arrested on suspicion of being concerned in a butcher wagon highway robbery case. Proof of guilt could not be brought home to Sam, and he was let go; but he was a marked man. Some months after a Broadway store was broken into, the burglars surprised, two of them captured, the third making his way to the roof, and, when pursued, emptying his pistol at the officer, none of the balls taking effect, however. I always suspected Sam of being that man, and, in his fright, now he has confessed to it."

"Will he not get away out of the city?"

"Not a bit of it; he is too much scared for that; besides, he is shadowed. Look there!"

At that moment Sam disappeared around the corner of a street, and a man in a long overcoat, with collar turned up (it was in winter) came into view, stood still a brief second, threw a salute in the direction of the Inspector, which was returned, accompanied by a low chuckle on the part of the Inspector, and the mysterious figure in the flowing ulster disappeared in the direction Sam had taken.

The New Cop and the Streetwalkers [18]

. . . All the streets in New York at night—that is, Sixth, Seventh, and Eighth Avenues and Broadway—were crowded with women of the town looking for customers. A few had invaded Fifth Avenue, but they were explorers. And over on the East Side the same condition existed. Only there the women wore a badge. You looked at their feet. Black shoes with red heels. It wasn't a bad scheme. That way you were saved the humiliation of speaking to a decent woman when you thought she was something entirely different. They used to tell the story of the ambitious young cop on his way up, who was transferred from East Fourteenth Street to the Tenderloin. For a while he didn't seem to accomplish much. Patrolmen were supposed to bring in streetwalkers once in a while. Their graft was needed. One night a roundsman stopped him on the street and wanted to know why he was not doing anything.

"Why don't you arrest some of these streetwalkers?"

The new policeman was astonished. He pointed to two well-dressed women and said: "Are them whores?"

Them was. He looked at their shoes. No red heels. But he took them to the station house. The desk sergeant looked at him for a minute and grinned and said: "Well, my man, what you got there?"

The new cop swelled with the importance of a civic duty nobly done and said: "Why, Sarg., I brought in a couple of streetwalkers in citizens' dress!"

[18] From *The Fun I've Had,* by Bayard Veiller, pp. 38–39. Copyright, 1941, by Bayard Veiller. New York: Reynal & Hitchcock.

11

An Honest Living

"Do you ever go into the department stores to study [shop girls]?" some one asked [O. Henry]. "Indeed not," was the reply. "It's not the salesgirl in the department store who is worth studying; it is the salesgirl out of it. You can't get romance over a counter."— Robert H. Davis and Arthur B. Maurice

Yorkville Yard Singer [1]

Irish Dick was quite representative of the Yorkville yard singers of forty years ago. I met him one day at the Adler & Ekstein Bakery factory, in East Seventy-fifth Street, off Avenue B (now York Avenue), where among my duties was the sale of stale bread to those who could not afford to buy fresh loaves in the local bakeries. Irish Dick turned up once and asked me for a loaf of bread on credit. He was a tall, lean red-haired man, very friendly and affable. I was accustomed to poor people and his frayed clothing did not evoke pity. But he did look hungry, and I found his gaiety and Irish brogue irresistible. When the bosses were not around, I made a habit of adding a few extra loaves and forgetting to take the money; so I readily complied with Irish Dick's request. He became a regular customer and I soon found out how he earned his living. Once I was singing at the top of my voice when he came in, and he offered me the honor of becoming his partner. For the next few months I neglected my work at the bakery, and became a back-yard singer.

[1] By Leo W. Schwarz, New York City, 1953.

Dick was an open-hearted and independent spirit. Perhaps he ended up on the Bowery—or Broadway—but he was then a province and a principality in himself. No money-grubber, either; he loved to sing because, as he put it, it was God's will, and he sang only to be enabled to enjoy "the Lord's nectar." He hated the rich, the cops and the Limeys; he loved the poor, horses and music. He seemed to be satisfied with a loaf of bread, a drop of nectar, though I suppose he supplemented his diet with the "free lunch" which every corner saloon generously offered in those days.

He was also a shrewd judge of horseflesh and human nature. He sang only in the back yards of the tenements, and his choice of yards and his timing were perfect. We were never doused with pails of water—or worse—as some of the back-yard singers were. We took our place toward the rear of the yard, in front of the ailanthus tree (what the kids used to call the "stink tree"), and I generally opened with *Ain't It All A Goldarn Shame*. I once used "Goddam" for "Goldarn," but he lectured me that cursing was irreverent and insulting to ladies. He taught me to hold the notes on e's and r's and create an exaggerated tremolo when I got to "While the rich keeps getting richer, it's the poor that gets the blame." Then he would harmonize on the refrain. If the women were not hanging out wash on their lines, he would sing a quasi-religious song like *Jerusalem the Golden*, but if they were, then he filled the air with a heart-rending ballad on the Chicago Fire or the Blizzard of '88. By that time a few coins wrapped in toilet paper would hit the ground, and if he thought these were forerunners of more, we offered a fine duet of *Meet Me in St. Louis, Louis*. He picked up the loot while I finished with a lively short popular song like *Come to Sleep, My Baby* or *Come, Josephine, in My Flying Machine*. If the women were not generous, he never cursed them out; rather, he sympathized, making a humane remark about the hard lot of poor women. Or he would quote St. Patrick: "The Lord could not do all his work on earth so he created mothers."

Chimney Sweep [2]

. . . [Chimney sweeps] live on their honest earnings and with all their smoke, and dirt, and soot, and rags, are entitled to more respect than

[2] From *What I Saw in New York;* or a Bird's Eye View of City Life, by Joel H. Ross, pp. 66–68. Entered . . . 1851, by Joel H. Ross. Auburn, New York: Derby & Miller.

any man of whiter skin who wears finer cloth which he refused to pay for.

And what is still more—these chimney sweeps are not only useful members of the community, giving us sweet houses, and clean puddings, but they are as happy apparently as any class with which I am acquainted.

Some of them sing, as they go through the streets announcing their calling, with a voice clear enough and musical enough to be admired; and it is sometimes quite amusing to hear them, though they are often as difficultly understood as the bobolink. But I must give the reader a specimen of such songs as can be understood and appreciated.

Here goes old sweep what's got no money—
Here goes old sweep as sweet as honey.

I know not but the old "sweep" who fortunately hit upon this song, the music of which I regret that I am unable to give, has made enough from his concerts, to retire, for I have not heard his ditty for several years.

Early in the morning they commence singing and traveling from street to street, carrying on their backs their tools. And since they have either become so fat, or chimneys have become so lank that the sweeper cannot ascend them, as formerly, he is under the necessity of increasing his soot-gatherers, which consist of an old blanket, or its equivalent, a bundle of rods, brushes, scrapers, and a rope.

They enter the apartment where the chimney is to be swept, and first hang up their blanket before the fireplace to prevent the escape of as much dust as possible. Then the brush and scrapers are sent on an exploring expedition. These are so attached to a stick as to operate on all sides. But as the handle is only about four feet long, it must be spliced or never reach the top of the chimney. Accordingly the bundle of rods, of which I have spoken, are brought into requisition, each of which has a socket on one end, to receive the end of the next rod, and so in a little time, even sooner than the reader will find the end of the story, the brush finds the top of the chimney, and the sweeping commences.

The rope to which I alluded, is fast at one end to the brush, and as the operator sends up his many-jointed broom-handle, he holds fast to said rope, occasionally winding it around the rods to hold them together, and thus the chimney is soon swept. The "Sweep" then gathers up the soot, carries it out, and receives for each flue, two or three York shillings, and leaves the house "as sweet as honey."

When Trade Was Musical[3]

. . . The houses of this period [the early nineteenth century] were built with a covered porch or stoop (properly stoob), a seat on either side extended from the door to the street, and here on pleasant evenings the family assembled to enjoy the balmy air and the pleasant chat of passing friends; while sitting here they often partook of refreshments which could be obtained in great variety at Vauxhall and other places in the neighborhood. In summer a man came around trundling a wheelbarrow on which was placed a furnace of charcoal for the purpose of keeping the boiler of green corn hot which he had for sale. The man sang—

Hot corn! Hot corn! Here's your nice sweet corn all pip - ing hot.

Later in the season the same man brought hot ginger-bread, and when new corn meal came, then he brought new corn meal pudding and cream. After eating these substantials the people retired to an early rest, and rose the next morning strong and vigorous for the duties of the day.

About this time street cries were numerous and were often accompanied by a song. A man brought clams around every week and he sang—

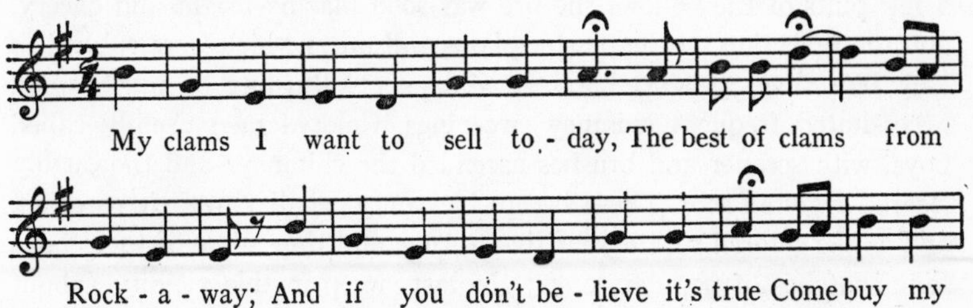
My clams I want to sell to - day, The best of clams from
Rock - a - way; And if you don't be - lieve it's true Come buy my

[3] From *The Evolution of Stuyvesant Village (New York City)*, Tenth to Bleecker Streets, Broadway to Second Avenue, and Around There, by A. A. Rikeman, pp. 46–47, 60–61. Mamaroneck: Press of Curtis G. Peck. 1890.

clams and then you'll know. Come you that have money and
I that have none. Come buy my fine clams and let me go home.

Then when apples were ripe and ready to fall, a man came around trundling a wheel-barrow, on which was a keg.—He sang with a peculiar nasal twang—Sweet Cider, Sweet Cider,—'tis equalized to wine yet people call it Cider.

Indeed things generally found expression in song, not that there were many regular tunes, for they were so full of the rhythm and beauty of nature, that the songs sang themselves.

* * * * *

What were called tin plate stoves were used up to 1840; these stoves were oval, consumed wood, and stood on iron legs about eighteen inches from the floor, over the fire was the oven and on the top of the stove was one opening making altogether a three story arrangement. Then coal stoves were introduced for heating purposes; the Franklin stove was most generally used. Sitting rooms and parlors were provided with grates, but in kitchens the old fashioned wood fires were still in vogue; the kitchen fire was not allowed to go out, at night the embers were covered with ashes, and in the morning the ashes were removed, the back log brought forward and broken in two and a new back log put on, then with an armful of wood thrown on the back log of yesterday and a few puffs of the bellows the fire was soon blazing bright and cheery, and the reflection on the pewter plates and mugs which were rubbed to look like silver produced a beautiful effect. Burning so much wood necessitated frequent chimney sweepings. Colored men usually called boys, with scraper and brushes ascended the chimneys and thoroughly cleared away all soot. These sweeps had a cry peculiar to their vocation, and as the colored race is sensitive to tune and time some of these boys sang snatches of popular songs; the last sweep in this vicinity (about 1842) sang—

Sweep oh sweep ——! Sweep — de chim - ney
From de bot - tom to de top. — Sweep oh sweep ——!
Home! Home! —— Sweet, sweet home! There's
no —— place like home! — There's no —— place like —— home.

Street Girl Peddlers [4]

. . . The "mint girls" traveled through this locality in particular, and others in general, selling their mint from willow baskets that hung on a white-spotted calico sleeve that covered a white dainty arm. Well do I remember the sweet voices that sang out "Red-dish-shees," "Mint and Strawberries," and the pretty mouths and lips associated with those voices.

Who has not heard the story of the old fire laddie who, in mischief, called after one of these pretty peddlers, giving certain information as to her stockings, but gave her credit for her smartness in reply? Things have changed, and the sweet voice, sweet face, and sweeter gossip have been driven off, to make way for brown-skinned Dutch girls, with dark-spotted calico frocks and gay aprons, who, to your questions, make billingsgate replies, and think no broad remark an insult, as they sell their goods.

Catherine Lane was at one time a favorite resort for old colored "aunties," who with their cedar-stave pails filled with smoking-hot ears

[4] From *Reminiscences of Old Fire Laddies* and Volunteer Fire Departments of New York and Brooklyn, Together with a Complete History of the Paid Departments of Both Cities, by J. Frank Kernan ("Florry"), pp. 56-58. Copyright, 1885, by J. Frank Kernan ("Florry") and Michael Crane. New York: M. Crane.

of golden corn, and dressed in a clean gown and apron, would nightly sit on the corner curbstone and in a rich, melodious voice sing out:

"Hot corn, hot corn—
Here's your lily-white corn;
All you that's got money
(Poor me that's got none)
Come buy my lily hot corn,
And let me go home."

I can still see the large gold hoop-rings that hung from their ears, far below the yellow, blue, and red striped bandanna, so nicely plaited and folded over their shiny, well-combed hair. It was often a question in the mind of the old fire laddie on his way home nights whether to luxuriate upon a lily-white corn or a nice baked pear, which the tidy "aunties" carried around in a deep glazed earthenware dish, floating deliciously in a warm bath of home-made syrup. Who eats hot corn now, from a street peddler? Not I, nor you. Water Street sailors, or those who have not as yet eaten their peck of dirt, may do it.

Many an old fireman remembers the time when he has eaten crullers from a Park Row stand, hot corn from a cedar pail, or relished a small plate from Holt's cellar on Fulton Street, made famous in by-gone times as the place of all places that never closed. If the old jail bell rang for a down-town fire on the East Side, toward morning, not a fire laddie but was sure of his coffee and hash in that renowned diving-bell. Many a one of its patrons now are owners and dwellers in a brown-stone house.

How ridiculous it would look at this time in an old "Vamp," whose age has made his top-knot and beard of the same color, to be seen stooping over a hot-corn pail, looking for a big ear to rub over the salt he holds in the palm of his hand.

A New York Cartman[5]

Thirty-five years ago I commenced business in New York as a licensed cartman. I continued in that business for the next twenty years following, and during that time I had the honor of carting quite a number of well-dressed young men to the old City Bridewell, that used to

[5] From *Recollections of an Old Cartman,* by I. S. Lyon, ex-cartman, Boonton, New Jersey, from the Newark Journal, pp. 3–5. Newark, N. J.: The Daily Journal Office. 1872.

stand in City Hall Park. I was at first what was then technically called a "catch cartman," the business of which was to grab the first job that offered—provided that the compensaiton was satisfactory. I afterwards got promoted to what the lower crust cartman derisively termed a "fine arts cartman." This fine arts business required a spring cart, and other fixtures suitable for removing pictures, looking glasses, and all other kinds of household furniture, with care and dispatch. This business was quite lucrative at first, but, like everything else that has money in it, it was soon overdone. Being among the first to start in it, I obtained some advantages which I retained to the end. This employment, naturally enough, called me in every direction all over the city—more especially in those locations occupied by those who were then termed the "big bugs." I always tried to do my work well and faithfully—and by so doing I not only gained, but also retained, the patronage of many of the best families in the city. Gentlemen having thousand-dollar pictures and mirrors to remove, were sometimes a little particular into whose hands they entrusted them; and why shouldn't they?

Thirty-five years ago nearly all the New York cartmen were strictly honest and upright men, and did their business on the square. They were true as steel and could be trusted. Gideon Lee, one of New York's old-time Mayors, once paid the city cartmen a very high compliment. Old Gideon, I believe, was a cartman himself in his younger days. He said that "during his whole term of office, as Mayor of the city, but *one* cartman had been brought before him charged with crime and that he very readily proved himself *not guilty*." But I have been informed, whether correctly or not I cannot say, that most of the New York cartmen of the present day are not a whit better or more honest than the Broadway merchants and Wall Street brokers. If this be really true, from my soul I pity them. But, after all, how can it be expected that they should retain their old-time honesty when all the rest of the world are thieves? Like all the rest of us, they are but human. A man must be something more or less than human at the present time if he is expected to keep his fingers out of his neighbor's pockets.

A New York cartman, above all others, should be an honest, intelligent, and upright man—for he must necessarily be entrusted with untold wealth in one shape and another. I recollect having on my cart one afternoon property valued at half a million of dollars, be the same more or less. It consisted of a collection of about thirty dingy-looking old oil paintings—said to be the grandest productions of some of the so-called old masters. I never once doubted the genuineness of their *antiquity;* but, although I had plenty of money in my pocket at this time, I wish to have it distinctly understood that I did not purchase them at that price. And right here permit me to remark—not under oath, however—that I acquired a very high character for honesty and square dealing during the twenty years that I followed carting; indeed, so *high* that I have not yet, with all my subsequent practice, become a very expert thief, which fact almost debars me from obtaining my rightful dues in this thieving and grab-game age.

The business of a catch cartman calls him in every direction all over the city, into the damp and loathsome vaults of the dead, and all through the stately marble palaces of the living, into the attics of six-story hotels and down to the fish-smelling wharfs, whence the "people" go down to the sea in ships. His daily beat comprises not only the city proper but all the surrounding country for twenty miles or more round about. Everybody trusts the cartman—oftentimes with secrets that they would not have divulged for the world—and it is very seldom that their trust is betrayed. His cartman's frock and his honest open countenance is a sufficient passport for him to go unchallenged wherever he pleases, and there is no one to say to him, "Thus far mayest thou go and no further." And no matter where he goes, whether it be into the vaults of a bank or a lady's dressing room, everybody supposes that *it's all right* and that he has been sent there by somebody on business, and no one questions him for being there. Oftentimes ladies of the *very highest* standing—sometimes standing as *high* as five feet six in their gaiters—confide secrets to their cartman such as they would not dare intrust to their husbands, and much less to their servant girls. A cartman who has established a good character for honesty and intelligence is looked upon by most businessmen as a person of more than ordinary importance and treated accordingly.

During the last two weeks in April of each year the cartmen begin to put on a few extra airs, and look and act with more importance than at any other time during the year. Everybody then calls him *Mr.* Cartman, and when the first day of May arrives then "stand from under!" He then becomes very domineering, and everybody feels that it is their interest, if not their duty, to bow and cringe to him, for on that day of all the year it is generally admitted that a cartman may charge any price that he pleases. Through a long continued practice this has become a fixed custom, which no one presumes to call in question, although there is no law in existence that justifies this assumption. All the goods and personal property, as well as a large proportion of the real, contained within the city limits have passed through the hands of the New York cartmen at one time or another, and I fully believe that, were the truth of the case known, more wealth passes through the hands of the city cartmen every year than is handled by the whole board of Wall Street brokers.

It is generally supposed that a cartman should know everybody and everything—here, there, and everywhere—past, present, and to come. He must know the exact locations of all public and business places—theaters and hotels, factories and workshops, shipping points and railroad depots—what time this ship sails and what time that train starts, and whether there are any *runaway couples* on board of either. He must know in what streets all the churches and justices' courts are located; to what denomination each church belongs, and who preaches in them; the name of the presiding justice in each court, and how large a fee it will require to bribe each of them. He must know where to find all the colleges and schoolhouses, the names of the professors in this college and of the teachers in that schoolhouse; who lives here and who lives there; when this man is going to move and where that man has moved to. He is likewise expected to know all the doctors, both quack and regular, and which can make the largest blue pills, and which can saw off your leg without your knowing it. Also, all the choice city scandal, and who has been fortunate enough to see the elephant; who is going to elope with this man's wife and who is going to run away with that man's daughter. In fact, it is generally expected by all those who know nothing themselves that the New York cartman should be an encyclopaedia and an intelligence-office combined; and if he don't happen to know all this and a great deal more, he is set down as a know-nothing and asked why he don't go to school and learn his A,B,C's. But almost any sharp, wide-awake cartman, who has taken out the first renewal of his license, would be able to answer all these questions correctly and a great many more which it would not be prudent for some gentlemen, who value their domestic peace, to ask.

The Stage Driver Makes Change [6]

Many of the [stage] drivers are very communicative on the subjects of their profession, and not a few tell some good stories of "slouches," "bums," and "beats," the names given to those gentlemen whose prin-

[6] From *Lights and Shadows of New York Life;* or, the Sights and Sensations of The Great City. A Work Descriptive of the City of New York in all its

cipal object in this world is to sponge upon poor humanity to as great an extent as the latter will permit. One of the cheapest ways of "getting a ride" is to present a five or ten dollar bill; very few drivers carry so much money, as they hardly ever have that amount on their morning trips; the bill cannot be changed, and the owner of it gets "down town" *free.*

Apropos of this method, a talkative Jehu said to me one morning, "When I was a drivin' on the Knickerbocker," a line that ran some twenty years ago [as of 1879] from South Ferry through Broadway, Bleecker, and Eighth Avenue, to Twenty-third Street, "there was a middle-aged man that used to ride reg'lar; all the fellows got to knowin' him. Well, he'd get in and hand up a ten dollar note—you know the fare was only six cents then—and we never had so much 'bout us, so, of course, he'd ride for nothin'; well, that fellow stuck me five mornin's straight, and I sort o' got tired of it; so on the six' day I went to the office and says to the Boss, 'There's a man ridin' free on this line. All the fellows knows him; he gives 'em all a ten dollar note and they can't break it. He's rid with me these last five mornin's, an' I'm goin' for him today, I want ten dollars in pennies, an' six fares out. If he rides I'll git square with him.' So the Boss he gives me nine dollars and sixty-four cents all in pennies—you know they was all big ones then—an' they weighed some, I tell you. When I got down to Fourteenth Street he hailed me. Then the fares used to pay when they got out. So he hands up this note; I looked at it—it was on the 'Dry Dock'—an' I hands him down the pennies. Well, how he did blow about it an' said how he wouldn't take 'em. Well, says I, then I'll keep it all. Well, he was the maddest fellow you ever seen; he was hoppin'! But he got out an' some one inside hollers out, 'Put some one on the other side or you'll capsize,' an' he thought it was me. He jumped on the sidewalk an' he called me everything he could lay his tongue to, an' I a la'ffin' like blazes. Says he, 'I'll report you, you old thief,' an' I drove off. Well, I told the Boss, an' he says, 'Let him come, I'll talk to him,' but he never made no complaint there."

Said another: "A lady got in with me one day an' handed up a fifty

---

Various Phases; with Full and Graphic Accounts of its Splendors and Wretchedness; its High and Low Life; its Marble Palaces and Dark Dens; its Attractions and Dangers; its Rings and Frauds; its Leading Men and Politicians; its Adventurers; its Charities; its Mysteries, and its Crimes, by James D. McCabe, pp. 218–221. Entered . . . 1879 . . . by J. R. Jones. Phila., Pa.; Chicago, Ill.; St. Louis, Mo.: The National Publishing Co.

cent stamp. I put down forty cents. I don't never look gen'rally, but this time I see a man take the change an' put it in his pocket. Pretty soon a man rings the bell an' says, 'Where's the lady's change?' Well, I thinks here's a go, an' I points to the man and says, 'That there gentleman put it in his pocket.' Well, that fellow looked like a sheet, an' a thunder-cloud an' all through the rainbow. He never said nothing but pulled out the change, gave it up, an' then he got out an' went round a corner like mad. Some don't wait like he did tho', but gits out right off. One day a chap got out an' another follered him, and they had it out on the street there, an' we all was a looking on."

Sometimes the drivers make "a haul" in a curious way. Said one: "A man handed me up a fifty dollar bill one night. I handed it back four times, and got mad because he wouldn't give me a small bill. He said he hadn't anything else, and I could take that or nothing, so, I gave him change for a dollar bill, and kept forty-nine dollars and ten cents for his fare. He didn't say anything, and after a while he got out. Why, the other day a lady gave me a hundred dollar note, and when I told her I thought she'd faint. 'My goodness!' said she, 'I didn't know it was more than one.' Such people ought to be beat; they'd be more careful when they lose a few thousand."

"Some fellows," said another driver, "give you ten or fifteen cents, an' swear they give you a fifty cent stamp, an' you have to give them change for fifty cents, or they'll may be go to the office an' make a fuss, an' the bosses will sooner take their word than yours, an' you'll get sacked."

One of the most laborious ways of "turning an honest penny" was brought to my notice by one of these knights of the whip. Said he: "Has you been a-watchin' of my business this morning? P'r'aps you ain't took notice of the money I'm takin' in? No, I guess not." The latter remark was followed by a rough laugh, in which I thought there was distinguishable a little more than mere merriment, especially when I heard a mumbled imprecation. He continued aloud: "I ain't seen any yet myself." Soon the bell rang, and a ticket was passed up. "Well," said he, "he's goin' it strong, to be sure; this here's the fourteenth ticket I've had on this trip." An explanation being solicited, the fact was revealed that there was a man inside who made a practice of buying twelve tickets for a dollar, then seating himself near the bell, he would take the fares of every one and give the driver a ticket for each, that is, receive ten cents and give the driver the equivalent of eight and one-third cents, thereby making ten cents on every six passengers. "You see," said the driver, "what a blessin' those sort of fellers is. Here I don't have no trouble whatsomever; he makes all the change for me, and 'spose my box should blow over, nothen's lost." From time to time as the tickets were handed up he would cheer the toiler inside with such expressions as "Go it boots," "How's the cash?" "How does the old thing work?" always loud enough to attract the attention of the "insides."

This strange individual interested me so much that I made some inquiries about him, at first supposing him to be crazy or otherwise terribly afflicted; but he is considered sound, is the third in a well-to-do firm, and is far beyond the need of having recourse to any such means for increasing his capital.

The Horse-Car Conductor[7]

You want a sort of running account of my daily work and what is required of us when we first go on the road? Well, we have to furnish our suits. If it is summer time the suit costs us from $14 to $16, while the winter apparel is worth several dollars more. Then we have to procure an overcoat, and some of us are required to make a deposit on the bell-punch. Of course that is repaid us whenever we leave. Then we must have a watch, and one that will keep good time. We have to regulate our watches by the large clock in the depot, and any variation makes it all the more difficult for us to run on time. Our clothes must be kept clean, and we are expected always to present a neat appearance and get down to the depot in the morning about five minutes before our car starts. The mats, which I took up the night before and which the driver has shaken, I put in their places. And just here let me say that we are compelled to keep our car clean and have the windows washed whenever they need it. I sweep out the car the last thing at night and before running in with the other cars, in order to avoid scattering dust over them. I am supposed to have full control over the car, and the driver is, to a certain extent, under me. If there is any trouble between us we can make it unpleasant for each other,

[7] From *New York by Sunlight and Gaslight,* A Work Descriptive of the Great American Metropolis, its High and Low Life; its Splendors and Miseries; its Virtues and Vices; its Gorgeous Palaces and Dark Homes of Poverty and Crime; its Public Men, Politicians, Adventurers; its Charities, Frauds, Mysteries, Etc., Etc., by James D. McCabe, pp. 242–247. Copyright, 1881, by Douglass Brothers. Philadelphia, Pa.

but I have the privilege to report any misconduct or disobedience, and the conductor is generally sustained.

Before starting out I take a certain amount in change, which is charged against me by the cashier. Some men turn their cash in at the end of each trip, but most of us wait until night, and hand the account for the entire day in at once. At the close of every trip I make out my report, specifying on this card the amount. As a general thing, my account comes out square, but once in a while I find myself out a few cents. It is rare that I find a surplus in my favor. Occasionally I will give too little change, or mistake one of those twenty-cent pieces for a quarter, thus cheating the passenger, but usually the other way. For a long time we were sold on those twenty-cent coins, and learned to be cautious. Then once in a while, when the car is full and we are making change rapidly, a three-cent piece or one of those small half-dimes will get in between other change which we hand to a passenger. Of course we are "docked" in those cases. The same way with counterfeit money —we have to run the risk and bear the loss. I got stuck on a five dollar note not long ago. The receiver handed it back to me the next day and charged me with it. I had to get rid of it as best I could. They are pretty lenient with us, however, and we do not often suffer.

There is a difference as to the time given for meals and stops by the lines. I have about two minutes at the lower end of the trip and from seven to fourteen at the upper. In the evening we get from fifteen to twenty. About fifteen minutes is allowed us for meals—that is, we have that time between trips at noon and night, but if we are behind time, that is taken off and we have so much less to eat in. We generally manage to have full time, however, for eating. Our meals are brought us by our children or wives, and are placed in the conductors' room at the depot. Some of the men live close enough to run home and get a bite. We get very little time to see our families, I tell you, except when we get our day off. Some of the roads let you have whatever day you ask for, and supply your place with one of the extras. An "extra" is a man who is substituted and generally has been taken off the regular force for disobeying orders. Slight disobedience, such as neglect to clean your car, often places you on the extra list, while gross carelessness will discharge you. You get no pay on your holidays, while you are paid from $2.00 to $2.50 a day while on duty. The "trippers," as those men are called who only run three-quarters of a day, get $1.50. I know the pay is not so poor, compared with many other occupations, but then we have so little time to ourselves, or for sleep. I only get five hours a day sleep, and I am terribly tired when the work is over. It is very hard to awaken me in the morning, so soundly do I sleep. All the chance we get to sit down is between trips or on this board seat, which we pay for ourselves, and that is not over comfortable, as you can see.

Our life is pretty monotonous, and yet all sorts of scenes occur to give it variety. If it was not for that, I could not stand it, and so most of the men say. We have all kinds of people, and articles of every description travel with us. The washerwoman gets on with her basket of clothes; the tailor brings in a bundle; the emigrant rides with a big bag or small trunk; the lady has a dozen small packages, and the caterer carries dainties for a party. Now and then a funny thing happens that sets the car in a roar of laughter. A man got in the morning after the election in Indiana and Ohio and purchased a paper. When he read the result, he rolled the paper up and fired it the length of the car, narrowly missing a dozen heads and striking a small boy with a pail of milk here on the platform. A German got on board the other day, who could not speak a word of English. Fortunately, I understand German a little, and was able to make out that he wanted to get out at Twenty-second Street. When we reached there I told him, putting my hand up to pull the bell, as he had several immense bundles. He shook his head, and drew my hand back, so we went on. I tried to find out what he meant, but he laughed and said nothing. Suddenly, when we were moving quite fast, he gathered up his luggage, shook hands with me, and before I could comprehend his movements, jumped off. He turned over and over, his bundles flew in every direction and his hat rolled into the gutter. At first I thought he was hurt, but he sat up in the street, kissed his hand to me, and laughed loud enough to be heard a block off.

We conductors have our annoyances also. It is hard to tell who worry us the most, but I guess the women do. Some of them are so nervous and fidgety, never knowing where they want to go, and asking every minute if we have reached there. They get out on the platform before the car stops, and often have to be held back from jumping off. They start out to shop sometimes, and forget their purses. After riding a block or two they suddenly discover the lack of money, and either declare there are pickpockets in the car or else are in tribulation lest we will put them off right away. On rainy days we have to raise their umbrellas and wait for them to get their dresses adjusted. Then those of them who go marketing bring huge baskets, which we have to lift on and off. Still, we ought to be courteous, and I think most of us are, though the ladies do not often take the pains to thank us for any extra attention. The worst lot we have to deal with are the young clerks and store boys, who ride regularly back and forth from business. They put on any quantity of airs and try to occupy the entire car. One of them always sits out here on my seat, even though there is plenty of room inside. They smoke when they shouldn't, and then want to know when the rule was made prohibiting it. They get in the way, jostle the other passengers, declare we do not give them the right change, and make themselves disagreeable generally. The newsboys are forbidden on many of the cars after nine o'clock in the morning, yet persist in jumping on after that time. The small boy steals a ride while we are forward in the car, and rainy days we get thoroughly drenched, particularly if the storm beats down the street. Only now and then are we able to stand inside and avoid the wet. Then we have the chronic grumblers—men and women—who want the windows up and down at the same time. We put them up, and some lady begins to shiver and some man turns up his coat collar and looks daggers at us; we put them down, and at once there are complaints that the air is stifling. Then there are those who annoy us by charging that they left articles in the cars, very valuable in most cases, which we have taken, but which, strange to say, are generally found at home or in some store. I might mention the drunken characters and the noisy ones who ride with us, but the list I have named embraces the majority of troublesome persons.

We cannot complain generally of bad treatment by the companies. They relieve us when we are sick, allow us a day to ourselves, and pay what they promise. Many of us are sorry we ever took the position, for an entirely different reason, and that is, that the place is regarded as a degrading one by so many, and we are excluded socially because of our occupation. Some of us are of good families, but the hard times compelled us to do anything that would secure us a competence and was not actually disreputable. Yet we are mostly looked down upon.

The Cabby's "Run-Around" [8]

. . . There was [a] band of nighthawks operating the fleet of scooped-out and sea-going hacks. The scooped-out hack was the open Victoria, while the sea-going vehicle was the closed hack, more like a brougham.

[8] From *The Girl from Rector's,* by George Rector, pp. 136–137, 138–139. Copyright, 1927, by Doubleday, Page & Company; 1926, 1927 by The Curtis Publishing Company. Garden City, New York.

By permission of Louise Fraser Lensky and Loew's Incorporated.

Like Robin Hood's band, they were a merry bunch of outlaws who trimmed the rich—but failed to donate to the poor. There were fifteen or twenty outside of Rector's every night, rain or shine. Their scale of prices depended on their victim's condition of sobriety and knowledge of geography. Their tactics originated the famous expression "run-around." A man who is giving you the run-around is trying to stall you off by using evasive methods.

A stranger got into a Rector cab one night and asked to be driven to the Hotel Astor, which had just been built and was directly across the street. The cabby was Gas-House Sam, who sensed that his fare was ignorant of the location of the hotel. So Sam click-clicked to his horse and away they went around the block, passing the hotel at the start and passing it again on the completion of the lap. Sam looped the hotel eleven times before he pulled his steed up on its thin haunches and helped his fare out. The charge was three dollars and the run-around proved that a long ride is costlier than a short walk.

* * * * *

Bounding Dick, Tenderloin Bill, and Frank the Gyp stopped whipping their horses years ago. I do not know what these men did for a living after the taxicab succeeded the oat burner. One cab driver's specialty was rolling drunks. This meant that he sought inebriated fares, whom he proceeded to drive through the park to a dark spot and then frisk. If the victim howled, the cabby never objected to going direct to a police station and being searched. Nothing was ever found on him and he was always discharged.

But so many complaints were lodged against him by fleece-lined customers who had lost their fleeces that an investigation was made and it was discovered that all his customers were paying for two cabs instead of one. Every time he started for the park with a fare, he was followed by another driver in an empty cab, who would drive by the first cab in the park just in time to be handed the victim's watch and money. After the driver came back from his triumphant trip to the police station, the two would divide the plunder. His last drive was a little longer than he reckoned on, for it landed him up in Sing Sing. His horse got a suspended sentence.

This cabby was a fine actor, for after having been given a clean bill of health at each police investigation, he would turn on his accuser and demand his money for the trip. On one occasion his accuser spent the evening in a cell because he failed to dig up the price of the ride. . . .

The Honest Junkman [9]

In front of Lincoln Hall's marriage canopy, a bower of stiff artificial calla lilies entwined in intensely dark-green leaves, the fervent chairman of the United Junkmen's Association of Brooklyn, Inc., thundered for justice for the trade. Anti-noise laws, he bellowed, had ruined the calling. The microphone tinnily protested his ardent assault, set up a metallic whine at every syllable. Two hundred tired-looking, middle-aged men in work clothes listened in bewildered silence. The bull-voiced chairman darted a finger at the fifth row back.

"Mr. Friedman," he cried, "how many years you are in the junk business?"

A tall, thin man, sunken cheeks gray with stubble, stood up. He seemed embarrassed in the sudden limelight.

He mumbled, "Twenty-two years. Twenty-two years I am in the junk business."

A murmur breathed through the wedding chamber. Other junkmen twisted in their seats to face Mr. Friedman. The chairman thundered another question.

"Was you ever stopped in the streets by policemen, Mr. Friedman?"

The thin man said, "Please, Mr. Chairman. I am an honest junkman."

With eager passion the stertorous chairman pressed his point.

"Why are they stopping you now, please, Mr. Friedman, if you are an honest junkman?" he demanded triumphantly.

"Because I am ringing bells," the thin man said bitterly.

An angry undertone rumbled from the swart throats. The craggy-browed chairman caught the undertone at the crest. The microphone plates danced again under his tirade.

He shouted, "Eighteen years I am hollering junk in the streets. Eighteen years I am ringing my junk bells. Last week in our meeting we had five tickets in here. Why?" No one answered. "Why?" he persisted. "Because illegitimate junk peddlers steals a bicycle. It's a sickness with these illegitimate fellas. A disease what you call. For them illegitimate fellas we catch the blame."

[9] From *The Eight Million,* Journal of a New York Correspondent, by Meyer Berger, pp. 297–301. Copyright, 1942, by Meyer Berger. New York: Simon and Schuster.

Some one stood up to put in a word. The chairman sat him down with a magnificent wave of his hand. The chairman spoke with heavy dignity.

"Please," he said. "Please give me the courtesy. I am talking. In this city," he rumbled, "you got maybe 8,500 junkmen with license. Eight hundred—it could be one t'ousand—are bad and they are ruining you. Ain't you ashamed of your sweethearts and wives when you read a junkman took off a bicycle or maybe a suit of clothes off a line hanging? This thing we must correct. If you stick with us you will be recognized as decent gentlemen. You will be able to make maybe a couple pennies and bring home a loaf of bread, a bottle milk to support your family."

Hardened, work-soiled palms thundered applause. The chairman's brow was dewy. He glared fiercely down the side lines, emotionally caught by his own eloquence and the applause. During a brief recess a young peddler explained about the Junkmen's Association. He said it means to fight the anti-noise ordinance.

He said: "If we can't holler 'Junk, rags, furniture, old clo',' how can the housewives know we are there? If we cannot ring on our junk bells, how can they hear us?"

The association, he said, had caused to be made for its members large white buttons bearing each member's likeness. It wanted the men fingerprinted. It wanted to do away with unscrupulous dealers who send men out to steal, rather than to buy.

He said: "We want the peddlers should be polite to the housewife. We want the housewife to know we are for her protection."

* * * * *

Sometimes a peddler accidentally made a good buy. One man paid thirty-eight cents for brass that turned out to be $28.50 worth of gold. A Negro junkman found $73 in an old suit lining. Another peddler found $200 in an old hair mattress. One fellow bought an iron statue of President Garfield at the Vanderbilt estate on Long Island and it turned out to be bronze, worth, maybe, $200.

The energetic chairman ended the meeting with a lesson on politeness to customers. He picked his words carefully to make the lesson sink in.

"If a housewife has got an item wort' three dollars," he said, "and she wants, maybe, six dollars, be always a gentleman, a credit to the profession. Don't say to this worm, 'The hell wit' it.' Don't do this. Tip your hat. Be nice. Don't even slam the door. Say, 'Lady, t'ank you just the same.' This you got to do if you don't want the public to look on us like low class. We must be gentlemen, and we'll make money, even in a crisis."

The class in politeness roared noisy approval. Boots thumped the floor. Rough hands pounded heartily. The chairman beamed.

"Fellow gentlemen," he said, "the meeting is adjourned."

Dress Spies [10]

. . . Hundreds of keen-eyed, quick-witted young women . . . earn their living in the garment industry by helping to pirate dress designs. Some scout their employer's rivals. Others . . . concentrate on the high-fashion designers who originate the styles. These are high-class operators. There are perhaps two dozen in New York—young women whose blue-blooded family backgrounds give them unquestioned entree to the salons of the *haute couture* but whose anemic bank accounts do not permit them to buy there.

They attend exclusive fashion showings, purchase what seem to be the most likely or striking models and turn them over to the mass manufacturers who copy them or, in garment-center parlance, "knock them off." The spy's reward is usually keeping the expensive original.

There is nothing illegal in these quaint careers. Unlike France, which protects its important fashion industry with strict laws and punishes style pirates severely, the United States has no fashion copyright law. There is little that Mainbocher and other creative designers can do but drop known or suspected spies from their invitation lists. The average garment manufacturer sends out his own spies without one ethical qualm. It is only when a competitor sneaks a spy into his showroom and makes off with a sketch of his season's pet model that he feels there ought to be a law.

Although every garment manufacturer doesn't engage in piracy, the practice is undeniably widespread. On the whole, the men who have mass-produced the American woman into the best-dressed female in the world are pretty proud of their ability to knock them off as fast as the big designers here and abroad can think them up.

[10] From "Piracy on Fifth Avenue," by Jhan and June Robbins, *This Week Magazine,* June 5, 1949. Copyright, 1949, by New York Herald Tribune, Inc.

In New York's garment center, which is jammed into all the available space on Seventh Avenue between Thirty-fifth and Forty-first Streets, there are few laurels given or asked for original designs. Instead, manufacturers concentrate on producing a gown which, from a distance of ten feet—or twenty, if you are a woman—looks like a custom-made model.

* * * * *

Occasionally . . . manufacturers glean their ideas from the glossy pages of the better fashion magazines. But for the most part, they pin their faith on the spies and counterspies who dodge along Seventh Avenue, often carrying their loot in unobtrusive, brown paper bags that fool nobody.

Spy work is fast and efficient. A department-store manager was flabbergasted recently when buyers for his bargain balcony, budget shop and costume floor each turned up with the same dress, selling in three different price lines. Such occurrences embarrass the stores, make customers angry and make the original designers angriest of all. *Couturière* Nettie Rosenstein, some of whose creations are priced below $100, is not particularly perturbed by the copyists who produce for the bargain basement. But the spies whose bosses tag their pirated products confusingly near her own level—around $49.50—are the ones she'd like to get her hands on.

Unfortunately, none of the nation's top-flight designers has ever been able to think up a suitable punishment although one temperamental artist has been known to chase a suspected spy out of her workrooms and pursue her into the street, hysterically waving a pair of shears. Another laid a trap by designing what he considered a perfect dud—a dress that nobody would buy—and leaving it out where the spies could grab it. They grabbed it all right, but to his dismay the cheap copies of this deliberate horror sold about as well as anything else that season.

* * * * *

The garment manufacturer is not a piratical type. He is much more likely to be a timid, worried little man who goes with a surprisingly large number of his fellows for treatment of dyspeptic ulcers and for frequent psychiatric advice. These twin complaints are the health hazards of this highly competitive enterprise where more than 1,000 manufacturers are desperately jostling one another for their share of two billion dollars' worth of annual business and where each year from ten to fifteen per cent of the firms are eliminated by bankruptcy.

Worried over the financial future, none seem to want to guess what fifty-four million American women are going to choose to wear next and when they will feel like shopping for it.

It is indisputable that new trends in fashions, and the best interpretations of them, begin in the salons of the nation's topflight custom designers. And with any luck, a manufacturer's spies can make the rounds of the *couturier* houses and glean a dozen numbers that will style-lead the season.

One of the stories attributed to Designer Omar Kiam tells of a manufacturer who didn't trust even his best spy to pick the winners from an important Kiam opening. He went himself, in elaborate disguise —beard, dark glasses and a bulbous putty nose.

Feeling quite secure, he sat eagerly eying the pirouetting models and made several purchases. Then Kiam came by, dropped a hand on his shoulder, and said cheerily, "Hello, Sam. Enjoying the show?"

Pawnbroker on Eighth Avenue [11]

Berg, a short, nattily dressed, middle-aged man, has worked behind the counter of a pawnshop since he was a youth. "It's a very good business," he says. "It's not seasonal, and you can't suddenly lose everything. It's not a business where you can get hurt; people loan and redeem all the time." Berg's shop is open six days a week from 9 A.M. to 6 P.M., and patronized by a wide variety of city dwellers. Throughout the day he makes loans, records interest payments, redeems pawned articles, and sells a potpourri of merchandise with solicitous care. He is an expert on the loan value, that is, the resale value, of watches, diamonds, gold rings, cameras, violins, luggage, suits, overcoats, furs, antiques—and tears or frenzy don't move him. "In this business," he says, "you can't be a softie. You wouldn't last."

Berg is shrewd, direct, poker-faced, and suspicious. Though he is courteous, and on occasion sentimental, he doesn't cash checks, tests all precious stones and metals for genuineness, and is watchful for

[11] From "Pawnbroker on Eighth Avenue, A Portrait," by Donald Paneth, *Commentary,* Vol. 17 (March, 1954), No. 3, pp. 276–279. Copyright, 1954, by the American Jewish Committee. New York.

stolen goods and the artifices of patrons. He automatically compares each patron with the article being pawned, and if they don't seem to correspond asks for identification. (He also carries a $200,000 Lloyd's of London insurance policy against fire, theft, and holdup.) "There are people who sit up nights figuring ways to put it over on the pawnbroker," he says with some dismay. "They try to pawn diamonds that aren't diamonds, or they go into a credit jeweler's, put $1 down on a $75 value, and then hock it for $10, or they try to disguise a hole in a suit jacket with a black arm band. Some people are really thieves. They come in when we're busy, pull the tag off a suit on the rack, and try to hock it. Or they say, 'I just want to see what color it is outside,' and fly around the corner with it. Anyway, I'm very careful."

* * * * *

Thirty or forty people a day pawn articles with Berg, and on an average day he loans them about $800, in small amounts between $10 and $25. "I don't like to make big loans," he says. "I'd rather loan $100 to ten people than to one person—the higher the number of pledges, the greater the turnover and the interest." Trade is particularly brisk each day between 9 and 10 A.M., noon and 1 P.M., and 5 and 6. P.M. "There are always a few people," Berg explains, "waiting for you to open. Usually, they need money to get to work. Then, at twelve o'clock, we get business from the people who go out to lunch; they want money to bet on a horse, and they pawn personal items such as tie clasps or fountain pens. At five o'clock, the people who have a dinner appointment or lost their bets come in." Of the days in the week, Friday is consistently the busiest in the shop. "It used to be Saturday," Berg says, "but most people get paid on Friday now, and redeem their clothing so they can wear it over the weekend. They bring it back and pawn it again on Monday morning. They bring in a new suit, maybe, and I loan them $11 or $12; then, in a month, I cut it down to $10 or $11, and so forth. If they put up a fuss, I explain to them, 'Well, you're wearing the suit out.' "

His diverse patrons comprise the poor and the well-to-do, the obscure and the notable, the transient and the regular. They include longshoremen from Tenth Avenue, young boxers from Stillman's Gymnasium, music students from Carnegie Hall, lodgers from nearby rooming houses, rodeo contestants from Madison Square Garden, and entertainers from Broadway night clubs. "There are always new faces," he says. "We get a lot of transient trade from the hotels and furnished rooms; six months later, I receive a money order from a [Navy] address or California or out of the country. We're a block from Stillman's gym, and I find managers bringing in youngsters from all over the United States. They don't have too much money, and they come in and start pawning the watches they won as amateurs so they can get a room. Then, they have one or two fights and they're not doing too well and they pawn their outfits—skipping rope, gloves, and headgear. They usually don't redeem them. Now the Puerto Ricans are coming in and living on Ninth, Tenth, Eleventh Avenue. They have very little, and they become porters or bus boys or go on relief. A St. Christopher medal is the first thing they'll buy and the first thing they'll pawn. I also do a lot of business with theatrical people. They love to live high, and they don't work too steadily unless they're top. I've had some very well-known entertainers pawn with me; I can't disclose their names, but the public would be surprised. I get a better class of trade too—from the hotels in the vicinity, the Pierre, St. Moritz, Hampshire House, Park Sheraton, and from the apartment houses on Central Park West. It happens in the best of families. Maybe they have to raise a bail bond, or maybe they're living on an income, have been entertaining a little too freely, and need some money until their monthly check arrives. They pawn some very lovely jewelry."

Berg has many steady patrons who won't trade elsewhere. "They get used to the same shop," he explains, "and feel comfortable in it. I have a press agent, for instance, who pawns his pants twice a week, and a TV actor who leaves his tuxedo with me except when he needs it for a scene; the actor pays $25 a week alimony. I've known one woman twenty years. She was formerly a silent movie actress, and she still gets letters from Cecil B. De Mille, which I have seen myself. She's in her early fifties now, and occasionally gets bit parts in Broadway shows. When things get tough for her, she pawns a little diamond ring and pin. I've got one guy who works for an express company, and drinks; once a week, at the end of the week, he pawns a nail clipper and a scissors for $1. Another guy I've known twelve years. He runs around with women, and never has enough money; he pawns his golf clubs, a very expensive set, and his wife's jewelry. I've been seeing a lot of him lately."

He works snappily behind the counter. "The person needs money," he says. "And he wants that money, he doesn't want to chat with you. We try to get him in and out fast." He shrewdly adapts his manner to each person with whom he deals: he is friendly with the regular, good-natured with the alcoholic, ingratiating with the well-to-do, benevolent with the Negro or Puerto Rican. "I treat everybody like a lady or gentleman," he says, "if they're sincere and don't try to put anything over on me. I make them feel right at home, and explain to them that it's strictly business. I explain that they can redeem their article today, tomorrow, or a year from today. Of course, we have the cocky type: whatever he asks I should give him. There's always a little argument with this type, but I take him off his perch immediately. 'If you can't act like a gentleman, we won't do business with you.' Then we have the meek type. They come in very slowly, very quietly, and stand at the counter. They're ashamed, and afraid you'll get angry with them. 'Is this a pawnshop?' they'll say." Through a name for courtesy, Berg has tried to attract the well-to-do and well-known to his shop. "The better class of trade," he says; adding, "Well, it's nice to do business with nice people. They're more understanding. Not that I don't want to do business with the other type, they're my livelihood."

* * * * *

Berg and Murray, his manager, a short, reserved, pipe-smoking man who has worked for him twelve years, wait on trade; another employee, Ray, is stock clerk. "Berg likes to handle the pledging himself," Murray says. "And he likes the place to be efficient and clean. Sometimes he flares up and says something. 'What'dya let the customer out for?' He feels he might have made the sale if we'd turned him over." Most of Berg's patrons need money quickly, often desperately, to pay rent, or buy food, or pay a bill. And his interest rates, though fixed by New York State, are correspondingly high: 3 per cent (per month) on $1 to $100 for the first six months, and 2 per cent for the following six; over $100, the rate is 2 and 1 per cent respectively. "It may sound a little exorbitant," Berg says, "but it's not. There's the upkeep of the business, and it's the same rate as seventy years ago." The amount of the loan he makes, however, is fixed by habit and tradition, not law. For example, he usually lends 50 cents to $3 on an alarm clock, $2 to $8 on a drafting set, $5 to $15 on an overcoat, $10 to $35 on a violin, $20 to $50 on a rifle, $50 to $200 on a fur coat. Occasionally, his loans are larger: $150 on a Leica camera or $300 on an old, rare violin or $800 on a diamond clip. "We keep it down," he acknowledges. "There are so many different opinions as to value—and we want to get our money back if it's not redeemed. Sometimes, if a person really seems to need the money I loan a little more. I once had a fella come in with his wife's fur coat. I offered him a loan of $90, and he told me he needed $125 for a hospital bill. I said no. But he started pleading, and I noticed tears come to his eyes. Then I began to weaken, and ask him questions, and he takes out the bill. Well, I loaned him $125. That was three years ago, and he's still paying interest on the coat; he hasn't been able to take it out yet. So I helped a fella out, and I'm getting a return on my money."

Gold and silver rings, diamonds, violins, objects of art are the most difficult articles upon which to fix a loan value. And Berg is extremely cautious when accepting them in pawn. He carefully tests all rings and diamonds. "I can judge by the weight of a ring if it's gold or gold-filled," he says. "I get a feel in my finger tips. But I don't allow my men to do this, I insist that they test it. Filing it a little in an inconspicuous place, and putting on an acid; if the acid turns green it proves the article is brass." Determining the value and genuineness of diamonds is more complicated. Berg goes over each diamond with a Diamond Point Pencil (it will scratch glass or sapphire but not another diamond) and measures its circumference and depth with a precision gauge. He chiefly encounters diamonds of three grades; brown, the cheapest, yellow, mediocre, and blue-white, valuable. "Some people," he says, "try to color a yellow diamond with an indelible pencil. Give it a 'Silver Cape,' a bright color. The only way to discover that is to wash a diamond with alcohol, which removes the indelible film. We wash practically every diamond with alcohol. Then we have a doublet-diamond—the top is diamond and the bottom is zircon, the nearest and hardest thing to a diamond. If you look into the center of that diamond, it's dead, it has no life." Unlike many other pawnbrokers, Berg is also familiar with the characteristics—and approximate value—of violins and objects of art. "A pawnshop takes in an awful lot of violins," he says. "We get quite a few from students at Carnegie Hall who either run short or quit. Now I'm no expert, I don't know the real value of a fiddle—a Strad or Guarnieri—but I know what to look for. How beautiful the stain is. Whether it's a healthy fiddle, cracked or repaired. How fine the scroll's been done." Similarly, he accepts china, bric-a-brac, and antiques in pawn. "Venetian glassware," he says, "Italian china, Royal Copenhagen china, Meissen and Dresden figures. As long as I can remember, I've loved anything old."

He records each loan in a ledger, on descriptive cards, and on the pawn ticket, which is small, pink and white, and oblong. "THIS TICKET GOOD FOR ONE YEAR ONLY," it says. "This Ticket may be renewed by paying the interest due." Each evening the descriptive cards are mailed to the Police Department, which checks them for stolen goods; Berg in turn receives daily lists of stolen goods from the police. "Every pawnshop gets a few characters with stolen goods," he says. "But I don't try to compete with the Police Department. If I think an article's stolen, I say, 'Do you mind if I check this?' I give the guy a chance to go, and he runs out of the store. This happens a dozen times a year, but as long as I'm behind the grill I don't get nervous." Many of the articles which are legitimately pawned are eventually redeemed, while the remainder are sold at auction or by Berg himself. "There are some people," he says, "who wouldn't think of shopping anywhere else. But we also get a lot of celebrities. I sold Joe Howard a diamond ring in '43 or '44. And Kid Gavilan. I sold him a guitar. I paid special attention to his hands. I have a small hand, but his hand was smaller than mine. It made you wonder where he gets all the power from."

Uncle Jim, the Sandwich Man [12]

They call it "The Bowery of the West Side"—that part of Eighth Avenue between Fourteenth and Twenty-third Streets. Fifteen years ago the name would have been more fitting, for today [1905] the original Bowery cannot vie with its successor in originality, variety, or picturesqueness. To see the liveliest, lightest, and almost the noisiest street in town, one must now wander through lower Eighth Avenue after dark, preferably on a Saturday evening.

* * * * *

[Here is one] colored business man who deals in sandwiches—spelled with a "t"—at a stand beside a saloon. The sandwich man is a well-known character roundabout, and everybody knows him as "Uncle Jim," the avuncular pre-nomen being a title of respect due to his gray hairs. Among his friends is a police captain, whose home is in a side street towards Ninth Avenue. When the cold weather set in a week or so ago, the captain sighted Uncle Jim and called to him: "Well, I'm ready to give you that present I promised."

[12] From "The Bowery of the West Side, Eighth Ave. Alive with Interesting Scenes, New Home of the 'Ole Cloes' Man— Restaurant and Café Life in the Quarter—Picturesque Incidents of a Stroll Through the Region on a Saturday Night," *New York Evening Post,* October 28, 1905.

He was referring, as he explained in telling the incident, to an offhand promise he had volunteered when the old Negro did him a favor some time last spring.

"What shall it be?" he continued. "Would you rather have a ton of coal or a jug of whisky?"

Uncle Jim scratched his head, and appeared to be thinking deeply. After a minute's pause, he said sheepishly: "Cap'n, don't you know I burns wood at my house?"

The Counterman and the Bagel [13]

. . . In a gaudy midtown cafeteria . . . the customer got himself a tray and picked up two bagels en route to other fodder. He stopped at Hot Meats presided over by a swarthy pirate clutching a gleaming knife big as a cutlass.

"Slice these bagels for me," the customer said.

The counterman looked at him disdainfully. This was like asking Dook Snider of the Dodgers to swat flies with his best bat, or an admiral to chop liver with his sword.

"This here knife," the counterman said, "ain't for slicing bagels. This is for cutting a nice fat corned beef, or a turkey. Go to Sandwiches. Down there, he's got a knife for cutting bagels."

"Maybe," the customer sneered, "your knife ain't sharp enough to cut a bagel."

The counterman leered. "Kindly lay your neck down on the block," he suggested, "and I'll show you *sharp*. . . ." His tone changed, "Move along, mister," he snapped. "People is waiting behind you."

"I don't move," the other said doggedly, "until you cut the bagels. You need a specialist to cut bagels, like an operation? Give me the knife, I'll do it myself."

Color crept up the counterman's neck. "Mr. B.!" he bawled suddenly.

A neat party answered the cry, gliding swiftly to the point of unrest. This was Mr. B., the manager. "What seems the trouble, gentlemen?" he murmured.

[13] From "Carver Spurns Bagel As the Unkindest Cut," by Murray Robinson, *The New York World-Telegram and The Sun,* April 27, 1954. Copyright, 1954, by New York World-Telegram Corp.

"*He,*" the counterman said, pointing with his shiv, "wants I should cut his bagels with my meat knife, and I say, 'Positively no,' and he's holding up the line."

"And I ain't moving," the stubborn patron said, "until the bagels are sliced. I'm entitled."

Mr. B. pondered briefly. "Gentleman," he told the bagel man, "I got a proposition: I will personally take the bagels to the bagel-slicer, have them sliced, and bring them back here. A deal?"

"A deal," the customer said, "but the bagels got to be sliced exactly in half. Anything I hate, it's a lopsided-cut bagel."

Mr. B. soon glided back with the sliced bagels. "He's got a pretty good eye down there," the customer said, drawing a critical bead on the bagels, "even though I seen better. This is about a 60–40 cut. It'll do."

He looked triumphantly at the Hot Meats artist—and the latter looked back just as triumphantly. He hadn't given in, either.

When the bagel man had gone, the next customer ordered pastrami—a foeman worthy of the counterman's steel—and said: "I see you're a man of principle."

"Principle, maybe," the counterman said, executing a riposte at the pastrami. "But tell you the truth, I was afraid to slice those bagels. You run across a bad bagel, it's like rock, like cement—and there goes your best knife! A good knife is harder to find than a good customer—or a soft bagel."

"A Nickel a Shtickel" [14]

. . ."A real Jewish delicatessen" in New York, where it assumes its most specialized form, can mean at least three different things. . . .

* * * * *

. . . The most primitive is the *shlacht* store, generally found in the market sections of the great old Jewish settlements on the lower East

[14] From "The Jewish Delicatessen," by Ruth Glazer, in *Commentary on the American Scene*, edited by Elliott E. Cohen, pp. 191, 192–194, 196–198. Copyright, 1945, 1947, 1948, 1950, 1951, 1952, 1953, by The American Jewish Committee. New York: Alfred A. Knopf.

Originally published in "From the American Scene" in *Commentary.*

Side, in Brownsville, and in the East Bronx. Now and then one will crop up like a poor relation on Upper Broadway or even the Grand Concourse.

Its essence is in its simplicity. Around the walls of what is generally a small square store are ranged open wooden counters. Suspended from hooks hang salamis, cold pastramis, rolled beefs, and bundles of frankfurters. On the walls are a few shallow shelves containing a meager supply of the traditional accessories—beans, ketchup, some crackers, sometimes soup. The proprietor stands in the midst of this dominion using now one counter, now another, depending upon the location of the particular meat called for. The main attraction of these stores—for there is little of the warmth and geniality of the other types in this form—lies in their cut-rate prices, sometimes as much as one-half of the going rate. Generally the meat is "Jewish" but not kosher. A nice distinction, which has grown in popularity.

* * * * *

. . . [The second type is] the kosher delicatessen! Facing a clear glass (sometimes, it must be confessed, not so clear) lies a succulent variety of rosy and warm meats in a never-varying order. You may visit every delicatessen in New York and not one will fail to have *first* in line its battery of ten or fifteen salamis, on the little raised platform facing the glass, ranged in three or four rows, one on top of the other; followed by rolled beef, the tongues, a few cold pastramis (for decoration, since pastrami is always served hot, sliced to order, from a steam box); the two trays of frankfurters—one of "specials," the short fat ones, one of the "regulars," the long thin ones; and finally a turkey. A smaller and rarer variety of frankfurter . . . [comes] in two sizes: the cocktail frankfurter, about as big as your thumb, and the "lilies," about half that size. "Lilies," research reveals, is short for "lilliputians." Sometimes the pans of cole slaw and potato salad are incorporated into this display. More often they are on the "back bar," the narrow counter behind the proprietor. Lying on the wooden cutting board is the inevitable corned beef which is always just about one-half gone. And invariably on the glass-topped counter is a plate with small chunks of salami. In the old days the plate always carried a sign, "A Nickel a Shtickel." (A most convenient—and profitable—way of disposing of the ends of the salami, too.) This immortal rhyme succumbed during the [Second World] war to the free verse of "Have a Nosh—10c." The poetic spirit of the industry was not to be quenched by this loss, however. A substitute slogan appeared all over the city right after the outbreak of the war: "Send a Salami to Your Boy in the Army."

* * * * *

My father's third alternative, the non-kosher, but Jewish delicatessen, is now probably the most numerous. This type differs, deliberately, in only the most subtle ways from the kosher delicatessen. It looks exactly the same, smells exactly the same, and the pastrami sandwiches lack neither juiciness nor flavor. But the neon kosher sign is missing from the window. For many years proprietors of this new type of delicatessen were in the habit of substituting the word *wurshtgesheft* in Hebrew characters. This formidable word strung across half the window would seem to leave no room for doubt in the minds of the uninitiated that this was a very kosher delicatessen indeed. But, finally, in response to pressure by a group of rabbis acting on behalf of the kosher delicatessen storekeepers, a city ordinance forbade this practice as misrepresentation. The new terminology which is rapidly gaining favor in the trade is "kosher style."

While the kosher delicatessens will serve only tea or soda pop in bottles as beverages, in the non-kosher delicatessen you can get coffee with cream, and butter on your bread if you insist on it. But the resistance by the proprietors has been fierce. In the six years that I spent behind a delicatessen store counter I rarely heard the cry, "Hot pastrami. Butter the bread." When it happened, we would ask to have the individual pointed out. My father, whose respect for tradition was very strong, would refuse to engage in such obscene practices, and would generally tell the waiter—"Give her a pat of butter, and let her butter the bread herself." Added to the display of meats in the *wurshtgesheft* is also a real roast beef (a non-kosher cut of meat). Most will not go so far as to include a ham, but I have seen even that in stores located in the newer neighborhoods.

In earlier years the menu of the delicatessen was simplicity itself: franks and beans, any kind of delicatessen meat fried with eggs, sandwiches, and that aristocrat of dishes—a plate of cold cuts (consisting principally of hot meats). As time has gone by, the list of dishes available from the kitchen now covers three or four pages of a printed bill-of-fare. "Delicious home-cooked meals, kosher style, like mother used to make" is a sign featured in most delicatessens today.

* * * * *

Since dairy dishes are not forbidden in the kosher-style store, a full selection of salads, fruit with sour cream, cheese and fish dishes is offered. All are served with bread and butter. But my mother could never get used to the idea of cutting a swiss cheese on the machine where a salami had lain but a moment before. After a while we all decided that we absolutely had to have another slicing machine—for the corned beef. We finally got one which was admirably suited for the purpose, tilted at just the proper angle to maintain even pressure against the blade and with a little trough for escaping juice. The "corned beef machine" was used exclusively to slice cheese. "You can cut corned beef so much better by hand," my mother would explain.

"Wiseguys" [15]

. . . A few waiters will steal the chandeliers off the ceiling if they think they can get away with it, and as a result every waiter has to be carefully watched. Larcenous lackeys are known as "wiseguys." One of the "wiseguy's" dodges is to have a sturdy leather pocket sewn inside his jacket. While in the kitchen, the "wiseguy" will sneak a steak and plop it into the secret pocket, and then he will secrete a baked potato. Outside, in the dining room, he swipes one of the dirty dishes from a serving pantry, quickly wipes it clean, removes steak and potato from pocket, and throws both on a plate and serves it to a customer. Then he makes out his own check. To prevent this, no waiters at the Hurricane may carry blue pencils or books of checks.

Another device is the switching of checks, for which the "wiseguy" requires a drunken customer. The waiter, let's say, has two chits for two tables. One for $15, one for $8. The customer who should get the $8 chit is slightly high. So the waiter presents him with the $15 tab, which the victim cheerfully pays. Then the waiter presents the same $15 check to his other party. Total collected: $30. Total coming to the house: $23. Net profit to wiseguy: $7. To prevent this, the rule at the Hurricane is that the payment for each check must be turned over to the cashier (who sits in the kitchen) not longer than ten minutes after totalizing. The cashier stamps the time of addition and the time of payment on the back of the check. The waiter can only hocus a customer if he can hold several dinner checks for twenty

[15] From "Headaches of a Headwaiter," *Never Whistle in a Dressing Room, or Breakfast in Bedlam*, by Maurice Zolotow, pp. 175–176. Copyright, 1944, by Maurice Zolotow. New York: E. P. Dutton & Company, Inc.

minutes or so until he has two uneven checks and one drunk. There are also two food checkers in the kitchen who make a note of every article of food the waiters remove. And the waiters can't buy their own jackets either. The management, in a spirit of enlightened selfishness, provides them with nice white coats and also takes care of all the laundering.

The Tipsy Tipper [16]

. . . Headwaiters get handsome tips from most customers, but the gentlemen of the press don't tip them much, and take their best tables, besides. Joe Lopez, headwaiter at the Copacabana, is a man whose talent in this direction must be greatly envied and admired. One night when he was working at the Stork Club a tipsy gentleman leaving the club asked him what was the biggest tip he had ever received.

"One hundred dollars, sir," said Joe.

"Well, here," said the drunk, handing him $150, "the next time anybody asks you that question, tell him it was $150 and that I gave it to you."

"Yes, sir," said Joe, "thank you, sir."

The drunk then paused in the doorway and said, "By the way, who gave you that $100 tip?"

"You did, sir," said Joe.

Joe, with that smile that has endeared him to millions, or at least to members of his own family, was putting the yard and a half into his wallet, and the drunk shrugged and went on.

Buckers [17]

Outsiders never seem to understand what hack drivers mean by buckers. I have never seen the term properly used in any of the news-

[16] From *I Am Gazing Into My 8-Ball*, by Earl Wilson, p. 181. Copyright, 1943, 1944, by the *New York Post;* 1945, by Earl Wilson. New York: Doubleday & Co., Inc.

[17] From *Hacking New York*, by Robert Hazard, pp. 16–22. Copyright, 1930, by Charles Scribner's Sons. New York.

paper articles I have read on the subject. The newspaper reporters call them "hackers," "backers," etc. As I understand it, the term came into use in this way. In the early days there were only a few places where one had a chance to get passengers, the hotels, railroad terminals, and steamer piers. There wasn't enough business to offer any good chance to pick up calls cruising. The hotel owners, etc., claimed the right to dictate who should solicit business at their doors and sold to companies the privilege of standing for calls at their doors, and for a time got away with it. The few places that were not so controlled were worked by independents, who formed groups and kept outsiders from working those stands by slugging them. Quite naturally the best fighters gravitated to the stands, and the less capable fighters were left out. These tail-enders then formed the Twentieth Century Brown & White Taxicab Owners Association and cut the rate from the previous forty cents a mile for two passengers and sixty cents for more than two to a straight thirty cents a mile. They painted their cabs brown and white so as to make them easily distinguishable. These low-rate cabs were so much in demand that they could get more business cruising the streets than the others could get on the best stands. Now, playing a line had become known as bucking a line, probably because it involved considerable trouble—one had to be able to fight, and other cab drivers were always attempting to crash (cut in in front of you)—so when cruising became profitable, the old timers, who stuck to the high rate and played the lines, became known as buckers.

Although a great many of the old closed lines have been broken up and are at present worked by low-rate cabs, the term is still in use to designate the old timers who run at as high a rate as possible and who get the business more or less by fighting for it. They play the waterfront more than anything else now. Most of them belong to an association and they own their own insurance company for bonding their own cars.

The Brown and White Taxicab Association registered their color scheme as a trade mark and fought the imitators through the courts for several years, clear up to the Supreme Court, and lost. Up to the time they lost, a membership in the organization was worth over two hundred dollars, but as soon as they lost, everybody painted brown and white, and a membership was worth nothing. The Taxi License Bureau kept the buckers with the high-rate clocks from using the brown and white color simply by refusing to license them, although they hadn't a vestige of legal authority. At this time over half of the taxicabs were Fords and most of the remainder were old second-hand cars of good makes, Packards, Renaults, Lancias, Deloney-Bellvilles, etc. A hackman with a nice new Ford was at the top of the heap.

Just as the Brown and Whites had almost wiped out the buckers, the Yellow Cab Company came into New York with a fleet of brand-new Yellow cabs, and they took the business away from everybody else almost overnight. Then everybody went to painting yellow in imitation, and a great many sold their old cars and bought new Yellows, as the Company operating the cabs was independent of the manufacturers.

When about half the hack drivers in the City were paying installments on new Yellow cabs, the Mogul Checker Manufacturing Company came into the City and started several fleets. Their cabs were designated by a checker stripe. They took the business away from the Yellows just about as quick as the Yellows had taken it away from the Brown and Whites. I understand that that summer the Yellow Cab Company took back over two thousand cabs whose owners were unable to make payments, and I know of a number of owners who ran for five or six months without paying any notes, simply because the Company apparently didn't have a place to put the cabs if they seized them.

Well, the Mogul Checkers had everything all their own way for the best part of two years, and finally they had sold cabs to about half the independents in town, when the old Twentieth Century Association was revived and again cut the rate, this time to twenty cents a mile. This time they painted their cabs a bright red with a stripe of white, black and gold. Immediately they took the business away from everybody else. Mogul Checker fleet owners were going broke in every direction.

Just before the Twentieth Century cut the rate, another outfit had invaded the field—the Luxors. They went into the hands of the receivers soon after the Twentieth Century came out.

The Twentieth Century, of course, was unable to keep imitators from using their color, and in a very short time there were more imitations on the street than there were genuine Twentieth Centuries. More money was being made at twenty cents a mile than had been made previously under the high rates, and there were so many of them on the street that those who didn't follow suit were starved out in short order; even the Yellow Cab Company had to come to it.

Due to the lack of a successful trade mark, the Twentieth Century would have lost out if they hadn't organized their own insurance company, which has been very successful, has kept the insurance rates down for their own members and has forced the insurance companies to lower their rates.

I doubt if there is any business in which there is greater uncertainty and any more ruthless competition.

Educating the Meter [18]

When the authorities finally decided to enforce the taxi bonding law I decided to fix the meter so it would run a little faster to make enough more to pay for the bond. There are a good many ways to make a meter run fast. The old Popp clocks were the easiest. All you had to do was to put the trunk strap around the cable tube and pull the strap tight so as to bend the tube out of line a little. The tighter you pulled the strap the faster the meter ran. The old Pittsburgh meters would jump if struck on top with a hammer. A good many of the old timers carried a hammer and a block of wood alongside of the seat. The block of wood was to put on top of the meter so the hammer wouldn't cave the case in. Most of them were very skillful with the hammer. They could strike just hard enough to make the clock register just what they thought the passenger would stand for. There were a lot of taximeter repair shops where for ten dollars you could get a clock educated, that is, fixed to run fast. The meters were all sealed by the License Bureau, but the mechanics at the shops were very good at opening up the seals and putting them back so that they looked all right.

The trouble with the educated meters was that they always ran the same and you were liable to have trouble if you picked up someone who knew how much the fare ought to be. I decided to try and fix mine so that I could let it run at the legitimate rate if desired or faster if the passenger looked right. I took the meter off and took it home and opened it up. It was a very complicated device. It cost a hundred and sixty dollars, but I wondered how they made it for less than a thousand. It took me quite a while to figure it all out. Then I made a small rachet dog to fit onto one of the gears and drilled a very small hole through the bottom of the case at the back where it wouldn't show and

[18] *Ibid.*, pp. 174–180.

ran a very fine wire through the hole and fastened it to the dog. When I pulled the wire it registered ten cents, but otherwise the meter ran just as before. It worked fine. The wire was so fine it didn't show at all and the partition in the cab prevented the passenger from seeing my hand when I reached out to pull the wire. With the wire I easily made enough more money to pay the forty-five dollars a month for the bond.

After several months the meter got out of order, as they do every so often. I kept putting off getting it repaired and used the wire altogether to make the meter work. It was quite a bother to keep track of the distance and pull the wire at the right time. Sometimes I would forget for quite a while and then would have to pull the wire three or four times in succession to catch up. A man picked me up at Chatham Square to go to Washington Heights. I started up the Bowery and what with ducking around trucks and L pillars I got a little careless about pulling the wire. The passenger said, "Hey! what's the matter with your meter? It jumps twenty or thirty cents every block or so. It will cost a fortune to go to Washington Heights at this rate."

I said, "Why, the clock has always been all right. I'll watch it and if it's fast I'll make it right with you."

I counted the blocks very carefully after that and pulled the wire at the right time. Presently the passenger said, "It seems to be working all right now. I guess I must have been mistaken. I'm sorry; I thought it was running fast but I guess it's all right."

After the Twentieth Century Taxi Owner's Association cut the rate to twenty cents a mile the public got to riding so much that most of the passengers knew what the clock should read better than the driver. The lady says, "Your meter is fast. I made this same trip yesterday for forty-five cents." It became necessary to be very careful in sizing up the passenger.

It was a good deal of trouble to reach out and pull the wire, so I tried other ways of fixing the clock. The meter contains a unit like an ordinary clock, with a spring and balance wheel to run the meter when the car is standing and register waiting time. The speed at which it runs is regulated by the length of the hair spring on the balance wheel. I took the little wedge out that holds the hair spring and cut about an inch off of the spring and put the wedge back. The best of that is that there is nothing there to prove that the meter was tampered with. After that the meter ran at a terrible gait. You could hear it going clickety click. The waiting time registered as though you were going twenty miles an hour all the time. The only trouble was that if you got stuck in traffic on Fifth Avenue, in the Forties, say, it was liable to run up a dollar going five blocks and the passengers would let out an awful yelp.

My next device was the best of all. I found that when a certain very delicate catch failed to work, the meter would register just double, that is, it would quit registering the nickels and throw a dime every time. I fastened a short length of spring wire in there so that when the flag was put straight down, a projection on the shaft the flag turns on would strike the wire and push it over so it would touch the little catch and keep it from working. The wire looked as if it got left there by accident. When the flag was thrown a quarter turn the meter was legitimate, but thrown a half turn, that is straight down, it ran double.

After that the main thing was to size up the passengers. It works like this. You get a call at Penn Station, say, for somewhere in East New York. You say, "How would you rather go, Bedford or Flatbush?" The fare says, "I don't know, you're supposed to know the way." So down she goes on double.

Hackie's Holiday [19]

Ever since a New York taxi driver named James Maresca wrote a best seller entitled *My Flag Is Up,* I haven't run into a hackie who hasn't got similar literary aspirations.

Accordingly, the moment I step into a cab alone, and the meter's flag is set at half-mast, I waste no time in striking up a conversation by saying, "Well, my friend, have you written any good books lately?"

I asked that question of a hackie named Harry in front of the Astor, and since I was paying a visit to a sick friend about three dollars away, I hoped Harry was the talkative type. He was.

"Funny you asked me about writin' a book, bud," he said, weaving his head and his cab from side to side. "I wuz just thinkin' about what happened to me one night last week."

"Wha hoppen?" I asked.

"Well, I'm rollin' down Park, empty, when a character lifts a pinky and hails me. The regular Adolph Menjou type. Y'know, kid, soup and fish, high hat, white scarf, gloves—the works. I grind the brakes to a

[19] From *Champagne before Breakfast,* by Hy Gardner, pp. 194–195. Copyright, 1954, by Hy Gardner. New York: Henry Holt and Company.

stop, not wanting to miss what smells like a good tip, and the gentleman parks himself in the back.

" 'Where to, sir?' I says, giving him the respect to which his appearance entitles him.

" 'Twice around Central Park, Harry, my chum,' he answers, getting my name from my license, 'and take it easy—I'm dressed for a blowout, not a wake.'

"He doesn't so much as open his yap till we're on the last leg of our second lap around the Park and I shut my trapper too, figuring if the guy wants to commiserate with himself, let him commiserate.

"Suddenly he pops the question. 'You seem like a nice sort, Harry,' he starts off. 'How about your getting into your formal duds and doing the town with me tonight?'

" 'Can't,' I snapped back. 'Gotta hack till four in the morning. Besides I ain't got no tuxedo.'

" 'Think nothing of it,' he said. 'Pull over to Eighth and 40th Street—a friend of mine there's got the biggest stock of rented tuxedos in town. Of course it's understood I pay all checks, including whatever your meter might total at the end of a successful night's tour of duty.'

"So I'm crazy," Harry says, "I take him up on the proposition, get shaved, massaged, dressed to kill, park my cab in a private garage, and I'm on the town. This fellow right away hails a cab and says, 'To the Waldorf, driver.'

"From the Waldorf we got to the Stork, where my friend nods to a few celebs. Bert Lahr and Morton Downey smile back at him. We have a couple of French 75's made with Mumms, pay the check, and tip while the waiter curtsies and my pal says, bored-like, 'Let's blow—it's like a morgue around here.'

"We hit everything in town worth hitting, night clubs, bars, meet and dance with a couple of dolls.

"Finally it's time to start pulling into the garage. Mr. Moneybags says, 'Righto—it almost slipped my mind. Let's return to my suite for a nightcap.'

"Whilst sipping the nightcap I slip off the monkey suit and get back into my work clothes—into which's pants mine host has slipped a double sawbuck to compensate for what I might have earned if I hadn't run into him.

" 'I sure envy you, mister,' I said, preparing to leave. 'You're really living. Maybe you got a job for me in your racket—this driving a hack year after year is wearing and tearing on a fellow and I'd love to get into something else.'

" 'No, Harry,' he said sort of odd-like, 'I know just what you mean, but I'm afraid I can't do anything for you. You see, I'm not a year-round playboy. I only enjoy an evening like this once a year—I pack my entire vacation into one night.'

" 'Well, how do you like that?' I chuckled. 'If being a rich guy ain't your regular racket, what *do* you do for a living?'

" 'What do I do for a living?' was the reply. 'The same as you do, Harry, I drive a hack!' "

The Taxi Driver and J. P. Morgan [20]

My old pal the late J. P. Morgan was a customer of mine, I only hauled him four or five times, long periods in between but I treasure him as an old customer an friend. First time I got him I didn't know it was J. P., on the outside he looked like a business gent of some kind but I sorter sensed that I had a customer what was away above the average an I took more than a mere liking for him instanter.

When he says, take me to the Manhattan Club I figured I had sensed right. The man, the way he carried himself, why, I felt like I was looking at a fine book, not a fine cover but something fine inside an I felt like I'd like to open that book an see how she reads. Anyway, I gits him to the club an it was warm an cloudy, he pays me off then cocks his head skyward, looks like more rain don't you think so he says.

Now them simple words ain't much in theirselves but somehow I sensed volume after volume in them. Ain't it wonderful how much can flash through a guys noodle in a split second. Think I, here's a gent who rates high in the world, most likely hes gotta war chest bulging over.

Yeah, I sensed all this. This big man was asking a little mans opinion, only a big man can do that, lotta folks, would say, now I gotta agree with what this here gent says or he won't like me. I didn't figure that way at all, it wasn't the way to open the book.

Anyway I says to him, yer all wrong, it ain't going to rain.

No, he says, what makes you think so, I sensed his interest right away. Perhaps he was thinking this here is an unusual taxi-driver, chances are he don't know who I am but anyway, he interests me, in a

[20] From *I'm Lucky at That,* by David Betts, the Taxi Philosopher, pp. 249–251. Copyright, 1930, by David Betts. Garden City, New York: Doubleday, Doran and Company, Inc.

way, he's even contradicting me which don't never happen, most unusually, most unusual, I saw right away that I'd got this here book, J. P. Morgan, open and had read some of it although I didn't know then it was J. P. and anyway it wouldn't a made no difference if I had.

No I says she ain't going to rain no more today. See them flowers in the park, "Madison Square."

Yes, fine, ain't they, says he, you bet I says, you love flowers an I love flowers. When you an me was kids, I says the pair of us wouldn't hesitate to stick a brick up in a dark spot sos the parson would stumble over it an skin his sneezer, but neither of us would trample on flowers.

I see I has the book wide open, J. P. first laughs, then smiles, I see I'd got him awful interested an he was looking kid-like in the face, he wasn't used to being talked to in this way an I'd found out what he was hungry for, real human stuff, something what didn't include pale high-hats an the like. I felt as pleased as he for giving him what he craved for an neither of us thought of our different stations in life.

Anyway I says to him, you'll notice them flowers is sorta perked up, sorta holding their heads up like they was saying we don't need no more water, we're feeling fine.

Yes, he says, they do sorta give you that idea when you look at em close.

Well, I gotta be going I says, figuring his time was valuable an he was forgetting an like the gentleman he was, from his shoes up, he sticks out his mit and we shakes an as he goes through the door that serious-faced gentleman turned and smiled as I thought he would, an later on when I'se in the Penn Depot. the cop says, do you know who I put on your cab, I don't I says, that was J. P. Morgan he says, an later on in the afternoon the sun had busted through an I wondered if J. P. noticed that an what would he be thinking an the all biz made me feel danged good, yeah I give him two or three more kid yarns after that an he never forgot me after a long missing spell.

The Hooker [21]

As good a place as any to get the feel of the port is the office of the Kennedy Towing Line at 32 South Street. It is the last old-fashioned tugboat office left. The bigger lines have gone down to buildings like

[21] From *Back Where I Came From,* by A. J. Liebling, pp. 25-30. Copyright, 1938, by A. J. Liebling. New York: Sheridan House.

24 State and 17 Battery Place, where they employ female stenographers and rub elbows with transatlantic steamship companies. But a potbellied iron stove still overheats the Kennedy office from early fall until late spring, and a gay blue and white portrait of the tug *Idlewild,* with more paint than perspective, provides its chief adornment. Of the six Kennedy boats two were built before 1875. It is Tom Wilson's favorite office for yarning.

Tom is the senior tugboat master of the harbor, with a voice on him like the Staten Island Ferry boat and a chest like an oil drum.

"I am seventy-four years old," he roars, "and I can jump out of that window and jump right back again." The office is on the second floor. "When they put me together they put me together right," says Tom, heaving on a handful of snow white hair. "Every hair drove in with a nail. None of your shin plasters.

"I went tug-boatin' when I was eighteen, aboard of the *Leonard Richards,* the twin of that *Idlewild* in the pitcher. Where did I go to sea from? The First Ward. Tugboat captains was the cream of society in them days. They wore high hats and gold watch chains and Prince Albert coats and striped trousers, and they never touched the wheel without kid gloves. They would steal the sight out of your eyes.

"The *Leonard Richards* was a Hooker. What was a Hooker? Why, a tug that cruised off Sandy Hook for schooners, of course. Just the same as a Gater was a tug that hanged off Hell Gate, and a Lugger was a tug that lugged ships to their berths after the Hookers and the Gaters brought them in, whether the ships was pine wooders from the South, or brickers, or whatever they might be.

"Them days there was more ships than now, and plenty of sail. The most part of them had no regular agents ashore to hire tugs, and there was no radio, anyway, so the agents wouldn't a'knowed when they was coming in. The first tug that seed a ship he made up to her and the two captains paced their deck awhile and called each other this and that and at last they struck a bargain, or they didn't, and you sheered off and he run up the American flag for another tug.

"But the tug that got out first had the best chance. So sometimes at night the captain would shake you by the shoulder and say, 'Get up and cast off with no noise,' and you would try to give the other boats the shake and get out to sea before they was wise. You would go out without lights, by Rockaway or South Beach or Coney Island, where you knowed there was nothing you could hit only maybe an oyster boat, and you wouldn't stop for that.

"Sometimes when you would get out in the stream you would hear the whistles tooting if they suspicioned you, and the whole gang would be after you.

"Then, if the old man was wise, he would switch his running lights. He would put his red and green lights astern and his white light on the bow, and it would look like he was coming in instead of going out. But if the other guy was wise he wouldn't take none of that—just give her more medicine.

"We would cruise off the Hook two or three days. We would carry that much coal, but only water for twenty hours, steady steaming; but we could get water at the Hook, but not coal. How far did we go? Halfway to Ireland, boy—halfway to Ireland. Ten per cent of what he got was for the captain, besides what he could steal, and if he didn't get no tow he didn't get no wages.

"Thirty or forty hours at a stretch working was nothing. The first command I got, after I got my license in 1883, I asked my owner for some bedding so's the men could lay down. 'I didn't hire them men to sleep,' he says. I can work thirty hours right now without squealing, and on my hoofs, too.

"Then when you would get out there sometimes there would be a good wind and they would sail right past you, and maybe offer you a line.

"But when the wind died they had a different tune.

"Once I picked up a French bark off Fire Island, and I couldn't make a price with him. I follied him and I follied him, and at Long Beach, sure enough he goes ashore. Now I had him, I figured, and he would pay me a damn good price to pull him off. Up comes a nor'west gale, and what does the sucker do but back her off under sail! Ah, well, heartaches in every trade.

"But one time they wouldn't bargain was the war. That was the golden age. All I had to do was cruise down by the Highlands on a calm day and take my pick of the schooners and barks that was bringing supplies to New York. I would make up to the one that looked the best bet.

" 'Morning, Captain,' I would tell the old man. 'Seed anything of a submarine around here?'

" 'My god!' he would say. 'So close to New York?'

" 'Shelled a ship up by Hoffman's Island this morning,' I would say.

" 'How much to take me in?'

" 'Fifteen hundred dollars.'

" 'You're a pirate. I'll not pay it.'

" 'Very good, Captain. Sorry we can't do business, Captain. But I ain't got no time to waste out here. I don't want to lose this little craft or the few lives I got on board.'

"I'd start off, and five minutes later he'd be signaling for me to come back and tow him at my price.

"When I'd get him up to Quarantine I'd drop him. 'If you want to go any further,' I'd say, 'get a local. This is an express.' "

It was during the war that Tom performed his greatest feat of pilotage.

The Swash Channel, between Homer Shoal and Flynn's Knoll, two treacherous shallows, is charted good for twenty feet of water.

"I took a five-masted bark, the *Orleans,* up there, drawing twenty-four and a half," Tom said pridefully. "When I got her through Morgan, the captain nearly went crazy.

" 'Why the hell did you take her through there?' he asks.

" 'I knowed the tide, and I knowed the spot. You didn't bump, did you?'

" 'No, but if that hawser had parted, or if something had gone wrong with that little boat, she would have been left dry and broke her back sure.'

"The reason I done it, of course, was I saved three miles instead of going round by the Main Ship Channel, and I was running short of water."

Tom says he never *knew* a harbor thief.

"I knew some that had the name of it," he said, "but I could not give you their pedigree. There were stories of some fellows that would go out in a schooner and make a price to bring her in. Then they would wait until night, and any tug they found at the end of a pier they would just take it and do the job and get their cash, and then leave the tug at the nearest slip, and think no more of it.

"But taking gear, now, that is something else again. Anything that was not nailed to the boat, in the old days, the owner was not considered entitled to it."

Blow-Outs [22]

Only the engineers and contractors actually engaged in the work could tell of the thousand other problems encountered and solved during the

[22] From *Fifty Years of Rapid Transit, 1864 to 1917,* by James Blaine Walker, pp. 264–266. Copyright, 1918, by James Blaine Walker. New York: The Law Printing Co.

construction of the subways. Almost every section had its own peculiar obstacles. For instance, in tunneling under the East River the contractor had to combat the water under the river bed while he was pushing the tubes across. The hydraulic shield and compressed air were invoked. The shield was pressed forward a few feet a day, the workmen, or "sand-hogs," excavating the material in front of it and installing the cast-iron rings of the tubes under its protection, the water in the material above being driven out by compressed air introduced into the workings through pipes connected with compressors on the surface.

Two of the most remarkable accidents ever recorded in compressed air work happened during the construction of the subway tunnels under the East River, and the second, although eleven years later, was almost a duplicate of the first. In each case a man was blown out of the tunnel by the force of the air, through the river bed and through the water to the surface and yet came out alive.

The first accident occurred in 1905 during the construction of the Battery-Joralemon Street tunnel of the first subway. As frequently happens, a "blow-out" took place. That is, the compressed air found a weak spot in the roof of the tunnel and began escaping. In such cases the usual treatment is for the men in the tunnel to heave bags of sand or clay into the vortex and thus stop the leak. On this occasion Dick Creedon, a workman employed by the contractor, attempted to plug the air hole with a bag of sand. The pressure of the air was so strong, however, that the "blow-out" sucked both bag and man into the vortex and forced them through thirty feet of sand and silt up into the waters of the river. On reaching the surface Creedon began swimming and was soon picked up by a boat, apparently none the worse for his marvelous experience. The "blow-out" was repaired by dumping tons of sand from scows immediately over the break.

The second of these accidents occurred in 1916 in the Whitehall-Montague Street tunnel of the Dual System subways, also under the East River. A "blow-out" occurred in the north tube a short distance out from the Brooklyn shore. The shield had just been shoved ahead for the placing behind it of another ring of the tunnel tube. Four workmen were about to place the top "breasting" board in its new position just ahead of the shield when there was a rush of air and three of the four disappeared. They were sucked into the vortex and through twelve feet of sand to the river bottom. One of them, Marshall Mabey, shot up through the water and into the air on the top of a geyser which eyewitnesses thought reached a height of forty feet above the surface. When he dropped back into the water he began swimming and was soon picked up by a boat sent out from the contractor's dock. He was practically unhurt. His companions were less fortunate. One was found unconscious in the river forty minutes after Mabey was rescued, but efforts to resuscitate him were unavailing. The body of the other was not recovered until the next day. It is supposed they were struck by some hard substance in their passage through the river bottom and either killed or made unconscious and then drowned. The break was repaired by placing a blanket of clay in the river bottom.

Chapin of the *World* [23]

The classic example of the cold, efficient city editor is, of course, the late Charles E. Chapin, who died in 1930, in Sing Sing Prison, where he had been sent after he had shot and killed his wife, Nellie Beebe Chapin, as she lay asleep in their hotel room in New York. Today, men who develop traits and methods similar to his are said to be marked with the "Chapin stigmata."

He was rather generally hated in the office of the *Evening World,* which he ruled with more power than most city editors have, but his professional ability was respected, and with good reason. The oldest story of him is of how Irvin S. Cobb, then on the staff, heard that Chapin was ill and looked up from his typewriter to remark, "I trust it's nothing trivial."

* * * * *

Chapin as city editor fired 108 men. . . .

He had no patience with amateurs, incompetents or bunglers. He knew his job and expected the men to know theirs. He could spot a four-flusher at a great distance and he prided himself on the variety of ways in which he fired men. Once a reporter was late telephoning a story. Chapin barked at him: "Your name is Smith, is it? You say you work for the *Evening World,* do you? You're a liar. Smith stopped working for the *Evening World* an hour ago."

A reporter who was late for work told Chapin a complicated story of having scalded his foot in the bathtub. A few days later Chapin

[23] From *City Editor,* by Stanley Walker, pp. 4, 6–7. Copyright, 1934, by Stanley Walker. New York: Frederick A. Stokes Company.

fired the reporter, explaining, "I would have fired you earlier but I wanted to see how long you could keep on faking that limp." A young man asked Chapin "what to do next" while he was covering a big fire. "Go pick the hottest place and jump into it," advised the tyrant. Sometimes, however, he fired people without meaning to. The old-timers could tell when a "firing" was real and paid no attention to the other kind. One younger man took Chapin at his word when the great man told him he was fired, and did not report at the office next day. He received a telegram from Chapin, saying, "If you are not back at work by Thursday morning, you are fired."

It was difficult to fool the old man. Once the Criminal Courts reporter missed a ferry from Staten Island and telephoned to the office from the ferry house at 9 A.M., reporting that he was on the job at the courthouse. "Cover the flood," ordered Chapin. "What flood?" "There must be a terrible flood at the Criminal Courts building," said Chapin. "I can hear the boats whistling."

Chapin was a good but cantankerous judge of writing. He once fired a man for using the word "questionnaire," which at that time had not been admitted to the dictionary. On another occasion, a reporter, writing of the finding of a body floating in the East River, referred to the "melancholy waters."

"Pretty good phrase, that," said Chapin.

He was overheard; thereafter, for days, the Harlem River, the Gowanus Canal and Spuyten Duyvil all developed "melancholy waters." Chapin issued a warning that the next man who used the phrase would be fired. A young reporter, Dwight Perrin, who later became city editor of the *Tribune* and after that assistant managing editor of the St. Louis *Post-Dispatch,* had not heard of the warning, and the next day his first story was that of a suicide whose body had been picked up in the Hudson. Perrin started his article, "The melancholy waters of the Hudson—"

Chapin was furious.

"You're fired," he said. " 'Melancholy waters!' Now, look here, in all sense, how could the waters of the Hudson be melancholy?"

"Perhaps," suggested Perrin, "it was because they had just gone past Yonkers."

"Not bad," said Chapin "You're hired."

12

Playtown and Playboys

Let me remind you that the symbol of an island of pleasure, presided over by a beckoning female, is almost a constant of the human imagination.—Alistair Cooke

Pulling or Riding the Goose [1]

[A] favorite game [of Dutch New York in the seventeenth century] was "Pulling the Goose." A goose with its head well greased was stretched across a road, and the sport was for a man to try to catch the bird by the head and carry it off as he rode on horseback at a gallop or drove beneath the bird in a cart going at full speed. This was also called "Riding the Goose." A variation of the game was made by stretching the rope across a ditch or canal or stream, under which a boat was swiftly rowed, and the man, standing on a plank, tried to carry off the bird in the same way. . . . If he missed, the plank tipped and he fell into the water; and then he had to swim back to the boat and repeat the attempt. There were always several contestants, and the game was extremely popular. It belonged especially to the Shrove Tuesday pastimes, and was frequently prohibited in New Amsterdam and Albany. . . .

* * * * *

Cats and hares were also used for this cruel sport. . . .

[1] From *Dutch New York,* by Esther Singleton, pp. 293, 295. Copyright, 1909, by Dodd, Mead and Company. New York.

Clubbing the Cat [2]

Prizes were offered for "Clubbing the Cat." This game generally took place on the square in front of the inn, or on the bowling-green, where from two heavy spiles driven into the ground a strong rope was stretched. In the center of the rope hung a lightly cooped barrel in which was a live cat. At the appointed hour all who wished to throw the club gave their names, and paid an entrance fee. It was also agreed that the winner should pay for three or four bottles of wine, and the landlord gave each of the players a bottle. When a sufficient number of players had entered, the name and number of each was written on a board with chalk, and drawing took place. Then a line was drawn on the ground or a long pole was laid down to show the distance from which the "throwing" was allowed. Now number one stepped forward with his club, which he threw with great force at the barrel. The winner was he who broke the cask and let the cat escape. Sometimes the cat, too dazed or frightened to jump out of the barrel when it was split open, only fell out. In every case the winner was always he whose throw made the cat leave the barrel; and as soon as the cat was out, it was chased, and he who caught it got a bottle of wine as a prize. Sometimes a peacock or goose was used; and sometimes, instead of a barrel, the bird was simply tied to a rope and killed.

"Saint Nick" [3]

A set of jingles scribbled as a jest by one member of patrician New York society re-formed a legend and created a national myth. Saint Nicholas

[2] *Ibid.*, pp. 292–293.

[3] From *The Social Ladder,* by Mrs. John King Van Rensselaer, in Collaboration with Frederic Van de Water, pp. 132–134. Copyright, 1924, by Henry Holt and Company. New York.

The General Theological Seminary, where Clement C. Moore taught, occupies the block between Twentieth and Twenty-first Streets, Ninth and Tenth Avenues. When Moore broke up his patrimony into building lots and had streets cut through to form Chelsea village, he gave his old apple orchard to the General Convention of the Protestant Episcopal Church on the condition that it build a seminary there.

Moore is buried in Trinity Church Cemetery (now divided by Broadway), which extends from Riverside Drive to Amsterdam Avenue between 153d and 155th Streets.

—Santa Claus—is known to the children of The Netherlands as a stalwart young man who rides about the world in December on a white horse, followed by a black servant. He leaves gifts at the homes of good boys and girls, and in addition supplies poor but virtuous maidens with dowries.

The Santa Claus of the reindeer, the sack full of toys and the chimney-descending propensities is a purely American character. He was created in an idle moment by a grave professor in the General Theological Seminary whose masterly books on the Oriental languages have long been forgotten, while the verses he wrote to amuse his children still endure. Clement C. Moore was a member of the old New York aristocracy and a professor of great erudition. He was also wealthy, and the property upon which the theological seminary now stands was his gift to the institution he served. One Christmastide he wrote "A Visit from St. Nicholas" to please his children. His wife, without his knowledge, sent the verses to a newspaper.

Like Byron, Professor Moore awoke to find himself famous. Unlike the English poet, he did not relish his fame. His verses ran from one end of the country to the other. His picture of the "jolly old elf" became graven for all time on the hearts of American children. The books he had devoted years of his life to writing were too erudite to arouse much interest, but his jingle became a classic. He became known as the creator of the American Santa Claus. Each Christmas Eve in New York children gather about the grave of Clement C. Moore, professor of Oriental languages, and sing carols to the memory of the man who made the American Santa Claus.

New Year's Calls [4]

There was another solemn rite sacred to these days—New Year's calls —with which we celebrated the beginning of a New Year. It was a custom, I understand, which came down to us from our Dutch forebears —those immaculate souls now preserved in an odor of sanctity which endows them with all the virtues and graces denied them in the flesh.

[4] From *Valentine's Manual of Old New York, 1926,* edited by Henry Collins Brown, pp. 47–52. Copyright, 1925, by Henry Collins Brown. New York: Valentine's Manual, Inc.

At all events the ceremony incidental to these festivities included an enormous amount of eating, drinking and sprinting—particularly drinking. There has come down to us also from the early records of this city, competent evidence of the occasional disastrous results of the unrestrained holiday merriment in the following item:

CORONER'S VERDICT (1786)

"That the said Tatum's death was occasioned by the freezing of a large quantity of water in his body, that had been mixed with the rum he drank."

Those of us who were specially favored of this world's goods indulged in the luxury of a carriage for the day. The carriage could hold six. On ordinary days it did duty as part of a funeral cortege. Its cost was $5.00, except on New Year's when it was advanced to $6.00. This was divided pro rata among the occupants. It was considered very recherché to have only four in the coach.

Weeks before "der tag" much patient thought was bestowed upon a very vital detail—the calling card. These were the product of a genius who deserves immortality. Some of them bore charming winter scenes with real snow produced by ground glass. Others were decorated all around with beautiful silk fringe in all colors of the rainbow. They were masterpieces of decorative art and a basketful of these strange devices would be today of extraordinary interest. They were greeted with exclamations of wild delight by the recipients; we were supposed to leave one card apiece for the young ladies upon whom we called. As a rule the ladies received in groups, and as long as you knew one of the group, that was sufficient to justify a call. Custom decreed that you must break bread with your hostess and partake of some liquid refreshment. Lemonade was the most favored beverage but wine became popular toward the end and I think the Demon Rum had considerable to do with the final disappearance of the custom.

It was not unusual to make ninety or a hundred calls which, of course, meant madly rushing in and out and no small amount of fatigue when a heavy snow fall intervened as sometimes happened; our Colonial friend Tatum, just mentioned, fell asleep in the snow. The men boasted of the numbers of calls they made and the ladies counted up the total of their cards. All the old sociability and its neighborliness which I imagine was the original charm of the custom gradually disappeared during the hectic period of its closing days. Then one year there was no calling, and no observance whatever. There was apparently no prearrangement of anything else. The practice simply ceased. Baskets were placed on door knobs to receive any cards that callers might leave. But the houses were closed—and so ended with all its faults one of the oldest and pleasantest customs on Manhattan Island.

Fun at Coney Island [5]

STEEPLECHASE

Coney's biggest boom and glory arrived with the development of the amusement park. Up to that time, rides and games were scattered everywhere, at some points crowding the beach to the water's edge. The amusement park was the department-store idea: a wide assortment of products in one enclosure.

Sea Lion Park was the first try. Its chief exhibit was a team of forty sea lions who juggled balls and performed aquatic feats. It also unveiled a strange new ride called "Shoot-the-Chutes," as well as a water ride, cages of live wolves, and a ballroom. But the big leap came with one man, George C. Tilyou, whose Steeplechase Park is the Island's surviving large-scale amusement area. Today, it covers twenty-five acres, half of them enclosed in a huge glass-and-steel pavilion.

Tilyou started with a single ride, and an idea. The ride was the famous "Steeplechase," a mechanical horse race in which eight (later four) double-saddled horses on iron rails circled the entire park. Racing fans would bet on their favorite horses, and hecklers along the half-mile way encouraged or abused the "jockeys." It is still popular today. To this ride, Tilyou added others. He brought the World's Largest Ferris Wheel from the Chicago Exposition. There was something very close to the modern cyclorama in his "Trip to the Moon." He introduced "Down and Out," a screwlike slide down a dark almost vertical chute which emptied onto "The Human Pool Table," where sixteen flat spinning discs whirled its human cargo. The usual roller coaster and ballroom, plus a wide variety of thrill rides, filled the original five-acre pavilion. Two of its historic items (still operating today) were "The Chanticleer," a European attraction featuring two Giant Chickens weighing half a ton each, and the hand-carved "Giant Carousel" orig-

[5] From "Coney Island," by Norman Rosten, *Holiday,* Vol. 18 (September, 1955), No. 3, pp. 86, 88–89, 90–91. Copyright, 1955, by the Curtis Publishing Company. Philadelphia.

inally built for Kaiser Wilhelm at a cost of a quarter of a million dollars.

Tilyou had an idea to go with his park: a continuous round of entertainment for a single admission. A "combination" ticket was good on all rides. You could stay as long as you liked. It was an immediate hit.

A group of us youngsters would stand, some thirty years later, around exit gates of Steeplechase, stopping people as they left: "Ticket, mister, can we have your ticket?" That round blue ticket with the numbered edge, 1 to 35—paradise! There were always enough unpunched rides to keep going for a while, once we got in. We would dash away, jeering at the gatemen who chased us. We knew the unguarded spots of the carefully fenced grounds.

The thirty-five ride combination ticket went up from fifty cents to a dollar in 1940, and in 1942 a new system was instituted: eight rides for a dollar; the next eight rides also cost a dollar. Today, while this rate still holds for weekends, the weekday customer gets fifteen rides for the first dollar.

Steeplechase started an era of mass entertainment. A couple would enter the Park, rent "clown" suits to protect their clothes, and frolic with tens of thousands. To this day, one of the great draws is Steeplechase's public stage. Innocent visitors walk out from the wings into a series of sharp surprises: falling scenery, moving floors, electrically-wired railings, compressed-air tricks (woe to the lady without firm undergarments!)—all to the delight of the seated audience. Coney invited you to see the clowns—yourself or others. The trick mirrors showed you fat, lean, crooked, stunted, elongated, balloon-headed, pinheaded—and you laughed. You came to laugh and it gave you what you came for.

LUNA

Steeplechase was only the beginning. The new century had hardly begun when a new fanfare was heard. "*Announcing:* Thirty-nine Supreme, Stupendous, Spectacular, Sensational Shows! By day a Paradise—at night Arcadia." A quarter of a million electric lights were switched on, and Luna Park opened its gates on May 2, 1903. Within two hours, over forty thousand persons were milling inside the twenty-two-acre park, at ten cents' admission.

The lights of the baroque kaleidoscopic tower changed color every second, while the lighted spires, domes, and battlements were (the program says so) "not surpassed even by the stars." The flat-bottomed boats of the Shoot-the-Chutes sped down a watery runway and bounded over the surface of the lagoon.

Housed in separate buildings were such attractions as "Eskimo Village," "Trip to the North Pole," "Monkey Theatre," "Infant Incubator," "Canals of Venice," "Chinese Theatre," "Hagenbeck's Wild Animals" and the newest in scenic railways: "Dragon's Gorge."

Luna introduced the spectacle show. Entitled "Fire and Sword," it had the following climax, as related in a guidebook of that period: ". . . down the mountain slopes gallop horses carrying shouting, shooting soldiers. Towers fall and destruction and death are dealt mercilessly. Finally the guns set fire to the buildings and from the windows of the houses roll great sheets of flame. Women can be seen pinned in by cruel fires. In the midst of the conflagration, the general's daughter is caught by the flames and she dives from the tower into the lake with her clothes blazing. Rescues follow one after another until the floors within the city's palaces tumble to earth, leaving charred and blackened walls. The realistic massacre together with many other features of real warfare at close quarters combine to form the most wonderful stage spectacle in world's history."

So runs the libretto, but how this was staged—presumably as a continuous performance—is beyond my powers to guess.

DREAMLAND

As Luna tried to top Steeplechase, it was natural that Luna should be challenged in turn. A year later, almost to the day, the last of the playland "giants" flared up on the Coney landscape. Dreamland (three and a half million noninflationary, highly inflammable dollars' worth of it) seemed to be the last word. Its columns and arches were magnificent, and its Beacon Tower, more massive and Western than Luna's, rose three hundred and seventy-five feet and gave off an awesome illumination at night. Inside Dreamland's vast acreage, a quarter of a million people could move about easily.

A lot of the old attractions were there, made to look new, and what couldn't be disguised was boldly pirated. So Dreamland had its own wild-animal show (Frank Bostock's), an infant incubator, a scenic railway, Shoot-the-Chutes, and without even the faintest blush, the old stand-by "Canals of Venice." (Didn't Mike Todd, the modern showman, a half century later, wow 'em with his "Evening in Venice" at Jones Beach?) Dreamland did have some elements of a new look, however. There was "The Midget City," with its population of three hundred Lilliputians; "Coasting Through Switzerland," against a background of snow-peaked Alps; "The Chilkoot Pass," sliding its patrons down the rugged Alaskan landscape. Santos-Dumont's airship took people for rides over the ocean, and somewhere else in the park a submarine took them under it.

To satisfy all tastes, a mammoth show, "Creation," vied with a two-hundred-thousand-dollar epic, "Fall of Pompeii," before your eyes, with Marie Dressler selling peanuts (a publicity stunt) at a concession nearby! The Dreamland Ballroom, built on the Iron Pier over the ocean, was the largest in the world. The side show featured Jolly Trixy, the Fat Girl, "so fat it takes seven men to hug her." The cataclysmic trend reached its climax in one of Dreamland's big thrillers: "Fighting Flames." Here the audience saw a six-story building set on fire, saw firemen fight the flame, real smoke, actual rescues, screams, escapes, melodrama.

Seven years later, in 1911, the greatest spectacle of them all occurred: Dreamland burned down. Newspapers announced the end of Coney Island, but when the smoke had lifted, most of it was still there, and doing business as usual. Fire had earlier destroyed a part of Steeplechase, which was rebuilt. And fire was to be the end of Luna, some thirty-three years later. What burns better than papier-mâché and wood? Dreamland was never rebuilt, nor was Luna Park. Luna's acreage is now a parking lot; some of its roller coaster is still visible—the torn edge of a painter's mural.

TUNNEL OF LOVE

Fire and water (Freud might have something to say here) from the beginning played a large role in Coney's fun history. Water rides were and still remain among the most popular attractions. These subterranean journeys through dimly lit canals—"The Tunnel of Love," "Canals of Venice," "The Old Mill" and others—were built upon the knowledge that darkness was a stable and popular commodity. Outdoor nautical runs like "Shoot-the-Chutes" were undoubtedly more dramatic, but lacked the mesmeric effect of the underground. If you wanted a long three-minute kiss, this was the place. Gondolas moved slowly and silently in shallow troughs, propelled by the flow of the water. Along the route, and breaking the darkness, were scenes designed to entertain or terrorize the observer drifting by.

I recall tableaux ranging from the pastoral to the violent: A beach picnic, an Indian scalping a colonist, George Washington at Valley Forge, an ape crushing a maiden in his arms. To our intrepid band of juvenile scouts, the water ride offered unusual opportunities to offset summer boredom. We would stand at the rail as the boats entered the cardboard caverns, calling out:

"Hey, mister, don't get your feet wet!"

"Lady, are *you* going to be sorry! Kiss, kiss, kiss!"

"You'll never get out of there alive, ho-ho!"

We tried other antics inside the canal—yodeling, imitating female distress calls ("Don't, *please* don't! Stop or I'll scream . . ."). There was also the old trick of stopping your boat and letting the boat behind bump into you, tying up traffic along the line.

One day, however, one of our Apaches got a brilliant idea. A half hour later, a boat moved along the tunnel and stopped before the George Washington tableau. Three boys leaped on the catwalk, raised the boat from the water and disappeared with it around the side of the tableau. Several moments later another boat, holding two romantically enraptured couples, slowly moved into view. Its occupants saw, sprawled on the "snow," ragged soldiers of Valley Forge listening to George Washington's exhortation. The wax figures appeared amazingly lifelike, even if several were costumed a bit on the modern side. Suddenly there was a sharp scream from one of the girls. She had seen one of the soldiers yawn, another wink lasciviously, a third slowly turn his head. The girl screamed again. Her escort leaped up; the boat tilted against the wooden sides of the canal, and moved on into the darkness again, followed by the eyes of three modern Valley Forge reinforcements. Wild laughter, then silence. Several minutes later, three boys sailed out of the labyrinth into the sunlight, and serenely departed.

CRAP GAME

But the old is always the new, and the beach is the oldest attraction of all. It is the place for picnics, for the romping of children, for romance; the place described, as far back as 1880, as being "where you may do pretty much as you like, and be reasonably sure of not attracting an unpleasant amount of notice." This is the real heart of Coney.

At night, the beach has its groups of stragglers—those reluctant to go home, those returning for the slight sea breeze or to sing around a guitar, or to enjoy the darkness. Of course, it is never really dark on the beach on a summer night: there is too much spillway from the boardwalk light.

I remember another scene from the past, an evening when our nimblest boy spy rounded up a few of us with the electric words: "I found something good!" We grinned: Was it a new break in the Steeplechase fence, a better knothole in Stillman's baths? He told us: "Some people under a turned-over life boat on the beach. Let's go!"

On the way, we each picked up some stones. As a preliminary maneuver, we galloped over the boat, falling into the sand nearby. There was silence from under the boat. Then, we threw a few stones against the wooden shell; no response.

"Let's throw some lighted newspaper under it," suggested one small demon.

Our scout crept up to the boat and hissed, "Look out, the cops!" The boat tipped up sharply and a sailor scrambled out. Before our scout could take off, the sailor had him by the leg.

"Let go, I didn't do nuthin'," he shouted.

"Shut up," said the sailor. "For God's sakes, stop yelling! I ought to beat your skin off. Now go on home, will you?" But he kept a sharp grip on the scout.

"I'll call a cop," said the scout.

The sailor said, "I'll beat you up, you fresh kid."

Our scout glared back at him. "Go on, I dare you."

The sailor hauled our man over to one side. "Listen, kid, suppose I give you a buck, would you vanish and never come back?"

Our scout hesitated. "What about the other guys?"

The sailor took out his wallet, "A buck for you, another buck for your friends. Now beat it, huh? We got a crap game goin' under there." Our scout seized the bills and ran. The sailor brushed the sand from his shirt and crept back under the boat. We dashed toward the boardwalk stairs, toward the games, shouting back at our beneficiary, "Thanks, pal. We won't forget you, pal!"

Hot Dog Day at Coney [6]

On Sunday, July 23, 1939, Coney Island observed Hot Dog Day, to capitalize on the favor shown the tidbit by the King and Queen of Britain during their American visit earlier that year, and to mark the golden wedding anniversary of the sausage and the roll.

An audience of several hundred persons gathered in Feltman's Gardens for the ceremonies, which started with a proclamation by C. J.

[6] From *Sodom by the Sea,* An Affectionate History of Coney Island, by Oliver Pilat and Jo Ranson, pp. 244–246. Copyright, 1941, by Oliver Pilat and Jo Ranson. New York: Doubleday, Doran and Company, Inc.

Hilbert, president of the Coney Island Chamber of Commerce, to the effect that the hot dog, "discovered or invented" at the resort in 1889, had become a symbol of democracy. Two hundred youngsters from St. John's Orphan Asylum, lured to the affair on the promise of something to eat, yelled "hurrah" repeatedly when Hilbert finished. They thought food was coming. They turned glum as Hilbert was succeeded by Willets H. Shotwell, assistant commissioner of public works, representing Borough President Ingersoll of Brooklyn.

"It is difficult to measure the contribution the hot dog has made to the fame and popularity of this great resort," declared Shotwell. "Why, Coney Island is even shaped like a frankfurter! I venture to say that if the hot dogs consumed here during one season were laid out link to link they would stretch as far as the miles of railroad which bring millions of visitors to the Island."

Some of the more restless orphans began climbing over benches, and two boosted themselves into a poplar tree as Milton Berle, Broadway master of ceremonies, skipped to the center of the platform.

"Only for the hot dog would I get up so early," said Berle. "I came right from bed to wurst."

Groans arose from the adults, but Berle continued: "This is no time for clowning. We must get down to business. Let our slogan be 'E Pluribus Hot Dog.'"

Attendants produced a purple robe and crown, which Berle donned before reading the following petition:

To George VI, by the grace of God, of Great Britain, Ireland and all the British dominions beyond the sea, King, Defender of the Faith, Emperor of India.

WHEREAS, from humble beginnings, through its own merits and in keeping with the American way, the hot dog, a native of the United States, has attained a new world-wide eminence, and

WHEREAS, it has contributed to the friendship between two great democracies, Great Britain and the United States, and

WHEREAS, it has established the picnic table as a new vehicle for international diplomacy, and

WHEREAS, your Majesty, relishing the hot dog, partook of it, skin and all, and ate thereof a second portion at the famed picnic in Hyde Park during your sojourn in these United States, and

WHEREAS, your illustrious predecessor, King James I, did create a precedent at Houghton Castle in 1609, and did there confer knighthood on the loin, making him forever Sirloin,

NOW, THEREFORE, do we the undersigned, friends of the hot dog, hereby humbly petition that your Majesty remember the hot dog in forthcoming honors and do on the occasion of your birthday, and following the precedent of James I, confer knighthood upon the hot dog and dub him Sir Hot Dog.

Berle proceeded to fly in the face of logic and thus place the ceremony firmly in the Coney Island tradition. Without waiting for a reply from King George VI, or in fact waiting to send the petition, Berle knighted a sample hot dog on his own account, then popped half of the regal meat into his own mouth.

This was too much for the orphans, who began to bang on the benches. They were diverted only slightly by the presentation of a highly imaginative painting of the 1889 marriage between the frankfurter and the roll by the sea.

"All I can say upon receiving this portrait," said Charles Feltman, grandson of the founder, "is that I shall give it a place of honor in our restaurant, so that the people who come to Coney Island may gaze upon this beauty which is more than skin deep."

Charles Feltman gazed around him in despair. Everybody had spoken his lines with determined vivacity. On paper the lines had seemed funny enough, yet they had raised little laughter. Concluding that the pangs of hunger were marring the effectiveness of the ceremony, the host gave a signal of the hand. Waiters thereupon rushed heavily laden trays into the gardens, and everybody ate hot dogs.

Where the Walls Have Eyes [7]

. . . Even in the closed rooms of the [Coney Island] bathing houses the feminine sense of propriety cannot divest itself of the well-founded uneasiness. It is well known that walls sometimes have ears; but the walls of these bathing houses only too often have eyes. And these eyes are not accidental cracks or knot-holes, but holes bored there on purpose. These cabins are eagerly sought for by a certain class of male

[7] From *The Dark Side of New York Life and Its Criminal Classes from Fifth Avenue down to the Five Points,* A Complete Narrative of the Mysteries of New York [by Gustave Lening], pp. 401–402. Entered . . . 1873, by Fred'k Gerhard. New York.

visitors, who pay the proprietors large sums if they engage to put in the neighboring cabin a pretty lady. . . .

Six-Day Bike Races [8]

Acting on a humane impulse, New York legislators outlawed the brutal one-man six-day bike races in 1898, seven years after they were introduced in the old Garden. The next year, the riders came off their high wheels, or bone-shakers, and paired off into teams. Mounted on the new safety bikes, they started a series of six-day races which gave the Garden much of its flavor and most of its aroma for the next quarter of a century. For the six days and nights of each race, two dozen paid insomniacs pedaled endlessly around a pine track while thousands of paying insomniacs screamed and babbled in a dozen tongues, and sometimes fell into fitful slumber. It was hard to say who was goofier, riders or customers.

"Once we thought a rider was screwball champ," Harry Mendel said today. Mr. Mendel was connected with the Squirrel Cage for thirty years in the old Garden on Madison Avenue and the present Garden on Eighth Avenue before the races were taken off the calendar in 1939. "This rider," Mr. Mendel said, "was from Holland. The other riders were always screaming for more dough. This one took what we gave him, always. It wasn't too much. Then it came out why he didn't mind traveling from Holland for peanuts. He was smuggling diamonds in his bicycle tubes."

The bike race crowds were made up of plain bike nuts, sightseers, slummers, show people, show-offs, song-pluggers, cabaret bands, Broadway characters and their ladies, hoodlums, cops, pickpockets, and coat-snatchers. In a thick gray haze which often hid the riders, the sleepless ones ate sandwiches and hot dogs and drank everything from champagne to vino. The smoke of fine Havanas mingled with those of cheroots and countless cigarettes. The only egress for the fumes was the huge movable skylight in the Garden roof. Sometimes it was opened. Some bike fans literally stayed the week in the old Garden. You could do it for a dollar admission—if you could live a week without air.

[8] From "When Bike Race Fans Paid for a Week Without Air in Smoke-Choked Old Garden," by Murray Robinson, *New York World-Telegram*, January 3, 1947. Copyright, 1947, by New York World-Telegram Corp.

The pickpockets and coat-snatchers looked forward eagerly to Six-day Week. Conditions were ideal for gathering boodle in the bedlam. About forty years ago, Detective Sergeants John Reith and John McMullen, who knew their dips, were stationed just inside the Garden entrance to head off the light-fingered set. They commandeered the cloak room. When a pickpocket bustled happily through the gate, Sergeant McMullen would fetch him a kick in the shin with his brogan. The dip would ricochet over to Sergeant Reith, who would grab him by the neck and seat of pants and heave him into the cloak room. When they had the cloak room full, the sergeants called the wagon. Some nights, the wagon called at the Garden a half dozen times.

Despite the sergeants' watchfulness and that of their successors among them, Frank Casazza and Dick McKenna and Johnny Broderick and Big Jack Smith, the six-day dips managed to make a nice score inside the Garden. Seasoned bike fans never took off their overcoats. If they did, they went home without them, so fast were they grabbed. The disappearing coats became the subject of a running gag. Peter Prunty, the announcer, would remove his hard hat and begin, "The ten o'clock score is—"

"Forty-three overcoats," a voice from the gallery would finish.

When the pickings were lean, the pickpockets would release balloons among the sleepy fans. When the latter reached up to keep the balloons aloft, their watches, wallets, and tie pins disappeared.

Maurice Brocco ("B-r-r-r-ro-co!") was the most popular rider with the crowds in the old Garden. They roared his name through the night.

The early morning hours were blazing high noon at the six-day races. That's when the show people and show-offs crowded the best boxes and offered prizes—"premes," they were called—for sprints. And when Jo-Jo, the Dog-Faced Boy, did his stuff. A guy in the gallery would wake up and roar, "Jo-Jo!" Jo-Jo, a gnome-like character, would bellow, "Ma-a-a-a-ah!" in a hoarse, flat voice. That was Jo-Jo's contribution to the six-day race. He was considered a card.

Mike Delores, the Mad Hatter of Danbury, was another Squirrel Cage regular. He was the rider's favorite. He offered big premes.

"One Saturday afternoon," Mr. Mendel recalled, "the Mad Hatter put up $2,400 in premes. But the biggest single preme was offered by William Fox, the movie magnate—$500 for one sprint. "In one of the last races in the old Garden, Peggy Joyce put up $1,000 in premes. She stood up in her box and waved her arms at the crowd. They were up to the elbows in ice. The band played, 'Pretty Peggy with Eyes of Blue.' The crowd loved her. When she left, Johnny Broderick and Big Jack Smith escorted her out. They were afraid the mob loved her ice more."

In the infield, in the pre-radio days, were the song-pluggers. More or less, they entertained the six-day customers. When they started a song that didn't sound promising, the gallery whistled them right down.

"The song pluggers paid $500 a week to the Garden promoters," Mr. Mendel said. "They had to bring their own pianos. They brought the pianos in first. The track was built around the pianos. The song-pluggers lived a hard life. They had to compete with Jo-Jo, the bikes, and the all-week guys staggering around the infield half asleep. The infield, by the way, was called the 'promenade' on the tickets. Fancy. Once," Mr. Mendel recalled with a smile, "a ballroom dance team put a red carpet in the infield. They were going to give an exhibition. They never got around to it. But the sleepwalkers used to roll it out and put on wrestling matches at four A.M."

It was the custom of the ragtime and jazz bands to visit the old Garden after their cabaret chores. They put on impromptu concerts in the boxes.

"The announcer gave them a good build-up," Mr. Mendel said. "At about two A.M., he'd announce, 'The Memphis Five has just left Harlem.' A few minutes later, it was, 'The Memphis Five has just reached Seventy-second Street.' And so on until they showed up. Sometimes two bands played at the same time. Who could tell the difference?"

The races were sent off by political and stage celebrities. When Al Smith, then sheriff, pointed the starting gun at the roof one night, he cracked, "This is the only time I get to fire a gun." Texas Guinan fired six shots instead of one.

The riders were supposed to get their sleep in the cavernous basement of the old Garden. But conditions were not ideal. The thoughtful management had installed a shooting gallery near their dingy quarters. They had no baths. When they wanted to bathe, an old tin tub was supplied.

It was sheer chaos below deck in the old Garden during six-day week—target rifles cracking, dice and card games going full blast, foreign riders screaming at trainers in near-English and practical jokers running hog-wild.

"Once," Mr. Mendel said, "they tied Eddie Madden, a trainer, to a bench while he slept. So, from then on, the trainers hid away in dark holes in the basement to sleep. That's why Reggie McNamara, a few races later, didn't eat for twelve hours. He couldn't find his trainer. The guy had Reggie's store teeth in his kick when he hid away and overslept."

Charley Ebbets and His Field [9]

Not so long ago, in a furnished room located within the shadow of Ebbets Field, home of the Brooklyn Dodgers, a sixty-five-year-old man was found dead. And all you could discover in the newspapers of the big city about that man's passing was a tiny item buried deep down at the bottom of a page.

Said that news squib: "Charles Ebbets, Jr., sixty-five-year-old son of the founder of the Brooklyn Baseball Club, died yesterday, penniless and forgotten after nineteen years of fighting to collect his share of his father's million-dollar estate."

Behind that tiny item lay hidden an ironic, tragic baseball story—stranger than fiction.

It began many years ago with old Charley Ebbets, when much of the bustling metropolis of New York, and most of Brooklyn, was cow pasture. Charley Ebbets had a son. The little boy was weak and pale and sickly. One day, in 1883, his father was persuaded to take a job with a new Brooklyn ball club as a bookkeeper. For if he did so, he would be able to move away into the country, and his sickly son would have plenty of opportunity to grow up out-of-doors.

Thus began the story of Charley Ebbets of baseball fame. In time, he prospered. He became more than just a bookkeeper for the Brooklyn ball club. He became its business manager—making out players' contracts, paying off help, superintending the road trips. Charley Ebbets had a great ambition—to build up some business for his son, Charles, Jr., to inherit. Because of that boy, he finally bought the baseball club.

Charley Ebbets called his team the Brooklyn Superbas. Because he yearned to see his son inherit more than just a small-time baseball club, old Charley began to dream fantastic visions. He saw a brand-new ballpark, to be called Ebbets Field, built way out in the Brooklyn countryside. To make his dream come true for his son, he began to design the ballpark and arrange for building it.

[9] From *Bill Stern's Favorite Baseball Stories,* pp. 26–28. Copyright, 1949, by Mac Davis. New York: Pocket Books, Inc.

Friends told Ebbets he was crazy to build out in the wilds, but he would reply: "I'm building this new ballpark for my son. Mark my words, some day Ebbets Field will be in the heart of Brooklyn, and thousands of fans will come to see the team play baseball. Some day, the Brooklyn club will be so famous that Ebbets Field will be too small to handle the crowds!"

That used to get a lot of laughs! Charley Ebbets was a funny man. Why, at the time, he even had ideas that baseball was only in its infancy, and believed that some day it would become so popular that millions would see baseball games during a season. He had a further novel idea about giving out rain checks!

Old Charley Ebbets, with his funny ideas about baseball and its future, worked hard and tried his best to make a success—all for his son. And also for that boy, Charles, Jr., he stuck to his dream. In 1912, he saw Ebbets Field built. The Brooklyn ball club had a new home, a beautiful park seating more than thirty-five thousand fans! The club prospered and became famous all over the nation as the Brooklyn Dodgers. Before Charley Ebbets died, he saw baseball prosper until it became the national pastime for millions of Americans!

But with his death, the ballpark which he had built for his son, Charles, Jr., became entangled in legal difficulties. The Ebbets clan began to fight over old Charley Ebbets' estate. And it was discovered that he had left his son, Charles, Jr., no money.

For nineteen years, Charles Ebbets, Jr., fought desperately to collect his share of his father's million-dollar estate. But he never succeeded. He died alone, forgotten, penniless—in a little room located in the shadow of Ebbets Field—the very ballpark that had been built by his father, only because of him.

Eccentric Rooters [10]

. . . For several seasons, in recent years, Ebbets Field—home grounds for many screwball fans—was graced by the presence of a man who appeared to dislike the Brooklyns. Each time the visiting team scored

[10] From *Low and Inside,* A Book of Baseball Anecdotes, Oddities, and Curiosities, by Ira L. Smith and H. Allen Smith, pp. 18–19. Copyright, 1949, by Ira L. Smith and H. Allen Smith. Garden City, New York: Doubleday & Co., Inc.

or executed a double play or got a good hit, this gentleman would cry out, "There goes yer ole baaaall gaaame!" (He seems to have disappeared the last couple of years—probably assassinated.)

Eccentric rooters were not lacking in the earlier days of baseball. In 1900 the New York press took notice of a Polo Grounds rooter who sat in the stands day after day and periodically declaimed in a loud and penetrating voice, "Well! Well!" It is recorded that the management finally barred him from the park on the grounds that his reiteration of "Well! Well!" was making nervous wrecks out of several ballplayers.

During the same period, Brooklyn had to put up with a fan who, day after day, sat in the stands and sang a meaningless song. He sang it steadily, resting only during the minutes in which the teams were changing sides. The lyrics of his song went:

In again and out again;
Out again and in again;
Up again and down again;
Down again and up again.

Wilbert Robinson [11]

In the vast body of baseball legend the name of Wilbert Robinson occupies a special position. Scores of flavorsome tales have him for protagonist. Most of the Robinson stories are familiar to the dyed-in-the-wool fan. . . . There is one little incident, however, which turned up in the old newspaper files, and which we feel will bear repeating.

One afternoon, just before his Brooklyn Dodgers were to take the field, Uncle Robbie sat on the bench with pencil and paper, getting his starting line-up written down for the plate umpire.

Someone observed that, after writing down three or four names, a worrisome hesitation overtook the fabulous Brooklyn manager. He glanced around as though for help and then spoke to a player who was sitting near him. The player shrugged and shook his head. Uncle Robbie then resumed his writing. The nature of the perplexity that had come upon him was brought to light later in the day.

[11] *Ibid.*, pp. 210–211.

In writing down the line-up, Uncle Robbie had arrived at one of the outfield positions, where he wanted to play Oscar Roettger. He started to write Oscar's name, then realized that he had no idea how to spell "Roettger." Turning to the player nearest him, he asked: "How the devil do you spell Oscar's last name?"

The player didn't know. So Uncle Robbie wrote down "Cox." And Dick Cox played right field that afternoon in place of Oscar Roettger.

Giant Fan Number One [12]

"You can't heckle professional comedians with standard insults," explained [Jack] White [the comedian who died in 1942]. "A professional knows all the standard toppers. You've got to knock off an *ad lib,* so you catch them unprepared." White estimated he had at least 12,000 standard insults catalogued in his memory. He said he had only been successfully squelched by three people: Myron Cohen, a Seventh Avenue garment manufacturer [then], dancer Paul Draper, and sports writer Jimmy Cannon. Cohen has been taking out-of-town buyers around to night clubs for so many years that he has memorized more insults than any man living, save White. And Cannon can think of more squelches per minute than anybody around. "The trouble with Cannon," said White, "is his timing. He doesn't know how to wait for his laughs." Cannon's best squelch involved the Giants. White was famous around New York, as Giant fan number one. During the season, he never missed a ball game at the Polo Grounds. He was a regular at the Polo Grounds since 1908, when he and some friends used to climb over a fence and get thrown out by an usher named Bum O'Neal; O'Neal was so used to White sneaking into the Polo Grounds that for years even after White could afford to pay his $2.20, he would throw White out anyway. White sat in the upper stands, section 33, overlooking third base, with about fifty or sixty other regulars who never miss a game, including such regulars as Jim Barton, William Gaxton, Ray Bolger, Toots Shor, Victor Moore, Jimmy Durante. White himself admitted that he first developed his technique

[12] From *Never Whistle in a Dressing Room,* or Breakfast in Bedlam, by Maurice Zolotow, pp. 82–84. Copyright, 1944, by Maurice Zolotow. New York: E. P. Dutton & Company, Inc.

of insult-and-injury by heckling umpires and members of the Chicago Cubs and Brooklyn Dodgers at the Polo Grounds. Baseball veterans credit White with having invented most of today's widely used insults against umpires and rival players, insults like "we're chipping in for a pair of glasses for the umpire." White himself was a semipro ball player around 1910, played Class B baseball with teams like the Bronx Athletic Club, the Crotona Parks, the Brophys. White generally played left field.

Anyway, White was such a fanatical Giant rooter that he always posted a winning Giant score in huge letters on a sign over the bandstand in his night club. But when the Giants lost, White refused to recognize a reality. He posted a sign reading: "NO GAME TODAY." Well, one time the Giants dropped a double-header to Brooklyn. That night, White had his usual "NO GAME TODAY" sign up.

Cracked Cannon that night: "Jack, you ought to put a sign up there reading 'NO TEAM TODAY.'" White, for one of the few times in his life, was stopped cold.

"Wake Me Up When Kirby Dies" [13]

Something more than sixty years ago [as of 1902] the attention of theatre-goers was directed to a young actor who appeared at intervals in the Chatham Theatre. He was J. Hudson Kirby. His acting had not much merit, but he persisted in a theory that made him famous. It was his idea that an actor should reserve all his strength for scenes of carnage and death. The earlier acts of a play he passed through carelessly, but when he came to death-scenes he threw himself into them with such force and fury that they came to be the talk of the town. Some of the spectators found the earlier acts so dull and tiresome that they went to sleep, taking the precaution, however, to nudge their neighbor, with the request to wake them up for the death-scene. And for long years after Kirby's time, the catch-phrase applied to any supreme effort was "Wake me up when Kirby dies."

[13] From *When Old New York Was Young,* by Charles Hemstreet, pp. 151–152. Copyright, 1902, by Charles Hemstreet. New York: Charles Scribner's Sons.

The Barker at Huber's [14]

. . . [At] Huber's [Dime] Museum, [at 106 East Fourteenth Street] with the freaks on the platform and its still more curious actors on the little stage, there used to be a remarkable "barker". . . . He looked like a bankrupt count of the grand old school of pomade and wax. All day he wore evening dress of the same epoch, and he barked in verse in a fearful and wonderful manner something like this . . . :

"Ladies and gents,
for only ten cents
you can see all the sights.
And there on your right
is the great fat lady;
she's a healthy baby
weighing three hundred pounds;
she's six foot around.
Her husband is the living
skeleton—see him shivering.
The dog-faced boy
will give you all joy,
and the tattooed man
does the best he can.
The human horse
is wonderful, of course,
and I'll show to you
the boxing kangaroo.
The lady lion tamer
will please every stranger. . . ."

Get the Hook [15]

At Miner's Bowery Theatre in New York . . . were given the first amateur nights in burlesque. Here the aspirants for footlight fame

[14] From *The Real New York,* by Rupert Hughes, p. 96. Copyright, 1904, by the Smart Set Publishing Company. New York and London.

[15] From *The Actor's Fair Bulletin.* Cited in *Burleycue,* An Underground History of Burlesque Days, by Bernard Sobel, pp. 223–224. Copyright, 1931, by Bernard Sobel. New York: Farrar & Rinehart, Inc.

were given the opportunity to show their goods. The audience was at liberty to give full expression to their approval or dislike to the offerings of the contestants for the prizes. One Friday night, in October, 1903, at Miner's Bowery, a particularly bad amateur was inflicting upon a patient audience an impossible tenor solo. Despite howls, groans, cat-calls, the artist persisted in staying on, when Tom Miner, who was running the show, chanced to see a large old-fashioned, crook-handled cane which had been used by one of the Negro impersonators. Quickly, he had Charles Guthinger, the late stage manager, lash it to a long pole. With this, he stepped to the wings without getting into sight of the audience, deftly slipped the hook around the neck of the singer and yanked him off the stage before he knew what happened.

The next amateur who was giving an imitation of Booth announced that he would next imitate Mansfield to follow, when a small boy yelled, "Get the Hook!" The audience roared and the actor fled in dismay.

Many later stars including Fannie Brice, Joe Cook and George White endured the ordeal of the hook. . . .

"This Little French Novelty" [16]

The audience stirred and rose, but before many men could struggle out to the aisles they were halted by a harsh and authoritative voice.

It grated through a microphone beside the orchestra pit, where the candy butcher had appeared even as the main curtain came down.

"One moment, ladies and gentlemen!" he commanded. "Do not leave the theatre. This completes only the first portion of our entertainment this afternoon. The second half will be presented immediately. If any among you require cigars, cigarettes or refreshing fruit drinks, may I call your attention to the concessionaire's counter just inside the theatre before you reach the lobby!"

His admonition grew slightly desperate as some of the patrons (practiced burlesque-goers, no doubt) kept retreating up the aisles.

"But those of you who wish to remain in your seats," he continued, in a more ingratiating tone, "will be rewarded by a free gift of this little French novelty—where formerly such secret devices was confined

[16] Reported by George and Mary Milburn at the Hudson Theatre, Union City, New Jersey, 1952.

to the private collections of wealthy collectors of these devices, such as J. P. Morgan and other millionaires who could afford the price."

Some of the departing men halted in the upper aisles and edged into back seats to listen.

"Now, ladies and gentlemen," the spieler went on, "I'm not standing up here before you trying to insult your intelligence by claiming that I'm trying to give away no rare and priceless article for free. I'm in business to make a profit, just like ever'body else. I'll admit it.

"But lemme just explain you what happened: I've got a personal contack in Paris, France, friends, and he writes me here a while back that this little novelty is very popular in Paris, France and maybe could be slipped through the U. S. customs by way of Tia Juana, Mexico. He says, 'You can make a fortune introducing this little device to the American public.'

"So I cables back to him, 'O.K.! Send me one gross of that little French novelty on, and I'll see where the American public reacks to it.'

"So the shipment comes through outa Tia Juana, Mexico, last Monday just before our show opened, and I offered them in this country for the first time at one dollar each—and I wanna tell you, folks, they sold like hot cakes at one dollar each. Why, I had men come to me after the show, when they seen what it was they passed up, begging me to sell 'em this little French article of entertainment.

"But I couldn't do it. And you wanna know why? Because when the police found out what was goin' on, they moved in, and warns me it's against the law in this state to sell amusing little French devices of this here particular kind and description.

"Now, ladies and gentlemen, I just couldn't figure out where they could do that to me, because I know you folks coming here to see our show are all broad-minded, and myself I couldn't see where it was gonna cause no adult-minded person harm to take this little French device home and amuse himself with it. But you know and I know and we all know that it don't do no good to arger with the police when they lay the lawr down. So I just says, O.K., and I packs these little French novelties up and I takes them back to my hotel room with me.

"But last night I got to thinkin' about it, and I thinks to myself, well maybe they got a lawr against selling these here little French novelties, but they haven't got any lawr against me giving them away for souvenirs to broad-minded people who appreciates a good laugh like you folks who come to this show.

"So it's an inspiration to me in the middle of the night. It so happens that I know an important executive and he's one of my closest pals—in fact—he's head advertising manager of Pan-American Chocolate Company. So I puts in a call to New York and explains my idea to him, and he says he thinks I've got an inspiration there, in fact he gets all enthusiastic and says he will back me up to the extent of allowing me to present this little French novelty as a free gift, merely as part of the advertising campaign they're putting on for their famous candy bar.

"So that solved my problem.

"No, friends, I'm not coming before you this afternoon as a gold-brick artist. I want you to be satisfied. Just so you won't think you're getting a pig-in-a-poke, I wanta show you right out in front here what this little French novelty consists of. So I hold it up here for your inspection. There are two beautiful French models joined here. Now I don't wanta take them apart—you can do that yourself. But if you will just take these pictures apart and reverse them, placing them together in full juxtaposition—and move this little French novelty before a light—any kind of light, electric, candle, or even just a match—you will get a good idea of what certain women do under certain circumstances. It leaves nothing to your imagination!

"Now may I impress upon you again, I am not *selling* this little French novelty—I am merely giving it away. Nobody can stop me from passing this little French souvenir out to you with each and every ten-cent chocolate bar you buy.

"The boys will pass this French device among you, free of charge, as they pass up the aisles selling this famous brand of chocolates—at ten cents a bar—and anyone who wants to buy a chocolate bar, I'd appreciate it if you'd raise your hand, because this here advertising manager of the chocolate company is standing in back of the theatre to see how my experiment goes, and you sure would help me by showing you're with me!"

A surprising number of white palms flashed up in the darkness of the theatre. Surprising, because such specious appeals to lickerish customers from burlesque candy butchers have been used, with only the slightest variation, for more than fifty years.

I signaled the man as he passed my seat in the box on his way to the balcony. I paid him ten cents and he handed me a five-cent bar of a well-known milk chocolate (Nestlé's) and with it two little slips of paper, stapled together, on which were printed two rather smudged half-tones of half-dressed burlesque stars. Although the backs were blank, these were photographs that could have been clipped out of any popular magazine or tabloid newspaper.

(Later, purely in the interest of scientific research, I brought this little French novelty home and tried it out on an electric light bulb, a candle, and a match, and it never did show me what the candy butcher insinuated that it would.)

The Girl in the Champagne Bath [17]

The most notorious party of the twenties took place after midnight of February 23, 1926, in the Earl Carroll Theatre. It landed the host in the federal penitentiary in Atlanta. And it was a newspaper sensation for months. No party since the "Girl-in-the-Pie" supper given by the millionaire Henry W. Poor in the mid-nineties created so much scandal; and yet, if James Huneker's description of the Poor party in *Painted Veils* is to be relied upon, the party at the Earl Carroll Theatre was like a small-town church social in comparison, and so I have always suspected that the Poor shenanigans were exaggerated. I attended the Earl Carroll party and found it inordinately dull, decorous, and tawdry. I have seen much wickeder stags held for the benefit of the volunteer firemen's associations in small towns.

In a letter I have from Huneker, dated January 4, 1921, he says that "the bacchanalian episode" he describes in *Painted Veils* "is an exact transcription of the famous dinner given by the late Henry W. Poor for the sculptor Augustus Saint-Gaudens at the studio of an amateur photographer, James Laurence Breise, on Sixteenth Street, near Fifth Avenue. The affair made an enormous scandal, and the yellow journals had their usual carnival of mud slinging. Names were duly printed and the little girl of the pie became a marked character."

The Poor episode, as Huneker describes it, involved not merely a tableau of nearly nude women who served formally attired male guests with champagne and canapés after their posings were concluded, nor the pièce de résistance at the supper table in which a very young and beautiful girl, entirely nude, arose from an enormous pie and danced on the table, but a dance in which the guests and the nude entertainers participated in a manner that seemed to shock the professedly blasé Huneker, as he narrates it.

[17] From *We Were Interrupted,* by Burton Rascoe, pp. 234–238. Copyright, 1947, by Burton Rascoe. Garden City, N. Y.: Doubleday & Company, Inc.

The "girl-in-the-champagne-bath" party was given by Earl Carroll for a Texas oil millionaire, W. R. Edrington, who had backed a number of Earl Carroll *Vanities* (imitations of the Ziegfeld *Follies*) and had built the theater for Carroll. The audience was mixed; about a third of the guests were women, among whom was Countess Vera Cathcart. The countess was very much in the newspapers at the moment, because she had been detained on Ellis Island by the immigration officials on the quaint and ambiguous charge of "moral turpitude" (it seems she had made a trip with the Earl of Craven without a chaperon). Carroll had taken advantage of the publicity, on her release, and had announced that he was starring her in a musical. I recognized none of the other women except Dorothy Knapp, whose pictures were often in the papers at the time.

The reception was on the stage, where there were two bars, one for beer on tap and served in seidels, the other for hard liquor cocktails, and wines. A table in between was attended by carvers who sliced hams, chickens, bologna, and cheeses for sandwiches. Members of the cast of the current *Vanities,* including the stately showgirls, mingled with the guests and made themselves available for the dances, for which a full orchestra supplied the music.

After the reception on the stage, the guests, about five hundred of them, were asked to take seats in the orchestra for the show. I sat with Philip Payne, then the managing editor of the *Mirror*. I recognized a great many newspapermen, including drama critics, columnists, editors, and desk men as well as reporters, but I recognized only two of the other male guests, Irvin S. Cobb and Harry K. Thaw. The show began with some vaudeville skits, brief and ordinary. The most audacious of the acts of the evening was not the bath incident; it was a Charleston contest in which various members of the chorus participated for cash prizes and consolation prizes of lingerie. The award was made on the strength and duration of the applause from the audience. The first prize of $100 was won by a very pretty young girl, very fresh and innocent-looking, dressed in the ordinary street clothes of flappers of the period, in contrast with the other contestants, who wore abbreviated chorus costumes. The winner, however, wore black silk stockings and girdle with garter straps. But she had omitted to put on panties. Carroll put a damper on the spirits of the clappers and made them look very much disturbed by saying he was glad "that little girl got the prize, because she is going on the operating table at ten o'clock in the morning for the removal of a cancer in her breast. She needs the money."

Carroll then announced that a beautiful girl would take a bath in champagne on the stage and that those who wished to drink from the bathtub should line up to the right of the theater; cups would be given them and the champagne would be drawn from a faucet in the tub's outlet until it was gone. Two attendants then erected a screen in the center of the stage while a bathtub on a mobile trestle was rolled from the wings behind it. A tall, dark girl, wrapped in a huge bathrobe, came out, acknowledged the applause, stepped behind the curtain and, from the neck up, could be seen getting into the tub. Then the screen was removed. A line began to form at the right as one chap walked up from the first position, dipped his cup into the tub, and walked off-stage very awkwardly and in obvious embarrassment, not having glanced in the direction of the bather.

Then the girl's head slumped as though she had collapsed. There was immediate confusion on the stage as Carroll and others rushed to the tub and lifted the girl out, meanwhile covering her with towels and robes. The line withdrew and the audience sat mystified, not knowing whether this was all part of the act or not. Then Carroll came forth and announced that the girl had fainted but had revived. He said her act was to conclude the show and that he was sorry but the party was over. He thanked all for coming.

Entrance to the theater had been through the stage door in an alley; the front entrance was barred and darkened. Phil Payne on our way out stopped to inquire about the girl. Carroll said she was a little hysterical but would be all right; she had suffered from the chill of immersion. (Incidentally, I was told the liquid was ginger ale in champagne bottles.) Then, whether Payne's next words were spoken on impulse, in which he forgot that all newspapermen had pledged themselves not to print a word about the party, or whether he shrewdly took advantage of Carroll's confusion of mind, I don't know, but this dialogue ensued:

"This would make a whale of a story for you, Earl. Can I break it?"

"Sure, sure, sure," said Carroll, his head bobbing around to return salutes of his departing guests.

"What's the girl's name?" asked Payne, taking a used envelope and a pencil from his pocket.

"Joyce, Joyce, Joyce—Joyce Kilmer."

Payne was about to write that name down when I said, "For God's sake, Phil, that can't be the girl's name. Joyce Kilmer is the name of the poet who wrote 'Trees' and was killed in the war."

Payne repeated almost my exact words to Carroll, who asked at random, "Anybody know the girl's name?" A chorus girl stepped forward and said, "Her name is Joyce Hawley." She watched Payne write it down. We left.

The next morning the *Mirror* played the story on pages one, two, and in runover columns, with pictures. No other morning paper referred to the party. The afternoon newspapers carried follow-ups and the story was splurged sensationally for weeks. But Payne became something of a pariah among newspapermen, who did not know that Carroll had specifically, in my hearing, granted Payne permission to print the story. Payne was deemed to have violated one of the sacred unwritten rules of the profession, of never breaking a story when under pledge not to do so. Payne, a simple, sensitive, sentimental, and very ingenuous soul, in spite of his job as managing editor of a sensational tabloid newspaper (it was said of him that the reason he was so successful as a tabloid editor was that he believed everything he printed), was depressed by the outcome, and it was possibly for this reason that he decided, at the last moment, to board as a passenger the *Mirror's* airplane which was going to try to break the time record for a transatlantic flight. The plane was lost somewhere in the ocean without trace.

As a result of the scandalous publicity about the party, Prohibition enforcement agents were obliged to act. Carroll was arrested on a charge of possessing and dispensing alcoholic beverages at the party. He denied the charges, against the advice of his counsel, so I was informed. Witnesses were called and the fact was overwhelmingly established that liquor was dispensed that night at the theater. Forgotten was Joyce Hawley, forgotten too was the original charge of violating the Volstead Act. Carroll was indicted and found guilty of perjury. He was sentenced to the federal penitentiary in Atlanta for a year, of which he served less than three months, in very comfortable quarters, where he was allowed to entertain visitors.

Anthony Comstock and "September Morn"[18]

A very conspicuous and to New York most entertaining figure in those days was the celebrated Anthony Comstock. . . . As head of the So-

[18] From *New York at the Turn of the Century, 1899–1916,* by Wirt Howe, pp. 17–18. Toronto, Canada: Privately Printed, 1946.

ciety for the Suppression of Vice he did the city a splendid service in combating the forces of evil in its midst. But his spirit was too puritanical and unyielding for the increasingly liberal standards and humor of the town; he often went too far, and his worthy efforts passed from being considered a benefit to being regarded first as a nuisance and then as a sort of standing joke.

This seems a good place to allude to an episode in his activities that occasioned no end of amusement at the time and is memorable as a sad commentary on how the rigid density of old age may cast a shadow on a useful career, for it occurred some years later when the good man was no longer young. There appeared one day in the window of an art shop a reproduction of a small painting by the French artist Paul Chabas, bearing the innocent title "September Morn." It disclosed a nude maiden standing ankle-deep in the water of what appeared to be the seashore at daybreak. Her pose was modest, the workmanship of the painting was excellent, the entire conception charming, and, to the rest of us, as innocent as the picture's name. Nevertheless, the Comstock Society, as it was called, descended on the audacious dealer, Ortiz by name, seized the offending work of art, and arrested its owner who was duly tried for displaying an obscene drawing and as promptly acquitted.

The only result of the farce was an immediate appearance all over the town of myriad reproductions of the picture, in shop windows, on post cards and advertisements, and the dissemination of as many jokes of every degree of off-coloration, and the eclipse of Comstock. New York enjoyed itself hugely for a time, but the overzealous reformer never lived down the ridicule that descended on him, and when he died perhaps more persons in Gotham connected his name with that rosy little daughter of the autumn morn than with any of his many praiseworthy achievements for the betterment of civic conditions.

The St. Regis' Prices [19]

. . . When the St. Regis was first opened, it was rumored that the prices charged exceeded anything New York had ever experienced, and the following story went the rounds: A man returning from some

[19] *Ibid.*, p. 12.

race track after a day of ill fortune encountered a friend and said to him: "I'm broke and hungry, Bill." "Here's $10,000," responded the generous Bill. "Go up to the St. Regis and get yourself a cup of coffee."

The unfortunate one entered the dining room and found that for $9,000 he could obtain a chop with peas, which would leave him $1,000 for a tip to the waiter, so he placed his order. The latter presently returned with a plate in the center of which appeared one pea. Said the famished guest: "Where is the chop?" "There it is," answered the waiter with dignity, "under the pea." "Oh," replied the guest humbly, "I beg your pardon; I thought that was a crack."

So many were the jokes of this kind that the hotel management actually took alarm and issued a formal statement that its prices were not higher than those at equally good resorts. They no longer are so. Other hotels' prices and New York's willingness to pay have caught up with them.

Big Spenders[20]

In the days before the Depression was finally accepted by the big spenders as a hard fact and not just a sort of overnight joke in bad taste, money had a strangely unreal quality on Broadway, at least. Texas Guinan, the rowdy but shrewd old gal who was, until the mob got mad at her, "The Queen of the Night Clubs," used to greet each arriving patron with the raucous shout: "Hello, Sucker!" This was considered hilarious, even when the time came to pay a tab which proved that Texas wasn't kidding with her salutation.

The various Texas Guinan emporia, all of which somehow fell into the same pattern—open, do turnaway trade, be closed by the prohibition agents—were always among the most expensive gay spots. Texas featured pretty girls and lots of them. Talent was something for somebody else to appreciate. The big spenders, the good parties, made a beeline for wherever Texas was in action. Remembered is a night in one of the Guinan deadfalls when a man at a ringside table was moaning and complaining.

[20] From *No Cover Charge,* A Backward Look at the Night Clubs, by Robert Sylvester, pp. 172–173. Copyright, 1956, by Robert Sylvester. New York: The Dial Press.

"I feel terrible," he told the doll sitting with him. "I lost $337,000 in the market today."

A waiter serving an adjoining table sneered.

"These drunks," he said contemptuously, "will cry over any little thing."

There was another typical big spender of the day who used to claim that it cost him $1,000 to fix a cigarette lighter in Texas Guinan's. His story was that his girl couldn't make her lighter work and he took it apart. He spilled the inflammable fluid on her expensive fur coat. A lighted cigarette set the coat on fire. Waiters proceeded to ruin it with water and a small fire extinguisher. The jolly spender had to go for $1,000 for another coat.

Arnold Rothstein and Arnold Reuben [21]

I would not like to create the impression in these recollections of my husband that his life was a solemn procession of bets, lendings, borrowings, fixings, headaches, craps, patent medicines, coffee and cakes. He had a great deal of fun out of life, according to his idea of fun. Hardly a day passed that he failed to play a practical joke on some one.

He had a definite gift for mimicry, for instance, and could successfully imitate not only male but female voices. From this he derived a lot of pleasure.

Here is a sample of one of his jokes. There was a time that Lillian Lorraine, who was once one of the most toasted actresses of Broadway, and famous in the Ziegfeld Follies, lived in an apartment near Reuben's.

For the benefit of those who are not familiar with New York, I might explain that Reuben was the man who made a delicatessen store a Broadway institution. He put in booths, and served huge sandwiches at fancy prices, and attracted to his place the same sort of persons who once frequented Jack's, Rector's and other famous restaurants.

21 From *Now I'll Tell,* by Carolyn Rothstein (Mrs. Arnold Rothstein) with an introduction by Donald Henderson Clarke, pp. 140–143. Copyright, 1934, by The Vanguard Press, Inc. New York.

One night Arnold was standing at the desk in this place which ostensibly was a delicatessen shop, but which really was a restaurant which catered to the night life of Broadway. He was, as was not unusual for him, awaiting a telephone call. I don't think Arnold ever was five minutes away from a telephone if he could help it.

Arnold picked up the receiver. It was Miss Lorraine ordering a chicken sandwich and a bottle of milk. Arnold, imitating Reuben's best manner, told her the order would be served promptly.

Hanging up the receiver, Arnold went outside to a pay station, called up Reuben, imitated Miss Lorraine's voice, and ordered six dozen club sandwiches, a can of fresh caviar (I don't know how much that is by the ounce), a gallon of dill pickles, and twelve quarts of milk.

When this order reached Miss Lorraine, there was a great excitement. Miss Lorraine, as an artist, had a temperament.

Those who do not find their humor in practical jokes may not appreciate this, but I can assure you that Arnold found great pleasure in the situation.

At another time he called Reuben on the telephone, giving the name of a noted actress. He ordered three hundred sandwiches and a barrel of herrings to be delivered at an address in West Forty-ninth Street. Reuben took charge of this order personally and found the address was the horses' entrance of Madison Square Garden.

These two practical jokes of Arnold's may, or may not, be fair samples. He was always at them. But whether or not a person approved of practical jokes, it is a fact that Arnold had a reputation for humor, and a quick tongue.

According to close friends of Arnold's, he was the originator in real life of a humorous idea which later was tricked up and used as a blackout in a successful musical production on Broadway.

A gambler acquaintance of Arnold's called him on the long distance telephone, reported that he was broke, and asked Arnold to send him five hundred dollars so that he could pay his debts and get back to New York. Arnold replied: "I can't hear you."

The seeker after a loan repeated his request several times, to which Arnold always answered: "I can't hear you."

After a few minutes of this, and jiggling of hooks and complaints from the other end of the line, my husband's own operator intervened to say: "But, Mr. Rothstein, I can hear him distinctly."

"All right," Arnold said, "then you give it to him."

And he hung up the receiver.

The Origin of the Dutch Treat Club [22]

[The Dutch Treat] Club originated seventeen years ago [as of 1924] in a very unpretentious way. At that time Tuesday was Regular Contributors' Day at the editorial office of *Life*—the day of the week when J. A. Mitchell looked over the drawings and sketches of his stand-by artists. Every Tuesday morning *Life's* anteroom would be thronged with clever illustrators chatting together sociably as they waited their turns to be ushered into the sanctum of "J.A.M.," and writers waiting similarly for interviews with Thomas L. Masson, the literary editor. Since many of these contributors lived in the suburbs, it was natural that, being in town for the day, they should feel like having a good time in each other's company. And so the "gang" got the habit of lunching somewhere together, each paying for his own meal. *Life* contributors brought friends who had no connection with that magazine. Numbers grew till one Tuesday the bunch organized themselves officially as the Dutch Treat Club, with Masson as President. Among those founder members were James Montgomery Flagg, Rupert Hughes, Julian Street, Ellis Parker Butler, Frank Ward O'Malley, and the Irwin brothers, Will and Wallace. The member who christened the club was George Barr Mallon, then city editor of *The Sun.*

From the Algonquin Archives [23]

In his days as a general reporter Alexander Woollcott was assigned to write a "Sunday special" on an obscure West Forty-fourth Street hostelry, the Algonquin. He found it "a little, unpretentious hotel, tucked away on a side street" and occasionally patronized by such diverse notables as Rollo Ogden, William T. Tilden II, Evangeline

[22] From "Where Celebrities Foregather," by Ronald Armstrong, *Little Old New York,* Vol. II (July-August, 1924), No. 10, p. 3. New York: Thirty-Fourth Street Midtown Association, Inc.

[23] From *A. Woollcott, His Life and His World,* by Samuel Hopkins Adams, pp. 118–119, 121–122, 125, 126, 127. Copyright, 1945, by Samuel Hopkins Adams. New York: Reynal & Hitchcock.

Booth, and Raymond Hitchcock. Douglas Fairbanks visited it in the way of trade, before his acting days, to sell soap to the management, and returned later to buy luncheon for Mary Pickford.

Its genesis as an intellectual oasis in the arid Philistinism of Broadway dates from a telephone call, Woollcott to Adams to Broun, for a luncheon. Where? There was a place next door, said Woollcott, then staying at the City Club, where they had a good apple pie. The trio formed a weekly luncheon date, F.P.A. coming up from his downtown office every Saturday. To them presently gathered Ross and Winterich, ex-*Stars and Stripes*, Robert Benchley, and the Pemberton brothers, Brock and Murdock. Frank Case, proprietor of the Algonquin and later an author in his own right, moved them from their quiet corner to more spacious accommodations.

Thus began the famous Round Table, which was to burgeon in an atmosphere of intellectual stimulus, wisecracks, and no-limit poker, and to endure through more than a decade as a landmark for highbrow rubberneckery. . . .

Celebrities, future celebrities, and near celebrities joined up: Marc Connelly, Deems Taylor, Frank Sullivan, John Peter Toohey, Howard Dietz, John V. A. Weaver, Irving Berlin, Donald Ogden Stewart, Raoul Fleischmann, Russel Crouse, George S. Kaufman, David Wallace, Robert Sherwood, occasionally Harold Gould, J. M. Kerrigan, Sidney Blackmer, and a sprinkling of Broadway stars and rounders. A Ladies Annex attached itself to the group: Edna Ferber, Margolo and Ruth Gillmore, Alice Duer (Mrs. Henry) Miller, Jane Grant, Ruth Hale, Beatrice (Mrs. George S.) Kaufman, Dorothy Parker, Neysa McMein, Margaret Leech, Elsie Janis, and Alison Smith, afterward Mrs. Russel Crouse.

Leadership in the group went, by tacit consent, to F.P.A., due to his reputation, already national, his wit, and in some degree to his financial status as by far the highest paid newspaperman of the lot. . . .

* * * * *

. . . Subsequently [their] scintillations would appear in one or another of the newspaper columns, which prompted an outsider to suggest that the members lived by taking in each other's joshing.

To the rapidly expanding Round Table publicity, Frank Case attributed the adoption by the newspapers of the by-line. Seeing their own well-paid writers quoted by name in other mediums, the editors concluded that they might as well get the benefit of their staff men's wit—such paragraphs as "Frank Sullivan was heard to observe recently," or "As Bob Benchley said to a certain self-exploiting actor at the Algonquin." Messrs. Sullivan and Benchley were invited by their superiors to "save it for home use."

* * * * *

The Algonquin preserves [this] Kaufman item among its unwritten archives, the call made by the young playwright upon a theatrical producer notorious for his habit of answering the bell of his apartment stark naked. He was in this condition when Kaufman arrived. The caller, after a moment's hesitancy, said: "I beg you pardon, Mr. H——, but did you know that your fly is open?"

* * * * *

Half the wisecracks of the next ten years were attributed to the Algonquin. Here were conceived, by common, but not too reliable, rumor, Dorothy Parker's quip: "If all the girls who attended the Yale Prom this year were laid end to end, I wouldn't be a bit surprised"; Irvin Cobb's epitaph for a beauty of notoriously general liaisons: "Here lies Polly Simpkins: asleep—alone—at last"; Frank Adams' example of a sentence embodying the word "meretricious": "Meretricious 'n Happy New Year"; and Heywood Broun's unprinted surgical lyric, composed on a hospital cot after a minor operation:

* * * * *

There was a young man with a hernia
Who said to his surgeon "Gol-dernya,
When carving my middle
Be sure you don't fiddle
With matters that do not concernya."

* * * * *

The Algonquin profited mightily by the literary atmosphere, and Frank Case evinced his gratitude by fitting out a workroom for Woollcott, Broun, and Adams, and a poker room for the whole membership.

With increasing fame, the Round Table became culturally self-conscious. There had not been a Cave of the Wits in New York since the 1850's, when there foregathered in Pfaff's beer cellar the High Bohemia of the period: Thomas Bailey Aldrich, William Cullen Bryant, FitzGreene Halleck, Bayard Taylor, Henry Clapp, Edmund Clarence Stedman, Walt Whitman, and Artemas Ward. Granted that the Algonquin wits were closer akin to Ward than to Whitman, nevertheless the Round Table was to revive the intellectual glories of the beer hall and give to the intelligentsia of New York an inspiration and a focus. . . .

* * * * *

Upstairs the literati played poker. Anywhere from five to a dozen of the regulars, together with accessions from the outer world, would sit down after dinner on Saturday night and stick to it until Sunday afternoon. Thanks chiefly to F.P.A.'s paragraphings, the Thanatopsis Literary and Inside Straight Club became almost as fabulous a feature of contemporary life as the Round Table. The game was table stakes: that is, there was no limit on any bet except the amount which lay on the table before the bettor. If he chose to shove in his whole pile on a pair of deuces, that was his privilege. Most of the players were of modest financial status; one hundred dollars was a big evening's loss or gain in the early days. Indeed, it was a week's salary or more for all but one or two.

* * * * *

Various traditions, customs, and observances grew up around the table, one of the most popular being the practice of signalizing a flagrantly misplayed hand by all rising and intoning to the strains of the "Englishman" song from *Pinafore*:

"He remains a god-dam fool."

* * * * *

The Thanatopsis died of the dollar. What caused the slower dissolution of the Round Table is not so clear. There was some inevitable scattering of the people who made up the circle. Aleck, himself, quit New York for the country. Others lost interest. The Round Table, as such, ceased to function in 1932. Any barbarian from outer darkness may now loll in that once hallowed spot. Some trailings of Sophisticate glory still persist, however. A handful of the old lot remains faithful to the place; alone of the New York hotels, it preserves a literary aura.

One of the most nostalgic of the Woollcott reminiscences embalms it under the title, "Wayfarer's Inn."

The Girl from Rector's [24]

In his hey-day on Broadway, Mizner lived at Rector's, where many other playwrights of the day were to be found. Here lived Paul Potter, whose play *The Girl from Rector's* really ruined the million-dollar hotel which George Rector and his father had made one of the great hostelries of the world.

Potter had completed the translation of a French farce for Al Woods and the title was undecided. One day Woods arrived at the hotel for a conference with Potter on the forthcoming production. It was raining and as Woods stepped out of his cab a beautiful young girl leaped out of a hansom cab and ran for the door of the restaurant. In those days skirts were worn to the heel, but this shapely and exquisite lady took no chances with the muddy pavements. Skirts high, rippling laughter, the most gorgeous legs and hosiery imaginable made an immediate and dazzling impression on the producer. In later years he could never recall whether he paid the cabman, but when he arrived at Potter's rooms he announced the title of the new play, *The Girl from Rector's.*

It was one of the first of the naughty French type of plays and though it aided Rector's to the pinnacle of success briefly, the association of the name with the play gradually gave the hinterlands the impression that Rector's was the most daring and emotionally dangerous place in New York. The transient trade—bossed by wives from a distance—stopped coming there.

Diamond Jim Brady

HIS STOMACH [25]

. . . A famous eater . . . was Diamond Jim Brady. I can affirm and testify, after looking over the books of that dim era, that Diamond Jim was the best twenty-five customers we had!

[24] From *The Fabulous Wilson Mizner,* by Edward Dean Sullivan, pp. 227–228. Copyright, 1935, by The Henkle Co. New York.

[25] From *The Girl from Rector's,* by George Rector, pp. 14–20. Copyright, 1927, by Doubleday, Page & Company; 1926, 1927, by The Curtis Publishing Company. Garden City, New York.

By permission of Louise Fraser Lensky and Loew's Incorporated.

You will probably recall him as the man who offered Hopkins—I mean the college and not the actress—one hundred thousand dollars in gold if the Hopkins surgeons could give him a new stomach—one from an elephant preferred. The Johns Hopkins surgeons could not perform the feat, but I understand that Diamond Jim left the hospital a magnificent sum for prolonging his life several years.

He was an odd character, and the first of the successful salesmen who utilized the bright lights of Broadway to promote the sale of his commodities. His name was derived from his jewelry, and when Diamond Jim had all his illumination in place, he looked like an excursion steamer at twilight. He had powerful diamonds in his shirt front that cast beams strong enough to sunburn an unwary pedestrian. He had diamonds in his cuffs and actually wore diamond suspender buttons, fore and aft. The fore may have been good taste, but the aft were parvenu. He wore diamonds on his fingers and there was a rumor that he had diamond bridge work. His vest buttons also were precious stones, and I think that when remonstrated with for his excessive display of gems, Mr. Brady remarked, "Them as has 'em wears 'em."

Although his business life led him among the bright lights, Diamond Jim never smoked or drank. But how he ate! He loved to be surrounded by handsome men and beautiful women at the table, and it was no unusual thing for us to lay covers for eight or ten guests of Mr. Brady. If they all kept their appointments, fine! And if nobody showed up but Diamond Jim, fine! Mr. Brady proceeded gravely to eat the ten dinners himself.

It is possible to obtain some idea of his terrific capacity by his average menu under normal conditions. When I say he never drank, I mean intoxicating beverages. His favorite drink was orange juice. I knew just what he wanted, and before he appeared at the table I always commandeered the most enormous carafe in the house. This was filled to the brim with orange juice and cracked ice. He tossed that off without quivering a chin. It was immediately replaced with a duplicate carafe, to be followed by a third, and possibly a fourth before the dinner was over and the last waiter had fainted in the arms of an exhausted chef.

The next item was oysters. Mr. Brady was very fond of sea food. He would eat two or three dozen Lynnhaven oysters, each measuring six inches from tip to tail, if an oyster has either. Wilson Mizner, observing Diamond Jim eating oysters, remarked, "Jim likes his oysters sprinkled with clams." Observing the same diner from a near-by listening post, Mr. Mizner also continued his observations with "Jim likes his sirloin steaks smothered in veal cutlets."

After Diamond Jim had nibbled daintily on three dozen papa oysters, it would be an even bet that he would order another dozen or so just to relieve the monotony. Then would follow a dozen hard-shell crabs, claws and all. There was no soup, which discounts Mizner's statement that Jim fanned the soup with his hat.

Diamond Jim was a gentleman, even though he did wear his napkin around his neck. But this was not due to lack of etiquette, but rather to the conformation of Mr. Brady's topography. A napkin on his knee would have been as inadequate as a doily under a bass drum. Diamond Jim's stomach started at his neck and swelled out in majestic proportions, gaining power and curve as it proceeded southward. Therefore the only place where a napkin would have done him any good was around his neck. And there he wore it. It looked like a bookmark in a tome of chins.

After the crabs, then would come the deluge of lobsters. Lobsters were Rector's specialty and I took special pride in serving none but the finest. Six or seven giants would suffice. Diamond Jim ate them like an expert and cracked their claws like a man. There was no waste except the actual bony structure, which was dropped gracefully aside. A bus boy removed the débris as rapidly as it accumulated. . . .

* * * * *

. . . Then he would order a steak and toy with it until it vanished. But steaks and chops were not his hobby. He loved sea food. Coffee, cakes, and pastry would follow. He selected his cakes carefully—in handfuls. When he pointed at a platter of French pastry he didn't mean any special piece of pastry. He meant the platter.

Then he would order a two-pound box of bonbons from the candy girl and pass them around among his guests. If any guest took a piece of the candy, Diamond Jim would then order another two-pound box for himself. In fact, so great was his love of sweets that he bought a controlling interest in the biggest of candy factories of that time.

He tipped very liberally, because he loved life and wanted everybody to enjoy life with him. I never saw the man do an unkind thing during all the years I knew him. There is no exaggeration in the details of his dinner, because I served him many and he relished every one. He was more of a gourmet than a gourmand, if you can perceive the line of demarcation between the two. If there is any reader who thinks that I am taking a ghoulish delight in rehashing the account of Diamond Jim Brady's personal habits, all I can say is that I wish I could have enjoyed Rector's cuisine as Diamond Jim did. Furthermore, he was a man who spent his money lavishly. Anybody could get a thousand from him in the days when a thousand dollars was an incredible sum. If you don't think it was, just hark back to the diaries of Rockefeller and Ford and read their stories of how they saved their first thousand. Today a thousand is nothing.

His friends used to remonstrate with him and caution him against the many leeches who preyed on him. Even I, although merely a servant seeking to please my patrons, took advantage of our friendship and said, "Mr. Brady, you shouldn't encourage these people. They haven't the slightest intention of paying you back. They are trimming you."

Mr. Brady said, "H'm"—he was munching candy—"what do you mean?"

I replied, "Just what I said. They are making a sucker out of you."

He answered me with the retort that proved the business acumen that lay under that massive frame. His rejoinder was a thorough analysis of his entire character, which was a desire to be a free spender and at the same time know what he was accomplishing with his money. He had no illusions about the butterflies who hovered around the gleaming torches in his shirt front. He knew them far better than they knew him, because every night he wasted with them was not a night wasted for him. He piled up millions while spending thousands.

What he answered was: "Being a sucker is fun—if you can afford it."

* * * * *

I almost forgot to add that when Diamond Jim had dinner in Rector's it was the usual prelude to an evening at the theatre. On the way to the show he would stop his car at a store and purchase another two-pound box of candy manufactured by the company he controlled. That would be finished before the curtain rose, and it was nothing unusual for him to buy another box between acts. After the show he would return to Rector's for a midnight snack.

HOW HE KNEW WHEN HE HAD HAD ENOUGH TO EAT[26]

. . . People said that Diamond Jim Brady had eaten more than two hundred ears of corn at one sitting. They said that he thought nothing of eating a whole leg of lamb, or an entire ham for his entrée at dinner. The stories finally piqued the curiosity of one railroad mag-

[26] From *Diamond Jim,* The Life and Times of James Buchanan Brady, by Parker Morell, pp. 235–236. Copyright, 1934, by Parker Morell. New York: Simon and Schuster, Inc.

nate's wife and she decided to get the truth of things by inviting him to dinner at her home.

In all fairness to the curious hostess it must be admitted that she really lived up to her share of the bargain, for knowing that Jim was fond of sea food she saw that a shore dinner of truly gigantic proportions was provided. For more than two hours the unsuspecting guest fulfilled his duties. He ate everything that was set before him—to the sixth and seventh helping. Finally, when there was nothing more to be eaten, the hostess decided that the time had come to strike.

"You must be very proud of your appetite, Mr. Brady," she said sweetly.

"Yes, ma'am, I am," said Jim, without the slightest suspicion that he was being baited.

"And how do you ever know when your appetite is satiated?" even more sweetly.

"Why, ma'am, I'll tell you," Jim answered seriously. "Whenever I sit down to a meal, I always make it a point to leave just four inches between my stummick and the edge of the table. And then, when I can feel 'em rubbin' together pretty hard, I know I've had enough."

The lady's horrified gasp still echoes in the drawing rooms of upper Fifth Avenue.

HIS NEW STOMACH[27]

Broadway, of course, had a thousand different explanations for Jim's miraculous escape from the jaws of death. The details of his $220,000 gift had not been made clear to the public at large, and this caused all sorts of fantastic stories: the Baltimore surgeons had grafted the stomach of a pig into Brady. It wasn't the stomach of a pig, but the stomach of a cow, and henceforth he would have to live exclusively on green vegetables and grass. No, his new stomach was neither a pig's nor a cow's, but another human being's! He had paid $200,000 to the widow of a Baltimore working man for her husband's digestive organs. Each group professed to have the correct information, direct from someone who was very close to Jim.

When the Phoenix-like Brady returned to New York in August, 1912, it was to the accompaniment of more newspaper publicity than the arrival of any other man had occasioned since Dewey came back from Manila Bay. Every paper in town sent its best reporters to the Eighty-sixth Street house, there to be received by a beaming Jim who

[27] *Ibid.*, pp. 252–256.

steadfastly refused to part with any tangible facts for the edification of a palpitating public.

"The details of my restoration I would rather have told by Dr. Hugh Young, who devised the treatment," the *World* quoted him as saying. "He is in Europe now, and I'd rather not speak without his consent. All I know is that I thought I was dying, that Broadway, the theatres, the crowds, the restaurants that I love, would never see me again and here I am feeling as if my sixty years were only sixteen. I'm going to give a big dinner party at the Vanderbilt Hotel on Friday night to show that the cure is permanent."

And so, because the reading public demanded news—red-hot facts and figures—the *World* man dressed the story up. He went down into the kitchen and talked with Jim's cook and the result was that the next morning's front page blazed with the following:

HIS GOLD LINED STOMACH MAKES LIFE A JOY AGAIN
Diamond Jim Brady, as He Puts in a Lively and Lovely Day
at the Table, Says His Gastronomic Delight is Worth
the $220,000 He Paid for Cure.
Out, Pepsin! In, Pullet! Cantaloupe, Bacon, Broiled Bass, Turtle
Soup, and Guinea Hen Among Things He
Eats—Coffee and Cigars, Too!

Big, genial Diamond Jim Brady, millionaire several times over and possessor of the only $220,000 stomach in the world—rated by the sum he has just presented to the Johns Hopkins University for restoring his appetite, digestion and joy in life, said earnestly to a *World* reporter last night:

"They certainly handed me back a newly lined, high-powered, pliant, and pleasantly dispositioned stomach—the kind I had when I was twelve years old and could eat a raw turnip with relish. Why, if you roasted a full-size bull moose and just put me in front of it, I guess I could eat the whole thing, and you'd probably find me gnawing at the hoofs and antlers. And no pepsin powders afterwards, either."

Stomach trouble wouldn't have been so intolerable in the first place if Diamond Jim hadn't been so very fond of his "eats." — One of Broadway's gladdest gourmets he always was; never so highly pleased as when he was acting as host to a happy company in a fashionable restaurant. But it is heartbreaking to sit at the head of a board as a host who has to wear a smile that is a pain to expand and a stomach the same, only more so, and to see the delicious dishes with the wonderful sauces going the other way while you sip at weak tea, and nibble at a wisp of toasted stale bread.

Such had been Diamond Jim's fate for a long time. If he dared to partake of a delicacy or two, it was always with the apprehension of going up, soon afterwards, to talk it over with the angels. Once or twice he narrowly missed taking the big jump as they call it on Broadway. His daily menu got to be something like this:

BREAKFAST

Milk Toast (half a slice) Egg (white of one)
Pepsin and bismuth ad lib

LUNCHEON

Potato, one crushed in buttermilk Pepsin and bismuth ad lib

DINNER

Bacon (one rasher) Egg (one poached)
Lettuce (two sprigs) Tea, one-half cup (weak)
Pepsin and bismuth strong

But NOW! Get a battalion of waiters and a corps of cooks and slam good grub along ad lib to the joyous Diamond Jim Brady. And cut out the pepsin and bismuth entirely.

Yesterday—well, here is his day's bill of fare:

BREAKFAST

Canteloupe (full portion) Oatmeal Bacon and Eggs
Watercress Marmalade
Coffee (one pot) Cigars

LUNCHEON

Olives Clams Radishes
Broiled Bass
Asparagus Potatoes Tomatoes
Omelette Soufflé
Dessert
Coffee Cigars

DINNER

Olives Anchovies Radishes
Turtle Soup Broiled Bluefish
Potatoes Peas Spinach
Sweetbreads
Broiled Guinea Hen à la Bercy
Salad Ice Cream
Coffee Cheese Fancy Cakes
Cigars

His eyes were shining as brightly as his seventy-four horsepower diamond stickpin, or his incandescent cuff buttons, or his glittering waistcoat buttons, or his gem-encrusted fingers as he said:

"Two hundred and twenty thousand dollars isn't much to give for a new stomach when you need one as much as I did. I had to go through months of rigorous treatment to get it. That was no joke. But the reward is great stuff. I do not feel at liberty to go into the details of the treatment through which I have come out of the hospital a fully restored man, though I went there a wreck. But I do know that I made up my mind to give persons less fortunate than myself, and afflicted as I was, a chance for treatment."

Bet-a-Million Gates [28]

Gates' custom of betting on anything sometimes found peculiar expression. He and his friends developed a habit of betting on the course of the Stock Market as if it were a horse race. But probably the most bizarre tale that survives to exemplify Gates' habit of mind is of what followed one afternoon session of poker in his apartment. Gates, Lambert, Drake and several others had been playing for hours, when toward dark a heavy rainstorm came up, and to the jaded gamblers it provided something novel to occupy attention that had become strained from long contemplation of the familiar spots and "faces" of a pack of pasteboards.

The pelting of raindrops on the windowpanes made Gates' eyes brighten. Here was motion. He noted that some drops moved quickly down the glass, while others, for whatever reason, progressed more slowly to the sash below.

"Say, John," he suddenly remarked to Drake, "see them two raindrops? I'll bet that fellow on this side reaches the bottom before that one over there."

Ten dollars was the first stake, and then this jumped to one hundred. It was a new sport and it became lively. For some minutes, at least, the crowd staked hundred-dollar bills on the course and speed of rain-

[28] From *Peacocks on Parade,* A Narrative of a Unique Period in American Social History and Its Most Colorful Figures, by Albert Stevens Crockett, pp. 128, 130–132. Copyright, 1931, by the Sears Publishing Company, Inc. New York.

drops chasing down a windowpane, just as if they were at some racetrack, playing the ponies.

* * * * *

Gates had a son called "Charlie," a good-looking youngster, but born without much of that gray matter of whose possession his male parent gave evidence—the typical son of a rich man who had found fortune easy and swift and had spoiled his offspring. The indulgent parent had rented an office which, in the early days of the Waldorf, had done duty as a small dining or entertainment room, and put Charlie into the brokerage business with J. F. Harris, under the firm name of "Harris, Gates & Company," with the elder Gates as their "silent partner." It was said he put $500,000 into the business. During Wall Street hours, Gates would make Charlie's office his headquarters, and his operations were not confined to mere buying and selling, but included betting on just how much stock would go up within a certain number of hours—or even minutes—how fast one stock would move as compared with another, and so on. And that office was the scene of many a stiff card game after the close of the Stock Exchange.

Occasionally, but not often, some man who was not of the "bunch" would be invited to "sit in," particularly if one of the regulars happened to be out-of-town. The place came to be a great resort for visiting Westerners. Gates, "Ike" Ellwood, John Drake, and a few others of their set were great devotees of bridge, as well as poker, and in that office on Saturday afternoons a four-handed game was almost inevitable. Often what to an ordinary man would represent a huge fortune would change hands in the office of Harris, Gates & Company, during a few hours' play. At one of these games, only three members of the regular crowd being present, a prominent New York officeholder and politician, rated as a "crackerjack" player, was invited to "make a fourth."

By no means a person of wealth as his hosts counted theirs, caution made him inquire, as casually as he could, as he sat down to take his hand: "By the way, what are we playing for?"

"One a point," Gates answered tersely.

The New Yorker breathed more freely. The game began and continued. Foy, Gates' secretary, taking tabs, at the end figured the winnings and losses. The visitor, it developed, had come out three hundred and thirty points ahead.

"You'll get your check tomorrow—or rather on Monday," said Foy, as the visitor left—which promise, of course, was satisfactory to the politician.

When on Monday at breakfast he drew the check out of its envelope, he fell back in astonishment. There, in plain letters and figures, it ordered a certain bank to pay to him, or bearer, the sum of $33,000.

The winner, breaking into a cold sweat, cut short his breakfast. As soon as he could stand on his feet, he grabbed his hat and coat, commandeered a cab and rushed up to the Waldorf-Astoria, where he sought Foy, Gates' secretary. As the latter came out of the elevator, the politician greeted him excitedly, waving the check.

"Mr. Foy," he said breathlessly. "You have made a tremendous mistake here. Look! Why, this check calls for the payment of thirty-three thousand dollars!"

"Oh, no," Foy answered quietly. "There is no mistake. You were three hundred and thirty points ahead at the finish. Well, at a hundred dollars a point, doesn't that work out to thirty-three thousand?"

"My God!" exclaimed the lucky man. "It can't be true." He had not imagined for a moment that the points had counted more than one dollar each, at the outside.

He was not satisfied with Foy's assurance, but sought Gates. "Mr. Gates," he protested, "I don't feel right in taking this money, because, in a sense, I got it under false pretenses. I am a poor man, but if I had lost this sum of money, I could have scraped together enough, I guess, to pay my losses. But I can tell you it would have hurt like hell, and so I don't feel this check belongs to me."

"Cut it out," Gates replied. "We had the game, didn't we? You won, didn't you? You got the check, didn't you? Well, let's forget about it."

Out-of-Towners on the Town [29]

. . . One night club waiter captain has devised a system for identifying [out-of-towners], sectionally at any rate, by their teeth.

It has been the experience of this man, who is considered a comer at the Copacabana and whose blanket designation for all non-New Yorkers is "hoops," that the teeth of Westerners are large, square and white; that those of Midwesterners are somewhat darker and a little more horsy, although not buck. He found Southerners to have teeth

[29] From "Night Life: Brash, Bubbly and Boppy, Out-of-Towners are Known to Night Clubs by Their Recklessness and Their Teeth," by Gilbert Millstein. *New York Times Magazine,* April 29, 1956, Section 6, Part 2, pp. 56–57, 69. Copyright, 1956, by the New York Times Company.

that were both smaller and rather more tarnished than those of Midwesterners. He had no line, he said on New Englanders, "because they rarely open their mouths," and he declared of New Yorkers: "Their teeth are like their clothes—worked on. They have Brooks Brothers teeth."

Whatever the state of their dentition, or even of their finances, out-of-towners account for 30 to 75 per cent of the trade of New York's night clubs and they are cultivated with a tenderness of the kind formerly reserved only for celebrities, moneyed hoodlums and the late James J. Walker. The steady rise of the non-New Yorker in the ephemeral estimation of cabaret owners and headwaiters is the result of a number of things, one of which may be termed the factor of ironic democratization: taxes have decimated the ranks of local big spenders; tax-free expense accounts have made it possible for nonresidents to tarry at the fleshpots. While a good many New Yorkers have expense accounts, too, they use them, in the main, to entertain out-of-towners, thereby producing not much more than a grave exchange of economical amenities at high prices paid by other people. Any real money possessed by a New Yorker, after he has paid his taxes, furnished his home and sent his children to school, is apt to be spent on a vacation.

He never spends his vacation in New York night clubs, if only because he has a television set which will give him far more expensive entertainment for nothing. The out-of-towner is equally harried by taxes and comforted by television, but he is drawn to New York with an ineluctable fascination. (The city annually entertains in the neighborhood of 13,000,000 visitors.) "He comes to New York," a respected cabaret owner with a large clientele outside the metropolitan area observed recently, "to find what he hasn't got in his home town—and if he had it in his own town, he wouldn't patronize it. It isn't for real unless he's seen it in New York and can tell folks back home about it. It is," he concluded, "a good thing for us he feels that way."

The leveling-off process has been profound. The sightseeing-bus people, for example, who once shuttled resolutely between Grant's Tomb and Chinatown, and whose customers, although worthy and from out of town, were hardly regarded as the mainstay of the cabaret business, have added a carefully frenetic slice of night life to their itineraries. Tour 8 of the Gray Line runs the gamut for $14.75 per person and "There Is Nothing more to Pay." It includes: "Cocktail and Full Course Dinner" at the Copacabana at 6:45 P.M.; "One Drink of Choice" at Sammy's Bowery Follies, a downtown institution in which the raffishness of other days has been carefully reconstructed over sawdust, at 10:30 P.M.; and another "drink of choice" in the Hawaiian Room of the Lexington Hotel at midnight, to say nothing of floor shows in all three places. Everybody goes home at one.

In urging its patrons to "Get Set for Your Liveliest and Smartest 'Night Out' in New York City," the company adds in its brochure: "Unescorted ladies are of course welcome to join our night life party. (GENTLEMEN WILL WEAR COATS AND TIES.)" "The waiters don't hustle anybody—tips are part of the deal," a man named Eddie Blaine, who is Gray's director of sales and traffic, pointed out. "And may I say we are the salvation of the unescorted woman in New York," he added, noting that not long ago the firm had shepherded, among others, 300 ladies of the Desk and Derrick Club, an oil-industry employes' group.

Gray's closest competition appears to be Times Square Sightseeing Lines, Inc., which, by a coincidence also has a Tour 8. This is, however, really only an extension of its No. 7. No. 7 is a two-hour trip through the Bowery ("The Street of Forgotten Men"), Greenwich Village ("Nite Clubs and Artist Colony"), and the Lower East Side ("The most congested streets in New York"). In making No. 8 out of No. 7, the line added an after-dark visit to the R. C. A. Observation Roof and the Latin Quarter. At the Latin Quarter, the visitor, says the folder, "is regaled by the eye-filling floor show of the famous 'Latin Quarter.' A full course chicken (or fish) dinner is served," and, as far as the company is concerned, clients can hang around the club until closing time, which is 4 A.M. daily and 3 A.M. Sunday mornings. The price is $12.95, tip and tax in tab.

There is an impressive number of out-of-towners whose idea of strenuous goings-on in New York at night is in-person attendance at television shows, tickets for which are free but not always available. Not content with sitting in comfort before their screens, such people may spend important sums of money to get to some bleak studio or former theatre, there to stand on line ultimately to see, for instance, the filming of the Jackie Gleason show; Arthur Godfrey, Ed Sullivan, Steve Allen (for stay-up-lates fond of audience participation) and all the quiz shows, by means of which they may conceivably return home with more money than they brought.

As reported by the Convention and Visitors Bureau, the taste of out-of-towners is quite catholic, a man from Rapid City, S. D., having recently inquired about (a) the location of Ambrose Lightship; (b) the name of the manager of the Colony Restaurant (he was advised to write to the restaurant and find out); (c) what he might expect to find on Rikers Island; (d) where Governors Island is, and (e) where the Park Sheraton Hotel is.

Not all, or even most, non-New Yorkers spend their nights here going to television shows, looking up the manager of the Colony Restaurant or spilling out of rubberneck buses into night clubs. A great many of them go to night clubs in taxicabs or their own cars, after first having dined in such altitudes as the Pavillon or Twenty-one and gone to the theatre, where they were not forced to stand on line but for which tickets were not free, either. In any case, aside from their teeth, there are certain folk characteristics common to all. (These days, the clothes of the visitors are practically indistinguishable from those of New Yorkers, being equally well tailored, just as expensive and equipped, if the wearer cares, with shoulders as narrow as those affected by any Madison Avenue esthete.)

However recklessly they play on a visit to the city, out-of-towners tend to look slightly less knocked about than New Yorkers. "New Yorkers," according to a sociologist who works for a living running a night club, "are perpetually drunk—not with whisky, but with motion—with subways, buses, cabs." Out-of-towners will telephone ahead for reservations with greater regularity than city people; they will accept the edicts of a maître d'hôtel and the tastes of a waiter with greater docility.

Upon entering a night club, it is their habit to scrutinize the room first, for geographical reasons, and then to narrow their focus to a search for celebrities. The New Yorker already knows the room and looks for his friends. "This is where the out-of-towner gives himself away," the night club owner went on. "He can't case a room with aplomb; he can't quite hide that eager look. Sometimes a New Yorker has reason to look around but the way he does it is neither furtive nor with hope. It is secret and beautiful. He doesn't rush, but he can count the house before he is seated."

New Yorkers are Scotch drinkers. Non-New Yorkers almost invariably call for "a shot" and are invariably surprised if served rye instead of bourbon. They are inclined to get elated earlier than New Yorkers, but this is unquestionably because they are away from home with nothing much more on their minds than the problem of getting elated. They will not only take a waiter's advice, they will exchange the time of night with him, ask for recipes, take away menus, give him their card and display wallets bulging with other cards—car-rental cards, airline credit cards, gasoline credit cards, dining credit cards and fraternal organization membership cards.

City people will give a check a careful rundown and then tip 15 to 20 per cent on the total less tax. Out-of-towners tip on the total, which they do not examine with too great care, but have a habit, depending on the state of their psychic security and hometown mores, of either undertipping or overtipping.

Sidewalk Superintendents [30]

Two types of people put up buildings in New York—those who are glad to let you watch construction and those who aren't. Sidewalk superintendents can be a terrible nuisance, getting in the way of trucks, gear, and workmen, but their hearts are in the right place; the admiration they express by merely standing and staring consists largely of a frustrated desire to dig dirt, blast rock, pour concrete, weld steel, lay brick, and otherwise lend a helping hand, and we think it only fitting that their tireless vigils should be made as comfortable and rewarding as possible. To the best of our knowledge, Rockefeller Center provided the first occasion on which, by cutting a number of portholes in the fence that surrounded the site, builders gave formal encouragement to sidewalk superintending. The reason for this great step forward is said to have been that Mr. Rockefeller, himself a gifted sidewalk superintendent, was brusquely ordered to keep moving when, one morning, he paused at a gap in the fence and peered inside. Over the years, various benign property owners and builders have contrived similar points of vantage, but it remained for the House of Seagram, currently engaged in putting up a skyscraper on Park Avenue, between Fifty-second and Fifty-third Streets, to give sidewalk superintendents what is, in this country and especially in this city, the ultimate accolade; to wit, their own commercials.

In the gray fencing that encloses three sides of the Seagram site, six sets of Plexiglas portholes have been installed. There are three portholes to a set, and they're graduated in height to accommodate superintendents tall, short, and middle-sized. Above each set of portholes is a small but powerful loudspeaker, and out of it pours a stream of transcribed messages from such distinguished personages as Faye Emerson, Hy Gardner, and Danton Walker, who plug the about-to-be building and themselves. . . .

[30] From "The Talk of the Town," *The New Yorker*, Vol. XXXII (June 2, 1956), No. 15, p. 23. Copyright, 1956, by The New Yorker Magazine, Inc. New York.

13

Eight Million Stories

It is a fiery story that is unfolded here; only, it is not one story, it is eight million stories. . . . Yes! anything can happen in this most crazy and curious of towns. Even we who have lived here all our lives find that adventure lurks around every corner.—Charles Hanson Towne

The Fire Club Plays "Follow Your Leader" [1]

. . . Thomas H. Smith, besides being the greatest tea merchant of his day, was also the greatest *Spreeite* of his day. He was the President of a club called "The Fire Club." It held its meetings in Franklin Square on the corner of Dover Street. Boys have a mode of amusement called "Follow your leader." This was adopted by the Club of which Smith was President. Many men who are now aged and respected men, or dead, belonged to the "Fire Club," Joseph Foulke, a trader at Curaçao, a Dutch Island in the West Indies, and the Staggs. There was old Peter Stagg, cashier of the City Bank, and John and Benjamin Stagg. There was old Matthias Bruen, and many more whose names were on the

[1] From *The Old Merchants of New York City,* by Walter Barrett [Joseph A. Scoville], Vol. I, pp. 33–37. Entered . . . 1862, by Geo. W. Carleton. New York.

Club list. They gave grand suppers, and their entertainments were very expensive. They would invite a guest to these suppers, explain the rules, and if he refused to join, or could not carry out the idea, the fine was one dozen of champagne. These fines were occasioned by a refusal to follow the leader. On one occasion a great cotton merchant from New Orleans was a guest. He agreed to all the conditions. It was late in the evening, in the dead of winter. The ice in the East River was floating up and down with every flood or ebb of the tide. "Follow leader," shouted Smith, and out of the warm, luxurious club rooms poured the members of the Club. Out of the Square, around the corner into Dover Street. "Follow leader," and on rushed Smith, the President of the Club, with thirty men behind him, down Dover, past Water, past Front, into South, and thence on to the pier. One of Smith's own ships lay at the dock. A lighter lay inside of the main wharf. The ice was loose and dashed up around the vessels. "Follow leader," exclaimed Smith, as he plunged from the dock into the water. Some drew back, but others followed the leader, who succeeded in getting out of the ice water on to the lighter, and from thence to the dock; and shouting "Follow leader," he led off with frozen clothes, up Dover and into the room of the Club. Plunge, plunge, plunge, one after another, and so on until all had successfully accomplished the terrible and dangerous feat. The Southern cotton merchant was last. Some of the regular club members remained until they saw him reach the dock again safely, and there they left him shivering. He did not remain long. As he walked up from the dock, he noticed a large store open in South Street. He entered. It was a wholesale and retail ship stores. "I have met with an accident—give me a glass of cognac, hot, with sugar and water." It was done, and he drank it. "Do you keep gunpowder?" he asked. Receiving an affirmative reply, he bought and paid for half a keg, and then took his way to the club room. At the door was standing Mr. Lowe and Mr. Town, two members of the Club. The latter exclaimed, "Brave Southern stranger—you have passed the ordeal safely. You are now *leader,* and we are deputed to place the Club under your command, if you choose to exert your sacred privilege."

"Thanks, my friends, I shall do so, but I will not ask you to go out of the room this cold night. Let us drink!" and as he entered the room, he sought a side closet where hung his cloak. There he placed the keg, and then returned and took a seat at the long solid mahogany table. President Smith called the Club to order. The stewards for the night opened a dozen of champagne amid shouts, calls, and songs of the most stirring character. "Order, come to order!" exclaimed President Smith.

When order was partially restored, he said: "Members of the club, our guest has passed the icy ordeal. He has now the right of becoming leader for the balance of the night, or until a failure in our sacred rites. What says he?"

The cotton merchant took from his bosom a bundle of tow, and laid it on the table. All eyes were fixed upon him. "I accept the command. I will lead now. Wait until I give the word and do as you see me do." By this time, he had spun the tow into a string, that would reach from the table to the grate. He placed a tumbler on one end of the tow, to hold it on the table, and then passed the other to the pan under the grate, and made that fast with a piece of coal from the coal scuttle. Not a word was spoke. All felt that something unusual was to occur. Cotton Merchant now deliberately went to the closet and returning with the keg took his seat. Then he went to work and removed the hoops, until he could take out the head of the little keg. Not a soul moved. Then he took a very little of what appeared to be black sand in his hand, walked to the fire, and flung it in. The considerable explosion that followed startled all. "Powder, by Jupiter," exclaimed Smith. Cotton Merchant took the end of the tow line from the glass, and pushed it down deep into the powder in the keg, and then reseated himself. "Now, Mr. President and members of the club, I wish you to hear what I have to say.

"You have tried my pluck. I come from a hot climate, and you have made me go through an icy ordeal. It is my time now, but I will not be so cruel. I will give you a *fiery ordeal* to go through. If you stand it, you will never need more wine; and if you do not, the fines will amount to a small fortune, and you will have wine enough to last your club a year. Look at me." He walked to the fire, kicked off the coal lump, and placed the other end of the tow-line in the red-hot coals. Then he walked back, and as he brought his fist down upon the table said in tones of thunder as he sat down, "Keep your seats, and thus follow your leader." The fire curled up in fitful spouts from the burning tar—it burnt over the grate pan, and began to crawl along the carpet. It had eighteen feet to go. Sixty and odd single eyes watched the burning train. One rose from his seat, then another, finally one exclaimed, "We shall all be blown to old Nick," and made for the door. The panic increased. Down stairs the club members plunged like a flock of sheep. Even Old Smith, the President, was among the first to bolt from the room. Before the tow-line had burned as far as the table all were gone but the cotton merchant. As soon as he saw that he was alone, he placed his foot upon the burning tow, and extinguished it. Then he opened the window and emptied the keg into the snow, and again resumed his seat. He waited long for the return of the club members; one by one they did come back. There Cotton sat, until Smith took his seat as President. "Now call for the fines," he said, and a severe lecture he gave them for their follies and real cowardice. The club died long ago.

A Fortune in Gulf Stream Water [2]

After the rapid development of the petroleum industry in the early eighties, when large refineries were established at Bayonne and elsewhere around the front yard of New York, much complaint used to be made that the waters of the bay were being polluted by the deposits of the oil offal, particularly of a fluid called "sludge acid" that was supposed to be most obnoxious. I think it must have been to fish, certainly, for I can remember when there used to be oyster beds in the East River, and the sludge acid did for them. The outcries of the populace finally found their way to the legislature, as such complaints do at times, and an investigation was instituted at which many experts, Harvard graduates, chemists, scientists, and other Wise Men of the Earth were good enough to testify. These succeeded in establishing:

1. There was much sludge acid in the waters of the bay.
2. There was no sludge acid in the waters of the bay.
3. Sludge acid was an injurious and undesirable menace.
4. Sludge acid was an innocent substance that hurt nobody.

As a reporter I had faithfully recorded these important additions to the sum of human knowledge, and they came forcibly back to me with the next chapter unfolded now of the tale of a pilot-boat at sea.

Old sailors believed that the water of the Gulf Stream was highly medicinal and with other blessings was a certain specific against rheumatism. There used to be an old retired ship captain living on the hill back of Tompkinsville that suffered at intervals from this ancient and

[2] From *From Sandy Hook to 62°*, Being Some Account of the Adventures, Exploits and Services of the Old New York Pilot-Boat, by Charles Edward Russell, pp. 295–298. Copyright, 1920, by Charles Edward Russell. New York and London: The Century Co.

honorable foe of mankind. When the attacks came upon him he always turned in his thoughts to the healing waters of the Gulf Stream and wished he had a barrel of them.

In those days the usual anchorage for pilot-boats was not far below the captain's house, and he had made the acquaintance of several of the boatkeepers, including one that he chiefly admired, by name Michael Jonas. One day he limped down to the landing with a large jug that he gave to Jonas and asked to have it filled on the next trip with water from the ever precious Gulf Stream, the rheumatism being powerful bad that winter.

When the boat returned from her next trip the captain was at the waterside to welcome her.

"Mike, did you bring my Gulf Stream water?" he called out.

Jonas had to acknowledge that in the press of so many other things he had forgotten about the all-healing Gulf Stream, but the next time he would surely remember.

This happened the next four trips. Jonas, conscience-stricken whenever he saw at the wharf the anxious face of the old captain, tried various devices to fortify his memory. He tied a string around a finger, but the string always came off. He put up a chalk-mark above his bunk and the cabin boy, in the interest of orderliness, rubbed it out. He told his sailors to remind him, and they always spoke of it when the boat was a hundred miles from the Stream. It was easy enough to tell himself when on shore that this time he would surely remember, but when he was at sea, what with the work he must do and the responsibility for the boat and the observations three times a day and the log and the blame' sailors and the state of the yawl and the rip in the forestaysail and what not, it always got away from him.

At last, one afternoon when they were reaching up from the Narrows on their way in, he saw the pathetic figure of the captain waiting for him, and he felt that he could stand the thing no longer. He took the jug from its hook, wove a line upon it, and dropping it over the side away from the shore, filled it with the waters of the bay.

"It's all salty, anyway," he said to himself, "What's the diff?"

"Mike, did you get my Gulf Stream water?" queried his poor old friend the moment the boat came to anchor.

"You bet I did, Cap," said the shameless Mike, and held up the jug. The captain could hardly wait until the yawl had brought the treasure ashore.

Two days afterward the captain, already vastly improved in health, was rowed out to the pilot-boat in search of the boatkeeper.

"How did you like your Gulf Stream water?" asked Mike, inwardly skeptical but sincerely desirous to please.

"Great!" shouted the captain. "See what it's done for me already. I can dance a jig. But that ain't what I want to talk about now. Mike, come over where we can talk business. Mike, do you want to get rich? I've got the greatest thing in the world. Do you remember where you dipped up that Gulf Stream water? Got the exact spot right? Well, sir, then it's the surest thing in the world. Mike, keep it all to yourself and we'll go shares on it. I don't want but ten per cent for myself. You take all the rest. Mike, there's an oil well at the bottom of the sea where you got that water. All we've got to do is to go out there and scoop up the oil in barrels. Mike, it's worth millions."

"No Violets for Him"[3]

. . . The memorable event of [1888] for New Yorkers will always be the blizzard on March 11, 12, and 13. New York was isolated for several days. Our managing-editor got his Boston news by way of Ireland, sent orders therefor to Cape Ann by the Mackay-Bennett cables and received reply by the same route. All electric lights were out for two nights. I slept on a table in the *Herald* office. The snow drifted to such depths that many people had to tunnel from the basements of their dwellings. The day before that blizzard dear old Walt Whitman sent to me a pretty little verse, entitled "The First Violet of Spring." I marked it for the editorial page and went home early. It was a beautiful night. When the paper was on the streets next morning, the joke was on me. Town and country were in the grasp of the Storm King! Ten thousand gods of trouble were loosed! I didn't hear the last of "The First Violet" for many a day. Poor Walt felt badly about the mishap—as if he were to blame—and didn't want to accept the money I sent to him for the brief verse. When I last saw him, shortly before his death, he apologized for the upset of the Weather Bureau. Again, when I stood beside his tomb as a pallbearer, I tenderly recalled his self-abnegation and sorrow over the discomfiture of a poet and an editor by the Powers of all-potent Nature.

[3] From *The Book of New York,* Forty Years' Recollections of the American Metropolis, by Julius Chambers, pp. 119–120. Copyright, 1912, by Julius Chambers. New York: The Book of New York Company.

An example of what I had to endure will suffice. The following poem, written in mock Walt Whitman style, appeared in a contemporary:

TO J.C., PERSONAL AND AFFECTIONATE

"The weather to-day in New York and its vicinity promises to be generally fair and cooler, preceded by partial cloudiness near the coast. To-morrow, it promises to be slightly warmer and generally fair."—Weather Report in the *Herald,* March 12, 1888.

NO VIOLETS FOR HIM

Roaring, imperial beauty, Julius, icicicular, valvular,
coruscating, diamond-sheened, sun-dazzling,
Montana blizzard, Dakota blizzard—blizzard from Buffalo-land;
Julius, weather-prophet, stormy-eyed, accurate. Arctic in
sunshine, tropical amid the snows;
Herald-governing, salary-raising Julius!
Lord of the cable, the wire, the thin, clammy type, millions
of spray-like sheets;
No bananas, nor oranges, nor feathery pines, nor odoriferous
pine-cones;
Nor mint-juleps, fragrant with spices and fruit, cold with
hurried, tumbling ice—
But hyperborean night, sombre, deadening night!
O Julius, with the weather prophet's eye!

Walt Whitman

Days afterward, when I obtained the original copy, I recognized the handwriting as that of my beloved friend, John Russell Young. This shows the *camaraderie* and jollity that existed in the *Herald* office during the storm, when most of the editors and reporters slept upon tables, under their overcoats. In the press-room "blankets" were taken from the presses for wrappings.

The Murder of David Graham Phillips [4]

. . . The work that enslaved Phillips cost him his life. A crazed conception of one of the characters in *The Fashionable Adventures of*

[4] From *David Graham Phillips and His Times,* by Isaac F. Marcosson, pp. 303–304. Copyright, 1932, by Isaac F. Marcosson. New York: Dodd, Mead & Company.

Joshua Craig led to his assassination. The circumstance of his taking-off was as dramatic as any scene his imagination devised. His own words, "life is a minute and youth a second," put, by a curious coincidence, into the mouth of Joshua Craig, proved to be tragically prophetic.

Late in the summer of 1910, Phillips began to get anonymous, and sometimes threatening, letters abusing him for his cynical delineation of American society women, and particularly the type embodied in the heroine of *The Fashionable Adventures of Joshua Craig*. He had received hundreds of similar letters, signed and unsigned, while "The Treason of the Senate" was appearing. It is no unusual experience with a fearless writer who deals with controversial subjects, whether in books or magazines. He laid the new attack to the vaporings of a crank and went his way.

It later developed that all these letters had been written by Fitzhugh Coyle Goldsborough. Member of an old and well-known Washington family, he was a talented violinist and also an aspiring poet. From his youth he had been more or less eccentric. Highly temperamental and emotional, he began to brood over fancied wrongs, chief of which was the Phillips attitude toward the vagaries of women as expressed in his books. He appeared to regard it as a personal affront to his own conception of the sex. All this brooding upset his mind. He developed into a paranoiac whose complex was Phillips. It was evident from documents he left behind that he believed Margaret Severence, the leading female character in *The Fashionable Adventures of Joshua Craig*, to be a caricature of his sister. As a matter of fact Phillips had never heard of the Goldsborough family.

Goldsborough's diary showed that he had read most of Phillips's books, and furthermore had followed his progress. In order to exercise a closer personal espionage he rented a front room at the Rand School of Social Science in Nineteenth Street, where he could watch the Phillips apartment. In this way he became familiar with the movements of his quarry.

Because of the hours of work that he kept, Phillips and [his sister] Mrs. [Carolyn] Frevert usually had breakfast about noon. It was the author's invariable custom to take a long walk immediately afterward, first stopping at the Princeton Club, then located in the old Stanford White house at the corner of Lexington Avenue and Gramercy Park, to get his mail. His sister usually joined him later on, and they took their promenade together.

At 1:30 o'clock in the afternoon of Monday, January 23, 1911,

Phillips left the apartment to follow his usual schedule. He had circled the western end of Gramercy Park and was within a few doors of the club when Goldsborough, who had been lying in wait for him, pumped six shots into him, saying, "Now I have you." He then shot himself in the right temple and fell dead in the gutter.

Phillips was taken to Bellevue Hospital, where he made a strong fight for life. At first his physicians held out hope. The wound in the lung, however, proved fatal. He lingered until 11:10 o'clock Tuesday night. Just before he expired he said, "I could have won against two bullets but not against six."

Phillips received a public funeral. Hundreds of persons from every walk of life gathered at St. George's Church to honor the man and his work. It was a demonstration such as has been accorded to few authors in this country. The remains were laid to rest in Kensico Cemetery. Upon the simple Ionic cross that guards his grave are carved the words: "Father, forgive them, for they know not what they do." The forbearance which was the keynote of the Phillips character is here revealed in enduring granite.

An O. Henry Ending

I[5]

. . . The morning newspapers brought me the news of [O. Henry's] death. Next day, Franklin P. Adams called me up to say that the funeral would be at the Little Church Around the Corner, that those in charge had selected a squad of indefinitely prominent citizens as pallbearers, and that he, Adams, had intervened to put on the list "some of Bill's friends in his own game." Would I serve?

I reached the church a little early. Waiting at the gate, I found Richard Harding Davis, also a pallbearer and also dressed in the Prince Albert Coat and the top hat then appropriate to mourning. As we waited, three open automobiles drove up and stopped at the curb. They

[5] From *The Making of a Reporter,* by Will Irwin, pp. 202–203. Copyright, 1942, by Will Irwin. New York: G. P. Putnam's Sons.

In the early morning hours of Sunday (June 5, 1910), Dr. [Charles Russell] Hancock came to [William Sydney Porter's] hospital room [at the Polyclinic] thinking the end was near. When he had finished his examination the nurse switched off the brightest of the two lights.

Will, rousing, said cheerfully, "Turn it back on. I'm afraid to go home in the dark." He whistled a few bars of the comic song he had paraphrased.

Then he dropped off to sleep, and did not awaken.—Dale Kramer, *The Heart of O. Henry* (New York, 1954), p. 308.

spilled over with a laughing and gaily dressed party of both sexes. From the leading car jumped a man named Davidson, then an editor of *Collier's.*

"What are you fellow doing here in those clothes?" he asked.

"Funeral—pallbearers," we replied.

"Whose?"

"O. Henry's."

"For the Lord's sake!" exclaimed Davidson, and rushed back to the cars. A whispered colloquy and they drove away. Two minutes later, Davidson drove back alone.

"Wedding," he explained. "I'm best man and master of ceremonies. We had engaged the main church for eleven, but there must be some mistake. So I've lied to the bride about the delay and had her spirited away for fear she'll get superstitious. Go on with your funeral."

It was a warmish June morning. A lawn surrounds the Little Church and the building sits intimately on the earth, English-fashion, so that the stained-glass windows reach almost to the ground. They were open that morning, and I sat beside one of them. And the solemn, vibrant words of the Episcopalian burial service came to one ear while the other picked up the suppressed giggles of young and gay wedding guests, gathering on the lawn.

That was the feature of his own funeral which O. Henry would have liked!

II [6]

Immediately after the funeral service, O. Henry's body was removed to the Pennsylvania Station, for burial in North Carolina, his homeland.

The bride and groom were married at noon. The church gave no sign nor did Dr. Houghton make any reference to what had gone before.

* * * * *

In the train the next day on their way to Lake Mohonk, [Frederic C.] Thomas handed his wife the morning newspaper. Putting his finger on the account of O. Henry's funeral, he said:

"That's the girl that got ahead of you at the church."

"Why—isn't that strange—there wasn't a wedding—it was a funeral."

* * * * *

At just about the same hour that the bride and groom reached Lake Mohonk for their honeymoon, a widow reached Asheville with her husband's body.

[6] From *The Little Church Around the Corner,* by George MacAdam, p. 328. Copyright, 1925, by George MacAdam. New York and London: G. P. Putnam's Sons.

The Wedding of Tom Thumb[7]

When Tom Thumb was married, Barnum kept out of sight. It was not known that he had anything to do with the business. It was first intended to have the wedding in the Academy of Music on the ticket system, but the general would not submit to making a show of himself on that occasion, so that idea was abandoned. The bishop of New York was to have performed the ceremony. Grace Church was the fashionable altar at which high New York exchanged its vows. It required some finesse and great skill to obtain that fashionable church for the marriage of the Lilliputians. Barnum undertook to manage that himself. He was not known to the rector, so he went boldly into his presence and asked for the church. He said the wedding was to be of the most select character, tickets were to be given to the aristocracy, and the guests were to come in full dress. The rector reluctantly consented. He appended to the consent certain conditions, which were put in writing, and if any one of the conditions were violated, the rector had a right to revoke his consent. Two conditions were expressly insisted upon. The first was that the church should not be mentioned in connection with the affair, until the morning of the wedding, though all New York knew it ten days before. "And now," said the rector, "don't you let that Barnum have anything to do with this matter. Don't let him know that I have given my consent to have Grace Church used. I wouldn't have Grace Church and Barnum bound up together for a thousand dollars." Barnum consented to all the conditions, and signed them on behalf of the agent, in whose name the affair was conducted. Great was the chagrin of the rector to learn that he had not only been outwitted by Barnum, but had entertained, beneath his own roof, the great showman himself.

Buffalo Bill in New York[8]

While Colonel William F. Cody, "Buffalo Bill," clung to the old Hoffman House as long as his friend, Ed Stokes, was its proprietor, he used

[7] From *Sunshine and Shadow in New York,* by Matthew Hale Smith (Burleigh), pp. 347–348. Entered . . . 1868, by J. B. Burr and Company. Hartford.

[8] From *Old Waldorf Days,* by Albert Stevens Crockett, pp. 36–37. Copyright, 1931, by Albert Stevens Crockett. New York: Aventine Press.

to drop into the Waldorf Bar, and there one might discover him at a table surrounded by a lot of admirers.

Cody, with his wide-brimmed hat, long mustache and goatee, and in the old days wearing a Prince Albert coat, presented a handsome figure and one which eyes seldom failed to follow.

Men liked to invite Colonel Cody to "have one" with them, and it is not on record that he ever refused. In accepting such an invitation, he followed an invariable formula.

"Sir," he would respond heartily, "you speak the language of my tribe."

One day, some twenty years ago, Colonel Cody was found sitting on a bench that used to stand opposite the bill clerk's window. He looked worn out. "Just come from Arizona," he said, "and, mind you, after that long journey, I can't get a room. And here I've been coming to the Waldorf for years. They say the hotel's full, and I guess I had better get breakfast. But, say, when I found out I couldn't get a room, it suddenly came to me that I didn't have one single clean boiled shirt in my baggage and tonight I've got to go to a dinner where I just must wear a white shirt. I didn't want to buy a new one. Well, at the desk they connected me by telephone with the laundry. There they told me it would take two days. That wouldn't suit me. So I said to the fellow 'Look here, I've got to have a shirt tonight. If I don't get it, I'll run through your hotel naked.' And, by George, sir, he promised me a shirt."

Morgan's Money Bags [9]

. . . J. P. Morgan's symbolic money bags carved above the choir stalls of St. Thomas's [were] an architect's jest in stone that the public had not yet discovered. The *World* had been working up a story on the carvings of this fashionable Fifth Avenue church, beginning with the dollar mark over the bride's door. They had published large layouts and stories about the gargoyles in the portico. A newly appointed managing editor on the *Sun* sent Miss Mary Watts up to St. Thomas's with

[9] From *Ladies of the Press,* the Story of Women in Journalism, by an insider, by Ishbel Ross, pp. 431–432. Copyright, 1936, by Ishbel Ross. New York and London: Harper & Brothers.

a microscope to see if she could find anything that the *World* had overlooked. She was dismayed, for she knew their round-up had been thorough. At the church offices she was severely snubbed. A crowd was standing outside, having read about the carvings. The church officials were much annoyed over all this vulger publicity. Coming out of the office Miss Watts ran into an elderly woman who looked like a cleaner. She engaged her in conversation. She mentioned the vestrymen and asked if J. P. Morgan was one of them.

"No," said the woman, "but his money bags are up by the choir."

"What?" said Miss Watts. "Where?"

But the woman shut up like a clam. So Miss Watts went prowling along the choir stalls. It was not easy to trace the small carvings in the dim light of the church, but finally she found the three money bags with the initials, "J.P.M.". . .

Travers and the Pet Shop Man [10]

. . . On his way home after the business day was over [William R. Travers], being attracted by the display in the window of a bird fancier and dog dealer, from curiosity he was tempted to enter the place. One of the conspicuous objects that met his eye was a very large-sized parrot. Mr. Travers inquired of the proprietor of the establishment who was in attendance "i-i-if th-th-th-that p-p-parrot c-c-could t-t-talk?"

Its owner quickly replied, "If it couldn't talk better than you I'd cut its damned head off."

Mr. Travers for a long time afterwards made up his mind some time or other to get even with this dealer in animals and birds, and succeeded most effectually. His coachman made a complaint to him that the stable was overrun with rats. Mr. Travers said, "Well, you m-m-must hunt for a r-r-rat dog." The coachman made it known that Mr. Travers wanted a dog, and all those engaged in dealing in dogs overran Mr. Travers' house as ferociously as the rats had overrun the stable, to get him to buy a dog. Among the rest who responded was this identical man who kept the store where the parrot was. Mr. Travers recognized him at once, and told him, "I-i-if he w-w-would b-b-b-be d-d-

[10] From *Twenty-Eight Years in Wall Street,* by Henry Clews, pp. 410–411. Copyright, 1887, by Henry Clews. New York: Irving Publishing Co.

down at the s-s-stable in the m-morning with t-th-the d-d-dog, he would g-g-give him a tr-tr-trial and if he p-pr-proved to b-b-be a g-g-good r-rat c-c-catcher, would b-b-buy him."

Mr. Travers sent for his coachman and told him to catch three or four rats and put them in the bin, and he would be down in the morning to try the dog. So, good and early next morning Mr. Travers was on hand at the stable, and also the dog man and his terrier. Three rats having already been put into the bin, Mr. Travers ordered the dog put inside, as the man said he was ready for the fray, and the rats were so ferocious, and showed such determined fight, that they kept the dog at bay, and he took to the corner of the bin for protection. By and by the owner pushed him right on the rats, and after a pretty fierce tussle he did secure one of them and shook him until dead. This success encouraged a tussle with another, which, after a long fight, shared the same fate. The third rat, however, was determined to resist the dog, and did so nobly and fiercely, making a prolonged fight, which resulted in a draw, and it was hard to tell which was the worst hurt, the dog or the rat.

The owner of the dog then turned to Mr. Travers and said: "Now you see what a fine dog that is, won't you buy him?" Mr. Travers replied: "I d-d-don't w-w-want t-t-to b-b-buy the d-d-dog, b-b-but I'll b-b-buy the r-rat."

Mr. Travers, when he first saw the owner of this dog, remembered him in connection with the parrot. Since the rat fight, however, this same man has never ceased to remember Mr. Travers, so that honors remain easy between them. . . .

He *Was* Caruso [11]

The relationship of the [Fifth Avenue] Bank to the Metropolitan Opera Company has always been a close one, and most of the great singers have carried accounts there at one time or another—a fact equally true of many of the outstanding artists, writers, actors, and musicians of the last half century.

Caruso was a depositor. One day he came into the Bank at the noon

[11] From *A Window on the Avenue,* A Portrait of the Fifth Avenue Bank Office of the Bank of New York, 1875–1955, pp. 30–32. Copyright, 1955, by The Bank of New York. New York.

hour to cash a check and happened to go to a new teller. Forty-fourth Street and Fifth Avenue is a windy corner where anything can happen, and when an alert young paying teller sees a famous name like Caruso on a check, he instinctively becomes suspicious. In this case, the fact that the person on the other side of the wicket *looked* like Caruso only increased his doubts.

The more Caruso tried to convince the distracted teller that he *was* Caruso, the more convinced the latter became that he was a fraud. Then Caruso had an inspiration. Stepping back a few paces from the teller's window so that he would not blow the money around, he placed one hand on his breast and began to sing an aria from *Tosca.*

Long before he had finished, the teller began to count the money out in a panic. When he came to the end, Caruso bowed and took his money, while the customers and the clerks cheered.

"C.A.10" [12]

The pedestrian, as he walks along the streets of New York, pondering on its greatness and wondering at its wickedness, may frequently have noticed chalk-marks on the sidewalks. They look innocent enough—much like the work of a childish hand who had been playing the game of "hop-scotch." The children do make the most of these marks, but not always. Men sometimes make them; they desire an assignation with the lady of the establishment, and select this novel method of informing her of the time and place. A few uncouth figures, seemingly meaningless, can be placed upon the brownstone steps, and as easily deciphered the next day by the lady within, who possesses the required "key."

There is a case at present before one of the courts of New York, wherein the adultery of the wife is sought to be proved. Suspicion was first aroused in the husband's mind by frequently finding this cabalistic sentence in letters of chalk on his front stoop: "C.A.10." At first he attributed it to the boys in the neighborhood, and requested a policeman to watch for and arrest the culprits. But the officer was unable to

[12] From *The Women of New York* or the Under-World of the Great City, Illustrating the Life of Women of Fashion, Women of Pleasure, Actresses and Ballet Girls, Saloon Girls, Pickpockets and Shoplifters, Artists' Female Models, Women-of-the-Town, Etc., Etc., Etc., by George Ellington, pp. 351–352. New York: The New York Book Company. 1869.

find who placed the letters there, and so informed the gentleman.

This set the husband to thinking, and he resolved to watch, believing that there must be some meaning to the signs. About three o'clock one morning he saw a young man approach, and, after looking cautiously about, place the same sign upon the step. His suspicions were aroused. The next day he observed that his young and handsome wife took a trip to Jersey City, going at the hour of ten; also, on other occasions, at the hour designated by the figure placed on the step. The result was, that the husband tracked his wife to an assignation-house in Jersey City, where she was met by the young man who had marked the step with chalk at the unseasonable hour of three in the morning.

"Sweet Face at the Window"[13]

A few months ago the following personal advertisement appeared in one of our morning papers:

> "*Sweet face at the window.*—Will the beautiful young lady who smiles nearly every morning upon the gent who rides past her house on the Eighth Avenue cars have the kindness to address a note to 'Admirer, Station E,' stating when and how an interview may be had?"

Chancing to know the smitten youth who inserted this amorous "personal," we resolved to see what came of it. He was what is generally termed a quiet man, and the last person in the world to engage in a flirtation.

The next day he received nine different letters in answer to this advertisement, showing beyond a doubt that there was more than one "sweet face at the window" that smiled on some fortunate passenger or other every morning, and who undoubtedly imagined that her face was the one alluded to by this advertiser. Our friend was in a quandary. At last he decided to appoint a meeting with all of them at a well-known restaurant, where, unknown to all but the one he sought, he could have the opportunity for which he wished.

The evening came, and our friend entered the saloon and took a position at a table where he could observe all who entered. As the hour approached quite a number of ladies came in and took seats at various tables. They each bore on their "sweet faces" a look of expectancy, and

[13] *Ibid.*, pp. 481–483.

they placed themselves in good positions to see all who entered after them. Most of them had passed that period of life when women's charms are most enticing to men.

Finally, his eye fell upon the object of his search. He left the table and approached her. The meeting was as cordial as might have been expected. He led her back to the table and ordered more refreshments, while the rest of the fair ones looked on in wonderment. To a few the truth was plain, but our friend soon sought the open air with his fair companion, leaving the others to their fates.

She was really a fine-looking woman, with a good education and a quaint brilliancy of conversation which would have charmed any man of taste. The hours glided away to ten o'clock, when she said she must leave him. He talked to her with all the impassioned fervor of first love, but she treated all his protestations with the most delightful nonchalance and gayly laughed them away. He, however, was sincere and true, and tried to turn her from her lightness and frivolity to thoughts of home and marriage, but all to no purpose. Weeks and months passed away, and she seemed to enjoy the flirtation immensely. At last he awoke from the spell she had cast so bewitchingly round him, and openly accused her of trifling with his affections. She denied this with tears in her eyes, and said she loved him—thus paving the way for another six months' flirtation.

But there came a time when the mask fell. A gentleman, an entire stranger, called upon him one evening, [carrying a box]. He was, he said, the husband of the woman, and, as he was convinced that our friend was acting entirely in the dark, had come to make an explanation. Our friend was thunderstruck. The husband then opened the box and handed him all the presents he had sent his wife. The lover was cured. He patronizes another line of cars, and to this day never allows himself to be led into another flirtation.

Mr. McGuire's Mourning [14]

. . . Mr. McGuire, a quiet little man . . . wore mourning for the forty years Riggs [O'Rourke, the "Mayor" of Park Row] recalls him along Park Row.

[14] From "Park Row's Something New under the Sun," by Murray Robinson, *New York World-Telegram and The Sun,* July 27, 1954. New York. Copyright, 1954, by New York World-Telegram Corp.

"He was a charming guy," Riggs said, "even though he dressed like an undertaker. He read nothing but obituaries, and kept tipping his derby and muttering prayers for perfect strangers while he read them.

"Mr. McGuire's story is a love story. When he was young, he had a friend with a beautiful sister. Mr. McGuire fell in love with her on sight—but he never told her or even went out with her.

"She died suddenly, and that was when Mr. McGuire went into mourning. Reading obits was one way to remember her dying. That, and his custom of putting flowers on her grave on every holiday, including the Fourth of July."

For all his macabre obsession, Mr. McGuire was not a strict loner. He would occasionally invite others at the Park Row bars to drink with him, until a strange thing happened.

"The boys thought they noticed," Riggs said, "that anybody Mr. McGuire bought a drink for died soon after. They began shunning him. He brooded about this and soon shunned Park Row. . . ."

The Legend of the Mausoleum Musicale [15]

Melancholy autumn almost always brings drifts of weird and macabre stories to town. One that's picking up fascinating detail right now is about a New Yorker, recently widowed, who moved a grand piano into a mausoleum in a local cemetery where his wife's body is entombed. The legend is that out of deep grieving he enters the tomb at irregular intervals and softly plays touching and romantic melodies that his wife had always loved.

The people who run the cemetery say it isn't true, but that stories in somewhat the same vein keep cropping up. The one most often told, but with no more basis than the pianist legend, is about the husband who holds sentimental feast in the crypt with an empty seat at table for his wife. No well-run cemetery, it seems, would permit that any more than it would mausoleum musicales. The only sound you hear at night in New York graveyards is the rustling of autumn leaves.

[15] From "About New York," by Meyer Berger, *The New York Times*, October 23, 1953. Copyright, 1953, by the New York Times Company.

Hell's Kitchen [16]

Years ago on Thirty-ninth Street between Tenth and Eleventh Avenues there existed a combination "Beer Saloon and Restaurant" conducted by a German and his wife with the name of "Heil" and having a sign on the front reading "Heil's Kitchen" where patrons were served with various dishes, the most popular being pigs knuckles and sauerkraut accompanied by a very large glass of good beer, which was extremely to the liking of those in the neighborhood and from others.

[There was] an establishment of a similar character . . . on the south side of West Thirty-fifth Street, just east of Eighth Avenue, known as the "Halfway House," as many will recollect.

When the "rough" boys wished to partake of the above or other food they would call out to one another, "Let's go down to 'Hell's Kitchen,' " not pronouncing the name "Heil" properly, through an innocent error or by deliberate [mis]pronunciation, as it may have been more musical to their ears, and this name consequently had to be borne by the neighborhood to this day.

The Gate-Crasher [17]

In the old Fourth Ward of New York, where there was a big Irish population, there used to be a character who lived off of wakes. He watched the papers for death notices; and when a death occurred in his neighborhood he would put on his shabby best, drop round to the house of mourning, weep over the bier, even though the deceased had been a total stranger to him, extol the virtues of the departed—and then eat and drink until he could hold no more.

One night, according to Dick Malloy, the Tammany politician, the old chap reached a wake. He walked in with leaky eyes, to be met by the two stalwart sons of the dead man.

"You didn't know our father and he didn't know you," they told

[16] By John H. Knubel, letter to the editor, *New York Herald Tribune,* January 25, 1942. Copyright, 1942, by New York Herald Tribune, Inc.

[17] From "Sense and Nonsense," *The Saturday Evening Post,* Vol. 184 (May 4, 1912), No. 45, p. 75. Copyright, 1912, by the Curtis Publishing Company. Philadelphia.

him. "You only came to get some free drinks. Now you get out or we'll throw you out!"

The old man got out; but at the door he paused for a parting shot.

"I'd have you know," he said, addressing the coffined form, "that you're not the only corpse in New York tonight! There are others—and a blamed sight better-lookin' wans too!"

Pay As You Enter [18]

Proceeding from the subterranean apartments below to view the rooms in the upper stories, a class of tenant house occupants was stumbled upon, for the amelioration of whose condition the [legislative] Committee, [appointed to examine into the construction of tenement houses] hardly deemed themselves commissioned. The staid chairman was quietly taking the lead, not venturing hardly to ask a question without a prefatory apology, when, passing into a room on the fourth floor, he was proceeding to open the bedroom door.

"No, sir, don't you do it," uttered a big, coarse woman; "I don't care who you are—no one opens that door unless he pays first!"

The chairman did not open the door, but while he looked amazed, together with the other rural members of the Committee, the dozen female occupants of the room set up a general laugh, the import of which was unmistakable. The chairman beat a hasty retreat, followed by two other members of the committee and Mr. Downing.

The Ogling Corpse [19]

Newspapermen know these stillborn fantasies better than most. They are forever running down the tales of mystery and wonder that periodically flood the talk of the town.

There is the one of the dead man in the subway who sits with eyes fixed on a lady passenger. Offended by his crude ogling, this lady fi-

[18] From *Frank Leslie's Illustrated Newspaper,* Vol. I (March 29, 1856), No. 16, p. 246.

[19] From *1001 Afternoons in New York,* by Ben Hecht, p. 271. Copyright, 1941, by the Viking Press, Inc. New York.

nally slaps the dead man's face, whereupon the cadaver pitches out of its seat and much hysteria ensues.

The name of this finicky and mistaken lady has never been found, nor that of the defunct ogler, nor of the subway guard who witnessed it all. There is available always to the good reporter, however, a ring of hundreds on hundreds of citizens who heard the story from a neighbor whose aunt or uncle was on the train where it all happened.

The Man in the Middle [20]

[An] old, horse-drawn 'bus [was] toiling down Fifth Avenue in a blinding snowstorm. Everything silent, since the snow was already five or six inches deep. [A] middle-aged couple lived in Washington Square and had been to the theater—way up town, say at Thirty-eighth or Fortieth Street. They enter an empty 'bus—you remember those 'buses in the days when *Life* was constantly caricaturing them and their lean horses. They had straw on the floor; a driver on the box; a smoky oil lantern at the front; a tin box in which you put your fare; and a door which the driver opened with a string when you signaled that you wished to get out.

The 'bus, with the man and his wife, goes slowly through the snow

[20] By Edmund Lester Pearson. From "Shouts and Murmurs," by Alexander Woollcott, *The New Yorker,* Vol. 6 (March 15, 1930), No. 4, p. 34. Copyright, 1930, by the F-R Publishing Corporation. New York.

A few years ago the late Alexander Woollcott told [the story of the Man in the Middle] . . . in *The New Yorker* [February 22, 1930, p. 38]. Three weeks later (March 15, 1930) he had something interesting to report to *New Yorker* readers. This is his postscript:

"You have not traced the story of the girl and the dead man in the subway back far enough," writes my precious leader, Edmund Pearson, who is shortly to be recalled to Harvard to occupy the *Chair of Murder*. In its earlier version it was (pardon me) a better yarn. Finley Peter Dunne *fils,* who thinks that you and I are the two nicest old gentlemen in New York, with the longest memories, and that we used to walk down Broadway in the mellow twilights of 1815, chanting glees with Washington Irving and Fitz-Greene Halleck—Mr. Dunne, I say, would be shocked that you did not recall the grimmer story which came out in *The Bookman* about 1902, when, under the editorship of Harry Thurston Peck and Arthur Maurice, that was a most readable magazine —as it is now again in 1930. This story was a corker."

The editor cannot find it in *The Bookman* for 1902—or 1901, or 1903. —Ben C. Clough, *The American Imagination at Work* (New York, 1947), p. 356.

down as far as—well, Twenty-second Street—when three other passengers get on, two young fellows supporting a third, whose heels drag. They address him as Jim, and tell him to buck up. But Jim is far gone in liquor; or, as they said in the sprightly '80's, he has a jag. He can do nothing for himself. A few streets below, one of them again tells Jim to buck up, slaps him on the back and gets out. A little later, the other one repeats the advice to Jim, and he, too, gets out. Jim is still silent; still sullen; and still slumped in the seat. Then the man leans forward and takes a look at Jim. Instantly he gets up, pulls the cord, and says to his wife: "We get out here." And out he gets, followed by his indignant and scolding wife. They stand in the drifting snow, near the corner of Fourteenth Street, and the wife wishes to know if her husband is crazy. Seven blocks still to go, and get her out in this blizzard—what does he mean? Her husband says: "Did you see that young man?" No, she didn't. What has that to do with it? "Well, I did, and his throat was cut from ear to ear."

The Pigeons on the Subway Train [21]

Sitting opposite Miss Haas on a northbound subway train one evening sat a man calmly reading his paper with three pigeons resting on top of him—one on his head, the others on his shoulders. Miss Haas contemplated the situation until she could stand it no longer. She tapped his paper, and said, "Pardon me, but what on earth are you doing with those pigeons in the subway?" "Them?" said the man. "I really don't know, lady. They musta got on at 59th Street."

The Wooden Cat [22]

The Commandant at the Brooklyn Navy Yard—this was several years ago—returned from a trip to Washington one autumn afternoon to

[21] From *Try and Stop Me,* A Collection of Anecdotes and Stories, Mostly Humorous, by Bennett Cerf, pp. 327-328. Copyright, 1944, by Bennett Cerf. New York: Simon and Schuster.

[22] From "Manhattan Weirds," by Morris Markey, *Vanity Fair,* Vol. 36 (July, 1931), No. 5, p. 82. Copyright, 1931, by the Condé Nast Publications, Inc.

The folklore of a metropolis is rather likely to be on the somber side, since paved streets and shadowed corners and the stir of millions do not

find his wife waiting for him at the Pennsylvania Terminal. She had met him, she said, to prevent his going to the Yard and becoming immersed in business, as she had tickets for the opera that night and did not wish to be disappointed.

She also told him of an amusing little incident that had occurred while she awaited the arrival of the train. Wandering into a quiet corner of the great concourse, she had noticed a solitary telephone booth with a sign on its door, "Temporarily Out of Order." Glancing through the murky doors of the booth, she had observed some small object on the shelf beneath the telephone instrument.

"Look," she said, "what an odd little thing it was." And she held out to him a small cat, very shrewdly carved from wood, and painted the color of a tortoise shell. They smiled over the curious little toy, and she thrust it into her bag as they left the station.

Several hours later they were sitting in the opera house with the mad wild music of the Valkyries singing in their ears, when the Commandant's wife felt the touch of light fingers at the back of her neck. She shivered a little, and tried to hold her attention to the music, but the touch was extraordinarily stealthy, and in a moment it was repeated.

She whispered to her husband, who refused to take her very seriously, and murmured that people do not deliberately annoy you at the opera. But after a little time it was almost impossible to listen to the music at all, for the stealthy touch was repeated several times at the back of her neck, until it was obvious that there was a purpose in it. Yet the touch itself was so very slight that she hesitated to disturb the people about her by turning and glancing back.

At the intermission she confessed that she was so nervous that she could not return to her seat. "I know I am being perfectly absurd," she said, "but it was such an eerie thing to feel that light hand brushing against me. It felt like the fingers of a ghost."

They went home, without returning to their seats. But they had gone no more than a few blocks in the cab when she began to feel doubt that anything had touched her at all. It may have been, she admitted to her husband, merely the fancy of nerves that were a bit on edge.

When they reached their room at home, she threw her opera cloak

---

produce idylls. Mr. Markey has collected a handful of the most persistent urban legends—of the sort that usually are told with the familiar preamble: "You can really believe this because it happened to a very close friend of my Aunt Maria's."—Note by editor of *Vanity Fair*.

on the bed and immediately had the feeling that its collar was unusually heavy. She lifted it again and glanced up suddenly, and pulled a loose thread that her fingers found. A large double handful of diamonds and sapphires and pearls flooded out over her hands and glittered on the bed in a stunning heap. There were ear rings, brooches, pendants, and finger rings of exquisite beauty.

It is not astonishing that they slept hardly at all. Both were convinced, of course, that those wraithlike fingers at her neck had stuffed the jewels in her collar during the first act of the opera. The next morning they went to the police. The police had difficulty making anything at all of the bizarre situation until the Commandant's wife happened to mention the incident of the little wooden cat. At once the police were ready with an explanation.

"The cat was planted in that place," said one of the detectives. "They picked out an obscure place and planted it there. A woman was supposed to come for it, and by picking it up, identify herself to some one who was watching. She—this expected woman—was an employee of a fence for thieves, and it was the plan to give the stuff into her keeping at an opportune moment. The woman was probably a little late. You happened to find the cat, and those who were watching misunderstood. They followed you, and hit upon a very ingenious method of passing the stuff into your hands."

Most of the jewelry was identified by owners, but a considerable amount was not, and it now remains in the possession of the Commandant's wife, who had acquired an enduring affection for the small wooden cat.

The Pearl Necklace [23]

This "pearl necklace" story has been told at one time or another about every big department store in the country, although most narrators insist angrily that it happened "to their own cousin."

A lady and her daughter are sauntering down Fifth Avenue. In front of Tiffany's the young girl's "pearl necklace" breaks, and the

[23] From *Try and Stop Me,* A Collection of Anecdotes and Stories, Mostly Humorous, by Bennett Cerf, p. 185. Copyright, 1944, by Bennett Cerf. New York: Simon and Schuster.

pearls roll all over the street. She reclaims them, and suggests giving them to Tiffany's for stringing.

"We can't ask Tiffany's to restring things like that," protests the mother. "After all, the whole necklace cost only $12.98 at Blank's." Anyhow, they enter Tiffany's. The man at the repair desk takes one look at the loose pearls, asks to be excused for a moment, and returns with the general manager, who offers the startled lady fifty thousand dollars for the lot.

The explanation? The president of Blank's has smuggled in the strand of pearls for his wife by hiding them with a shipment of cheap imitations addressed to the store's bargain jewelry department. The special marking on the real pearls has been lost, and the strand mixed up with all the others. The honest lady brings them back to Blank's just in time to clear the saleswoman, who has been accused by the president of stealing the pearls for her own purposes.

Of course, a story like this *could* have happened in real life. Reasonable odds against it: 4,000 to 1.

Harpo Marx and the Doorman [24]

On a spring afternoon, Harpo [Marx] was deploying down Fifth Avenue encased in a bright yellow overcoat and topped by a blue hat with a little feather in it. Around his middle he wore a sash such as Brazilian maxixe dancers favor. His throat was bared, and the ends of a Byronic collar lay low on his chest. The details may sound a bit eccentric, but the ensemble was one of great elegance—particularly since it is Harpo's fancy when out for a stroll to arrange his plastic features so that he resembles exactly the late Kaiser Wilhelm.

In front of a very famous jewelry store, Harpo came to a resplendent halt. An argument was in progress between a taxicab driver and the doorman of this awesome emporium. The doorman was tall, blond, and uniformed. The taxi driver was none of these things. He was chiefly Jewish. And Harpo stood listening owl-eyed to the barrage of insults to which the doorman was treating the driver.

"Get away from in front of here, you dirty Jew," said the doorman.

[24] From *1001 Afternoons in New York,* by Ben Hecht, pp. 100–102. Copyright, 1941, by the Viking Press, Inc. New York.

"Go on before I break your dirty Jew head. There'll be a law soon keeping you and all Jews off this street. Go on, get back to the ghetto where you belong."

Harpo vanished from the scene. Fifteen minutes later our Preposterous Knight reappeared, walking on Fifth Avenue. His pockets were filled with five-and-ten-cent-store emeralds, rubies, and diamonds. He paused before the doorman and fixed upon him his finest Kaiser glare. The doorman bowed and opened the door obsequiously for Harpo and beamed ingratiatingly on this arrogant customer. Harpo glared back at him, barked once, and entered the store, leaving the flunky soul of the Nazi stirred to its depths.

Twenty minutes later Harpo emerged, and as he stepped into the street he tripped. The horrified door-opener saw this elegant customer fall flat on his face. And he saw something even more horrifying. Out of the pockets of this high-born shopper rolled a score of emeralds, rubies, and diamonds. They bounced across the pavement in all directions. They were the $3 worth of paste jewels Harpo had bought in the five-and-ten-cent store. But the doorman didn't know this.

With a cry of anguish the doorman threw himself to the sidewalk and darted wildly after the bouncing jewels. He scurried about on hands and knees for ten minutes. He retrieved rubies from the gutter, snatched emeralds from under the feet of startled pedestrians, and plucked diamonds from the pavement cracks. He tore his pants, scuffed his knees, and had his fingers stepped on. He arose after the ten minutes, out of breath but beaming, and approached the elegant customer with the rigid face.

"Please," he panted blissfully, "look quick. See if they are all here."

Harpo examined the jewels coldly as the doorman handed him the glittering handful.

"Yes," Harpo barked, "they are all here."

"Thank God!" said the doorman and mopped his brow and stood by vibrating joyfully.

Harpo strode to the curb. A cab was waiting. At its wheel sat the same Jewish driver at whom the Nazi flunky had been screaming insults a half-hour before. The doorman limped eagerly beside Harpo and opened the door of the vehicle with a happy bow.

Harpo paused before the opened door. He examined the jewels still in his hand and selected the largest diamond from among them. He handed it to the doorman.

"Here," said Harpo, "for your trouble."

The doorman gaped.

"And give this one to your best girl," said Harpo, selecting another huge diamond, "and to your dear mama this ruby."

To the cabby Harpo suddenly cried in a voice all business: "Drive me to the synagogue. I am late for my afternoon prayers."

The doorman was discharged later that afternoon for screaming at the assistant manager.

The Dead Cat [25]

. . . [A] legend . . . is batting around the town today. I heard it first from a writer named Charles Boswell who lives at 260 West 11th Street. Mr. Boswell believed the story and related it as follows:

A Brooklyn woman put her cat in a cat and dog hospital. It died and she called for its remains. She wished to bury the pet herself. The dead cat was put in a neat box and the lady started for home. On the way she stopped at Stern's department store in 42nd Street to make some purchases. While shopping she noticed suddenly that the box she had placed on the counter near her was gone. Store detectives began a search for the missing dead cat. Ten minutes later a woman was found slumped on the floor of a telephone booth. Beside her was the box, just opened, and the feline corpse staring out of it. The woman was dead. She was immediately identified as a notorious shoplifter for whom this and other emporiums had been gunning these last six months. She had obviously stolen the box, taken it to a telephone booth to open, sighted the dead cat, and fallen lifeless to the floor with a heart attack—the victim of macabre justice.

Mr. Boswell said the story had been told him by two actors in the apartment above his, Oscar Stirling and his wife, Edna Peckham, recently on view in *Kind Lady*. Mr. Boswell said these two knew the full truth of the story.

Interview with the Stirlings revealed that they had got the story from their Christian Science practitioner, a Mr. Charles Simmonds of 450 West 24th Street. Mr. Simmonds, a man not to be doubted, had told them the story as gospel.

Mr. Simmonds repeated this gospel. He had heard it, he said, from a woman who was a friend of the dead cat's owner. This woman was

[25] *Ibid.*, pp. 271–273.

Mrs. Katherine Luebbers of 28 Mile Square Road in Yonkers. Mrs. Luebbers would give me the names of all the people involved.

And Mrs. Luebbers turned out to be full of the dead-cat wonder. She did not know the name of the animal's owner, but the story had been told her by her son-in-law, Ronald Schaeffer, who knew all about it. And Mr. Schaeffer turned out to know everything about it. He had heard the story first-hand from a passenger on a commuters' train whose aunt knew the lady who owned the dead cat.

At Stern's the tale was firmly, and a little indignantly, denied by W. F. McCue, chief store detective. And at the West 54th Street police station there was no record of any feline or shoplifter corpses being reported.

By this time you may have heard the tale of wonder elsewhere. There are probably scores and hundreds of wonder-lovers broadcasting it from table to table and from office to office. And if you have nothing to do, like myself, take a few days off and play ring-around-a-rosy with this Dead-Cat-Come-to-Judgment rumor.

You will come upon no dead cat or stricken shoplifter, but you will get an instructive look into that well of rumor which is deeper and more crowded with fact apparently than that other well out of which no wars, massacres or religions are ever born.

The White Satin Dress [26]

A favorite story of New York literary circles a few years ago concerned a beautiful young girl in a white satin dress. It was one of those anecdotes which everybody swore had actually happened to his first cousin or next-door neighbor, and several narrators became very testy when they were informed that several other people's cousins had evidently undergone the same experience just a few weeks before.

At any rate, the legend maintained that a very lovely but poverty-stricken damsel was invited to a formal dance. It was her chance to enter a brand-new world. Who knew but that some rich young man would fall in love with her and lift her out of her life in a box factory?

[26] From *Try and Stop Me,* A Collection of Anecdotes and Stories, Mostly Humorous, by Bennett Cerf, pp. 284–285. Copyright, 1944, by Bennett Cerf. New York: Simon and Schuster.

The catch in the matter was that she had no suitable dress to wear for such a great occasion.

"Why don't you rent a costume for the evening?" suggested a friend. Not having thought of this before, the girl became hopeful, and that very night went to a pawnshop near her little flat, where for a surprisingly reasonable sum she rented a beautiful white satin evening gown with all the accessories to match. Miraculously, it fit her like a glove and gave her such radiance that upon her arrival at the party she created a minor sensation. She was cut in on again and again, and as she whirled happily around the floor she felt that her luck indeed had changed for the better.

Soon, however, she began to feel faint and nauseated. She fought against a growing discomfort as long as possible, but finally stole out of the house with barely sufficient strength to stagger into a cab and creep up the stairs to her room. She threw herself onto her bed, brokenhearted, and it was then—possibly in her delirium—that she heard a woman's voice whispering in her ear. It was harsh and bitter. "Give me back my dress," it said. "Give me back my dress! It belongs to . . . the dead. . . ."

The next morning the lifeless body of the young girl was found stretched out on her bed. The unusual circumstances led the coroner to order an autopsy. It was found the girl had been poisoned by embalming fluid which had entered her pores when she became overheated from dancing. The pawnbroker was reluctant to admit that he knew where the dress had come from, but spoke out when he heard that the district attorney's office was involved. It had been sold him by an undertaker's assistant who had taken it from the body of a dead girl just before the casket was nailed down for the last time.

The Richardson "Spite House" [27]

In the year 1882 one Hyman Sarner, a clothier, who owned several lots on East 82nd Street, wished to build apartment houses on his property,

[27] From "The Queerest House in This Country," by A. G. Van der Weyde, in *Valentine's Manual of Old New York,* edited by Henry Collins Brown, No. 5, New Series, 1921, pp. 224–226. Copyright, 1920, by Henry Collins Brown. New York: Valentine's Manual, Inc.

New York for a period of thirty-two years boasted the queerest house in this

which extended to within a few feet of Lexington Avenue. On the Lexington Avenue side was a very long and very narrow strip of land, absolutely valueless, he thought, for any building purpose, unless taken in conjunction with adjoining land.

Sarner ascertained that one Joseph Richardson was the owner of the narrow strip along the Avenue. He offered Richardson $1,000 for the land, but Richardson demurred, saying he considered the property worth very much more. He wanted $5,000. Sarner refused to pay this price and Richardson called his visitor a "tight-wad" and slammed the door on him.

Sarner then proceeded with the construction of his apartment house and arranged with the architect who drew the plans that there should be windows overlooking Lexington Avenue. When the houses were finished Richardson noted the windows and then and there determined upon his curious revenge.

"I shall build me," he said to his daughter, "a couple of tall houses on the little strip which will bar the light from Sarner's windows overlooking my land, and he'll find he would have profited had he paid me the $5,000."

The daughter, Della by name, unavailingly protested, as did also Richardson's wife, that a house only five feet wide would be uninhabitable.

The old man, who had acquired a reputation as a miser, was obdu-

---

country, if not in the entire world. This was the famous Richardson "Spite House," at Lexington Avenue and 83rd Street. The house extended north 104 feet on the avenue, but was only five feet wide. In general appearance it was not unlike a bicycle case set on end. The house attracted much attention during its brief existence, which terminated [in 1915].

The house was erected to satisfy a personal grudge and the owner lived fifteen years to enjoy the discomfort that it caused the man he wished to spite. The story of the "Spite House," as a result of much litigation in the courts, is voluminously told in the court records.

Soon after [Richardson's] death [in 1897, his daughter] "Miss Della" brought suit against her stepmother to dispossess her from her quarters in the "Spite House," "Miss Della" claiming that the aged miser's wife was merely a tenant and could be evicted upon due notice. Mrs. Richardson fought the case in the courts for many months.

In the year 1902 the "Spite House" was sold by the heirs to James V. Graham and Charles Reckling. . . . Later it passed into the possession of C. A. Stein . . . and in 1909 it again changed hands.

On August 20, 1915 [after changing hands two more times], the career of the strange house came to a sudden end when Bing & Bing . . . abruptly bought the old building, and in short order tore it down, as well as two adjoining houses, and erected in their place [a] big eleven-story apartment house.—A. G. V. der W., *ibid.*, pp. 224, 227.

rate. "Not only will I build the houses," he insisted, "but I will live in one of them and I shall rent to other tenants as well. Everybody is not fat and there will be room enough for people who are not circus or museum folk."

So, within a year, the house was built. It effectively blocked out the light from all the side windows on Sarner's property, and old Mr. Richardson was happy. The Richardson "Spite House" was four stories in height and was divided into eight suites, two on each floor. Each suite consisted of three rooms and bath, running along the Lexington Avenue side of the structure.

Only the very smallest furniture could be fitted into the rooms. The stairways were so narrow that only one person could use a stair at a time. If a tenant wished to descend or ascend, from one floor to another, he would, of necessity, have to ascertain that no one else was using the stair. The halls throughout the house were so narrow that one person could pass another only by dodging into one of the rooms until the other had passed by. The largest dining table in any of the suites was eighteen inches in width. The chairs were proportionately small. The kitchen stoves were the very smallest that are made.

Richardson, with his wife, Emma—she was the old man's second wife—occupied a suite on the ground floor. "Miss Della," as she was known, the daughter, who followed the example of her penurious father in her mode of life, declined to live in the "Spite House," declaring that it was "too swell" a structure for her. She was now far along in years and preferred to remain where she had long lived in a dwelling called "the Prison House" on East Houston Street. She was seen by the neighbors only in the early morning, when she swept the steps, visited the grocery store for some bare necessities and returned to immolate herself in her "prison house," where she refused to see any visitors.

"Miss Della" was almost as wealthy as her father. She was as avaricious and parsimonious as the old man and owned much property in New York City.

Joseph Richardson died in 1897 at the age of eighty-four. He left his property—including, of course, the famous "Spite House"—to his widow and the two children, one of whom was the "Miss Della" of "Prison House" fame. The builder of the "Spite House" was buried in a coffin which he had had made thirty-two years earlier and which he had always stored in a room of the house where he lived.

Twenty-three Skidoo [28]

. . . Standing on what was traditionally the windiest corner of the city, [the Flatiron Building] was facetiously considered a good vantage point for the glimpse of a trim ankle, in the long-skirted, prewar era; policemen used to shoo loungers away from the Twenty-third Street corner, and the expression "twenty-three skidoo" is supposed to have originated from this association.

Skyscraper Contest [29]

William Van Alen, architect of the Chrysler Building, and his former partner, H. Craig Severance, became rivals when each was commissioned to design the world's tallest building. When the Chrysler tower seemed likely to terminate at 925 feet, the builders of the Bank of the Manhattan Company structure [or Manhattan Company Building] at 40 Wall Street (designed by Severance and Yasuo Matsui) decided to halt their operations at 927 feet. Meanwhile, steel workers were secretly assembling the rustless steel sections of the Chrysler spire which, when lifted through the dome and bolted into place, brought the building to its triumphant height of 1,048 feet. Subsequently the Empire State Building stole the laurels.

An East Side Boy Buys a Suit [30]

I remember—why, it's a small thing. You see, I made five dollars and I had a five-dollar bill. The boss gave me five dollars. I went down with

[28] From *New York City Guide,* A Comprehensive Guide to the Five Boroughs of the Metropolis—Manhattan, Brooklyn, the Bronx, Queens, and Richmond, prepared by the Federal Writers' Project of the Works Progress Administration in New York City, pp. 204–205. Copyright, 1939, by the Guilds' Committee for Federal Writers' Publications, Inc. New York: Random House, Publishers.

[29] *Ibid.,* p. 224.

[30] As told by B. Meisler. Recorded by Tony Schwartz, New York, 1955. Transcribed by B. A. Botkin.

the five dollars and I kept it in my [pocket]. I didn't trust my pocket, but I had my hand in my pocket too. And I kept on going. I remember like this very day. I passed by Canal Street. You see, that was Saturday afternoon. So I was standing. I see, you know, suits with canes. Looked to me very nice. I looked. I was thinking myself, "Gee, when I could work myself up to buy a suit, that would be wonderful." I was a young kid, about fifteen.

So all of a sudden I felt somebody pushed me right in the store. I looked at him. "What kind of business—?" He said, "Wait a minute, wait a minute, don't be afraid." He said, "You need a suit." He put on, he fixed me. The way he put on the suit was, I don't know, foolish. You see, when he put me on, he didn't let me fit on the suit but just like that, from outside. "So you see how your pants is just good." Of course, I bend myself. The pants was just nice. The same thing, he fitted me [the jacket].

I remember it was a light suit. He packed it up and I asked the man, "How much is the suit?" "Well, I'll give you a bargain—thirty-nine fifty." So I told him if I had thirty-nine fifty, I'll go back in Europe. He said, "Thirty-nine fifty," and I kept on walking. While I was walking, he kept on shooting five dollar bills off—five, ten. So he asked me, "How much?" "So I'll tell you what I'll do," I told him. "I've got five dollars in my whole possession. I'll give you two seventy-five." "Aw, you're crazy." So while I was going till the door, I opened up the door, he hold me my jacket. He said, "All right, come in, sold."

He wrapped up the suit. He said, "Don't stay here too long, 'cause the boss he might come in. I'm giving you a present." He gave me two twenty-five in change, and I kept on running. You know what I mean—from I was surprised, such a bargain. So I made a mistake. Instead of running in 521 Grand Street, I went up 523 on the same floor and I banged the door open. I didn't knock—just banged the door. So a woman was almost naked. You see, she kept on yelling. So I found out that this is not my apartment. So to make it short, I had a lot of trouble. And they took me in next door. So I went up next door in my apartment. I used to live in a room and I started to fit on the suit. I see the suit doesn't fit at all. It's up till here—you can't button it. I'm just like in a strait jacket. So I'm running back. Don't laugh. I was taking the suit back. I was mad and I wanted to go back to the same place.

I went in one place, they wanted to sell me a suit. But in one place I was sure, I was sure that's the place. I was more than sure. I was coming in. I said, "What kind of a suit you sold me?" He said, "What you mean? *Zei nisht kein greener.* [Don't be a greenhorn.]" He said, "I'll ship you out to the other side. What are you making trouble here?" "So give me back my money." So one guy he felt sorry for me. He tells me this way. He said, "Listen here. Money back you can't get it. You got a big buy. Go across the street in the park. Go in the park there. You see people going around down there, they're going around trying selling suits. Now your suit you'll get a good buy."

So I went over in the park and I tried to sell that suit. So one man comes in to me, a young man. *Zogt er zu mir,* [he said to me], "What have you got to sell?" "Here's a suit—the suit is worth a lot of money. I want to sell it. Give me five and it's yours." He said, "Oh, that suit is worth fifteen dollars." "So, well, give it me." *Zogt er,* "I'll tell you what I'll do. I'll sell you the suit."

So I made with him a bargain. If he'll sell me the suit, we'll go half and half. So he took me the suit, and he tells me to sit down on the bench. I'm still waiting for him. The cop waked me at midnight, about three o'clock in the morning, and chased me out from the park. And I didn't have the suit and the money was gone.

Country Boy on the Town [31]

A roughcut cowhand, six feet tall under his ten-gallon hat, was sauntering around a large department store during one of his infrequent trips to the big city. The salesgirl asked politely if there was anything else she might help him with. "No, thank ya, ma'am, I reckon not. I never seen so much I could do without."

* * * * *

A country boy on his first visit to New York discovered the Automat. He got two dollars' worth of nickels, [and a] tray . . . and, beginning at the door, proceeded to drop nickels in the slots and fill the tray with piles of food. Finally, when his tray got as loaded as a salesman on the last day of the convention, an Automat attendant stopped him and said: "Hey! You can't put any more on that tray. Why don't you go to a table and start eating what you have?"

The boy from the country looked at him scornfully.

"Oh yeah," he said. "And quit while I'm winning?"

[31] From *Stories I Like to Tell,* 306 of the Best Jokes and Anecdotes I Have Heard in Twenty Years of Radio and TV, by Arthur Godfrey, pp. 148, 149. Copyright, 1952, by A. M. L. Enterprises. New York: Simon and Schuster.

Two Hundred and Fifty-seven Apples[32]

A beery man with hoary chin stubble approached an applecart at Fulton Ferry in Brooklyn at ten o'clock one morning about thirty years ago. He said to the peddler, "Will you let me eat all the apples I can for a quarter?" Apples then sold at twenty for twenty-five cents—more than most men could eat—and it seemed a shame to take the money. Perhaps the apple vendor had no conscience. Anyway, he took the twenty-five cents and the customer dug into the heap.

At two o'clock that afternoon . . . the beery man was still eating apples. . . .

. . . Off the barge slip some two hundred stevedores and waterfront loafers milled about the apple vendor's cart. The apple mound that had been four feet high at ten o'clock that morning was now a valley between the low pushcart walls. The face of the beery man was very flushed but he munched steadily.

Silver and grimy banknotes swapped hands. A little man with dirt ingrained in his facial seams kept tabs. Each time an apple was reduced to core, he marked the cobblestone pavement with a piece of white chalk. At six o'clock, when the sun roofed Manhattan on the opposite riverbank with autmnal red and gold, the count was two hundred and fifty. The watchers hoarsely cheered this news. The poor apple peddler was crushed.

"I got to go now," he said.

He put his hands to the cart handles. The stevedores made rumbling noises in their throats. The cart did not move.

Night filtered its first layer of dusty powder on the river. Lights came on in Manhattan's graying towers. Trolley cars and El trains blossomed with weak yellow incandescents. They moved like toys through the spider-web structure of Brooklyn Bridge. The river darkened and turned gelid black. The beery man continued to munch stubbornly.

It was full night when the cart was emptied. Brittle stars quivered over the river. The bridge, an arc of glowing dots, reproduced itself on the onyx waters, as on a black mirror. River craft trailed serpentine reflections, red and green, in their own ripples.

[32] From *The Eight Million,* Journal of a New York Correspondent, by Meyer Berger, pp. 3–5. Copyright, 1942, by Meyer Berger. New York: Simon and Schuster.

Two hundred and fifty-seven apples. The stevedores and the loafers noisily and triumphantly bore the bloated champion across the cobbled drayway toward a waterfront saloon.

The poor apple man moved off in the dark. His empty cart rattled on the cobblestones and the street lamp distorted his image in long and melancholy shadow. I wondered what he would tell his wife and children when he got home. "I sold two hundred and fifty-seven apples for twenty-five cents," he would say. Twenty-five cents was a day's cart hire.

The Bell-Ringing Fish [33]

"Fish is brain food," Fritz Strohschneider, a waiter and a friend of mine told me, "but around cities they is brainier. It is just like people, the city fish is more slicker as the country fish.

"I don't go fishing more," he went on without encouragement, "since they exploded Heinrich Heine.

"In the old days it was so nice on Sunday to fish for tommys from the docks. Tommys and eelses. On 96th Street dock we used to sit, me and my friend Jake Poppberger, with a case of beer and our clarinets. It was the most convenient fishing.

"Each one would have four, five lines. The lines are tied to wires and on each wire there is a bell. When a fish bites, the bell rings, like an elevator. You pull him up and it is sport.

"So one Sunday we was sitting on the dock, and we had eight lines out. Suddenly, along comes Heinrich Heine.

"It seems between those bells was musical gradations, by chance of the length of the wires, and as I am sitting tuning my clarinet, so I hear played wonder good on the bells the scale. 'Do, re, mi, fa, sol,' and the rest of it. 'My God, Jake,' I says, 'what is this for a fish?'

"Back it comes the other way the scale—being a fish the scale was its specialty—and then 'dingle, dingle'—it was trying to pick out 'Annie Laurie.'

"Jake wanted to pull up the line, but I said, 'What, you would murder a musician?'

[33] From *Back Where I Came From,* by A. J. Liebling, pp. 45–47. Copyright, 1938, by A. J. Liebling. New York: Sheridan House.

"We looked down it shouldn't be boys in a boat under the pier, but there was nothing. The next Sunday we came to the same spot. We set the lines and soon it gave *'Ich Weiss Nicht Was Soll Es Bedeuten.'* Then I named the fish Heinrich Heine. So we played on our clarinets and Heinrich Heine would accompany us.

"Every Sunday new tunes we were teaching him, and sometimes he even offered for us original compositions. So nice it was in the sunset to sit there with a case of empty beer bottles and play 'Love's Old Sweet Song.' "

Fritz sighted. He flicked listlessly at an imaginary speck of dust with his towel.

"I never saw Heinrich Heine," he said. "I don't know whether he was a tommy or whether an eel. But in a way I helped kill him. Among the tunes we taught him was *'Die Wacht Am Rhein.'* We didn't mean no harm. It was before America went to war. Scotchers, Englishers, Irishers used to come down to the pier. It made them mad to hear the fish play so nice the German antler.

"But when this country went in the war a battleship came in the river. A bright Sunday morning Heinrich Heine commenced to play. 'Ta-tum-tee-um-tee-um-Die Wacht Am Rhein.' The battleship shot a torpedo and exploded Heinrich Heine. Since then I go no more fishing."

The Talking Horse[34]

The Dodgers were playing an important game with the Giants. First the Dodgers and then the Giants were in the lead. "Lippy" Durocher was walking back and forth. After all, it was almost the end of the season, and every game counted more than percentages showed. About the seventh inning, with the score tied, a horse strolled up and tapped Durocher on the shoulder. "Hey, Lippy," he said, "why don't you send me in? I can bat." Durocher glanced up and snarled, "Go away and don't bother me. I'm having enough troubles."

Now it was the last half of the eighth inning, and the Dodgers went

[34] By Bernard Cohen, Indiana University. From *Hoosier Folklore,* Vol. VI (September, 1947), No. 3, p. 108. Copyright, 1947, by the Hoosier Folklore Society. Indianapolis: Published quarterly for the Hoosier Folklore Society by the Indiana Historical Bureau.

Contributed, November, 1945, by Ernie F. Postlewaite, who heard it from Bud Granger, a member of the San Francisco Seals, a professional baseball club.—Ernest W. Baughman.

out in the field. One of the players made an error, and the Giants scored again. Finally the Dodgers came to bat. It was their last chance, and Durocher had reached a state of bad nerves. The horse came trotting up again. "Come on, Lippy; let me go in. What can you lose? The chances aren't very good and I am." Durocher showed his teeth in a snarl. "You irritate me. Go peddle your milk like a good boy." The horse sadly walked away.

The first man up flied out and Durocher became desperate. He stood up and yelled at the horse, "Hey, you, come over here! You might as well try it." The horse came trotting out and stepped up to the batter's box. The first pitch was low and wide for a ball. The second was a perfect pitch, and the horse took a swing at it. He connected, full force, and the ball flew into the stands for a home run. Durocher started jumping up and down, and waving his arms. "Run, you fool; don't just stand there." The horse turned around and laughed. "Don't be silly. If I could run, I wouldn't be playing baseball."

Casey Stengel and the Sparrow [35]

The story of Casey Stengel and the sparrow has been told in many variations. Usually it is warped around so that it becomes a piece of deliberate screwball behavior on the part of Stengel. Newspaper accounts of the incident, written in 1918 right after it occurred, would seem to contradict these versions.

Stengel was a great hero in the few years he played with the Dodgers; then he was traded to the Pirates. On that day in 1918 he came back to Brooklyn as a member of the Pittsburgh club. Technically he had now gone over to the enemy, yet the Brooklyn fans held him in such high esteem that it was a sure thing they would salute him with cheers on his return.

He did not bat in the top of the first, but was the first man scheduled to hit for Pittsburgh at the beginning of the second. He walked out of the dugout when the time came, selected a bat, and strode to the plate. The Brooklyn fans got to their feet and cheered him mightily. Arriving at the plate, Casey turned and faced the stands and lifted his

[35] From *Low and Inside,* A Book of Baseball Anecdotes, Oddities, and Curiosities, by Ira L. Smith and H. Allen Smith, pp. 212–213. Copyright, 1949, by Ira L. Smith and H. Allen Smith. Garden City, New York: Doubleday & Co., Inc.

cap from his head in acknowledgment of the salute, and a bird flew out of his hair, circled the diamond once, and then disappeared into the sky. A great roar went up from the multitude—old Casey hadn't disappointed 'em!

The fact appears to be that Mr. Stengel was as greatly startled as the fans had been when a bird flew out of his thatch. For the moment, however, he made no effort to disillusion his admirers, being content to let them think he had rigged the bird trick in their honor.

Later on he told his story of what had happened. When he had gone to his position in right field in the first inning, he saw an injured sparrow wobbling along at the base of the wall. He walked over and picked it up and was trying to decide what to do with it when he noticed that the ball game had been resumed and he needed to get down to business. He quickly placed the stunned bird under his cap and went to work as an outfielder. He swore later on that he had completely forgotten about the sparrow when he came in from the field and went to bat. Nonetheless, the bird story has been widely repeated as an example of Stengel's showmanship.

The Library Lions [36]

There once was a girl named Mary.
The lions didn't roar when she walked by the Library.

Bop Jokes [37]

. . . The boppers developed a language of their own. Things were "cool" and cool things "gassed" the initiates and anything that was particularly cool was actually "crazy."

[36] From *Hard Lines,* by Ogden Nash, p. 53. Copyright, 1931, by Ogden Nash. New York: Simon and Schuster.

An allusion to the popular saying that the lions (in front of the New York Public Library on Fifth Avenue at Forty-second Street) roar whenever a virgin passes.

[37] From *No Cover Charge,* A Backward Look at the Night Clubs, by Robert Sylvester, pp. 287–288. Copyright, 1956, by Robert Sylvester. New York: The Dial Press.

A whole literature of "bop jokes" was soon being reported in the press, on the stage, and over the radio. There was one very popular legend about the bop musician whose apartment was just under a minister's. The bopper played piano night and day. The minister knocked on his door and asked if the bopper must practice even while he was composing a sermon. The bopper insisted that it was a compulsion.

"Do you know the golden rule?" asked the reverend.

"Whistle the first few bars," said the bopper, "and I'll fake the rest."

It was also widely reported that two boppers walked past a film house advertising Somerset Maugham's *Quartet*. A few blocks down the street they passed another small film house offering Maugham's *Trio*.

"Let's dig this crazy combo," said one. "It's fading fast."

Other odd doings of the boppers were daily reported. Seeing an Indian charming a cobra with the traditional flute, one bopper admitted: "I don't dig the tune, man, but that cat's got a crazy music stand."

And there was also the incident of the two boppers walking through a cemetery. They noted the carefully tended lawns, the fresh flowers, the elegant marble stones.

"Man," says one, "these cats really know how to live."

"It's a Wonderful Town" [38]

It's the same in New York as in many other towns. There are old people who do not go out so much in the town any more, because they are tired and because they think the best days of New York, the glory and excitement, are gone. But they have a lot to remember. There are younger people who do not know or care what the best days were; for them, the town was never more alive and exciting than now. And there are others, still younger, who live in the hope that all children have—for children are hopeful; they take the easy, beautiful present for granted—that the best days of New York are still to come.

For instance, some day another airplane may smash into the Empire

[38] From "John Lardner's New York, Love and Adventure on all the Bridges, while Cats Sit in Windows Snarling at Pigeons," *Look, America's Family Magazine,* Vol. 16 (December 30, 1952), No. 27, p. 6. Copyright, 1952, by Cowles Magazines, Inc. New York.

State Building. There are New York children—I know a few—who curse their lots at having been too young to see or appreciate the last collision of a plane with the tower, a few years ago. But it will happen again—youth has confidence. Meanwhile, because the movie *King Kong* has been replayed in many places in recent days, there is a happy substitute vision of New York for the city's children and for children everywhere: of the great gorilla swarming across the face of the Empire State, which trembles and sways in his clutch. New York needed a Gothic symbol like Kong, for the young and susceptible—just as Paris needed Quasimodo in Notre Dame, and the Phantom terrorizing the Opera; and as London needed its memories of the princes murdered in the Tower, and of the heads of lords and queens on poles and pikestaffs.

Perhaps one day a giant ape *will* swing from the Empire State Building, or a Martian huntsman will land there with his hound pack, in hot pursuit of a space cadet. There are people in our town who will snarl and mutter and write to the *Times,* because the great event has spoiled their television reception from WNBT and WCBS and WJZ and WPIX and WABD. But in their time, they looked for romance and adventure, too, each in his own way, innocent or quizzical or cockeyed. It's a quality that the town gives to those who live in it.

Once, twenty-five years ago, a New York saloonkeeper sat at the big wooden "house" table in his place, talking with an old patron and friend. The friend was one who, in a business way, built sensational scenic effects for the stage—dizzy mountain heights, tours through hell, sawmills where virtuous girls were cut in half. But he put this dull trade behind him when he drank.

"It's my experience," he said, "that the number of red-haired women seen in New York in any given period of time is equal to the number of white horses."

"No!" roared the saloonkeeper. "There are more white horses."

They set out, with pencils and pads, to tour the town by cab, to the Battery and back. The count that first time, as I remember, was 187 red-haired women to 168 white horses. The figures varied and criss-crossed as, once a year, year after year, the survey was renewed. Each year, a reporter from the newspaper office above the saloon wrote a story about the investigation. One year, however, the reporter, the saloonkeeper, and the sawmill-builder stayed in the saloon and counted red-haired women and white horses by intuition. The hunt remained indoors from then on, and, finally, it was disbanded. The saloonkeeper by now was an older man than he had been.

"What the hell is the use of even thinking about it?" he said. "Today, it takes you an hour to move from 40th Street to 30th Street. The traffic has driven the white horses and the red-haired girls off the streets."

* * * * *

Once, I knew a young fellow in town—he was a ticket-scalper's assistant—who wore the mayor's castoff clothes. Derbies, striped pants, cutaways and spats, they were, mostly, for this was the best-dressed mayor we ever had. We have had some fine, colorful mayors in New York. One said, "You said a mouthful, queen," to the queen of Belgium. One was shot at while boarding a ship. One read the funny papers over the radio. The well-dressed mayor, in partnership with Grover Whalen, was great at civic receptions; and whenever there was a reception, the young scalper with the mayor's old clothes showed up, and stuck his head into the newspaper photographs between the mayor and the king, the prizefighter or the Channel-swimmer who was being greeted. New York was a wonderful town for him. I could imagine his feelings of pain and shock one day not long ago when Rudy Halley, the crime-fighter and economizer in the city government, denounced civic receptions and their pomp and panoply.

"Why don't we have just a handshake and a bugle call?" said Rudy Halley.

* * * * *

New York is a town in which pet cats sit in apartment windows gnashing their teeth at pigeons they can never catch . . . where there is a colony of gypsies, and a colony of Mohawk Indians . . . where men who have never seen South Bend, Indiana, do snake-dances in Leon & Eddie's the night before a Notre Dame football game. Last month, a youth proposed to a girl on the Williamsburg Bridge, and the girl said no. The youth climbed on a girder and threatened to jump. The girl ran to a telephone to call the police.

"There's a man trying to jump off the George Washington Bridge!" she cried. She had the wrong bridge by ten miles, but the cops noted the location of the call and went to the right bridge and saved the youth. If they'd gone to the George Washington Bridge, they'd have found love and adventure there too. It's a wonderful town.

Index

Names of authors, editors, and informants included are set in caps and small caps.

ABOUT THE EDITOR

EVER SINCE Ben Botkin went out to Oklahoma in 1921 to teach English at the state university, he has been interested in the folkways and traditions, ballads and legends, that make Americans tick. From collecting play-party songs among his students he turned to editing four volumes of the regional miscellany, *Folk-Say*, whose title, coined by him in 1928, has given us a new word, folksay, first included in the *American College Dictionary* in 1947. In the sense of folk history folksay is best exemplified by *Lay My Burden Down* (1945), a collection of slave narratives from interviews with former slaves by members of the Federal Writers' Project, for which he served as folklore editor in 1938–1940. From 1942 to 1945, he was chief of the Archive of American Folk Song in the Library of Congress. In a half-dozen treasuries, beginning with *A Treasury of American Folklore* (1944–1955), he explored the folklore of American regions.

A study of city folklore begun on a Guggenheim Fellowship in 1951 culminated in *Sidewalks of America* (1954) and now in *New York City Folklore*, his seventeenth volume. A former president of the American Folklore Society, honorary vice-president of the New York Folklore Society, and chairman of the executive committee of the Workshop for Cultural Democracy, he was honored in June, 1956, by the University of Nebraska with the degree of doctor of letters as a "successful interpreter of the legends which have helped us understand our cultural heritage." He has contributed to various periodicals and encyclopedias and taught or lectured in a number of Western and Eastern universities. A Bostonian by birth, he has made his base for the past eleven years in Croton-on-Hudson, with frequent cross-country trips in search of new sources of social history and studies in popular culture.

ABOUT THE EDITOR

EVER SINCE Ben Botkin went out to Oklahoma in 1921 to teach English at the state university, he has been interested in the folkways and traditions, ballads and legends, that make Americans tick. From collecting play-party songs among his students he turned to editing four volumes of the regional miscellany, *Folk-Say,* whose title, coined by him in 1928, has given us a new word, folksay, first included in the *American College Dictionary* in 1947. In the sense of folk history folksay is best exemplified by *Lay My Burden Down* (1945), a collection of slave narratives from interviews with former slaves by members of the Federal Writers' Project, for which he served as folklore editor in 1938–1940. From 1942 to 1945, he was chief of the Archive of American Folk Song in the Library of Congress. In a half-dozen treasuries, beginning with *A Treasury of American Folklore* (1944–1955), he explored the folklore of American regions.

A study of city folklore begun on a Guggenheim Fellowship in 1951 culminated in *Sidewalks of America* (1954) and now in *New York City Folklore,* his seventeenth volume. A former president of the American Folklore Society, honorary vice-president of the New York Folklore Society, and chairman of the executive committee of the Workshop for Cultural Democracy, he was honored in June, 1956, by the University of Nebraska, with the degree of doctor of letters as a "successful interpreter of the legends which have helped us understand our cultural heritage." He has contributed to various periodicals and encyclopedias and taught or lectured in a number of Western and Eastern universities. A Bostonian by birth, he has made his base for the past eleven years in Croton-on-Hudson, with frequent cross-country trips in search of new sources of social history and studies in popular culture.